COMMERCIAL REPORTS

AREA STUDIES SERIES

EDITORIAL DIRECTOR Professor J J O'Meara
RESEARCH UNIT DIRECTOR T F Turley
ASSISTANT DIRECTOR S Cashman

CHIEF EDITORIAL ADVISERS

P Ford
Professor Emeritus, Southampton University
Mrs G Ford

SPECIAL EDITORIAL CONSULTANT FOR
THE UNITED STATES PAPERS

H C Allen
Commonwealth Fund Professor of American History, University College, London
Director of the London University Institute of United States Studies

RESEARCH EDITORS
Johann A Norstedt
Marilyn Evers Norstedt

This Series is published with the active co-operation of
SOUTHAMPTON UNIVERSITY

IRISH UNIVERSITY PRESS AREA STUDIES SERIES

BRITISH PARLIAMENTARY PAPERS

UNITED STATES OF AMERICA

40

Embassy and consular
commercial reports
1898–99

IRISH UNIVERSITY PRESS
Shannon   Ireland

PUBLISHER'S NOTE

The documents in this series are selected from the nineteenth-century British House of Commons *sessional and command papers*. All of the original papers relating to the United States of America are included with the exception of two kinds of very brief and unimportant papers. Omitted are (1) random statistical trade returns which are included in the larger and complete yearly trade figures and (2) returns relating to postal services, which are irregularly presented, of tangential USA relevance, and easily available in other sources.

The original documents have been reproduced by photo-lithography and are unabridged even to the extent of retaining the first printers' imprints. Imperfections in the original printing are sometimes unavoidably reproduced.

This reprint is an enlargement from the original octavo format.

© 1971 Irish University Press Shannon Ireland
Microfilm, microfiche and other forms of micro-publishing
© *Irish University Microforms Shannon Ireland*

ISBN 0 7165 1540 7

Printed and published by
Irish University Press Shannon Ireland
DUBLIN   CORK   BELFAST   LONDON   NEW YORK
T M MacGlinchey *Publisher*   Robert Hogg *Printer*

Contents

IUP Page Number

For ease of reference IUP editors have assigned a continuous pagination which appears on the top outer margin of each page.

Commercial Reports

F.O. annual series no. 2030: report on New Orleans and District, 1897
1898 [C.8648–52] XCIX 9

F.O. annual series no. 2031: report on Charleston and District, 1897
1898 [C.8648–53] XCIX 41

F.O. annual series no. 2038: report on Galveston and District, 1897
1898 [C.8648–60] XCIX 77

F.O. annual series no. 2081: report on New York, 1897;
Providence, 1897
1898 [C.8648–103] XCIX 107

F.O. annual series no. 2082: report on Baltimore, 1897;
Norfolk, 1897; Richmond, 1897
1898 [C.8648–104] XCIX 153

F.O. annual series no. 2085: report on Chicago, 1897; Denver, 1897; St. Louis, 1897
1898 [C.8648–107] XCIX 189

F.O. annual series no. 2115: report on Portland, Oregon, 1897;
Astoria, 1897; Tacoma, 1897; Seattle, 1897; Port Townsend, 1897
1898 [C.8648–137] XCIX 209

F.O. annual series no. 2147: report on Boston, 1897; Portland, Maine, 1897
1898 [C.8648–169] XCIX 255

F.O. annual series no. 2152: report on California, 1897
1898 [C.8648–174] XCIX 297

F.O. annual series no. 2206: report on New Orleans, 1898;
Pensacola, 1898; Mobile, 1898
1899 [C.9044–32] CIII 353

F.O. annual series no. 2210: report on Texas, 1898
1899 [C.9044–36] CIII 381

Continued

Contents

Continued

IUP Page Number

F.O. annual series no. 2220: report on Charleston, 1898; Savannah, 1898; Brunswick, 1898; Darien, 1898
1899 [C.9044–46] CIII 421

F.O. annual series no. 2237: report on Baltimore, 1898; Norfolk, 1898; Newport News, 1898
1899 [C.9044–63] CIII 453

F.O. annual series no. 2239: report on Chicago, 1898; St. Louis, 1898; Denver, 1898; St. Paul, 1898; Omaha, 1898
1899 [C.9044–65] CIII 491

F.O. annual series no. 2256: report on New York, 1898; Providence, 1898
1899 [C.9044–82] CIII 527

F.O. annual series no. 2257: report on Galveston, 1899 (first quarter)
1899 [C.9044–83] CIII 571

F.O. annual series no. 2295: report on Portland, Oregon, 1898; Astoria, 1898; Tacoma, 1898; Seattle, 1898; Port Townsend, 1898
1899 [C.9044–121] CIII 581

F.O. annual series no. 2314: report on Boston, 1898; Portland, Maine, 1898
1899 [C.9044–140] CIII 629

F.O. annual series no. 2349: report on San Francisco, 1898; Los Angeles, 1898; San Diego, 1898
1899 [C.9496–20] CIII 667

F.O. annual series no. 2352: report on Philadelphia, 1898
1899 [C.9496–23] CIII 705

As most commercial reports are extracted from larger papers, the reader should note that a particular report may lack a proper title page.

FOREIGN OFFICE.
1898.
ANNUAL SERIES.

Nº 2030.

DIPLOMATIC AND CONSULAR REPORTS ON TRADE AND FINANCE.

UNITED STATES.

REPORT FOR THE YEAR 1897

ON THE

TRADE OF NEW ORLEANS AND DISTRICT.

REFERENCE TO PREVIOUS REPORT, Annual Series No. 1869.

Presented to both Houses of Parliament by Command of Her Majesty,
FEBRUARY, 1898.

LONDON:
PRINTED FOR HER MAJESTY'S STATIONERY OFFICE,
BY HARRISON AND SONS, ST. MARTIN'S LANE,
PRINTERS IN ORDINARY TO HER MAJESTY.

And to be purchased, either directly or through any Bookseller, from
EYRE & SPOTTISWOODE, EAST HARDING STREET, FLEET STREET, E.C., and
32, ABINGDON STREET, WESTMINSTER, S.W.: or
JOHN MENZIES & Co., 12, HANOVER STREET, EDINBURGH, and
90, WEST NILE STREET, GLASGOW; or
HODGES, FIGGIS, & Co., Limited, 104, GRAFTON STREET, DUBLIN.

1898.
Price Twopence.

[C. 8648—52.]

New Series of Reports.

Reports of the Annual Series have been issued from Her Majesty's Diplomatic and Consular Officers at the following places, and may be obtained from the sources indicated on the title-page:—

No.		Price.	No.		Price.
1910.	Philadelphia	1½d.	1970.	Beyrout	1d.
1911.	Rio Grande do Sul	3½d.	1971.	Yokohama	1½d.
1912.	Quito	1d.	1972.	Warsaw	½d.
1913.	San José	1d.	1973.	Sofia	1½d.
1914.	Dunkirk	1d.	1974.	Madrid	2d.
1915.	Samoa	1d.	1975.	Vienna	2d.
1916.	Bordeaux	2½d.	1976.	Erzeroum	1d.
1917.	Porto Rico	1½d.	1977.	Berlin	1½d.
1918.	Galatz	1½d.	1978.	Adis Abbaba	1d.
1919.	Christiania	½d.	1979.	Tamsui	1d.
1920.	Copenhagen	3d.	1980.	Odessa	2½d.
1921.	New York	2½d.	1981.	Brindisi	2½d.
1922.	San Francisco	3½d.	1982.	Macao	1d.
1923.	Kiukiang	1d.	1983.	Pakhoi	1d.
1924.	Harrar	½d.	1984.	Peking	2d.
1925.	Berne	1½d.	1985.	Mexico	1½d.
1926.	Mannheim	1d.	1986.	Canton	1d.
1927.	Fiume	1½d.	1987.	Naples	1½d.
1928.	Oporto	1d.	1988.	Port Said	1½d.
1929.	Hangchow	1d.	1989.	Algiers	3½d.
1930.	Boston	2½d.	1990.	Vienna	1d.
1931.	Tahiti	1d.	1991.	Valparaiso	1½d.
1932.	Manila	1½d.	1992.	Gothenburg	2½d.
1933.	Caracas	1d.	1993.	St. Michael's (The Azores)	1d.
1934.	Hamburg	3d.	1994.	Antwerp	1d.
1935.	Portland	3d.	1995.	Tangier	1½d.
1936.	Malaga	2½d.	1996.	Swaziland	1d.
1937.	Tokio	1½d.	1997.	Swatow	1d.
1938.	Genoa	3d.	1998.	St. Petersburg	4½d.
1939.	Palermo	3d.	1999.	Dar-al-Baida	1½d.
1940.	Santiago de Cuba	1½d.	2000.	Dantzig	2d.
1941.	Noumea	1d.	2001.	Algiers	1½d.
1942.	Frankfort	3½d.	2002.	Rome	2d.
1943.	Chungking	1½d.	2003.	Bangkok	1d.
1944.	Ichang	1d.	2004.	Nagasaki	1d.
1945.	Hankow	1½d.	2005.	Hiogo and Osaka	1½d.
1946.	Guatemala	1½d.	2006.	Jeddah	2d.
1947.	Syra	1d.	2007.	Paris	1d.
1948.	Taganrog	2d.	2008.	Meshed	2½d.
1949.	Loanda	2½d.	2009.	Chiengmai	1½d.
1950.	Panama	2½d.	2010.	Stettin	1½d.
1951.	Shanghai	2d.	2011.	Vera Cruz	1d.
1952.	Aleppo	1½d.	2012.	Kiungchow	1d.
1953.	Ispahan	1½d.	2013.	Christiania	2½d.
1954.	Tonga	1d.	2014.	Warsaw	1d.
1955.	Nice	1d.	2015.	Hakodate	1d.
1956.	Granada	1d.	2016.	Buda-Pesth	2d.
1957.	Söul	1d.	2017.	Batoum	1d.
1958.	Cadiz	1½d.	2018.	Bushire	2d.
1959.	Chinde	½d.	2019.	Tegucigalpa	½d.
1960.	Stockholm	2d.	2020.	Montevideo	1d.
1961.	Zanzibar	1d.	2021.	Tainan	1d.
1962.	Tokio	1½d.	2022.	Copenhagen	½d.
1963.	Asuncion	1½d.	2023.	Odessa	1½d.
1964.	Baghdad	1½d.	2024.	Munich	1½d.
1965.	Réunion	1d.	2025.	Valparaiso	1½d.
1966.	Chefoo	2½d.	2026.	Berlin	2½d.
1967.	Newchwang	1d.	2027.	Rouen	1½d.
1968.	Tabreez	½d.	2028.	Stockholm	1½d.
1969.	St. Paul de Loanda	1d.	2029.	Belgrade	1½d.

No. 2030.

Reference to previous Report, Annual Series No. 1869.

UNITED STATES.

NEW ORLEANS.

Consul Vansittart to the Marquess of Salisbury.

(Received at Foreign Office, February 3, 1898.)

My Lord,

I HAVE the honour to transmit herewith my Annual Trade Report for 1897, as well as those from Mr. Howe, Her Majesty's Vice-Consul at Pensacola, and Mr. Barnewall, British Vice-Consul at Mobile.

I have, &c.
(Signed) A. G. VANSITTART.

Report on the Trade and Commerce of the Consular District of New Orleans for the Year 1897.

TABLE of Contents.

	PAGE
New Orleans—	
Review and general remarks	2
Bank clearings	3
Trade of the year	4
Total commerce of the port	4
Imports and exports	4
Grain trade	5
Lumber trade	6
Manufactures	7
Coffee	7
Sugar	8
Rice	8
Cotton	9
Railroad business	13
Street railways	14
Wharves	15
Health statistics	15
Drainage	16
Shipping	17

(78)

UNITED STATES.

Table of Contents—continued.

	PAGE
Pensacola—	
Trade	21
Between Pensacola and Liverpool	21
New trade to Continent and Japan	21
Louisville and Nashville railroad and new trade	22
Imports	22
Population and industries	23
General remarks	23
Agriculture	24
Annexes:—	
A.—Return of principal articles of export	24
B.— ,, imports and exports by countries	25
C.— ,, shipping	25
Mobile—	
Trade and commerce	26
Lumber and timber	27
Cotton	27
Grain	27
Fruits	27
Shipping	27
Iron and coal	28
Annex and shipping returns	29

Review and general remarks.

Although prices in general were not satisfactory during the past season, the consumption of general supplies were not up to expectations, and profits were exceedingly small, yet statistics show that New Orleans handled a larger volume of merchandise, and that most of the staple crops upon which this city depends for the success of her trade were marketed in greater volume than during the preceding season. Her only misfortune was, in common with other great commercial centres of the country, to have handled a large volume of business at little profit.

The cotton crop, on which the prosperity of this city and the country tributary to it mainly depends, was considerably larger than during the previous year. A most gratifying fact connected with the marketing of the cotton crop was the increase in the amount of the staple handled by factors, the improvement in this respect being very considerable.

The sugar crop of Louisiana, which contributes so largely to the commercial importance of New Orleans, was also much larger than during the previous year, some 300,000 barrels more of sugar than last season being handled, and prices were satisfactory to producers.

The rice crop was unfortunately almost a complete failure, the yield being barely a third of what it had been in the previous season.

As regards the foreign commerce of the port, both exports and imports increased greatly, a gain of 21 per cent. as compared with previous season.

The gain in exports was due largely to cotton and grain. The grain shipments were especially conspicuous, and it is but a few years since New Orleans became prominent as a grain port. The gain in imports amounted to nearly 600,000*l.*, the total movement aggregating 3,262,983*l.*

In the matter of improvement in exports the fact should be noted that New Orleans passed Baltimore during the year, taking the third place, and standing next to Boston as the third largest exporting port in America.

The shipping of the port not only increased 19 per cent. over the previous year, but improved in the size and quality of the vessels employed. The increase in the ocean tonnage of the port being 184,571 tons in the vessels entered, and of 203,196 tons in those cleared on a total of 387,767 tons.

The total increase in the railroad tonnage of the port was 271,556 tons in the freight received, and of 144,463 tons in that despatched, making a total increase in the railroad business of 416,019 tons, or 9·3 per cent., and in value of 3,600,116*l.*

There were few failures of consequence which, all things considered, augurs well, and notwithstanding the fact that the first two months of the present business season, September and October, were practically lost, owing to yellow fever and quarantine restrictions, the end of the calendar year arrived with every evidence that all the ground lost during the quarantine period has been recovered. Certainly the splendid exhibition of recuperative power which New Orleans has made since the close of the quarantine trouble, should encourage the people to look forward with confidence to a prosperous season during 1898.

It should be noted that, out of 19,979,963*l.* representing the total value of all exports from New Orleans to foreign countries during the year ended December 31, 1897, something over 8,000,000*l.* represented the total value of the exports to Great Britain from this port.

A comparison of the credit clearings of the associated banks for the 12 months of the commercial year gives the following figures:— *Bank clearings.*

Season.	Bank Clearings.
	£
1896–97	86,684,900
1895–96	99,763,236
Decrease	13,078,336

The exact comparison of the foreign commerce of the port is shown by the following figures giving the value of the merchandise, imported and exported, as taken from the returns of the Collector of the port of New Orleans:— *The foreign commerce of the port.*

Year.	Imports.	Exports.	Customs Receipts.
	£	£	£
1896–97	3,262,983	20,106,821	589,300
1895–96	2,813,100	17,241,700	353,300
Increase	449,883	2,865,121	236,000

UNITED STATES.

Trade of the year.

The trade of the year showed an improvement in nearly all lines. The corn exports were 3,045,730 bushels, against 19,910,416 bushels the previous year, and 2,584,037 bushels in 1894-95.

The cotton exports were 2,012,384 bales, as against 1,641,502 bales the previous year, an increase of 370,882 bales; and the value of provisions exported rose from 164,036*l.* to 262,363*l.*

Total commerce of the port.

The total commerce of the port for the 12 months was—

1896-97.

	Tonnage.	Value.
		£
Receipts by rail and river	4,986,620	31,756,277
By coastwise vessels	544,303	13,044,024
By foreign vessels	736,341	3,262,983
Total receipts	6,267,264	48,063,284
Shipments by rail and river	1,843,692	17,372,042
Exports, coastwise	517,847	10,208,056
„ foreign	1,398,813	20,106,821
Total shipments	3,760,352	47,686,919
Grand total of commerce	10,027,616	95,750,203

The totals for the past few years have been as follows :—

Season.	Value.
	£
1890-91	106,352,823
1891-92	99,293,148
1892-93	105,566,126
1893-94	96,701,413
1894-95	91,131,886
1895-96	83,916,181
1896-97	95,750,203

Imports and exports.

The imports and exports of New Orleans, including coastwise, has been as follows for the past three years :—

Year.	Value.	
	Imports.	Exports.
	£	£
1895	16,053,165	22,585,174
1896	16,014,530	24,481,923
1897	16,807,007	30,314,877

NEW ORLEANS.

The grain trade. The grain trade of this city has risen in the past six years from a comparatively insignificant part of the commerce of this port to one of its most important, and this city stands to-day third in exports, being exceeded only by Baltimore and New York.

From September 1, 1896, to August 31, 1897, 33,904,482 bushels of cereals were shipped from the port of New Orleans to European ports. Last year's total exports up to September 1, 1896, was a little over 22,000,000 bushels, so it will be seen that the increase of this year over last is something like 12,000,000 bushels.

The facilities for handling grain at this port were increased during the past year by the erection of the Stuyvesant and Port Chalmette elevators. The grain was carried by some 435 ships, of which 340 were British.

While during the last 12 months the movement was confined almost entirely to maize, the shipments this year will be more diversified, consisting of wheat, maize, rye, and oats.

Latest returns of the movement of grain. The following return has just been issued by the New Orleans Grain Committee. The receipts of grain are as follows:—

	Quantity.
	Bushels.
Receipts of grain in 1897	43,000,000
,, ,, 1896	32,900,000
Showing an increase in quantity of ..	10,100,000
The total exports of grain of all kinds were ..	41,500,000
Same period last year ..	29,000,000
Increase for 1897 ..	12,500,000

The last returns show that for the month of December, 1897, the total grain export rose to 5,405,955 bushels, being an increase over the same month of 1896 of more than 3,000,000 bushels, or of 140 per cent. The export of oats for the month of December, 1897, amounted to 321,310 bushels, and of rye, 34,500 bushels, a great increase as compared with the corresponding period of 1896. The total grain exports of New Orleans for the year ended December 31, 1897, were 39,624,908 bushels.

The following comparative statements are interesting, as showing the shipments of grain to British ports, with the amounts in bushels:—

(78)

UNITED STATES.

1896-97.

Destination.	Quantity.			
	Corn.	Wheat.	Oats.	Rye.
	Bushels.	Bushels.	Bushels.	Bushels.
Liverpool	9,761,211	1,329,513	33,668	..
Hull	1,314,657	241,800	..	..
Lynn	231,932	..	..	..
Manchester	543,620	..	..	..
Queenstown	2,260,027	..	..	..
Cork	123,023	..	..	25,000
Birkenhead	279,702	..	..	..
Dublin	237,634	..	..	..
Belfast	1,570,589	..	..	..
Bristol	145,586	..	..	..
Leith	43,000	..	..	..
Total	16,510,981	1,571,313	33,668	25,000

1895-96.

Destination.	Quantity.		
	Corn.	Wheat.	Oats.
	Bushels.	Bushels.	Bushels.
Liverpool	5,899,942	751,482	..
Falmouth	336,820	..	..
Ipswich	243,968	..	..
Hull	116,800	..	..
Lynn	94,000	..	..
London	166,782	..	..
Manchester	239,000	..	..
Queenstown	628,439	..	..
Cork	125,000	..	..
Kingstown	20,000	..	..
Birkenhead	262,874	..	..
Dublin	154,775	..	..
Total	8,288,400	751,482	..

Lumber trade.

The fiscal year closed on June 30, 1897, shows a gain of 25 per cent. in the lumber export of the South over the preceding fiscal year. The sum total of shipments for the fiscal year ending June 30, 1896, was, in superficial feet, 905,980,008, while that of the fiscal year ending June 30, 1897, registers a total, in superficial feet, of 1,133,234,546, or a gain in superficial feet of 227,254,538. New Orleans and Louisiana have shared in the lumber business very heavily, and, indeed, have been the very centre of it.

The State of Louisiana possesses the greatest cypress lands in the country. As an exporting point for the timber from this region of country, New Orleans, during the recently-closed fiscal year has shipped to Austria-Hungary, Belgium, Denmark,

France, Germany, Italy, the Netherlands, Portugal, Spain, England, Ireland, British Honduras, Costa Rica, Guatemala, Nicaragua, Cuba, Norway and Sweden, and Scotland 22,312,000 feet of timber, logs, &c.; and 94,352,000 feet of boards, deals, and planks, and to the same countries, excepting those which are non-wine producing, 9,433,900,000 staves. Germany is the heaviest importer from this port. It alone received 7,192,000 feet in timber, logs, &c.; and 30,488,000 of boards, deals, and planks. Mexico is looked upon as a rich prospective field for the export from southern ports, and especially from New Orleans, of yellow pine and cypress.

While there have been fluctuations in the trade of New Orleans, its manufactures have steadily advanced and it has become more and more a manufacturing city. Especially marked is the improvement in the character of its products. Formerly its industries were of the cruder kinds, the cleaning of rice, sawing of lumber, &c. It now possesses an ample supply of skilled labour, and manufactures a large variety of articles, supplying most of the home demand, and supplying large quantities of manufactured products to the interior. *Manufactures.*

In 1870 there were only 63 different industries enumerated in the census; 89 in 1880; 145 in 1890; and 202 in 1897.

The following are the statistics of factories, capital, hands, and output each year:—

Year.	Number of Factories.	Capital.	Hands Employed.	Value of Output.
		£	Number.	£
1870	554	1,085,828	4,411	1,690,087
1880	915	1,713,078	8,404	3,761,781
1890	2,152	4,573,120	23,504	8,554,103
1896	2,246	9,422,524	38,812	13,452,900

During the past season arrivals of Brazil coffee in New Orleans amounted to 295,000 bags, as against 163,000 in the year previous. New Orleans came next to New York in the amount of her imports of coffee, with a total of 374,000 bags. Next to New Orleans came Baltimore with 185,000 bags, and then San Francisco with 108,000 bags. Notwithstanding the growing popularity of the milder grades of coffee from Mexico and Central America, the demand for Brazilian still holds its own. *Coffee.*

The following table gives the figures of imports for the past four years:—

Season.	Quantity.	Value.
	Lbs.	£
1896-97	49,979,785	1,170,750
1895-96	34,942,253	1,106,681
1894-95	47,374,931	1,490,548
1893-94	43,993,671	1,544,221

UNITED STATES.

The following is a comparative statement of the imports of coffee at the port of New Orleans for the year ending June 30, 1897, as compiled by the Auditor's Department, New Orleans Custom-house:—

Countries.	Quantity.	Value.
	Lbs.	£
Belgium	19,890	400
France	31,998	1,162
Germany	12,642	140
England	43,609	1,710
Netherlands	68,544	1,735
Guatemala	131,132	5,007
Honduras	195,226	6,460
Mexico	9,901,605	333,667
Brazil	39,435,399	817,374
British Honduras	3,200	100
Nicaragua	2,681	54
Venezuela	133,859	3,480
Total	49,979,785	1,171,289

During the season 1895–96 only 9,660 lbs., valued at 400*l*., were imported from England; and 48,505 lbs., valued at 1,530*l*., from the British West Indies.

Sugar. The crop of 1896–97 is reported at 282,000 tons. There was imported from January 1, 1897, to December 31, 1897, about 64,000 tons of sugar, and received of domestic sugar about 230,000 tons.

During the past year the price improved, and planters made handsome profits. Many plantations are now being brought into use again, and there are indications for a very large acreage next year.

The main characteristics of the operations in sugar production in Louisiana during the past seasons have been the constant endeavour to reduce the cost of working, and labour-saving contrivances have been adopted wherever possible, and economy in heat generation and evaporation, together with a more complete extraction, has been continually kept in view.

The average value of sugar per lb. during 1896–97 was 3·16 c. (1¾*d*.), as against 2·92 c. in 1895–96, and 2·60 c. in 1894–95.

It is now thought that the protection provided by the customs tariff is sufficient to make the manufacture of sugar profitable.

Rice. Rice ranks third among the great staple products of Louisiana, and has marketed as much as 2,000,000 bags in a single season. At present the greatest part of the Louisiana crop of rice comes to New Orleans for the final preparation, where there are 12 large mills. In the State, besides, there are 26 other mills of fair capacity. The milling capacity of New Orleans is more than adequate for the supply, as it can pound as much as 170,000 bags per month.

NEW ORLEANS.

The rice crop of the past season was an utter failure, being the smallest yield experienced in more than 12 years. The total yield, allowing for rice held back for seed consumed in the country, and used by country mills, was about 550,000 sacks, as compared with 1,500,000 sacks last season.

The milling capacity of city mills has remained about stationary, but improved machinery has been introduced, which has really increased the ability of the mills to turn out goods.

Reducing the rough rice to barrels of clean (three sacks to the barrel) the record of crops for a series of years past is as follows:—

Year.	Total Crop.
	Barrels.
1890-91	386,561
1891-92	450,999
1892-93	664,139
1893-94	313,466
1894-95	264,946
1895-96	442,528
1896-97	150,649

Prices ruled much higher than during the preceding season, rough rice bringing on an average of 6s. 2d. per barrel more than the preceding year. Clean rice also brought very much higher prices, and the better grades were very scarce for a large part of the season.

The quality of the rice was, on the whole, good. The main cause of the poor crop of 1896-97 was the long drought.

Whilst reporting on the cotton trade of New Orleans, I have thought it necessary to allude, in a general way, to the whole crop of the Southern States, by which only a proper estimate can be made.

Cotton.

According to the last annual report of Mr. Hester, the Secretary of the New Orleans Cotton Exchange, the cotton crop of the United States for the year ending August 31, 1897, amounts to 8,757,964 bales, showing an increase over the crop of 1895-96 of 1,600,618, a decrease under that of 1894-95 of 1,143,287, and an increase over that of 1893-94 of 1,208,147 bales. Five-sixths of the excess was in the groups known as the "other Gulf and Atlantic States," Texas (including Indian territory) showing an increase in round figures of 258,000 bales, the Gulf States (Arkansas, Louisiana, Mississippi, and Tennessee) of 669,000, and the Atlantic States (Alabama, Georgia, Florida, North Carolina, and South Carolina) of 674,000 bales.

No unusual or startling features have been developed in the course of the market, and although the year's production was larger than generally expected, after the disastrous results of the extreme hot weather, and drought of July and August, and the trade and financial outlook in this country were generally unsatisfactory, these were offset by the fact that prices kept unusually steady.

Cotton prices.

Based on a fair average for the United States, the highest point touched was $8\frac{1}{8}$ c. ($4\frac{1}{4}d.$) per lb., and the lowest $6\frac{1}{16}$ c.; the average for the season being $7\frac{32}{100}$ c. ($3\frac{3}{4}d.$). Both the extremes noted were exceptional, the general range having been between 7 c. and $7\frac{3}{4}$ c. per lb. The average commercial value of the crop has been 36 dol. 76 c. (7l. 11s. $7\frac{1}{2}d.$) per bale, against 41 dol. 9 c. (8l. 9s. 2d.) last year, 30 dol. (6l. 3s. 9d.) year before last, and 37 dol. 50 c. (7l. 14s. $8\frac{1}{2}d.$) in 1893-94, and the total value of the crop compares with the past five years as follows:—

COMMERCIAL Crop.

Year.	Quantity.	Value.
	Bales.	£
1896-97	8,757,954	68,384,966
1895-96	7,157,346	58,819,069
1894-95	9,901,251	59,407,506
1893-94	7,549,817	56,623,627
1892-93	6,700,365	56,953,102
1891-92	9,035,379	67,765,342

Cotton growth.

As was the case last year, this year's commercial crop contained part of the growths of three seasons.

In considering the actual growth of the current year, Mr. Hester, Secretary of the New Orleans Cotton Exchange, arrives at the following calculation:—

	Quantity.
	Bales.
Commercial crop of 1896-97	8,758,000
Less old cotton left over from 1895-96	165,000
	8,593,000
Plus growth of 1896-97, marketed in 1895-96	166,000
Grown, not marketed in 1896-97	100,000
	8,859,000
Deduct August receipts of new cotton of the growth season 1897-98	84,000
Actual growth of 1896-97	8,775,000

Showing, as it happens, a difference between the commercial crop and actual growth of only 17,000 bales. The stocks of old cotton left over in the South on plantations, at counted and uncounted towns, and in the hands of Southern spinners, aggregate less than at this time for years. The Southern country has seldom been so depleted of its cotton. As a general thing, from $2\frac{1}{2}$ to 3 per cent. of the crop can be counted as being left over; this year there is but little more than 1 per cent.

The following table shows the amount of cotton, in bales, exported from New Orleans to the principal European countries, from August 1, 1896, to July 31, 1897, inclusive:—

New Orleans, export of cotton.

Country.	Quantity.		Value.
	Bales.	Lbs.	£
England..	850,704	426,977,670	6,147,409
France ...	431,770	217,229,891	3,102,320
Germany	384,392	192,587,361	2,779,874
Italy ..	157,754	77,461,274	1,124,947
Spain ..	80,552	39,124,456	595,863
Ireland ..	31,622	15,867,667	205,223
Belgium..	26,766	13,653,577	195,627
Total	1,963,560	982,901,896	14,151,263

TOTAL Exports of the United States.

Year.	Quantity.				Total.
	Great Britain.	France.	Continent and Channel.	Canada, Overland.	
	Bales.	Bales.	Bales.	Bales.	Bales.
1896-97	3,018,462	702,632	2,250,289	80,617	6,052,000
1895-96	2,299,182	465,870	1,861,116	81,040	4,707,208
1894-95	3,443,574	774,476	2,500,911	99,316	6,818,277
1893-94	2,859,114	587,299	1,775,784	65,690	5,287,887

Included under Continent are exports to Mexico, Japan, and China, which amount to:—

30,180 against 39,298 last year from Southern ports to Mexico; and 61,106 from San Francisco, Portland, and other ports to Japan and China, as against 37,578 last year.

For the first time in its history, the cotton consumption of the South has passed the million bale mark, the returns by Southern cotton mills for the year closed showing as the total number of bales consumed, 1,042,671, an increase of 137,970, as against 1895-96. As a whole there is cause for satisfaction at the general results of the year's business. In face of two successive seasons of trade depression and uncertainty, the cotton spindles of the South have increased in round numbers 675,000, or say 21 per cent.; while the aggregate of the bales consumed is greater by 180,000, equal to 25 per cent.

Cotton consumption of the South. Mills, &c.

The following table shows the progress made during the past eight years:—

UNITED STATES.

Year.	Consumption.	Increase.	Decrease.
	Bales.	Bales.	Bales.
1889-90	546,894	65,719	..
1890-91	604,661	57,767	..
1891-92	686,080	81,419	..
1892-93	743,848	57,768	..
1893-94	718,515	..	25,333
1894-95	862,838	144,323	..
1895-96	904,701	41,863	..
1896-97	1,042,671	137,970	..

Net increase in eight years, 561,496 bales.

The record for the past year does not indicate so great an impetus in the building of new mills, a natural consequence, perhaps, of the uncertainties incident to a national election year.

MILLS.

	Number.
Total number of mills last year	475
Crossed out, merged into other concerns, and burned	12
	463
New and uncompleted mills added to list	19
Total number of cotton mills in the South	482

Last year the number of mills added was 55.

SPINDLES.

	Number.
In the South, total in operation	3,419,663
,, idle	143,148
New, not completed	289,180
Grand total	3,851,991

This shows an increase of spindles, old, idle, and not complete, over last year of 158,753, and a gain of spindles at work during more or less of the past year of 463,267.

The total consumption in all the mills (old and new) for the year was 1,042,671 bales, against 904,701 for the season of 1895-96, and 862,838 for that of 1894-95, an increase over last year of 137,970 bales, and over the year before of 179,833.

NEW ORLEANS.

CONSUMPTION United States. (American Cotton.)

	Quantity.	
	1896–97.	1895–96.
	Bales.	Bales.
Total consumption in United States	2,847,351	2,504,972
Of which—		
Taken by spinners in Southern States	1,042,671	904,701
,, ,, Northern States	1,804,680	1,600,271

Mr. Hester's, Secretary of the New Orleans Cotton Exchange, latest analysis of the cotton movement for the four months of the season from September 1 to December 31, inclusive, shows that, compared with the crop movement of 1894, Texas, including Indian territory, has brought into sight this season, in round figures, 272,000 bales less, while other Gulf States, which include Arkansas, Louisiana, Mississippi, Tennessee, Missouri, Oklahoma, have marketed 205,000 more, and the group of South Atlantic States, which includes North and South Carolina, Georgia, Florida, Alabama, and Virginia, show an increase of 332,000, in other words, all the States outside of Texas and Indian territory have increased over the big crop year 537,000, against a decrease for Texas and the Indian territory of 272,000, which leaves the net increase in the total crop marketed of 265,000.

Mr. Hester's latest returns of cotton, from September 1 to December 31, 1897.

There has, further, been exported to Europe so far this season, 6,137,144 bales of cotton, as against 5,838,567 bales last season.

The countries included in the sales of cotton, and the quantity sold to each are:—

Country.	Quantity.
	Bales.
Great Britain	2,846,717
France	772,096
Continent of Europe	2,518,331

The railroad business of the past year was as follows:—

Railroad business.

UNITED STATES.

1896–97.

	Quantity.	
	Forwarded.	Received.
	Tons.	Tons.
Southern Pacific..	505,783	537,476
Texas and Pacific	175,993	420,629
Illinois Central ..	249,544	1,134,769
Louisville and Nashville	272,278	334,645
New Orleans and North Eastern	198,148	369,009
Yazoo and Mississippi Valley ..	99,095	474,843
Minor roads	30,000	130,000
Total	1,530,841	3,401,371

The railroad business is steadily increasing, and the importance of New Orleans as a railroad centre is becoming more marked, as the following table shows:—

Year.	Quantity.		Total.
	Forwarded.	Received.	
	Tons.	Tons.	Tons.
1889–90	1,486,516	1,969,681	3,456,197
1890–91	1,491,226	2,064,516	3,555,742
1891–92	1,452,600	2,398,368	3,850,968
1892–93	1,403,538	2,554,484	3,958,022
1893–94	1,412,541	2,601,531	4,014,072
1894–95	1,374,667	2,731,932	4,106,599
1895–96	1,386,378	3,129,815	4,516,193
1896–97	1,530,841	3,401,371	4,932,212

Street railways. New Orleans has, during the last three years, been engaged in the task of changing its street railroad line from the old slow mule car system to electricity. This has been a very expensive task, costing between 2,400,000*l.* and 3,000,000*l.* The work is now practically completed, and the street car system of the city challenges comparison with any in the country. There is hardly likely to be any material increase in the street railroad mileage for some years, as it is sufficient for the present needs of the city.

The present condition of the several street railroads is as follows:—

Lines.	Track Miles, Electric Lines.
New Orleans and Carrollton	15·32
Crescent City	50·18
New Orleans, City and Lake	57·05
St. Charles Street	16·04
Orleans	9·62
Canal and Claiborne	14·65
Total	162·86

There are also one steam road and three small lines operated by mules, which bring the total mileage up to 170 miles.

The wharves, at present, are leased to the Louisiana Construction Company, the lease expiring in 1901. It is generally admitted that the city would be glad if it could get rid of the wharf lease, and it is now aiming to do so. A dock commission was created by the legislature in 1896, having control of the wharves, with the understanding that it would seek in some way to secure them for the city, and then establish some system that would allow them to be used free. Although the task is a difficult one, it is confidently expected that New Orleans will ultimately enjoy the blessing of free wharfage.

In the meanwhile, the Illinois Central Railway Company has, at considerable expense, carried out its pledge of free wharves, building at the foot of General Taylor Street a handsome system of wharves, warehouses, and grain elevators under the name of the Stuyvesant Docks. The wharves are everywhere in a fair condition except between Canal and Julia Streets, where new stringers and planks are wanted.

A dredge-boat has been contracted for by the wharf lessees, and they have promised that the 25 feet of water at the wharves called for by their contract will be secured long before it is needed by the shipping.

The private wharves of the Illinois Central Railway Company, at Stuyvesant Docks; of the Southern Pacific, at Algiers and Gretna; the Texas and Pacific, at Westwego; the North Eastern, the New Orleans and Western, at Port Chalmette, have all been recently improved and put in good condition for business.

PERCENTAGE of Deaths for the Year ending December 31, 1897.

Description.	Estimated Population.	Number of Deaths.	Rate per 1,000.
Whites	195,000	4,268	21·89
Coloured	80,000	2,462	30·77
Total	275,000	6,730	24·47

UNITED STATES.

Taking the population of New Orleans at 275,000 inhabitants, the mortality for the past year was 24·47 per 1,000. There died in New Orleans in 1897 some 6,730 persons, and it is pleasing to note that the mortality, in spite of the yellow fever, was less, as compared with the 7,594 deaths of the previous year.

The reasons given for this improvement, under adverse circumstances, are:—better garbage system, the paving of streets, and the improved sanitary condition of the city in general.

The number of deaths from yellow fever reached 298.

Dr. Loeber's report on the yellow fever in the Touro Infirmary contains an interesting statement, viz., that there were four students and 15 nurses engaged in tending the yellow fever patients (numbering some 105) in the infirmary; that not one of the 19 was immune, and yet none caught the disease. He says still further that, of 100 or so patients other than yellow fever sufferers and attendants, there was not one who became infected.

The following table gives the principal causes of deaths:—

Description.	Number of Deaths.
Yellow fever	298
Pneumonia	365
Bright's disease	368
Malarial fevers	206
Senile debility	233
Old age	36
Cholera infantum	175
Enteritis	221
Cancer	169
Bronchitis	166
Typhoid	141
Diarrhœa	87
Dysentery	62
Meningitis	86
Influenza	65
Diphtheria	37
Killed and murdered	37
Infantine debility	77
Apoplexy	192
Accidents	169
Measles	1
Suicides	40
All other causes	3,469
Total, 1897	6,730
„ 1896	7,594

Drainage. Probably by far the most important public project ever undertaken in New Orleans is the drainage of the city, which is now under way. Feeble attempts have been made from time to time to improve its drainage system, but the work heretofore has been mainly patchwork, upon which much money was expended with very little beneficial result to show for it. Five years ago the proposition for a complete drainage system was first broached, and an advisory drainage board was created, a preliminary survey made of the city and a plan of drainage prepared. This called for 1,600,000*l.*, but the largeness of the sum staggered the public of New Orleans, and the drainage proposition made little headway. The present system is very unsatisfactory. It renders the city easily susceptible to rain overflows; makes the soil and the climate damp; it affects public health unfavourably and increases the death-rate. The legislature, in response to the prayers of the people, created a drainage commission, and gave it full power over the drainage system, with the right to issue bonds. The drainage commission advertised the contract, and it is now settled that the National Contracting Company will do the entire work, operating the pumps and other machinery by electricity, for little over 200,000*l.* The Company, which has announced its intention to push the work as fast as possible, has further agreed to employ only home labour, and to pay a minimum wage of 6*s.* 2*d.* a day.

There has been a marked increase in the shipping coming to New Orleans during the year, and the tonnage is larger than for any previous year. There are three facts to be noted with regard to vessels arriving, all of which speak favourably for this port. *Shipping.*

1. That New Orleans has increased its maritime connection, and vessels now run from here to more ports than ever before. Formerly cotton and other goods were shipped to Liverpool, Bremen, or other Great Continental cities, and distributed by them; now they go direct to the minor ports. There have been steamship lines established during the year to Belfast and Dublin, Genoa, Trieste, Copenhagen, and Antwerp.

2. There has been a marked disposition to concentrate the steamships dealing with this port into companies, with fixed schedules, regular dates of leaving, &c. The bulk of the business is now done by the regular lines instead of by "tramps." Thirty years ago there were practically no regular lines. The United States Bureau of Navigation could enumerate only 12 four years ago, but to-day there are 31.

3. The tendency has been to bring larger and better vessels to New Orleans than formerly. There are now in the regular lines doing business with New Orleans: 13 steamers of over 4,000 tons each, two of between 5,000 and 7,000 tons, and two of over 8,000 tons, which would have been regarded as "monsters" a dozen years ago, and there are altogether, including vessels trading with this port, but not belonging to the regular lines, 23 steamers of over 4,000 tons running between New Orleans and other ports.

A special feature of the shipping of New Orleans of recent years has been the increase in the size of vessels coming here, due to the jetties and the deeper water which the harbour now possesses. The larger vessels mean cheaper freight rates. *Size of vessels.*

The coastwise business between New York and New Orleans has shown great activity and improvement during the past year. The placing of the new and fast steamer "Creole," in the Cromwell line, has stimulated an active rivalry between the two New York lines in the matter of speed, and has resulted in reducing the time between the two ports to less than four days. *Coastwise traffic.*

(78)

UNITED STATES.

Jetties.

When the jetties were constructed, it was thought they would afford all the water that would be necessary for the commerce of New Orleans, but it is now seen that they do not suffice for the changes that have taken place. Deeper water is needed for the large vessels which enter this port. With a channel of 32 feet, it is thought the annual tonnage of this city would soon pass the 3,000,000 ton limit. The statistics of last year's commerce are a strong argument in favour of the jettying and improvement of South-west Pass, so as to give the Mississippi Valley a channel of 32 feet to the Gulf.

Shipping figures.

There entered during the year 1897, 1,275 vessels of 1,930,998 tons, and cleared 1,285 vessels of 1,963,040 tons.

This shows an improvement of 19·8 per cent. as compared with the previous year, of 28·2 per cent. compared with 1895, of 26·1 per cent. compared with 1894, and of 35·2 per cent. compared with 1893.

It is interesting to compare the year 1876 (which was in ante-jetty days) with the year 1897, just ended. In 1876, no less than 1,294 vessels entered New Orleans, as compared with 1,275 in 1897; and in number of vessels the commerce of this city was better then than it is to-day, but when the tonnage is considered it is very different. In 1876 it was only 951,737 tons; whereas at the present time it is 1,930,998, or more than twice as much. The vessels entering this port in 1876 averaged 732 tons each; last year they averaged 1,522 tons. The improvement in size, and generally in draft also, has been constant.

The following table shows the increase in number and tonnage of vessels entered and cleared during the past eight years:—

Year.	Cleared. Number of Vessels.	Cleared. Tonnage.	Entered. Number of Vessels.	Entered. Tonnage.
1890	1,193	1,457,879	1,193	1,457,879
1891	1,214	1,544,060	1,212	1,542,267
1892	1,364	1,676,327	1,359	1,667,331
1893	1,266	1,461,561	1,231	1,461,954
1894	1,165	1,511,227	1,146	1,566,642
1895	1,164	1,606,827	1,193	1,615,640
1896	1,205	1,609,759	1,205	1,665,927
1897	1,285	1,963,040	1,275	1,930,998

The following tables, marked Annex A, give various returns in connection with the shipping at the port of New Orleans during the year 1897:—

NEW ORLEANS.

Annex A.—RETURN of all Shipping at the Port of New Orleans during the Year 1897.

ENTERED.

Nationality.	Steam. Number of Vessels.	Steam. Tons.	Sailing. Number of Vessels.	Sailing. Tons.	Total. Number of Vessels.	Total. Tons.
British	466	955,575	...	...	466	955,575
American	187	122,736	17	5,442	204	128,178
Norwegian, &c.	218	110,973	3	2,120	221	113,093
Spanish	58	135,056	3	3,110	61	138,166
German	37	60,281	5	6,707	42	66,988
Italian	3	4,384	4	2,602	7	6,986
French	14	26,814	...	...	14	26,814
Danish	10	18,127	...	...	10	18,127
Mexican	2	1,010	...	...	2	1,010
Dutch	4	9,240	...	...	4	9,240
Portuguese	...	...	11	7,866	11	7,866
Austrian	2	2,035	3	2,814	5	4,849
Russian	...	...	1	363	1	363
Greek	1	1,656	...	...	1	1,656
Total	1,002	1,447,887	47	31,024	1,049	1,478,911
,, for the year preceding	...	...	...	...	1,025	1,294,340

NOTE.—The above figures do not include American coastwise tonnage: 234 vessels of 469,234 tons.

CLEARED.

Nationality.	Steam. Number of Vessels.	Steam. Tons.	Sailing. Number of Vessels.	Sailing. Tons.	Total. Number of Vessels.	Total. Tons.
British	470	967,755	...	...	470	967,755
American	173	109,838	7	2,626	180	112,464
Norwegian, &c.	225	109,121	1	470	226	109,591
Spanish	63	146,834	3	3,029	66	149,863
German	35	56,315	9	12,195	44	68,510
Italian	2	2,739	7	5,172	9	7,911
French	12	22,408	...	...	12	22,408
Danish	11	21,380	...	...	11	21,380
Mexican	3	1,368	...	...	3	1,368
Dutch	4	9,046	...	...	4	9,046
Portuguese	...	...	9	6,513	9	6,513
Austrian	13	23,825	3	2,814	16	26,639
Russian	...	...	1	363	1	363
Greek	1	1,656	...	...	1	1,656
Total	1,012	1,472,285	40	33,182	1,052	1,505,467
,, for the year preceding	...	...	...	...	980	1,282,271

NOTE.—The above figures do not include American coastwise tonnage: 240 vessels of 470,142 tons.

UNITED STATES.

TABLE of British Shipping Entered and Cleared at the Port of New Orleans during the Year 1897, compared with 1896.

ENTERED.

Year.	Steam. Number of Vessels.	Steam. Tons.	Sailing. Number of Vessels.	Sailing. Tons.	Total. Number of Vessels.	Total. Tons.
1897	466	955,575	...	...	466	955,575
1896	395	784,833	4	4,977	399	789,810

NOTE.—71 more ships entered than last year, 1896.

CLEARED.

Year.	Steam. Number of Vessels.	Steam. Tons.	Sailing. Number of Vessels.	Sailing. Tons.	Total. Number of Vessels.	Total. Tons.
1897	470	967,755	...	...	470	967,755
1896	391	773,016	2	2,746	393	775,762

NOTE.—79 more ships cleared than last year, 1896.

CARGOES Carried in British Ships from January 1, 1897, to December 31, 1897.

Articles.		Quantity.
Cotton	Bales..	1,417,800
Cotton products—		
Cotton seed oil-cake	Sacks..	421,080
„ meal	„ ..	988,112
„ soap stock	Barrels	20,845
„ oil..	„ ..	85,802
Corn	Bushels	20,144,172
Wheat	„ ..	10,495,157
Flour	Sacks..	341,057
Cotton seed	„ ..	76,103
Staves	Pieces	7,932,757
Timber	„ ..	1,539,690
	Logs ..	12,158
Lumber	Feet ..	9,602,833
Lard	Packages	121,919
Tallow	Tierces	4,007
Rosin	Barrels	6,174
Molasses	„	24,952
Pig-iron	Tons ..	29,710
Copper	Bars ..	20,562
Lead ore	Sacks..	17,706
Spelter	Plates	96,019
	Tons ..	3,547
Tobacco	Hogsheads	1,792
Cattle, livestock	Head..	1,996

PENSACOLA.

The following are the more important lines of vessels trading between New Orleans and other ports:—

	Number of Vessels.	Tonnage.
West Indian and Pacific line; British; Liverpool and West Indian and South American ports	17	70,638
Harrison line; British; Liverpool	18	60,028
Hamburg-American line; German	11	26,680
Forenede Gulf-Baltic line; Copenhagen	8	15,053
Orthwein's Gulf ports line	44	75,369
Prat's line; Spanish; Barcelona	5	11,108
Head line; British; Belfast	5	18,088
Pinillo's line; Spanish; Barcelona and Genoa	8	25,338
Chargeurs Réunis; French; Havre	3	9,029
Prince line; British; Rotterdam, Antwerp, and Genoa	10	20,876
Larrinaga line; Liverpool	6	10,937
Freitas line; Continental ports	12	19,626
Compania Bilbania line; Mediterranean ports	8	13,480
Elder, Dempster, and Co.; British; Bremen and Antwerp	5	16,866
Holt line; British; Havre	11	18,320
Glynn line; British; Liverpool	8	16,783
La Fleche line; Spanish; Liverpool and Continental ports	3	6,610
Serra line; Spanish; Liverpool	7	12,100
Cuban line; London and Antwerp	4	7,427
Southern Pacific—		
American; New York	12	43,665
American; Texas; Cuban and Central American ports	5	5,497
Total Southern Pacific	17	49,162
Cromwell line; New York	5	10,667

PENSACOLA.

Mr. Vice-Consul Howe reports as follows:—

Respecting the amount and character of the trade of Pensacola during the past year I am able to state that the business of the port exceeded in volume that of the year 1896—referred to in my last annual report as beyond all former years in Pensacola's business annals. *Good business year.*

In the year 1895, under the auspices of the Louisville and Nashville Railroad Company, a line of steamers was established to ply at short intervals between Pensacola and Liverpool, loaded with products from the Western States, in grain, flour, tobacco, and other articles brought here by this railroad. Also to load cotton and other articles coming here from the adjacent Southern States for shipment. These exports have continued to increase, and have been lately further developed and added to by shipments of similar cargoes to the Continent. Among the latest exportations and the new places made available for trade, *Line of steamers.* *Increased exports.*

(78)

Pig-iron and cotton to Japan.

are ports in Japan to which shipments of pig-iron and cotton from the inland southern places, notably, pig-iron, from the manufacturing town of Birmingham, Alabama, have been sent through Pensacola. The large iron British sailing ship, "Lord Wolseley," loaded here nearly a full cargo of pig-iron of 3,000 tons, and the British steamer "Hounslow," cotton and pig-iron, during the year, respectively, for Yokohama and Kobe, Japan.

Grain elevator.

During the past year the Louisville and Nashville Railroad Company added to its other late additions of warehouses and other equipments on its wharves towards facilitating the loading of cargoes to be exported from Pensacola, by erecting a large grain elevator. The structure has a capacity of 500,000 bushels. The building is of wood covered with iron, and cost about 175,000 dol., equal to about 35,000l. The erection of this building, said to be one of the best in this country, not only marks a new era in Pensacola's export trade, but also opens another southern channel through which the grain, wheat, and corn of the West can be sent forward. It is thought that the grain elevator, in connection with two large import and export warehouses on the wharf of the Louisville and Nashville Railroad, will so increase the business of Pensacola as to make it a most formidable rival of the large shipping centres of the north.

Increases, export trade. Another channel for grain exports.

Business compared with former years.

In comparing the business of Pensacola now with that of former years, the onward strides in the trade of the port will be apparent. Until the recent new departures in exports through Pensacola, the only export trade of the place hitherto, with the exception, occasionally, of cotton shipments, was entirely composed of pitch-pine timber, in its various preparations, this wood being obtained from the forests of Florida, and from surrounding timber regions; hence it will be seen how much more important the port now becomes with its new business in exports, which bids fair to grow to very large dimensions.

Port increased in importance.

British interests.

With Pensacola's trade British interests are in many ways concerned. In addition to former, and still as active, trade in exports of pitch-pine cargoes, the bulk of which business has always passed through the hands of British houses at home and abroad, in the new export lines British capitalists and shipowners will also participate.

Coal.

The exports in coal during the past year were about equal to the quantity exported in the year 1896. During the year six British steamers called here to coal. It is expected that in time Pensacola will be a port of call for steamers homeward bound from adjacent ports requiring bunker coal.

Imports. Fruit.

Salt.

Pyrites (sulphur ore).

The imports to Pensacola are rather limited in articles from foreign countries. From some of the British islands in the West Indies cargoes of fruit continue to be received here. From Liverpool a few cargoes of salt are imported yearly. During last year several shipments of pyrites (sulphur ore) were received at Pensacola to go forward to the iron manufacturing town of Birmingham Alabama, to be used in the smelting works there. From Mexico came several shipments of sisal grass, which went forward to factories in the northern and western towns. The chief articles of daily requirement in trade, such as flour, salted meats, dry goods, clothing, liquors, articles of grocery, &c., continue to be imported from the large northern and western markets, as well as from New Orleans and other large southern cities, and amount to several millions of dollars yearly. Among these articles some goods of British manufacture, imported direct by the large houses north and south, find their way to Pensacola. The articles and values of exports and imports from and to foreign countries during the year will be seen among the tables hereto annexed. *Sisal grass. Chief articles.*

British shipping at Pensacola in the year 1897 was up to its highest previous yearly average. British steamers and sailing vessels did the largest proportion of the carrying trade to the United Kingdom and foreign ports during the year. The steamers took each over two tons in cargo to their one ton net register tonnage. *Shipping.*

The population of Pensacola has largely increased within the last few years, and may now be put at between 15,000 and 16,000 inhabitants. As regards the industries of the place there are several steam mills at Pensacola and its vicinity for the manufacture of pitch-pine timber for exportation, as well as for local requirements. A large number of persons are employed in these mills at good daily wages. An important industry at Pensacola is the fishing business. Several firms own fleets of small schooners, which make regular trips out in the Gulf, returning to port when their catch of fish is sufficient. Many of the fish are brought in alive in tanks, and are shipped away to near and distant towns, put up in ice. This business not only gives a handsome return yearly to the capitalists engaged in it, but also provides employment for a large number of persons. There are some cigar factories here, and they use a good deal of the tobacco grown in the tobacco districts of Florida. In unskilled labour the loading of vessels contributes largely to the support of a number of the people by the continued employment throughout the year, in greater or lesser magnitude, as the business goes on, of the men of the different labour societies, both white and coloured, at good daily wages. Those employed in skilled labour, carpenters, masons, workers in iron, &c., appear mostly to find remunerative employment. In fact, as I have from time to time remarked in these reports, the labouring classes at Pensacola appear to move along without privation or visible stint in their regular yearly routine. *Population and industries. Steam saw-mills. Fish business. Cigar factories. Employment in skilled and unskilled labour.*

The health of Pensacola was good during the past year, and particularly may it be noted in this connection that for some weeks at the close of the year yellow fever prevailed at New Orleans, and even at nearer places to Pensacola, but this town escaped the dread disease. *Health.*

A street railway, to be operated by electricity, is now being constructed at Pensacola, which will be an improvement and convenience to the town, taking the place, as it will, of the slow- *General remarks.*

UNITED STATES.

going horse cars hitherto in use. New buildings for private residences, as well as for business purposes, have been built in this town during the past year, and continue to be erected. Financially, the prosperity of the people here seems to be very good.

Agriculture. As there is not sufficient material at this post to warrant a separate report on agriculture, I will only say that Pensacola's suburban growth of fruit and vegetables continues to supply the inhabitants of the town. Also poultry, milch cows, and good milk are in abundance here. Good beef and mutton are obtainable daily, coming here from the western markets, and preserved on arrival in cold storage compartments of the ice factories at Pensacola.

Annex A.—RETURN of Principal Articles of Export from Pensacola during the Years 1897-96.

Articles.		1897. Quantity.	1897. Value. £	1896. Quantity.	1896. Value. £
Pitch-pine lumber	Super. feet	158,013,360	395,033	157,961,584	394,904
Sawn pitch-pine timber	Cubic feet	12,011,290	300,283	11,375,608	284,390
Hewn ,, ,,	,,	339,321	7,774	526,224	12,059
Cotton	Bales	91,011	663,622	51,878	540,396
Tobacco	Hogsheads	7,534	116,778	7,933	122,962
Coal	Tons	118,011	98,337	123,967	103,306
Pig-iron	,,	21,369	44,519	6,091	12,690
Corn	Bushels	424,767	43,742	373,334	38,889
Wheat	,,	219,134	41,088	...	...
Flour	Sacks	17,345	14,454	33,890	28,242
Other articles	...	...	75,265	...	46,277
Total	...	...	1,800,895	...	1,584,115

NOTE.—Exchange: 4 dol. 80 c. per 1*l*.

Annex B.—TABLE showing Total Value of all Articles Exported from and Imported to Pensacola from and to Foreign Countries during the Years 1897–96.

Country.	Exports. 1897.	Exports. 1896.	Imports. 1897.	Imports. 1896.
	£	£	£	£
United Kingdom	1,071,332	892,622	445	825
British possessions	12,798	19,017	450	90
Mexico	93,167	128,140	94,451	15,203
Italy	82,991	51,764	179	21
Netherlands	77,652	57,752	..	..
France	73,075	67,695	..	..
Brazil	55,666	104,547	23	..
Germany	52,460	12,175	5,261	5,021
Japan	50,370	..	..	..
Belgium	34,584	27,934	604	..
Argentine Republic	34,434	55,751	..	..
Egypt	16,674	9,730	..	..
Portugal	14,517	3,560	..	..
Uruguay	11,108	5,165	..	..
Spain and colonies	10,782	28,441	..	2,963
Austria	8,023	9,257	..	..
Russia	2,914	..	..	..
Denmark	2,529	2,758	..	..
Tunis	1,627	2,496	..	..
Venezuela	..	503	..	..
Total to foreign countries	1,706,703	1,479,307	..	..
Total to ports in the United States	94,192	104,808	..	..
Grand total	1,800,895	1,584,115	101,413	24,123

Annex C.—RETURN of all Shipping at the Port of Pensacola during the Year 1897.

ENTERED.

Nationality.	Sailing. Number of Vessels.	Sailing. Tons.	Steam. Number of Vessels.	Steam. Tons.	Total. Number of Vessels.	Total. Tons.
British	40	32,101	98	162,200	138	194,301
American	55	35,408	35	24,976	90	60,384
Swedish and Norwegian	106	100,602	10	10,311	116	110,913
Italian	81	59,498	...	...	81	59,498
Spanish	...	...	20	37,698	20	37,698
German	11	10,406	10	6,628	21	17,034
Russian	24	17,032	...	...	24	17,032
Austrian	5	3,072	2	3,435	7	6,507
Portuguese	6	3,859	...	...	6	3,859
French	4	1,970	1	1,834	5	3,804
Netherlands	1	1,284	2	2,739	3	4,023
Danish	1	765	...	...	1	765
Total	334	265,997	178	249,821	512	515,818
,, for the year preceding	307	233,000	168	225,003	475	458,003

UNITED STATES.

CLEARED.

Nationality.	Sailing. Number of Vessels.	Sailing. Tons.	Steam. Number of Vessels.	Steam. Tons.	Total. Number of Vessels.	Total. Tons
British	42	35,250	97	161,217	139	196,467
American	63	35,911	36	25,090	99	61,001
Swedish and Norwegian	104	99,141	13	14,183	117	113,324
Italian	81	58,637	...	...	81	58,637
Spanish	...	...	21	37,207	21	37,207
German	11	10,422	11	8,391	22	18,813
Russian	25	17,930	...	...	25	17,930
Austrian	4	2,453	3	3,998	7	6,451
Netherlands	1	1,284	2	2,739	3	4,023
French	4	2,070	1	1,834	5	3,904
Portuguese	5	3,334	...	...	5	3,334
Danish	1	765	...	...	1	765
Total	341	267,197	184	254,659	525	521,856
,, for the year preceding	312	246,387	164	226,563	476	472,950

NOTE.—Of the American steamers given above as entered and cleared, the steamship "Pensacola" made 22 trips out loaded with coal to Texas and Mexico. The other steamers were small vessels engaged in towing barges of coal to Mexico and Texas.

MOBILE.

Mr. Vice-Consul Barnewall reports as follows:—

Trade and commerce. The increase in the general business has been most gratifying, and should inspire business men with renewed energy.

Foreign trade. The foreign trade of Mobile one year ago proved to be a record year, but the magnitude of that of the fiscal year ended June 30, 1897, eclipsed that of the year previous by over 3,000,000 dol. (600,000*l*.), 40 per cent. The comparative figures of the trade for the last three fiscal years are here given:—

	Value. 1896–97.	Value. 1895–96.	Value. 1894–95.
	£	£	£
Exports	2,026,230	1,399,215	1,034,460
Imports	169,625	188,115	200,185
Total	2,195,855	1,587,330	1,234,645

Of the exports, England received for the three years 1,284,680*l*., 744,250*l*., 580,660*l*., or 75 per cent. of the exports to Europe, 63 per cent. of the total exports. Germany took about one-third as much.

Cotton, lumber, and timber continue to be the leading articles of export, followed by flour, corn, and wheat. This last-named item appearing for the first time in the export figures:—

Articles.		Quantity.		
		1896–97.	1895–96.	1894–95.
Flour	Barrels ..	26,848	53,644	13,102
Corn	Bushels ..	2,588,730	842,725	75,085
Wheat	,, ..	440,355	..	..

In lumber the increase in the exports shows nearly 10,000,000 feet, half of which went to the United Kingdom. In timber a phenomenal increase is observable in sawn timber, a gain of nearly 3,000,000 cubic feet, there having been a most unprecedented demand throughout the year. Prices ranged from 10 to $12\frac{1}{2}$ c. (5d. to $6\frac{1}{4}d$.) per cubic foot.

Lumber and timber.

Prices.

While the increase shown is very large, there is every reason to believe that during the coming season the bulk of the lumber and timber exports will be even larger than this season, because of the opening of the Mobile, Jackson, and Kansas City Railroad at the beginning of the new season; and there is no doubt that this road will bring to Mobile thousands of feet of lumber and timber for export during the next season. It is destined to become an important factor in the upbuilding of Mobile's lumber and timber trade, for it traverses one of the finest bodies of virgin timber in the south, the natural outlet of which is at the port of Mobile.

Last year's net receipts of cotton were: 209,876 bales, average weight 499·62 lbs., price per lb. 7·84 c. For the season just closed: 303,608 bales, average weight 507·35 lbs., price 7·10 c. The value of receipts last year, 1,644,165l.; this year, 2,187,305l.

Cotton.

COMPARATIVE Receipts for Two Years.

Grain and feed.

Articles.	Quantity.	
	1896–97.	1895–96.
	Sacks.	Sacks.
Corn	1,276,868	751,378
Oats	136,108	113,369
Wheat	232,697	..

In staves there is a heavy increase, 366,425 pieces in 1896–97, against 147,978 in 1895–96.

Staves.

Of the imports, fruits form a leading feature; bananas, cocoa-nuts, pine-apples, oranges, lemons, and plantains.

Fruits.

The total number of vessels up and down the channel is reported: steamships, 644; ships and barks, 288; schooners, 224. Vessels drawing 13 to 23 feet continue to go down the channel

Shipping.

Iron and coal.

without material detention. There is a six-sectional dry dock capable of handling a 1,000 ton vessel.

The growth of the manufacture of iron and the production of coal in the south, though of comparatively recent date, is none the less interesting and striking. In 1880 the south made 397,000 tons of pig-iron; in 1896, out of a total production of 1,700,000 tons, Alabama produced more than half. The first pig-iron of any consequence produced in Alabama was in 1872, in which year the total production of the State was 11,171 tons. The production in 1880 was 68,925 tons; in 1885, 203,069 tons; in 1890, 816,911 tons; in 1895, not including charcoal iron, 854,667 tons.

Pig-iron.

Coal.

The production of coal in Alabama was:—

Year.	Quantity.
	Tons.
In 1870	11,000
1875	67,200
1880	380,000
1885	2,492,000
1890	4,090,409
1896	5,745,617

The output of coal in the Southern States in 1895 was 33,198,694 tons, including West Virginia—Alabama producing, as will therefore be seen, more than one-sixth. The total production of the United States was about 180,000,000 tons, the South producing about 15 per cent.

Alabama stands to-day fourth as an iron-producing State in this country, the product of Illinois (which is third) for 1896 exceeding that of Alabama by only about 3,000 tons. In the production of iron ore Alabama stands third. One of the most notable features in connection with the manufacture of iron in Alabama is the nearness of the material entering into its manufacture, and the apparent inexhaustible supply of same.

These industrial developments could not have been possible without a great growth of another interest in the South, that is the railroad interest. Since 1880, the mileage has been increased by the addition of over 25,000 miles. Over 200,000,000*l.* has been spent in building new roads and the improvement of old ones; cheaper transportation, from 60 to 80 per cent., has resulted.

MOBILE.

Annex A.—RETURN of all Shipping at the Port of Mobile during the Year 1897.

ENTERED.

Nationality.	Sailing. Number of Vessels.	Sailing. Tons.	Steam. Number of Vessels.	Steam. Tons.	Total. Number of Vessels.	Total. Tons.
British	77	28,576	74	118,714	151	147,290
Norwegian	61	61,035	159	73,500	220	134,535
American	48	18,185	...	...	48	18,185
Russian	12	6,743	...	...	12	6,743
Italian	9	5,801	...	...	9	5,801
Dutch	1	1,369	...	...	1	1,369
Austrian	...	...	1	1,360	1	1,360
Turkish	1	612	...	...	1	612
German	...	...	3	1,717	3	1,717
Swedish	5	4,757	...	...	5	4,757
French	1	452	...	...	1	452
Colombian	...	...	1	229	1	229
Total	215	127,530	238	195,520	453	323,050
Coastwise	...	...	...	...	28	16,555
Grand total	...	...	...	...	481	339,605
Total for the year preceding	...	...	...	...	478	355,447

CLEARED.

Nationality.	Sailing. Number of Vessels.	Sailing. Tons.	Steam. Number of Vessels.	Steam. Tons.	Total. Number of Vessels.	Total. Tons.
British	76	31,724	76	120,456	152	152,180
Norwegian	61	59,132	168	83,128	229	142,260
American	42	14,748	1	428	43	15,176
French	1	452	...	...	1	452
Turkish	1	612	...	...	1	612
Dutch	2	2,820	...	...	2	2,820
Italian	11	8,599	...	...	11	8,599
Russian	14	7,166	...	...	14	7,166
Swedish	4	3,642	...	...	4	3,642
Danish	1	450	...	...	1	450
Austrian	...	...	1	1,360	1	1,360
German	1	1,352	3	1,717	4	3,069
Total	214	130,697	249	207,089	463	337,786
Coastwise	...	...	...	...	32	16,873
Grand total	...	...	...	...	495	354,659
Total for the year preceding	...	...	...	...	482	360,343

LONDON:
Printed for Her Majesty's Stationery Office,
By HARRISON AND SONS,
Printers in Ordinary to Her Majesty.
(75 2 | 98—H & S 78)

FOREIGN OFFICE.
1898.
ANNUAL SERIES.

Nº. 2031.

DIPLOMATIC AND CONSULAR REPORTS ON TRADE AND FINANCE.

UNITED STATES.

REPORT FOR THE YEAR 1897
ON THE
TRADE OF CHARLESTON AND DISTRICT.

REFERENCE TO PREVIOUS REPORT, Annual Series No. 1857.

Presented to both Houses of Parliament by Command of Her Majesty,
FEBRUARY, 1898.

LONDON:
PRINTED FOR HER MAJESTY'S STATIONERY OFFICE,
BY HARRISON AND SONS, ST. MARTIN'S LANE,
PRINTERS IN ORDINARY TO HER MAJESTY.

And to be purchased, either directly or through any Bookseller, from
EYRE & SPOTTISWOODE, EAST HARDING STREET, FLEET STREET, E.C., and
32, ABINGDON STREET, WESTMINSTER, S.W.; or
JOHN MENZIES & Co., 12, HANOVER STREET, EDINBURGH, and
90, WEST NILE STREET, GLASGOW; or
HODGES, FIGGIS, & Co., Limited, 104, GRAFTON STREET, DUBLIN.

1898.

[C. 8648—53.] *Price Twopence Halfpenny.*

New Series of Reports.

Reports of the Annual Series have been issued from Her Majesty's Diplomatic and Consular Officers at the following places, and may be obtained from the sources indicated on the title-page:—

No.		Price.	No.		Price.
1911.	Rio Grande do Sul	3½d.	1971.	Yokohama	1½d.
1912.	Quito	1d.	1972.	Warsaw	½d.
1913.	San José	1d.	1973.	Sofia	1½d.
1914.	Dunkirk	1d.	1974.	Madrid	2d.
1915.	Samoa	1d.	1975.	Vienna	2d.
1916.	Bordeaux	2½d.	1976.	Erzeroum	1d.
1917.	Porto Rico	1½d.	1977.	Berlin	1½d.
1918.	Galatz	1½d.	1978.	Adis Abbaba	1d.
1919.	Christiania	½d.	1979.	Tamsui	1d.
1920.	Copenhagen	3d.	1980.	Odessa	2½d.
1921.	New York	2½d.	1981.	Brindisi	2½d.
1922.	San Francisco	3½d.	1982.	Macao	1d.
1923.	Kiukiang	1d.	1983.	Pakhoi	1d.
1924.	Harrar	½d.	1984.	Peking	2d.
1925.	Berne	1½d.	1985.	Mexico	1½d.
1926.	Mannheim	1d.	1986.	Canton	1d.
1927.	Fiume	1½d.	1987.	Naples	1½d.
1928.	Oporto	1d.	1988.	Port Said	1½d.
1929.	Hangchow	1d.	1989.	Algiers	3½d.
1930.	Boston	2½d.	1990.	Vienna	1d.
1931.	Tahiti	1d.	1991.	Valparaiso	1½d.
1932.	Manila	1½d.	1992.	Gothenburg	2½d.
1933.	Caracas	1d.	1993.	St. Michael's (The Azores)	1d.
1934.	Hamburg	3d.	1994.	Antwerp	1d.
1935.	Portland	3d.	1995.	Tangier	1½d.
1936.	Malaga	2½d.	1996.	Swaziland	1d.
1937.	Tokio	1½d.	1997.	Swatow	1d.
1938.	Genoa	3d.	1998.	St. Petersburg	4½d.
1939.	Palermo	3d.	1999.	Dar-al-Baida	1½d.
1940.	Santiago de Cuba	1½d.	2000.	Dantzig	2d.
1941.	Noumea	1d.	2001.	Algiers	1½d.
1942.	Frankfort	3½d.	2002.	Rome	2d.
1943.	Chungking	1½d.	2003.	Bangkok	1d.
1944.	Ichang	1d.	2004.	Nagasaki	1d.
1945.	Hankow	1½d.	2005.	Hiogo and Osaka	1½d.
1946.	Guatemala	1½d.	2006.	Jeddah	2d.
1947.	Syra	1d.	2007.	Paris	1d.
1948.	Taganrog	2d.	2008.	Meshed	2½d.
1949.	Loanda	2½d.	2009.	Chiengmai	1½d.
1950.	Panama	2½d.	2010.	Stettin	1½d.
1951.	Shanghai	2d.	2011.	Vera Cruz	1d.
1952.	Aleppo	1½d.	2012.	Kiungchow	1d.
1953.	Ispahan	1½d.	2013.	Christiania	2½d.
1954.	Tonga	1d.	2014.	Warsaw	1d.
1955.	Nice	1d.	2015.	Hakodate	1d.
1956.	Granada	1d.	2016.	Buda-Pesth	2d.
1957.	Söul	1d.	2017.	Batoum	1d.
1958.	Cadiz	1½d.	2018.	Bushire	2d.
1959.	Chinde	½d.	2019.	Tegucigalpa	½d.
1960.	Stockholm	2d.	2020.	Montevideo	1d.
1961.	Zanzibar	1d.	2021.	Tainan	1d.
1962.	Tokio	1½d.	2022.	Copenhagen	½d.
1963.	Asuncion	1½d.	2023.	Odessa	1½d.
1964.	Baghdad	1½d.	2024.	Munich	1½d.
1965.	Réunion	1d.	2025.	Valparaiso	1½d.
1966.	Chefoo	2½d.	2026.	Berlin	2½d.
1967.	Newchwang	1d.	2027.	Rouen	1½d.
1968.	Tabreez	½d.	2028.	Stockholm	1½d.
1969.	St. Paul de Loanda	1d.	2029.	Belgrade	1½d.
1970.	Beyrout	1d.	2030.	New Orleans	2d.

No. 2031.

Reference to previous Report, Annual Series No. 1857.

UNITED STATES.

CHARLESTON.

Consul de Coëtlogon to the Marquess of Salisbury.

(Received at Foreign Office, February 3, 1898.)

My Lord,

I HAVE the honour to forward herewith my Annual Trade Report and those of Brunswick and Wilmington Vice-Consulates, also Annual Return of British Shipping at Charleston, S.C., for 1897.

I have, &c.
(Signed)   H. DE COËTLOGON.

Report on the Trade and Commerce of the Consular District of Charleston for the Year 1897.

TABLE of Contents.

	PAGE
Charleston—	
General remarks	1
Cotton	6
Phosphates and fertilisers	9
Rice	13
Naval stores	15
Lumber	17
Fruits and vegetables	19
Shipping and navigation	21
Miscellaneous	24
Brunswick, Ga.	26
Wilmington	30

The total trade and commerce of the port of Charleston during the commercial year of 1896–97, which ended August 31, 1897, amounted to 75,740,261 dol., which, compared with 67,265,129 dol. for the previous year, shows an increase last season of 8,475,132 dol.; a review of the official figures indicates

Total trade and commerce.

an increase in cotton trade of 4,459,000 dol.; in fertilisers, 1,272,491 dol., and in the wholesale trade of 2,132,000 dol.

Increase. In the yearly exports the gain was equal to about 28 per cent., and the imports were nearly double those of the year before. The improvement thus shown while material in itself is, nevertheless, considerably less than was anticipated from the favourable indications at the beginning of the year, the total results being considerably below Charleston's highest trade year of 1890-91, when the volume of business aggregated 98,000,000 dol.

British shipping, which handles most of the foreign exports from this port, also shared proportionately in last year's moderate increase, as will be seen by reference to the annual return of British shipping at Charleston for 1897, attached to this report; the arrivals last year being 72 vessels with a net tonnage of 119,118 tons, compared with 56 ships of 78,859 tonnage the previous year.

Decreased trade. On the other hand, there was some falling-off in the value of trade in several other branches of regular business, but it is observed that the decline was more in prices realised than in amount of trade done. Charleston has not yet, however, recovered from the ill-effects of the general trade depression that has prevailed throughout the Southern States for the past five years.

Causes of decrease. The business of the port was also considerably hampered and restricted during the months of September, October, and November last, owing to the rigid quarantine regulations which were adopted by the local authorities in order to guard against the introduction of yellow fever from the several Mexican Gulf coast towns, where it existed in an epidemic form during the months mentioned; the embargo placed on persons and freight having the effect of diverting much business to competing ports with less rigorous quarantine rules, which, under other circumstances, would probably have come here in the regular course o trade.

Yellow fever quarantine regulations.

Low cotton prices. Low prices for cotton that prevailed during last October and November also contributed to lessen the export business of the port, limiting the demand for foreign shipping, and causing freight rates to be unusually dull during several of the best weeks of the cotton season. Luckily, however, the dulness in cotton freights was, to some extent, offset by the securing of several contracts of Western grain and flour by Charleston railways and shipbrokers which enabled them to load cargoes according to charters without serious inconvenience or delay to ship-interests.

First grain exports. It may be worthy of mention that these grain exports were the first shipments of the kind that have ever been made from Charleston to foreign countries, and they have brought into use this season, for the first time, the new grain elevator of the South Carolina and Georgia Railway Company, which was alluded the British steamer "Verbena," which cleared from the Charleston custom-house for Liverpool with a cargo of wheat, pig-iron, and cotton on October 22, 1897; this shipment was followed later by other mixed cargoes of wheat, flour, pig-iron, and cotton for Liverpool and Bremen.

The aggregate grain shipments, however, from Charleston do not as yet form a very important item in the year's business, so far as comparative quantity and values are concerned, but they are significant as the starting point of a new branch of industry, and also as being the realisation of what has been a commercial dream of this community for many years past; indeed it has been impossible for Charleston to handle Western grain with profit until the recent completion of the jetties gave a deep water entrance to the harbour capable of accommodating grain-loaded ships.

It is a source of gratification to report that there has been a still further increase in the depth of water on Charleston Bar during the past year; the official figures furnished to the public by Captain F. V. Abbot, late United States Engineer in charge of the jetty works here, September 1, 1897, giving the maximum depth of $24\frac{1}{4}$ feet, from deep water inside the harbour, to the deep sea outside the bar, an increase of nearly a foot since the previous year. *Increased water on Charleston Bar.*

The only inconvenience that shipping now appear to have is in the insufficient water in some of the city docks, several vessels having lately grounded in the soft mud in the docks so firmly that it required the assistance of one or more tugs in order to float them out of dock into the stream when loaded and ready for sea. *Too little water in the docks.*

This matter will doubtless be remedied by proper dredging operations before another season, unless it is deemed more advisable to extend the present docks to deep water further out in the stream, where there is an abundance of water for the class of ships now coming here.

As usual British shipping has maintained the position it has held for many years, as first in the foreign carrying trade from this port, and has perhaps derived some additional advantage recently from the noticeable falling-off in arrivals of Spanish sailing vessels, owing to the Cuban difficulties and the possibility of war between the United States and Spain, which had a naturally disturbing effect on the commercial relations of the two countries. A few Italian vessels, mostly small sized sailing craft, with two or three steamers as exceptions, continue yearly to take cargoes, and occasionally a Norwegian, German, or Austrian flag is to be seen; but, as stated, the bulk of the business continues to be done n British bottoms; the local coastwise carrying trade excepted, which is still in the hands of American vessels under existing navigation laws. *British shipping leads.*

The continued growth of the cotton manufacturing industry in the States of South Carolina, North Carolina, and Georgia, situated in this Consular district, continues to attract the attention of those interested in this business, and some facts are herewith *Cotton manufacturing.*

(79)

UNITED STATES.

given from the most recently published reports furnishing statistics on the subject. South Carolina is now operating more spindles than any of the other Southern States, North Carolina being second and Georgia standing third on the list.

South Carolina. At the end of 1897 South Carolina had in operation 54 cotton mills with nearly 1,000,000 spindles, and consuming yearly 148,767,042 lbs. of cotton, equal to about 327,000 bales, or say 40 per cent. of the total crop produced in the State during the year, estimating the same at 800,000 bales in round numbers.

North Carolina. North Carolina had 150 mills; the total number of spindles, however, was smaller, but will probably reach 1,000,000 also when mills now being built are completed. Roughly speaking, therefore, it may be said that the two Carolinas have, at the end of 1897, each about 1,000,000 spindles and 25,000 looms in actual operation manufacturing cotton goods.

Total Southern mills. The relative growth and importance of the industry is apparent from the fact that the total number of cotton mills in the Southern States are 375 mills with 3,197,000 spindles, and manufacturing 500,000,000 lbs. of raw cotton yearly. This shows that the Carolinas have nearly double the number of mills and spindles of all the other States in the South combined, and consuming about three-fifths of the yearly quantity of raw cotton taken by Southern mills.

Georgia. Georgia, which is by far the most important other Southern State manufacturing cotton, after the Carolinas, has a number of splendidly equipped mills and abundant water-power at Augusta and Columbus, and in that State are situated most of the cotton mills and spindles not above enumerated in the figures given for the Carolinas; the three States combined practically embracing the principal cotton manufacturing industries of the South.

Woollen mills, &c. In addition to the foregoing cotton mills there are also, at present in North Carolina, the following other textile manufacturing establishments, namely: 16 woollen mills with 5,038 spindles, and 234 looms; 25 cotton hosiery mills with 1,410 knitting machines; four bleacheries and four dyeing and finishing mills; but there are no woollen mills as yet in South Carolina.

Tobacco. The South Carolina tobacco crop is grown principally in the counties of Florence, Sumter, Clarendon, Williamsburg, and Darlington, situated in the Peedee section of the State. This crop has become, within the past two or three years, one of the three staple annual products of which cotton and corn are the other two.

Tobacco Boards of Trade have been organised in the towns of Florence and Timmonsville, well-equipped warehouses have been established at Darlington, and experienced men from the North Carolina and Virginia tobacco districts are now engaged in the management of the new and growing South Carolina industry.

New crop. The tobacco crop of 1897 commenced to be marketed in September last, and this feature of the business was attended with less difficulty to planters than had heretofore been the case owing to previous want of experience and acquaintance with curing, grading, and methods of selling advantageously at warehouse auction sales.

Growers this season are, more than ever, sellers, and as the building up of home tobacco markets, with the consequent advantages resulting therefrom to the growth of tobacco in this State, must necessarily depend much on the planters themselves, it is obvious that great benefit is derived from good local markets where growers can easily haul their own products to warehouses, sell, store, or return them home should quotations for the day be low, or other unsatisfactory conditions exist at the time ; moreover, freight rates to distant points are thus avoided, together with the drawbacks and inconveniences of making preliminary arrangements and dealing with strangers.

Home markets.

Advantages.

Taken altogether, the present status of the new industry in South Carolina is satisfactory, and prospects for future growth seem encouraging and appear deserving of the attention it is receiving from capitalists and planters alike, inasmuch as it is what is called a money crop ; always convertible, like cotton, into cash in the markets of the world.

Satisfactory conditions.

Reference has been made on several occasions in reports from this Consulate to the experimental tea farm conducted by Dr. Charles U. Shepard, at Pinehurst, near Summerville, South Carolina, 22 miles from Charleston, under the auspices of the United States Government.

Tea raising.

The results appear to show that it is possible, under such careful cultivation as Dr. Shepard has given to the plants under his charge, to produce in this climate a fairly good quality of tea so far as appearances go. The product of the South Carolina farm has been sold in this city for two or three years for 1 dol. per lb. (equal to about 4s.). The beverage made from this article, however, had a slightly yellowish, muddy colour, and a somewhat weedy taste to the palates of the writer and several of his friends who had tried it, in comparison with the ordinary grades of Chinese and Ceylon teas sold in this market.

Qualities.

During the past year, Secretary Wilson, of the Agricultural Department of the United States, received an interesting report from an accomplished horticulturist whom he sent to Summerville to investigate the Carolina tea industry with the view of ascertaining the prospects of profitably growing the tea plant in this country should it be decided to introduce it as an industry.

The report states that the labour question is the most important one to be considered in the matter. It is estimated that it costs about eight times as much to pick 1 lb. of tea in South Carolina as it does in China or Japan. The profitable production of the leaf also depends upon the amount of rainfall and the moisture in the soil. In districts where there is sufficient heat and rain, the plants yield from 15 to 20 pickings yearly.

Labour question.

In the South Carolina fields which were inspected the conservation of moisture, by drainage, was increased by systematic surface culture which prevented, to a considerable extent, the evaporation of moisture from the upper stratum of soil, and

UNITED STATES.

a gain equivalent to about 10 to 15 inches of rainfall is thus secured.

Cultivation costly. It would seem from this that it is hardly practicable to successfully compete with cheap Oriental labour, notwithstanding the fact that some of the processes here have been done by machinery; the picking of the leaves, however, requires discrimination in selection and must be done by hand.

It was ingeniously sought to meet the difficulties of the labour problem on the Carolina tea farm by establishing a small coloured school, and tea picking was included in the curriculum, and the **Negro instruction schools.** young negro scholars, after some instruction, proved to be fairly good pickers. Only the most delicate leaves were selected in order to compete more readily with the imported article. Choice seeds were brought from all foreign countries, especial care being **Vegetation of plants.** taken to select specimens from high altitudes. In the experiments at Summerville a germination of one-third the seeds was considered a good average, and the total loss of an entire importation of seeds would occasionally occur. The most promising variety used here was brought from Darjeeling and came from an elevation of about 3,000 feet, and combined hardiness with a good-sized and delicate leaf. With the careful pruning and treatment received the report seems to indicate that the plants on the Carolina farm should have **Vigour of plants short lived.** maintained their original strength and vigour for 40 years instead of four as was the case; and careful pruning is well known to be the most costly process in the manipulation of the plant.

Prospects. As to the future of tea raising in the United States, the report goes on to show that the promoter of the Carolina farm still has great faith in the ultimate success of tea culture in this country, and urges the establishment of schools of instruction for the development of knowledge as to the proper methods of profitable tea culture.

Cotton.
Receipts. During the last cotton year of 1896–97, ending August 31, 1897, the total receipts of all grades of cotton at the port of Charleston were 403,326 bales, compared with 292,336 bales for the previous year, showing an increase for last season of 110,990 **Prices.** bales. The highest prices paid during the year were 8 c. per lb. for middling uplands on September 10, 1896, and the lowest figures for the same class of cotton were $6\frac{1}{2}$ c. on December 14, 1896. After this date values improved slightly, and on January 15, 1897, reached $7\frac{1}{4}$ c.; receding again to a fraction below 7 c. until March 10, from which time until the close of the cotton year on August 31, 1897, prices fluctuated between 7 and $7\frac{3}{4}$ c.; the final quotations being 7 c. at the end of August.

Exports. Comparative exports of cotton from Charleston during the year ending August 31, 1897, were as follows:—To foreign countries, 263,312 bales, compared with 192,304 bales for the previous season; and to domestic ports and interior towns of the United States, 147,530 bales last year, and 76,806 bales the year before; making the grand total of exports both foreign and coastwise, last year 410,842 bales, compared with 269,110 bales for the year before; these figures showing an increase during the past season

CHARLESTON.

in the foreign exports of 71,008 bales, and in domestic of 70,724 bales. Of last year's foreign exports 71,423 bales went to Liverpool, and the remainder, 191,889 bales, to Continental European ports, mostly to Bremen, Barcelona, and Genoa; there having been no shipments direct to France throughout the year. *Increase.*

The total net receipts of cotton at all American ports last season were 6,829,100 bales, compared with 5,420,246 bales for the year before, an increase for the last season of 1,408,854 bales. Of the above mentioned receipts, the following are the figures for the five cotton ports in this Consular district, namely:— *Total receipts, &c.*

Charleston received 403,326 bales last year and 392,336 bales the year before; Savannah, 845,533 bales last year, and 782,996 bales the year before; Wilmington, 234,664 bales last year, and 176,447 bales the year before; Brunswick, 121,475 bales last year, and 74,340 bales the year before; and Port Royal, 70,971 bales last year, and 77,906 bales the previous year; all of these ports showing material increases last season with the exception of Port Royal whose decrease is attributable to some changes that took place during the year in the management of the Port Royal and Augusta railway, resulting from the sale and final adjustment of the affairs of that road, which have been in the courts for several years.

Carolina sea island cotton opened late in September, 1896, at 20 c. per lb. for medium fine grades, and prices remained at about this figure until November, when the market declined to 17 c. for this grade; the decline in extra fine and fancy crops being even more marked than in medium fines in comparison with opening prices. *Sea islands.*

Georgias opened at 14½ c. per lb. for extra choice qualities, but large receipts in December forced prices down to 11½ c. at the end of the year. *Prices.*

Florida sea island cottons sent to this market were of rather poor quality and met with slow sale, and at the close of last season on August 31, 1897, the greater part of the unsold Florida sea island cotton remaining on hand was held at Savannah.

Crop accounts were very conflicting at the beginning of last September with reference to the new crop then nearly ready to market, but the outlook at that time appeared to indicate that there would be an average yield for South Carolina and Floridas, with perhaps a slight decrease in Georgias during the new season of 1897–98. There was a comparatively large stock on hand when the new season opened, and with a good yield the probabilities all seemed to point to low prices, it being estimated that even should the new crop be 10,000 bags less than for the previous season the available supply would, notwithstanding, be about the same, counting stocks held in the several markets and by spinners, rendering it most unlikely that prices would show much improvement over the year before. *Crop prospects.*

The receipts, exports and stock of South Carolina, Georgia, and Florida sea island cotton during the year 1896–97, as *Receipts and exports.*

UNITED STATES.

compared with the previous season of 1895–96, was as follows:—

RECEIPTS.

	Quantity.	
	1896–97.	1895–96.
	Bales.	Bales.
Carolina sea islands	10,700	9,851
Georgias and Floridas	367	123
Texas	97	645
Stock on hand, Sept. 1, 1896	572	2
Total	11,736	10,621

Exports. EXPORTS of Sea Islands from Charleston during the Year ending September 1, 1897, and for the previous year.

	Quantity.	
	1896–97.	1895–96.
	Bales.	Bales.
Exports	10,809	10,049
Stock, sea islands	927	572
Total	11,736	10,621

Of the exports last year, 8,655 bales went to foreign countries; Liverpool receiving 7,022, France 1,633, and the remainder to ports of the United States.

Total crop. The total crop of sea island cotton, including Carolinas, Georgias, and Floridas, for the cotton year ending September 1, 1897, amounted to 101,970 bales, compared with 92,053 bales for the previous year, showing an increase last year of 9,917 bales. These figures do not include 97 bales of Texas sea islands received here last season, and 645 bales received during the season before from the same State.

Later cotton figures. In addition to the foregoing facts the following figures will show the extent of Charleston's cotton trade from 1 September, 1897, to December 31, 1897, which period forms the first four months of the next commercial season of 1897–98, and will be included in next year's report.

Receipts. The total receipts of upland cotton at this port, from September 1, 1897, to December 31, 1897, were 350,620 bales of uplands, and 8,405 bags of sea islands; compared with receipts, during the corresponding four months of the previous year, of 307,961 bales of uplands, and 9,573 bags of sea islands.

Exports. The exports during the same period were 310,356 bales of uplands, and 3,070 bags of sea islands, compared with exports during the last four months of the previous year of 285,992 bales of uplands, and 3,857 bags of sea islands. Of the above-mentioned exports, last year the proportion going to foreign countries was 230,873 bales of uplands, and 1,726 bags of sea islands; of which Liverpool received 67,635 bales of uplands, and 1,726 bags of sea islands, the rest of the foreign exports going to continental European ports—mostly Bremen, Barcelona, and Genoa.

Phosphates and fertilisers

The business of manufacturing fertilisers from phosphate rock is, like the sea island cotton trade, largely confined to Charleston; this being the largest fertiliser manufacturing centre in the United States. Much of the money used in the manipulation of fertiliser products is supplied by capitalists here, where the goods are stored and shipped to consumers as required throughout the active business season, usually lasting from the beginning of October to the end of April.

During the past commercial year the entire Southern country has suffered from general trade depression, which has naturally affected the fertiliser industry. Indeed the business is subject to many risks; large sums of money have to be expended in manufacturing and handling the goods which must be put out at a venture, dependent for profitable returns on the extent and value of crops.

Shipments.

Shipments of fertilisers from Charleston last year were 374,494 tons, compared with 257,715 tons during the previous season of 1895–96; being a gain last year of 116,779 tons, nearly 50 per cent. The total output of the mills is estimated to have been nearly 400,000 tons, some of the companies manufacturing from 20,000 to 80,000 tons yearly, and using in the process such materials as sulphur, kainit, blood, tankage, cotton-seed meal, potash, and phosphate rock, all of which are cash articles.

These figures show that last season's fertiliser business was large, and manufacturers were fairly well satisfied with the results of the year's operations, and when the new season opened, September 1 last, they were busily engaged in overhauling buildings, works, machinery, acid chambers, and wharves, and putting the same in good order for the next year's trade, which was expected to be large, and possibly to exceed any previous year.

Probable consumption large.

It is expected that the State of Georgia alone will use this season 400,000 tons of commercial fertilisers, more than the quantity consumed by any other two States combined, much of which will be supplied by Charleston mills. North Carolina's consumption closely approximates 200,000 tons, the result being that nearly the whole of last year's South Carolina product of 400,000 tons was sold when the new season opened on September 1, 1897.

Comparative statement.

The following comparative statement of shipments of fertilisers from the three principal ports in this Consular district of Charleston, Savannah, and Port Royal, will show the relative importance of each, and also give some idea of the total business.

Shipments and sales.

SHIPMENTS and Sales of Fertilisers for the last Two Years.

From—	Quantity.	
	1896.	1897.
	Tons.	Tons.
Charleston	257,715	374,494
Savannah	90,000	120,000
Port Royal	35,000	35,000
Total	382,715	529,494

Chemical imports.

The imports of chemicals used in the manufacture of fertilisers at Charleston, during the year ending August 31, 1897, were 107,828 tons, valued at 810,941 dol.; compared with 58,938 tons, imported the previous year, with a valuation of 433,400 dol.; showing an increase last season of 48,890 tons, of 377,541 dol. value. The principal chemical imports consisted of:—

	Quantity.
	Tons.
Kainit	42,349
Brimstone	8,900
Muriate of potash	5,289
Sulphur pyrites	20,570
Nitrate of soda	1,095
Manure salt	718
Sulphate of potash	121
Sulphur ore	28,786

In addition to the above imports of chemicals at Charleston, there were also imported to Savannah 120,000 tons, and to Port Royal 35,000 tons during the season.

Of the above-mentioned imports, the bulk of the pyrites and sulphur ore came from Spain and Portugal; the brimstone from Italy; the kainit, potash and manure salt from Germany, and the nitrate from the nitrate beds of Chili; little or nothing now being imported direct from Great Britain.

Phosphate rock.

The depression in phosphate trade last year was not confined to South Carolina, but extended to Florida, Tennessee, and other mining regions. In this State river mining operations were considerably interfered with by unfavourable legislation, and concessions in the way of reduced royalties on rock have come too tardily to save the industry from serious loss, and much trade has gone to other competing States. The Coosaw Company, the largest in the State, has closed down its works and suspended operations indefinitely, the Farmers Company have also gone out of the business, and another company failed during the past autumn to pay expenses, and was also obliged to stop work.

It is estimated that the present mining capacity of the United States is equal to 1,000,000 tons of phosphate rock a year. The variety of the rock is considerable, and the mining equipment extensive and capable of indefinite improvement, and seems likely to meet any demand for the future arising from the further growth and development of industry. *Mining capacity.*

There are two classes of mining operations now carried on in this State, land and river mining. What is known as land rock is taken from land mines where the phosphate deposits are found from 6 to 15 feet below the surface of the ground. Land rock is generally used in local fertiliser manufacturing for supplying the American demand, there being little or no shipments of fertilisers from this port to foreign countries, the foreign demand, to the present time, having confined itself almost exclusively to crude or dried rock in its unmanufactured state. *Mining classes. Land rock.*

River rock is dredged from the rivers of the State, the principal supply being obtained from the beds of the Coosaw, Bull, and Beaufort rivers, situated in Beaufort, South Carolina, and this variety is mostly shipped to foreign countries, where it forms the basis for commercial manures manufactured abroad. *River rock.*

Phosphate rock is found along the margins of most of the navigable rivers in this State, and also in the river beds; much of it is convenient to main lines of railways, and can be delivered cheaply and quickly alongside of steamers and sailing vessels for shipment to other countries.

The royalty now payable to the State on phosphate river rock is 25 c. (about 1s.) per ton, a reduction from 50 c. per ton having been made a year ago. Notwithstanding this reduction, however, there was a great falling-off in the amount of royalties received last year by the State, which amounted to 121,602 dol., compared with 174,400 dol. for the previous season, a decrease last year of 52,798 dol. The mining companies also sustained heavy losses, owing to the combined ill-effects of low prices, keener competition of Florida and Tennessee phosphate products, and the attitude of the State authorities heretofore shown toward the mining companies. *Royalty*

Since the State Board of Phosphate Commissioners were finally induced to reduce the royalty to 25 c., it appears probable that new people with means and experience may go into the Coosaw River before long to mine rock, it being understood that the Empire Phosphate Company will operate in this territory, which was formerly worked by the Coosaw Company.

The shipments of phosphate rock from the port of Charleston during the year ending September 1, 1897, were only 2,240 tons to foreign countries, but to ports and places in the United States they amounted to 126,779 tons. Shipments from Beaufort *Shipments.*

were 82,376 tons foreign, and 5,044 to places and ports in the United States.

Sources of supply. The total amount of phosphate mined in this country last year was 993,507 tons, of which South Carolina supplied 445,047 tons; Florida, 516,460 tons; Tennessee, 25,000 tons; and North Carolina, 7,000 tons. The total valuation of this whole product at present prices is estimated at 3,600,000 dol., equivalent in sterling to about 720,000*l.*

Tennessee rock. The phosphate rock which has been discovered in Tennessee has within the past three or four years come forward as a strong competitor with the Carolina and Florida product. It, however, varies greatly from the Carolina and Florida article. Tennessee rock is darker in complexion and denser; it does not require washing and drying, and as a general rule is of good grade, but its analysis does not run uniformly, often differing considerably in the same deposits. After it is crushed it grinds easily and also slacks up in drying.

Many of the deposits are situated, however, in places more or less remote from railway and steamboat transportation facilities, this being particularly the case with the early discoveries which were made in Swan Creek, Trotty's Bend, Centreville, and Blue Creek, but the newer discovered fields in Davidson, Hickman, Rutherford, and White counties, are more advantageously located, being all very near the railways.

Accessibility and convenient means of transportation are also enjoyed by miners operating in Maury County. Mines also have been brought to public notice in the neighbourhood of Mount Pleasant, and these, together with mines in Bradley, Marshall, Sevier, Perry, Lewis, Wayne, and Decatur Counties, are near the Tennessee River, and it seems likely that operations at these places may be conducted profitably, and possibly develop considerable business on account of shipments to New Orleans, St. Louis, Pensacola, and Norfolk.

North Carolina. It is difficult to get accurate information of the phosphate rock mined or used in North Carolina, as the business is comparatively small in that State. The shipments of phosphates from other States are large, and manufacturers use rock from South Carolina, Florida and Tennessee in manufacturing their goods. There is a large consumption of commercial manures throughout the State of North Carolina, approximating 200,000 tons during the past year.

Florida competition. Florida is by far the most important and dangerous rival that South Carolina has to contend with in the phosphate business; varied and valuable deposits have been discovered and are now worked in that State, each good of its kind, and in qualities are as follows:—hard and soft rock, land and river pebble, and river rock.

Cost of mining. The cost of mining most of the Florida rock is comparatively small when contrasted with mining operations elsewhere; and in order to meet competition and build up the business that State no longer requires a royalty on rock mined within its domain. The growth of the Florida industry has been somewhat retarded by the inconvenient distances of some of the deposits from railways and water courses of a navigable character; the difficulty and cost of transportation having acted as a check on what would, otherwise, have been a larger output for the year.

Outlets for shipments. The principal outlets at present, by water, for shipments of Florida rock are by way of Jacksonville, Fernandina, Brunswick, Savannah, Tampa, Punta Gorda and Key West, and, as railway facilities are now being extended, miners are gradually becoming relieved from the unfavourable conditions under which they have hitherto contended. Most of the Florida rock is shipped to foreign countries; as yet she does not manufacture fertilisers, and consequently has not, in this respect, come into competition with Charleston's large fertiliser industries; but owing to the cheapness and good quality of the rock it is expected that, in time, numerous fertiliser-manufacturing establishments are sure to be established in the State, which will then be able to compete with South Carolina's fertiliser business as it does now in the phosphate-rock trade.

Algerian phosphates. The harmful effect of the phosphates of Algiers and Tunis on the South Carolina industry have not been so apparent during the past year as the competition nearer home from Florida and Tennessee; although the unfavourable influence has been material in affecting prices in foreign markets for American shipments with which the African mines compete. From the latest reports received it appears that those mines have made but slow progress during the last year, and have not kept pace with the development of similar new industries in this country. There seems to have been a want of harmony among the companies engaged in the business, and political interference from which they have also suffered has tended to restrict and hamper the successful prosecution of the work. Notwithstanding all drawbacks, however, it is claimed that the Algerian and Tunis mines turn out 300 tons of phosphate rock daily, and that the output last year was 142,340 tons, which it is expected will be increased next season to 175,000 tons. **Output.**

Most of last year's output was shipped to the following countries:—England, France, Italy, Germany, Austria, Japan, Belgium, and Spain; quantities shipped being in the order named, and varying from 54,005 tons sent to England to the smallest shipment, which was 250 tons taken by Spain.

Later figures. The market for phosphate rock at the end of the year closed firmer with quotations for crude of 3 dol., at mines, per ton; hot-air dried 3 dol. 25 c. per ton, f.o.b. vessels in Ashley River; 3 dol. 45 c. per ton, f.o.b. City. Ground rock in bulk 5 dol. 50 c. per ton, f.o.b. vessel at city.

Exports. The total exports of phosphate rock from this port from September 1 to December 31, 1897, were 29,950 tons, compared with 32,904 tons for the previous year, of which none went abroad.

Rice. Weather was very favourable for field work during the greater part of harvest season for the Carolina rice crop of 1896-97, and cutting of grain, which commenced earlier than usual, progressed

Crop conditions.

steadily without interruption from storms and floods, until all the early planting was gathered in and stacked in the fields.

That part of the crop, however, that was planted in June did not fare so well, having sustained some damage from a severe blow which occurred late in the season, before the grain had matured sufficiently to be ready for the sickle.

Fortunately the unfavourable weather was only of short duration, although it was quite sufficient to destroy a number of buildings on some plantations, in addition to the material injury done to the late crop, which, however, amounted to a small portion only, of the total yield; the final result being that the rice crop of the Atlantic Coast was, last season, about equal to its predecessor, while the Carolina rice yield, which constitutes the bulk of the Atlantic Coast crop, was slightly in excess of the previous season.

Favourable prices.

The Louisiana rice crop last year was comparatively small, which naturally had a favourable effect on prices realised for the Carolina product, and as the supply was unequal to the demands of this country, importations of foreign grown rice were unusually large during the year. Good prices were obtained throughout the season for Carolina rice, the higher grades of what is known as "head" rice being in particularly good demand at remunerative figures, quotations ranging from $4\frac{1}{2}$ to 5 c. per lb.

Receipts. Carolina rice.

Receipts of rough rice at South Carolina mills during the business year ending August 31, 1897, were 1,007,908 bushels compared with 959,118 bushels for the previous year, an increase last year of 48,790 bushels in Carolina rice receipts.

Louisiana.

The Louisiana rice crop last season amounted to 2,558,292 bushels, compared with 7,466,721 bushels the previous season, showing a decrease last year of 4,908,429 bushels.

Total American crop.

The total crop of rice produced in the United States last year was 3,966,200 bushels, and for the year before 6,875,339 bushels, a falling-off last year in the total American crop of 2,909,139 bushels.

First shipments.

The first shipments of last year's rice crop were received at Charleston, from Waverly Mills, on August 18, 1896, and consisted of 30 barrels; this was followed a few days later by 18 barrels more from the same mills. The first cargo of rough rice, 1,500 bushels in quantity, arrived on August 22 from Pon Pon River, and a second shipment of 1,500 bushels more, from the same plantation, was also received on the 29th of that month; these shipments were followed by others when the season was fairly open in September and receipts soon became general.

New crop.

The new crop for the current season of 1897–98 was about two weeks late, the first cargo of rough rice having been received on September 2, 1897, from Ashepoo River, while the first receipts of cleaned new crop rice arrived from Waverly Mills next day, September 3 last. At that time the new crop was well under way, weather conditions had been favourable both on the Atlantic and Gulf Coasts and the indications generally pointed to good results for the new season, because even should the next crop be larger than last year, prices are likely to be fairly good, as in any case the crop produced will be insufficient to meet the requirements of this country, whose importations of rice from foreign countries depends on the amount of the American product.

The total quantity of rice milled of the crops of South Carolina, North Carolina, Georgia, and also the same for Louisiana, and the whole crop of the United States, with which they may be compared, are as follows:— *Milled rice.*

Rice crop.

	Season of 1896–97.
	Barrels.*
CROP OF SOUTH CAROLINA.	
Milled at Charleston	65,660
,, Georgetown	26,628
Total, South Carolina	92,288
CROP OF GEORGIA.	
Milled at Savannah	27,272
CROP OF NORTH CAROLINA.	
Milled at Wilmington, Washington, and Newbern	8,500
Total, Atlantic coast crop	128,060
,, Louisiana crop	215,618
Grand total for the United States	343,678

* Barrels of 300 lbs. net weight.

The total receipts of rice at Charleston from September 1, 1897, to December 31, 1897, were 34,602 barrels, compared with 40,188 barrels for the same period of the previous year. *Later rice figures. Receipts.*

The exports during the same time last year were 23,992 barrels in comparison with 25,912 for the year before. There were no foreign exports last year, all the rice above named having been either shipped to places in the United States or consumed here.

At the end of the year the market closed firm with quotations for prime grades ruling at $5\frac{1}{4}$ to $5\frac{3}{4}$ c. per lb. *Closing prices.*

The naval stores business for the past 12 months was rather small, but fair prices were obtained for resin and spirits of turpentine, and such transactions as took place were, under the circumstances, considered satisfactory by dealers and producers. *Naval stores.*

Receipts at Charleston for the year ending August 31, 1897, amounted to 5,283 casks of turpentine and 56,293 barrels of resin. *Receipts.*

The market opened last year at $21\frac{1}{2}$ c. per gallon for spirits of

16   UNITED STATES.

Prices.

turpentine, and gradually advanced until September 1 when 26½ c. was offered for spirits in machine-made barrels, and 25½ c. for turpentine in oil and country-made barrels.

Quotations for resin ruled firm during the past year, the average price for B, C, D, and E grades being 1 dol. 25 c. per barrel; but towards the end of last August the demand was not very good, and offering prices for B resin was only 1 dol. 10 c. per barrel, and for C, D, and E grades 1 dol. 15 c. a barrel.

Very little fine resin is now received in this market owing to the fact that what little virgin pine timber now remains in the State is held firmly by owners who are unwilling to let the trees be cut at any price; consequently the business has greatly fallen off for the past few years in this section for want of timber, low prices and more attention having been given to cotton planting and other products.

It is not improbable, however, that in the event of better prices being obtainable in the future old pine trees will again be worked over, and what virgin timber still remains in the State may be brought into the market.

Exports, coastwise

Exports of spirits of turpentine and resin to coastwise ports and places in the United States for the past year in comparison with the previous one were:—

Exports to—	1896–97.		1895–96.	
	Turpentine.	Resin.	Turpentine.	Resin.
	Casks.	Barrels.	Casks.	Barrels.
New York	5,039	32,163	5,651	25,452
Interior by railway	363	..	525	124
Total	5,402	32,163	6,176	25,576

Foreign exports.

The foreign exports from Charleston, during the past commercial year, compared with the previous season, with the names of countries and amount of shipments to each, were as follows:—

CHARLESTON.

Exports to—	1896-97.		1895-96.	
	Turpentine.	Resin.	Turpentine.	Resin.
	Casks.	Barrels.	Casks.	Barrels.
Rotterdam	..	3,330	..	2,404
Hamburg	..	..	300	3,000
Trieste	..	..	..	2,378
Glasgow	..	..	1,000	909
London	300	5,329	1,896	1,542
Liverpool	..	..	..	5,107
Bremen, direct	..	1,000	..	2,000
„ viâ Savannah	..	2,348	..	6,891
Bristol	..	..	941	6,114
Middlesboro'	..	3,602	..	..
Cardiff	..	..	..	2,961
Manchester	..	..	..	2,400
Hull	..	3,292	..	..
Stettin	..	2,808	..	..
Lübeck	..	1,391	..	..
Genoa	..	1,000	..	..
Bowling	..	3,344	..	..
Porto Rico	15	..	..	..
Total	315	27,444	4,137	35,706

The receipts of the naval store at Charleston from April 1 to December 31, 1897, were 3,484 casks of turpentine and 23,523 barrels of resin, compared with 7,530 casks of turpentine and 39,177 barrels of resin during the same period of the previous year.

Later statistics. Receipts.

The exports from April 1 to December 31, 1897, were 3,336 casks of turpentine and 30,969 barrels of resin, compared with exports during the previous year of 6,822 casks of turpentine and 39,326 barrels of resin. Of the resin exports, 15,346 barrels went to foreign countries, of which Liverpool took 11,533 barrels, the remainder going to North European and other ports.

Exports.

At the end of 1897 the market closed firm for both turpentine and resin, quotations for turpentine being 30½ c. per gallon, and for resin prices ranged from 1 dol. 10 c. per barrel for A, B, and C grades up to 2 dol. 40 c. and 2 dol. 90 c. for window glass and water white.

Closing prices.

Lumber trade during the past year shared, to some extent, in the general business depression from which the country has not yet quite recovered. Prevailing prices were too low for the business to be profitable to manufacturers, and it was only by the strictest economy that any small margin of profit could be realised. The industry, however, has been maintained on a footing that will enable merchants to take advantage of any rise in prices, or improvement of business conditions, if they should occur in the near future. The local lumber trade has not been equal to former years, during the past season, owing to fewer buildings being erected.

Lumber.

Good facilities are now possessed by this port for handling

Good facilities.

UNITED STATES.

shipments of lumber from interior mills which places the trade in a position to favourably compete in prices with other southern ports, this being especially the case in regard to Charleston's waterway communications, which in numbers of cases have enabled dealers here to secure orders that more southerly ports could not execute profitably under existing railway arrangements, on which they were solely dependent.

The advantage in this respect has been especially apparent in handling square edge and sound lumber and sawed trolley railway ties.

Prospects. The prospects at the end of last season were not very encouraging for next year, but an increased demand was hoped for by dealers on account of the passage by the United States Congress of the Dingley Tariff Bill which it was thought might have the effect of improving business next spring.

Exports. Comparative exports of lumber, timber, and cross-ties from the port of Charleston for the year ending August 31, 1897, as compared with the previous year, were as follows:—

EXPORTS, COASTWISE.

Exported to—	Quantity.	
	1896-97.	1895-96.
	Feet.	Feet.
New York	34,918,629	53,873,767
Boston	14,644,613	6,966,000
Philadelphia	917,164	3,774,000
Baltimore	2,254,000	1,649,000
Other American ports	8,900,540	8,844,327
Total coastwise	61,634,946	75,107,094

EXPORTS, FOREIGN.

Exported to—	Quantity.	
	1896-97.	1895-96.
	Feet.	Feet.
West Indies	1,442,000	2,190,685
Other foreign ports	33,000	..
Total foreign	1,475,000	2,190,685

GRAND TOTAL.

	Quantity.	
	1896-97.	1895-96.
	Feet.	Feet.
Grand total, coastwise and foreign	63,109,946	77,297,779

Lumber and timber. Later figures. At the end of the year there was a light demand for well manufactured stock with a fair export trade. Closing quotations were, for merchantable lumber, 14 to 16 dol. per 1,000 feet for city sawed; for railroad square and sound, 12 to 14 dol.; for raft timber, 8 to 11 dol; dock timber, 4 dol. 50 c. to 6 dol. 50 c.; and for shingles, 4 to 7 dol. per 1,000.

Exports. The coastwise exports, from September 1 to December 31, 1897, were, in round numbers, 20,000,000 feet, compared with 15,000,000 feet during the corresponding four months of the previous year; and the exports abroad for the last four months were 496,000 feet, compared with 275,000 feet for the year before.

Fruits and vegetables. Charleston's trade in fruits, principally strawberries, and vegetables last season was the most favourable one for the past three years. The shipping season, which ended July 31, 1897, was noted not so much for its large yield as for the fairly good prices generally obtained for shipments and for the unusual length of the shipping season.

The results of the year left a considerable sum as net profit in the hands of farmers who raise early fruits and vegetables, and this money, which is mostly put into circulation here has had a good effect on the general business of the community.

Favourable conditions. It is reported that farmers paid up their obligations last season better than perhaps they have ever done before, they also purchased supplies more liberally than heretofore, and have been more disposed to look out for and adopt new and improved tools and implements in their business, and in various other ways also are making proper efforts to keep up with the times and with the competition of other ports.

The figures which are herewith given in reference to this industry are taken from carefully compiled statistics prepared by Mr. L. Sahlman, president of the Truck Farmers' Association of Charleston and vicinity, the best available source from which accurate and comprehensive data are obtainable on the subject, and may be interesting to British producers in Jamaica, Bermuda, &c., who compete for the early vegetable trade in American markets.

It will be observed also that the details given are somewhat fuller than usual, and several matters are mentioned that have not been alluded to before in these reports.

UNITED STATES.

Autumn crop. The autumn crop of beans was the largest ever produced in Charleston County, but unfortunately prices obtained in Northern markets were so low that only the first shipments brought fair returns, and it is estimated that fully 10,000 baskets of beans were left ungathered to rot away in the fields.

Shipments. Shipments and home consumption of early autumn crop products, duly classified, with quantities and values added, were:—

Shipments of Autumn Crop.

Shipped North.		Quantity.	Value.
			Dollars.
Beans	Baskets	84,500	63,000
Peas	,,	1,000	1,500
Lettuce	,,	2,150	3,225
Potatoes	Barrels	1,000	3,025
Beets	,,	1,750	3,500
Total	..	..	74,250

Consumption. Consumption at Charleston of autumn crop vegetable products last year were:—

Items.		Quantity.	Value.
			Dollars.
Cabbage	Crates	2,000	5,000
Irish potatoes	Barrels	9,300	18,600
Sweet potatoes	,,	73,150	73,150
Beets	Bushels	12,000	9,000
Carrots	Baskets	7,100	5,375
Turnips	Bushels	30,300	15,150
Miscellaneous vegetables	Baskets	67,301	67,000
Total	..	..	193,275

Spring crop The spring crop here was late last year, but the same conditions prevailed in most other competing sections. In North Carolina the crop was much delayed by frost and rain, which gave Charleston shippers the advantage of a clear field for a short time.

Then the extensive floods in the Mississippi valley had the effect of destroying much of the early Louisiana and Alabama crops, in the neighbourhoods of New Orleans and Mobile, and this created a demand in the Southern States usually supplied by those places, and at the same time contributed to keep up prices in Northern markets to which most Charleston shipments go.

Taken altogether, therefore, growers in this section were, for a time, exceptionally favoured by the floods, rain and frost blocking off competitors both to the north and southward, and they reaped considerable advantage therefrom.

Shipments to northern and near-by markets of spring crop **Shipments.** fruits and vegetables during the season of 1897 were as follows:—

Items.		Number.
Strawberries	Quarts	775,480
Asparagus	Boxes	25,100
Cabbage	Crates	125,582
Potatoes	Barrels	164,860
Lettuce, beans, beets, cucumbers, &c.	Baskets	233,200
Tomatoes	,,	9,000
Okra	,,	3,000
Sweet potatoes	Barrels	1,200
Mutton corn	Baskets	1,000
		Dollars.
Total estimated value of above shipments		1,993,996

Consumption at Charleston of the spring crop consisted of **Consumption.** 350,000 quarts of strawberries, 11,000 barrels of sweet potatoes, and 165,000 packages of miscellaneous vegetables; the total value of the home consumption of the spring crop being 170,000 dol.

The total number of vessels arriving at this port during the **Shipping and** business year ending August 31, 1897, were 742, of all nation- **navigation.** alities, with an aggregate net registered tonnage of 924,560 tons; being an increase last season of 105,658 tons.

The arrival of vessels of all nationalities during the year ending December 31, 1897, according to the harbour-master's report made up to the end of the year, were 804 vessels, with a tonnage of 1,021,826 tons, compared with arrivals during the same period of the previous year, of 742 ships, of 813,553 tons, showing an increase last year of 62 vessels, and 108,273 tonnage.

Of last year's arrivals the nationalities of the ships were as **Nationalities.** follows:—

Nationality.	Number of Vessels.
American	695
British	72
German	6
Norwegian	24
Italian	2
Spanish	8
Austrian	1
Swedish	1

Full details of British shipping are given in the annual return
(79)

of British shipping at Charleston for the year 1897, attached to this report.

Freights.

Coastwise freights during the first half of the year 1897 were the lowest recorded in the history of sailing vessels at this port. There was some little improvement, however, in the latter part of August last, when better rates were quoted, but the improvement was not sufficient to cause any material increase in the offers of tonnage. One beneficial effect of the low rates was to bring about the shipment of several cargoes of Carolina phosphate rock during last summer which otherwise would have gone from Florida. Large shipments of cross-ties and lumber were also made on account of prevailing low freight rates.

Freights for coastwise shipments on September 1 last were as follows:—Dry cross-ties to New York, 14 c. for 44 feet ties; to Boston, 15 c. Lumber, to New York, 4 dol. to 4 dol. 25 c. per 1,000 feet. Phosphate rock, from city docks to New York, 1 dol. 60 c. per ton; to Baltimore, 1 dol. 40 c.; to Philadelphia, 1 dol. 40 c. The rates for shipments from up the river points above the city averaged about 25 c. per ton additional to the above-mentioned rates.

Foreign freights.

Foreign freights were quiet and steady during the first part of the past year, with an increasing demand early in September, which slackened off, however, in October, owing to low prices for cotton, and for awhile there was rather more tonnage than was needed for freight offered, brokers and shippers being obliged to figure closely in order to secure paying freights for cargoes of vessels under charter. In this they seem to have been fairly successful, as no reports of breach of charters or claims for demurrage have been made by ship-masters during the season.

CHARLESTON.

Return of British Shipping at the Port of Charleston, S.C., in the Year 1897.

Direct Trade in British Vessels from and to Great Britain and British Colonies.

Entered.

Total Number of Vessels.			Total Tonnage.			Total Number of Crews.	Total Value of Cargoes.
With Cargoes.	In Ballast.	Total.	With Cargoes.	In Ballast.	Total.		£
3	15	18	22,746	7,162	29,908	470	1,563

Cleared.

Total Number of Vessels.			Total Tonnage.			Total Number of Crews.	Total Value of Cargoes.
With Cargoes.	In Ballast.	Total.	With Cargoes.	In Ballast.	Total.		£
17	1	18	27,370	1,348	28,718	333	619,100

Indirect or Carrying Trade in British Vessels from and to other Countries.

Entered.

Countries whence Arrived.	Number of Vessels.			Tonnage.			Number of Crews.	Value of Cargoes.
	With Cargoes.	In Ballast.	Total.	With Cargoes.	In Ballast.	Total.		£
Brazil	1	1	2	1,042	837	1,879	46	20,320
Chile	1	...	1	1,049	...	1,049	16	5,000
Germany	16	1	17	37,518	1,567	39,085	541	100,950
Italy	1	...	1	1,297	...	1,297	23	1,200
Spain	14	...	14	21,557	...	21,557	314	33,460
Portugal	7	2	9	8,540	...	8,540	...	...
United States	...	4	4	...	15,803	15,803	286	...
Total	40	8	48	71,003	18,207	89,210	1,226	...

Cleared.

Countries to which Departed.	Number of Vessels.			Tonnage.			Number of Crews.	Value of Cargoes.
	With Cargoes.	In Ballast.	Total.	With Cargoes.	In Ballast.	Total.		£
Germany	17	...	17	29,229	...	29,229	448	833,000
Spain	6	...	6	8,364	...	8,364	204	233,800
United States	...	20	20	...	17,920	17,920	462	...
Total	23	20	43	37,593	17,920	55,513	1,114	1,066,800

24 UNITED STATES.

Miscellaneous manufactures.

During the past business year Charleston's general manufacturing industries (fertilisers excluded) have barely held their own on account of the difficulties they had to contend with growing out of the business depression that prevailed throughout the country since 1892. The fertiliser trade, the chief manufacturing industry of this port, being a conspicuous exception, as elsewhere reported in this review.

Charleston cotton mills.

The most important event, perhaps, in local manufacturing circles during the year, was the reorganisation of the old cotton mills under the new name of the "Charleston Mills," with a capital of 350,000 dol., after the old plant had remained idle for nearly a year. This mill is advantageously situated within the city of Charleston, on the western bank of the Cooper River, and in close proximity to the North-Eastern and Charleston and Savannah railway stations, enabling the mill to procure its raw material from any part of the cotton producing section of the Atlantic or Gulf States, for a considerable part of which product Charleston is the natural geographical outlet, this giving it the benefit of favourable freight rates both for supplies purchased and goods shipped. The mill can thus select such cotton as is most advantageous to spinners, that having a long staple with very little waste.

The capacity of the mill is 28,000 spindles, and it is equipped principally for the manufacture of coarse goods. The building is an imposing one, constructed of brick, in an excellent state of preservation. The machinery and equipments have been thoroughly examined and overhauled, comparing favourably with most of the up country mills, and requiring an expenditure of only about 15,000 dol. for necessary improvements, and it began operations under its new management free from debt or other encumbrance.

Labour difficulties.

Great difficulty was experienced by the old cotton mill in securing steady labour, it never having been able to procure a sufficient number of native Charlestonians for the work, and was consequently obliged to import much of its help at heavy expense. In view of this the new management deemed it advisable to try the experiment of employing negro labour as well as white, there being a population in Charleston of about 35,000 coloured persons. The directors were of opinion that from this source they would be able to secure the required number of steady operatives at moderate wages, enabling them to earn good dividends to stockholders, and at the same time, should negro labour prove successful, confer a benefit on the whole community by employing an over-abundant class of labour, much of which at present goes to waste or worse.

Coloured labour experiment.

The experiment of utilising coloured labour in cotton mills is being watched with much interest by textile manufacturers all over the country, as the general opinion heretofore has been that there are racial peculiarities which render the African too careless, clumsy, and somnolent to be safely entrusted with delicate and intricate machinery requiring care and constant attention.

CHARLESTON.

Shuttle block making. The most recent addition to the smaller manufacturing industries of this port was the establishment of a plant on Southern wharf for the manufacture of shuttle blocks to meet a demand that comes principally from Liverpool, Havre, and Barcelona. The new factory is operated by the Southern Hardwood Manufacturing Company, the work now being done consisting of shuttle block making alone, but later on the company proposes to add turning machinery to its present equipment and may also increase considerably the capacity of the mill.

Details, &c. of manufacture. The plant now in operation consists of a thirty-horse power electric motor turning three saws which are run for the purpose of sawing the blocks out of the rough logs, brought from the forests in lengths of about 8 feet and of various diameters, ranging from 6 to 18 inches. The first sawing cuts the logs into proper lengths for the shuttles, the second set cuts the round pieces into halves or quarters, and the third sawyers trim the blocks into shape. About 1,200 are now made daily, differing in size according to orders, from $12\frac{1}{2}$ inches long by $1\frac{3}{8}$ inches square to 23 inches long by 3 inches square. After the blocks are cut the ends are dipped in boiling wax, to prevent splitting, and they are then stacked up in a room to dry for some days. The woods used are persimmon and dogwood, which are considered the only desirable kinds available for shuttle manufacture. In the making of these blocks it is necessary to use only straight-grained wood entirely free from knots, and there is, consequently, much waste material, which, however, makes excellent fuel, that the company expect to sell as part of their product. When first cut the shuttle blocks are perfectly green and quite heavy, but after standing in piles for a time before shipment, they are thoroughly seasoned and ready for turning when they reach Europe. They are not sold as lumber but are shipped carefully packed in coffee sacks, and are sold at so much per thousand blocks.

The various sizes are for shuttles used in weaving different kinds of coarse and fine goods, the silk looms taking the smaller shuttles. There is always a good demand for shuttles, and the orders for blocks are well in advance of production.

Ample supply of wood. There is an abundant supply of dogwood and persimmon tree wood near Charleston, and it is easily obtained in quantities required; it is mostly brought to town in small boats from adjacent river landings, and some also comes down by railway from more distant points. The shuttle saws have as yet only been turning a short time, but a considerable quantity of blocks have already been shipped, and the company are now filling a large order for Liverpool.

Good prospects. Everything appears to be working smoothly with this new industry, and there are good prospects for future growth from the above-mentioned modest beginning with which it has started.

Shoe and knitting mills. The shoe and knitting mills, two of the more recent additions to Charleston's manufacturing industries, are reported to have done a good business last year, and are in good shape to begin the new year.

UNITED STATES.

Bagging factory.

The bagging factory lost a little more time than usual during the season in cleaning up, making repairs, and building an addition to their mill, which reduced the output somewhat; but prices, however, were about half a cent higher per pound for bagging than the previous year, resulting in a very slight difference in the total annual value of the two years product.

Established industries.

In the other well-established manufacturing industries of the city there was little or no change, all did fairly well, and are in good condition at the close of the year.

BRUNSWICK.

Mr. Vice-Consul Torras reports as follows:—

Since rendering you my last report, I am again pleased to be able to state that business still continues to improve, and that the commercial outlook for the future is bright.

Health.

The health of the city has been and is very good, which points to the fact that drainage was all that was necessary to render this one of the most healthy of Southern cities.

Commerce.

No goods of any consequence are directly imported into this Consular district from British ports, with the exception of salt from Liverpool and tropical fruits from the Bahama Islands. The exports are mentioned in the enclosed tabulated statement, where it will be noticed that the exportation of cotton from this port has increased from year to year until during the past year an increase of almost 24 per cent. has been attained over 1896, and hopes are entertained that business will continue to increase, as this port is considered one of the cheapest on the Atlantic coast, and consequently is preferred to other ports by the owners of steam and sailing ships.

Navigation.

The enclosed statistics also show the increase of tonnage at this port to be $13\frac{3}{8}$ per cent. over that of 1896.

American schooners are subject to a charge of 1 dol. for harbour-master's fee, foreign vessels paying an average of 10 dol., these schooners when in the coasting trade are allowed to purchase an annual licence at the rate of 25 c. per ton which exempts them from paying the customary pilotage fees, other vessels pay pilotage fees at the approximate rate of 3 dol. per foot of draught each way.

St. Simon's bar.

This bar, which was mentioned in my last report, contrary to the expectations of many has retained its depth of 24 feet.

Exports.

The surrounding country at the back of this port, and the neighbouring States of Alabama, Kentucky, Tennessee, Virginia, and Florida furnish this market with an abundant supply of cotton, pig-iron, phosphate, tobacco, cereals, flour, resin, turpentine, and valuable hard woods, the increased exportation of all of which has been remarkable during the past year.

Industries.

The principal industry of this port and surrounding country is saw-milling. There are a large number of saw-mills which send by rail to this port quantities of yellow-pine lumber; there

Table 1.—THE Actual Figures showing the Great Increase in the Volume of the Exports and Imports of the Port of Brunswick, Ga., 1897.

Month.	Imports.			Exports.												Total Volume.
	Vessels Arrived.	Tonnage of Arrivals.	Value.	Vessels Sailed.	Tonnage of Sailings.	Cotton.	Yarn.	Pig-iron.	Phosphate.	Turpentine.	Rosin.	Timber.	Lumber.	Cross-ties.	Shingles.	Value.	
			Dollars.			Bales.	Bales.	Tons.	Tons.	Barrels.	Barrels.	Feet.	Feet.	Pieces.	Pieces.	Dollars.	Dollars.
January	32	25,050	470,000	34	30,499	17,341	840	3,360	1,665	3,423	17,442	371,000	8,343,000	77,449	1,281,000	988,136	1,458,136
February	49	34,723	380,200	35	29,386	6,558	290	3,237	3,570	1,408	37,793	9,000	5,921,000	118,500	..	630,081	1,010,281
March	45	39,412	609,100	42	31,208	17,169	261	2,814	4,830	592	18,372	373,000	9,313,000	57,666	450,000	959,606	1,568,706
April	60	45,778	411,710	51	42,079	16,710	341	3,150	4,232	4,360	19,189	410,000	11,826,000	203,577	996,550	1,096,679	1,508,389
May	52	39,982	419,300	49	36,547	512	159	92	4,000	7,770	16,376	1,014,000	10,214,000	193,581	1,646,800	471,071	890,371
June	43	35,204	443,300	38	34,460	4,394	87	1,400	3,048	7,782	33,625	528,000	8,849,000	188,918	1,047,100	636,102	1,079,402
July	35	22,982	300,600	45	30,377	..	99	..	1,250	8,543	14,357	967,000	14,117,000	44,100	1,453,300	417,934	718,534
August	41	28,245	368,000	34	22,650	4	60	..	2,946	4,490	9,741	172,000	8,180,000	79,525	1,593,000	312,392	680,392
September	44	39,717	416,600	35	29,486	16,291	224	600	8,522	6,101	25,692	525,000	8,241,000	30,569	890,000	939,800	1,356,400
October	51	50,008	585,400	57	51,125	26,344	200	2,400	2,340	8,666	34,164	619,000	13,956,000	201,201	610,000	1,460,641	2,046,041
November	44	38,887	734,600	42	40,333	46,749	..	3,296	6,403	4,179	22,081	266,000	10,462,000	103,506	1,570,000	1,806,242	2,540,842
December	54	43,876	664,300	48	43,439	49,169	23	3,850	3,914	6,405	15,615	618,000	11,613,000	140,112	388,000	1,969,975	2,634,275
Total	550	443,161	5,803,110	510	421,589	201,541	2,584	24,199	46,720	68,719	264,447	5,812,000	121,041,000	1,388,704	11,925,750	11,688,659	17,491,769

NOTE.—Not enumerated in the table of exports are 212 bales of wool, 25 cases of baking powders, 5,182 barrels of cotton-seed oil, 1 pony, 15 tons of guano, 200 barrels of flour, 206 tons of corn, 10,000 laths, 1,960 cases of oysters, and 113 barrels of tar.

(79—To face p. 27.)

are few factories of any other description and those of little consequence.

Timber. The pitch-pine of this State has been cut so recklessly and improvidently for the last 8 or 10 years, that the large trees suitable for lumber are now only to be found at some distance from the railroads, and extensive branch lines will have to be and have been put down in consequence.

Agriculture. Cotton is the principal agricultural product of this State, and the next in importance, rice; the men employed on these farms are paid at the rate of 50 c. per day.

Taxes. The rural property is taxed 1 per cent. on the estimated value of the land.

Manure. The land is fertilised by a composition, of which phosphate is the base, and the other component parts, potash, ammonia, kainit, and animal manure, the cost of which is estimated at 15 dol. per ton.

Labour strike at docks. During the recent strike the strikers demanded an increase of 25 c. per day of 10 hours, and after nearly a month of idleness they returned to work at the original rate of pay, with the exception of a few working in holds of ships whose positions were considered of sufficient importance to entitle them to an increase of wages.

Shippers. The shippers at this port find it difficult to insure foreign vessels with American insurance companies; cargoes for European ports shipped on good class vessels are charged about 5 per cent.

Freights. Freights on lumber for the north of Europe have obtained an average of 90s. per standard of St. Petersburg; for the Mediterranean about 86s., and for River Plate and other South American ports about 96s.

British tonnage. It is expected that the tonnage of British steamers loading at this port during 1898 will be double that of 1897.

UNITED STATES.

TABLE 2.

Arrivals—Nationality.			Exports—Foreign and Domestic.			Comparative—1896 and 1897.			
Nationality.	Vessels Arrived.	Tonnage.	Month.	Foreign.	Domestic.	Subject.		1896.	1897.
American	359	282,367	January	Dollars. 594,736	Dollars. 393,400	Arriving	Tonnage	384,215	443,164
British	65	82,966	February	382,821	247,260	Sailing	"	370,350	421,589
Norwegian	50	35,216	March	713,356	246,250	Cotton	Bales	153,787	201,541
Spanish	45	24,552	April	772,729	323,950	Pig iron	Tons	10,619	24,199
German	1	868	May	230,521	240,550	Phosphates	"	38,911	46,720
Russian	7	3,928	June	439,102	197,000	Naval stores	Barrels	293,645	328,166
Swedish	8	5,038	July	216,234	201,700	Lumber	Feet	118,572,000	126,853,000
Dutch	1	654	August	111,720	290,672	Cross-ties	Number	1,026,078	1,387,702
Italian	9	4,757	September	653,000	286,800			Dollars.	Dollars.
Portuguese	5	1,733	October	819,566	641,075	Imports	Value	4,951,296	5,803,110
Danish	2	1,415	November	1,439,392	366,850	Exports	"	10,714,106	11,688,659
French	..	..	December	1,528,025	441,950				
Total	552	443,494	Total	7,901,202	3,787,457	Total volume		15,665,402	17,491,769
						Increase			1,826,367

BRUNSWICK.

RETURN of British Shipping at the Port of Brunswick, Ga., during the Year 1897.

Direct Trade in British Vessels from and to Great Britain and British Colonies.

Entered.

Number of Vessels.			Total Tonnage.			Total Number of Crews.	Total Value of Cargoes.
With Cargoes.	In Ballast.	Total.	With Cargoes.	In Ballast.	Total.		£ s. d.
3	26	29	233	41,722	41,955	715	281 1 8

Cleared.

Total Number of Vessels.			Total Tonnage.			Total Number of Crews.	Total Value of Cargoes.
With Cargoes.	In Ballast.	Total.	With Cargoes.	In Ballast.	Total.		£ s. d.
24	...	24	38,094	...	38,094	599	782,214 7 6

Indirect or Carrying Trade in British Vessels from and to other Countries.

Entered.

Countries whence Arrived.	Number of Vessels.			Tonnage.			Number of Crews.	Value of Cargoes.
	With Cargoes.	In Ballast.	Total.	With Cargoes.	In Ballast.	Total.		£
Martinique	...	2			2,423		40	...
Holland	...	2			3,936		61	...
Cuba	...	2			1,545		31	...
Madeira	...	1			1,439		22	...
Canary Islands	...	4			5,289		88	...
United States	...	10			12,957		228	...
Brazil	...	6			4,828		80	...
Argentina	...	2			1,554		24	...
Germany	1	...		1,623	...		23	...
Algiers	...	1			1,522		21	...
France	...	1			324		7	1,500
Total	1	31	32	1,623	35,817	37,440	625	1,500

Cleared.

Countries to which Departed.	Number of Vessels.			Tonnage.			Number of Crews.	Value of Cargoes.
	With Cargoes.	In Ballast.	Total.	With Cargoes.	In Ballast.	Total.		£ s. d.
Holland	5			5,724			98	16,497 18 4
Germany	15			22,200			342	316,459 17 3
St. Thomas	2			291			15	657 3 1
Martinique	1			200			6	458 6 8
Russia	1			1,066			21	23,458 15 0
Brazil	2			1,921			29	3,628 19 7
Argentina	3			1,849			30	3,464 17 4
France	1			1,290			22	1,041 13 4
United States	...	1		...	1,623		23	...
Total	30	1	31	34,541	1,623	35,164	586	365,667 10 7

UNITED STATES.

WILMINGTON.

The books of the Produce Exchange show that during the calendar year 1897 the port receipts have been as follows:—

Articles.		Quantity.
Cotton	Bales..	296,440
Spirits turpentine	Casks..	35,390
Resin	Barrels	164,042
Tar	,,	60,929
Crude turpentine	,,	10,302

Exports. During the year the foreign and domestic exports have been as follows:—

Articles.		Quantity.
Cotton	Bales..	276,911
Spirits turpentine	Casks..	34,108
,, ,,	Cases..	185
Resin	Barrels	164,283
Tar	,,	61,313
,,	Cases..	2,908
Crude turpentine	Barrels	10,456
Pitch	,,	4,703
Lumber	Feet ..	30,344,461
Shingles		4,665,658
Peanuts	Bushels	64,086
Cotton goods	Packages	5,115
,, yarn	,,	368
Paper stock	,,	1,061

Foreign exports. During the year the foreign exports have been as follows:—

Articles.		Quantity.
Cotton	Bales..	249,374
Spirits turpentine	Casks..	6,479
	Cases..	100
Resin	Barrels	156,146
Tar	,,	8,545
Pitch	,,	768
Lumber	Feet ..	10,710,890
Shingles		2,452,400

The exports by the month were as follows:—

January.—Cotton, 17,432 bales; spirits turpentine, 1 cask; resin, 17,843 barrels; tar, 31 barrels; pitch, 36 barrels; lumber, 1,679,027 feet; shingles, 969,800.

February.—Cotton, none; spirits turpentine, 200 casks and 100 cases; resin, 8,109 barrels; tar, 1,925 barrels; pitch, 700 barrels; lumber, 1,143,336 feet; shingles, 205,000.

March.—Cotton, none; spirits turpentine, none; resin, 25,766 barrels; tar, 4,956 barrels; lumber, 1,621,451 feet; shingles, 455,450.

April.—Cotton, 6,560 bales; spirits turpentine, 6 casks; resin, 8,596 barrels; tar, none; lumber, 1,241,978 feet; shingles 25,000.

May.—Cotton, none; spirits turpentine, none; resin, 5,447 barrels; tar, none; lumber, 685,807 feet; shingles, none.

June.—Cotton, none; spirits turpentine, 2,204 casks; resin, 12,644 barrels; tar, 15 barrels; pitch, 20 barrels; lumber, 508,059 feet; shingles, 46,200.

July.—Cotton, none; spirits turpentine, 1,003 casks; resin, 12,210 barrels; tar, 1,106 barrels; lumber, 1,032,877 feet; shingles, none.

August.—Cotton, none; spirits turpentine, 1,300 casks; resin, 8,883 barrels; tar, 2 barrels; pitch, 2 barrels; lumber, 1,079,359 feet; shingles, 42,000.

September.—Cotton, 38,674 bales; lumber, 130,313 feet.

October.—Cotton, 75,951 bales; resin, 11,678 barrels; tar, 10 barrels; pitch, 10 barrels; lumber, 890,221 feet; shingles, 522,975.

November.—Cotton, 58,467 bales; resin, 13,970 barrels; lumber, 584,606 feet; shingles, 73,300.

December.—Cotton, 52,290 bales; spirits turpentine, 1,765 casks; resin, 31,000 barrels; tar, 500 barrels; lumber, 113,856 feet; shingles, 112,675.

LONDON:
Printed for Her Majesty's Stationery Office,
By HARRISON AND SONS,
Printers in Ordinary to Her Majesty.
(75 2 | 98—H & S 79)

DIPLOMATIC AND CONSULAR REPORTS.

REPORT FOR THE YEAR 1897

ON THE

TRADE AND COMMERCE OF GALVESTON AND DISTRICT.

REFERENCE TO PREVIOUS REPORT, Annual Series No. 1894.

Presented to both Houses of Parliament by Command of Her Majesty,
MARCH, 1898.

LONDON:
PRINTED FOR HER MAJESTY'S STATIONERY OFFICE,
BY HARRISON AND SONS, ST. MARTIN'S LANE,
PRINTERS IN ORDINARY TO HER MAJESTY.

And to be purchased, either **directly** or through any Bookseller, **from**
EYRE & SPOTTISWOODE, EAST HARDING STREET, FLEET STREET, E.C., and
32, ABINGDON STREET, WESTMINSTER, S.W.; or
JOHN MENZIES & Co., 12, HANOVER STREET, EDINBURGH, **and**
90, WEST NILE STREET, GLASGOW; or
HODGES, FIGGIS, & Co., Limited, 104, GRAFTON STREET, DUBLIN.

1898.

[C. 8648—60.] *Price Twopence.*

CONTENTS.

	PAGE
GALVESTON—	
Introduction	5
Improvement of trade	5
Gain to British shipping	6
Bank clearances	6
Position of Galveston among United States ports	6
British trade	6
Decrease of British trade	6
Less cotton exported to Great Britain	6
Increase in other articles	6
Comparative standing of Great Britain	6
Decrease off-set by carrying trade	7
General foreign trade, total value of	7
Standing of various countries	7
Imports	7
Value of imports	7
Imports from Great Britain	7
„ Germany	8
„ France	8
„ Mexico	8
„ other countries	8
Exports	9
Total value of exports	9
Cotton	9
Cotton-seed oilcake and meal	9
„ oil	9
Wheat	9
Maize	9
Wheat flour	9
Lumber	9
Lead	9
Logs	9
Borax	9
Spelter	9
Cattle	9
Exports to Great Britain	9
„ Germany	10
„ France	10
„ The Netherlands	10
„ Belgium	10
„ Denmark	11
„ Italy	11
„ Mexico	11
„ other countries	11
Shipping and navigation	11
Total tonnage of shipping	11
Tonnage of foreign shipping	11

(92)

CONTENTS—continued.

	PAGE
GALVESTON—continued.	
Shipping and navigation—continued.	
British shipping	11
Cargoes of British vessels	12
Freights	13
Public health	13
Dengue epidemic	13
Death rate for year	14
Immigration	14
Railways	14
Figures as to Texas railways	14
Improvement of terminal facilities at Galveston	14
Pittsburg and Gulf Railroad	14
Cotton business, 1896-97	14
United States crop for season	15
Prices	15
Texas crop	15
Percentage of deliveries from various groups of cotton growing States	15
Receipts of cotton at various United States ports	16
Exports of cotton from various United States ports	16
Cotton business, 1897-98	16
Phenomenal crop	17
Comparative small Texas crop	17
Prices	17
Increase of receipts at Galveston	17
„ Galveston exports	17
Receipts at Galveston	17
Comparative standing of Galveston	17
Receipts and exports at Galveston	18
Grain trade	20
Grain-laden British vessels	20
Table of grain exports	20
Public works	20
Improvement of wharf front	21
New grain elevators	21
Contemplated improvements	21
Harbour improvements	21
Completion of South Jetty	21
Work of dredger	21
Depth of water	21
Expenses of improvement	21
Tables of imports, exports and shipping	22
SABINE PASS—	
Trade and commerce	28
Shipping and navigation	28
Population and industries	28
Public health	29
Public works	29
General remarks	29
Shipping return	30

NOTE.—Calculations are made throughout this report at 5 dol. to the 1*l.* sterling.

No. 2038. **Annual Series.**

Reference to previous Report, Annual Series No. 1894.

Report on the Trade and Commerce of Galveston and Consular District for the Year 1897 *by Mr. Consul Nugent.*

During the year 1897 the general domestic trade of Galveston has shown a steady improvement over 1896, and in some respects very marked, as compared with the past few years.

Owing to the Dingley Tariff, recently brought into force, much greater activity than usual was displayed in filling stocks of various goods, and owing further to the establishment of a new steamship line from New York, and the competition resulting therefrom, rates by sea were very much lower, and in consequence wholesale dealers largely availed themselves of favourable conditions to import merchandise from that city.

Both the wholesale grocery trade and the wholesale dry goods business materially increased during 1897, the former showing a gain of 15 per cent. in value, and the latter some 40 per cent. Both benefited largely by the low ocean rates from New York, and also by the enforced quarantining of New Orleans during the yellow fever epidemic.

Owing to these conditions a good deal of the trade, formerly tributary to St. Louis and New Orleans, has been captured by Galveston and bids fair to stay here.

There was but one noticeable business failure in Galveston during 1897 and none at all amongst wholesale houses, whilst retail trade was very good during the year.

Turning to the foreign trade of Galveston a fair improvement in the total value over 1896 was shown.

The imports, however, undoubtedly owing to tariff restrictions show a decline, and were, in fact, less in value than in any year since 1892, excepting 1894–95.

As I have had occasion to remark in previous reports Galveston is at present "une quantité négligeable" as regards direct foreign imports. Her rise as a deep water port is, at present, too recent to interfere with established importing ports.

When the existing contracts for imports viâ New Orleans and the railways leading out therefrom expire, we may hope to see a material increase in direct foreign exports, but hardly until then.

The foreign imports amounted to only 128,849*l*. in 1897, as against 158,981*l*. in 1896.

Examining the figures of the exports, however, the striking increase of the business of the port during 1896 is seen to have been kept up.

Marginalia: Introduction. Improvement of domestic trade. Improvement of foreign trade.

(92)

GALVESTON.

The value of the exports from Galveston during 1897 was 12,000,943*l*., as against 11,288,866*l*. in 1896 and 7,106,425*l*. in 1895, or a gain of more than 6 per cent. for the year, and this, too, with a largely diminished price of cotton, the principal commodity exported.

Gain to British shipping. — This gain has largely benefited British shipping; the cargoes exported in British vessels during 1897 being valued at 10,268,069*l*. as against 9,121,882*l*. in 1896, a gain of 12·5 per cent., and the number and tonnage of British ships both showing a big increase.

Exports of cotton, grain, cotton-seed products, lead, spelter, &c., have all increased, and, as far as the business of the port is concerned, 1897 may be summed up as the heaviest exporting year Galveston has ever known.

Bank clearances. — Increased business has had an effect on bank clearances, these being 287,688,100 dol. for 1897, as against 262,101,680 dol. in 1896.

Position of Galveston among United States ports. — Galveston ranked in 1897 as the fifth exporting port in the United States, and the eleventh in point of bank clearances.

For the year ending June 30, 1897, the gain in exports from the United States Atlantic ports was 10·25 per cent., whilst the Gulf ports increased in exports no less than 37·40 per cent.; or to put it another way, of the total increase of exports from the whole country of 168,380,000 dol., 58 per cent., or nearly 100,000,000 dol. worth, was shipped from southern ports.

The facts I have stated above all show that Galveston obtained her fair share of the increased export business.

British trade. Decrease of British trade. — Although the general trade of Galveston increased in 1897, that done with Great Britain and the Colonies shows a decided decrease, falling from 6,838,468*l*. in 1896 to 5,739,688*l*. in 1897, or a decrease of 16 per cent.

Less cotton exported to Great Britain. — This decrease was almost entirely due to the comparatively small quantity of cotton shipped from here to Great Britain during the present season, and this too in spite of a phenomenally heavy crop.

Whilst cotton exports to Germany and France have increased, those to Great Britain have decreased and are actually less this season, with the immense excess received here, than last season with its smaller crop. Of course, only a certain amount can be taken by Lancashire spinners, and what is not sent from Galveston goes from other ports, so that perhaps there is no great actual loss to British trade as a whole, but only a shifting of the point and time of export, and an allowing of this country to carry the cotton until needed.

Increase in other articles. — Except in cotton, however, trade with Great Britain has increased, but the decrease of some 1,300,000*l*. in cotton during 1897 can only be off-set by a gain of some 400,000*l*. in other exports, so that British trade, on the whole, has, as I before remarked, diminished, whilst that with France and Germany has increased.

Comparative standing of Great Britain. — The total shrinkage will be best seen when it is stated that in 1894 Great Britain did 57·88 per cent. of the total trade of this port, 58·53 per cent. in 1895, and 60·31 per cent. in 1896.

In 1897 the percentage was only 47·84, whilst France had increased from 11·93 per cent. in 1896 to 17·22 in 1897, Germany remaining at about the same figure, viz., 21·60 per cent. in 1896 and 21·26 per cent. in 1897. A study of the tables of percentages following will show this in detail.

As an off-set, however, against the decrease in actual imports and exports to and from Great Britain must be placed the carrying trade done in British ships. As before remarked, this increased 12·5 per cent., and out of a total foreign trade of 12,129,792*l*. at least 10,300,000*l*. was done in vessels under the British flag.

Decrease off-set by carrying trade.

The total value of the trade to and from Galveston during 1897 was 12,129,784*l*., as against 11,447,847*l*. in 1896, thus showing an increase of rather over 5½ per cent.

General trade. Total value of general foreign trade.

The imports amounted to 128,849*l*. and the exports to 12,000,943*l*.

The following table shows the percentage of the total trade done by each of the principal countries interested.

Standing of various countries.

TABLE showing Percentages of Total Trade at Galveston, by Countries, during the Years 1896–97.

Country.	1896. Value.	1896. Percentage.	1897. Value.	1897. Percentage.
	£		£	
Great Britain and Colonies	6,905,621	60·31	5,793,509	47·84
Germany	2,472,331	21·60	2,579,031	21·26
France	1,356,088	11·85	2,088,820	17·22
Netherlands	281,193	2·45	658,926	5·43
Belgium	75,266	0·66	506,925	4·18
Mexico	30,773	0·27	109,923	0·90
Denmark	149,151	1·30	160,571	1·32
All other countries	177,224	1·56	232,089	1·85
Total	11,447,647	100·00	12,129,794	100·00

The total value of direct imports from abroad into Galveston during 1897 was 128,849*l*., as against 158,981*l*. in 1896, or a decrease of 19 per cent.

Value of imports.

Of the total of 128,849*l*., 70,238*l*. represented the value of articles subject to duty, and 58,611*l*. that of those entered free.

The principal dutiable articles were cement, chemicals, manufactures of flax, hemp, and jute, rice, and beetroot sugar, whilst amongst those free of duty the most important were coffee, sheep dip, jute and jute butts, sisal grass and manufactures of wood.

The imports from Great Britain and Colonies were valued at 53,820*l*. in 1897, as against 77,153*l*. in 1896.

Imports from Great Britain.

The following table shows the value of the principal imports from the British Empire in 1897, as compared with 1896.

(92)

GALVESTON.

Imports from British Empire.

Articles.	Value.	
	1897.	1896.
	£	£
Bags for grain, made of burlap*	3,295	..
Cotton ties*	..	32,155
Paper stock (old bagging)*	1,007	4,140
Salt*	1,533	6,909
Jute and jute butts*	25,868	16,417
Sheep-dip	3,041	1,825
Chemicals and compounds	2,115	163
Earthenware (plain and decorated crockery)..	3,625	4,218
Flax, hemp, and jute (manufactures of)	4,461	1,740
Iron and steel (manufactures of)	1,037	2,185
Ale and porter	950	1,520
All other articles	6,888	5,881
Total	53,820	77,153

* Free of duty.

Note.—Cotton ties and salt were dutiable during part of 1897, and free during 1896.

The chief falling-off was in cotton ties (owing to the recently imposed duty), and the heaviest gain was in jute from India.

Imports from Germany. The imports from Germany decreased from 50,369*l.* in 1896 to 44,127*l.* in 1897. The chief articles imported were, cement, value 16,388*l.*; chemicals, 5,601*l.*; rice, 3,247*l.*, and beetroot sugar, 12,645*l.*

There was an increase in the value of the cement imported, but a large fall in that of the sugar.

Imports from France. Imports from France were valued at 2,074*l.* in 1897, as against 3,768*l.* in 1896, and consisted chiefly of wines, preserved fruits, and fish.

Imports from Mexico. The imports from Mexico amounted to 16,663*l.* in 1897, as compared with 15,117*l.* in 1896, the chief items being sisal grass, 12,635*l.*, and timber, 3,993*l.*

Imports from other countries. Standing of various countries. The only other items of note imported during 1897 were coffee from Porto Rico, 2,881*l.*, and cement from Belgium, 7,253*l.*

The following table shows the percentage of the import trade at Galveston for 1896 and 1897 by countries.

Tables showing the imports in detail are also annexed.

GALVESTON.

TABLE showing Percentage of Imports at Galveston, by Countries, during the Years 1896-97.

Country.	1896. Value.	1896. Percentage.	1897. Value.	1897. Percentage.
	£		£	
Great Britain and Colonies	77,153	48·53	53,820	41·77
Germany	50,369	31·68	44,127	34·24
France	3,768	2·37	2,074	1·61
Mexico	15,117	9·50	16,663	12·93
Belgium	7,858	4·94	7,602	5·90
All other countries	4,716	2·98	4,563	3·55
Total	158,981	100·00	128,849	100·00

The total value of the exports from the port of Galveston during 1897 was 12,000,943*l*., as compared with 11,288,866*l*. in 1896, or an increase of about 6⅓ per cent. *Exports. Total value of exports.*

Cotton, as usual, was the leading commodity exported, and during 1897 the largest amount ever shipped from this port left Galveston, viz., 1,374,942 bales, valued at 8,988,313*l*., as compared with 1,182,601 bales, value 9,419,062*l*. in 1896. *Cotton.*

Although the quantity was larger, yet, owing to cheap prices, the value was less.

Other cotton products, such as cotton-seed oilcake and meal were exported in 1897 to the amount of 164,863 tons, value 650,418*l*., as against 136,648 tons, value 593,376*l*; also cotton-seed oil to the value of 236,364*l*., as compared with 94,344*l*. in 1896. *Cotton-seed oilcake and meal. Cotton-seed oil.*

As regards cereals there was a striking increase in the amount of wheat exported during 1897, viz., 7,372,636 bushels, value 1,352,399*l*., as compared with 3,440,494 bushels, value 414,702*l*. in 1896, while the exports of maize decreased, being only 4,073,019 bushels, value 260,695*l*., as against 6,222,282 bushels, value 402,615*l*. in 1896. *Wheat. Maize.*

On the whole, however, the grain trade shows considerable expansion for the year.

Wheat flour shows a slight falling off, only 49,878 barrels, value 40,888*l*., being exported in 1897, as against 56,195 barrels, value 42,578*l*., in 1896. *Wheat flour.*

Other exports of note that increased in 1897 over 1896 were lumber, value 29,624*l*., as against 13,332*l*.; lead, 45,124*l*., as against 13,196*l*.; logs, 23,374*l*., as against 10,120*l*.; borax, 57,045*l*., as against 23,153*l*.; and spelter, 112,394*l*., as against 88,663*l*. *Lumber. Lead. Logs. Borax. Spelter.*

The most notable of new exports in 1897 was cattle, value 62,882*l*. *Cattle.*

Although there was a great falling-off in the exports to Great Britain and Colonies, yet the British Empire was, as usual, the best of Galveston's customers, 47·83 per cent. of the total exports going thither. *Exports to Great Britain.*

GALVESTON.

The total value of the merchandise shipped to Great Britain and Colonies in 1897 was 5,739,688*l*., as against 6,838,468*l*. in 1896, as will be seen from the following table.

Exports to British Empire.

Articles.	Value. 1897.	Value. 1896.
	£	£
Cotton	4,795,981	6,118,165
Cotton-seed oilcake and meal	76,061	89,451
Maize	89,651	128,922
Wheat	505,653	210,924
" flour	15,698	2,206
Lumber	9,918	2,106
Cotton-seed oil	6,614	13,894
Logs	1,276	880
Spelter	110,393	87,567
Lead	38,354	8,676
Borax	57,045	25,153
Copper and copper-matte	18,816	14,876
Cattle	3,780	..
Sundries	10,448	135,648
Total	5,739,688	6,838,468

It will be seen that the greatest decrease was in cotton, viz., some 1,300,000*l*.; whilst there was a total gain in other exports of some 400,000*l*.

Exports to Germany. The export trade to Germany rose from 2,421,962*l*. in 1896, to 2,534,904*l*. in 1897, but was only 21·13 per cent. of the total exports in the latter year, as against 21·45 per cent. in 1896.

The chief items exported were cotton, 1,799,912*l*.; cotton-seed oilcake and meal, 403,329*l*.; wheat, 163,577*l*.; maize, 82,940*l*.; lumber and logs, 29,024*l*.; cotton-seed oil, 8,550*l*., and staves, 45,813*l*.

Exports to France. The exports to France were 17·40 per cent. of the total export trade of 1897, as against 11·98 per cent. in 1896, and rose from 1,353,250*l*. to 2,086,747*l*.

The chief items were cotton, 1,861,776*l*.; wheat, 128,911*l*.; cotton-seed oil, 59,220*l*.; maize, 16,323*l*.; and lead, 6,770*l*.

Exports to the Netherlands. The exports to the Netherlands again largely increased during 1897, being 658,926*l*., as against 281,193*l*. in 1896.

The principal exports were cotton, 97,881*l*.; cotton-seed oilcake and meal, 74,396*l*.; maize, 45,253*l*.; cotton-seed oil, 110,905*l*., and staves, 56,926*l*.

Exports to Belgium. The exports to Belgium rose from 65,968*l*. in 1896 to 499,323*l*. in 1897, a striking increase.

The chief items taken by that country were cotton, 223,066*l*., and wheat, 272,155*l*.

GALVESTON.

The exports to Denmark also increased during 1897 to 160,571*l.* from 149,151*l.* in 1896.

The principal of these were cotton-seed oilcake and meal, 84,196*l.*; cotton, 35,278*l.*; wheat, 14,280*l.*; and maize, 26,528*l.*

The exports to Italy were 113,996*l.* in 1897, as compared with 36,289*l.* in 1896, the chief items being cotton, 94,300*l.*, and cotton-seed oil, 12,920*l.*

The exports to Mexico increased from 15,656*l.* in 1896 to 93,260*l.* in 1897. They were chiefly made up of cotton, 61,825*l.*, and cotton-seed oil, 23,995*l.*

Other exports in 1897 to be noted were flour to Cuba, 15,802*l.*, and to Porto Rico, 6,357*l.*; cattle, 59,102*l.*, to Cuba; and cotton, 18,294*l.*, to Russia.

The following table shows the standing of the chief countries as regards exports during 1896 and 1897, whilst a table showing the exports in detail is annexed.

TABLE showing Percentage of Exports from Galveston, by Countries, during the Years 1896–97.

Country.	1896. Value.	1896. Percentage.	1897. Value.	1897. Percentage.
	£		£	
Great Britain and Colonies	6,838,468	60·57	5,739,688	47·83
Germany	2,421,962	21·45	2,534,904	21·13
France	1,353,250	11·98	2,086,747	17·40
Netherlands	281,193	2·49	658,926	5·50
Denmark	149,151	1·32	160,571	1·34
Belgium	65,968	0·58	499,323	4·16
Russia	81,505	0·71	18,294	0·15
Italy	36,289	0·32	113,996	0·94
Mexico	15,656	0·14	93,260	0·77
All other countries	45,624	0·44	95,234	0·78
Total	11,288,866	100·00	12,000,943	100·00

According to the statement issued by the United States customs authorities the total tonnage entered at Galveston increased largely during the year 1897, being 979,261 registered tons, as against about 800,000 registered tons in 1896.

The foreign tonnage entered was 609,498, both that and the domestic showing considerable increase.

The foreign tonnage cleared amounted to 627,870 registered tons, and comprised 276 British, 24 German, 18 Norwegian, and 26 Spanish vessels.

The enlarged business of the port in 1897 brought a corresponding increase in British shipping, the movement of which was the heaviest ever recorded in one year.

During 1897 there were 276 British vessels entered at Galveston, their combined tonnage being 505,959 registered

GALVESTON.

tons, against 230, of 395,607 tons, in 1896, so that there was an increase of 20 per cent. in numbers, and of 27 per cent. in tonnage.

The average tonnage per vessel was very high, viz., 1,830.

There were 34 British vessels having full or partial cargoes, but only 13 brought cargoes direct to Galveston, the remainder having cargo in transit.

The number of vessels arriving direct from Great Britain or a British colony was 121. Of the others 36 arrived from Brazil, 20 from Portuguese colonies, 20 from Spanish colonies, 15 from U.S. Colombia, 13 from other United States ports, 12 from Argentina, 11 from Mexico, and the remainder from various other countries.

During 1897, 277 British vessels cleared from Galveston, as against 229 in 1896. Their combined registered tonnage was 509,023 tons, as against 391,934 in 1896. Of these 277 vessels 101 were destined for the United Kingdom, 70 for Germany, 42 for France, 26 for the Netherlands, 12 for Belgium, 11 for Denmark, and the remaining 15 for other countries.

Cargoes of British vessels.

The total value of the cargoes exported in 1897 in British shipping was 10,268,071*l*., as compared with 9,128,882*l*. in 1896, or an increase of 12·5 per cent.

The following tables show the value of the cargoes shipped to the various countries in British bottoms during 1897, as compared with 1896, and the chief items for the same two years:—

Country.	Value. 1896.	Value. 1897.
	£	£
Great Britain	5,170,762	4,781,039
Germany	2,128,184	2,158,371
France	1,380,035	2,090,762
Holland	184,165	636,152
Denmark	85,112	157,643
Belgium	65,968	375,932
Italy	41,891	48,142
Mexico	12,433	15,278
Cuba	..	4,750
Russia	53,332	..
Total	9,121,882	10,268,069

The following is a list of the principal exports in British vessels during the year 1897 as compared with 1896:—

GALVESTON.

Articles.		Quantity.	
		1896.	1897.
Cotton	Bales	987,389	1,175,876
Cotton-seed meal	Sacks	1,964,010	2,339,035
" oilcake	"	186,962	364,472
Wheat	Bushels	2,886,159	6,434,742
Maize	"	4,897,472	3,645,623
Cotton-seed oil	Gallons	1,097,983	363,925
Walnut lumber and logs	Pieces	29,854	70,365
Spelter	Plates	297,386	220,376
Borax	Sacks	23,364	37,724
Copper matte	"	28,261	16,727
Lead	Bars	35,987	85,320
Lumber	Feet	203,621	399,477
	Pieces	138,972	316,768
Cedar logs	"	2,602	6,589
Staves	"	101,015	4,100,501
Flour	Sacks	..	25,773
Ixtle	Bales	..	5,733
Zacatan	"	..	4,268
Canaigre root	"	..	6,780

Early in the year 1897 cotton freights had reached the unusually low figure of $\frac{1}{8}d.$, whilst wheat was correspondingly low at 2s. $7\frac{1}{2}d.$, and tonnage for cotton-seed meal and cake at 16s. Freights.

There was a good rally in April, and at the close of the latter part of May the freights quoted were $\frac{3}{16}d.$ for cotton, and 3s. for wheat. At the beginning of September cotton had reached a $\frac{1}{4}d.$, cotton-seed meal was quoted at 17s., and wheat at 3s. $1\frac{1}{2}d.$

From this time on to the close of December, cotton freights gradually increased, finally reaching $\frac{9}{32}d.$, closing at $\frac{17}{64}d.$, whilst cotton-seed meal and cake had touched 18s. 6d., finishing at 18s., and wheat had ranged from 3s. 3d. to 3s. 6d., which was quoted generally at the end of the year.

The low freights in October were occasioned by the stagnation of business, owing to the yellow fever scare, and the consequent accumulation of berth and chartered steamers waiting for cargoes (at one time there were 64 steamers in port), and it is needless to say that as soon as the apprehensions proved groundless, things quickly assumed their normal condition.

During the summer and autumn of 1897 Galveston was visited by a widespread epidemic of "Dengue" or breakbone fever. As many as 20,000 or 25,000 cases were treated, but the mortality was almost "nil." Public health. Dengue epidemic.

Coinciding as it did in point of time with the epidemic of yellow fever at New Orleans, and showing, in some cases, symptoms very similar to that dread disease, it was thought prudent to send a Government expert here to pronounce on the nature of the malady, and he announced that he found eight well defined cases of yellow fever.

The effect of this statement was to cause a total cessation of business, and a strict quarantine against Galveston. However, as none of the patients died, and the fever did not rage much longer, the quarantine was very shortly afterwards raised, and the flow of business resumed.

Excepting this epidemic the health of Galveston during 1897 was good, and the rate of mortality low.

Death-rate for year. The death-rate for 1897 was 13½ per cent., on an estimated population of 50,000.

Immigration. During 1897 there were 1,357 passengers from foreign countries landed at Galveston. Of these, 1,233 were of the immigrant class, and were chiefly brought in German vessels. The bulk of them were farmers and unskilled labourers, of whom the majority settled in Texas.

Although the number of immigrants is, as yet, comparatively speaking, small, the outlook at present is not unfavourable for immigration business, as the lines bringing them are now regularly coming to Galveston.

Railways. Figures as to Texas railways. According to the figures issued by the Railway Commissioners of Texas for the year ending June 30, 1897, there were 68 railways in operation in the State during that year with a total length of 9,484 miles, excluding yard track and sidings.

There was an addition of 46 miles of new line during the year.

The aggregate earnings of these 68 lines amounted to 37,340,226 dol., or some 2,000,000 dol. more than in 1896. The working expenses were 29,173,938 dol., or 78 per cent. of the earnings, a slight decrease.

The net earnings increased by 894,741 dol. over 1896, and the amount carried was 16,342,302 tons, as against 14,510,919 tons in 1896.

Improvement of terminal facilities at Galveston. As regards the port of Galveston, the most important railway matters during 1897 were the means taken to increase the terminal facilities of the town, and the completion of the Kansas City, Pittsburg and Gulf line to Beaumont.

As regards the former, much good work has been done by all the railways entering Galveston in building new sidings, filling in land, &c., and it is hoped that no further block of trains such as occurred here in last October, thereby greatly delaying the shipping of cargoes, will again occur. With the advent of deep water the business here has so largely increased that the railways cannot afford to have fault found in respect to terminal facilities, without running the risk of losing business.

Pittsburg and Gulf Railroad. The Kansas City, Pittsburg, and Gulf Road is of great importance to Galveston. Through its connection with the International and Great Northern, and with the East and West Texas Line, it virtually brings another trunk line into this port. Much new territory has been opened to Galveston merchants by giving them the same rates from here to points on this line as from New Orleans.

Cotton business, 1896-97. The cotton crop of the United States for the year ending August 31, 1897, amounted to 8,757,964 bales, valued at 321,924,834 dol., as compared with 7,157,346 bales, valued at

294,095,347 dol., for the year closing August 31, 1896. The increase for the year was 1,600,618 bales. Five-sixths of this gain was shown by the groups known in the cotton world as "other Gulf States" and "Atlantic States," the increase for Texas being only in round figures 258,000 bales. *United States crop for season.*

Prices were steady throughout the season, ranging from 7 c. to 7¾ c. per lb., though both higher and lower prices were exceptionally quoted. *Prices.*

The average commercial value of the crop per bale was 36 dol. 76 c., as against 41 dol. 9 c. for the season of 1895–96.

The following table shows the details of the Texas crop, which includes cotton grown in the Indian territory:— *Texas crop.*

	Quantity.	
	1896–97.	1895–96.
	Bales.	Bales.
Receipts at Texas seaboard	1,430,602	1,055,094
Shipped inland to Mexico and points west of Mississippi River	94,167	71,355
Shipped by rail via St. Louis and Cairo	172,727	234,511
Receipts at New Orleans (exclusive of Galveston)	538,210	605,991
" points on Mississippi River, north of St. Louis, bound eastward	11,848	22,631
Total	2,247,554	1,989,582

The proportion of the crop produced by the various groups of the cotton growing States during the last two seasons was as follows, viz.:— *Percentage of deliveries from various groups of cotton-growing States.*

	Quantity.	
	1896–97.	1895–96.
	Bales.	Bales.
Texas	2,248,000	1,990,000
Other Gulf	2,831,000	2,162,000
Atlantic	3,679,000	3,005,000
Total	8,758,000	7,157,000

The net receipts of cotton in bales at the different United States ports, and the detailed exports from these ports, during the seasons of 1896–97 and 1895–96 are shown in the following tables. The gain made by this port will be noticed, even though the Texas crop was not so heavy in proportion as the crop made elsewhere. The proportion of the crop of this State received at Galveston, viz., 61 per cent., was higher than ever before known, whilst New Orleans and Galveston were as usual the only two ports handling over 1,000,000 bales of cotton:— *Receipts of cotton at various United States ports.*

GALVESTON.

Net Receipts of Cotton at United States Ports.

Ports.	Quantity. 1896-97.	1895-96.
	Bales.	Bales.
New Orleans	2,128,315	1,809,864
Galveston	1,376,357	1,001,175
Mobile and Pensacola	371,222	227,379
Savannah	845,353	782,996
Charleston	402,317	292,288
Wilmington	234,664	176,447
Norfolk	738,286	344,124
Baltimore	61,255	45,038
New York	107,885	98,557
Boston	162,429	154,521
Philadelphia	53,097	45,414
West Point	50	143,838
Newport News	9,707	15,472
Brunswick	121,475	74,340
Port Royal	70,971	77,906
El Paso, Texas	100	300
Laredo, Texas	13,759	24,293
Eagle Pass, Texas	10,131	9,492
Texas City, Texas	54,245	54,019
Other minor points	67,482	42,883
Total	6,829,100	5,420,346

Table showing Exports of Cotton from United States Ports for 1896-97.

From—	Great Britain.	France.	Continent and Channel.	Total.	Total, 1895-96.
	Bales.	Bales.	Bales.	Bales.	Bales.
New Orleans	851,111	427,595	705,463	1,984,169	1,619,068
Galveston	743,026	201,591	286,225	1,230,842	706,090
Mobile and Pensacola	210,200	...	42,301	252,501	119,510
Savannah	48,263	15,334	372,543	436,140	366,116
Charleston	78,339	...	191,889	270,228	200,717
Wilmington	95,431	...	111,363	206,794	132,531
Norfolk	148,320	5,200	46,755	200,275	53,822
Baltimore	81,319	8,801	82,923	173,043	147,407
New York	330,700	44,111	306,657	681,468	698,316
Boston	234,519	...	1,169	235,688	275,716
Philadelphia	12,353	...	449	12,802	8,969
West Point	...	...	...	...	8,930
Newport News	9,382	...	325	9,707	14,629
Brunswick	103,370	...	21,791	125,161	74,340
Port Royal	71,529	...	...	71,529	77,906
El Paso, &c.	...	...	100	100	400
Laredo	...	...	13,759	13,759	24,293
Eagle Pass	...	...	10,131	10,131	9,492
Texas City	...	...	...	...	53,019
San Francisco	600	...	56,446	57,046	34,897
Total	3,018,462	702,632	2,250,289	5,971,383	4,626,168
Last year (1895-96)	2,299,182	465,870	1,861,116	4,626,168	...

Cotton business, 1897-98. Early in the present cotton season a phenomenally heavy crop was predicted, and this prognostication has been verified.

There seems to be no doubt that the production this season will exceed even the famous crop of 1894-95, when 9,900,000 bales were marketed, as the present estimate for the total crop of this season is from 10,500,000 to 11,000,000 bales. This enormous excess over the average has been largely grown in the Atlantic and Gulf States, excluding Texas. In this State, whilst the production has been heavy, it has not kept up with the strides of the cotton grown elsewhere. *Phenomenal crop. Comparative small Texas crop.*

Of the big crop of 1894-95 Texas produced one-third, but it is doubtful whether more than 3,000,000 bales will be marketed from this State this present season.

This abnormal production has, of course, had its effect on prices, which have ruled very low since September. At the beginning of that month middling cotton was $7\frac{1}{8}$ c. per lb., but at the end had dropped to $6\frac{1}{4}$ c. *Prices.*

By the end of October the price had gone down to $5\frac{3}{4}$ c., since which time it has varied from $5\frac{3}{4}$ c. to $5\frac{3}{8}$ c. The price of middling cotton on September 1, 1896, was $7\frac{1}{2}$ c., and at the end of the year, $6\frac{3}{4}$ c., or about 1 c. per lb. higher than at present.

In spite of the Texas crop being less in proportion than that produced in other States, and of the greatest production in this State being in the northern portion, and hence less likely to come to Galveston, this port has received more cotton than ever before known. *Increase of receipts at Galveston.*

Nearly 70 per cent. of the Texas crop to date has come to Galveston, and the difference between the amount handled here and at New Orleans is very much less than of late years.

Up to November, 1897, Galveston was the largest cotton exporting point this season, and it is only lately that New Orleans has passed her.

The exports to domestic ports, owing to the establishment of a new line to New York, and the presence here of the Morgan Line steamers during the time New Orleans was quarantined, have nearly doubled during the present season, whilst those to France and Germany have largely increased, Great Britain alone falling behind. *Increase of Galveston exports.*

The following table shows the receipts at Galveston during the last five seasons, up to February 1:— *Receipts at Galveston.*

Year.	Receipts to Date.	Receipts for the Season.	Texas Crop.
	Bales.	Bales.	Bales.
1893-94	904,374	1,021,724	1,824,922
1894-95	1,433,288	1,659,999	3,275,933
1895-96	758,372	1,001,075	1,989,582
1896-97	1,162,799	1,376,355	2,247,554
1897-98	1,606,577	..	..

The receipts here thus far this season and to the same date last season are compared in the following table, as well as those *Comparative standing of Galveston.*

GALVESTON.

for the same periods at New Orleans, Savannah, and Charleston, and the percentage of increase shown in each case.

	Galveston.	New Orleans.	Savannah.	Charleston.
	Bales.	Bales.	Bales.	Bales.
Receipts to February 1, 1898	1,606,577	1,977,341	964,021	402,055
Receipts to February 1, 1897	1,162,799	1,707,097	700,319	345,192
Percentage of increase..	38·16	15·83	37·65	16·47

Receipts and exports at Galveston.

The following table gives the receipts, foreign and coastwise exports, and stocks from September 1 in each of the last five seasons up to February 1.

The marked increase will be noticed.

Year.	Receipts Net.	Exports. Foreign.	Exports. Coastwise.	Stock, February 1.
	Bales.	Bales.	Bales.	Bales.
1893–94	904,374	636,225	135,135	137,073
1894–95	1,433,288	1,081,262	179,334	162,731
1895–96	758,372	489,051	155,326	113,448
1896–97	1,159,765	990,271	140,371	107,323
1897–98	1,606,577	1,129,835	274,746	214,072

The following tables show the standing of Galveston this season as compared with other cotton exporting ports of the United States up to the date of writing, and also the exports of cotton, in detail to the same date.

GALVESTON.

Ports.	Quantity.	
	1897–98.	1896–97.
	Bales.	Bales.
Galveston	1,606,577	1,162,799
New Orleans	1,977,346	1,707,097
Mobile	288,558	248,113
Savannah	964,021	700,319
Charleston	402,055	345,192
Wilmington	286,063	229,380
Norfolk	471,072	608,032
Baltimore	46,475	47,159
New York	93,693	95,145
Boston	135,885	126,229
Philadelphia	52,198	28,482
West Point		50
Newport News	7,120	9,559
Brunswick	155,923	84,427
Texas City	..	43,073
Port Royal	45,038	60,202
Other ports	79,247	41,577
Total	6,611,271	5,536,835
Difference	1,074,436	

TABLE of Receipts and Exports at Galveston, 1897–98, up to February 1, 1898.

RECEIPTS

	Quantity.	
	1897–98.	1896–97.
	Bales.	Bales.
Net	1,606,577	1,162,799
Other ports in district	174	36,904
Gross total	1,606,751	1,199,703

EXPORTS—FOREIGN.

Destination.	Quantity.	
	1897–98.	1896–97.
	Bales.	Bales.
Great Britain	597,602	630,107
France	242,817	157,148
Continent	280,916	216,175
Channel	8,500	861
Total	1,129,835	1,004,291

GALVESTON.

Exports—Coastwise.

Destination.	Quantity.	
	1897–98.	1896–97.
	Bales.	Bales.
New York	231,688	134,231
Morgan City	..	129
Other domestic ports	43,129	8,050
North, by rail	9	37
Total	274,826	142,447

Grain trade. Increased business. The trade in grain at Galveston which may be said to have only begun in 1893 shows a further increase for 1897 over 1896.

A total of 11,445,655 bushels was shipped, as against 9,662,776 bushels in 1896. Of this amount, 7,372,636 bushels were wheat and 4,073,019 bushels maize, as against 3,440,494 bushels and 6,222,282 bushels respectively in 1896.

The grain was principally shipped to Belgium, Denmark, France, Germany, Holland, and England.

Grain trade well established. There seems little doubt but that the grain trade at Galveston has become firmly established, and that this port is destined to be a prominent factor in the business ere long.

Increase in storage capacity. The storage capacity has been increased during the year by the construction of one new grain elevator and the enlargement of another and is now 2,300,000 bushels, as against 1,400,000 in 1896.

Grain-laden British vessels. Table of grain exports. There were 149 full or partial grain cargoes shipped in British vessels during 1897, as against 126 in 1896.

The following table shows the amount of grain shipped to February 1, from the beginning of the present season, September 1, and there is, at present, a stock of 729,250 bushels of wheat and 660,897 bushels of maize in port.

Destination.	Quantity.	
	Maize.	Wheat.
	Bushels.	Bushels.
England	123,500	3,066,059
Germany	292,992	784,800
Holland	654,500	1,516,660
France	374,800	1,078,600
Belgium	26,000	1,260,273
Denmark	76,000	229,285
Total	1,547,792	7,935,677

Public works, &c. The chief improvements during the year were on the wharf front.

GALVESTON.

The piers, which were destroyed by fire in 1896, were rebuilt, and sheds for merchandise added.

A number of old wooden structures on the wharves have been removed to make room for railway lines and sidings, and a great improvement has taken place in this respect. Other extensive improvements of this nature are contemplated in the near future.

A grain elevator of the capacity of 700,000 bushels was completed and is now in use, and another of 600,000 bushels capacity is now nearly finished.

A new dredger was built during 1897, and has been used for filling up land for building more wharves.

Other contemplated improvements are the cutting in two of various wharves with a long frontage on the channel by slips, so as to accommodate more vessels, and the systematising of the terminal facilities, which were found lacking during the rush of business last October. There seems a desire on the part of all concerned to leave no stone unturned to provide this port with the latest and best shipping facilities.

Early in 1897 the south jetty was completed to its full proposed length of 34,800 feet, and, for the present, no further work will be put upon it unless it is decided to extend it to the 30 foot curve. From the beginning of 1897 until work upon it ceased, there were put into the south jetty about 4,509 tons of rip rap stone, and some 15,516 tons of granite. Much more work was done on the north jetty; 1,200 feet being added.

The railway is now built to the extreme proposed length of the jetty, viz., 25,907 feet, and the apron is complete to the same point.

There remains but 300 feet to be completed with the outside granite blocks, so that both jetties are expected to be entirely finished before very long.

The work on the north jetty was delayed by a severe storm last March.

There were 42,334 tons of rip rap and 43,368 tons of granite put on the north jetty during 1897.

As regards the dredging of the channel, work was carried on during the whole year by the Government dredger, but was not pushed with such activity as in 1896, when it was considered necessary to endeavour to have at least a depth of 24 feet in the channel before the opening of the cotton season in September.

The total amount removed in 1897 by the dredger was 756,711 cubic yards.

In January, 1897, the survey showed a depth of 25 feet at mean low tide; whilst at present the depth is 26½ feet, or a gain for the year of 1½ feet.

The total amount appropriated for the work up to July, 1897, was 1,695,633*l*., whilst up to the same date 1,639,734*l*. has been expended.

GALVESTON.

Imports at Galveston during the Year 1897, Free of Duty.

Commodities.	Great Britain.	Germany.	France.	Mexico.	Porto Rico.	British East Indies.	Belgium.	All other Countries.	Total Value, 1897.	Total Value, 1896.
	£	£	£	£	£	£	£	£	£	£
American manufactures re-imported	55	2,519	...	...	...	...	40	...	2,614	2,209
Art works of American artists	...	...	39	...	...	...	...	...	39	104
Books and printed matter	61	5	...	...	...	...	...	...	66	136
Bags for grain, made of burlaps	3,295	...	...	...	...	...	...	47	3,342	...
Coffee	...	...	...	...	2,881	...	...	...	2,881	4,214
Chemicals (sheep dip)	3,041	...	...	...	...	...	...	...	3,041	...
Fertilizers (muriate of potash)	...	681	...	...	...	...	...	...	681	214
Fibres (jute and jute butts)	...	...	...	...	...	25,868	...	...	25,868	16,417
,, (bagging for cotton)	...	...	...	...	...	287	...	...	287	...
Household and personal effects	70	40	...	16	...	...	20	...	146	530
Mineral waters	...	177	...	...	...	...	...	...	177	74
Paper stock (old bagging)	1,007	...	...	...	...	...	...	...	1,007	4,140
Salt	1,533	...	...	...	...	...	...	...	1,533	6,909
Scientific apparatus for schools	...	131	...	...	...	...	...	...	131	268
Vegetable fibres (sisal grass)	...	...	...	12,635	...	...	...	...	12,635	10,010
Wood (timber, logs, and manufactures)	...	5	...	3,993	...	...	...	...	3,998	2,801
Miscellaneous articles	18	127	...	4	...	...	...	16	165	34,414
Total value of free imports for 1897	9,080	3,685	39	16,648	2,881	26,155	60	63	58,611	...
,, ,, ,, 1896	45,127	3,257	123	15,087	...	16,418	5	2,423	...	82,440

GALVESTON.

Imports at Galveston for the Year 1897, Paying Duty.

Commodities.	Great Britain.	Germany.	France.	Mexico.	Porto Rico.	British East Indies.	Belgium.	All other Countries.	Total Value, 1897.	Total Value, 1896.
	£	£	£	£	£	£	£	£	£	£
Asphaltum	...	...	...	...	...	...	...	778	778	...
Books and printed matter	76	1	...	...	...	...	...	...	77	71
Breadstuffs	44	...	...	...	...	...	...	49	93	26
Cement (Portland in barrels)	392	16,388	...	...	...	...	7,253	...	24,033	13,573
Coal and coke (bituminous)	661	...	...	...	...	...	48	46	755	765
Chemicals and compounds	2,115	5,601	...	15	...	...	4	...	7,735	163
Cotton (manufactures of)	455	152	...	...	...	...	...	66	673	737
Earthenware (plain and decorated)	3,626	402	...	...	...	...	...	88	4,116	4,684
Fibres (manufactures of flax, hemp, and jute)	4,461	14	...	...	...	...	...	...	4,475	1,750
Fruits and nuts (preserved and prepared)	65	5	...	...	...	...	...	47	117	320
Fish (sardines and others)	130	...	286	...	...	...	...	25	441	565
Glass	9	64	71	...	...	...	237	15	396	915
Iron and steel (manufactures of)	1,037	730	...	...	...	...	...	...	1,767	2,757
Metals (manufactures of)	415	36	...	...	...	...	...	...	451	64
Malt liquors (ale and porter in bottles)	950	9	...	...	...	...	...	...	959	1,529
Oil (olive)	3	...	...	...	...	...	...	31	34	574
Provisions (dairy products and meats)	8	...	...	...	...	...	...	87	95	79
Rice	...	3,247	...	...	...	...	...	...	3,247	4,311
Rice meal	...	...	...	...	...	...	...	...	...	...
Sugar (beet above 16 D.S.)	...	12,645	...	...	5	...	...	475	13,125	39,103
Spirits (distilled)	50	...	...	...	...	...	...	...	50	166
Salt	466	...	...	...	...	...	...	...	466	...
Vegetables (preserved and prepared)	524	19	...	...	...	...	...	13	556	751
Wines (still and sparkling)	...	384	1,411	...	...	...	...	83	1,878	772
Wood (manufactures of)	5	5	1	...	...	...	...	...	11	85
Wool	282	97	31	...	...	...	...	...	410	262
Miscellaneous	2,031	643	235	...	587	...	...	4	3,500	5,484
Subject to duty for 1897	17,805	40,442	2,035	15	592	26,155	7,542	1,807	70,238	76,541
Free of duty for 1897	9,080	3,685	39	16,648	2,881	...	60	63	58,611	82,440
Total imports for 1897	26,885	44,127	2,074	16,663	3,473	26,155	7,602	1,870	128,849	...
,, ,, 1896	60,455	50,369	3,768	15,117	...	16,698	9,298	3,276	...	158,981

GALVESTON.

Exports from Galveston for the Year 1897.

Destination.	Cotton. Quantity. Bales.	Cotton. Value. £	Cotton-seed Oilcake and Meal. Quantity. Tons.	Cotton-seed Oilcake and Meal. Value. £	Wheat. Quantity Bushels.	Wheat. Value. £	Maize. Quantity. Bushels.	Maize. Value. £	Wheat Flour. Quantity. Barrels.	Wheat Flour. Value. £	Lumber. Value. £
Great Britain and colonies	734,178	4,795,981	19,337	76,061	2,791,225	505,653	1,439,950	89,651	19,192	15,698	9,918
Germany	273,973	1,799,912	102,384	403,329	899,035	163,577	1,209,723	82,940	...	...	11,139
France	285,569	1,861,776	2,742	10,376	692,028	128,911	234,971	16,323	...	...	766
Netherlands	14,300	97,881	18,447	74,396	1,438,273	267,823	765,913	45,253	4,109	2,831	1,946
Belgium	36,349	223,066	600	2,060	1,476,075	272,155	...	...	350	200	472
Denmark	4,975	35,278	21,353	84,196	76,000	14,280	422,462	26,528	...	...	100
Mexico	8,711	61,825	...	...	...	...	...	...	...	...	2,270
Cuba	...	...	...	...	...	...	...	...	18,280	15,802	63
Spain	...	...	...	...	...	...	...	...	...	...	...
Italy	14,334	94,300	...	...	...	...	...	...	...	...	...
Russia	2,553	18,294	...	...	...	...	...	...	...	...	...
Austria	...	...	...	...	...	...	...	...	...	...	...
Porto Rico	...	...	...	...	...	...	...	...	7,947	6,357	250
Total for 1897	1,374,942	8,988,313	164,863	650,418	7,372,636	1,352,399	4,073,019	260,695	49,878	40,888	26,924
,, 1896	1,182,601	9,419,062	136,648	593,576	3,440,494	414,702	6,222,282	402,615	56,195	42,578	13,332

Exports from Galveston for the Year 1897—continued.

GALVESTON.

Destination.	Cotton-seed Oil. Quantity.	Cotton-seed Oil. Value.	Lard. Value.	Lead. Value.	Logs. Value.	Borax. Value.	Spelter. Value.	Cattle. Value.	Staves. Value.	Copper Ore. Value.	Sundries. Value.	Total, 1897.	Total, 1896.
	Gallons.	£	£	£	£	£	£	£	£	£	£	£	£
Great Britain and colonies	135,500	6,614	...	38,354	1,276	57,045	110,393	3,780	4,167	18,816	6,281	5,739,688	6,838,468
Germany	157,520	8,550	1,177	...	17,885	...	...	...	45,813	...	582	2,534,904	2,421,962
France	1,063,409	59,220	...	6,770	565	...	2,001	...	...	...	39	2,086,747	1,353,250
Netherlands	1,992,413	110,905	...	...	318	...	...	...	56,926	...	647	658,926	281,193
Belgium	10,100	440	...	...	...	...	...	...	...	...	930	499,323	65,968
Denmark	2,500	140	...	...	...	...	...	...	...	...	49	160,571	149,151
Mexico	692,599	23,995	...	...	3,230	...	...	...	...	...	1,940	93,260	15,656
Cuba	...	...	...	...	...	...	...	59,102	...	...	80	75,047	10,344
Spain	...	...	...	...	...	...	...	...	...	...	...	...	27,280
Italy	193,800	12,920	...	...	...	...	...	...	...	...	6,776	113,996	36,289
Russia	...	...	...	...	...	...	...	...	...	...	...	18,294	81,305
Austria	242,500	13,580	...	...	...	...	...	...	...	...	...	13,580	...
Porto Rico	...	...	...	...	...	...	...	...	...	...	...	6,607	8,000
Total for 1897	4,490,341	236,364	1,177	45,124	23,274	57,045	112,394	62,882	106,906	18,816	17,324	12,000,943	...
,, 1896	1,832,830	94,344	5,433	13,196	10,120	23,153	88,663	...	...	14,876	153,216	...	11,288,866

GALVESTON.

TABLE of Shipping Engaged in the Foreign Trade at Galveston during the Year 1897.

ENTERED.

Nationality.	In Ballast.		With Cargo.		Total.	
	Number of Vessels.	Tons.	Number of Vessels.	Tons.	Number of Vessels.	Tons.
American	5	1,314	6	983	11	2,297
British	242	440,470	34	65,489	276	505,959
Danish	1	1,540	...	...	1	1,540
German	3	2,913	21	37,548	24	40,461
Greek	1	1,805	...	...	1	1,805
Mexican	1	117	...	...	1	117
Norwegian	12	12,974	6	2,993	18	15,967
Russian	2	884	...	...	2	884
Spanish	25	39,072	1	1,396	26	40,468
Total	292	501,089	68	108,409	360	609,498

CLEARED.

Nationality.	In Ballast.		With Cargo.		Total.	
	Number of Vessels.	Tons.	Number of Vessels.	Tons.	Number of Vessels.	Tons.
American	2	801	14	19,052	16	19,853
British	9	10,005	268	499,018	277	509,023
Danish	...	...	1	1,540	1	1,540
German	...	...	23	37,854	23	37,854
Greek	...	...	1	1,805	1	1,805
French	...	...	1	1,042	1	1,042
Mexican	...	...	1	117	1	117
Norwegian	...	...	21	18,383	21	18,383
Russian	...	...	2	884	2	884
Spanish	...	...	24	37,369	24	37,369
Total	11	10,806	356	617,064	367	627,870

GALVESTON.

RETURN of British Shipping at the Port of Galveston in the Year 1897.

Direct Trade in British Vessels from and to Great Britain and British Colonies.

Entered.

Number of Vessels.			Total Tonnage.			Total Number of Crews.	Total Value of Cargoes.
With Cargoes.	In Ballast.	Total.	With Cargoes.	In Ballast.	Total.		£
11	110	121	20,351	212,443	232,794	3,514	...

Cleared.

Total Number of Vessels.			Total Tonnage.			Total Number of Crews.	Total Value of Cargoes.
With Cargoes.	In Ballast.	Total.	With Cargoes.	In Ballast.	Total.		£
101	...	101	201,372	...	201,372	3,142	4,781,039

Indirect or Carrying Trade in British Vessels from and to other Countries.

Entered.

Countries whence Arrived.	Number of Vessels.			Tonnage.			Number of Crews.	Value of Cargoes.
	With Cargoes.	In Ballast.	Total.	With Cargoes.	In Ballast.	Total.		£
United States of America	7	6	13	11,080	8,952	20,032	346	...
United States of Colombia	11	4	15	23,620	6,761	30,381	538	...
Belgium	2	2	4	3,926	3,004	6,930	111	...
Brazil	...	36	36	...	61,858	61,858	939	...
Portugal and colonies	...	20	20	...	36,739	36,739	524	...
Spain and colonies	...	20	20	...	33,946	33,946	489	...
Argentine Republic	...	12	12	...	23,473	23,473	326	...
Mexico	1	10	11	2,098	14,241	16,339	277	...
France	...	5	5	...	9,016	9,016	131	...
Italy	...	4	4	...	7,246	7,246	102	...
Uruguay	...	3	3	...	4,832	4,832	70	...
Guatemala	...	1	1	...	2,168	2,168	43	...
Other countries	2	9	11	4,414	15,791	20,205	321	...
Total	23	132	155	45,138	228,027	273,165	4,217	...

Cleared.

Countries to which Departed.	Number of Vessels.			Tonnage.			Number of Crews.	Value of Cargoes.
	With Cargoes.	In Ballast.	Total.	With Cargoes.	In Ballast.	Total.		£
Germany	70	...	70	124,056	...	124,056	1,815	2,158,371
France	42	...	42	80,923	...	80,923	1,231	2,090,762
Netherlands	26	...	26	46,445	...	46,445	656	636,152
Belgium	12	...	12	20,220	...	20,220	311	375,932
Denmark	11	...	11	17,952	...	17,952	270	157,643
Italy	1	...	1	1,656	...	1,656	23	48,142
Mexico	4	2	6	5,056	1,138	6,194	137	15,278
Cuba	1	1	2	1,338	1,397	2,735	51	4,750
United States of America	...	6	6	...	7,470	7,470	146	...
Total	167	9	176	297,646	10,005	307,651	4,640	5,487,030

Sabine Pass.

Mr. Vice-Consul Roland reports as follows:—

Trade and commerce.
During the year ended December 31, 1897, the total clearances through the custom-house at this port, comprising all classes of rigs and nationalities, were:—107 vessels, registered 76,097 tons, 1,348 crews, carrying cargoes of 65,223,038 superficial feet of long leaf yellow pitch pine, lumber, and timber, of the value of 513,924 dol. United States currency, of which 26 vessels registered 58,223 tons, 451 crews, with cargoes representing a value of 51,170*l.* were under the British flag. These figures would have been largely augmented but for the unusual demand for tonnage for the exportation of cotton and grain, which class of freights obtain better transportation rates than is admissible for lumber and timber. The exports at this port are exclusive of long leaf yellow pitch pine, lumber, and timber, and this being a sub-port to Galveston and not a port of entry there are no imports. I am informed that a Bill is pending before the United States Congress, with a view to separating this port from Galveston, and making it an independent full port of entry, in which event, considering the improved facilities already accomplished and in prospect, a large importation of all classes would follow.

The market prices of long leaf yellow pitch pine is based on the supply, demand, and a classification covering quality, dimensions, &c. The f.o.b. prices are at present: rough lumber 10 dol. per 1,000 superficial feet; dressed lumber, 14 dol. per 1,000 superficial feet; sawn timber 11 c. per cubic foot on 40 foot basis; hewn timber, 11 c. per cubic foot on 100 foot basis.

Shipping and navigation.
On September 12, 1897, this port was visited by a hurricane doing considerable damage to the shipping at that time in the harbour. The British ship "Otterspool," the only British vessel at that time in the harbour, sustained injuries, most of which were repaired here.

The appointment of a harbour-master took effect early in the year, and the addition of this port officer facilitates the handling and despatching of vessels. The facilities for loading and discharging have been materially improved by the construction of a slip 700 by 180 feet, and another slip 1,000 by 200 feet is now in the course of construction. The value of cargoes exported in British bottoms was 51,170*l.*, an increase on the year 1896 of 37,134*l.*

Population and industries.
The population of this port is approximately 1,000 having increased by about 500 during the year. The employment of the people is almost exclusively handling lumber and timber, and their wages run from 2 dol. to 7 dol. 50 c. per day, the latter being that paid for skilled labour in handling and stowing timber. During the greater part of the months of September and October much inconvenience to shipping and business in general was occasioned by quarantine regulations existing between nearly all of the Gulf ports, on account of the yellow fever

SABINE PASS.

at New Orleans and adjacent points. There was not a case of yellow fever at this port, and extra precautions were taken both by State and Federal quarantine officers and the Board of Health to prevent its introduction. There has been very little sickness here and the rate of mortality is very low. *Public health.*

Under the available appropriation by the United States Congress, the channel at this port has been straightened and widened, and the extension of the jetties is now in progress, all of which contemplates an expenditure of about 1,050,000 dol. The quarantine station has been moved 2 miles further from town, and better facilities exist for the fumigation and inspection of vessels. *Public works.*

A telephone communication was established early this year between this point, Orange, Beaumont, and Port Arthur, and recently a telegraph line has been constructed, connecting us with Beaumont, where connection is made with all points.

Port Arthur is the southern terminus of the Kansas City, Pittsburg, and the Gulf Railroad, 780 miles south of Kansas City, Missouri, the second largest railroad centre in the United States. Port Arthur is located in Sabine Lake, which has an outlet to the Gulf of Mexico through Sabine Pass, 14 miles inland. Port Arthur will be connected with Sabine Pass Harbour by the Port Arthur Channel, 7 miles long, 183 feet wide, and 26 feet deep, of which $1\frac{1}{2}$ miles have been dredged to a depth of 20 feet. This channel is expected to be completed in nine months, ready for commerce to all parts of the world. Contracts have been let by this railroad company, aggregating 2,500,000 dol. for the channel, docks, and railroad terminals. It may be of interest to note that this railroad taps the largest grain producing section of the United States; also the cotton belt of Louisiana. The exportation of grain and cotton will be made feasible through this port in the near future. *General remarks.*

This railroad has established a regular line of steamships out of this port, the Atlantic and Mexican Gulf Steamship Company, their vessels making bi-monthly trips.

SABINE PASS.

RETURN of British Shipping at the Port of Sabine Pass during the Year 1897.

Direct Trade in British Vessels from and to Great Britain and British Colonies.

	Entered.						Cleared.					
Total Number of Vessels.			Total Tonnage.			Total Number of Crews.	Total Value of Cargoes.	Total Number of Vessels.			Total Tonnage.			Total Number of Crews.	Total Value of Cargoes.
With Cargoes.	In Ballast.	Total.	With Cargoes.	In Ballast.	Total.			With Cargoes.	In Ballast.	Total.	With Cargoes.	In Ballast.	Total.		
...	3	3	...	4,771	4,771	66	£ ...	9	...	9	27,277	...	27,277	219	£ 28,301

Indirect or Carrying Trade in British Vessels from and to other Countries.

Entered.

Countries whence Arrived.	Number of Vessels.			Tonnage.			Number of Crews.	Value of Cargoes.
	With Cargoes.	In Ballast.	Total.	With Cargoes.	In Ballast.	Total.		
Mexico	...	9	9	...	2,729	2,729	75	£ ...
Argentine Republic	...	3	3	...	5,329	5,329	69	...
Portugal	...	2	2	...	2,333	2,333	36	...
South Africa	...	1	1	...	2,179	2,179	29	...
Brazil	...	4	4	...	4,996	4,996	72	...
Total	...	19	19	...	17,566	17,566	281	...

Cleared.

Countries to which Departed.	Number of Vessels.			Tonnage.			Number of Crews.	Value of Cargoes.
	With Cargoes.	In Ballast.	Total.	With Cargoes.	In Ballast.	Total.		
Mexico	8	...	8	4,468	...	4,468	65	£ 4,394
Argentine Republic	2	...	2	10,182	...	10,182	34	2,882
Portugal	1	...	1	490	...	490	7	696
South Africa	1	...	1	2,557	...	2,557	20	2,504
Guatemala	1	...	1	363	...	363	13	355
Germany	1	...	1	3,752	...	3,752	28	467
Uruguay	1	...	1	829	...	829	14	672
Holland	1	...	1	4,894	...	4,894	29	7,292
Belgium	1	...	1	3,411	...	3,411	22	3,608
Total	17	...	17	30,946	...	30,946	232	22,870

No. 2081 Annual Series.

DIPLOMATIC AND CONSULAR REPORTS.

UNITED STATES.

REPORT FOR THE YEAR 1897

ON THE

TRADE AND COMMERCE OF NEW YORK AND DISTRICT.

REFERENCE TO PREVIOUS REPORT, Annual Series No. 1921.

Presented to both Houses of Parliament by Command of Her Majesty,
MAY, 1898.

LONDON:
PRINTED FOR HER MAJESTY'S STATIONERY OFFICE,
BY HARRISON AND SONS, ST. MARTIN'S LANE,
PRINTERS IN ORDINARY TO HER MAJESTY.

And to be purchased, either directly or through any Bookseller, from
EYRE & SPOTTISWOODE, EAST HARDING STREET, FLEET STREET, E.C., and
32, ABINGDON STREET, WESTMINSTER, S.W.; or
JOHN MENZIES & Co., 12, HANOVER STREET, EDINBURGH, and
90, WEST NILE STREET, GLASGOW; or
HODGES, FIGGIS, & Co., Limited, 104, GRAFTON STREET, DUBLIN.

1898.

[C. 8648—103.] *Price Twopence Halfpenny.*

CONTENTS.

	PAGE
NEW YORK—	
General remarks	5
Strikes	6
New tariff	6
Treasury gold balance	6
Agricultural produce	6
Mining—	
Gold	7
Silver	7
Copper	7
Lead	7
Spelter	7
Production of pig-iron	7
Railways	7
Exports and imports	7
New York money market	8
,, banks	8
,, clearing-house returns	9
Clearings outside New York	9
New York Stock Exchange	9
,, produce exchange	9
Sterling exchange on London	10
Failures	10
State banks of deposit and discount—	
Number	14
Capital	14
Assets and liabilities	14
Improved condition	14
Legislation	14
Recommendations	15
Deposits in savings banks	15
Debt of State of New York	15
New York City debt	15
Law enabling aliens to hold land	16
Freights—	
Grain	16
Cotton	17
Petroleum	17
Timber and deals	17
Sugar	17
Cattle	17
General cargo	17
Shipping at New York	17
New lines and vessels	18
Diversion of trade from New York	18

(149)

4

CONTENTS—continued.

	PAGE
NEW YORK—continued—	
Public works—	
Canals	19
Ship canal	20
New bridge over East River	21
Harbour channel of New York	21
Kill van Kull	22
Improvements of North River	22
Railroads goods traffic	22
Electricity as a motive power	22
Vital statistics	23
Immigration	23
Strikes in State of New York	24
Labour conditions	25
Electric light and water plants	25
Wages	26
Farming interests	26
Wages	26
Depreciation in value of farms	26
Comparative prices of staple commodities	27
Trade and commerce—	
Anthracite coal	27
Iron and steel	27
Steel rails	28
Tin-plate	28
Export of manufactures	28
Production and manufacture	28
Dry goods	28
Cotton goods	28
Silk	30
Woollen goods	30
Flax	31
Leather	31
Hides	31
Imports and exports	31
Cattle	32
Cheese	32
Scotch herrings	32
Grocery	32
Beet sugar	32
Tables of exports and imports	32
African exports	32
Delegates from Central and South America	33
Prohibition of import of sealskins	33
Return of principal articles of export	34
„ „ import	35
Value of imports and exports by countries	36
Specie	37
Grain shipments	38
Return of shipping	39
„ number of seamen	40
PROVIDENCE, RHODE ISLAND, trade report	41

No. 2081. **Annual Series.**

Reference to previous Report, Annual Series No. 1921.

Report on the Trade and Commerce of the Consular District of New York for the Year 1897

By Mr. Consul-General Percy Sanderson.

(Received at Foreign Office, April 16, 1898.)

The year 1897 was one of marked improvement although it opened under somewhat depressing conditions. The markets were in an unsatisfactory state, with prices of iron and steel extremely low, and combinations for the maintenance of prices failing in their object, the trade in cotton goods was far from prosperous; there was a sharp fall in the price of wheat in the month of January; traffic returns were disappointing, and railroad dividends were reduced in consequence; and the prospect of a new tariff law led to uncertainty in respect of trade in general. After the first quarter, however, matters began to improve, and in July the contrast became apparent between the abundant harvest in the United States and the crops in Europe and in other leading exporting countries. Stocks of wheat were down to a very low point, and the price rose rapidly, the demand being enormous. From this time forward a tide of prosperity set in, for practically the whole country with the exception of the South. The Western farmers were able to dispose of all the wheat they could gather at prices, in many instances, twice and three times as large as they had been able to obtain before, and as a result they began paying off mortgages on their farms and largely increased their purchases of supplies, &c. Trade in the manufacturing centres in the East reaped the benefit of much of this increased demand, and the additional traffic swelled the revenues of the railroads, whose earnings at the end of the year showed a very marked increase over those for 1896. The South unhappily formed an exception to this general recovery in business; floods in the spring caused great loss of life and property, and at one time it was estimated that 20,000 square miles were under water. Later on, in September, yellow fever broke out, and during two months, trade over a wide district was seriously interfered with by rigid quarantines. It was estimated at first that the cotton crop would be a small one; there was, however, a much larger yield than had been expected, the return being probably above an average, but

General remarks.

NEW YORK.

Strikes.

the prices were extremely low. Taken as a whole the year may be said to have been a satisfactory one, the value of the exports was the largest on record, that of the imports in excess of 1896, and the value of the total foreign trade showed an increase of more than 8,600,000*l.* over the highest previous total in 1891.

Labour troubles were less prominent than in recent years, but there was one very large strike of bituminous coal miners in Pennsylvania and Ohio, Indiana, and Illinois, in which it is calculated that about 150,000 men were engaged; the strike lasted from the beginning of July till about the middle of September, when it was ended by concessions on both sides.

New tariff.

The discussions in Congress over the new tariff were less protracted than usual. The new Congress was convened in extra session at the beginning of March, and the Bill was passed by the House of Representatives on the 31st of that month. In the Senate delay was caused by alterations, but an agreement was arrived at in July, and the new tariff became law on the 24th of that month.

Treasury gold balance.

While the Government receipts were not equal to the disbursements, there has never been any anxiety respecting the reserve of gold in the Treasury. This has been very large; in October offers of gold for legal tenders were refused, and on December 31, 1897, the balance was 160,911,547 dol.

Agricultural produce.

Taking the crops throughout the United States the yield was most satisfactory. Wheat was one of the largest crops that has ever been raised, the return showing over 530,000,000 bushels, an increase of more than 100,000,000 bushels when compared with that of last year. The yield of Indian corn was 1,903,000,000 bushels, somewhat less than in 1896 and in 1895 but still a large crop. Oats, 689,000,000 bushels, a trifle less than last year, but above the average. Prices in all cases were higher than last year, and as regards wheat, higher than for six years past. The cotton crop has probably been a very large one judging from the fact that 8,500,000 bales had already come into sight on February 1, 1898, but the price has been very low; in August it was quoted at $7\frac{5}{8}$ c., or a trifle over $3\frac{3}{4}d.$ per lb., and at the end of the year it had fallen to $5\frac{1}{2}$ c., or $2\frac{3}{4}d.$ a lb.

The following table shows the average prices received by farmers and planters all over the country during the last six years as reported by the Agricultural Department:—

AVERAGE Prices received by Farmers and Planters.

Articles.		1897.	1896.	1895.	1894.	1893.	1892.
		Cents.	Cents.	Cents.	Cents.	Cents.	Cents.
Wheat	Per bushel	80·8	72·6	50·9	49·1	53·8	62·4
Rye	,,	44·7	40·9	44·0	50·1	51·3	54·8
Oats	,,	21·2	18·7	19·6	32·4	29·4	31·7
Barley	,,	37·7	32·3	33·7	44·2	40·6	47·2
Indian corn	,,	26·3	21·5	26·4	45·7	36·5	39·4
Cotton	Per lb.	...	6·6	7·59	4·6	6·99	8·4

For purposes of rough calculation the cent may be taken as equal to a halfpenny.

The gold production of the United States shows a progressive **Mining:** increase, the estimate for 1897 being 2,975,067 ozs., valued at **Gold.** about 12,300,000*l.*, as compared with 2,568,132 ozs., valued at 10,617,600*l.*, in 1896, and 2,254,760 ozs., valued at 9,322,000*l.*, in 1895. Every State in which gold is mined with the exception of Utah appears to have returned an increase.

The production of silver is still very large; the quantity mined **Silver.** in 1897 is put down at 56,117,000 ozs., in 1896 at 58,489,000 ozs., and in 1895 at 46,331,000 ozs.

The production of copper is returned at 217,000 tons, of which **Copper.** it is calculated that 128,850 tons were exported. In 1896 the return showed about 12,000 tons less.

The lead production in 1897 was 194,000 tons, or nearly **Lead.** 20,000 tons more than in 1896. That of spelter about 100,000 **Spelter.** tons, comparing with about 78,000 tons in 1896.

The total production of pig-iron throughout the United States **Production of** is returned at 9,652,680 tons in 1897, as compared with 8,623,127 **pig-iron.** tons in 1896, and 9,446,308 tons in 1895. This is the largest output in any calendar year. The increase in the production was progressive, and on December 31, 1897, there were 188 furnaces in blast, producing 226,608 tons per week, as compared with 154 furnaces, producing 159,720 tons per week, at the corresponding date in 1896. The production was kept up notwithstanding the low price which ruled, and the stock at the end of the year was about 875,000 tons, or only 37,000 tons more than at the end of 1896, the total consumption being estimated at 9,780,000 tons. This includes an import of about 155,000 tons of iron and steel, being considerably less than in any previous year, and comparing with an import of 1,783,000 tons in 1887.

The earnings of the railways were poor during the first part **Railways.** of the year, and in several instances dividends were reduced, but there was a great improvement during the last six months, when the heavy grain movements and the revival in trade increased the receipts in some cases enormously. The railroads in the north-west and south-west reaped the greatest advantage, but those in the Eastern manufacturing districts were favourably affected although in a minor degree. Several of the lines converted their bonds, which were running at a high rate, into new ones bearing a lower rate of interest, for the most part about $3\frac{1}{2}$ per cent.

The value of the total exports of merchandise from the United **Exports and** States during 1897 amounted to upwards of 1,099,000,000 dol. **imports.** (about 220,000,000*l.*), nearly 94,000,000 dol. more than in 1896, when the value of the exports was the highest known up to that period. This is largely accounted for by the higher price of wheat and the increase in the export of breadstuffs, 170,500,000 bushels of wheat and flour, as compared with 155,000,000 bushels in 1896, and 188,500,000 bushels of Indian corn, as against 132,000,000 bushels in 1896. The shipments of cotton, 6,458,622 bales, were nearly 428,000 bales in excess of those of 1896, but the values stand at about 20,000,000 dol. less in consequence of the low price. For the same reason there is a reduction in the value of petroleum exported; on the other hand there is an increase in the value of provisions, and of "all other exports," which include manufactured goods. The value of the imports amounted to about 742,630,000 dol., or about 148,526,000*l.*, being more than 61,000,000 dol. in excess of those for 1896. The importations were very heavy in the early part of the year, especially in the month of April, in anticipation of higher duties under the new tariff. The value of the excess of exports over imports was nearly 356,500,000 dol., or about 71,300,000*l.*

The exports of gold exceeded the imports by a little over 51,000*l.*, whereas in 1896 there was an import of gold on balance amounting to nearly 9,500,000*l.*

In silver the returns show an export balance of over 5,000,000*l.* as compared with about 6,760,000*l.* in 1896.

New York money market.
At the commencement of the year there was great ease in the money market, so much so that in January the banks entered into an agreement not to lend below 2 per cent. at call, while the trust companies were lending at 1½ per cent. In March and April there were very heavy custom-house payments, but money returned from the interior and no effect was produced by these payments nor by the gold exports during April, May, and June. The tendency of rates was rather downwards until September, when reviving trade and the demand for money for moving the crops made their influence felt for a short time. In October there was a return to the former ease, and it was only in December that firmness was developed on the payment of the large sums connected with the purchase of the Government interest in the Union Pacific Railroad on which they had foreclosed.

The rate for call money was nominally 2 per cent. till the middle of September when there was a slight rise; at the end of September and during the first half of October the range was between 3 and 4 per cent., from this point it fell to 2 to 2½ per cent., and from the middle of December till the close of the year rates varied between 3 and 5 per cent.

On the Stock Exchange the rates followed the same course, but were, as a rule, slightly lower.

The rates for choice 60 to 90 day commercial bills with two signatures were from 3 to 3½ per cent. during the greater part of the year, in August, November, and December 3½ to 4 per cent., and in September and October 3¾ to 4½ per cent.

New York banks.
The following table shows the position of the New York clearing-house banks at different periods of the year; the rate of conversion being 5 dol. to the 1*l.*:—

NEW YORK.

Week ending—	Loans.	Deposits.	Specie.	Legal Tenders.	Reserve to Deposits.	Surplus Reserve.
	£	£	£	£	Per Cent.	£
January 2	98,275,180	106,157,000	15,268,460	17,928,180	31·27	6,657,380
February 6	99,502,720	113,792,360	15,911,900	23,444,200	34·58	10,902,000
March 6	100,412,360	115,492,220	17,012,340	22,972,100	34·62	11,111,380
April 3	100,546,540	113,845,300	17,197,660	20,796,980	33·37	9,533,300
May 1	101,166,340	115,372,780	17,465,960	21,160,760	33·48	9,783,520
June 5	102,383,740	116,251,020	17,862,180	20,264,740	32·79	9,064,160
July 3	106,541,580	120,996,740	18,099,320	20,426,840	31·83	8,276,960
August 7	109,912,480	125,246,460	18,425,960	21,086,080	31·54	8,200,420
September 4	113,858,240	128,351,880	18,484,680	20,426,120	30·31	6,822,820
October 2	114,398,680	123,870,640	18,433,020	15,604,720	27·51	3,110,080
November 6	114,807,160	126,468,620	20,435,200	15,418,200	28·34	4,236,240
December 4	119,548,800	133,255,720	20,897,960	16,840,560	28·32	4,424,580
,, 31	121,556,320	135,012,840	20,946,140	15,964,820	27·33	3,157,740

The surplus reserve represents the excess over 25 per cent. of the deposits, and the returns give the average of each week, not the actual figures for the day mentioned.

The maximum and minimum of deposits were: maximum 113,000,000*l*. as compared with 105,000,000*l*. in 1896, and minimum 106,000,000*l*. as compared with 87,700,000*l*.; the maximum and minimum of reserve 11,830,000*l*. and 2,300,000*l*. in 1897, and 8,036,000*l*. and 1,646,000*l*. in 1896.

The New York clearing-house returns show an increase of over 15 per cent. as compared with 1896, the figures being 33,427,027,000 dol. or about 6,685,405,000*l*. in 1897, and 28,870,775,000 dol. or about 5,774,155,000*l*. in 1896. This increase occurred entirely in the third and fourth quarters of the year. These figures are the largest since 1892, and no proper comparison can be made with that and former years, inasmuch as sales of shares on the Stock Exchange were included up to May 1892, but since that time they have been cleared independently through the Stock Exchange clearing-house. Since March 5, 1896, the cotton exchange has also been clearing its own transactions. *New York clearing-house returns.*

The clearings outside of New York amounted to 23,976,091,000 dol. or about 4,800,000,000*l*., being an increase of 6·7 per cent. as compared with 1896. During the first half of the year there was a decrease, but during the last five months the increase was very marked. *Clearings outside New York.*

The number of shares sold on the New York Stock Exchange was 77,324,170 in 1897 as compared with 54,654,096 in the previous year. The total of the new issues of both bonds, 87,720,000 dol., and stocks, 53,275,000 dol., was far below the average, but when the old issues newly quoted and those replacing old securities are included, the total has only been exceeded twice during the last 13 years. *New York Stock Exchange.*

On the produce exchange the total of sales exceeded those of 1896 by about 14 per cent., but fell considerably below those of 1895. There was an increase in flour, wheat, maize, oats, barley, malt and rye, and calculating the barrel of flour as equivalent to 4½ bushels of grain, the total sales amounted to about 1,477,322,000 bushels as compared with about 1,286,000,000 bushels in 1896. There is still the same complaint as last year of the *Produce exchange.*

NEW YORK.

railway rates from Chicago and Buffalo favouring Philadelphia, Baltimore, Norfolk, Newport News, and Boston, to the detriment of New York trade.

Sterling exchange on London.

Sterling exchange on London was lower than in 1896. The following table gives the posted rates, highest and lowest, for each month in the year. These are fractionally higher than the rates at which the bulk of business is done.

TABLE showing the Posted Rates of Sterling Exchange for the Year 1897.

Month.		At 60 Days.	At Sight.
		Dollars.	Dollars.
January	highest	4·86	4·88½
	lowest	4·84	4·87
February	highest	4·86	4·88
	lowest	4·85	4·87½
March	highest	4·86½	4·88½
	lowest	4·85½	4·87½
April	highest	4·87½	4·89
	lowest	4·86½	4·88
May	highest	4·87	4·88½
	lowest	4·86½	4·88
June	highest	4·87	4·88½
	lowest	4·86½	4·88
July	highest	4·87	4·88
	lowest	4·86½	4·88
August	highest	4·87	4·88
	lowest	4·84	4·86½
September	highest	4·85	4·87
	lowest	4·83	4·85½
October	highest	4·84	4·86½
	lowest	4·82½	4·85
November	highest	4·84	4·87
	lowest	4·83	4·86
December	highest	4·84	4·87
	lowest	4·82½	4·85½

Under ordinary circumstances the rate for bills payable on demand which admits of the export of gold from New York to London is about 4·88 dol. for bars and 4·89 dol. for coin, and the rate at which gold coin can be imported without loss is about 4·835 dol. per 1*l.* sterling.

The rate of exchange adopted in this report is the London Stock Exchange rate of 5 dol. to the 1*l.* As the true value of the 1*l.* sterling at par is 4·8665 dol., the Stock Exchange valuation is about 2¾ per cent. below par, and accordingly the present quotations of American securities are about 2¾ per cent. higher than in New York, a bond worth 100 in the United States being quoted at 102¾ in London.

Failures.

The following taken from the tables prepared by Messrs. R. G. Dun & Co., shows the number of commercial failures in the Consular district as well as those in the whole of the United States in 1897 as compared with 1896.

	Number of Failures.		Amount of Liabilities.	
	1897.	1896.	1897.	1896.
			£	£
New York	1,871	2,173	6,196,047	9,322,428
Connecticut	350	296	483,806	419,864
New Jersey	132	193	382,178	640,966
Rhode Island	109	125	318,332	544,204
Delaware	47	57	42,260	128,220
Whole of United States	13,351	15,088	30,866,414	45,219,367

These figures show a very marked decrease both in the number of failures and in the amount of liabilities, the exception being in the State of Connecticut, where there has been a slight increase in each case. As regards the whole of the United States, the number of failures decreased about 11 per cent. as compared with 1896, and the liabilities by 32 per cent.; the figures for the State of New York are of a very similar character. In the year 1896 the number of failures in the United States was 15,088 and the average liabilities for each failure 14,992 dol. In 1897 the number was 13,351, and the average liabilities 11,559 dol., but if the half-years be taken the average liabilities during the first half-year of 1897 were 13,441 dol., and during the second half-year 9,593 dol. being the smallest for any six months since 1890. The number of failures, however, 6,530, was much about an average, and the inference seems to be that the improvement in trade conditions during the latter part of 1897 was of more benefit to those in a large way of business than to the small trader.

In the tables published by Messrs. R. G. Dun & Co. showing the insolvencies by branches of trade, the only exceptions to a decrease in the amount of liabilities are foundries and manufacturers of iron and nails, where the number of failures was 108 against 114, but the liabilities 1,189,167*l*., as compared with 1,014,232*l*. in 1896, and manufacturers of cotton and lace and hosiery, 59 against 67, but a very large increase in liabilities, 1,960,143*l*., as compared with 529,868*l*. in 1896. The remaining manufacturers and trades show decreases of which the largest are, among manufacturers, woollens, carpets and knitted goods, lumber, carpenters and coopers, clothing and millinery, and liquors and tobacco; among traders, clothing and furnishing, dry goods and carpets, and shoes, rubbers and trunks.

The figures published by Bradstreet's differ slightly from the above as regards the totals. They classify the failures according to their primary causes under eleven heads. Eight of these heads imply faults of those failing, namely, incompetence, irrespective of other causes; inexperience, without other incompetence; lack of capital, including trying to do too much business for the capital employed; granting of unwise credit; speculation outside of regular business; neglect of business due to doubtful habits; personal extravagance; fraudulent disposition of property. The remaining three heads refer to failures not due to the faults of those failing, namely, disaster (flood, fire, failure of crops, commercial crisis); failure of others, apparently solvent debtors; special or undue competition. The following summaries are taken from these tables:—

NEW YORK.

Number of Failures in the United States, with Amount of Liabilities and Percentage of Total.

	1897.				1896.				1895.				1894.			
	Number.	Per Cent.	Liabilities.	Per Cent.	Number.	Per Cent.	Liabilities.	Per Cent.	Number.	Per Cent.	Liabilities.	Per Cent.	Number.	Per Cent.	Liabilities.	Per Cent.
Incompetence	1,610	12·3	3,261,154	10·3	1,892	12·5	6,867,114	13·6	1,781	13·7	3,104,309	9·8	1,794	14·1	3,054,586	10·4
Inexperience	734	5·6	465,065	1·7	688	4·6	767,905	1·6	518	4·0	556,382	1·7	538	4·2	855,144	2·1
Lack of capital	4,108	31·4	7,489,597	23·6	4,699	31·1	10,194,538	20·7	4,305	33·2	8,424,695	26·1	4,385	34·6	7,833,272	25·8
Unwise credits	456	3·5	1,684,305	5·3	653	4·4	1,905,452	3·5	603	4·6	1,687,407	5·1	532	4·2	1,060,509	3·5
Speculation	106	0·8	1,614,421	5·1	182	1·2	2,118,435	4·3	146	1·1	1,203,064	3·7	108	0·8	884,125	3·0
Neglect	311	2·5	320,659	1·1	345	2·3	435,255	0·9	333	2·6	430,556	1·3	321	2·5	389,297	1·3
Extravagance	159	1·2	226,584	0·7	140	0·9	539,616	1·1	128	1·0	425,108	1·6	135	1·1	300,070	1·0
Fraud	1,339	10·2	3,724,960	11·6	1,305	9·2	2,760,028	5·7	1,154	8·9	2,105,998	6·9	1,022	8·0	1,947,446	6·4
Disaster	3,312	25·3	10,072,005	31·7	4,153	27·5	18,444,749	37·4	3,229	24·9	10,677,113	33·6	3,295	25·9	11,694,960	39·0
Failure of others	266	2·0	1,962,437	6·1	397	2·7	4,499,445	9·2	299	2·3	2,569,468	8·1	317	2·5	1,876,472	6·2
Competition	683	5·2	918,557	2·8	550	3·6	842,266	2·0	462	3·6	611,438	2·0	277	2·1	404,823	1·3
Total	13,083	...	31,739,744	...	15,094	...	49,383,803	...	12,958	...	31,745,588	...	12,724	...	30,309,704	...

NEW YORK.

These figures as regards their totals show a great similarity between the years 1897 and 1895. There is, however, a considerable decrease in the liabilities under the head of "lack of capital," and a large increase in those under the head of "fraud."

Of the 15,008 failures in 1897 in the United States and Canada the percentages were, according to "Bradstreets," of traders having 1,000*l.* capital or less, 88·9 per cent. as compared with 80 per cent. in 1896; with 1,000*l.* to 4,000*l.* capital, 7·6 per cent. in 1897 and 13·7 per cent. in 1896; with 4,000*l.* and less than 10,000*l.* capital, 2 per cent.; with 10,000*l.* to 20,000*l.* capital, 0·6 per cent.; with 20,000*l.* to 100,000*l.* capital, 0·6 per cent.; and with 100,000*l.* capital and over, 0·03 per cent.

State banks of deposit and discount. Number.

The report of the Superintendent of Banks for the State of New York for the fiscal year ended September 30, 1897, shows that the number of State banks of deposit and discount transacting business was 212, being one less than the number at the corresponding period in 1896. During the year one bank failed, one went into voluntary liquidation, and one converted its business into a purely private and personal one; on the other hand, two new banks were organised. The total amount of capital of these 212 banks was about 6,114,000*l.*, as compared with a capital of about 6,244,000*l.* in 1896, and the assets and liabilities amounted to about 65,855,000*l.*, an increase of nearly 11,100,000*l.*, or upwards of 20 per cent. Of this increase 8,600,000*l.* was due to an increase in general deposits, two-thirds of which accrued between June and September, 1897. In commenting on this improved condition of the banks the Superintendent remarks that this year the published reports reflect the actual position more accurately than they did formerly when a large amount of collateral security that was not easily realisable had been thrown upon them; worthless items have been eliminated, much has been written down, and the tendency is for values to improve.

Capital.

Assets and liabilities.

Improved conditions.

The total resources of all the institutions under the supervision of the department are given as follows:—

	Amount.
	£
Banks of deposit and discount, September 15, 1897 (about)	65,855,000
Savings banks, July 1, 1897 .. .. „	167,934,000
Trust companies, July 1, 1897 .. .. .. „	88,693,000
Safe deposit companies, July 1, 1897 .. .. .. „	986,000
Foreign mortgage companies, January 1, 1897 .. „	4,685,000
Building and loan associations, January 1, 1897 .. „	10,898,000
Total	339,051,000

The increase, as compared with 1896, is about 27,500,000*l.* The securities and cash held by the Superintendent in trust for the protection of depositors amounted to about 808,000*l.*

Legislation.

There were only two changes made in the banking laws by the legislature of 1897; one adding to the list of stocks and bonds authorised as investments for the deposits in savings banks; the other providing that when receivers have been appointed for a bank all actions to enforce the liability of stock-holders shall be taken in the name of such receivers, but if they refuse to proceed upon a proper request by a creditor, then that creditor may take proceedings himself.

Recommendations. — The Superintendent recommends that the banking law be carefully and thoroughly revised in the near future. He points out that the sections of the Act referring to individual banks are incomplete, in that they contain no specific requirements for the amount of capital to be paid in, and he favours an interpretation of the law in the sense that no new individual banks should be authorised. He renews the recommendation made a year ago, that a deposit of money or securities should be required from building and loan associations to be held in trust as a guarantee that these institutions will satisfy the assessments levied upon them for the support of the department and for the cost of their examination. He considers that some amendment is desirable in the law providing for the incorporation of associations for lending money upon a pledge or mortgage of personal property, under which 36 associations had been formed; the law as at present framed merely requires the Superintendent to approve the bond which each is required to file annually, and to receive the annual reports which they must make, but does not provide for any examination.

Deposits in savings banks. — He also refers to the position of deposits in the savings banks; first, in reference to a demand that a list of savings banks accounts which have remained untouched for a number of years should be published or made accessible to enquirers. This he strongly deprecates on the ground that anyone with the right to such information can have no difficulty in obtaining it now, whereas it should be withheld from those who have no real concern with it, such as the drunken or worthless husbands of women depositors or predatory attorneys who would be apt to use it for their own purposes. Secondly, as to whether such deposits are liable to assessment for taxation as personal property. A case is now pending in the Law Courts which will lead to a decision on this subject, but the Superintendent urges that immediate measures should be taken by the legislature for the specific exemption of such deposits from assessment for purposes of taxation.

Debt of State of New York. — The debt of the State of New York amounted on September 30, 1897, to 5,765,660 dol., of which 495,000 dol. was for the Adirondack Park, and the remainder for the canals. This sum, equal to about 1,153,200*l*., compares with 2,320,660 dol. or about 464,200*l*. at the same date in 1896. The tax-rate for the purposes of the State Government is 2·67 dol. per 1,000 dol., as compared with 2·69 dol. in 1896–97.

New York City debt. — The position of the funded and temporary debt of the City of New York on December 31, 1897, as compared with December, 1896, is given below:

	December 31, 1897.		December 31, 1896.	
	Currency.	Sterling.	Currency.	Sterling.
	Dollars.	£	Dollars.	£
Funded debt..	223,018,034	44,603,607	195,907,690	39,181,538
Sinking fund..	86,170,758	17,234,152	77,630,491	15,526,098
Net funded debt	136,847,276	27,369,455	118,277,199	23,655,440
Temporary debt	5,069,245	1,013,849	2,433,327	486,665

The valuations of the year 1897 were, real estate, 1,787,186,791 dol.; personal estate belonging to residents, 251,988,384 dol.; belonging to non-residents, 47,524,295 dol.; shareholders of banks, 81,936,386 dol., making a total of 2,168,635,856 dol. or about 433,727,171*l*. as compared with 421,296,981*l*. in 1896. All the items show an increase except that of shareholders of banks. The rate of taxation was upon the assessed valuation of real and personal estate 2·10 per cent. as against 2·14 in 1896, and upon the assessed valuation of personal estate of such corporations, &c., as are not subject to local taxation thereon for State purposes, 1·834 per cent. as compared with 1·8276 in 1896. The total taxes were 45,332,402 dol. (about 9,066,500*l*.) as compared with 44,900,330 dol. (about 8,980,066*l*.) in 1896. The following are some of the items of appropriation: State taxes and common schools for the State, about 1,100,000*l*.; city debt interest, 1,131,000*l*.; redemption, 583,200*l*.; public works, 704,000*l*.; public charities, 258,000*l*.; police, 1,397,000*l*.; street cleaning, 600,000*l*.; fire department, 487,200*l*.; board of education, 1,186,300*l*.; judiciary, 373,000*l*.; asylums, reformatories, and charitable institutions, 305,400*l*.

Law enabling aliens to hold land in the State of New York.

A law was passed on May 19, 1897, enabling any citizen of a State or nation, which, by its laws, confers similar privileges on citizens of the United States, to take, acquire, hold and convey lands of real estate in the State of New York in the same manner and with like effect as if such person were, at the time, a citizen of the United States.

Freights.

Business in the freight market was good on the whole during the year 1897; the unsatisfactory state of the market in the East Indies, Australia, and the River Plate attracted tonnage usually engaged in trade to those countries; but the export from the United States was large, and notwithstanding this accession and increased carrying capacity of vessels of the regular lines, a good demand was maintained for most classes of vessels.

Grain freights.

The export of grain continued active throughout the year and freights were satisfactory although at no time reaching a very high figure. They were at their lowest in March and advanced gradually till they reached their highest point in November, viz., 4s. per quarter for Cork. As in the previous two years grain shipments have somewhat decreased in New York, ports in Virginia, Baltimore, and Philadelphia being favoured of late in preference to New York. This is attributed to the difference in railway rates which still continues, to high charges for loading and discharging at New York, and to the difference in the load line for North Atlantic ports in winter. There has been an unusually large amount of small grain such as barley, buckwheat, and oats shipped from New York, and during the autumn oats formed part cargo of a large proportion of grain shipments. All grain shipments were made by steamers.

Cotton freights were steady although the crop was very large; charterers engaged tonnage in good time and the maximum rates were 45s. per steamer's net register ton from Gulf ports, and 40s. from Atlantic ports to a direct port in the United Kingdom or on the Continent. The outbreak of yellow fever in the South during the months of September and October exercised an adverse influence on freights which might have reached a higher point if cotton shipments had not been checked. The bulk of shipments was made by steamer, a few cargoes only being shipped to Russia by sailing vessels. *Cotton freights.*

During the spring and early summer months the Standard Oil Company shipped petroleum largely in cases by steam vessels to the far East, but later in the year they took up tonnage in sailing vessels some months ahead and so kept up their stocks more economically. The export of petroleum for Europe continues to be regulated by the tank steamers of this company, and charters made for petroleum in barrels were necessarily low to make competition possible with shipments in bulk. *Petroleum freights.*

Timber freights were active, and during the spring steamers were employed in this business; later, however, the better rates obtainable for grain and cotton left the shipments in the hands of owners of sailing vessels. In deals an unusually large business was done, and a number of steamers were engaged for consecutive voyages. *Timber and deal freights.*

Sugar, as during the preceding year, was imported in small quantities, owing to the continuation of the troubles in Cuba. The greater part came by vessels of the regular lines. *Sugar freights.*

The shipments of cattle were slightly in excess of those of last year, but they were almost entirely taken by vessels of regular lines, and there was practically no demand on the general market. *Cattle freights.*

There has been a very large increase in the number of steamers despatched with general cargo of every description, specially locomotives, rails, bridge and railroad material, to China and Japan, and this business seems likely to increase. Japan is at present the principal consumer, and is now in the market for a large quantity of cotton to supply her factories. *General cargo.*

The return of shipping at New York shows an increase of 98 vessels and nearly 560,000 tons in the entrances, the figures being 4,324 vessels of 7,518,351 tons in 1897, and 4,226 vessels of 6,959,925 tons in 1896. The clearances show 4,664 vessels of 7,334,647 tons compared with 4,012 of 6,698,508 tons. *Shipping at New York.*

British tonnage shows an increase in the entries of 69 vessels and 331,226 tons, the total being 2,156 vessels and 3,771,463 tons, rather more than 50 per cent. of the whole. United States tonnage, 1,087,932 tons, is about 30,000 tons less than in 1896; German, 1,320,914, has increased 112,251 tons as compared with the previous year; Dutch, 323,822, shows an increase of about 8,000 tons; French, 295,500, an increase of 8,000 tons; Norwegian, 246,032, an increase of 65,000 tons; and Belgian, 193,828, an increase of about 14,000 tons.

New lines and new vessels.

A new line of steamers, the Wilsons and Leyland-Furness line, has been formed, carrying passengers as well as cattle, horses and general cargo, between New York and London. The White Star, the North German Lloyd, and the Hamburg-American lines, have all increased their fleet by very large vessels, and at the end of the year a commencement was made of running steamers regularly once a month to Calcutta by way of the Red Sea and Aden with general cargo, and returning with jute. These steamers occasionally proceed beyond Calcutta.

Diversion of trade from New York.

An enquiry conducted by the Chamber of Commerce of the State of New York into the diversion of trade from this port shows that the total exports from the United States in 1897, were valued at 1,127,800,000 dol., as compared with 1,023,300,000 dol. in 1896, whereas from New York they fell from 491,600,000 dol. in 1896 to 467,500,000 dol. in 1897. As regards this apparent loss it may be mentioned that there was a decrease of 64,400,000 dol. in the total shipments of coin and bullion, of which 62,000,000 dol. fell to New York, so that if the item of coin and bullion be excluded the exports have really increased by 38,000,000 dol. Taking the different items, however, it is found that while there was a large increase in the exports of cotton (69,000,000 dol.), breadstuffs (56,500,000 dol.), and provisions (25,000,000 dol.), the export under these three heads from New York diminished by about 4,000,000 dol. There was an increase in the export from New York of nearly 20,000,000 dol. in the value of locomotives and cycles, but the proportion to the whole export from the United States fell from 54·8 per cent in 1896 to 51 per cent. in 1897. The committee of the Chamber of Commerce, who conducted the enquiry in addition to commenting on the differential rates established by the railways and on the terminal charges, make two recommendations, first, to deepen and widen the channel into the harbour, certainly to a depth of 35 feet at low water, and a width of 2,000 feet; and second, that the Erie Canal and connecting locks and waters be deepened, so as to admit of barges coming through the lakes and canal without breaking bulk. They also drew attention to the difference in the load-line which allows of vessels from other ports carrying additional cargo in winter, representing a difference of from 600 to 2,000 dol. in freight to be earned, an amount which is considered a sufficient inducement to vessels to accept somewhat lower freights from other ports in preference to loading at New York.

Notwithstanding the above figures, it is pointed out in Bradstreet's that New York continues to hold the first place as

NEW YORK.

an exporter of breadstuffs and provisions, and that in the matter of provisions the export from New York exceeded in value that from Boston, which comes second on the list, by over 5,000,000*l*. As regards cattle, the largest export was from Boston, 154,406, showing a decrease of over 3,900; that from New York was 135,217, showing an increase of nearly 11,600 as compared with 1896.

The report of the Superintendent of Public Works of the State of New York shows that 3,617,804 tons (of 2,000 lbs. each) of freight were carried on the canals of the State during the year 1897, being 97,090 tons less than in 1896, and 117,490 tons more than in 1895. The tonnage of 1897 is, however, only 79·7 per cent. of the average of the 10 preceding years, which again is lower than that of the 10 years previous to them. *Public works. Canals.*

The amounts carried by the different canals were as follows:—

	Quantity.
	Tons.
Erie Canal	2,584,906
Champlain Canal	797,637
Oswego Canal	53,537
Black River Canal	71,447
Cayuga and Seneca Canal	110,277

The total east-bound tonnage was 2,448,361 tons, of which 1,232,211 tons were through freight, and 1,216,150 tons way freight. The westward tonnage amounted to 1,169,443 tons, of which 499,682 tons were through freight and 669,761 tons way freight. The tendency is towards a decrease in through traffic, and a larger business in way freight.

The goods carried are classified as follows:—

	Quantity.
	Tons.
Products of the forest	896,971
,, agriculture	789,783
,, manufactures	152,388
,, merchandise	250,872
All other articles	1,527,790
Total	3,617,804

As compared with 1896 there was a large increase in Indian corn, stone, lime, and clay, and in ice; a larger decrease in wheat, oats, flax seed and anthracite coal.

The report states that the past season was not a prosperous one for boatmen, freight rates being unusually low, and many individual boatmen preferring to tie up their boats rather than run them at the prevailing prices. The reasons given are, *first:*

the rapid deterioration of the canals as a waterway for transportation of freight; this is being remedied by the improvements now being carried out; *second:* the construction and condition of the canal boats and the method of traction adopted; the number of boats is given as 2,332, of which 1,117 carry grain and are rated as 1, 2, and 3, and the remainder are classed as boats for lumber, coal and other coarse freight; it is said that the majority of the whole number are old and rotten, and that many of them are propelled by mule power; *third:* the large terminal charges in the harbours of the cities of Buffalo and New York. As a remedy for the two latter, the Superintendent proposes a change in the present law so as to admit of the formation of canal transportation companies with a capital exceeding 50,000 dol., and legislation authorising the Canal Board, on the recommendation of the Superintendent of Public Works, to fix and determine from time to time the terminal charges which shall be levied or collected by elevator and storage companies.

The appropriation of 9,000,000 dol. (1,800,000*l.*) made for the purpose of improving the Erie, the Champlain, and the Oswego Canals, has been found insufficient for completing the work, and it is estimated that a further sum of 7,000,000 dol. (1,400,000*l.*) will be required. The improvements take in 454 miles of canal, the channel of the Erie and Oswego Canals having to be deepened from 7 feet to 9 feet, and the locks lengthened to double boat length, and the depth of the Champlain Canal having to be increased from 6 feet to 7 feet. The original estimate was for considerably more than the sum appropriated, and it was calculated that the material excavated from the canal bottom, could be used in raising the embankments, but it was found to be unfit for this purpose. The providing of new material for raising the embankment added considerably to the cost, but in addition, as the excavation proceeded the canal walls fell in in many places, and foundations of bridge abutments were weakened and gave way. The old slope walls have to be rebuilt in many places, and new culverts have had to be constructed. The report shows that out of the 454 miles, 307 are under contract, covering what are believed to be the most difficult portions of the proposed improvement, which can probably be completed at the opening of the navigation in 1899 if the further sum of 7,000,000 dol. is made available.

The shrinkage of canal business has been pretty constant during the last 30 years, and the tonnage has gradually fallen from an average of about 6,000,000 tons to something under 4,000,000 tons. During 1896 there were 32,252,000 bushels of grain carried from Buffalo to New York by canal, and 64,370,000 bushels by rail. During 1897 there were only 22,117,500 bushels carried by canal against 98,806,600 bushels carried by rail. The rate on wheat by canal was 2·8 c. per bushel as compared with 3·7 c. in 1896.

Ship canal from great lakes to

A preliminary examination has been made for a ship canal from the great lakes to the navigable waters of the Hudson River wholly within the United States, and of a sufficient capacity to transport the tonnage of the lakes to the sea. In the report on this subject three routes were stated to be possible. First: from Lake Erie by the Upper Niagara River to the vicinity of Tonawanda or Lassalle, thence by canal with locks to the Lower Niagara River to some point on Lake Ontario, through Lake Ontario to Oswego, up the Oswego and Oneida Rivers to Oneida Lake, through the lake and across the divide to the Mohawk River, and down that river to the Hudson at Troy. The second route follows the line of the Erie Canal from Lake Erie and the Niagara River through to the Hudson, or this line so modified as to provide a continuously descending canal from Lake Erie to the Hudson. The third route coincides with the first from Lake Erie to Lake Ontario, running thence through Lake Ontario to the St. Lawrence River, and down that river to some point near Ogdensburg, crossing the State of New York to Lake Champlain, up the lake, and then following in general the route of the Champlain Canal to the Hudson at Troy. The relative merits of these routes are discussed in the report, and the first is considered the best, but the cost of construction is estimated at about 40,000,000*l*., and the cost of maintenance at about 400,000*l*. a year. It is stated that such a canal would have no military value, and that it is not advisable that its construction should be undertaken by the general Government. The opinion is expressed that if, beyond the improvements now being carried out under existing plans, the Erie Canal be further improved so as to be made navigable for 1,500-ton barges, necessary alterations being made in its alignment so as to give a continuously descending canal from Lake Erie to the Hudson, and the Mohawk River be canalised, this would enable freight to be transported from East to West at a cheaper rate than by a ship canal, and that the cost would be approximately one-fourth that of a ship canal.

Hudson River.

The construction of a new bridge over the East River was commenced in May, 1897. The Bill providing for a commission to build this bridge was passed in May, 1895, but delay occurred owing to difficulties in purchasing property along the line to be occupied, and it further was found necessary to purchase a charter which had been granted in 1894 for the building of a bridge. The new bridge will in appearance resemble the Brooklyn Bridge, but the piers will be of steel instead of stone, the approaches on each side will be about 600 feet longer, and the space between the two piers will be about 1,600 feet, or very slightly in excess of that of the Brooklyn Bridge; the width, however, will be 118 feet as compared with 85 feet. The designs provide for six lines of rails, two for an elevated railway, and four for surface railroad cars, with all necessary approaches, switches and terminals. The cost is estimated at 12,000,000 dol. (2,400,000*l*.), as compared with 15,000,000 dol. (3,000,000*l*.) for the Brooklyn Bridge.

New bridge over the East River.

The need for a deeper channel in the harbour of New York in view of the constantly increasing draft of modern steamships was again brought to notice by the New York Board of Trade

Harbour channel of New York.

(149)

Kill van Kull and Staten Island Sound.

Improvements of the North River.

Railroads goods traffic.

Electricity as a motive power.

The endeavour is to obtain an increase in the depth of the channel from 30 to 35 feet, and that the width should be increased to 2,000 feet. A report has been made to the United States Government by the Engineer Corps and the Lighthouse Board recommending these improvements.

There is a plan for deepening the Kill van Kull and Staten Island Sound, and eventually for opening an inland waterway from New York to Washington, and it is understood that the United States Harbour Board, which has charge of the operations about the Sound, will recommend an increase in the appropriation for dredging.

The five new piers on the North River, which were alluded to in the last report, are now in course of construction. They are to be 125 feet wide with slips 250 feet wide between them so as to give room to warp the largest vessels into them under all conditions of tide.

During the year 1897 the total tonnage of all classes of merchandise sent westward from New York city by rail and consigned to or beyond Buffalo, Salamanca, Pittsburg, Bellaire, &c., was 1,383,907 tons of 2,000 lbs.; that arriving in New York city from the places above noted or from points west of them amounted to 6,746,851 tons. The railroads carrying these goods are the New York Central and Hudson River; Erie; Pennsylvania; Baltimore and Ohio; West Shore; Delaware, Lackawanna, and Western; Lehigh Valley; New York, Ontario, and Western; and, as regards goods arriving only, the Chesapeake and Ohio Railroad.

These amounts show an increase of about 100,000 tons in goods sent westward, and an increase of upwards of 1,600,000 tons in goods received from the West, the figures in 1896 having been 1,290,373 tons despatched and 5,077,651 tons received.

Electricity as a motive power is being largely introduced for the tramways in New York, several of the lines having lately adopted the underground trolley system. It has also been introduced on the New York, New Haven and Hartford Railroad, on a portion of which trains are being run by means of a third rail. This rail is shaped like a flattened "A" and rests on wooden blocks, which it overhangs, and so protects them from moisture; it is placed in the centre between the two other rails and through it passes the electric current of 500 volts which propels the cars. With a view to avoiding accidents it is fenced in at the stations, and, where the line crosses a road, a break occurs in the rail, the current being carried underground. The power-house is at Berlin, in the State of Connecticut, with four cities within a distance of 13 miles. The third rail is laid to New Britain and thence to Hartford, a total distance of about 13 miles; the line so equipped was opened for traffic on May 24, and has proved a success. The system is to be extended to Bristol, a distance of about seven miles; the Waterbury, Meriden, and Connecticut River Railroad are likely to adopt the same system, and it has been spoken of in connection with the elevated railroads of New York city. An electric locomotive is in operation on the Shore Road at Hoboken, New Jersey.

NEW YORK.

The vital statistics of the City of New York for the past two years are given as follows:— *Vital statistics.*

	Number.	
	1897.	1896.
Births	54,089	55,632
Still-births	3,574	3,542
Marriages	20,365	20,513
Deaths	38,877	41,622

Of the deaths reported 15,394 were of children under five years of age, which compares with 16,807 in 1896.

Cause of Death.	Number.	
	1897.	1896.
Small-pox	24	1
Measles	391	714
Scarlet fever	500	402
Diphtheria	1,376	1,555
Croup	214	208
Whooping cough	308	435
Typhoid fever	299	297
Diarrhœal diseases	2,515	2,874
Puerperal fever	169	198
Cancer	1,217	1,141
Phthisis	4,843	4,994
Other tuberculous diseases	848	932
Congenital debility	2,460	2,710
Diseases of nervous system	3,344	3,358
Heart diseases	2,346	2,396
Bronchitis	1,089	1,292
Pneumonia	4,621	5,383
Diseases of digestive organs	3,057	3,040
Bright's disease	2,059	2,195
Acute nephritis	440	490
Accident	1,782	2,641
Homicide	65	71
Suicide	436	384

The cases of contagious diseases reported were diphtheria, 10,496; croup, 400; measles, 9,118; scarlet fever, 7,699; typhoid fever, 1,004; small-pox, 73.

The population was estimated on July 1, 1897, at 1,990,562, and the death-rate for the year is given as 19·53 per 1,000, as compared with 21·52 in 1896.

The immigration returns show a large decrease in the total of 1897, as compared with 1896, the numbers being 172,420 and 233,394 respectively. The numbers from Austria-Hungary decreased by 17,000, from Italy 11,000, from Russia 10,000, and from Germany 7,000. From Great Britain there was a diminution *Immigration.*

of 1,700 and from Ireland 3,300. The immigration from the different countries is noted below, but owing to the records having been burnt in a fire which occurred at the Immigration Office at Ellis Island, it is impossible to give the destinations:—

Country.	1897. Male.	1897. Female.	1897. Total.	1896. Total.
	Number.	Number.	Number.	Number.
Great Britain	4,627	2,373	7,000	8,706
Ireland	7,430	10,987	18,417	21,749
Austria-Hungary	13,593	11,444	25,037	42,154
Belgium	425	271	696	913
Denmark	927	632	1,559	2,348
France	1,179	796	1,975	1,926
Germany	7,854	6,807	14,661	21,895
Greece	1,428	58	1,486	1,636
Italy	39,177	17,631	56,808	67,581
Netherlands	441	238	679	1,352
Norway	2,315	1,557	3,872	5,520
Portugal	705	850	1,555	2,002
Roumania	329	300	629	713
Russia and Poland	11,317	9,194	20,511	30,404
Spain	226	32	258	202
Sweden	4,765	6,141	10,906	13,709
Switzerland	862	503	1,365	1,849
Turkey	81	35	116	97
Other countries	3,095	1,795	4,890	8,638
Total	100,776	71,644	172,420	233,394

In addition to the above 1,421 persons, 1,303 males and 118 females were rejected, on the following grounds:—1,094 as paupers or likely to become a public charge, 305 as contract labourers, one as an idiot, six as insane, and 15 on account of disease.

Strikes. The report of the State Board of Mediation and Arbitration shows that during the year ended October 31, 1897, there were 243 strikes of which the Board had definite knowledge as compared with 246 in 1896. Many of these were of short duration, lasting only a few hours or a few days. Among the more important may be mentioned the steam-fitters' strike, and the tailors' strike, both of which occurred in New York.

The steam-fitters' strike was the result of a disagreement between different trades in New York City as to whether plumbers or steam-fitters should do certain work on a college building then in course of erection. The strike began on March 10 and threatened to result in a general strike in the building trades, involving 60,000 to 75,000 mechanics, but it was eventually settled by arbitration at the beginning of April.

The tailors' strike began on May 17, and is said to have involved some 20,000 to 24,000 workers in New York and Brooklyn. The men claimed that an agreement had been violated which had been entered into by the contractors in the autumn of the previous year, whereby a scale of wages was fixed for the term of one year, piece-work was to be abolished and the day's work was not to extend beyond 10 hours. The contractors on the other hand stated that no agreement had been made, and that wages were higher at the time than they had ever been. The requirements of the men resolved themselves finally into a demand for rates of wages ranging from 9 to 18 dol. per week of 59 hours, and for the manufacturers to sign an agreement that they would not employ any contractor who violated a contract in these terms. The strike was eventually settled at the beginning of June for the most part by individual agreements, the terms conceded being a 10 hours day and wages varying according to the work from 9 to 16 dol. (equal to about 1l. 17s. to 3l. 6s.) a week. The United Brotherhood of Tailors have since issued a notice to the clothing manufacturers that at a given time in 1899 the clothing workers would refuse to work for any contractor or middleman. There were other strikes among the cloakmakers, tailors, &c., during the year, and in fact, no year passes without a few strikes of this nature.

From the report of the Commissioner of the Bureau of Labour Statistics of the State of New York it appears that on March 31, 927 labour organisations reported a total membership of 142,670, of whom 2·98 per cent. were women; on June 30 the number of unions reporting was 975, the membership 151,206, and the percentage of women 2·67; and on September 30, unions 1,009, members 167,454, of whom 5,702 or 3·41 per cent. were women. As regards idleness, on March 31 there were 43,361 members, or 36·6 per cent., out of work; on June 30 the number had fallen to 27,738, or 18·1 per cent.; and on September 30 they were further reduced to 23,230, or 13·9 per cent. The average number of days worked was for the first quarter 58 for men and 63 for women; for the second quarter, 69 for men and 57 for women; and for the third quarter, 67 for men and 66 for women. The average earnings were 155 dol. 6 c. (31l.) for men and 85 dol. 63 c. (17l. 2s. 7d.) for women during the first quarter; 159 dol. 12 c. (31l. 16s. 6d.) for men and 81 dol. 39 c. (16l. 5s. 7d.) for women in the second quarter; and 174 dol. 40 c. (34l. 17s. 8d.) for men and 91 dol. 80 c. (18l. 7s. 3d.) for women in the third quarter. *[Labour conditions.]*

The second part of the Commissioner's report deals with the position of electric light and power, gas, and water plants in the State, and states that answers to inquiries were received from 97 electrical companies, 26 combined electric light and gas, two combined electric light and water, 61 gas, and 96 water companies. In addition returns were obtained from four electric light, five combined electric light and water, and 71 water supply plants all belonging to municipalities. The cost of producing electricity for lighting purposes seems to vary from 2½ mills to a little over 10¾ mills per ampère, the average price being estimated by a New York private corporation at 9 mills, something less than a half- *[Electric light, electric power, and water plants.]*

penny, per ampère. The selling price per incandescent light ranges from 40 c. (1s. 8d.) per month in Oswego to 1 dol. 50 c. (6s. 3d.) in Amsterdam, New York. For municipal arc lamps 6 dol. (25s.) a month are charged in Lockport, and 50 c. (2s.) a night in New York. Prices for electric power range from 25 dol. to 90 dol. yearly per horse-power (5l. to 18l.).

The cost of producing gas ranges from $31\frac{1}{2}$ c. (1s. $3\frac{3}{4}d$.) per 1,000 cubic feet in Utica to 1 dol. 49 c. (6s. $2\frac{1}{2}d$.) in Cohoes, the average being about 53 c. (2s. $2\frac{1}{2}d$.); the lowest price to consumers is 1 dol. 20 c. (5s.) per 1,000 cubic feet in New York, Brooklyn, and Buffalo; the highest, 2 dol. 50 c. (10s. 5d.) in Kingston, Middletown, and Renssalaer.

Wages. The average yearly wages paid were as follows:—Electric light and power plant, public, 612 dol. 50 c. (122l. 10s.), private, 672 dol. 47 c. (134l. 10s.); combined electric light and gas plants, 627 dol. 61 c. (125l. 11s.); combined electric light and water plants, 444 dol. 29 c. (89l.); gas plants, 621 dol. 90 c. (124l. 8s.); water plants, public, 519 dol. 44 c. (104l.), private, 364 dol. 80 c. (73l.). These figures do not include salaries paid to officers.

Farming interests. The third part of the report is devoted to the farming interests of the States, and the details were obtained from reports received from 1,255 stations in different counties.

Wages. The table relating to wages paid to farm labourers shows as daily wages: With board and lodging, summer, 99 c. (4s.); winter, 74 c. (3s.). Without board and lodging, summer, 1 dol. 22 c. (5s.); winter, 91 c. (3s. 10d.). Monthly wages: With board and lodging, summer, 18 dol. 8 c. (3l. 12s. 6d.); winter, 13 dol. 87 c. (2l. 15s. 6d.). Without board and lodging, summer, 23 dol. 20 c. (4l. 13s.); winter, 14 dol. 95 c. (3l.).

Depreciation in value of farms. The report points to the rapid and serious depreciation in the market value of the farms, which is estimated by the owners at from 50 to 75 per cent. during the last six years. The Commissioner comes to the conclusion that, notwithstanding that over 660,000l. has been expended by the State during the last 11 years for the avowed purpose of promoting agricultural interests, the farming industry is in a most deplorable condition with very poor prospects of recovery or improvement in the immediate future. No interest appears to have been realised on farm investments during 1894, 1895, and 1896, and it seems that where there were no mortgages requiring payment of interest a farmer was considered almost miraculously fortunate if his income from products could be made to pay the cost of production, even with stinted allowance for household expenses and by starving the soil. Some of the causes are stated as follows:—Low prices of farm products and high prices of farm labour; indebtedness; poor roads, making distant markets inaccessible; heavy charges of middlemen and for commission; high rates for railway transportation; and the competition of Western and Southern producers. In 1880 the value of farms was estimated at about 211,240,000l., and of farm products at about 35,605,000l.; the figures of the census of 1890 were: farms about 193,606,000*l*., and farm products about 32,320,000*l*., and over 34 per cent. of the farms were encumbered to the amount of over 43 per cent. of their total value.

The general tendency of prices of leading staple products as shown by Bradstreet's index of 98 staple articles was towards steadiness and strength, and although they were at a comparatively low point in June and July this showed considerable improvement on the prices at the same date in the previous year, while it is necessary to go back to January, 1895, to find an index number for that month equal to January 1, 1898. The index numbers are as follows :—

Comparative prices of staple commodities.

	1897.	1896.
April 1	74,915	67,189
July 1	72,999	67,182
October 1	79,111	72,178
	1898.	1897.
January 1	80,149	75,044

Of 98 staple articles comparing as to price on January 1 and December 1, 1897, there were 27 which showed an advance, 23 a decline, and 48 remained unchanged.

There has been an advance in prices of live-stock, provisions, fresh and dried fruits, hides and leather, raw and manufactured textiles (with the exception of cotton and cotton goods, manila, hemp, and jute), lead and tin, chemicals, and miscellaneous products; metals showed a decline.

During December prices of groceries and provisions, coal and coke, mineral and vegetable oils, and building materials were steady; there were advances in cereals, food products, naval stores, glass, and tobacco; while lower prices ruled for cotton goods, fresh fruits and raisins, pig-iron, steel rails, copper and lead, and some drugs and chemicals.

The amount of anthracite coal which was brought to market in 1897 was only 41,637,864 tons, as compared with 43,177,485 tons in 1896, and 46,511,477 tons in 1895, and prices continued unsatisfactory.

Trade and commerce. Anthracite coal.

The circular price for stove coal was 4 dol. 25 c. for the first six months and 4 dol. 50 c. for the last six months, but there is reason to believe that the actual prices ruled between 3 dol. 90 c. and 4 dol. 3 c. during the whole year with the exception of January when they were lower.

The prices for iron and steel were very low, and taking a number of leading articles they will be found the lowest for the last seven years. Prices declined in the early part of the year, there was a certain recovery in July or August which continued till October or November, and then a reaction set in. Steel billets were quoted at 15 dol. 75 c. to 16 dol. at the beginning of

Iron and steel.

the year, at 13 dol. 70 c. to 14 dol. 50 c. in May, at 16 dol. 45 c. to 17 dol. 50 c. in October, and at 15 dol. to 15 dol. 50 c. at the close of the year. Steel rails dropped heavily in price on account of the collapse of the steel rail pool in February. The price in 1896 was 28 dol., it was fixed at 25 dol. in 1897, but dropped to 16 dol. in February, and for the rest of the year was 18 dol. to 19 dol. The average price of Bessemer pig-iron was 10 dol. 13 c., as compared with 12 dol. 14 c. in 1896; of steel rails 19 dol. 58 c., as against 28 dol.; of steel billets 15 dol. 8 c., against 18 dol. 83 c. Notwithstanding the low price the total production of pig-iron in the United States in 1897 exceeded that of 1896 by upwards of 1,000,000 tons, and in the case of steel rails the effect has been to encourage exports. Considerable quantities of American steel rails were sold to a railway in India, and in addition to exports to Sydney, Mexico, and Japan, it is stated that an order for 1,000 tons was received at the end of the year from England.

Steel rails.

Tin-plate. The importation of tin-plate at New York decreased slightly, viz., from 59,789 tons in 1896 to 58,349 tons in 1897. For the year ended June 30, 1897, it is estimated that the total production of tin-plate and terne-plate in the United States was about 447,000,000 lbs., the consumption about 552,000,000 lbs., and that the average annual capacity of production of the mills completed and in process of construction was 650,000,000 lbs. The imports of tin-plate at New York, 58,349 tons, valued at 532,000*l*. show a reduction of about 2½ per cent. in quantity and 10 per cent. in value.

Export of manufactures. As regards the exports of manufactures of iron and steel, the articles which show the most notable increase are pig-iron, bars and rods of steel, steel rails, wire, nails, and bicycles. As regards locomotives the total export from the United States is returned at 348, valued at about 611,000*l*. in 1897, compared with 312, valued at about 592,000*l*. in 1896.

Production and manufacture. The centre of production for crude iron is apparently moving westward, where the iron ore is described as being purer and richer, easier to smelt, and producing a better article. On the other hand, the eastern mills manufacturing structural plate, pipe and bar iron, and wire, are likely to continue to do a good business. In the wire trade large profits are said to have been made in 1897, and at the close of the year it was understood that arrangements had been made for a large combination of mills in different parts of the country with a capital of about 10,000,000*l*.

Dry goods. The import of dry goods at New York under the heads of cotton, silk, and woollen manufactures are returned at a value of about 15,230,000*l*. during the calendar year 1897, as compared with 14,494,000*l*. in 1896 and 20,530,000*l*. in 1895. As compared with 1896 there has been a slight increase in the importation of cotton goods and a somewhat larger one in silks, but again a decrease in the value of woollens.

Cotton goods. The stock of cotton goods on hand at the beginning of the year was large, and in January there was very little demand; in February a purchase of 750,000 pieces of print cloths advanced the price of this class of goods, but the improvement was of short duration and buying became so slack that in the middle of April several of the manufacturers found their mills overstocked and decided to sell by auction even at a sacrifice. A sale of nearly 20,000 packages of staple cotton goods was held on April 14, and the prices realised, being only from 5 to 8 per cent. below the regular wholesale prices, led to the anticipation of a better market. During July, August, and September an extensive business was done for all but the export trade; prices remained low at first in consequence of the anxiety of sellers to reduce their stocks, but as the holdings decreased, to a certain extent in consequence of the curtailment of production, a rise was established, and in September the highest point was reached in staple cottons, being about 5 per cent. above the bottom. Buying then suddenly ceased, yellow fever in the south checked purchases in that important consuming district, and the remainder of the year was marked by curtailed business and declining prices.

In cotton dress fabrics the sales were probably larger than in 1896 in both printed and woven patterned goods, but prices were unsatisfactory; and the prices of such staple goods as indigo blues, blacks and greys, shirting, &c., were lower at the end of the year than they had ever been before. In ginghams production has been materially reduced, but this has not conduced to better prices than before; there are, however, indications that these may come into favour again. In print cloths the stock at the beginning of the year was 2,300,000 pieces, and notwithstanding the large purchase made in February, as noted above, and a curtailment of production extending over three months it had increased to 2,390,000 pieces at the end of the year.

The total production for the year is given as 10,748,000 pieces in 1897, as compared with 10,055,000 pieces in 1896; the highest price was $2\frac{11}{16}$ c., as compared with 3 c. in 1896, and the lowest, that which ruled at the close of the year, $2\frac{1}{4}$ c., as compared with 2·4375 c.

The statements of the Fall River mills show that the average dividends were about 3 per cent., reductions of wages were determined upon and the outlook was considered unsatisfactory. Complaints are made of the competition which comes from the south where labour is cheaper and the hours are longer; so long as only heavy coarse yarn fabrics were produced the Fall River mills were not materially affected, but during the last two years there has been a steady expansion of the output of print cloths and fine yarn goods in the south and a growth in the appreciation of buyers for southern-made goods. The total number of spindles in the country is returned at 17,356,537 in 1896–97, an increase of 545,341 as compared with the former year; of these 13,900,000 were in the north, and 3,456,537 in the south, the latter showing an increase of over 445,000. During the first half of the year the export demand for heavy-weight sheetings, drills, and coarse coloured cottons was very good; later, however, the fall in the price of silver checked the demand for China, and an increase in the Canadian tariff on the import of cotton goods probably led to the very heavy falling-off in the export of cotton cloth to the Dominion. The total exports of cotton cloth from the United States during the calendar year 1897 amounted to about 285,700,000 yards, as compared with about 281,200,000 yards in 1896; to the United Kingdom 9,300,000 yards, a decrease of 2,100,000 yards; Canada 14,400,000 yards, a decrease of 21,100,000 yards; China 133,500,000 yards, an increase of 26,500,000 yards; British East Indies 11,300,000 yards, an increase of 8,100,000 yards; Africa 18,700,000 yards, an increase of 4,200,000 yards. The exports from New York amounted to 197,200,000 yards as compared with 194,300,000 yards in 1896. The total imports of cotton-manufactured goods into the United States from Great Britain during 1897 were valued at about 2,740,000*l*., as compared with 2,397,000*l*. in 1896.

Silk. From the returns of the Silk Association of America it appears that the imports of silk manufactures were larger during the past year than in 1896, but below those of 1895; the values being given at 4,633,300*l*. in 1897, 3,947,000*l*. in 1896, and 5,464,600*l*. in 1895. There was an increase to the extent of about 400,000*l*. in the value of piece-goods imported, and of about 100,000*l*. each in ribbons and laces; there was a decline, however, of about 60,000*l*. in the value of velvets. The principal articles are: Piece-goods, 2,569,000*l*.; velvets, 333,150*l*.; ribbons, 277,400*l*.; laces, 571,000*l*.; and silk and cotton goods. These figures include imports amounting to somewhat less than 7 per cent. of the whole at Boston, Chicago, and Philadelphia, in addition to those at New York. The imports of raw material, viz., raw silk, waste, silk noils, and pierced cocoons at all ports in the United States increased very largely, the figures approaching very closely to those of 1895. The amounts and values are given as follows:—1897, 11,786,021 lbs., 6,206,000*l*.; 1896, 5,661,630 lbs., 2,970,000*l*.; 1895, 11,070,941 lbs., 6,240,000*l*. The shipments of raw silk from Hong-Kong amounted to 10,876 bales, as against 3,811 in 1896; those from Shanghai to 15,152 bales, against 6,113; and from Japan 38,497 bales, compared with 15,925 in 1896.

It is stated that owing to the high rates of duty, more especially on the cheaper grades of French silks, it is probable that French firms from Lyons will set up factories in the United States.

Woollen goods. The trade in woollen goods showed no animation at the beginning of the year, and the chief feature of the first three months was easier prices for heavy-weight fabrics for men's wear, and forced sales of staple goods, clay worsteds particularly, at lower prices than had been known before. As the tariff began to assume a definite shape, and it became certain that a duty would be levied on raw wool, and that the duties on manufactured goods would be materially increased the market grew firmer, and when the tariff bill passed the demand became more active than for some time past. This demand was met in the first instance without any very material rise in price, the manufacturers being in possession of cheap wool, but as orders came in to the full extent of their production prices were gradually advanced. At the close of the year the rise as compared with prices at the opening was in clay worsteds 16 oz., nearly 40 per cent.; in serges 12 oz., 25 per cent.; in cheviots, 14 oz., over 40 per cent., and in wool cassimeres nearly 40 per cent. It is considered probable that these high prices will lead to a demand for cotton mixed worsteds and other cheap fabrics.

The imports at New York show a large increase in the importation of unmanufactured wool, namely, 49,909 tons valued at 2,456,000*l*., as compared with 26,313 tons valued at 1,274,500*l*. in 1896. The total imports of unmanufactured wool imported in 1897 amounted to about 160,000 tons, more than double the importation of 1896, and about 57 per cent. of this came from Great Britain. The import of woollen goods at New York shows a reduction of about 125,000*l*. in value, equal to rather more than 2 per cent.

Flax. The imports of manufactures of flax and hemp show a value of about 3,200,000*l*., an increase which brings them nearly up to the figure of 1895.

Leather. New York was at one time the principal market for leather, but since the organisation of the United States Leather Company the most extensive sales are made in Boston. Stocks in New York were low in January, and they were not increased subsequently to any appreciable extent. Prices advanced in August and the tendency was upward to the close of the year. Union sole leather is in extensive use as a material for shoes; large and increasing quantities of it are sold to cutters, who make it up into the shapes and sizes required for the shoe factories; more of the business was done last year than in any previous one. Large quantities of kid are used, and during the year the demand at times exceeded the supply. There were very small quantities of calf-skins available and prices rose; coloured kid and patent leather met with ready sales throughout the year. The export of leather from New York was much the same as in 1896.

Hides. Hides were high in proportion to the value of leather throughout the year and to the rates obtainable for shoes. Green hides fluctuated from $8\frac{1}{2}$ c. in April to $11\frac{1}{4}$ c. in December. Dry hides advanced somewhat but only to the extent of the duty imposed by the new tariff. The imports of skins were valued at about 4,666,000*l*., an increase of nearly 30 per cent. as compared with 1896, but about 1,000,000*l*. less than in 1895; the exports of furs and hides were valued at about 525,000*l*. or about half the amount of 1896. The imports of gloves and manufactures of leather are returned at about 1,546,000*l*., an increase of over 50 per cent.

Imports and exports. As regards articles not mentioned above, there was a considerable increase in the imports of chemicals and indiarubber on the free list, and a large reduction in sugar on the dutiable list. In exports, bacon and ham, 4,555,000*l*., increased about 30 per cent.,

Cattle.

and in the amount and value of cereals, but a considerable reduction in the value of illuminating oil.

The export of cattle has again increased by about 11,000 head at New York, and amounted to over 135,000 in 1897, about 19,000 less than the export from Boston.

Cheese.

In cheese the imports have increased nearly 10 per cent. in quantity, but decreased about $4\frac{1}{2}$ per cent. in value; the exports, on the other hand, have increased both in quantity and in value.

Scotch herrings.

The trade in Scotch herrings tends to increase as this article becomes better known; hitherto the preference has been for salted mackerel except among the poorest classes, but Scotch herrings are now to be found in the stores of the large wholesale grocers; and the opinion is expressed that if care be exercised in the selection of the fish and in the packing sales will increase. The import at present amounts to about 25,000 to 30,000 barrels per annum.

Grocery.

The trade in grocery is reported to have been good throughout the year, but the improvement was most marked during the last three months.

Beet sugar.

A commencement has been made of the manufacture of beet sugar in the State of New York, the machinery was brought into the State from Canada and so far the experiment has proved an undoubted success. The owners of the factory, which has been set up at Rome, distributed in the autumn of 1896 seed gratis to 860 farmers on condition that they should bring in the whole of their crops for purchase on the basis of 5 dol. a ton for beets up to the standard; the pulp is sold back to them as food for cattle at 2 dol. a ton. The crop was about 15,000 tons and the amount of sugar made 643,800 lbs., on which the State paid a bounty of 1 c. a lb. The area under beet cultivation was about 1,000 acres, and contracts have been made for three times that area for the present year. There is a prospect of another beet sugar factory being established at Batavia in this State if contracts can be made with the farmers for the growing of beets. The soil appears to be adapted for this cultivation, the percentage of sugar obtained being in some cases as high as 16·6 per cent.

The estimated consumption of sugar in the United States is 2,000,000 tons per annum, and in the matter of imports, bounty fed beet sugar being now subject to a countervailing duty, it is estimated that cane sugar, on the export of which no bounty is paid, enjoys an advantage of about $\frac{1}{8}d$. per lb. The import at New York showed an increase in the free but a considerable decrease in the dutiable classes.

Tables of exports and imports.

Tables are annexed of the principal articles of export and import, and as regards the latter a distinction has been maintained between articles entering free and those subject to duty, but it should be borne in mind that by the change of tariff which came into force on July 24, 1897, articles which had been on the free list, notably wool, became subject to duty.

African exports.

The returns of the total exports from the United States to

Africa show a slight falling-off in the calendar year 1897 as compared with 1896, the values being about 3,343,000*l*., against about 3,406,500*l*.; those to British Africa have also decreased from 2,642,000*l*. to 2,515,000*l*. The exports from New York to British Africa amounted to about 1,980,000*l*. in 1896 and about 1,845,000*l*. in 1897. The principal articles of export were manufactures of iron and steel, wire and bicycles, machinery and agricultural implements, cereals and breadstuffs, tinned provisions and lard, drugs and medicine, boots and leather, hardware, boards, furniture and manufactures of wood, and illuminating and lubricating oils.

During the month of June delegates from Mexico and the Central and Southern American Republics visited New York by invitation to discuss the means of extending trade between the United States and their countries. Their recommendations were the establishment of new steamship lines, the supply of banking facilities, and the adoption of the long credit system on the same lines as those of English and German houses, and that the tariff laws should be modified. The modification which has since been made in the tariff is not in the sense suggested, and may affect the import of wool from Argentina. *Delegates from Central and South America.*

In the month of December an Act was passed by Congress prohibiting pelagic sealing by American citizens and regulations were issued in consequence, providing that no seal-skins, raw, dressed, dyed or otherwise manufactured be admitted to entry in the United States unless accompanied by a certificate of the United States Consul to the effect that they were not taken from seals killed within the prohibited waters, and this applies as well to passengers' personal effects as to goods forwarded as merchandise. All articles manufactured from seal-skins must have the linings so arranged that the pelt of the skin, on which the name and address of the manufacturer must be marked, can be exposed for examination. Articles of seal-skin taken out of the United States will be readmitted on a certificate of ownership from the collector of customs of the port of departure. This must be obtained before leaving on the voyage, and articles for which no certificate can be shown are liable to seizure and destruction. *Prohibition of import of seal-skins.*

NEW YORK.

RETURN of Principal Articles of Export from New York during the Years 1897-96.

Articles.		1897. Quantity.	1897. Value.	1896. Quantity.	1896. Value.
			£		£
Agricultural implements	...	...	801,205	...	722,375
Bacon and ham	Tons	137,619	4,555,640	101,161	3,488,435
Beef—					
Fresh	,,	68,713	2,257,746	72,974	2,404,903
Canned	,,	10,058	364,708	13,218	470,983
Cured and salted	,,	13,101	299,228	16,766	393,679
Barley	Bushels	8,916,452	629,967	7,997,070	591,529
Books, maps, &c.	...	...	292,199	...	290,361
Butter	Tons	8,577	539,368	9,615	605,477
Carriages, and parts thereof	...	...	298,504	...	313,402
Cattle (live)	Number	135,217	2,674,948	123,563	2,417,616
Cheese	Tons	17,509	711,376	13,865	533,720
Copper	,,	81,708	3,908,535	92,942	4,056,417
Cotton—					
Raw	,,	156,319	5,165,244	169,574	6,215,434
Cloths	Yards	197,222,076	2,055,752	194,317,463	2,186,362
Cycles	...	...	1,105,296	...	557,983
Drugs and patent medicines	...	...	991,984	...	1,072,973
Flax (seed)	Bushels	...	...	3,849,979	623,587
Flour	Barrels	4,717,867	3,947,533	4,817,435	3,602,868
Fruit	...	...	869,820	...	655,745
Furs and hides	...	...	524,679	...	1,039,422
Hardware	...	...	678,275	...	581,778
Hops	Tons	4,086	295,164	5,764	257,026
Horses	Number	30,442	841,624	17,533	497,460
Indian corn	Bushels	33,226,359	2,200,446	19,100,058	1,398,357
Indiarubber (manufactures of)	...	...	163,600	...	222,535
Instruments (scientific)	...	...	467,788	...	418,343
Iron and steel manufactures	...	...	1,567,277	...	1,476,267
Lard	Tons	124,787	2,890,724	111,330	2,675,699
Leather	...	...	1,391,202	...	1,374,874
Machinery	...	...	2,644,563	...	2,586,186
Oats	Bushels	34,714,008	1,851,148	15,880,250	831,486
Oil—					
Illuminating	Gallons	497,237,227	5,237,468	491,260,824	6,263,139
Lubricating	,,	41,629,492	1,115,592	39,570,692	1,088,397
Cotton seed	,,	16,325,231	889,500	11,860,302	655,822
Oil-cake and meal	Tons	92,976	421,744	90,686	366,620
Paper	...	...	497,176	...	289,340
Paraffin and paraffin wax	Tons	45,468	836,395	39,554	723,589
Pork	,,	18,871	435,857	18,108	407,470
Rye	Bushels	5,797,516	557,347	3,568,858	300,708
Sewing machines	...	...	570,857	...	546,352
Specie and bullion	...	...	15,031,311	...	20,807,283
Steam engines	Number	228	355,920	...	...
Tallow	Tons	13,869	236,232	21,106	373,130
The oil	,,	33,371	838,179	32,401	920,247
Timber	...	...	425,198	...	517,106
Tobacco (leaf)	Tons	...	2,937,616	61,754	2,337,166
Wheat	Bushels	25,105,887	4,587,983	18,476,263	2,710,092
Wood (manufactures)	...	...	286,690	...	894,723

NEW YORK.

RETURN of the Principal Articles of Import into New York during the Years 1897–96. Classified in accordance with the Tariff in Force January 1, 1897.

Articles.		1897. Quantity.	1897. Value. £	1896. Quantity.	1896. Value. £
FREE.					
Art works	...	...	336,936	...	605,281
Argols	Tons	7,284	264,409	9,183	431,116
Books	...	...	255,151	...	264,460
Burlaps	...	...	645,536	...	663,797
Chemicals	...	...	2,100,231	...	971,208
Cocoa, and shells of	Tons	10,831	521,344	10,948	476,522
Coffee	,,	316,476	13,017,693	245,035	13,799,762
Cork, wood, or bark	...	...	233,840	...	210,010
Cotton (unmanufactured)	Tons	7,328	356,895	3,565	197,115
Feathers and down (crude)	...	...	279,780	...	390,187
Fruits	...	...	347,778	...	345,029
Gum	...	...	1,232,398	...	1,098,590
Indiarubber	Tons	17,573	4,067,382	14,422	2,982,145
Jute, manilla, and sisal grass	,,	110,019	964,250	103,549	964,367
Liquorice root	,,	20,357	152,529	32,463	231,513
Matting	...	...	337,223	...	441,074
Oils	...	...	500,693	...	465,609
Skins	...	...	4,666,397	...	3,673,925
Silk (raw)	Tons	1,403	1,916,604	486	806,536
Soda (nitrate of)	,,	...	...	79,133	491,654
Spices	,,	14,825	445,962	10,361	277,802
Sugar	,,	71,505	938,228	41,672	617,315
Tea	,,	27,756	1,483,303	25,768	1,485,529
Tin bars and pigs	,,	22,544	1,214,494	16,380	960,939
Wool	,,	49,909	2,456,247	26,313	1,274,555
DUTIABLE.					
Cheese	Tons	4,741	253,540	4,318	264,537
Chemicals	...	...	769,455	...	633,747
China	...	...	904,756	...	1,027,555
Coal-tar colours	...	...	670,421	...	488,845
Dry goods—					
Cotton (manufactured)	...	...	4,925,240	...	4,764,802
Silk	...	...	4,522,112	...	3,821,814
Woollen	...	...	5,782,675	...	5,907,775
Fish	...	...	479,237	...	440,730
Flax and hemp (manufactured)	...	...	3,196,376	...	2,765,473
Fruits and nuts	...	...	1,622,566	...	1,991,228
Furs	...	...	606,939	...	582,818
Glass	...	...	644,321	...	905,009
Gloves and manufactures of leather	...	...	1,546,367	...	991,013
Jewellery and precious stones	...	...	1,084,618	...	1,052,263
Metals	...	...	545,276	...	573,874
Paper, and manufacture of	...	...	443,983	...	431,920
Specie and bullion	...	...	5,615,860	...	18,146,793
Sugar	...	...	7,822,892	...	10,251,232
Tobacco (leaf)	...	...	1,313,065	...	1,324,520
Tin-plates	Tons	58,349	532,219	59,789	591,999
Wines and spirits	...	...	1,275,243	...	1,172,060

NEW YORK.

TABLE showing Total Value of all Articles Exported from and Imported to New York from and to Foreign Countries during the Year 1897.

Country.	Exports. £	Imports. £
Great Britain and Ireland	31,396,615	18,019,705
British possessions	5,394,278	6,107,540
Germany	8,981,359	13,865,675
France and possessions	5,143,777	10,764,319
Belgium	3,754,577	1,829,870
Spain and possessions	1,895,871	3,228,992
Netherlands	4,445,743	2,215,830
United States of Colombia	611,883	882,286
Central American States	502,102	933,492
Italy	1,982,738	3,323,017
Brazil	2,222,619	12,040,701
China	1,595,776	2,502,334
Denmark and possessions	641,648	115,366
Venezuela	602,674	1,695,345
Portugal	277,775	602,674
Argentine Republic	918,924	901,221
Mexico	883,864	2,132,391
Hayti	651,840	283,986
Sweden and Norway	659,680	320,481
Japan	1,179,318	1,750,677
Chile	387,366	535,905
San Domingo	202,056	423,538
Uruguay	141,876	635,936
Austria	637,499	1,029,867
Russia	629,282	555,923
Peru	186,955	80,973
Other countries	3,349,672	6,527,482
Total	79,277,788	93,305,526

NEW YORK.

Table showing Countries to and from which Specie was Imported and Exported during the Years 1897–96.

Country.	1897. Imports. Currency. Dollars.	1897. Imports. Sterling. £	1897. Exports. Currency. Dollars.	1897. Exports. Sterling. £	1896. Imports. Currency. Dollars.	1896. Imports. Sterling. £	1896. Exports. Currency. Dollars.	1896. Exports. Sterling. £
Great Britain	5,558,511	1,111,702	45,434,186	9,086,837	47,865,419	9,573,084	59,267,462	11,853,492
France	2,502,306	500,461	15,802,328	3,160,465	18,713,535	3,742,707	11,696,008	2,339,202
Germany	3,287	657	12,257,201	2,451,440	3,683,571	736,714	28,536,172	5,707,234
Cuba	2,807,173	561,434	...	...	7,384,150	1,476,830	52,035	10,407
Mexico	12,375,456	2,475,091	2,000	400	8,226,005	1,645,201	66,641	13,328
Other countries	4,832,569	966,513	1,660,844	332,168	4,861,288	972,257	4,418,100	883,620
Total	28,079,302	5,615,858	75,156,559	15,031,310	90,733,968	18,146,793	104,036,418	20,807,283

TABLE showing Shipments of Grain from the Port of New York to Great Britain and the Continent of Europe, with the Nationality of the Vessels, for the Years 1897-96.

| | Steam Vessels. | Sailing Vessels. | 1897. | | 1896. | |
Nationality of Vessels.			Total Number of Vessels.	Total Number of Bushels.	Total Number of Vessels.	Total Number of Bushels.
Great Britain	842	11	853	83,563,448	631	46,601,699
Belgium	34	...	34	3,542,718	32	3,118,798
Netherlands	78	...	78	3,894,280	75	3,820,173
Germany	169	...	169	15,307,409	162	10,748,033
France	37	...	37	1,671,796	27	1,187,990
Portugal	19	...	19	1,473,265	17	1,215,592
Denmark	23	3	26	1,066,699	27	1,264,934
Italy	1	...	1	85,237	1	21,315
Spain	3	...	3	421,379	1	73,062
Norway	35	2	37	3,121,055	6	588,447
America	10	7	17	1,138,158	8	513,365
Austria	5	...	5	290,206	4	138,005
Nicaragua	...	...	...	...	1	50,550
Total	1,256	23	1,279	115,575,650	992	69,341,962

The grain shipments by steam and sail for 1897 were as follows:—

| Name of Grain. | Total Quantity. | |
	1897.	1896.
	Bushels.	Bushels.
Wheat	33,624,005	21,594,416
Maize	30,982,268	16,181,019
Rye	5,405,672	3,438,708
Oats	34,409,704	15,681,095
Barley	8,539,013	7,743,930
Buckwheat	1,694,410	1,164,416
Flax seed	920,572	3,538,378

NEW YORK.

RETURN of all Shipping at the Port of New York during the Year 1897.

ENTERED.

Nationality.	Number of Vessels.			Tonnage.		
	Sailing.	Steam.	Total.	Sailing.	Steam.	Total.
Great Britain and Colonies...	576	1,580	2,156	364,964	3,406,499	3,771,463
United States	536	322	858	262,287	825,645	1,087,932
Austrian	...	18	18	...	35,303	35,303
Belgian	...	59	59	...	193,828	193,828
Brazilian	2	1	3	1,668	767	2,435
Dutch	9	135	144	14,152	309,670	323,822
Danish	11	31	42	5,760	54,967	60,727
French	4	113	117	1,676	293,824	295,500
German	68	444	512	82,202	1,238,712	1,320,914
Greek	...	1	1	...	1,501	1,501
Haytian	2	...	2	370	...	370
Hawaiian	3	...	3	3,050	...	3,050
Italian	63	3	66	48,881	4,384	53,265
Nicaraguan	...	1	1	...	1,347	1,347
Norwegian	33	222	255	28,033	217,999	246,032
Portuguese	3	23	26	1,111	42,798	43,909
Spanish	4	55	59	1,255	74,302	75,557
Swedish	2	...	2	1,396	...	1,396
Total	1,316	3,008	4,324	816,805	6,701,546	7,518,351

CLEARED.

Nationality.	Number of Vessels.			Tonnage.		
	Sailing.	Steam.	Total.	Sailing.	Steam.	Total.
Great Britain and Colonies...	956	1,533	2,489	389,738	3,366,005	3,755,743
United States	612	326	938	240,454	826,572	1,067,026
Austrian	...	8	8	...	15,623	15,623
Belgian	...	58	58	...	193,852	193,852
Brazilian	1	...	1	834	...	834
Dutch	13	133	146	20,169	304,844	325,013
Danish	11	33	44	5,554	56,774	62,328
French	4	105	109	1,691	282,499	284,190
German	61	393	454	72,203	1,138,094	1,210,297
Haytian	3	...	3	555	...	555
Hawaiian	4	...	4	4,589	...	4,589
Italian	55	3	58	46,864	4,384	51,248
Norwegian	34	230	264	30,013	204,834	234,847
Portuguese	4	22	26	1,355	40,378	41,733
Spanish	3	55	58	654	83,414	84,068
Swedish	4	...	4	2,701	...	2,701
Total	1,765	2,899	4,664	817,374	6,517,273	7,334,647

NEW YORK.

RETURN of the Number of Seamen who have been Engaged, Discharged, Left Behind, Reported Dead, or Deserted, or who have been Relieved at the British Consulate-General, New York, and showing the Total Number of British and Foreign Sailors who were Engaged, Discharged, &c., from British Ships, with the Amount of Wages paid at the Consulate-General to Seamen on discharge from their Ships, and from Hospital or Jail; and also showing the Number of New Agreements entered into during the Year 1897.

Seamen.									Nationality.		Wages.			Agreements.
Engaged.	Discharged.	Left Behind.			Dead.			Deserted.	Relieved.	British.	Foreign.	Total Number of Seamen.	Paid on Discharge from Vessel.	Paid on Discharge from Hospital or Jail.	Total Wages Paid.	Number Opened
		In Hospital.	In Jail.	Total.	At Sea.	On Shore.	Total.									
8,883	8,004	200	7	207	31	20	51	1,461	247	9,162	9,691	18,853	Dol. c. 363,981 55	Dol. c. 2,028 7	Dol. c. 366,009 62	150

Providence, Rhode Island.

Mr. Vice-Consul Stockwell reports as follows:—

The course of trade and business in this Vice-Consular district for the year 1897 in some respects was disappointing, and in others encouraging and helpful. The era of exceptional prosperity predicted as a result of a change of national administration did not come, at least not to the extent anticipated. Compared with the business of the previous year, however, that of 1897 was more extensive and more satisfactory generally. If the volume of trade was small, or less than expected, it was carried forward on a sure basis, and on lines that lead up to increase and greater prosperity.

A prominent factor declares that a significant feature of general business is the fact that the earning power of the invested dollar has gradually decreased the margin of profit in the manufacture of textiles, jewellery, machinery, &c., the yield from stock investments has been scaled down, and keen competition continues the process of weeding out houses in the trade. The big trusts, the aggressive mercantile establishments with unlimited capital, are pushing the smaller concerns to the wall, and leading up to a concentration of business that is not cheerful for the consumer to contemplate. And yet the wage-earner continues to dress well, to live well, and to get some comfort if not luxuries out of his daily toil.

During the last 29 years there were only four years when the average rate of discount on commercial paper taken by banks in this city fell below 5 per cent. In the quarter of a century from 1869 to 1894 a lower average than 5 per cent. was reached only once, in 1885, when 4·91 per cent. was recorded. In 1894 it was 4·60 per cent.; in 1895, 4·99 per cent.; in 1896, 6·17 per cent.; and in 1897 the average was 4·63 per cent. So far as bank earnings go, the year 1896 was the record year since the panic of 1893. During the 25 years preceding 1894 the average rate of discount for the entire period was exactly 6 per cent. *Money.*

The bank clearings in 1897 amounted to 266,741,400 dol. The clearings in 1896 amounted to 256,286,200 dol. *Bank clearings.*

The total receipts at the custom-house for the year amounted to 192,541 dol. 58 c. The tonnage of the port is 33,155 tons. *Port statistics.*

The total revenue of the State in 1897 was 1,405,680 dol. *State revenue.*

The permanent school fund amounts to 293,452 dol., and the appropriation by the State in 1897 for educational purposes was 220,800 dol. A new normal school building is in process of construction and near completion. It is proposed to open in this building a free textile school—something new in this State. *Education.*

Improved highways are the order of the day throughout a large part of this country. The city and State are now mending the ways as rapidly as the people will provide the funds by city ordinance or legislative enactment. During the year three half-mile macadam roads have been built to show the people what *Improved highways.*

good roads ought to be. In all, this year and last, 12 such half-mile roads have been built at a cost of 89,154 dol., and the State wants no more at this price.

Railways. The number of railway corporations in the State is 24. The capital stock of steam roads is 98,409,275 dol.; of street roads, 10,522,000 dol. The total receipts of the steam roads were 35,586,929 dol.; of the street roads, 1,962,917 dol. The net earnings of the steam railways were 5,586,154 dol. 35 c.; of the street roads, 667,001 dol. The number of passengers carried by the steam roads was 48,929,602; by the street roads, 38,769,424. The steam roads carried 3,635,580 less passengers than in 1896.

Breachway, Block Island. An important aid to navigation, referred to in the report of last year, is the breachway at Block Island (comprising the town of New Shoreham, State of Rhode Island). During the year 1897 18,205 vessels made use of this harbour of refuge in mid-ocean opposite and 15 miles distant from Point Judith, where storms are more destructive, perhaps, than at any other point on the Atlantic coast.

Public improvements. It is proposed to make a channel 25 feet deep and 400 feet wide through Providence River and Narragansett Bay to the ocean about 30 miles away. This work is now in progress as provided for by an Act of Congress passed in 1896. This is a work of great importance, and will result in an increase of maritime commerce.

The State House, referred to in other reports, is still in process of construction. It is estimated that the total cost will be not less than 3,000,000 dol.

Terminal facilities referred to in previous reports were brought to completion, ostensibly, in the fall of the year, and the railway companies prepared to take possession and to start trains from the new station, but the Supreme Court enjoined the railway companies from occupying the station, because, as set forth by the people, the station had not been built according to plan and agreement. The railway companies still use the old terminals, and the new ones remain unoccupied.

Manufacturing. The woollen and worsted industry has been active and satisfactory throughout the year. The advance in wages in some cases has been about 10 per cent. Mills have been running uninterruptedly, and the market has been active.

The cotton industry, however, has been much depressed and disturbed at all points. Wages are 10 per cent. less, and as a result strikes have occurred and are still in progress at the close of the year.

Trades. Mechanical trades have been and continue active, particularly all that relate to building operations. At the present time there is an era of " home building " on the part of the well-to-do middle classes. Instead of investing earnings in wild mining schemes of the west, or in bonds of states and municipalities that appear to be in favour of cheaper silver, and possibly of legal repudiation of obligations, they are building modest structures for their own or others' use, and hence a great many dwelling-houses were erected in 1897, giving all trades employment at the old scale of prices.

The jewellery industry (200 establishments in this city) had a more prosperous year in 1897 than in any during the previous decade, according to the report of leading manufacturers.

The manufacture of mill machinery, except cotton, of tools, engines and boilers, has been fairly active, and wages of the preceding year have been sustained. In all mechanical trades there has been no reduction of wages for skilled workmen.

Every part of the country may see the result of unwise immigration. This State and city make no exception. According to the story of some of the emigrants, they left comfortable homes and steady employment in England to come to this country in the hope of bettering if not making their fortunes. The fabulous stories told by interested persons, perhaps emigration agents, led the emigrants to sell at a sacrifice, or to give away, their belongings, and to hasten to this country. *Immigration.*

For example, one emigrant said that he was told that there was such a demand for labourers in all trades that emigrants were met at the place of landing by those in need of help, and engaged on the spot at their own prices. The result of many families coming to this country has been, first, great and overwhelming disappointment; second, want; and third, often terrible distress, ending in pauperism.

If the uneasy labourer in England could know the history of some English families that have emigrated to this country, he would cling to what he has, even if it be only a crust.

RETURN of Foreign Shipping at the Port of Providence during the Year 1897.

ENTERED.

Nationality.	Sailing Number of Vessels.	Tonnage.
British	58	6,445
American	18	4,947
Italian	1	747
Total	77	12,139
,, 1896	98	13,651

PROVIDENCE.

Cleared.

| Nationality. | Sailing. ||
	Number of Vessels.	Tonnage.
British	47	4,827
American	10	1,683
Total	57	6,510
„ 1896	82	9,895

Return of Principal Articles of Export from Providence during the Year 1897.

Articles.	Value.
	£
Iron and steel	848
Miscellaneous	20
Total	868

Return of Principal Articles of Import into Providence during the Years 1897–96.

| Articles. | Value. ||
	1897.	1896.
	£	£
Dry goods	44,632	39,514
Chemicals	16,081	15,808
Metals	16,330	22,229
Wool	27,961	..
Lumber	14,135	29,571
Liquors	3,290	3,566
Precious stones	39,864	34,566
All others	26,982	30,722
Total	189,275	175,976

TABLE showing the Total Value of all Articles Exported from and Imported into Providence from and to all Countries during the Years 1897-96.

Country.	Exports. 1897.	Exports. 1896.	Imports. 1897.	Imports. 1896.
	£	£	£	£
Austria	..	..	6,927	8,600
Belgium	..	..	440	7,789
British East Indies	..	..	5	107
British West Indies	..	..	4,952	7,085
Canada	868	..	15,688	29,483
Cuba	..	..	1,576	2,819
Denmark	..	..	3	..
England	..	..	74,154	47,277
France	..	..	45,021	38,335
Germany	..	..	16,136	16,677
Hayti	..	..	..	1,032
Ireland	..	..	5,586	310
Italy	..	..	2,785	1,987
Japan	..	..	18	262
Netherlands	..	..	592	550
Portugal	..	..	112	207
Russia	..	..	4,005	..
Scotland	..	..	2,342	3,699
Spain	..	..	408	6,306
Sweden and Norway	..	..	112	124
Switzerland	..	..	3,358	3,302
Turkey in Asia	..	..	5,055	..
Other countries	..	..	..	25
Total	868		189,275	175,976

LONDON:
Printed for Her Majesty's Stationery Office,
By HARRISON AND SONS,
Printers in Ordinary to Her Majesty.
(75 5/98—H & S 149)

No. 2082 Annual Series.

DIPLOMATIC AND CONSULAR REPORTS.

UNITED STATES.

REPORT FOR THE YEAR 1897

ON THE

TRADE, &c., OF BALTIMORE.

REFERENCE TO PREVIOUS REPORT, Annual Series No. 1883.

Presented to both Houses of Parliament by Command of Her Majesty,
MAY, 1898.

LONDON:
PRINTED FOR HER MAJESTY'S STATIONERY OFFICE,
BY HARRISON AND SONS, ST. MARTIN'S LANE,
PRINTERS IN ORDINARY TO HER MAJESTY.

And to be purchased, either directly or through any Bookseller, from
EYRE & SPOTTISWOODE, EAST HARDING STREET, FLEET STREET, E.C., and
32, ABINGDON STREET, WESTMINSTER, S.W.; or
JOHN MENZIES & Co., 12, HANOVER STREET, EDINBURGH, and
90, WEST NILE STREET, GLASGOW; or
HODGES, FIGGIS, & Co., Limited, 104, GRAFTON STREET, DUBLIN.

1898.

[C. 8648—104.]   *Price Twopence Halfpenny.*

CONTENTS.

	PAGE
BALTIMORE—	
General remarks	5
Exports and imports	5
Export of steel rails to Calcutta	5
Receipts at custom-house	6
Grain trade	6
Bank clearances	7
Wholesale dry goods	7
,, clothing	8
Canned goods	8
Boot and shoe trade	8
Leather trade	9
Pig-iron, product of district	9
Cattle, sheep, horse, and pig trade	9
Raw cotton	10
Tobacco	10
Coffee	11
Coal	12
Shipping and navigation—	
Shipping of consular district	12
Merchant seamen deserters	13
Shipbuilding	13
Baltimore Channel	14
Lightship inside Cape Henry	14
Telegraphic shipping intelligence from Cape Henry	14
Winter North Atlantic Load Line	14
Railways—	
Pennsylvania Railway, mileage, earnings, and expenses	15
Cost of 1st class passenger carriage for Pennsylvania Railway	15
Baltimore and Ohio Railroad, mileage, earnings, &c.	15
,, ,, experiments with electricity as a motive power	16
Baltimore Street	16
Public buildings—	
New Court-house	16
Addition to Maryland Penitentiary	16
Licences	17
Immigration Bureau	17
Population	17
Cost of living	17
Buildings, total number of	17
Oysters	18
Fish	18
Injury to fisheries by proposed sewage system	18
Terrapin	18
Incorporated enterprises	19
Savings banks	19
Vital statistics	19

(135)

CONTENTS—continued.

	PAGE
BALTIMORE—continued—	
Annexes—	
1.—Return of principal articles of export for 1896–97	21
2.— „ „ import for 1896–97	22
3.—Statement of the values of exports and imports from 1886–97 inclusive	22
4.—Table of the total value of articles exported or imported from and to foreign countries during 1897	23
5.—Table of receipts and exports of grain for 1895–97	23
6.—Statement of prices of wheat, maize, oats, and rye for 1897	24
7.— „ „ flour for 1897	25
8.—Return of all shipping for 1897	25
9.—Table of ocean freights	26
10.—Statement of cost of yearly licences	27
11.—Table of immigration	28
12.— „ monthly sterling exchange for 1897	28
NORFOLK, VIRGINIA—	
Development of Norfolk	29
Dismal Swamp Canal	29
Investments by railways	29
Cotton	29
Shipping	30
Pea-nuts	30
New buildings	30
Lumber	31
Saw mills	31
Bank statement	31
Population	31
Annexes—	
1.—Table of principal articles exported and imported during 1897	32
2.— „ all shipping for 1897	33
RICHMOND, VIRGINIA, trade report	33

NOTE.—The rate of exchange used is 5 dol. to the 1*l.*

No. 2082. **Annual Series.**

Reference to previous Report, Annual Series No. 1883.

Report on the Trade, Commerce, and Navigation of the Consular District of Baltimore for the Year 1897

By Mr. Consul Fraser.

(Received at Foreign Office, April 12, 1898.)

Although it was confidently expected that with the discontinuance of the uneasiness and uncertainty connected with the Presidential election, business, which had been very much depressed for several years, would at once begin to improve, it was not until the year had well advanced that any material change for the better was observable. General remarks.

The doubtfulness of the tariff question for the first six months of the year kept business within very narrow channels, in fact, reduced it down to actual needs.

It is believed that if it were not for the great European demand for, and the consequent rise in the price of, grain, 1897 would have shown a repetition of the stagnation in trade which characterised the three previous years.

The wholesale clothing trade of Baltimore which would seem to reflect the state of trade in this district, was the first branch of business to show an increase, and the great advance in the bank clearances was another indication of a recovery from adverse conditions.

As a whole, trade for the past year has been a great improvement on the preceding one, and it is confidently expected that 1898 will present a still greater increase.

With the exception of two or three years during the past thirteen, exports have yearly increased until they reached in 1897 almost three times the value of 1885. The constant increase in the export of grain has greatly contributed towards this result. There has been in the past year a heavy increase in the exports of provisions, lard, and illuminating oil, and an augmentation in copper and tobacco, which have, with the enormous export of grain, made it the greatest year for exports in the existence of Baltimore. A noticeable figure in the exportation during 1897 was that of steel rails to Calcutta, which is said to be the first shipment of the kind from the United States to India. They were made at a steelworks in the vicinity of Baltimore, and are of the double T variety and reversible. There have been shipped Exports and imports.
Heavy increase in exports.
First shipment of steel rails from United States to India.

7,016 tons of the value of 132,300 dol., being an average price per ton of 18 dol. 85 c. or 3*l*. 15*s*. 4*d*. Fittings for the rails valued at 7,000 dol. have also been shipped. There has also been exported to East London, South Africa, 1,684 tons of the same kind of rails the value of which is given at 31,500 dol.; and also fittings costing 4,305 dol.

Imports, gradual decline of, but increase for 1897.
Imports have been gradually declining since 1891, although there was an increase of about 900,000 dol. in the past year over 1896. In 1897 the principal articles which decreased were tin-plate, over 16,000,000 lbs.; nitrate of soda, about 6,000 tons; and cement, over 38,000,000 lbs. Coffee increased over 11,000,000 lbs., and tin bars and pigs about 400 tons, which, together with a considerable increase in numerous other commodities, brought the gain up to the sum mentioned.

Receipts at custom-house.
The receipts in 1897 at the Baltimore custom-house amounted to 2,287,111 dol., of which all but 87,700 dol. was received for duties. This was an increase of only 25,000 dol. over 1896, when the sum collected was 2,262,007 dol.

Grain trade.
The year 1896 was an improvement on the previous year in the receipts and exportation of grain. The past year was a still greater improvement, and Baltimore has now risen to the front rank in the trade. It has the largest exportation of maize in the United States, and is second in wheat exports.

Business hampered by speculators.
The volume of business done in 1897 exceeded any previous year, although it is stated, that, if it were not for the alleged manipulation of the Chicago wheat market by speculators, business in that cereal would have been much greater. To this cause is also attributed the falling-off in flour exports. The want of ability on the part of the transportation companies to carry the grain offered, is given as another reason why the business is retarded, and from this cause alone, it is said, the quantity handled was lessened between 8,000,000 and 10,000,000 bushels during the past year. The receipts of flour for 1897 decreased 706,633 barrels and the exports of it 740,042 barrels; oats also decreased 2,742,909 bushels in receipts, and 1,649,422 bushels in exports from 1896. The increase, however, in the receipts of wheat, amounting to 10,303,967 bushels; of 16,787,853 bushels of maize; and of rye, 2,280,224 bushels; and also in exports of wheat of 8,714,183 bushels; in maize, 16,665,826 bushels; and in rye, 2,167,229 bushels, much more than offsets the losses. The volume of trade in 1896 was more than 50 per cent. over 1895, and 1897 over 1896 was 35 per cent. The export of rye has increased from "nil" in 1895 to 3,195,974 bushels in 1897, and whole cargoes of it have been exported during the past year to Germany, Belgium, and Holland.

Rye exports very large.

Reduction of fee for grain inspection.
The Directors of the Baltimore Chamber of Commerce have reduced the fee charged for grain inspection from 50 to 15 c. a 1,000 bushels, and this is expected to make the port a still more attractive one for the shipment of grain.

The fact that the rate charged by the railway companies for the carriage of grain from Chicago to Baltimore is 3 c. per 100 lbs., less than that charged to New York, has been brought to the attention of the Inter-State Commerce Commission. No change has, however, been made, and it was pointed out to the Commissioners that the present differential rate was established by a commission after a very expensive railroad war, and that the better terminal facilities for the handling of grain at Baltimore, and the fact that it is 187 miles nearer Chicago than New York, entitle it to the continuance of the reduced rate.

Annex 5 gives a detailed statement of the receipts and exports of grain for the years 1895, 1896, and 1897, and Annexes 6 and 7 the prices of grain and flour respectively for 1897.

The bank clearances for the year were the greatest ever known at Baltimore, and appended are the figures for the past 10 years:— *Bank clearances.*

Year.	Value.
	Dollars.
1888	620,587,729
1889	650,583,571
1890	753,095,093
1891	735,714,652
1892	769,355,899
1893	705,733,232
1894	673,443,512
1895	695,707,281
1896	720,089,733
1897	795,688,363

The wholesale dry goods trade being, to a certain extent, with the Southern States, was affected by the yellow fever epidemic there and by the low price of cotton, but the rise in the price of cereals gave an impetus to it, and the results for the past year are considered fairly satisfactory. The volume of business was greater than in 1896, and there was a gradual growth throughout the year with the exception of the months of September and October. The low price of cotton brought the manufactured article down to the lowest prices in the history of the trade. The enhanced prices of woollens, however, under the new tariff bill counterbalanced this to some extent. Woollens have risen fully 20 per cent., and it is expected that they will still further advance—possibly 15 per cent. There does not appear to be any present hope of immediate improvement in the cotton goods market. It is expected that the coming year will be an advancement on the past three years and any change will undoubtedly be for the better, now that the tariff question has been set at rest for some time to come. British manufacturers appear to be holding their own, except as regards hosiery, linens, and laces. The first-named article of British make has almost disappeared from the trade, as few, if any, reach this market, whereas, *Wholesale dry goods.*

formerly, thousands of dozens were sold. The German article has replaced the British, and it cannot be learned that any effort whatever has been made to regain the trade. It would seem that German hosiery of the lower grades is shipped at almost cost price to meet a certain rate in the tariff, the manufacturer depending on the higher grades for his profit. Saxon linens have not yet to a very great extent supplanted the British articles, but inroads have been made, and it would be well for the home manufacturer to come more into touch with the wholesale trade and ascertain what the requirements are, so as to prevent his falling into the same position as the hosiery producer. These remarks apply with equal force in the case of continental manufactured laces.

Wholesale clothing. The wholesale clothing trade, which is one of the largest industries of Baltimore, shows an improvement in the past year of about 25 per cent. The excellence of Baltimore clothing has given it a larger range of territory than any other product of the city, but in the Southern States, where it has a large sale, the business was reduced about 10 per cent. in the past year by the yellow fever epidemic and the depression in the cotton market. The capital invested is estimated at nearly 6,000,000 dol. About 12,000 hands are employed who received last year in wages about 2,250,000 dol.

Canned goods. The canned goods trade is another very large industry of Baltimore. The goods canned are principally peas, beans, tomatoes, corn, peaches, and pineapples, the latter imported from the Bahamas, and a small quantity sent from Florida.

The year opened with the poorest prospects, and the packers, having no faith in the market, decided not to pay as high prices as formerly for green peas, and they were sold at lower prices than ever before known. The packers accordingly placed their pack on the market at prices far below anything on record, and they sold out the entire pack before the season closed.

Tomatoes, however, at the beginning of the packing season began to advance in price, and by November they had attained a rise of nearly 30 c. on each dozen cans. The corn market has been depressed for the last two or three years by, it is said, the large amount of stock on hand, but this is believed to have now been removed to a great extent by the small pack of 1897, which is given as the smallest known for years.

The close of the year found the market in a healthy condition as to supply and price. But the rise in the price of wheat unquestionably benefited the whole canned goods industry, and at the close of the year prices had advanced from 10 to 20 per cent. It does not appear possible to obtain statistics of the trade, but from what can be gathered it would seem that the output for 1897 was about 20 per cent. less than for 1896.

Boot and shoe trade. The manufacture of boots and shoes is a large industry of Baltimore, and the trade extends from Pennsylvania to the Gulf of Mexico, and westward to the Mississippi. In the South, however, larger sales are made, but the yellow fever there during the summer had a very depressing effect on the trade, as it had on the wholesale clothing business.

There are four large factories in Baltimore each capable of turning out by the aid of the most approved machinery, about 100,000 pairs of shoes annually. The sole leather and a considerable portion of the upper leather used is American tanned, the very finest of the upper leather being imported from England, France, and Germany. The cost to equip a factory of the first class with the latest description of machinery is about 8,000*l.*

It is estimated that the volume of business in the leather trade increased about 20 per cent. over 1896, and the amount of business done is said to be about 20,000,000 dol. The prices of No. 1 scoured oak backs ranged from 28 c. to 33 c. Belting butts brought from 28 c. to 35 c., and packer hides ranged from 8 c. to 11½ c. At the end of 1897 it was estimated that the manufacturers' stock in hand was one-third less than at the close of 1896. *Leather trade.*

The following table gives the production for 1896 compared with 1886 of pig-iron in the several States of the Baltimore Consular district. *Pig-iron products in Consular district of Baltimore*

States.	Quantity.	
	1896.	1886.
	Tons.	Tons.
Maryland	79,472	27,234
Virginia	386,277	139,509
West Virginia	108,569	88,052
Kentucky	70,660	48,968
Total	644,978	303,763

The export of cattle from Baltimore has increased enormously since its inception in 1879, when the shipments were only 2,675 head, of the value of 267,500 dol. *Cattle, sheep, horses, and pigs.*

During the year 1897, 58,003 cattle, valued at 5,800,300 dol., were exported, being a decrease of about 1,800 head from the previous year.

There was, however, an increase of 6,261 in the number of sheep exported in 1897 over 1896. Horses declined slightly in shipments, the number for 1897 being 861, against 894 in 1896.

The loss in the shipments of cattle from Baltimore to the United Kingdom is exceedingly small, amounting in the case of one of the steamship lines to only ·085 per cent. This certainly speaks well for the management, equipment, and suitability of the steamers—which are all British—engaged in the trade. Although a very large number of pigs are received at Baltimore, none are exported alive. They are very much subject to sea-sickness; the mortality is high; the insurance companies will not take a risk upon them; and altogether they are very undesirable as freight in the live state. They are shipped as pork, of which 2,889 tons, valued at 455,612 dol. were exported in 1897. The Union Stock Company of Baltimore reports the following receipts at its yards for the past two years:—

Nature of Stock.	Receipts.	
	1897.	1896.
Cattle	161,078	147,809
Sheep	387,019	392,917
Pigs	823,061	798,003

Raw cotton.

In the beginning of 1897 the local official quotation for cotton was 7 c. per lb., and in August it rose to $8\frac{1}{2}$ c., the highest for the year. The closing quotation for the year was $5\frac{5}{8}$ c., which was a fall of $2\frac{7}{8}$ c. on the highest official quotation.

In the receipts and exports, &c., there has been little change for the past two years—a slight rise in favour of 1897. They were:—

	Quantity.	
	1896.	1897.
	Bales.	Bales.
Receipts	263,889	278,777
Exports, foreign	171,426	176,616
Coastwise trade	65,000	59,800

It is estimated that the cotton mills in the vicinity of Baltimore used 64,000 bales.

Tobacco.

The receipts of Maryland tobacco in 1897 reached the large number of 34,873 hogsheads, an increase of 5,244 over 1896. The crop was somewhat larger than in the preceding year, and this and the fact that a larger quantity of new crops came into market in the autumn than has been the case for many years, are given as the reasons for the increase.

There was a surplus of common tobacco which continued to sell at the extremely low prices of the previous year—1 c. to $1\frac{1}{2}$ c. —until the autumn, when it was found that the crop of " Burly " would prove very short. A great demand then set in and the accumulated stock was soon sold out at advanced prices.

The prices of 13 c. to 14 c. obtained for the medium and better grades of tobacco were considered very satisfactory to the growers.

As in 1896, the French Government awarded contracts for about 11,000 hogsheads. In the last three months of the year the new ground leaf crop of nearly 2,500 hogsheads was exported to Europe at satisfactory prices.

About 8,000 hogsheads composed the crop of Ohio which, as usual, was sold almost entirely in Baltimore, and met a fair demand. Its colour and quality were excellent, and 90 per cent. of it was "fire cured." Fine grades brought very good prices. The stock of "air cured" was in little demand until the discovery of the shortage in "Burly," when a moderate request set in which has since continued.

The following is a statement of the receipts and shipments at the inspection warehouses in Baltimore:—

	Growth.			Total.
	Maryland.	Ohio.	Virginia and Kentucky.	
	Hogsheads.	Hogsheads.	Hogsheads.	Hogsheads.
Stock on hand on January 1, 1897	12,206	6,227	12	18,445
Received in 1897	34,873	8,043	..	42,916
Total	47,079	14,270	12	61,361
Shipments in 1897	38,228	6,283	6	44,517
Stock on hand on January 1, 1898	8,851	7,987	6	16,844

Coffee.

There was an increase in the receipts at Baltimore of 55,458 bags of coffee in 1897 over the previous year. The quantity received in 1896 was 147,608 bags, against 203,066 bags in the past year. A considerable amount—the quantity of which cannot be ascertained—was imported by steamer viâ New York.

In the beginning of 1897 No. 7 coffee was quoted at $10\frac{1}{8}$ c. per lb.; it declined to 8 c. by the end of March, and after a further decline of $\frac{3}{4}$ c. it closed at the end of April at 8 c. During the summer there was a gradual decline until the end of September, when the price reached 7 c. A short period of activity followed and the price rose to $7\frac{1}{8}$ c. to $7\frac{1}{4}$ c. The price then went down, and at the end of November it reached $6\frac{1}{4}$ c. to $6\frac{1}{8}$ c., the lowest of the year. At the close of 1897 the price was $6\frac{5}{8}$ c. to $6\frac{3}{4}$ c.

The following comparative table is given of the charges made at Baltimore and at New York in the handling of coffee:—

Service.		Rate—	
		At Baltimore.	At New York.
		Dol. c.	Dol. c.
Sampling	Per 1,000 bags	1 50	10 0
Labour on wharf. New York, 30 c. per hour, average charge 15 hours on each 1,000 bags	..	0 50	4 50
Skimming	Per bag	0 10	0 15
New bags	Each	0 12	0 15
Storing and delivering	Per bag	0 4	0 4
Storage per month	,,	0 2	0 4

Coal. — The exports of bituminous coal from Baltimore for the past year amounted to 70,034 tons, valued at 33,611*l.*, compared with 51,818 tons for 1896. The average price per ton in 1897 was 9s. 7d. The shipments are principally to Mexico, Cuba, and the Danish West Indies, and it is stated that if any efforts were made to increase the trade the export would be much greater. Anthracite coal is not exported, and is reported to be lessening in demand and is being substituted by oil, gas, and in some districts by wood, as fuel, but this does not appear to reduce the price of it to private consumers, to whom it is sold at 26s. per ton, 6s. dearer than at New York, although Baltimore is much nearer the coal fields.

Shipping and navigation. — The total foreign tonnage of the port of Baltimore for the year 1897 was 1,846,362, an increase of 336,112 tons over 1896. Of the 874 foreign trade vessels entered at the port in the year 1897, 696 were British, with a registered tonnage of 1,287,276 tons. This is an increase over 1896 of 131 British vessels and of 241,003 tons, and greatly exceeds the number and tonnage of British vessels which have entered the port during the past 17 years. German vessels come next in number with 106, all steamers, aggregating 417,209 tons gross. Compared with 1896 this is a decrease of two vessels and an increase of 45,917 tons gross. Appended to Mr. Vice-Consul Myers report is a return of the shipping at Norfolk, Virginia. It shows that 443 British vessels of a tonnage of 794,881 tons entered, and 452 vessels aggregating 814,510 tons cleared during 1897. In consequence of there being no British Consular officer resident at Newport News for several years, it appears that correct returns of the shipping there cannot be obtained. It has, however, been ascertained at the custom-house that 380 British vessels of a total tonnage of 658,048 tons cleared in 1896, and that 431 vessels, with a tonnage of 799,249 tons, left the port in 1897. In the Consular district of Baltimore there were cleared in 1897, 1,580 British vessels having a tonnage amounting to 2,903,526 tons, which is 80 per cent. of the whole carrying trade of the district.

There are nine regular lines of British steamers trading

between Baltimore and the United Kingdom or the Continent, and the principal part of their cargoes consists of grain, cattle, and dressed beef. They are the "Johnston" line to Liverpool, the "Atlantic Transport" to London, the "Donaldson" to Glasgow, the "Lord" to Dublin and Belfast, the "Neptune" to Rotterdam, the "Empire" to Leith, the "Puritan" to Antwerp, the "Blue Cross" to Glasgow, Newcastle, Hull, Bordeaux, and Havre, and the "Bristol Channel" line to Avonmouth. The first five named have a weekly service, and the others sail fortnightly and monthly. The "Earn" line trades regularly to Cuba, bringing iron ore to Baltimore and returning with coal. The "Munson" line have steamers at irregular periods to Cuba and Mexico. The fruit trade with the West Indies is carried on almost entirely by Norwegian steamers under charter to American Companies. There are no British passenger steamers sailing to or from Baltimore, and the "North German Lloyd" and "Hamburg American" lines have a monopoly of that branch of business. They brought to Baltimore 967 cabin passengers and 7,571 immigrants last year, an increase of 204 cabin, but a decrease of 4,147 immigrants. A return of all shipping at Baltimore is contained in Annex 8, and Annex 9 is a statement of the ocean freights for 1897.

Merchant seamen deserters. The treaty of June 3, 1892, between Great Britain and the United States respecting merchant seamen deserters appears to have had much effect in reducing the number of desertions from British ships. 578 seamen deserted during the past year, about 3 per cent. of the whole number of British seamen that had arrived at the port. It has also been instrumental in putting a stop to vexatious lawsuits for recovery of wages which were formerly brought against shipmasters by men who had quitted their ships. Since the treaty came into operation the power given to arrest deserters has only been made use of at this port on six occasions and no warrant has been asked for in the past three years. The expenses connected with the arrest of a deserter at Baltimore are very large—averaging from 4l. to 6l., according to the difficulty of arresting him—and that has doubtless had the effect of preventing applications for warrants being made by shipmasters. The expenses are made up in this way: Commissioners' fees, 10 to 15 dol., according to length of examination; United States marshal's fees for arrest, attending examination and taking prisoner to jail, 8 to 9 dol.; imprisonment, 50 c. a day.

Shipbuilding. 39 vessels of various types were constructed at Baltimore during 1897, the majority being small vessels for the coasting trade. The total tonnage was 8,377 tons, valued at 631,175 dol. The twin-screw torpedo-boats "Rodgers," "Winslow," and "Foote," each 160 feet long, 16 feet beam, and with a speed of 24½ knots an hour, have been built for the United States navy. The torpedo-boat "Plunger," 85 feet in length, with a diameter of 11 feet 5 inches and a displacement when floating light of 155 tons, and with the superstructure awash 167 tons, is practically finished for the United States Government, but many details have yet to be completed. Her motive power when afloat consists of twin quadruple expansion engines with twin screws, and when submerged a 70 horse-power motor fed by 48 electric storage batteries. The funnel telescopes before submerging, and a cover is clamped down air and water-tight. The armament consists of five automobile torpedoes, which, however, can only be fired from above the water. There has also been built the submarine boat "Argonaut." She is designed to be used as a wrecking vessel, but it is claimed that she can readily be transformed into a torpedo boat. She is 36 feet long and 9 feet in diameter and built of iron. The power for driving the propeller is a 30 horse-power gasoline engine when she is on the surface, or partly so, and a dynamo when submerged. A search-light is affixed to the pilot-house and is intended to be used when the boat is under water. By the use of water tanks in the floor of the boat it is stated she can be kept at any desired depth. Wheels propelled by a motor are affixed to her and on which the inventor claims she can be carried along the bottom of the sea provided it is suitable. Air is supplied through hollow iron masts when she is submerged, and in the event of the water being deeper than the masts a hose is attached to them and floated in a boat. At very great depths air is supplied from storage tanks. The newspapers report that a successful test of the boat was made in the Patapsco River, near Baltimore, on December 15 last.

Baltimore Channel. The Government engineer in charge of the deepening and widening of the channel approaches reports that by the end of June next, when the appropriation made by Congress of 400,000 dol., together with the annual grant of 50,000 dol., shall have been exhausted, there will be a depth of 30 feet from Fort McHenry to the bay end of the channel with a width of 250 feet in the straight sections and about 750 feet in the angles or turns. The engineer, however, estimates that it will require an additional sum of 800,000 dol. to be expended so as to obtain a uniform depth of 30 feet throughout the channel, and if even this sum was at once appropriated it would take two years to complete the work. Although the very pressing necessity for a lightship inside Cape Henry on the upper part of the middle ground has repeatedly been brought to the attention of the Government, nothing has yet been done. The Chamber of Commerce is endeavouring to make arrangements for a better service of shipping intelligence by telegraph from Cape Henry.

Lightship needed inside Cape Henry. Telegraphic shipping intelligence from Cape Henry.

Winter North Atlantic Load Line. Considerable anxiety is felt in Baltimore as to the result of the petitions and representations sent to the Board of Trade from New York and Philadelphia asking that the rules relating to the Winter North Atlantic Load Line be altered so as to raise the freeboard of vessels sailing for Europe from ports south of 37° 30′ N. to that required of vessels departing from ports to the northward of that latitude. It is contended on behalf of Baltimore that the difference in draft—some 4 to 5 inches—allowed to ships trading here, is offset by the fact that they load in almost fresh water, and that they will consequently immerse much more quickly. When a steamer has reached the open sea, 170 miles from Baltimore, it is claimed that with the consumption of coal, stores, &c., and the additional buoyancy of the water, she will have risen 3 to 4 inches; and in some cases, depending on the build of the ship, will have eliminated the allowance made to her under the rules. It is also claimed that a steamer leaving Cape Henry will not be subjected to the same stress of weather as one leaving a northern port, until she reaches the course taken by the latter, when her freeboard will, from the further consumption of coal, &c., be equal if not greater than the other ship.

It is felt, in view of these considerations, that if any change is made, especially the extension of the Winter Load Line down to Cape Hatteras, as is suggested, the port will be placed at a very great disadvantage with the numerous grain shipping ports to the southward.

The Pennsylvania and the Baltimore and Ohio are the principal railways having stations in Baltimore. *Railways.*

The first-named operates 8,977 miles of main line, 1,725 miles of second line, and 4,269 miles of sidings, including all east and west of Pittsburg. Its gross earnings for 1897 were 90,716,620 dol., the operating expenses 60,327,309 dol., and net earnings 30,389,311 dol. It has declared a yearly dividend of 5 per cent. from 1894 to 1897 inclusive. *Pennsylvania railroad operates 8,977 miles main line. Earnings and expenses.*

The following detailed statement of the cost of constructing a first-class passenger carriage for the Pennsylvania Railroad may be of interest:—Wheels and axles, 66*l.*; trucks on which the car rests, 106*l.*; air brakes, 26*l.*; 25 fixtures for seats, 10*l.*; three bronze lamps, 2*l.* 14*s.*; two gas tanks, 17*l.*; chandeliers, 10*l.*; screws, 10*l.* 4*s.*; springs for seats, 8*l.* 12*s.*; basket racks, 15*s.* 8*d.*; sash levers, 8*l.* 8*s.*; bronze window lifts, 4*l.* 16*s.*; gold leaf for woodwork, 2*l.* 18*s.*; window fasteners, 3*l.* 2*s.*; two stoves, 15*l.* 10*s.*; and tin for roof, 8*l.* 4*s.* There were used in the construction of the car 2,480 feet of poplar, 3,434 feet of ash, 1,800 feet of white pine, 2,350 feet of yellow pine, 450 feet of hickory, 400 feet of cherry, 500 feet of oak, and 439 feet of maple veneer, 13 gallons of varnish, 45 lbs. of glue, 3,000 lbs. of iron besides 800 lbs. of iron castings, 69 yards of scarlet and 54 yards of green plush, 61 yards of sheeting, and 243 lbs. of hair. The cost of these was 312*l.* 16*s.*, and the labour was 252*l.* 8*s.*; making the total cost of the car about 865*l.* *Detailed cost of 1st class passenger carriage. Total cost, 865l.*

The total mileage of the Baltimore and Ohio Railroad on July 1, 1897, was 2,046 miles, of which 774 miles are west of the Ohio River. It operates from Baltimore to Philadelphia and Baltimore to Chicago, and has viâ the Baltimore and Ohio South West a direct route to Cincinnatti and St. Louis. It reaches New York over the tracks of the Central Railroad of New Jersey. The last dividend of the stock was paid on November 15, 1894, and the line passed into the hands of receivers on February 29, 1896. Its gross earnings for 1897 were 25,582,123 dol., and the *Mileage of Baltimore and Ohio Railroad. Earnings and expenses.*

operating expenses were 20,012,094 dol., leaving the net earnings 5,570,029 dol. The income from other sources was 1,040,716 dol., making a total income of 6,610,745 dol., from which there has to be deducted 7,779,111 dol. fixed charges; the net earnings Washington branch, 16,755 dol.; and payments to retire bonds, 131,130 dol.; total, 7,926,996 dol., leaving a deficit of 1,316,251 dol.

Experiments with electricity as a motive power.

This railway has recently been experimenting with electricity as a motive power. Electric motors weighing about 80 tons each were some time ago brought into use to haul goods trains through the belt tunnel around Baltimore, and they were so successful that now they are used to draw all trains in the tunnel. The annoyances of smoke, soot, and coal gas which existed under the old system when steam locomotives were used have been therefore entirely removed.

Experiments made with electric motors on turntables were equally successful. It usually requires four men to turn a locomotive, and while they are doing so their regular work is abandoned. In operating a 60 foot turntable, the current being taken from the power plant, it was found that on an average it cost less than a farthing for each time the table was turned. It is calculated that the yearly saving is about 141l.

Baltimore street railways.

There are 283 miles of street railways in Baltimore operated by three companies:—The City Passenger with 65 miles; the Central, 37 miles; and the Consolidated with 181 miles. The overhead electric trolley system is almost entirely used as the motive power, and horses have been totally superseded. The cost per car mile when horses were used by the Consolidated Company was $6\frac{1}{4}d.$; by cable traction, $8d.$; and electricity, $4d.$ Owing to the city being built on numerous hills, and the streets consequently having high gradients and also very sharp curves it was found that when the cable was used it soon became worn and often necessitated its being replaced monthly. It is possible by the system of transfer tickets from one branch of the Consolidated Railroad to another to ride between 75 and 80 miles for the small sum of $2\frac{1}{2}d.$ The dividend declared by the City Passenger Company in 1897 was $10\frac{1}{2}$ per cent.; by the Central, 6 per cent.; and by the Consolidated Company, 9 per cent. The street railway companies are required to pay yearly to the city a tax of 9 per cent. upon their gross receipts. In 1897 the sum paid by the three companies was 50,546l. They also paid a tax of 1l. on each of the 517 cars in service. A further sum of 26,304l. was paid to the tax department as taxes on the real estate and stock of the companies, making in all 77,367l. handed over to the city during the past year.

Public buildings. New courthouse.

There is in course of construction for the use of the State and municipal courts, a four storey building of white marble with a granite base, for which an appropriation of 2,750,000 dol. has been made. It is expected that it will be completed in 1899.

Addition to Maryland Penitentiary.

An addition to the Maryland Penitentiary which will cost over 1,000,000 dol. is also in course of construction.

BALTIMORE.

Licences. The sum of 139,856*l*. was received for 18,304 licences issued at Baltimore during 1897. This was a decrease compared with the previous year of 139 licences and of 296*l*. The revenue received from liquor licences of every description alone for the past year was 110,006*l*., of which the city received 82,505*l*., and the State 27,501*l*. or a quarter. The Liquor Licence Commissioners granted 2,241 applications for licences last year, but only 2,150 were taken out. A statement of the licences of each class issued, with the rate, will be found in Annex 10.

Immigration State Bureau. A State Bureau of Immigration, having its office in Baltimore, was established two years ago for the purpose of securing desirable settlers for Maryland. Part of its work consisted in securing information throughout the State regarding the character and adaptability of the soil, the different kinds of products grown, the schools, churches, and other institutions. The facts thus ascertained were extensively advertised in Europe and the West, in English, German, and Dutch, by pamphlet, newspapers, maps, &c., and the results obtained are considered highly satisfactory. A colony of Hollanders has settled at Wilhelmina, Caroline County, and a smaller one in Dorchester County, besides colonies of settlers from the Western States. The appropriation of 10,000 dol. by the State for the work of the bureau is now exhausted, but the results secured appear to warrant its continuance. A total of 1,562 persons, excluding colonists from the West, were induced by the efforts of the bureau to settle in Maryland, the majority being labourers; tailors, of whom there were 51, coming next in number.

Falling-off in number of immigrants. There was a considerable falling-off in the number of immigrants arriving at Baltimore during 1897 as compared with the previous year. A table showing the nationality of the arrivals for the past two years is given in Annex 11.

Population of Baltimore. According to the census taken by the police in 1897 the total population of Baltimore is 500,723, an increase of 45,296 over the police census of 1890. There are 242,017 males and 258,706 females divided into 422,761 whites, 77,478 coloured, and 484 Chinese and Japanese. Since 1890 the coloured population has increased 6,445. The increasing respect for the marriage relationship among them has, it is stated, tended to this result.

Cost of living increased. With the increase in population the cost of living has been enhanced, and with the exception, perhaps, of house rent, the prices of food, coal, gas, &c., equal, and in some cases exceed, those of the metropolis of the country. The requirement by almost every person engaged in trade in Baltimore that he pay an annual licence fee ranging from 1*l*. 1*s*. to 100*l*. 4*s*., has, it can be safely said, the effect of raising the price of the necessities of life.

Buildings in Baltimore. A police report published in May, 1897, gives the number of buildings of all kinds in Baltimore as 104,090, divided as follows:—Dwellings, 85,936; business houses, 9,316; stables, 7,085; manufactories, 1,050; churches, 400; and educational buildings, 303. Compared with 1895 there is an increase of

(135)

BALTIMORE.

1,737 dwellings, 1,337 business houses, 245 stables, 49 educational buildings, 9 manufactories, and 2 churches, a total of 3,379.

Oysters. The oyster trade of Baltimore still continues to maintain its position as one of the city's leading industries. Hundreds of families along the Chesapeake Bay depend upon the trade for their livelihood. Two steamers and 13 sailing vessels are owned by the State of Maryland and used for the protection and encouragement of the oyster fisheries. The prices ranged from 75 to 85 c. per bushel for extra grade, to 40 to 60 c. per bushel for the second quality. It is reported that there is no longer any profit in the canning of oysters, and the demand seems to be lessening; that there is no prospect of oysters being sold for that purpose at a lower price than they have been, and that there is no hope of a larger demand for this luxury. Legislation has been asked for by those interested in the industry that the close season be extended so as to include April and September (it is now from May 1 to the end of August), as it is alleged that during these two months small oysters are taken out of the State to be planted and afterwards brought back and sold in Baltimore to the injury of the trade.

Longer close time demanded.

Fish. About 136,000,000 fish, consisting of shad, white and yellow perch, trout, bass, and carp, have been propagated at the Maryland State hatcheries, and distributed throughout the State during the years 1896 and 1897. It is considered that fish culture has been most beneficial in the increase of the supply of food fish, and has long passed the experimental stage. The propagation of German carp has been shown to be a mistake, and has been abandoned. The proposed new sewage system for Baltimore, if it will, as contemplated, have its outlet in the Chesapeake Bay, must it is believed have a very serious effect on the oyster and fish industry. Notwithstanding, scientific assurances are given that after precipitation or other effective treatment of sewage, it will have no injurious effect on oysters and fish.

Proposed sewage system for Baltimore will injure fisheries.

Terrapin. The terrapin is a tide-water tortoise, and the diamond-backed species, *malaclemmys palustris*, of the Atlantic coast of the United States, and for which Maryland has long been famous, is in great danger of becoming extinct. It is given the name of diamond-backed from the lozenge-shaped figures on its back. During the existence of slavery it was so numerous that on the bill of sale of a slave it was usually stipulated that he was not to receive terrapin more than twice a week. Now it is considered a great delicacy and brings very high prices, and only the rich can indulge in the luxury. Small terrapin can be produced at little cost, and the Maryland Commissioners recommend the establishment of hatching stations along the marshy shores of the Chesapeake Bay and its tributaries, and in this way they believe the supply will be fully restored. Sexes are called "bull" and "cow," and the small ones are little bulls and heifers respectively. Cullings are those under 5 or 6 inches in length—it is unlawful to catch them of less size—and 18 or 24 make a dozen. Those over 6 inches are called counts, and 12 are a dozen. The counts containing eggs are more valuable, and bring about 48 to 50 dol. a dozen.

It appears from the records of the Baltimore Superior Court that 160 corporations, with an aggregate capital stock of 49,601,100 dol., were formed in the city during the year 1897. Of this number, 133, with a capital of 5,490,000 dol., were mercantile and business enterprises, the remaining 27 being building and saving associations and land companies, with an aggregate capital of 44,111,100 dol. The latter sum, however, represents the extreme limit of stock authorised to be issued. *Incorporated enterprises.*

The following is a statement of the business done by the Baltimore savings banks in the year 1897:— *Savings banks.*

	Amount.		Total.	
	Dol.	c.	Dol.	c.
Resources, January 1, 1897	48,793,847	28		
Received from depositors during year	14,438,358	61		
Interest and dividends received	2,401,954	90		
			65,634,160	79
Paid to depositors, including principal and interest	13,168,751	67		
Paid expenses	154,762	28		
State and city taxes	126,315	83		
Premium credits	693,702	57		
			14,143,532	35
Resources, January 1, 1898	..		51,490,628	44

	Number.
Depositors, January 1, 1897	143,913
Accounts opened during the year	23,250
„ closed „ „	18,923
Depositors, January 1, 1898	148,240

There was an increase in resources in 1897 over 1896 of 2,696,781 dol. and of 4,327 depositors. Of this increase 1,269,606 dol. represents the excess of amounts deposited over sums withdrawn by the depositors, and the balance of 1,427,175 dol. was brought about by the accumulation of interest receipts in the banks. *Increase in depositors and deposits.*

The total number of deaths in Baltimore for 1897 is reported as 9,329, of which 7,163 were white and 2,166 coloured. The death-rate for the former per 1,000 of the population was 16·61, and for the coloured 28·88, or 18·43 for the whole. This is a decrease from the preceding year of 590 deaths, but the Commissioner of Health reports that a far greater reduction could be made if the sanitary condition of the city was improved and increased. *Vital statistics.*

(135)

BALTIMORE.

Not a single case of small-pox was reported to the Health Board during the past year.

Consumption was by far the cause of the greater number of deaths, 1,047 having fallen victims to it. Believing that the germs of the disease are carried about in the air from the dried expectoration of persons suffering from it, the city authorities at the request of the Health Commissioners have made it a criminal offence to expectorate in public conveyances, side-walks, or places of public assembly.

There is no compulsory law for the registration of births, which are given at 8,800 for 1897, of which 7,382 were white and 1,418 coloured. These figures are believed to not nearly represent the correct number, as doctors and midwives fail to make returns. This would give 17·12 per 1,000 of the white, and 18·90 of the coloured, and 17·39 of the whole population. 706 still-births were reported during the year. The total mortality under five years was 3,510. 1,180 persons died in gaols and public institutions. The number of bodies received at the morgue in 1897 was 294, of whom 20 were unidentified, and 189 were buried by the city. The following is a list of the principal causes of death, with the number of deaths from each, in the years 1896 and 1897:—

Causes of Death.	Number. 1896.	Number. 1897.
Measles	27	16
Scarlet fever	31	53
Diphtheria	249	347
Croup	32	13
Whooping cough	87	42
Typhoid fever	188	189
Typho-malarial fever	16	20
Diarrhœa	113	99
Dysentery	82	57
Cholera, infantum	412	401
„ morbus	22	14
Consumption	1,122	1,047
Pneumonia	884	759
Bronchitis	253	243
Influenza	60	88
Bright's disease	228	203
Cancer	344	316
Disease of the heart	476	478
Sun and heat stroke	105	11
Appendicitis	25	33
Accident	177	87
Child birth	26	10
Abortion	2	6
Pernicious anæmia	11	12
Cerebro spinal fever	32	22
Illuminating gas	13	9

BALTIMORE.

Annex 1.—RETURN of Principal Articles of Export from Baltimore during the Years 1897-96.

		1897.			1896.		
Articles.		Quantity.	Value.		Quantity.	Value.	
			Currency.	Sterling.		Currency.	Sterling.
			Dollars.	£		Dollars.	£
Agricultural implements	...	...	277,663	55,532	...	86,738	17,347
Animal foods	Tons	22,325	336,412	67,282	...	...	...
Bacon and hams	,,	21,592	3,426,454	685,290	7,315	1,422,695	284,539
Bark, and extract of for tanning	...	...	95,272	19,054	...	142,736	28,547
Beef—							
Fresh	Tons	4,651	713,755	142,751	4,704	800,334	160,066
Canned	,,	3,113	663,554	132,710	8,340	2,081,939	416,387
Cured and salted	,,	1,954	269,676	53,935	12,341	1,684,439	336,887
Barley	Bushels	14,231	6,397	1,279	64,352	21,837	4,367
Books, maps, &c.	...	...	56,735	11,347	...	48,502	9,700
Casings for sausages	...	...	488,659	97,731	...	521,066	104,213
Carriages and parts thereof	...	...	21,680	4,336	...	2,720	544
Cattle, live	Number	58,003	5,800,300	1,160,060	59,833	5,842,600	1,168,520
Chemicals	...	...	161,470	32,294	...	232,808	46,561
Copper, ingots, bars, &c.	Tons	39,460	9,830,604	1,966,120	37,649	9,188,711	1,837,742
Cotton—							
Raw	,,	38,926	5,697,675	1,139,535	36,962	6,194,332	1,238,866
Cloths	Yards	707,999	106,124	21,224	921,504	127,009	25,401
Cycles and parts	...	...	14,625	2,925	...	5,350	1,070
Drugs and patent medicines	...	...	4,915	983	...	5,925	1,185
Flour	Barrels	2,325,803	9,937,253	1,987,450	3,065,845	11,262,839	2,252,567
Fruit	...	...	303,295	60,659	...	296,997	59,399
Furs and hides	...	...	22,564	4,512	...	34,936	6,987
Glucose	Tons	8,795	369,071	73,814	4,465	208,405	41,681
Hair	...	...	145,736	29,147	...	197,284	39,456
Hardware	...	...	1,076	215	...	3,245	649
Horses	Number	861	132,922	26,584	894	117,035	23,407
Indian corn	Bushels	43,048,008	13,287,413	2,657,482	26,382,182	8,472,374	1,694,474
Iron and steel manufactures	...	...	842,366	168,473	...	205,120	41,024
Lard	Tons	44,470	6,423,455	1,284,691	40,669	6,003,979	1,200,795
Lead	,,	557	35,253	7,050	...	...	...
Leather	...	...	28,098	5,619	...	9,257	1,851
Machinery	...	...	99,132	19,826	...	50,014	10,002
Oats	Bushels	5,270,096	1,308,778	261,755	6,919,518	1,690,067	338,013
Oil—							
Illuminating	Gallons	65,263,498	3,715,922	743,184	45,276,688	2,736,284	547,256
Lubricating	,,	872,431	109,418	21,883	779,414	94,216	18,843
Cotton-seed	,,	526,636	140,141	28,028	612,243	212,204	42,440
Oilcake and meal	Tons	64,445	1,417,861	283,572	56,830	1,367,314	273,462
Oleomargarine oil	,,	11,488	2,377,748	475,549	12,924	2,195,064	439,012
Paper	...	...	28,577	5,715	...	29,435	5,887
Paraffin and paraffin wax	Tons	2,711	243,021	48,604	2,329	228,729	45,745
Pork	,,	2,889	455,612	91,122	1,644	216,047	43,209
Rye	Bushels	3,195,974	1,501,299	300,259	1,028,745	444,690	88,938
Sewing machines	...	...	3,088	617	...	11,514	2,302
Sheep	Number	49,379	387,644	77,528	43,118	327,222	65,444
Starch	Tons	8,810	524,449	104,889	5,678	430,064	86,012
Steel rails	,,	8,700	163,800	32,760	...	...	...
Tallow	,,	2,208	187,393	37,479	4,125	387,366	77,473
Timber	...	...	550,443	110,088	...	570,495	114,099
Tobacco—							
Leaf	Tons	36,261	5,873,132	1,174,626	34,002	5,748,936	1,149,787
Stems	,,	2,996	125,755	25,151	2,340	58,073	11,614
Wheat	Bushels	15,304,039	14,439,276	2,887,855	6,589,856	4,646,165	929,233
Wood (unmanufactured)	...	...	2,382,156	476,431	...	1,926,586	385,317

NOTE.—5 dol. to the 1*l*.

Annex 2.—RETURN of Principal Articles of Import into Baltimore during the Years 1897-96.

		1897.			1896.		
Articles.		Quantity.	Value.		Quantity.	Value.	
			Currency.	Sterling.		Currency.	Sterling.
			Dollars.	£		Dollars.	£
FREE.							
Art works		...	7,652	1,530	...	25,081	5,016
Books	...	...	19,993	3,998	...	21,304	4,260
Burlaps	...	...	99,683	19,936	...	83,783	16,774
Chemicals	...	...	655,283	131,056	...	592,504	118,500
Coffee	Tons	12,156	2,070,811	414,162	8,521	1,973,365	394,673
Fruits	...	...	513,815	102,763	...	305,797	61,159
Licorice root	Tons	4,104	145,863	29,172	1,519	53,470	10,694
Matting	...	...	216,752	43,350	...	104,262	20,852
Salt	Tons	14,312	58,229	11,645	20,789	63,052	12,610
Soda, nitrate of	,,	7,092	227,650	45,530	1,152	36,061	7,212
Tea	,,	59	19,633	3,926	82	34,068	6,813
Tin, bar and pigs	,,	1,452	434,469	86,893	1,030	300,085	60,017
Wool (unmanufactured)	,,	1,311	513,966	102,793	36	11,117	2,223
DUTIABLE.							
Cement	...	...	250,493	50,098	...	369,895	73,979
Cheese	Tons	83	25,706	5,141	64	24,229	4,845
Chemicals	...	...	373,176	74,635	...	433,047	86,609
China	...	...	613,886	122,777	...	572,750	114,550
Dry goods—							
Cotton (manufactured)	...	...	227,848	45,569	...	240,269	48,053
Silk (manufactured)	...	...	36,995	7,399	...	44,266	8,853
Wool (manufactured)	...	...	285,883	57,176	...	213,281	42,656
Fish	...	...	19,288	3,857	...	16,454	3,290
Flax	...	...	357,858	71,571	...	128,822	25,764
Fruits	...	...	301,380	60,276	...	401,356	80,271
Glass	...	...	44,750	8,950	...	103,034	20,606
Iron ore	Tons	292,613	369,483	73,896	368,561	577,135	115,427
Iron in pigs	,,	4,567	130,336	26,067	3,389	120,131	24,026
Iron and steel (manufactured)	...	...	158,787	31,757	...	71,252	14,250
Metals	...	...	21,360	4,272	...	20,862	4,172
Paper	...	...	33,452	6,690	...	53,529	10,705
Rice	Tons	4,611	175,697	35,139	3,427	112,014	22,402
Salt	,,	2,939	8,323	1,664	...	...	...
Sugar	,,	16,627	891,937	178,387	17,005	1,033,982	206,796
Tin-plates	,,	599	33,288	6,657	7,883	400,014	80,002
Tobacco leaf	...	...	36,943	7,388	...	117,096	23,419
Wines and spirits	...	...	83,243	16,648	...	43,025	8,605
Wool (unmanufactured)	Tons	85	27,665	5,535	...	...	...

Annex 3.—STATEMENT showing the Export and Import Values at Baltimore for the past 12 Years, also the Monthly Export and Import Values during the Year 1897.

Year.	Exports.	Imports.	Months during 1897.	Exports.	Imports.
	Dollars.	Dollars.		Dollars.	Dollars.
1886	46,810,870	11,785,113	January	5,832,534	904,618
1887	49,545,970	13,055,880	February	7,858,046	903,695
1888	45,099,334	12,098,629	March	7,973,928	964,986
1889	62,077,610	15,409,234	April	6,107,896	1,527,007
1890	72,120,083	15,339,312	May	6,173,032	1,122,075
1891	79,475,125	18,270,000	June	6,753,759	1,365,720
1892	93,126,389	14,258,570	July	7,014,121	713,402
1893	73,153,487	14,858,621	August	11,183,881	850,255
1894	63,961,279	11,749,927	September	10,872,628	697,514
1895	60,171,591	19,934,369	October	7,928,790	774,423
1896	81,508,836	10,208,741	November	9,209,161	679,321
1897	98,560,604	11,126,556	December	11,652,828	623,741

BALTIMORE.

Annex 4.—TABLE showing Total Value of all Articles Exported from or Imported into Baltimore during the Year 1897.

Country.	Value.	
	Exports.	Imports.
	Dollars.	Dollars.
Great Britain	43,094,539	3,265,918
Belgium	6,293,780	130,591
Brazil	1,754,979	2,069,518
Spain and Cuba	81,386	501,794
France	10,094,565	114,978
Germany	16,158,231	1,893,742
Netherlands	17,512,641	604,591
Mexico	244,833	39,059
Italy	..	501,072
Other countries	3,325,650	2,006,193
Total	98,560,604	11,126,556

Annex 5.—TABLE of the Receipts and Exports of Grain for the Years 1895–97.

RECEIPTS.

Articles.		Quantity.		
		1895.	1896.	1897.
Wheat	Bushels	4,834,118	7,592,041	17,896,008
Maize	,,	11,854,704	27,724,535	44,514,388
Oats	,,	2,895,724	10,428,850	7,685,950
Rye	,,	364,710	1,381,485	3,661,709
Barley and malt	,,	665,051	772,267	807,234
Total		20,614,307	47,899,178	74,565,289
Flour	Barrels	3,779,596	4,104,896	3,398,333

Exports.

Articles.		Quantity.		
		1895.	1896.	1897.
Wheat	Bushels	3,977,261	6,589,856	15,304,039
Corn	,,	9,645,758	26,382,182	43,048,008
Oats	,,	134,318	6,919,518	5,270,096
Rye	,,	..	1,028,745	3,195,974
Barley and malt	,,	..	64,352	14,231
Total		13,757,337	40,984,653	66,832,348
Flour	Barrels	2,539,981	3,065,845	2,325,803

Annex 6.—STATEMENT showing the Prices of Wheat, Maize, Oats, and Rye, in the Baltimore Market during the Year 1897.

Month.	Southern Wheat.				Western Wheat.		Southern White Corn.		Southern Yellow Corn.		Two White Oats.		Two Mixed Oats.		Two Rye.	
	By Sample.		On Grade.													
	Cents.	Cents.	Cents.	Cents.	Cents.	Cents.	Cents.	Cents.	Cents.	Cents.	Cents.	Cents.	Cents.	Cents.	Cents.	Cents.
January	87 to	97	82 to	95¼	86⅜ to	94¾	22 to	28¼	21½ to	28¼	24 to	26	21 to	22	41¼ to	44
February	87	92	82	91½	86½	91	26	29	26	27½	23	24¼	21	22	40	42
March	83	92	84¼	91	81½	90½	26½	31	26	30	23	26	21	23½	38½	40¾
April	73	85	84¼	91	72¾	83½	28½	31	26½	30	25	27	23¼	24	37½	42½
May	80	90	84¼	91	77	81½	31	34	29½	31	26	28½	23½	26	38½	41½
June	55	81	67¼	72	69¾	78	30	33	29½	33½	25½	28	23	25½	38	38¾
July	50	80	67	84½	69½	83¼	30	35	33	35	25	27	23	24	38¼	44½
August	80	107½	81½	107	83⅛	106½	34	38	35	39	23½	27½	20	24	44	56
September	89	104¼	87½	104	92¼	103¾	36	39	37	39½	24	26	21	23½	50	54
October	88	101	87½	101	92	100½	31	37½	31¼	38	26¼	27	22¾	23½	50	53½
November	90	101	91	100	95⅞	99⅝	30	35½	31	35	27	29½	23	27	52	53½
December	91	100	91¼	99¾	95⅝	99¼	27½	35½	27½	36	29	30	26½	28	51½	53¼
Range ..	50	107½	67	107	69½	106½	22	34	21½	39½	23	30	20	28	37½	56

BALTIMORE.

Annex 7.—STATEMENT showing the Prices of Flour in the Baltimore Market during the Year 1897.

Month.	Per Barrel.		
	Family.	Extra.	Super.
	Dol. c. Dol. c.	Dol. c. Dol. c.	Dol. c. Dol. c.
January..	4 25 to 4 85	3 25 to 4 15	2 65 to 3 30
February	4 25 4 60	3 25 3 90	2 65 3 0
March	4 10 4 60	3 10 3 90	2 60 3 0
April	3 94 4 65	3 0 4 0	2 60 3 0
May	4 0 4 65	3 0 4 0	2 50 3 0
June	4 0 4 40	3 0 3 75	2 50 2 75
July	3 75 4 40	2 90 3 75	2 50 2 85
August	4 0 5 0	3 0 4 25	2 60 3 25
September	4 50 5 20	3 40 4 65	2 75 3 50
October	4 50 4 85	3 40 4 20	2 75 3 50
November	4 40 4 85	3 35 4 25	2 70 3 25
December	4 40 4 75	3 35 4 20	2 70 3 20
Range	3 75 5 20	2 90 4 65	2 50 3 50

Annex 8.—RETURN of all Shipping at the Port of Baltimore during the Year 1897.

ENTERED.

Nationality.	Sailing.		Steam.		Total.	
	Number of Vessels.	Tons.	Number of Vessels.	Tons.	Number of Vessels.	Tons.
British	22	7,441	674	1,279,835	696	1,287,276
American (foreign)	122	50,020	34	16,921	156	66,941
German	...	...	106	417,209	106	417,209
Italian	13	9,918	2	2,833	15	12,751
Norwegian	1	344	87	61,841	88	62,185
Total	158	67,723	903	1,778,639	1,061	1,846,362
American coastwise	69	56,242	1,562	1,912,712	1,631	1,968,954

CLEARED.

Nationality.	Sailing.		Steam.		Total.	
	Number of Vessels.	Tons.	Number of Vessels.	Tons.	Number of Vessels.	Tons.
British	22	7,441	675	1,282,326	697	1,289,767
American (foreign)	117	53,409	32	16,190	149	69,599
German	...	...	106	417,209	106	417,209
Italian	13	9,918	2	2,833	15	12,751
Norwegian	1	344	87	61,841	88	62,185
Total	153	71,112	902	1,780,399	1,055	1,851,511
American coastwise	160	79,737	1,980	2,067,607	2,140	2,147,344

Annex 9.—Table of Ocean Freights from Baltimore for the Year 1897.

Months.	Steam Grain per Bushel.		Steam Grain per Quarter.									
	To Liverpool.		To London.		To Glasgow.		To Cork for Orders.		To Rotterdam.		To Antwerp.	
	d.	d.	s. d.	s. d.	s. d.	s. d.	s. d.	s. d.	s. d.	s. d.	s. d.	s. d.
January	3¼ to	3½	2 4½ to	2 9	2 7½ to	2 10½	3 3 to	3 6	2 9 to	3 0	2 7½ to	2 10½
February	3	3½	2 7½	2 9	2 6	2 10½	3 3	3 4½	2 7½	3 0	2 6	2 10½
March..	2½	3	2 3	2 9	2 0	2 6	3 0	3 3	2 6	2 9	2 6	2 7½
April	2	2¾	2 0	2 3	1 9	2 3	2 6	3 0	1 9	2 6	2 0	2 6
May	1	2¼	1 6	2 1½	1 0	2 0	2 4½	2 9	1 9	2 0	1 6	2 3
June	1	3	1 6	1 9	1 0½	2 6	2 4½	2 7½	1 6	2 6	1 9	2 0
July	2¼	4	1 6	2 .6	1 3	2 6	2 6	3 6	2 6	3 0	1 9	3 0
August	3¼	4	1 4½	2 1½	1 4½	2 0	2 6	3 4½	2 9	2 10½	2 6	2 10½
September	3¼	4	1 6	2 6	1 7½	2 3	3 4½	3 9	2 6	3 0	2 7½	3 0
October	4¼	4½	2 6	3 1½	2 3	3 0	3 6	3 7½	2 10½	3 1½	2 9	3 3
November	3½	4½	3 0	3 3	3 0	3 3	3 7½	4 0	3 0	3 1½	3 3	3 4½
December	4	4½	3 0	3 1½	3 1½	3 3	3 4½	3 10½	3 0	3 3	3 3	3 4½
Range	1	4½	1 4½	3 3	1 0	3 3	2 4½	4 0	1 6	3 3	1 6	3 4½

BALTIMORE.

Annex 10.—STATEMENT showing the Cost of Yearly Licences at Baltimore.

Description of Licence.	Cost.	Remarks.
	Dol c.	
Traders—		
Female	7 10	Any female taking out a licence pays this fee, irrespective of the value of stock
Stock value of—		
1,000 dol.	13 10	
1,500 „	16 10	
2,500 „	19 10	
4,000 „	23 10	
6,000 „	31 10	
8,000 „	41 10	
10,000 „	51 10	
15,000 „	66 10	
20,000 „	81 10	
30,000 „	107 10	
40,000 „	126 10	
Over 40,000 dol.	151 0	
Brokers, real estate—		
2 co-partners	26 0	
3 „	51 0	
Brokers—		
Exchange	101 0	
Bill	51 0	
Pawn	501 0	
Horse	51 0	
Stock, grain, coffee, cotton, sugar, and merchandise	31 0	
Cigarettes	11 0	A dealer in cigarettes must also take out a trader's licence
Billiards, 1st class	51 0	For 1st table
„ 2nd class	26 0	For 2nd table, and every additional one
Pedlar, foot	101 50	
„ 1 horse	151 50	
Liquor—		
Saloon or restaurant	251 0	
Hotel	251 0	In addition to this licence, an hotel-keeper must also possess a licence chargeable according to the rental of his premises, ranging from 26 dol. 10 c. for a rental of 100 dol. a year, to 451 dol. for a rental of 10,000 dol. and over
Retail grocer	251 0	
Wholesale grocer	251 0	
Bottles of fermented liquor	41 0	
Oysters, commission merchants	26 0	
„ measurers	20 0	
Chesapeake Bay fisheries—		
For fishing with net in Chesapeake Bay, below Poole's Island	5 25	
Exhibition	4 0	
Marriage	1 0	This charge is for the clerks' fees

NOTE.—Included in the above charges are the sheriffs' and clerks' fees, which range from 1 dol. to 1 dol. 50 c. for each licence.

BALTIMORE.

Annex 11.—TABLE showing the Nationality, &c., of the Immigrants Arriving at Baltimore during the Years 1897-96.

Country.	1897. Males.	1897. Females.	1897. Total.	1896. Total.
England	34	1	35	45
Scotland	4	..	4	5
Ireland	6	..	6	7
Austria	780	351	1,131	2,421
Belgium	1	..	1	..
Bohemia	177	199	376	..
British West Indies	15	9	24	29
British Guiana	1	..	1	..
Canada	2	1	3	..
Cuba	4	..	4	..
Denmark	6	1	7	5
Danish West Indies	1	..	1	..
Finland	1	..	1	..
France	1	1	2	..
Germany	1,058	1,234	2,292	3,667
Honduras	..	1	1	..
Hungary	826	477	1,303	1,730
Italy	1	..	1	..
Norway	2	..	2	1
Poland	..	1	1	..
Portugal	1	..	1	..
Roumania	21	26	47	26
Russia	1,243	1,077	2,320	3,782
Switzerland	2	4	6	..
Turkey in Asia	1	..	1	..
Total	4,188	3,383	7,571	11,718

Annex 12.—TABLE of the Monthly Sterling Rates of Exchange Ruling at Baltimore during the Year 1897.

Months.	60 Days. Highest.	60 Days. Lowest.	At Sight. Highest.	At Sight. Lowest.
	Dol. c.	Dol. c.	Dol. c.	Dol. c.
January	4 86	4 84	4 88½	4 87
February	4 86	4 85	4 88	4 87¼
March	4 86½	4 85½	4 88¼	4 87¼
April	4 87½	4 86½	4 89	4 88
May	4 87	4 86½	4 88½	4 88
June	4 87	4 86½	4 88½	4 88
July	4 87	4 86½	4 88	4 88
August	4 87	4 84	4 88	4 86½
September	4 85	4 83	4 87	4 85½
October	4 84	4 82½	4 86½	4 85
November	4 84	4 83	4 87	4 86
December	4 84	4 82½	4 87	4 85½

NORFOLK.

Mr. Vice-Consul Myers reports as follows:—

From the standpoint of material development the past year has been pre-eminently the greatest in the history of Norfolk. Millions have been spent by the transportation companies in improving their terminals, and in adding new facilities for the handling of the rapidly increasing volume of business.

Development of Norfolk.

A partial list of the improvements that have been made or under construction are as follows: the Norfolk and Western Railway Company has been reorganised, has purchased 1,000 additional cars, and has taken preliminary steps for the erection of a large elevator at its Lamberts Point terminus. The Southern Railway, amongst other large additions to its property, has built another pier and warehouse, covering 5 acres, giving 19 acres under roof, 2½ miles of wharf front, and 25 miles of track costing 200,000 dol.

The New York, Philadelphia, and Norfolk is building a large pier and warehouse, and is, with aid of other roads, building a belt line connecting all the roads and a bridge over the river above the Navy Yard, at a total cost of 550,000 dol. There are now 400 men employed on their construction.

The Seaboard Air Line has added to its shops, improved its warehouses and piers, and built a large number of cars: 300,000 dol.

The Old Dominion Steamship Company has built an additional pier and warehouses costing about 100,000 dol., and has added another new steamship line to its already splendid line, costing about 250,000 dol.

The Merchants' and Miners' Steamship line has also added to its warehouses and wharf property and built another fine steamer, expending about 350,000 dol.

The Virginia Beach Railroad has changed to a broad gauge at a cost of 150,000 dol., and has arranged to build 40 miles from Kempsville to the Carolina Sound, costing about 350,000 dol.

The Dismal Swamp Canal Company is deepening and widening that great waterway at a cost of about 750,000 dol.

Dismal Swamp Canal deepened, &c.

The River Front Railroad has been constructed in Portsmouth at a cost of 40,000 dol.

Electricity as a motive power has been applied to the Port Norfolk Railroad at a cost of 100,000 dol.

An aggregate of nearly 4,000,000 dol., invested by the railroads and transportation lines, is an evidence of their good faith in the future of the port of Norfolk and Portsmouth. The spirit of progress in other lines has also been manifested in liberal expenditures of money in improvements.

4,000,000 dol. invested by railways, &c., in Norfolk.

Norfolk now ranks as the fourth cotton port of the United States; the trade in this staple having been developed since 1865, prior to which the receipts were insignificant. During the 12 months ending August 31, 1895, the net receipts of

Cotton.

cotton at Norfolk were 472,540 bales, the total receipts in 21 years being 11,162,929 bales. The receipts for the year ending August 31, 1897, were 712,072 bales.

Exports of cotton.

The exports, coastwise and overland shipments and distribution have been as follows:—

	Quantity.
	Bales.
Exports to Great Britain, France, and Continent	200,275
Coastwise and overland shipments	534,778
Inland to Virginia and Carolina mills	4,933
Local consumption, five mills	4,193
Burned	538
Total distribution	744,717
Stock on hand	36
Total	744,753

Shipping at Norfolk.

The shipping of the port is naturally divided into foreign and coastwise, the foreign subdivided into regular established lines, charter lines, and tramp shipping, the charter lines being run by firms controlling no established and regular vessels, but depending on charter to keep up a fairly regular line of shipments to certain ports, while the tramp shipping is ready for any cargo to any port, provided rates are agreeable.

The large increase in receipts of cotton, lumber, staves, naval stores, coal, grain, tobacco, pig-iron, and steel billets, due to the concentration of railway systems at this port in the last few years, has given a tremendous impetus to foreign as well as coastwise shipping, and has drawn the products of the west and north-west and south in rapidly accumulating masses.

Formerly cotton was the chief article of export, but the extension of the railroad systems has changed this. Now grain leads in bulk, and coal and iron are close competitors.

Pea-nuts.

The handling of pea-nuts is an industry of which Norfolk has at the present a monopoly, one no doubt which she will continue to hold, from the fact of the city being the nearest distributing point for the region producing this nut.

Prior to 1876 the total crop of these nuts amounted to about 100,000 bags or 400,000 bushels. The principal source of the nuts is the tide water region of Virginia and North Carolina. Having become in demand, more attention in recent years has been paid to their culture, so that at present a full crop reaches about 2,800,000 bushels, and a sale is found for them all over the United States as well as Canada.

New buildings.

The value of buildings erected in the city for the year 1897 was 930,000 dol. This does not include the buildings erected in the suburbs of Portsmouth, Berkley, Port Norfolk, Pinners Point, Lamberts Point, South Norfolk, and several other places which have been rapidly developed during the year.

NORFOLK.

Lumber. Norfolk is the great centre and distributing point of an enormous lumber business, it being estimated that over 600,000,000 feet of boards and bill stuff is handled annually at this port. This is composed principally of what is known as the short leaf or "North Carolina pine," and comes from a territory comprising 40 counties in Eastern North Carolina, and 13 counties in Eastern Virginia, containing an area of about 14,500 square miles.

Pine is the principal product of this vast region, though white cedar, cypress and several other valuable lumber woods, including several hard woods, are milled in large quantities.

Number of saw mills. In this region there are more than 300 saw mills, one-fourth of which are equipped with dry kilns and all modern appliances. Several of the largest of these mills are located on the harbour very near the city, and most of them have their principal offices here, transacting their business and getting their supplies from this city.

The capital invested in these great plants aggregates more than 2,000,000 dol.

The average price for this lumber is 12 dol. per 1,000 feet rough, or 15 dol. per 1,000 feet dressed.

Bank statement. The following statement of facts concerning the capital, surplus, deposits, loans, discounts and other resources and liabilities of the banks will be of interest. These figures are compiled from bank statements published on December 20, 1897:—

	Amount.	
	Dol.	c.
Capital	1,699,900	0
Surplus and undivided profits	985,287	9
Individual deposits	5,921,210	50
Loans and discounts	5,655,667	1
Stocks and bonds	1,935,832	10
Currency, specie, and legal tender notes available for immediate use	507,875	95

Population. The population of Norfolk, taking in all the suburbs properly so-called, may be set at 100,000. With the rapid extension of Norfolk and of these suburbs, the whole may be considered one centre, especially in relation to the country at large. It may be added that by rail Norfolk is only 12 hours from New York.

NORFOLK.

Annex 1.—TABLE showing Principal Articles of Export and Import at the Port of Norfolk during the Year 1897.

EXPORTS.

Articles.		Quantity.	Value.
			Dollars.
Corn	Bushels	12,427,373	4,310,599
Cotton	Bales	111,993	3,180,321
Lard	Lbs.	45,760,837	2,305,790
Logs and lumber			1,648,848
Wheat	Bushels	987,691	886,615
Leaf tobacco	Lbs.	7,626,306	546,152
Pig-iron	Tons	53,438	534,397
Oils			378,862
Flour	Barrels	65,675	285,865
Staves and headings			240,255
Coal, bituminous	Tons	72,356	233,367
Cattle	Head	2,961	222,075
Meat products			203,080
Coke	Tons	52,862	170,284
Steel	Lbs.	4,716,485	95,225
Meal	Barrels	28,506	61,202
Cotton-seed oil	Gallons	191,000	47,750
Pea-nuts			4,502
Horses	Head	40	8,000
Miscellaneous articles			103,588
Total			15,466,777

IMPORTS.

Articles.	Value.
	Dollars.
Fertilisers	69,100
Kainit	57,173
Manure salt	55,428
Sulphate of ammonia	29,063
Brimstone	19,163
Salt	1,638
Wines	299
Wearing apparel	83
Miscellaneous articles	2,153
Total	234,100

NORFOLK.

Annex 2.—TABLE showing the Movement of all Shipping at the Port of Norfolk during the Year 1897.

ENTERED.

Nationality.	Sailing. Number of Vessels.	Sailing. Tons.	Steam. Number of Vessels.	Steam. Tons.	Total. Number of Vessels.	Total. Tons.
British	13	15,093	430	779,788	443	794,881
German	...	...	31	55,907	31	55,907
Spanish	...	...	29	49,047	29	49,047
Norwegian	...	...	18	33,281	18	33,281
American	17	11,518	1	478	18	11,996
Italian	12	7,377	...	...	12	7,377
French	4	1,542	...	...	4	1,542
Danish	..	...	3	4,777	3	4,777
All others	...	...	4	7,267	4	7,267
Total	46	35,530	516	930,545	562	966,075

CLEARED.

Nationality.	Sailing. Number of Vessels.	Sailing. Tons.	Steam. Number of Vessels.	Steam. Tons.	Total. Number of Vessels.	Total. Tons.
British	11	13,928	441	800,582	452	814,510
German	1	473	40	74,707	41	75,180
American	36	21,208	3	971	39	22,179
Spanish	...	...	30	50,202	30	50,202
Norwegian	...	...	22	38,442	22	38,442
Danish	2	959	4	6,948	6	7,907
Italian	9	5,717	...	...	9	5,717
French	3	1,162	...	...	3	1,162
All others	...	...	4	7,267	4	7,267
Total	62	43,447	544	979,119	606	1,022,566

RICHMOND, VIRGINIA.

Mr. Vice-Consul Brine reports:—

General trade. There are some welcome signs that business conditions throughout the country are on the mend, and Richmond is in the van of the movement. It cannot be said that there is any immediate prospect of a great return tide of prosperity, but the year 1898 promises to be better than its immediate predecessors.

Reports from the banks, from the manufacturers, from the jobbers, are to the same effect. Gradually more money from the banks is borrowed to resume or extend operations. Slowly factories which have been idle are beginning to work, and many large and important works which have been decided upon are waiting for the first coming of normal trade to be begun.

Manufacturing. While the commerce of the port of Richmond has been increasing at a rapid rate, the revenue collections are vastly improved, the railroad traffic has been keeping pace, and the city has been progressing in other ways. Richmond has increased her manufacturing establishments from 984 to 1,071 during the past

(135)

year, and while there has been a slight decrease in the number of hands employed, and in the amount of capital invested, the sales have exceeded by more than a million dollars those of 1896.

Banks. Very gratifying and significant is the handsome showing of the banks for the past 12 months. The total resources of the National, State, and Savings banks amounted to 17,727,140 dol., and, including two trust companies, aggregate 18,400,000 dol., showing an increase of 1,000,000 dol. over 1896, and of 4,800,000 dol. over 1890.

A comparative statement of the bank clearances for the past two years shows an increase in 1897 of 2,019,889 dol. 35 c.; 1896, 114,518,841 dol. 66 c.; 1897, 116,538,731 dol. 1 c.

Failures. There have been 52 failures during the past year, the total liabilities amounting to 1,074,300 dol., with assets aggregating 537,400 dol. This bears favourable comparison with 1896, and, indeed with any year during the past decade.

Jobbing trade. The volume of business in the Richmond jobbing trade during 1897 shows an increase over the previous record, which is due to renewed energy on the part of merchants, as well as increases in the prices of some commodities.

The annual sales of the trade were 526,970 dol. in excess of that year, and aggregating 30,413,032 dol.

Tobacco. The tobacco trade shows a very appreciable increase, and the dealers are most sanguine as to the future of this staple industry. The improved condition of the loose tobacco market is especially gratifying.

The planters of dark tobacco have found a fully high market in Richmond, with prices advanced over last year from 25 to 30 per cent. in medium and more common grades. Sun-cured averaged more than a dollar a hundred over last year's prices. For black wrappers and fine dark shippers much higher prices prevailed than in 1896. In brights there has been activity, and in prices a well-sustained market, with a full corps of buyers always on sales. Medium grades have ruled high, while, as elsewhere, the finer grades of cutters have not been so high, and fine wrappers not in such strong demand. The advance in the lower and medium grades has more than offset the decline in finer grades.

The inspections of hogshead tobacco and stock on hand have constantly decreased, and were the smallest in many years, and the same condition exists as to stocks of hogshead tobacco on hand. This decline is due largely to the inspection system in vogue in former solely loose markets — to direct sales from them — and to the fact that the largely-used western tobacco on this market does not pass local inspection, but is sold by western sample, and is taken directly to the factory. Loose trade would increase the local inspection.

The defective system of reporting private sales, the far most important data in the Richmond trade, does not admit of as good showing of the magnitude of the market as might be made. Other makrets, showing a recorded full strength in this respect, appear relatively to an advantage. Thousands of hogsheads are privately sold, not to say resold, and exported, &c., which are never reported. It is safe to say that the transactions in Richmond in tobacco amount yearly to more than 70,000,000 pounds, while credit is given for much less.

The work of deepening the James River Channel now being carried on by the United States Government, has been steadily proceeded with during the year. *James River improvement.*

Richmond has undoubtedly increased her export trade, but as the export takes place at other ports, principally Norfolk and Newport News, Virginia, it will be credited to those ports, this port and its sub-port West Point being practically no longer ports of entry or clearance for foreign-going vessels. *Export trade.*

RETURN of Articles Imported into Richmond, Virginia, during the Year 1897.

Articles.	Value.
	Dollars.
Farm and garden seeds	19,803
Guano	12,300
China and earthenware	7,695
Wine and spirits	3,979
Matches	2,489
Cigars	1,437
Miscellaneous	9,096
Total	56,799

RETURN showing Value of Articles Imported into Richmond, Virginia, during the Year 1897.

Country.	Value.
	Dollars.
Great Britain	16,852
France	14,171
Orchilla, West Indies	12,300
Germany	6,947
Norway	2,489
Italy	1,975
Cuba	1,437
China	338
Canada	290
Total	56,799

LONDON:
Printed for Her Majesty's Stationery Office,
By HARRISON AND SONS,
Printers in Ordinary to Her Majesty.
(75 5 | 98—H & S 135)

No. 2085 Annual Series.

DIPLOMATIC AND CONSULAR REPORTS.

UNITED STATES.

REPORT FOR THE YEAR 1897

ON THE

COMMERCE, &c., OF CHICAGO.

REFERENCE TO PREVIOUS REPORT, Annual Series No. 1853.

Presented to both Houses of Parliament by Command of Her Majesty,
MAY, 1898.

LONDON:
PRINTED FOR HER MAJESTY'S STATIONERY OFFICE,
BY HARRISON AND SONS, ST. MARTIN'S LANE,
PRINTERS IN ORDINARY TO HER MAJESTY.

And to be purchased, either directly or through any Bookseller, from
EYRE & SPOTTISWOODE, EAST HARDING STREET, FLEET STREET, E.C., and
32, ABINGDON STREET, WESTMINSTER, S.W.; or
JOHN MENZIES & Co., 12, HANOVER STREET, EDINBURGH, and
90, WEST NILE STREET, GLASGOW; or
HODGES, FIGGIS, & Co., Limited, 104, GRAFTON STREET, DUBLIN.

1898.

[C. 8648—107.] *Price Three Halfpence.*

CONTENTS.

Chicago— PAGE
    General remarks ... 3
    Imports—
        Art works ... 4
        Ginger ale ... 4
        Bone and horn, manufactures of ... 4
        Books, maps, music, &c. ... 4
        Brushes ... 4
        Cement ... 4
        Bicycles ... 4
        Cotton cloths, manufactures of ... 4
        Clothing, wearing apparel, and ready-made clothing ... 4
        Lace, edgings, embroideries, &c. ... 4
        Porcelain, china, bisque, &c. (plain) ... 4
            „   „   „   (ornamented) ... 4
        Emery grains ... 5
        Cutlery ... 5
        Tin-plates, terne, and taggers tin ... 5
    Exports ... 5

Denver—
    New buildings ... 5
    Real estate ... 5
    Clearing-house ... 6
    Banks ... 6
    Customs ... 6
    Post Office ... 6
    Manufacturing ... 6
    Taxable property, value of ... 7
    Public lands ... 7
    Agriculture ... 7
    Fruit ... 7
    Live-stock ... 8
    Dairy products and poultry ... 8
    Railways ... 8
    Iron and steel ... 9
    Coal ... 9
    Coke ... 10
    Stone ... 10
    Oil ... 10
    Mining ... 11
    Imports in 1897 ... 12
    Imports for past 10 years ... 12

S. Louis, Mo.—
    Review of year's business ... 13
    Grain trade ... 13
    Flour ... 14
    Manufacturing industries ... 14
    Grocery trade ... 15
    Foreign grain trade ... 16
    Lumber trade ... 17
    Foreign shipments of flour and grain ... 18
    Missouri productions marketed ... 19

No. 2085.   Annual Series.

Reference to previous Report, Annual Series No. 1853.

Report on the Commerce, &c., of the Consular District of Chicago for the Year 1897

By Mr. Consul W. Wyndham.

(Received at Foreign Office, April 13, 1898.)

The progressiveness, vitality, and energy of Chicago as a financial centre has been splendidly demonstrated during the past year. At the beginning of 1897 local financiers found themselves forced into the defensive position of seeking to maintain credit under the very trying conditions of panic and disaster which had befallen the city, as the year 1896 had been notable for bad business, financial crashes, and aggravation of hard times all over the country, the result of fear of what would happen if the silver party came into power. The agricultural class who are the chief producers of what this country has for sale in the world's markets, had for a long time been discouraged by the prices received for their products which barely met the cost of production.

General remarks.

The months of the year just passed by have seen an enormous enhancement in the value of all American agricultural products. Wheat has gone over the dollar mark (*i.e.*, 4s. 2d. to the bushel), so that the incumbrances of hard times have been largely removed, and the inhabitants of the country districts have had more money to spend.

With the consuming power of a great part of the population enormously increased, came the opportunities to the merchant and manufacturer, and with the safe retention of a sound money policy, business men have at last dared to look ahead and begin to plan such new ventures as mean a larger future employment of labour.

Nowhere has this been more evident than in Chicago, but there is still the depression to be combated, which always succeeds a period of unusual prosperity like that enjoyed by Chicago during the World's Fair.

Chicago although it is a port of entry for goods sent through in bond, receives a great part of its importations through business houses at New York, and other seaboard ports, and the same may be said of its exports, for goods of Chicago origin are sent to the seaports and are shipped as opportunities for cheap freight offer,

(144)

CHICAGO.

this renders it very difficult to obtain any reliable statistics of the enormous commerce of this large city, and even the Secretary of the Board of Trade here tells me it is almost impossible to get the actual figures as to the different countries to which the exports go or whence the imports come.

Imports. — The total value of imports as entered in the Chicago custom-house received in bond for the year 1897 amounted to 2,100,000*l*. This, however, does not include goods entered at other ports and sent on here.

Art works. — In the class of goods described as art works France and the United Kingdom appear to be the main source of supply, France sending about twice as much as the United Kingdom. The figures are for France, 510,100*l*.; Great Britain, 247,000*l*. Of this total Chicago imported through its own custom-house 21,800*l*. worth.

Ginger ale. — Ginger ale is imported almost exclusively from the United Kingdom, the total importation amounted in value to 41,428*l*. for the United States in 1897, of which this city received 893*l*. through Chicago customs.

Bone and horn, manufactures of. — The United Kingdom leads in supplying bone and horn goods, Chicago received 534*l*. worth out of a total importation amounting to 15,819*l*.

Books, maps, &c. — The three principal countries supplying books, maps, &c., are as follows: *i.e.*, United Kingdom, 344,686*l*.; Germany, 198,656*l*.; and France, 51,545*l*. Chicago's importation amounted to 29,509*l*.

Brushes. — France leads easily in brushes, sending in 1897 112,910*l*. worth, to 15,475*l*. from the United Kingdom, and 14,830*l*. from Germany. Chicago's share being 4,375*l*.

Cement. — German cement worth 3,161*l*. was imported last year, as against 1,531*l*. from Belgium, and 1,242*l*. from the United Kingdom.

Bicycles. — Although the United States are very large manufacturers of bicycles still during the past year the importation of this class of goods amounted to 36,888*l*. from Austria-Hungary, and the United Kingdom sent to the States bicycles and parts valued at 18,251*l*.

Cotton cloths, manufactures of. — Manufactured cottons were received last year from the United Kingdom amounting to 2,089,157 square yards valued at 50,800*l*. These are all unbleached, dyed, and coloured.

Ready-made clothing, wearing apparel, &c. — There is a very large importation of ready-made clothing, and it would seem incredible that to Chicago there should be 40,000*l*. of goods of this description imported in 1897, yet this is the figure shown in the Government books.

Lace, edgings, embroideries, &c. — Switzerland is the main supplier of lace, &c., the United Kingdom sending about one-half as much as Switzerland, whilst France and Germany send only one-fourth as much. In this class of goods there has been a noticeable diminution in British trade.

Plain porcelain, china, bisque, &c. *Decorated china, &c.* — 57,990*l*. represents the value of the supply of plain china, &c., of which the largest part was of British manufacture, and this trade could be further developed by active, pushing canvassers; on the other hand, whilst Great Britain leads easily in the plain china market, Germany sends the most decorated and ornamented china, &c., being far in advance even of France in its exports, Germany figures for 550,000*l.*, as against France 240,000*l.* and the United Kingdom 80,000*l.*

Emery is imported almost exclusively from the United Kingdom, the Chicago importation amounting in 1897 to 450*l.* <small>Emery grains.</small>

Of the 18,560*l.* worth of cutlery imported to Chicago only one-third came from the United Kingdom, the remaining two-thirds were of German manufacture. <small>Cutlery.</small>

There was about 58,000*l.* worth of tin-plates, terne, &c., imported during the past year, of which the greatest amount came from Canada and British Columbia. <small>Tin-plates, terne, taggers tin, &c.</small>

The chief articles of export are grain, flour, preserved provisions, cattle, &c. These are, however, shipped from the Atlantic seaports, and no statistics are obtainable here as to their ultimate destination. Furniture, office, and desk supplies are largely sent abroad from Chicago, and agricultural implements are largely manufactured and sent to Europe. Chicago is the collecting and distributing centre of a very large area of the Western States, and it is to Chicago as the headquarters that the traveller for foreign manufacturing houses comes, and it is also the home of the representatives of foreign business houses. A great number of British firms have agents here who secure a vast amount of custom for their firms, and it requires untiring energy and persevering push to keep up with the methods of doing business here. The agent who wants to succeed must be at work from daylight to dark or he will be left behind in the great scramble that is hourly going on in all and every kind of business here, personal solicitation and determined push are absolutely the only way in which a hold can be obtained, and kept when obtained, circulars are simply waste-paper and no one spares time to study them. <small>Exports.</small>

DENVER.

Mr. Vice-Consul Pearce reports as follows:—

The commercial record of Denver and the State of Colorado for 1897 shows considerable improvement over that of 1896. Prices ranged lower than in the previous year for nearly all varieties of staple goods and wares, but the increased volume more than compensated for the decline in prices.

The total number of building permits issued by the Inspector during the year was 768, and the value of the new buildings erected was 250,220*l.*, an increase over 1896 of 26,780*l.* It is claimed that the cost of building has been reduced one-half, as compared with five years ago, and that the buildings are of a much better class than those erected at that time. <small>New buildings.</small>

The transactions in real estate for the year amounted to 1,394,380*l.*, a decrease of 75,460*l.* from 1896. A number of large transfers were made in the months of November and December, in the business portion of the city. <small>Real estate.</small>

(144)

6 DENVER.

Clearing-house. The records of the bank clearing-house of Denver for 1897 show a total of 24,882,849*l*., an increase of 609,249*l*. over 1896.

Banks. The condition of the four national banks in Denver, at the close of the year, is given as follows:—

	Amount.
	£
Deposits	4,725,651
Loans and discounts	2,212,328
Resources	5,332,453

As compared with 1896 this shows an increase as follows:—

	Amount.
	£
Deposits	1,169,752
Loans and discounts	199,073
Resources	1,004,698

Customs. The Surveyor of Customs has issued the following report of the business transacted at the Denver office for 1897:—

	Amount.
	£
Free goods imported	3,000
Dutiable goods imported	24,000
Lead ore	168,000
Total	195,000
Goods exported	128,000
Duty collected	19,554

Post office. The gross receipts at the Denver post office for the year were 78,666*l*., a gain of 2,692*l*. over 1897.

Manufacturing. The value of the products of the manufacturing industry for the year shows a considerable gain over that of 1897. This is attributed in a great measure to the increased demand for mining machinery and farming implements.

Skilled mechanics have been generally steadily employed during the year.

Eastern manufacturers have established agencies here for the sale of improved machinery and modern electrical appliances for mining and other purposes, this together with the excellent local manufacturing industries makes Denver a distributing centre for the best mining and metallurgical appliances to be found anywhere.

The following is a summary of the manufacturing industry,

DENVER.

including the product of the smelting companies for the years 1896 and 1897:—

Year.	Number of Men Employed.	Amount of Wages Paid.	Value of Product.
		£	£
1896	13,103	1,305,140	8,113,400
1897	16,699	2,198,156	8,690,340

The total assessed valuation of taxable property in the State for the year was 39,457,302*l.*, a decrease of 856,410*l.* from 1896.

The volume of business transacted at the United States land offices in Colorado during the year indicates an increasing demand for agricultural and grazing lands. A large area of the State is still open for settlement.

Farming has made considerable progress during the past year. An exceptionally good harvest has materially helped to make this industry more than usually profitable.

It is estimated that there are 4,500,000 acres of cultivatable land in the State which can be irrigated by the various canal and ditch companies, and about one-half of this acreage was under cultivation during the year.

The estimated value of the agricultural products for the year is as follows:—

Articles.	Value.
	£
Wheat	800,000
Alfalfa	1,600,000
Clover and timothy	250,000
Natural grasses	600,000
Corn, oats, barley, and other grains	1,200,000
Potatoes	550,000
Garden products	900,000
Dairy and poultry products	700,000
Total	6,600,000

This shows an increase of 2,100,000*l.* over 1896.

Within the past 10 years the progress in horticulture in the State has been rapid, and a widespread fruit industry has been created. The counties of Montrose, Delta, Mesa, and Garfield in Western Colorado, and Fremont, Arapahoe, Jefferson, Boulder, Larimer, and Otero on the eastern slope of the mountains may be named as sections most extensively developed.

Statistics, as given by the Horticultural Inspectors, show 35,653 acres in orchard-bearing fruit, and the values of the crop in 1897 is estimated at 1,000,000*l.*, an increase of 428,000*l.* over 1896.

The acreage that is available and suitable for fruit lands is 845,491 acres.

(144)

DENVER.

Increase in the planting of fruit trees and vines during the year is estimated at 20 per cent.

Up to within about a year ago Colorado only produced sufficient fruit for its own consumption, but during the past year there was a considerable surplus, which found a ready market in several eastern States, owing to the recognised superiority in the quality of the fruit.

Melons and cantaloupes were produced on lands watered by the Arkansas River, in the southern part of the State, in immense quantities, and it is reported that 72,000 crates of cantaloupes and 228,000 water-melons were shipped to eastern cities.

Live-stock. During the year the live-stock industry has been more prosperous than for many years past. Early in the season there was a considerable advance in the price of cattle, and this, with the unusually large grass and hay crop, created a demand for feeding purposes. The result has been a large increase in the number and value of live-stock in the State.

Following is the estimated number and value:—

	Number.	Value.
		£
Cattle	1,000,000	4,000,000
Sheep	800,000	320,000
Hogs	50,000	70,000
Horses	187,800	900,000
Mules	7,000	24,600
Total	2,044,800	5,314,600

This shows an increase in value over 1896 of 1,150,600*l.*

The estimated value of live-stock handled in the Denver stock yards, 1897, compared with 1896, is given as follows:—

Year.	Cattle.	Sheep.	Hogs.
	£	£	£
1897	1,939,319	125,183	118,437
1896	1,373,531	54,192	84,805
Increase	565,788	70,991	33,632

Dairy products and poultry. The value of the dairy products for the year is estimated at 500,000*l.*

It is stated that there are good opportunities in the State for the investment of capital in this industry, as large quantities of butter are imported from adjoining States to supply the local demand.

The estimated value of the poultry and egg supply of the State for the year is 200,000*l.*

Railways. There has been no new railway construction during the year, and the assessed valuation of all the railroads in the State is practically the same as given in my report for 1896.

There has been no very great increase in business over the previous year.

STATEMENT of Production of Iron and Steel in Colorado during the Year 1897. *Iron and steel.*

Articles.	Quantity.	Value.
	Lbs.	£
Merchant iron	38,193,312	106,941
Castings	1,643,810	6,575
Cast-iron pipe	10,942,309	28,450
Spikes	4,416,735	14,575
Bolts and nuts	3,373,976	16,870
Total	..	173,411

This shows a decrease in value of 423,309*l*. from 1896.

During the year the iron mines, blast furnaces, and rail mill of the Colorado Fuel and Iron Company were not in operation, which accounts for the heavy falling-off in production.

The year 1897 was a good one for the coal operators of the State, and during the last few months of the year almost every mine in the State was worked to its full capacity to supply the home demand and that of adjoining States. *Coal.*

The output shows an increase of 143,687 tons over the output of 1896.

The total commercial value of the production, based on the retail price, is estimated at 1,800,000*l*.

DENVER.

TABLE showing Output of Coal by Counties during the Years 1896-97.

Counties.	Quantity. 1896. Tons of 2,000 lbs.	Quantity. 1897. Tons of 2,000 lbs.
Arapahoe	398	413
Boulder	504,947	585,370
Dolores	2,100	2,400
El Paso	32,016	23,916
Fremont	282,459	310,596
Gunnison	269,875	315,917
Garfield	227,280	213,693
Huerfano	365,648	350,980
Jefferson	18,105	13,600
Las Animas	1,331,115	1,424,196
La Plata	99,116	72,965
Larimer	..	6,000
Montezuma	2,000	2,000
Mesa	20,457	27,764
Park	33,887	..
Pitkin	162,071	148,700
Weld	22,159	18,810
Total	3,373,633	3,517,320

Coke.

TABLE showing Coke Production during the Years 1896-97.

Counties.	Quantity. 1896. Tons of 2,000 lbs.	Quantity. 1897. Tons of 2,000 lbs.
Garfield	76,312	50,265
Gunnison	50,440	68,385
Las Animas	195,091	179,461
La Plata	2,851	2,851
Total	324,694	300,962

Stone. The several quarries of the State produced during the year building and all other classes of stone and marble to the estimated value of 98,000*l*.

Colorado stone was used in the construction of several buildings at Omaha and Kansas City.

Oil. During the past year there has been but little new development of importance in the petroleum industry to report in this district. The production of crude petroleum of the Colorado field is about 2,000 barrels of 42 gallons per day. This product is manufactured into illuminating oil and lubricants, and a certain percentage of the by-products is sold for fuel, which is in demand for use in roasting furnaces in the reduction of metalliferous ores.

TABLE showing the Value of the Output of the Mines in Colorado during the Year 1897.

Articles.	Value.
	£
Gold	3,665,311
Silver	2,428,485
Lead	590,463
Copper	226,345
Total	6,910,604

This shows an increase in value over 1896 of 973,460*l*.

The average price of silver for the year was $59\frac{7}{10}$ c. per oz., as against 67 c. in 1896.

The Commissioner of Mines gives the number of men engaged in metalliferous mining as 29,215; number of accidents in mining 279, fatal 110.

Various estimates have been given in regard to the gold product for the year, but probably the most conservative and reliable figures are those furnished by Wells, Fargo, and Co., shown in the above table.

There have been no new discoveries of gold in Colorado of any importance during the year, but the product from the older districts has shown a marked increase.

Cripple Creek, which has been referred to in my reports of the last four years, must be especially mentioned in this particular. The exact figures representing the product for the year are not to be obtained. Various estimates have been given, but perhaps the most reliable data that can be furnished will show that 500,000 ozs. of gold representing a money value of at least 2,000,000*l*. has been produced from this district alone.

It is estimated that the yield of ore during the year, from the various mines in the Cripple Creek district, amounts to 275,000 tons of 2,000 lbs.; 100,000 tons were sent to the smelters at Denver and Pueblo, the balance, 175,000 tons, was treated at the chlorination and cyanide mills at Cripple Creek, Florence, and Colorado city.

Mining generally throughout the State has been prosperous during the year, and there has been an entire absence of strikes and labour troubles which were so prevalent in Colorado in 1896. The attempt which was made in that year by the Miners' Union to gain a strong hold in Colorado proved a failure; this is perhaps mainly due to the fact that the mining interests are spread over a large area, and not concentrated in one spot as in other localities where the Miners' Union has been able to dictate its own terms and conditions.

STATEMENT of Values of Imports from Great Britain Entered at the Port of Denver during the Year 1897.

Articles.	Value.
	£ s.
Indiarubber	20 4
Iron and steel	94 12
Jewellery	58 0
Wood, manufactures of	55 0
Earthenware	1,572 0
Cotton, manufactures of	126 16
Wool	607 0
Tobacco and pipes	72 12
Spirits	195 12
Wine	71 12
Tea	430 16
Effects	774 16
Toys	54 4
Seeds	22 4
Books	40 16
Plants	32 8
Silk	46 16
Total	4,275 8

RECORD of Imports from Great Britain for the past 10 Years.

Year.	Value.
	£ s.
1888	8,109 12
1889	17,585 7
1890	32,512 4
1891	26,008 16
1892	9,357 4
1893	6,603 16
1894	4,984 4
1895	6,481 4
1896	7,366 12
1897	4,275 8

During the year a large quantity of lead ore, representing about 12,000 tons of lead, passed through the custom-house here from British Columbia. The ore is treated by the Colorado smelters, and the lead shipped by way of Galveston to Liverpool and Havre. No duty is paid on this lead, it merely passes through in bond.

St. Louis.

Mr. Vice-Consul Western Bascomb reports as follows:—

It is not claimed that every line of trade is in a satisfactory condition as to values and profits, but there is a general belief that the tide has turned for the better and business is flowing in with excellent prospects for the future. *Review of the year's business.*

In making comparisons with former years, it should be borne in mind that values are much lower than in 1892 and previous years, consequently the volume of trade is not always determined by the amount of sales.

In many lines there has been a decline in values of 25 per cent. and over, so that the same aggregate of value represents a much larger quantity of goods than formerly. This is illustrated by enquiries made of a large grocery establishment, where the cashier reported a slight falling-off in sales, and the shipping clerk claimed it was the best year the house ever had.

Notwithstanding the wonderful progress made in the last 20 years in what is known as the productive industries, the contiguous territory is largely an agricultural country and prosperity depends largely upon the products of the farm and the ability to market those products. There was a marked improvement in agricultural products during 1897, the crops being abundant, and there was an excellent foreign demand for the surplus, and a revival of live-stock business. These conditions with the revival of manufacturing industries set the whole of commerce in motion and the impetus was felt in all directions.

St. Louis is favourably located to command a large portion of the grain trade of the West, having in addition to unsurpassed railway facilities for transportation, the Mississippi River furnishing a cheap water route to New Orleans, where ample facilities exist for storing and handling grain for ocean transportation. *Grain trade.*

The past year has not, however, realised what might have been expected from the large export demand for wheat or corn. The low stage of water in the river after harvest precluded cheap rates by water, and for some three months navigation was practically suspended at a time when the crops were moving.

Rail competition reduced freight to Gulf ports to such a low point as to prevent shipments viâ St. Louis to southern seaports, largely diminishing such shipments.

The receipts, however, were considerable aggregating 57,600,639 bushels, of which 15,000,000 bushels were on through bills of lading consigned by St. Louis dealers to the Atlantic seaboard. There were 6,500,000 bushels forwarded by river to New Orleans in addition to some 30,000,000 bushels by rail, besides 13,250,000 bushels to Atlantic seaports divided between New York, Baltimore, Newport News and Charleston.

It is promised by the engineers in charge of river improvements that the difficulties of river transportation will be greatly lessened

14 ST. LOUIS.

Flour.

another season, and a larger proportion of the surplus grain of the Mississippi Valley will pass viâ St. Louis to the Gulf.

The flour business of the year was not equal to former years, nor was it satisfactory, the high price of wheat curtailed the manufacture, and so-called "blended flours" (a mixture with corn flour) largely interfered with the southern trade. The receipts were 1,329,916 barrels, the amount manufactured in city mills 1,080,916 barrels.

Manufacturing industries

A comprehensive statement of the manufacturing industries of the city has been compiled in comparison with the census reports of 1880-90.

While these aggregate figures show a wonderful increase, it must be remembered that values in 1880 and in 1890 were much higher than at present, and that if the present output was valued on the same basis as in those years it would show a tremendous increase.

Year.	Number of Factories.	Number of Employés.	Amount of Wages Paid.	Value of Products at Factory.
			£	£
1880	2,924	41,825	3,548,706	22,866,675
1890	6,148	93,610	10,633,048	45,742,863
1897	7,237	127,902	14,205,200	61,500,000

Boots and shoes.

The boot and shoe trade has shown a remarkable advance. Manufactories were established here only seven years ago, and the volume of the product in 1897 was 5,200,000*l*. The receipts from other sources has also increased, 993,276 cases having been received during the year. The total sales are given as 7,171,200*l*., which placed this city as only second to Boston, the only city in the country which leads St. Louis in this line.

Dry goods.

The dry goods trade has received a great impetus the last half of the year, and has been very gratifying, the increase being estimated at from 12½ to 15 per cent., and the total sales at 10,000,000*l*.

Clothing.

While the clothing trade has not been very prominent, yet it is reported as increased in 1897 about 20 per cent., and the total sales to 500,000*l*.

Drugs.

St. Louis is one of the largest drug distributory centres in the United States, which includes chemicals, essential oils, patent and proprietary medicines, and druggist's sundries amounting to 5,000,000*l*. in 1897, one of the establishments being the largest of the class in this country. The business is reported to have increased in 1897 from 15 to 20 per cent.

Hats, caps, and gloves.

The hat, cap, and glove business is reported to have increased the past year 10 to 15 per cent., and the aggregate sales 700,000*l*. for the year 1897.

Wooden and willow ware.

It is claimed that over 50 per cent. of the wooden and willow ware business of the United States is done in St. Louis, and the business for 1897 shows a healthy increase over 1896.

St. Louis has for a long time been the leading manufacturing city for tobacco in the United States. The output for 1897 in the city proper was 58,796,408 lbs., and the first Missouri district, which includes St. Louis, 62,588,229 lbs. The value of the manufactured product was about 5,000,000*l*. Tobacco.

The trade in agricultural implements increased about 5 per cent., in vehicles 20 per cent., the total sales being 3,000,000*l*. Agricultural implements and vehicles.

This is an important hardware market, the sales being reported at 3,200,000*l*., in addition to iron, steel, heavy hardware reported as increased about 12½ per cent., with sales aggregating 1,400,000*l*. Hardware.

The output of glass from the city factories is estimated at 500,000*l*., and with window, plate and art glass from other points the total is estimated at 900,000*l*., and an increase of about 25 per cent. Glass and glassware.

The cotton business for the year ending August, 1897, showed a fair increase of about 24,000 bales. Cotton.

The wool trade shows a remarkable revival, the receipts being more than doubled over 1896, and greater than any previous year. They aggregate 30,865,400 lbs., valued at 1,600,000*l*. Wool.

The furniture trade in the year 1897 has been an improvement over the previous year, there being a marked increase in business, commencing in the spring and continuing throughout the year. Factories gradually added to their employés, and in the autumn they were all running full time, the actual output being about 1,100,000*l*., an excess over the previous year. The entire value of furniture and kindred lines handled being about 3,600,000*l*. The hands employed numbering upwards of 5,000 in the 50 factories. Furniture.

The export trade has probably doubled the past year, securing business from Mexico, Central and South America.

The Steam and Electric Car Furniture Factory has extended its business by opening offices in London, Japan, China, the Latin American republics, and in Africa.

There are 40 wholesale grocery houses in St. Louis with reported sales for 1897 of 11,000,000*l*., but representing a volume that would have sold for 16,000,000*l*. a few years ago. The grocery trade.

The comparative receipts and shipments of coffee for 1897 and 1896 are as follows:— Coffee.

Year.	Quantity.	
	Receipts.	Shipments.
	Sacks.	Sacks.
1897	320,005	279,685
1896	403,388	292,585

There being a large falling-off as compared with 1896, which is explained by a large accumulated speculative stock at the end of 1896, while a hand to hand purchasing has obtained in 1897, owing to constantly declining values.

Sugar.

The following is a comparative statement of receipts and shipments of sugar for the years 1897 and 1896:—

Year.		Quantity.	
		Receipts.	Shipments.
1897	Barrels	497,285	399,873
	Bags	497,525	223,217
	Hogsheads	1,447	631
1896	Barrels	448,105	293,759
	Bags	253,919	..
	Hogsheads	1,298	856

Since the new tariff came into effect but little foreign refined sugar has been imported owing to enormous importations previous to the imposition of the higher duty, the price having advanced about 20 per cent. during the year.

Rice.

The receipts and shipments of rice are as follows for 1896 and 1897:—

Year.	Quantity.	
	Receipts.	Shipments.
	Packages.	Packages.
1897	95,801	72,519
1896	87,090	64,610

The business being reported satisfactory and a gain over 1896.

Teas.

Teas have shown an improved distribution during the year, and larger receipts with a tendency to a higher appreciation of the better qualities.

Receipts for the past two years have been:—

Year.	Receipts.
	Packages.
1897	27,112
1896	16,157

Foreign grain trade in St. Louis.

6,465,983 bushels of grain were shipped by river to New Orleans for export. In addition to this 13,435,110 bushels was forwarded direct by rail for the Atlantic seaboard, largely to Baltimore and Newport News; something over 1,000,000 bushels going by the way of Charleston. In addition to this some

30,000,000 bushels of grain were bought and shipped by St. Louis exporters from western points direct by rail to New Orleans and Galveston, but did not pass through St. Louis, making the total export grain business of St. Louis for 1897 some 50,000,000 bushels.

The cotton business for the year ending August 31, 1897, was, gross receipts, 570,413 bales; net amount handled and sold in St. Louis, 114,897 bales. *Cotton.*

The lumber trade of St. Louis during 1897 shows more prosperity than did the trade of 1896. Not only was there a greater volume of business, but prices averaged higher, and especially in a wholesale way, the year ended with a rush. The business failures among the lumbermen were insignificant, and the losses sustained by lumbermen in failures were light, for lumber consumers were in fairly good state during the year. *City lumber trade.*

It was more especially the latter half of the year that showed the heavy volume of business, the receipts and shipments during that period being greater than during a similar period of any previous year in the history of St. Louis as a lumber market.

On the other hand, navigation was seriously deterred during the last three or four months of the year because of low water, a number of our river operators being unable to finish out their season contracts. From the upper river a decrease in receipts was expected, white pine no longer being as strong a commodity on this market as during former years. The past 10 years have shown a steady decrease in the amount of Northern white pine, and a steady increase in the amount of Southern yellow pine handled on this market.

The total receipts of lumber and logs by river and rail during 1897 aggregate about 820,000,000 feet, compared with 795,000,000 feet during the previous year. The shipments amounted to 467,000,000 feet, against 395,000,000 feet during 1896

The aggregate value of the State's total production of timber computed at prevailing prices will approximate 1,400,000*l*., in the production of which over 6,000 persons were employed. Almost every county in the State produced a sufficient amount of "native," or hardwood lumber, for local use, and a majority of the seventy counties south of the Missouri River each produced a large surplus. *Missouri State lumber interests.*

The following are the principal lumber-producing counties of South Missouri, the greater portion of their output being pine:— Carter, 26,811,000 feet; Pemiscott, 21,807,000 feet; Stoddard, 21,438,000 feet; Wayne, 25,794,000 feet; Shannon, 18,360,000 feet; Dunklin, 14,283,000 feet; Mississippi, 11,188,000 feet.

(144)

ST. LOUIS.

FOREIGN Shipments of Flour and Grain on Through Bills of Lading from St. Louis, by Railroad and River, for the Year 1897.

Destination.	Flour.	Wheat.	Corn.	Oats.	Rye.
	Barrels.	Bushels.	Bushels.	Bushels.	Bushels.
To England	167,920	223,066	169,071	7,000	...
Germany	3,945	...	...	...	...
France	...	...	...	...	...
Scotland	88,938	...	...	...	...
Ireland	49,375	...	...	3,690	...
Austria	...	...	...	...	...
Denmark	1,450	...	...	...	...
Norway	4,940	...	...	...	...
Holland	4,260	...	...	...	...
Belgium	10,221	...	...	...	...
Italy	330	...	...	...	...
Spain	650	...	...	...	...
Switzerland	...	...	...	...	...
Sweden	...	...	...	...	...
Iceland	...	...	...	...	...
Newfoundland	750	...	...	...	...
Canada	1,630	...	3,321	...	...
Cuba	37,790	...	...	...	...
Central America	5,420	4,000	...	...	...
South America	775	...	...	...	...
Mexico	...	...	33,907	...	...
Porto Rico	...	...	...	...	...
Seaboard for export	28,175	1,425,526	10,760,769	405,660	399,100
Total for export by rail	406,569	1,652,592	10,967,068	416,350	399,100
Total for export by river	...	1,815,623	3,827,963	631,429	190,968
Grand total	406,569	3,468,215	14,795,031	1,047,779	590,068

ST. LOUIS.

The surplus productions of Missouri actually marketed, as shown by the records of the railroad, express and boat companies, with their values, computed at prevailing current prices, were as follows:—

Articles.		Quantity.	Value.
Cattle	Head	1,016,760	7,625,700
Horses, mules	,,	104,361	834,880
Hogs	,,	3,142,074	4,398,903
Sheep	,,	319,372	223,569
Mixed live stock	Cars	4,068	740,376
Poultry	Lbs.	45,496,179	636,940
Butter	,,	4,232,189	118,501
Cheese	,,	575,342	10,356
Milk	Gallons	304,948	8,149
Eggs	Dozen	31,969,031	511,504
Flour	Barrels	4,645,614	3,623,579
Meal	Lbs.	8,443,484	16,884
Mill feed	,,	61,150,077	61,140
Apples	Bushels	3,334,746	33,432
Dried fruit	Lbs.	1,042,849	8,342
Small fruit	Crates	264,749	35,300
Small fruits	Baskets	88,249	5,204
Cotton	Lbs.	16,600,000	199,200
Cotton-seed products	,,	24,000,000	96,000
Wool	,,	2,871,000	114,840
Grass seed	Bushels	365,635	144,425
Broom corn	Tons	1,800	14,400
Castor beans	Bushels	27,275	4,364
Molasses and honey	Gallons	96,940	5,160
Vegetables	Lbs.	32,211,419	64,494
Fish	,,	1,010,715	10,167
Dressed meat	,,	1,052,859	16,946
Game	,,	1,440,649	8,644
Bacon, lard, tallow	,,	2,453,369	28,092
Hides	,,	9,396,218	122,150
Furs, feathers	,,	499,406	27,469
Canned goods	,,	5,246,767	26,234
Wine, cider	Gallons	392,410	66,379
Lumber, logs, piling	Feet	307,496,300	626,783
Post, cord wood	Cars	6,371	23,087
Cooperage	,,	2,634	79,020
Ties		2,759,676	110,387
Coal	Tons	2,420,147	548,340
Lead	,,	65,504	397,431
Zinc	,,	92,754	366,371
Chats	,,	97,620	7,809
Barytrs tiff	Lbs.	17,640,000	6,976
Lime, cement	Barrels	883,676	265,102
Granite	Cars	3,101	83,727
Stone	,,	3,913	123,400
Brick	,,	6,472	64,720
Gravel, sand, ballast	,,	17,914	32,225

The apparent shortage in dressed meats and meat products is due to the fact that most of the packing houses of Kansas city are in the State of Kansas, and those of St. Louis being on the Illinois side of the river, hence those States get the credit of Missouri's productions.

LONDON:
Printed for Her Majesty's Stationery Office,
By HARRISON AND SONS,
Printers in Ordinary to Her Majesty
(75 5 | 98—H & S 144)

No. 2115 Annual Series.

DIPLOMATIC AND CONSULAR REPORTS.

UNITED STATES.

REPORT FOR THE YEAR 1897

ON THE

TRADE AND COMMERCE OF PORTLAND AND DISTRICT.

REFERENCE TO PREVIOUS REPORT, Annual Series No. 1935.

Presented to both Houses of Parliament by Command of Her Majesty.
JUNE, 1898.

LONDON:
PRINTED FOR HER MAJESTY'S STATIONERY OFFICE,
BY HARRISON AND SONS, ST. MARTIN'S LANE,
PRINTERS IN ORDINARY TO HER MAJESTY.

And to be purchased, either directly or through any Bookseller, from
EYRE & SPOTTISWOODE, EAST HARDING STREET, FLEET STREET, E.C., and
32, ABINGDON STREET, WESTMINSTER, S.W.; or
JOHN MENZIES & Co., 12, HANOVER STREET, EDINBURGH, and
90, WEST NILE STREET, GLASGOW; or
HODGES, FIGGIS, & Co., Limited, 104, GRAFTON STREET, DUBLIN.

1898.

[C. 8648—137.] *Price Twopence Halfpenny.*

CONTENTS.

	PAGE
PORTLAND—	
Introductory remarks	3
Clearing-house returns	3
Exports: wire nails, raw cotton, steel rails, paper	3
Wheat	4
Flour	4
Other cereals: barley and oats	5
Hop trade	5
Fruit trade	5
Timber trade	5
Fish trade: salmon	6
Wool trade	7
Import trade	7
Coal	7
Tin-plate trade, lost	8
Cement; bags and bagging; hemp, &c.	8
British trade, review	8
Financial	9
Banks	9
Exchange	10
Failures	10
Insurance	11
Shipping and navigation	11
Tonnage engagements	11
Freights	12
Ports and harbours	12
Shipbuilding	13
Lights and buoys	13
Sailors	14
Seaman's institute	14
Population	14
Mining	15
Manufactures and industries	16
Fisheries	17
Beet sugar	17
Labour	18
Health: births and deaths	18
Public works; rivers and harbours	19
Canals	19
Railways	19
Agriculture	19
Orchards and fruits	21
Stock-farming	22
Dry dock needed	22
Assessment and taxation	23
Real estate	23
Klondike	23
Statistics	24
ASTORIA Report	26
TACOMA AND SEATTLE Report	31
PORT TOWNSEND	40

No. 2115.   Annual Series.

Reference to previous Report, Annual Series No. 1935.

Report on the Trade, Commerce, and Agriculture of the Consular District of Portland, Oregon, for the Year 1897

By Mr. Consul Laidlaw.

(Received at Foreign Office, May 17, 1898.)

The wheat harvest of 1897 throughout this district was the largest on record, and prices of agricultural produce were generally higher than for many years past. As a natural consequence the improvement in trade of this port and district was very remarkable. The following comparison of the clearing-house returns at Portland shows a satisfactory condition of business:— *Introductory remarks. Improved trade.*

	Amount.	
	1897.	1896.
	£	£
Clearances	14,859,050	12,481,779
Balances	3,027,757	2,723,965

Clearing-house returns

Farmers have paid off or largely reduced their indebtedness; cattle and sheep-owners have found a profitable market for their produce; the production of gold was largely increased, and all indications point to a continued improvement during 1898.

Details of exports are given in Annex B attached to this report, which shows an increase of 17 per cent. exclusive of transit and coastwise trade. Only a small proportion of the wheat surplus from the harvest of 1896 was carried into 1897, and therefore appears in the exports for that year, while large stocks have been carried over and will swell the exports for 1898 very much. *Exports.*

Attention is called to the export of wire nails to the value of 10,625*l.*, and raw cotton 17,919*l.*, shipped to Japan, and steel rails of the value of 3,438*l.* shipped to Korea. *Wire nails. Raw cotton. Steel rails.*

These goods were received from the Eastern States. The amount of paper, principally newspaper the product of Oregon mills shipped to Japan is increasing. *Paper.*

Note.—Calculations are made throughout this report at 5 dol. to the 1*l.* sterling.

PORTLAND.

Wheat.

The season was very favourable for wheat-growing, and the crop harvested was the largest on record. The export trade was, therefore, unusually brisk, and prices averaged much higher than for years past. Quality was generally a very good average, though there was some country damage. The following is a comparison of monthly average export values of Walla-Walla wheat during the last three years:—

Month.	1897. £ s. d.	1896. £ s. d.	1895. £ s. d.
January	1 9 1	0 18 11	0 14 11
February	1 8 0	1 0 6	0 14 11
March	1 7 8	1 0 3	0 15 10
April	1 7 3	0 19 10	0 16 4
May	1 5 6	0 19 6	0 17 6
June	1 3 7	0 18 0	0 18 4
July	1 3 1	0 17 5	0 17 4
August	1 8 1	0 17 5	0 17 0
September	1 8 2	0 18 6	0 15 4
October	1 7 1	1 2 6	0 16 5
November	1 6 10	1 6 8	0 16 6
December	1 5 5	1 6 9	0 16 11
Average	1 6 8	1 0 6	0 16 5

Valley and blue-stem wheat commands 1s. per quarter more than Walla-Walla. The total shipments both foreign and coastwise from the Columbia River, including clearances, were 1,076,209 quarters, valued at 1,440,477l.: coastwise shipments were 95,070 quarters.

The entire export of wheat from this Consular district to foreign countries were 1,511,630 quarters, and its distribution is as follows:—

Great Britain 75 per cent., France 13 per cent., Cape de Verdes for orders 10 per cent., South Africa and Japan 2 per cent.

The export by steamer is increasing very materially; steamers coal at Coronel and Cape de Verdes.

Flour.

The total shipments of flour from the Columbia River both foreign and coastwise were 469,944 sacks valued at 530,520l., which is considerably less in quantity but of higher value than in 1896. The shipments to foreign ports were as under:—

To—	Sacks (of 280 Lbs.).
Great Britain	125,863
Chinese ports	105,683
Japanese ports	41,666
South African ports	35,630
Other countries	3,183
Total	312,025

From the whole Consular district the total shipments of flour aggregated 805,500 sacks of 280 lbs.

In January patent roller extras sold at an average of 25s. 5d., and superifines at 16s. per sack. From February to April prices averaged 23s. 6d. and 15s. 7d.; May and June 21s. 10d. and 15s. 3d.; July 21s. 5d. and 12s. 10d.; August 24s. 4d. and 13s. 11d.; September and October 24s. and 15s. 4d.; November and December 22s. 5d. and 12s. 10d. for patent extras and superfines respectively.

Although the crops of barley and oats were quite large, the shipments, except coastwise, were very small, consisting of a few sacks of oats and bran to South Africa. *Other cereals.*

The year opened with light stocks and good prospects for the hop trade, though many contracts had been made at from 4d. to 4½d. per lb. As the season developed there were prospects of a large yield, and picking commenced in the last week in August. During the first part of September the weather was rainy and mould and lice did much damage, reducing the yield one-third, and the quality proved generally inferior, only 10 per cent. being classed as choice, 30 per cent. as prime brewing, 30 per cent. as common, and 30 per cent. mouldy and inferior. Oregon produced about 65,000 bales of 180 lbs. each, and Washington 32,000 bales generally of better quality than Oregon hops. Prices improved towards the close of the year, sales being made at 3¼d. to 7d., according to quality. Shipments were made by rail to New York and the United Kingdom in many cases, consigned to British dealers. Stocks at close of year large and generally of lower qualities. *Hop trade.*

Although prices of green fruits were generally very low, owing to heavy yield both in this district and in California causing a glutted condition of the principal markets (the middle Western States) yet, on the whole, a profit was realised as the cost of production is very small. Apples were an exception, the crop being large, and a good and profitable market was found for all sound fruit. There was a large quantity of fruit dried, more particularly of prunes, which sold at 4 to 5 c. (2d. to 2½d.) per lb. for good quality. *Fruit trade. Green fruit.* *Dried fruits.*

The timber trade with foreign ports was three times as much as during 1896, and several large British steamers were employed in the trade. Shipments were made as under:— *Timber trade.*

To—	Quantity.	Value.
	Feet.	£
Chinese ports	5,923,730	7,170
Japanese ports	4,473,543	7,249
Siberia	2,123,000	3,822
„ (railway sleepers)	..	821
Hawaiian Republic	609,000	916
East Indies	..	380
Total	..	20,358

(186)

PORTLAND.

The business was hampered by a difficulty in securing tonnage. There was more lumber cut at Portland than at any other place on the Pacific coast, but no correct statistics are obtainable of the coastwise trade. It is stated that Oregon mills produced 549,823,000 feet of lumber of an estimated value of 879,717*l.*, about 1*l.* 12*s.* per mil. feet board measure. Particulars of trade at other points in this district are given in the reports of the Vice-Consuls at Tacoma, Port Townsend, and Astoria, annexed to this report. The business was more profitable than it has been for a few years past.

Fish trade. Salmon, tinned.

Prices of tinned salmon were very low during 1897, and as the cost of production does not decrease in proportion the business could not be called profitable, though the product largely exceeded that of 1896. The Columbia River pack is now marketed principally in the Eastern States. The only direct foreign shipments were as under:—

To—	Cases (of 48 Lbs.).	Value.
		£
Great Britain	13,457	13,855
South Africa	1,300	975

The prices paid for raw salmon were: 4 c. (2*d.*) per lb. for Chinook, 2½ c. (1¼*d.*) per lb. for steelheads and bluebacks, and 1½ c. (¾*d.*) per lb. for silversides, and the average prices at which the tinned product was marketed were about as under:—

	Per Dozen.			
	Spring Catch.		Fall Catch.	
	From—	To—	From—	To—
	s. d.	*s. d.*	*s. d.*	*s. d.*
Flat 1-lb. tins	4 8	4 10	..	..
Tall „	3 7	4 0	..	..
Oval „	7 0	7 2	..	..
Flat ½-lb. tins	2 10	3 0	..	..
Tall 1-lb. „	..	..	3 0	3 4

The following is a summary of this business throughout the Consular district:—

	Quantity.	Value.
	Cases.	£
Columbia River (spring), Oregon	337,655	279,627
,, ,, Washington	139,269	114,966
,, (fall), Washington	5,508	3,580
,, ,, Oregon	70,289	45,680
Other rivers and bays in Oregon	68,683	44,281
Puget Sound (spring), Washington	370,900	291,870
,, (fall), Washington	120,200	78,130
Grays Harbour, Washington	20,000	13,000
Willapa Harbour, Washington	17,500	11,375
Total	1,150,004	882,509

Fresh and salt fish. There was shipped to the Eastern States from the Columbia River as nearly as can be ascertained the following:—

	Quantity.	Value.
	Lbs.	£
Fresh salmon	5,060,000	48,056
Salt salmon	930,300	9,303
Sturgeon	995,400	9,954
Halibut	950,000	9,506
Total		76,819

Wool trade. Prices of wool did not advance to the extent expected upon the raising of the tariff, but the growers made money at the prices secured, not to mention the large appreciation in value of sheep. The condition of the wool was superior and lower in shrinkage than in 1896. The clip of Eastern Oregon was about 21,000,000 lbs.; of the Willamette and Umpqua Valleys (principally combing wools), 800,000 lbs. The wool market opened at from $7\frac{1}{2}$ to 10 c. for Eastern Oregon and $12\frac{1}{2}$ c. for Valley. In August prices advanced to 12 to 13 c. for Eastern Oregon and 14 to 15 c. for Valley. The consumption of the nine woollen mills in Oregon was larger than for some time past and exceeded 2,500,000 lbs.

The clip of Washington is said to have been nearly 7,000,000 lbs., and that of Idaho 7,500,000 lbs.

Imports. A reference to Annex B shows an increase of 34 per cent. in value of imports through the custom-house, not taking into account the transit trade. The increase in coals, rice, tea, hemp and manila, sugar, caustic soda, spirits, silk, and matting are particularly noticeable, but of the last two articles only a small proportion is for local consumption. There was a decrease in earthenware, salt, and coffee, a heavy decrease in tin-plate, and no imports of pig-iron.

Coal. Imports of coal from Australia and British Columbia were larger than for years past but prices were low, Australian

PORTLAND.

averaging 17s., and British Columbia about the same. The following were the receipts:—

From—		Quantity.
		Tons.
Australia	.. ..	21,778
British Columbia	.. ..	4,778
Great Britain	.. ..	225
Atlantic ports	.. ..	1,450
Coast mines by sea..	.. (about)	10,800
„ by rail	.. „	16,900

Tin-plate trade lost. The duty on tin-plate was raised during the year to 1½ c. per lb., and although 62,932 boxes were received from Great Britain during the year, this trade may now be considered lost. All the roofing plates were of American make and the receipts of American for canning purposes were also considerable. Tin-plate mills in the United States are in a position to hold the trade as the quality produced is superior, and the tariff gives efficient protection. Lighter plates are now used in the canned goods trade, weighing usually 100 lbs. to the box; as light as 85 lbs. has been used to some extent. The average price of standard 100-lb. cake plates was 15s. 6d. At the date of writing this report there are practically no English tin-plates on the way, and American will be used almost exclusively in 1898. The consumption for canning purposes on the Columbia River alone exceeded 65,000 boxes. English tin-plates, I am informed, cannot at present be laid down under 17s. per box, while American sells at 13s. 6d.

Cement. Of the cement imported to this market 40,273 casks came from Belgium, 6,774 from Germany, and only 4,038 casks from Great Britain. The reason for the loss of this trade was given in my last report (Annual Series, 1897, No. 1935). There was a fair trade during the year, but the average market price did not exceed 10s. 6d. per barrel.

Jute bags and bagging. The direct imports of bags and bagging from Calcutta were not so large as last year, but the consumption was very much greater, and was supplied in a great measure by shipments viâ San Francisco. The harvest of wheat alone in this district required over 15,000,000, not to mention oats, barley, and hop cloth. Only a small percentage of the demand for sacks was supplied from the Washington penitentiary. The average price of standard size wheat bags was 5 dol. 25 c. (1l. 1s.) per 100 bags. Most of the imports were received before the duty of ⅞ c. per lb. and 15 per cent. ad valorem was imposed.

Hemp and manila. 120 tons of raw hemp and 1,252 tons of manila were imported for the cordage works, and 134 tons of jute. Efforts are being made to encourage the growth of hemp and flax in this State.

Window glass. All the window glass was imported from Belgium.

British trade. In looking over the list of imports I do not see anything encouraging for the British manufacturer. In salt, Great Britain largely monopolises the trade, but Salt Lake is competing for the trade with some success. In caustic soda and soda ash American manufacturers in the Eastern States are also developing strong competition.

All the paints entered at the custom-house come from England, and there seems to be an increasing demand for Scotch whiskies. Of the earthenware 80 per cent. was British and 15 per cent. German.

There was quite a large import trade from the United Kingdom in flax and hemp twines used for fish nets and sacking. In imported cutlery British manufacturers are still in the lead, the percentage of German being small this year, but the great bulk of the trade is for American goods. It is impossible to trace the amount of trade in the finer qualities of cotton goods and fine cashmeres, tweeds, meltons, and worsteds which are usually purchased in New York and shipped here by rail. These are generally of British manufacture. Most of the cheaper grades of woollens are either manufactured in Oregon or in the Eastern States, and nearly all of the hosiery is of German make. Britain leads the trade in all the finer qualities of linens, damasks, sheetings, &c., but German manufacturers are improving their goods. British manufacturers cannot compete with American domestics, calicoes, and dress goods.

A glance at Annex C attached to this report will show the preponderance of British trade with this district, particularly in exports.

Financial matters. Money has been plentiful throughout the year for commercial purposes, but there has not been much disposition to lend for long terms. In this district there are 74 national banks, the resources of which are as under, exclusive of deposits, loans, and discounts:—

States.	Number.	Capital.	Surplus.	Undivided Profits.
		£	£	£
Oregon	30	603,000	108,144	157,355
Washington	34	805,600	134,389	68,398
Idaho	10	48,000	49,375	26,854
Total	74	1,456,600	291,908	252,607

During the year one large national bank in Portland went out of business, and was succeeded by a branch of Wells, Fargo, and Co. There are now four national banks, two British, and seven savings and private banks. The condition of the national banks in Portland on December 15, 1897, and December 16, 1896, was as under:—

PORTLAND.

RESOURCES.

	Amount.	
	1897 (Four Banks).	1896 (Five Banks).
	£	£
Loans and discounts	504,256	679,301
United States bonds	305,060	305,060
Other stocks and bonds	445,716	225,226
Premiums on United States bonds	22,800	24,852
Real estate, furniture and fixtures	48,125	49,074
Redemption fund, United States Treasury	5,625	6,075
Due from other banks	177,076	68,875
,, reserve agents	135,686	75,521
Cash on hand	221,341	399,217
Total	1,865,685	1,833,211

LIABILITIES.

	Amount.	
	1897.	1896.
	£	£
Capital paid in	220,000	320,000
Surplus and profits, less expenses	157,621	163,740
Dividends unpaid	..	500
Circulation	85,288	120,920
Deposits, individual and bank	1,402,776	1,228,051
Total	1,865,685	1,833,211

Exchange.   From January to May exchange of 60 days commercial drafts varied between 4 dol. 84 c. and 4 dol. 86 c. per 1*l*., but the average was not over 4 dol. 84 c.; from May to September there was only a nominal market as little export business was carried on. From September till the close of the year rates were low, and the average rate was only 4 dol. 80¼ c. Bank exchange usually sold at two points higher.

Failures.   Dunn's Commercial Agency gives the following comparison of commercial failures in this district during the last two years:—

PORTLAND.

States.	1897. Number of Failures.	1897. Liabilities.	1896. Number of Failures.	1896. Liabilities.
		£		£
Oregon	169	131,388	178	332,880
Washington	136	106,047	149	378,389
Idaho	75	72,440	83	88,500
Total	380	309,875	410	799,769

The following is a statement of the insurance business in the State of Oregon, compiled by the State Commissioner for the year 1897:— *Insurance.*

	Gross Premiums.	Premiums Returned.	Losses Paid.	Net Premiums.
	£	£	£	£
Fire Insurance Companies	221,877	43,586	88,327	89,964
Life and accident ..	115,395	63,022	8,096	44,277
Marine and miscellaneous	3,953	454	123	3,376

In the shipping and carrying trade a much more cheering state of affairs presents itself, so far as British interests are concerned, for the flag of Great Britain is paramount, and the business was more profitable than for several years past, but even in this trade the German flag is oftener seen than heretofore, and a perusal of the shipping returns, Annex A, gives food for reflection when coupled with the fact that 14 foreign vessels, mostly German, were still on the way at the close of the year. *Shipping and navigation. British shipping.*

The percentage of British tonnage employed in the foreign trade was 81 per cent. against 88 per cent. last year. A new feature was the increased number of steamers of large capacity employed in the grain and timber trades. More life has been thrown into the China-Japan line of steamers, and the vessels have been carrying full cargoes inwards and outwards.

Engagements of tonnage, sail and steam, exclusive of coasting voyages were as under:— *Tonnage engagements.*

Cargoes.	Tons, Register. 1897.	1896.	1895.
Grain and flour..	140,117	131,381	138,356
Timber	17,596	14,976	8,419
Miscellaneous	3,175	3,516	843
Total	160,888	149,873	147,618

PORTLAND.

Freight.

The year opened with grain charters as low as 18s. 9d., and there was very little business done until June, rates having meanwhile advanced to 1l. 2s. 6d.: when it became evident that there would be a very heavy surplus for export, quite a large number of ships were chartered to arrive at from 1l. 5s. to 1l. 15s. In October 1l. 17s. 6d. was paid, and up to 2l. 2s. 6d for steamers, and before the close of the year 2l. to 2l. 2s. 6d. had been paid for sailing vessels.

The average rate during the year for iron or steel vessels to the United Kingdom, Havre, Antwerp, or Dunkirk was 1l. 12s. The following table shows the rates for arrived vessels during the year:—

Month.	Rates of Freight. From—	Rates of Freight. To—
	£ s. d.	£ s. d.
January	0 18 9	0 19 0
February, March	No trans	actions
April, May	..	1 1 3
June	..	1 2 6
July	No trans	actions
August, September	1 10 0	1 15 0
October	1 15 6	1 17 6
November, December	..	2 0 0

Coasting trade.

There has been an extreme scarcity of coasting craft, everything procurable having been chartered to carry passengers and freight to the Klondike Gold Fields, viâ Alaskan ports. At the date of writing this report the mad rush has to a great extent ceased, but may be resumed, should favourable reports be received, when the summer opens in that region.

Ports and harbours.

No work was done at the mouth of the Columbia River during the year, but in June a survey was made of the bar by the United States engineers revealing a 30 foot channel, 2,000 feet wide across the bar at mean lower low-water, with a 29 foot depth of over three-quarters of a mile. The engineers consider the channel is now established in what should be its permanent position. It is proposed to remove the wreck of the "Sylvia de Grasse" below Tongue Point in the Columbia River and the outer portion of the ledge on which it rests, and by dredging to open a water-way in front of Astoria 25 feet deep and 250 feet wide at the bottom. Some dredging was done and the channel materially improved. Dredging was continued on the various bars in the Willamette and Columbia Rivers below Portland, and 23 feet at low-water obtained. It is intended to continue this work until a channel of 25 feet in depth at low-water is obtained from Portland to the sea. There was little or no detention experienced by vessels passing up and down the river during the year. In another portion of this report notice is taken of Government work on other ports and harbours. The Port of Portland Commission is building a new dredge, and the harbour will be dredged in some places near the wharves where required as there has been some shoaling going on.

Numerous small craft have been built during the year, including two steam light vessels for the United States Government. Two torpedo boats are approaching completion, and a 30 knot torpedo boat has been contracted for by a firm here. A large suction dredger is under construction. *Shipbuilding.*

Some minor changes were made in lights and buoys of this district, and the following important changes are reported:— *Lights and buoys.*

On February 17, 1898, the first order fixed light on the southerly extremity of Cape Disappointment will be permanently discontinued and a light of the fourth order, showing red and white flashes alternately, interval between flashes 15 seconds, will be permanently established in its place. *Cape Disappointment light.*

On or about May 16, 1898, a fixed white light of the first order will be established in the lighthouse recently erected on the extreme westerly point of North Head, northerly side of the mouth of the Columbia River. *North Head light.*

The focal plane of the light will be 192 feet above mean highwater, and the light may be seen 20¼ miles in clear weather, the observers eye 15 feet above the sea. The light will be visible from all points of approach from seaward excepting from the northward to the eastward of S. by E. ⅞ E. The approximate geographical position of the tower is: lat. north 46° 17′ 52″, long. west 124° 04′ 48″. Bearings and distances from the tower are—

Cape Disappointment lighthouse, S.E. by E. ⅜ E., 1¾ miles.
Point Adams lighthouse, S.E. by E., 7⅝ miles.
Tillamook Rock lighthouse, S.S.E. ½ E., 22¼ miles.
Columbia River light vessel No. 50, S. ¾ W., 8⅝ miles.

On or about May 20, 1898, steam light vessel No. 67 will be established in 25 fathoms of water about 2½ miles S.W. ⅝ S. from Umatilla Reef, Flattery Rock, making off from Cape Alava, Washington, and about 4¼ miles west-north-westerly from the Cape. The vessel will show a fixed white light from each of a group of four lens lanterns encircling each masthead. In each lens lantern there will be a 100 candle power incandescent electric light; the focal plane of the lights will be 55 feet above the sea, and the lights will be visible 12¾ miles in clear weather, the observers eye 15 feet above the sea. If the electric light apparatus should become inoperative the lights will be a fixed white, but will be less brilliant than the electric lights. The vessel has a flush deck, two masts, schooner rigged and has no bowsprit; she has a smoke-stack and a fog signal between the masts. At each masthead, under the lens lantern, there is a white circular gallery. The hull is painted red, and "Umatilla Reef" in large black letters on each side, and "67" in black on each bow end quarter. During thick or foggy weather a 12-inch steam whistle will sound blasts of three seconds duration, separated by silent intervals of 27 seconds. The approximate geographical position of the vessel is: lat. north 48° 09′ 43″, long. west 124° 50′ 43″. Bearings from the proposed position of the vessel are— *Umatilla Reef light vessel.*

PORTLAND.

Destruction Island lighthouse, S.E. ¼ E., easterly 32¾ miles.
Cape Flattery lighthouse, N. ⅜ W., westerly 14¼ miles.

The importance of these lights cannot be over-estimated, and it is believed the North Head light will save many vessels from loss. It is a curious fact that many wrecks off the mouth of the Columbia River have been caused by the light at Cape Disappointment having been sighted, and the vessels drifting north have picked up the light at Willapa in mistake for that at Cape Disappointment, shut out by the North Head.

Sailors. Wages of sailors out of this port were 4*l*. for A.B.'s till the month of July, since which time 5*l*. has generally been paid. An attempt was made by the crimps at the beginning of the shipping season to exact an illegal bonus of 10*l*. per man, and against my advice this was paid in several instances. I recommended masters to take out warrants for arrest of all deserters, but for some reason they were averse to doing so. As soon as they began to take my advice the crimps ceased their exactions and reduced their demands to 2*l*., which has generally been paid throughout the year. The crimps also insist upon the men taking an advance of 40 dol., two months wages, the least allowed by law in the United States. I consider shipowners and masters are to blame for this state of affairs. In their unreasoning fear of detention the masters take the chance of arrest and punishment under the United States law for payment of any remuneration for the shipment of seamen. I have never known an instance where the provisions of this law were enforced. The following were the numbers and changes in crews of British vessels during the year:—

	Number.
Total number of crews	2,542
Deserted	396
Discharged	186
Engaged	429
Deaths reported	4
Sent to hospitals	21

The percentage of desertions to number of crews was 15¼ per cent. against 8 per cent. last year. If warrants were issued for the arrest of every deserting seaman I think it would check the practice very much.

Seamen's Institute. Something in the way of an institute has been carried on by the Seamen's Friend Society, but the work is hampered for want of funds. In view of the fact that the majority of seamen entering this port are British, I think it would be more successful if this beneficent work were taken in hand by the Missions to Seamen Society, which has done such effective work in the neighbouring port of San Francisco.

Population and industries. Health. Population of Oregon. From the best information at my command the population of the entire State of Oregon, which has an area of about 96,000 square miles, does not much exceed 400,000, though some

PORTLAND.

authorities during the past year claim over 420,000, which would be only 4·40 to the square mile. Of the population over one-fifth is within the confines of the city, which good authorities estimate contains 87,300 inhabitants. The principal industries of this State are agriculture, mining and fisheries, and such may be said of the neighbouring States of Washington and Idaho in this Consular district. In addition to the immense saw and flour-mill plants and the large woollen, pulp and paper-mills, manufactures are being developed in different directions, but are handicapped by these States being used as a dumping ground for the surplus products of manufactures in the Eastern States.

Population of Portland.

Oregon and Idaho are large gold-producing States, and the product of Washington is also considerable. Year by year there is a greater development of the resources of these States in this respect, but there is a lack of capital for the proper working of mines. The output of gold in Oregon is estimated as 722,000*l.* I believe this to be very much too high as the shipments by express given below were only 70 per cent. of that amount. Baker County produces nearly three-fifths of the whole.

Mining. Gold.

Most of the silver product came from the great mines in Cœur d'Alene district, Idaho. Some of the largest of these are under the control of British capitalists who are spending large sums in their systematic development. There is a lawless element amongst the miners which tends to weaken the confidence of those interested. The United States Assayer at Boise City, Idaho, has furnished me with a copy of his report of the product of that State for the year ending December 21, which is as under :—

Silver.

	Quantity.		Value.	
	Fine ozs.	Lbs.	1897. £	1896. £
Gold ..	192,813	..	425,066	464,740
Silver	5,493,975	..	1,420,664	1,294,953
Lead ..	..	118,606,600	900,247	590,676
Total ..	..	..	2,745,977	2,350,369

Wells, Fargo and Co.'s annual reports give the value of shipments of the precious metals during the last two years as under :—

State.	Gold.		Silver.		Ores and Base Bullion.	
	1897. £	1896. £	1897. £	1896. £	1897. £	1896. £
Oregon	480,959	390,041	9,000	19,357	2,380	5,000
Washington	94,390	76,670	14,000	34,100	5,232	..
Idaho	545,000	530,500	911,120	654,536	548,200	440,000
Total	1,120,349	997,211	934,120	707,993	555,812	445,000

Quicksilver. At Black Butte Lane County, Oregon, a valuable deposit of cinnabar has been opened, which reports say can be worked very economically at a cost of 10 c. per pound. This is probably an under statement, but the deposits are said to be very large.

Copper. There are said to be immense deposits of copper in the Seven Devils district in Idaho, which it is claimed rivals the richness of the mines of Butte, Montana, but it is a difficult country to open up, although the mines have been worked more or less for years. I learn that 120,000*l*. was paid during the year for one property. There are copper deposits all over these States embraced in this Consular district, but none of them are developed to any extent.

Lead. Lead was higher in price and the production was nearly twice as great as during 1896. Average value was about 15*s*. 2*d*. per 100 lbs.

Iron. There was little iron smelting done throughout the district. The furnaces at Oswego, near this place, were not in blast during the year.

Coal. There are numerous coalfields throughout the district, but the only workings at Oregon are at Coos Bay. Exports from that point were 85,129 tons. The following is given as the product of the Washington mines during the year:—

Location of Mine.	Owner.	Tons Mined.	Men Employed.
Roslyn	North Pacific Coal Co.	360,938	580
Caroonado	Carbon Hill Coal Co.	308,000	450
Wilkeson	Wilkeson Coal and Coke Co.*	82,741	212
Burnett	South Prairie Coal Co.	64,380	121
Issaquah	Seattle Coal and Coke Co.	101,966	275
Black Diamond	Lawson, Robbins, and Lawson	27,967	40
Cokedale	Skagit Coal Co.*	16,000	70
Black Diamond	Black Diamond Coal Co.†	75,000	200
Franklin	Oregon Improvement Co.†	96,400	250
Newcastle	Oregon Improvement Co.†	96,400	250
Renton	Renton Coal Co.†	21,000	30
Cle-Elum	Cle Elum Coal Co.†	30,000	32
All other mines†		96,000	188
Total		1,376,792	2,698

* The coal from these mines is nearly all coked.
† The product of these mines is estimated.

The average value at the mines seem to have been about 8*s*. per ton. There were no accidents or disasters of any magnitude during the year.

Manufactures. There are really no reliable statistics obtainable of the manufacturing industries of Oregon, with the exception of salmon canning factories and the larger saw-mills and flour-mills, and perhaps the woollen mills. Wild guesses are made at the product and extent of the trade, and are called estimates. My experience has been that these estimates are generally much exaggerated. Business has been brisk in all the above-named branches, and generally there is no doubt that there has been a very great improvement in the various industries.

PORTLAND.

Woollen mills. There are nine woollen mills in the State of Oregon, that at Oregon City being the largest mill west of the Mississippi working 14 sets of cards, and employing 275 hands. Another large concern is the Salem Woollen Mills Company, owning two mills. The other mills are smaller. All the mills have been running full time, and some of them night and day. All grades of blankets are made, the finer quantities being most beautiful goods. There has been a large and profitable demand for mackinaws and other heavy goods for the Klondike trade, and flannels, cheviots, tweeds, cassimeres, serges, and worsted goods are also made, usually of cheap to good quality, but really handsome and fine goods are now being made by some of the mills. Hitherto, the finest qualities of worsteds have been brought from eastern mills or imported from Great Britain.

Clothing. A new clothing factory was started in Portland during the year, employing over 150 operatives.

Mills. Flour-mills were shut up between seasons, but were fully employed the rest of the year, and the saw-mills generally ran full time. Pulp and paper-mills were well employed, and there was a good demand for leather and its products. The leather made in this State has an excellent reputation. Foundry and repair shops did a better business, the largest plant here employing 250 men, but shops generally were not fully employed. The meat-packing companies did a somewhat larger business than in 1896, and prices advanced considerably.

Rope and cordage. There is a thoroughly equipped rope and cordage factory here making all sizes. Raw material is imported from Manila, India and Mexico. The works were in steady operation during the year and supplied the trade of the north-west.

Fishing industry. According to the report of the Fish and Game Protector, there were 31 factories at work during the season packing salmon on the Columbia river and in Oregon coast streams and bays. The number of fishermen employed was 4,698, and of shoremen and operators at the factories 2,638; 1,845 boats were employed and 1,977 gill nets, besides traps and seines.

Beet sugar. A good deal of interest has been taken in the question of the manufacture of beet sugar, it having been proved that the soil and climate are eminently suitable for the cultivation of sugar beets, as the following data based on a long series of experiments by Prof. G. W. Shaw of the Experimental Station show:—

Results as to Quality.

County.	Weight of Beets.	Sugar.	Purity.
	Grains.	Per cent.	Per cent.
Washington	439	15·3	90·9
Clackamas	486	13·7	84·3
Union	609	16·6	86·8
Jackson	503	15·6	82·2
Other counties	523	14·3	84·4

PORTLAND.

Results as to Yield per Acre and Cost.

County.	Yield.	Cost per Acre.
	Tons.	£ s. d.
Washington	15·3	4 16 0
Clackamas	16·8	5 4 0
Jackson	14·9	undetermined
Union	23·2	2 4 10

These prices do not take into account cost or rent of land or cartage to factory. Other tests made last year from beets grown in Multnomah County and Clackamas County gave even better results. Arrangements have been made to erect a refinery at La Grande in Union County by Utah capitalists interested in the refinery at Los Alimetos, California, and it will be a duplicate of that factory, to cost 80,000*l*. It is estimated to consume 350 tons of beets, and to turn out 35 tons of granulated sugar per day with a season of 100 days. Prof. Shaw says the average for sugar beets is 2 per cent. more sugar in juice than in California. The factory has contracted with farmers to grow annually for five years 3,000 acres at 4 dol. (16*s*.) per ton. This business might be worthy of consideration by English capitalists, and is capable of great extension.

Labour. It has been estimated that the number of hands employed in various manufacturing industries in this State was 21,000, and the value of the product 10,000,000*l*. These figures are most probably exaggerated. It is claimed that this county, which practically means Portland, produced 6,000,000*l*. of this sum, and the number of hands employed was 12,000. There does not seem to have been such a surplus of labour as for some years past, but there is still great room for improvement, particularly in skilled labour. Common labourers have generally had little difficulty in securing employment at about 6*s*. per day. Building trade has been inactive. Farm labourers have been more in demand, and in view of prospective improvement in the state of agriculture this is likely to continue.

Clerks, &c. I cannot see any improved demand for the services of clerks and salesmen, who have great difficulty in securing steady employment, but there is a scarcity of good household servants, who can generally secure employment readily at good wages.

Births, deaths. Health. There were 1,083 births registered in this city during the year and 717 deaths, which gives a mortality rate of about 8·21, but the Health Office excludes deaths of persons brought here for treatment, and makes the rate 6·25, about one-third of that of San Francisco. This satisfactory condition is undoubtedly due to the pure water supply, and the systematic and energetic work of the city physician and Health Department. There has been a remarkable decrease in the number of cases of diphtheria and scarlet fever, and an increase in measles. A new and comprehensive health ordinance came into effect during the year. The principal causes of death during the year were:—Tuberculosis, diseases of the heart and pneumonia, 30 per cent. of the deaths resulting from these causes.

The annual report of Captain W. L. Fisk, of the United States Engineer Corps, shows that works of improvement are being prosecuted under his charge at Coquille, Coos Bay, Siuslaw, Tillamook, Columbia and Willamette Rivers, below Portland, and on the Willamette River above Portland. With the exception of those mentioned below, these works are only of local interest. Coos Bay is a harbour of some importance, and Empire City is the port of entry for Southern Oregon; its business is increasing and it has some foreign trade. {Public works. River and harbour works. Oregon.}

The projected improvement consists of two high tide jetties of stone extending seaward with an entrance width of 1,500 feet.

The north jetty has been built to 10,368 feet, and work during the year was confined to placing rock on it to raise it to high water level. There had been spent on this project at close of the fiscal year, June 30, 1897, 135,805*l*., and estimates for completion of the project are 388,282*l*. The least low water on the bar was 18 to 22 feet with an average tide of 5½ feet. Before improvements began the low water depths on the bar was sometimes 10 feet. Mention of the work on the lower Columbia and Willamette Rivers is made in another part of this report.

The river and harbour works mentioned below are under charge of Captain Harry Taylor, United States Engineers, and the information is derived from his annual report. {Washington.}

A contract has been let for the improvement of Grays Harbour mentioned in my report of last year (Annual Series 1897, No. 1935), and this valuable improvement will now go on.

At Everett Harbour, a harbour basin is being dredged together with a channel into the Snohomish River, the work will cost about 74,400*l*. The work is proceeding satisfactorily.

Since the canal and locks at the cascades of the Columbia were opened to navigation at the close of 1896, nothing has been done on the second lock for which provision has been made. {Canals. Cascades.}

Work has not been actually commenced nor has any definite plan been approved for the projected canal to connect Lakes Washington and Union with the waters of Puget Sound, although money has been appropriated by Congress for the purpose. {Lake Washington and Lake Union.}

But little railway work is in progress in this district. The Astoria Railway at the date of writing this report is nearly completed. {Railways.}

All the land necessary in connection with the construction of a boat railway round the obstructions of the Columbia River at The Dalles has not yet been acquired, nor have the detailed plans been approved by the United States engineers, so that active work is not likely to be commenced for some time to come. {Boat railway.}

The Oregon assessor's return of figures relating to agriculture for the year 1897 are given below:— {Agriculture.}

PORTLAND.

Assessor's returns. Oregon.

	Number.	Value.
		£
Acres of tillable land	3,441,559	6,360,135
,, wagon road lands	857,633	168,970
,, railroad lands	2,339,258	519,334
Acres, non-tillable land	7,111,749	3,288,100
Horses and mules	170,696	429,532
Cattle	394,181	813,442
Sheep and goats	1,745,256	350,188
Swine	100,384	33,850

Property is usually listed for assessment at about half its value, so that returns are largely under rated, but show a large increase over those of 1896.

Washington. I refer to Mr. Vice-Consul Alexander's report annexed for agricultural conditions in Washington. The season was remarkably favourable, and the crops with few exceptions were bountiful. The wheat yield was enormous and superior in quality and quantity to any ever before harvested in the State.

Idaho. I have found it extremely difficult to get any reliable data on the products of Idaho. A large quantity of wheat is grown in the northern counties, and is reported either through this port or Tacoma. The weather conditions were very favourable for all crops, in some counties wheat averaged 30 bushels of splendid grain to the acre. Stock continued in fine condition.

Oregon. Wheat is the staple crop of Oregon and yields from 15 to 40 or more bushels per acre according to conditions. Oats, barley and rye are grown largely, and corn over a limited area. Root crops and vegetables are luxuriant. Berries are wonderfully prolific. Apples, prunes, peaches, cherries and pears are largely exported. Sugar beets and flax, both for fibre and seed, grow well in many sections of the State. Hops are a staple crop. For nearly all these products weather conditions were favourable and crops very large, and as prices generally were good, the results to the farmers were the best for a series of years.

Cereals. The following figures give approximately the grain harvests of this Consular district, some of the estimates are probably exaggerated, but the wheat harvest is very nearly correct, and may be underrated:—

Articles.	Quantity.
	Bushels.
Wheat	35,000,000
Oats	9,550,000
Barley and rye	3,140,000

Wheat. A larger acreage than heretofore was put under wheat, and all conditions being favourable the heavy crop was got in with very little damage. The Willamette Valley, formerly the principal source of supply, has of recent years taken a very secondary place, its percentage of the harvest being less than one-fifth. Wheat growing was very profitable at the prices realised. As an instance, a person who rented 300 acres in Umatilla County is said to have cleared 26½ dol. (5*l.* 6*s.*) per acre after paying rent and all expenses. It is undoubtedly the case that many who were bankrupt realised enough to pay off their indebtedness and have money in hand. Fuller statistics are given under the head of exports in this report.

Oats were a good and profitable crop, generally above the average as to quality, though some damage was done by early rains. Prices were good and advanced towards the close of the year. The average was about 1 dol. 10 c. (4*s.* 5*d.*) per cental. Oats.

Cultivation of barley is not general. Sufficient brewing and feed barley was grown for home consumption and some exported. Crop was a good average one both as to quality and yield. Prices were profitable, averaging about 87 c. (3*s.* 6*d.*) per cental. Barley.

Good work has been done of late years by the Oregon State Board of Horticulture, and a constant war has been kept up against insect pests, as a consequence orchards are generally in good order. The year was a good one for fruit growers who had a heavy yield, and in spite of over-stocked markets, some of those who handled this produce well made money. There are nearly, if not quite, 40,000 acres of prune orchards in Oregon, of which 15,000 acres are in the Willamette Valley, 15,000 acres in Rogue River Valley, and 6,500 acres in the Umpqua Valley. About half are bearing. Orchards and fruits.

Flax has been grown for years for the seed, and while for some years the production has been light, farmers are largely encouraged to grow the plant not only for the seed but for the fibre. A linen thread manufacturer from Glasgow visited the State last year, and reporting on the samples of Oregon flax, said, "They were as fine as any grown in Ireland, being sound, good, and strong, with a splendid fibre, and that he believed it would yield as large a percentage as any flax produced in Ireland." I expect to see a large quantity grown in the future. Hemp seed is being distributed to farmers who are encouraged to grow the plant for its fibre, for which there is a good home market. Flax-seed and fibre. Hemp.

As it has been demonstrated that the sugar beet can be grown so successfully and profitably, a large acreage will be planted during 1898. Sugar beets.

The 1897 crop of potatoes in Oregon State was about 4,500,000 bushels, generally well grown and sound. There was a good demand at profitable prices. The crop was a good average throughout the three States embraced in this district, and the average price paid to farmers during the year was 50 c. (2*s.*) per cental, some realising 75 c. (3*s.*). I am told there is a profit in potatoes at 30 c. (1*s.* 2*d.*). Potatoes.

The experience of farmers in regard to hops during the past year was somewhat checkered, some did very well, and others lost their entire yield by mould and lice. Hops.

(186)

Stock-farming.

In sharp contrast with the Assessor's returns given elsewhere, a reliable agricultural paper gives the following returns of animals in Oregon at the close of 1897. I believe this is pretty nearly correct:—

	Number.	Value.
		£
Milch cows	130,000	538,200
Other cattle	479,000	1,628,600
Sheep	2,106,000	964,500
Swine	262,000	235,800

Stock came through the winter in very good condition, and losses on the ranches were exceedingly light. There has been a heavy demand for both cattle and sheep throughout the year at advancing prices, and large numbers have been driven out of the State. The increase in sheep will more than make up for this, but there is a short supply of beef cattle. Stock raising was more profitable than for many years past, and existing conditions are favourable for the business.

Cattle.

Sales of cattle on the ranches have been very large, and averaged about 2*l*. 16*s*. for yearlings, 4*l*. 10*s*. for two-year olds, and 5*l*. 8*s*. for three-year olds. A large packing-house gives the value as high as 6*l*. 2*s*.

Sheep.

Most of the sheep on the ranches of Oregon and Washington are graded merinos. There has been a decided increase in numbers in spite of the large flocks driven and shipped to other States. The business was very profitable, and values have advanced rapidly. The average price of sheep on the ranches was fully 10*s*.

Swine.

There was a good demand for all swine offered, and packing-houses paid an average price of 2*l*. per head for fat animals.

Angora goats.

Angora goats seem to be profitable. They are useful in keeping down the aftergrowth on lands partially cleared, need little care, and there is a good demand for their fleeces.

Horses.

There was a good demand for horses during 1897. Large numbers of all sorts were taken to Alaska for pack purposes and generally died during the winter. They increased very rapidly on the ranches in Eastern Oregon. The horses from that section are of the lighter breeds, have good feet and limbs, and great endurance. Western Oregon produces superior draft horses. Horse-breeding has not been profitable for some years past, but the business seems to be improving. There are over 200,000 horses in the State.

General remarks. Dry dock needed.

One of the greatest needs of this port is a floating dry dock, and I believe if interested British capitalists would look into the subject they would find a fair investment for money. Owing to the rise and fall of the river at different times of the year, a floating dock would be most suitable. It would naturally be built of wood, as being the material most readily obtainable and also cheaper. Considering the amount of tonnage annually visiting this port, much of which would dock if there were facilities for the purpose, I am inclined to think good interest would be made on the investment.

Assessed value of all property within the State of Oregon was 28,635,394*l*. in 1896, and 26,983,421*l*. in 1897. The valuation within this city during the same period was 9,295,183*l*. and 7,911,935*l*. respectively. Rate of taxation, 1·65 per cent. for State, county, and road purposes; city tax, 0·95 per cent. *Assessment and taxation.*

Not including street and sewer assessments paid by property owners, and receipts and expenditures of Water Commission given below, the total revenue of the city was 135,014*l*., and the expenditures 138,519*l*. *City finances.*

The bonded debt of the city of Portland is now 1,064,519*l*. Of this 101,300*l*. bears interest at 6 per cent., and the rest at 5 per cent. The annual interest charge is 54,521*l*., which is promptly paid. *Bonded debt.*

The Water Commission collected during the year 46,369*l*., and expended 49,332*l*., which included 9,000*l*. paid for East Portland plant, and 2,900*l*. interest on bonds. Water bonds are an especially favourite investment. *Water.*

Values of real estate are stronger than they were in 1896, but the sales were not large, transfers in Multnomah County not exceeding 840,336*l*. *Real estate.*

The rush of people to the Klondike goldfields gave an immense impetus to the outfitting trade both here and in Seattle and Tacoma, and a very large and profitable business was done. Steamers and crafts of all kinds were put into the trade whether seaworthy or not, and many large steamers are now on the way from Eastern States and other parts with the expectation of going into the trade, but at the date of writing this report the rush has ceased, and travel is light. Some believe there will be plenty of business on the opening of the Yukon River in June, but I am inclined to believe that unless extraordinary amounts of gold come out the fever has spent itself. I anticipate considerable distress will result to a good majority of those who have given up everything to go to that inhospitable region. Should the gold fever again return I think it well to warn the British public to be very cautious before they part with money to so-called transportation companies, as many people have been swindled during the past year through their blind trust in the specious statements made to them by agents of companies of all kinds which had no foundation, but often existed only upon paper. *Klondike.*

(186)

Annex A.—RETURN of all Shipping at the Port of Portland during the Year 1897.

ENTERED.

Nationality.	Sailing. Number of Vessels.	Sailing. Tons.	Steam. Number of Vessels.	Steam. Tons.	Total. Number of Vessels.	Total. Tons.
British	65	106,547	19	39,906	84	146,453
American, from foreign countries	4	3,404	1	392	5	3,796
American, from Atlantic ports	2	2,061	...	...	2	2,061
American coasting	31	9,408	141	145,493	172	154,901
German	8	12,971	...	...	8	12,971
Norwegian	2	2,625	4	7,933	6	10,558
French	2	3,356	...	...	2	3,356
Japanese	1	1,148	...	...	1	1,148
Total	115	141,520	165	193,724	280	335,244
,, for the year preceding	145	163,405	183	183,707	328	347,112

CLEARED.

Nationality.	Sailing. Number of Vessels.	Sailing. Tons.	Steam. Number of Vessels.	Steam. Tons.	Total. Number of Vessels.	Total. Tons.
British	68	113,297	18	35,890	86	149,187
American, to foreign countries	3	4,113	...	...	3	4,113
American coasting	45	13,974	140	142,739	185	156,713
German	6	10,373	...	...	6	10,373
Norwegian	2	2,625	4	7,933	6	10,558
Japanese	1	1,148	...	...	1	1,148
French	1	1,135	...	...	1	1,135
Total	126	146,665	162	186,562	288	333,227
,, for the year preceding	161	170,376	184	187,361	345	357,737

Annex B.—RETURN of Principal Articles of Export from Portland during the Years 1897-96.

Articles.		1897. Quantity.	1897. Value.	1896. Quantity.	1896. Value.
			£		£
Wheat	Quarters	907,774	1,254,144	862,185	1,002,547
,, flour	Sacks	312,025	350,997	426,240	370,020
Timber	Feet	13,129,273	20,358	4,036,000	7,052
Barley	Bushels	2,726	206	31,384	3,093
Canned salmon	Lbs.	62,400	975	97,598	2,066
Paper	,,	...	4,486	...	...
Wire nails (transit)	,,	1,891,000	10,625	...	...
Raw cotton ,,	,,	1,518,500	17,919	...	...
Steel rails ,,	Tons	984	3,438	...	...
Ammunition	...	...	1,612	...	...
Other articles	...	...	7,646	...	17,715
Total	...	...	1,672,406	...	1,402,493

RETURN of Principal Articles of Import to Portland during the Years 1897-96.

		1897.		1896.	
Articles.		Quantity.	Value.	Quantity.	Value.
			£		£
Coke	Tons	...	...	3,319	1,911
Coal	,,	25,879	10,449	14,755	5,446
Tin and tinplate	Lbs.	599,715	2,717	1,788,732	8,715
Rice and rice flour	,,	3,993,119	12,415	1,626,416	4,178
Earthenware and glass	...	...	8,845	...	12,721
Salt	Lbs.	6,136,600	2,357	7,505,600	3,446
Cement	Casks	51,086	12,230	58,079	13,621
Tea	Lbs.	861,025	25,140	400,874	10,628
Coffee	,,	135,500	4,256	151,499	5,284
Hemp, manilla and jute	Tons	1,506	19,045	350	5,992
Window glass	Lbs.	857,954	3,281	1,322,462	4,101
Bags and bagging	...	...	14,721	...	47,503
Sugar	Lbs.	2,500,297	13,029	2,310,292	11,908
Caustic soda	,,	345,304	1,168	169,879	594
Soda ash	,,	334,350	528	259,669	389
Chloride of lime	,,	7,895	35	69,197	221
Soda	,,	152,186	226	157,982	192
Sulphur	Tons	1,157	4,340	1,737	5,035
Manufactures of flax and hemp	,,	...	4,326	...	7,410
Pig-iron	,,	...	...	2,138	5,275
Bar and rough iron	,,	...	...	2,225	8,940
Raw and waste silk	Lbs.	142,696	86,771	57,664	12,937
Matting	Rolls	52,027	37,537	...	3,224
Oils	...	...	1,545	...	2,951
Spirits	Gallons	18,482	2,330	...	1,215
Paints	...	...	1,150	...	...
All other articles	...	...	27,292	...	34,529
Total	...	...	295,733	...	218,366
Transit entries—					
Tea	Lbs.	1,104,934	33,585	3,813,777	102,450
Matting	Rolls	40,375	36,728	...	...
Silk	Bales	1,543	131,056	...	...
Other articles	...	...	34,612	...	113,750
Grand total	...	...	531,714	...	434,566

PORTLAND.

Annex C.—TABLE showing Total Value of all Articles Exported from and Imported to Portland, Oregon, to and from Foreign Countries during the Years 1897-96.

Country.	Exports 1897.	Exports 1896.	Imports 1897.	Imports 1896.
	£	£	£	£
Great Britain	1,154,333	1,002,681	30,490	58,262
Belgium	..	..	13,725	14,079
British Columbia	1,052	6,319	4,239	2,681
China and Japan	184,615	244,218	203,929	60,624
China and Japan in transit	31,983	..	235,741	211,017
Australia	..	43,004	7,425	4,552
Korea	3,729	..	..	..
India and East Indies	..	..	21,243	65,675
India and East Indies in transit	..	..	240	1,167
Philippine Islands	..	..	3,931	5,992
Germany	..	..	7,761	8,967
Hawaiian Islands	7,057	13,744	67	138
South Africa	65,281	79,480	..	..
Chile	..	4,420	..	..
Asiatic Russia	4,642	8,200	..	102
West Indies	..	..	1,736	..
France	114,167	..	331	..
Cape de Verde	105,122	..	..	..
All other countries	425	427	856	1,310
Total	1,672,406	1,402,493	531,714	434,566

NOTE.—The foregoing returns of exports and imports do not include coastwise trade.

ASTORIA.

Mr. Vice-Consul Cherry reports as follows:—

General remarks. Notwithstanding the near completion of the railway between Astoria and lines connecting with the trans-continental railroads, the general business of the town and district is not as satisfactory as could be wished. This is consequent upon lower values of the chief product, tinned salmon, necessitating a reduction of 20 per cent. in prices paid for raw fish, an equal reduction having been made last year. A great change has also been brought about in the methods and management of salmon canneries, so that much less labour is required, and a good many of the working population have moved to the new mining camps of British Columbia, and Southern Oregon.

Real estate. Owing to these adverse conditions the price of all real estate in town and country has greatly fallen in the past year till it is now below its fair value, giving a desirable chance to investors. This is especially applicable to timber lands which can be had below their forest value.

ASTORIA.

There is a falling-off in every line of imports except cement, in which there is an important increase. *Imports.*

The total exports show a falling-off, but this is altogether in the exports of canned salmon and flour; wheat and lumber showing an increase. *Exports.*

There has been a decrease in number and tonnage of British vessels in the foreign trade as compared with last year. Last year 91 per cent. of the whole was British, while this year the ratio is 78 per cent. The average tonnage of British vessels this year is 200 tons over last year's average, and is 440 tons over the average of other tonnage in the foreign trade. *British shipping and navigation.*

The "Glenmorag" and "Potrimpos," on which I reported last year, have to all intents and purposes been abandoned, the unusually heavy storms of this winter having damaged them too severely. I am happy to state that no serious casualties have occurred during the past year. *Disasters.*

The agreement between the two corps of pilots of the States of Oregon and Washington worked well till on December 1, when the Washington pilots condemned the schooner they had rented, and for the remainder of the season contented themselves with the services of the tugs. It is understood that the Washington pilots have purchased a pilot schooner in New York, to be brought round for next season's work. In the meantime, the condemned pilot boat has been re-commissioned with a further force of Washington State Pilots. This will give three pilot boats for the coming year. *Pilot service.*

A small marine railway has been built, and has been used by several vessels during the latter part of the year, amongst them the United States lighthouse tender. The railway is large enough to accommodate vessels of 1,200 tons. It would, in my opinion, be a paying investment to construct a marine railway for larger ships, the chief materials, piling and lumber, can be had more cheaply here than anywhere else. At present there is nothing to accommodate large vessels between San Francisco and Esquimalt. *Improvements. Marine railway.*

A very comfortable and well-arranged hotel was completed at Flavel, five miles down the river, and was opened this summer as a seaside resort; it will be kept open all the year round, when the new fortifications are completed and occupied by their garrisons. *Hotel.*

The connecting railroad, the completion of which has been promised for each of the last five months of 1897, is not as yet completed, and, from what I can learn, will be ready for use but little before the contract time, *i.e.*, June 1, 1898. *Railways.*

Since the starting of a new line of British steamers between the Columbia River and Japan and Hong-Kong, the matter of a quarantine station has occupied attention. There is no station between San Francisco and Port Townsend, and in case of infection it would be necessary to take a vessel either to one or other of those ports. A good deal of correspondence has taken place between the local Chamber of Commerce and the proper department in Washington. *Quarantine station.*

Considerable sums have been expended at Chinook Point on *Government improvements.*

Fortifications. New lighthouse on North Head.

the north side and Point Adams on the south side of the river, in erecting fortifications of modern type to command the entrance to the river, and rifled cannon of the latest pattern have been placed in position.

The lighthouse on North Head, mentioned in my last report, is now completed, and will be in operation on or about March 1, 1898.

Entrance to Grays Harbour.

Tenders for the construction of jetties at the entrance to Grays Harbour have been received, and a Portland, Oregon, firm's bid has been accepted. The work is to be commenced this spring, and will consist of training jetties to narrow and scour out the entrance, giving an increased and permanent depth on the bar there, on the same principle that has been so successful at the entrance of the Columbia River.

Industries. Salmon fishing.

Notwithstanding the competition of the frozen fish purchasers for the markets of the eastern cities, salmon fishing has been much depressed. The price went down from 4½ c. (2¼d.) per lb. at the commencement of the season to 3 c. (1½d.) per lb. at the close. This makes a fall in the raw product of 40 per cent. in two years. A number of fishermen have left for the new mining regions of the Yukon River. So far no price has been fixed for the coming season; fully one-third less of new nets will be used, and old netting will be made use of as much as possible.

Salmon canning.

In this Vice-Consular district, it is estimated the product of tinned salmon was 563,000 cases, of 48 lbs. of fish each, made up as under:—

	Number of Cases.
Columbia River, spring catch	420,000
,, fall catch	63,000
Coast north of Columbia River	10,000
,, south of ,,	70,000
Total	563,000

The prices at the commencement of the season were poor, but towards the latter part showed great improvement, from which resulted a clearing out of all the stocks of cased salmon on hand.

Sturgeon fishing.

During the year the catch of sturgeon was very poor. It seems a great pity to allow this source of income and winter occupation for fishermen, in an otherwise dull time, to be destroyed by over fishing. The artificial propagation of salmon shows what can be done to replenish the Columbia River with an abundant supply of fish.

Logging.

After a number of years of depressed prices, demand for lumber steadily increased from the month of August to the end of the year; the price of logs has, of course, kept up with this demand, and it is now again a profitable pursuit. New logging camps are springing up in the fir and spruce forests of this district. Another large raft of piling and saw logs was successfully towed down to San Francisco last summer, making three successful ventures.

There has been a steady rise in price of sawn timber, giving good and profitable employment to the various mills, and also to the box factories. The exports abroad show a notable increase, especially from Grays Harbour, but the amount is very small indeed when the reasonable possibilities of the immense forest wealth of the district is considered. The output is somewhat hampered by the scarcity of suitable tonnage. *Sawn lumber.*

There has been an increased production in box-making, tanning and paper pulp factories. *Factories.*

Owing to want of coasting steamers between here and Puget Sound, the freight by river steamer and railroad is too high to allow the tin cans made at the local factory to be landed at the Puget Sound salmon canneries at a profit. I am informed that a branch of the parent concern is to be established at New Whatcom. The output for the local can-making plant was at least 20 per cent. better for 1897 than for 1896. *Can making.*

There has been fairly good employment for labour. The construction of the railway and fortifications employed a great number, but of course this is but temporary, and for this class of labour, work will be found on the construction of the Grays Harbour jetty. For steady employment for any class of labour the outlook is not promising. *Labour.*

The various crops in this county all had abundant returns, with good prices. But the district is not an agricultural one, and with the possible exception of potatoes does not supply the population. Hay made the best return, next to it was fruit. The want of good roads is a great drawback, some of the best and most easily cleared land is inaccessible during the winter months. No disease affecting horses or cattle showed itself in the district during the past year. A great deal of interest was taken in experimental growth of flax for fibre, to be used for the production of twine for use in salmon and other fisheries ; so far no reports have been received from Lisburn in the north of Ireland, to which samples were sent. *Agriculture.*

Astoria, owing to the causes already stated, has lost population, but the district, as a whole, has gained, and considerably, the gain being in native born citizens. Health has remained uniformly good. *Population and health.*

ASTORIA.

Annex A.—RETURN of all Shipping at the Port of Astoria, Oregon, during the Year 1897.

ENTERED.

Nationality.	Sailing. Number of Vessels.	Sailing. Tons.	Steam. Number of Vessels.	Steam. Tons.	Total. Number of Vessels.	Total. Tons.
British	69	113,211	18	38,866	86	152,077
American coasting	111	32,291	353	292,468	464	324,759
,, foreign	7	6,363	4	2,944	11	9,307
German	6	10,243	...	...	6	10,243
French	2	3,181	...	...	3	3,181
Japanese	1	1,148	...	...	1	1,148
Norwegian	...	...	5	8,873	5	8,873
Total	196	166,437	380	343,151	576	509,588
,, for the year preceding	226	186,836	409	337,239	635	524,075

CLEARED.

Nationality.	Sailing. Number of Vessels.	Sailing. Tons.	Steam. Number of Vessels.	Steam. Tons.	Total. Number of Vessels.	Total. Tons.
British	9	17,334	8	19,718	17	37,052
American coasting	108	31,631	297	286,730	405	318,361
,, foreign	6	3,336	3	1,375	9	4,711
German	1	1,916	...	...	1	1,916
Norwegian	...	...	1	2,302	1	2,302
Total	124	54,217	309	310,125	433	364,342
,, for the year preceding	163	88,878	370	315,674	533	404,552

Annex B.—RETURN of Principal Articles of Export from Astoria, Oregon, during the Years 1897–96.

Articles.		1897. Quantity.	1897. Value.	1896. Quantity.	1896. Value.
			£		£
Canned salmon	Cases	13,457	13,855	53,158	59,213
Wheat	Bushels	170,252	28,664	45,442	6,881
Flour	Barrels	...	...	8,258	5,084
Lumber	M. feet	5,533	9,594	3,652	8,537
Sundries	...	...	1,989	...	1,600
Total	...	...	54,102	...	81,315

ASTORIA.

RETURN of Principal Articles of Import to Astoria, Oregon, during the Years 1897–96.

Articles.		1897. Quantity.	1897. Value.	1896. Quantity.	1896. Value.
			£		£
Tin-plates	Boxes	56,935	26,835	82,862	39,824
Salt	Lbs.	...	...	22,400	16
Coal	Tons	3,202	1,599	3,725	1,924
Steel rails	Lbs.	...	...	14,560,563	30,542
Cement	Barrels	6,500	1,684	5,420	1,439
Sundries	...	...	143	...	4,556
Total	...	...	30,261	...	78,301

TACOMA AND SEATTLE.

Mr. Vice-Consul Alexander reports as follows:—

General remarks relative to the State. Many things have contributed to the prosperity of the State during the past year. First of all, the abundant harvest; and secondly, the finding of gold in the North-West Territory of Canada, which has given an impetus to the domestic trade of the Puget Sound district, especially to the town of Seattle, whose business has been substantially augmented by prospective fortune-seekers procuring their supplies here.

Health. The general health of the State has been good, no epidemic diseases of a serious nature having occurred.

There has been comparatively little cattle disease in this section of the country during the year; stock of all kinds have wintered well, and there has been no loss from this cause.

Very large shipments of beef cattle have been made to Chicago and other Eastern markets, the price obtained being sufficiently remunerative to warrant rail transportation, especially towards the end of the year when 2½d. per lb. was paid on foot. Large consignments of pigs were also made to those markets; and in addition, beef cattle, sheep, and pigs were sent to the Puget Sound country, the Alaska trade taking a large share. Sheep brought the high price of 16s. to 18s. a head alive. Horses are in great demand, from 4l. upwards being offered on the ranch according to quality and the purpose for which they are required.

Industries. The railway shipments from the State to Eastern points viâ the Great Northern, Northern Pacific, and Canadian Pacific Railways, amounted during the year to 7,671 truck-loads of timber and 17,540 truck-loads of shingles, as compared with 6,486 of timber and 14,194 of shingles in 1896. The shipments consisted of 122,736,000 feet of timber, as compared with 96,890,000 feet in the preceding year, and 2,806,400,000 shingles, as against 2,129,100,000 shingles. The cargo shipments for 1897 from the State were 407,060,923 feet of timber, 55,074,500 feet of lath, and 6,500,000 shingles. There has been a general increase in price.

Mining. The coal-mines of the State have been more steadily worked than in the past, the output being estimated at 2,000,000 tons, which is 280,000 tons more than in any previous year.

Fisheries. The run of salmon during the year 1897 was unusually large, and the salmon pack in the Puget Sound district shows a corresponding increase over that of last year, amounting to 494,026 cases valued at 370,000*l.*, as against 195,664 cases valued at 140,000*l.* in 1896. There were in addition 11,680,000 lbs. of fresh salmon sold, valued at 35,040*l.*; 3,720,000 lbs. of salted salmon, valued at 14,480*l.*; 672,000 lbs. of smoked salmon, valued at 80,604*l.*; while 420,000 fish, valued at 6,720*l.*, were shipped to British Columbia canneries. 12 canneries are now in operation in this district.

Agriculture. The past year has been a remarkably good one for the farmer, the crops exceeding all expectations. Crop statistics for the State may be estimated for the year at about as follows:—Wheat acreage 769,800, yielding 16,900,000 bushels at an average of 22 bushels to the acre; oats acreage 57,600, yielding 2,900,000 bushels at an average of 51 bushels to the acre; barley acreage 46,700, yielding 1,600,000 bushels at an average of 35 bushels to the acre. Some wheat land in the Palouse country yielded 50 bushels to the acre. The price of these products has been higher than for several years past, and the farmers have been benefited accordingly. The net price of wheat to the farmers ranged from 1*s.* 5*d.* to 3*s.* 3*d.* per bushel, the average being 2*s.* 10*d.* The average freight from the grain districts to tide-water was from 14*s.* to 17*s.* per ton of 2,000 lbs. The wheat crop was of an excellent quality on the whole.

The amount of wheat grown in the State and inspected by the State Grain Inspector was 11,603 truck-loads, of which amount 8,185 were inspected at Tacoma, 1,892 at Seattle, and 1,526 at Spokane; this, figuring at 754 bushels to the truck-load, would make 8,748,662 bushels. Almost all the wheat from the Walla Walla district graded No. 1, while much of that from the Palouse country only graded No. 2, being damaged and bleached on account of the late rains in September. The wheat has ranged from 54 to 65 lbs. to the bushel, with an average of 59 lbs.; very little fell as low as 54 lbs., and a good deal went up to 62 lbs. A few farmers in the eastern part of the State were, at the close of the year, holding their wheat, but the bulk of it has already been sold.

Dairying. The dairy industry is improving, but the supply of all the commodities is still not equal to the demand, which should be a great inducement for more capital to be invested in this industry and for farmers to give it greater attention. A good average price of 10*d.* has maintained for butter during the year. Milk has increased in value per gallon, but cheese and eggs are the same as last year.

Horticulture. The past year has been very good from a horticultural point of view, large crops having been gathered from the various varieties of fruits, which has had a tendency to keep down prices.

The crops have been fairly free from insects, blight and other fungus diseases. The enormous demand for evaporated fruits and vegetables for supplies for the prospectors going into the North-West Territory of Canada has created a new market for Washington growers, and many are engaging in this industry with apparent success; though, in some instances, the product has been poorly manufactured and has proved deficient in keeping qualities.

With decrease in production of hops, due to the overstocking of the market for the past few years, probably aided by the increased demand, prices have again advanced to a point which renders the crop a profitable one, the yield being so large — 1,500 to 3,000 lbs. to the acre — as to give the grower a good return for his labour. The total crop for 1897 is estimated at 31,528 bales, valued at 140,000l., the price being from 6d. to 7½d. per lb.

Hops.

The following figures are taken from the returns of the State Board of Equalisation for 1897 for the State of Washington:— Acres of land, exclusive of town lots, 14,941,061; acres of improved land, 2,275,594; value of lands, 14,452,952l.; value of improvements, 1,394,732l.; value of agricultural tools, &c., 175,686l.; live-stock: number of cattle, 237,967, valued at 512,124l.; horses, mules, and asses: 174,877, valued at 404,563l.; pigs: 83,617, valued at 25,085l.

Agricultural statistics.

Respecting commercial relations with China and Japan, very little need be said in addition to what was reported last year in connection with this trade. In addition to the regular steamships of the Northern Pacific Steamship Company, four chartered steamers have been employed for single voyages to cope with the requirements of the traffic during the summer months; at this time the question of the imposition of duties on tea, matting, and other products of China and Japan was under consideration by the Government; and importations that, under ordinary circumstances, would have been spread over an entire season, were hurried across within the second quarter of the year in the hope of arriving in the United States before the duty had been imposed. In consequence the volume of trade from the Far East for the remainder of the year was comparatively small. On the other hand, the exports of flour, raw cotton, machinery, wire nails, steel rails, electrical material, and manufactures of all kinds from the United States to Japan, China, and the East generally show a perceptible increase; and the capacities of the steamers connected with the Trans-Pacific lines have been taxed to the utmost on the westward voyage to afford the shipping facilities required. The quantity of steel rails brought across the American Continent by rail from the manufactories in the vicinity of Chicago, and exported viâ Puget Sound to Japan, has aggregated about 15,000 tons; and it is a remarkable circumstance that the American manufacturers, under the disadvantage of the expense of a 2,000 miles' transportation by rail, can successfully compete with English and Belgian firms selling rails in Japan. There has been some falling-off in the number of bales of cotton domestics, with other textile

Commercial relations. China and Japan.

Steel rails for Japan.

(186)

manufactures, passing through the Puget Sound ports for China, the exporters apparently finding cheaper shipping facilities by steamers running from New York viâ the Suez Canal. Exports from America have to an appreciable extent been curtailed by the dearth of opportunities for shipment across the Pacific, in consequence of the steam tonnage in the regular lines being insufficient to carry all the cargo offered, and the rates of freight not proving remunerative enough to induce outside steamers to run the risk of coming across from China or Japan in ballast for the return cargoes offering.

Japan. The Nippon Yusen Kaisha, the Japan Mail Steamship Company, whose American terminus is at Seattle, has greatly improved its service during the year, the company's boats having been carrying very full cargoes. As the principal articles of export and import to and from Seattle have been carried by this line, it might be well to refer to Annex B in the Seattle tables to show the enormous amount of business actually done by the company. A very large increase will be noticed in the cotton and textile manufactures, as well as in the iron manufactures, under which head are included the exportations of steel rails to Japan and Korea.

South Africa. The export of wheat, flour, and timber to South Africa has, during the year 1897, shown a decrease from that of the previous year; the uncertainty of future events in that country most probably being responsible for this interference with business.

Central America. The direct steamship service from Puget Sound to Central America has been withdrawn recently, the carrying trade evidently being found unprofitable by the projectors, and in consequence exports from this district are handicapped by being transhipped at San Francisco.

Alaska. The discovery of gold in the North-West Territory of Canada, contiguous to Alaska, and the return of successful miners in the summer of 1897, has proved of immense advantage to the district and towns of Puget Sound; the intending miners from the United States for the most part purchasing their outfits in Tacoma or Seattle, where many establishments have been opened for this special purpose. In addition to the steamships in the regular Alaskan trade, several transportation companies have been organised, induced by the prospective rush of fortune seekers into this territory. Some of these companies have made promises which it has been proved impossible to carry out on account of the conditions existing there; thereby causing great annoyance to those whose patronage they received, and, in some instances, resulting in litigation. Steamers with American register from all parts of the Pacific Coast of the North-West have been requisitioned for the trade, and, the steam tonnage not meeting the requirements of the traffic, dismantled sailing vessels have been loading timber, flour, and other provisions for the newly-established towns of Dyea, Skaguay, Wrangel, and other places where the prospectors cross the mountain ranges to the head of fresh water navigation on their way to the goldfields. It is not within the scope of this report to enter into the details pertaining to the future of the prospectors after their landing in Alaska.

TACOMA AND SEATTLE.

This Alaska business has created a large demand for new boats of all sizes and styles with which to navigate the Alaskan lakes and the Yukon River; and boat-building is now actively progressing in almost every town on Puget Sound, adding greatly to the prosperity of the country. It is estimated that some 60 vessels have been built in Seattle alone, of which about one-half are lighters designed for the Yukon River. Their carrying capacity is estimated at 20,000 passengers.

Among the local industries may be mentioned the Puget Sound Dry Dock Company, with their dock at Quartermaster Harbour, which had on their ways for repairs of one kind or another, 36 American steamships and 24 sailing vessels, 12 of the latter flying the British flag; making a total of 60 vessels during the year. *Dry dock.*

The Tacoma Smelting and Refining Company reports the business done at its smelter during the year as follows:—Ore received, gold, 19,656 ozs.; silver, 400,615 ozs.; lead, 6,295,904 lbs.; output, gold, 18,922 ozs.; silver, 392,447 ozs.; lead 5,250,786 lbs.: the total value being 158,808*l*. *Smelting works.*

Seattle adds to its many industries the Centennial Flouring Mill with a capacity of 750 barrels per diem. This mill is erected on the tide-flats, thus enabling steamers to take on cargoes direct from the mill. *Other industries.*

All the many industries of this town have increased their business and enlarged their capacities, especially the shipyards, iron foundries, and machine shops. The Moran Bros. Company built during the year the United States revenue cutter "Golden Gate," which is now doing duty in San Francisco Harbour, and the work compares most favourably in every particular with that done on the Atlantic coast, the boat giving complete satisfaction. This same firm has under construction torpedo-boat No. 9 for the United States Government, and it is expected that it will be completed during the early part of the coming year.

Grain freights from ports in the Puget Sound district to Europe have ranged from 22*s*. 6*d*. to 43*s*. 9*d*. per ton of 2,240 lbs., the average being 31*s*. 3*d*. To South Africa, 35*s*. to 45*s*., average 42*s*. 6*d*. Timber freights to Europe, 42*s*. 6*d*. to 65*s*., average 57*s*. 6*d*.; West coast of South America, 30*s*. to 40*s*., average 35*s*.; Australia, 45*s*. to 60*s*., average 55*s*. *Freights.*

The total business at the port of Tacoma during the year is estimated by the local authorities at 6,392,593*l*., of which the exports may be summed up as follows:—Foreign, 1,476,564*l*.; coastwise, 734,712*l*.; rail, 433,832*l*.; total 2,645,108*l*. *Exports and imports.*

The imports being:—Foreign, 1,212,189*l*.; coastwise, 324,315*l*.; rail, 2,210,981*l*.; total, 3,747,485*l*., indicating a falling-off again in the imports, but a very large increase in the export trade.

For the port of Seattle for the same period, the business amounted to 795,029*l*., of which 668,375*l*. were exports and 126,654*l*. imports; thus indicating an increase over the previous year, 1896, of 459,840*l*. in the exports and an increase of 79,680*l*. in imports. These figures cannot be taken as an accurate indication of the business of this town, the very large domestic business—probably over 2,000,000l.—and the rail shipments, of which no figures are obtainable, not being included.

The following table shows the number and nationalities of vessels which entered and cleared during the last year:—

Annex A.—RETURN of all Shipping at the Port of Tacoma during the Year 1897.

ENTERED.

Nationality.	Sailing. Number of Vessels.	Sailing. Tons.	Steam. Number of Vessels.	Steam. Tons.	Total. Number of Vessels.	Total. Tons.
British	32	59,763	34	51,207	66	110,970
American	8	3,937	12	6,962	20	10,899
German	1	2,174	...	...	1	2,174
Hawaiian	1	2,041	...	...	1	2,041
Total	42	67,915	46	58,169	88	126,084
,, for the year preceding	37	54,558	55	60,986	92	115,544

CLEARED.

Nationality.	Sailing. Number of Vessels.	Sailing. Tons.	Steam. Number of Vessels.	Steam. Tons.	Total. Number of Vessels.	Total. Tons.
British	38	70,193	28	47,338	66	117,531
American	13	9,821	8	5,338	21	15,159
German	4	8,294	...	...	4	8,294
Norwegian	2	2,939	...	...	2	2,939
Swedish	1	1,363	...	...	1	1,363
Total	58	92,610	36	52,676	94	145,286
,, for the year preceding	66	90,118	50	59,647	116	149,765

NOTE.—The entrances and clearances of American vessels do not include the domestic trade.

The following tables show the exports and imports for the past two years:—

Annex B.—RETURN of Principal Articles of Export from Tacoma during the Years 1897–96.

Articles		1897.		1896.	
		Quantity.	Value.	Quantity.	Value.
			£		£
Wheat	Bushels	3,976,419	681,637	2,954,904	432,965
Flour	Barrels	321,594	246,957	355,670	210,372
Timber	Feet	29,508,000	51,905	31,159,000	72,678
Textile manufactures	...	...	150,254	...	358,556
Cotton	Lbs.	6,901,000	86,447	3,636,300	59,293
Iron	...	..	34,678	...	51,052
Electrical supplies	...	...	11,610	...	18,030
Milk, condensed	Lbs.	556,300	9,132	688,200	10,753
Tobacco	...	..	20,582	...	...
Other articles	...	...	40,367	...	72,341
Total	...	...	1,333,569	...	1,286,040

RETURN of Principal Articles of Import to Tacoma during the Years 1897–96.

Articles.		1897.		1896.	
		Quantity.	Value.	Quantity.	Value.
			£		£
Free—					
Silk, raw	Lbs.	1,857,300	642,162	775,000	429,756
Tea	,,	200,000	2,838	899,000	15,104
Matting	Rolls	102,905	57,267	846	779
Ore	...	...	22,615	...	26,130
Wool	Lbs.	950,403	14,406	...	...
Other articles	...	...	8,122	...	10,689
Total	...	...	747,410	...	482,458
Dutiable—					
Sugar	Lbs.	1,830,000	9,386	2,748,000	18,189
Rice	,,	247,400	896	186,000	653
Ore	...	...	5,926	...	4,797
Liquors (malt, spirit, &c.)	...	...	2,320	...	1,126
Other articles	...	...	13,521	...	14,235
Total	...	...	32,049	...	39,000
,, free and dutiable	...	...	779,410	...	521,458

Annex C.—TABLE showing Total Value of all Articles Exported from and Imported to Tacoma to and from Foreign Countries during the Years 1897-96.

	Exports.		Imports.	
Country.	1897.	1896.	1897.	1896.
	£	£	£	£
Great Britain	66,762	131,645	1,442	14,013
Queenstown and St. Vincent for orders	625,349	272,189	..	..
British colonies and dependencies—				
Hong-Kong £148,248		115,503	24,509	23,213
Africa 23,828		105,149	..	..
Australia 14,969		33,321	..	..
Canada 3,754		2,820	31,263	39,527
India 27		14,797	3,189	3,014
Other countries ..		505	..	..
	190,826			
Japan	218,554	205,539	472,305	268,818
China	162,875	369,402	246,321	171,833
France	43,000	2,040	..	..
Africa, Portuguese	12,384	8,165	..	..
Sandwich Islands	5,589	..	..	..
South America—	£			
Chili 3,538		2,800	..	..
Argentine Republic 1,900		..	..	..
	5,438			
Other countries	2,792	22,165	381	1,040
Total	1,333,569	1,286,040	779,410	521,458

NOTE.—The domestic trade and goods for immediate transportation are not included in this table.

The following table shows the number and nationalities of vessels which entered and cleared during the last year:—

Annex A.—RETURN of all Shipping at the Port of Seattle during the Year 1897.

ENTERED.

Nationality.	Sailing.		Steam.		Total.	
	Number of Vessels.	Tons.	Number of Vessels.	Tons.	Number of Vessels.	Tons.
British	2	4,798	16	13,765	18	18,563
American	4	3,821	...	...	4	3,821
Japanese	...	...	12	26,470	12	26,470
Norwegian	1	1,468	2	1,680	3	3,148
Total	7	10,087	30	41,915	37	52,002
for the year preceding	19	23,656	94	102,849	113	126,505

TACOMA AND SEATTLE.

CLEARED.

Nationality.	Sailing. Number of Vessels.	Sailing. Tons.	Steam. Number of Vessels.	Steam. Tons.	Total. Number of Vessels.	Total. Tons.
British	3	5,366	16	10,929	19	16,295
American	19	15,957	1	91	20	16,048
Japanese	...	...	13	29,180	13	29,180
Hawaiian	3	3,893	...	...	3	3,893
Norwegian	...	...	3	2,520	3	2,520
Italian	1	1,354	...	...	1	1,354
Total	26	26,570	33	42,720	59	69,290
,, for the year preceding	27	17,495	40	24,973	67	42,468

NOTE.—The entrances and clearances of American vessels do not include the domestic trade.

The following tables show the exports and imports for the past two years:—

Annex B.—RETURN of Principal Articles of Export from Seattle during the Years 1897-96.

Articles.		1897. Quantity.	1897. Value. £	1896. Quantity.	1896. Value. £
Wheat	Bushels	444,346	69,106	478,181	68,402
Flour	Barrels	89,744	61,420	83,160	54,343
Timber	Feet	21,258	43,467	10,437,000	22,040
Cotton	Lbs.	108,057	275,335	213,826	19,683
Textile manufactures	Yards	10,048	91,264	...	...
Iron manufactures	...	...	61,245	...	7,978
Electrical supplies	...	...	11,157	...	1,570
Oils	...	...	6,950	...	...
Tobacco	...	...	6,337	...	...
Other articles	...	...	43,348	...	45,858
Total	...	...	669,629	...	219,874

RETURN of Principal Articles of Import to Seattle during the Years 1897-96.

Articles.*	Value. 1897. £	Value. 1896. £
Free	79,873	3,843
Dutiable	14,979	32,440
Total	94,852	36,283

* Articles not specified; exchange has been taken at 5 dol. to the 1*l*.

TACOMA AND SEATTLE.

Annex C.—TABLE showing Total Value of all Articles Exported from and Imported to Seattle from and to Foreign Countries during the Years 1897–96.

	Exports.		Imports.	
Country.	1897.	1896.	1897.	1896.
	£	£	£	£
Great Britain	11,989	96,954	..	4,819
Queenstown or Falmouth for orders	60,486	..	..	..
Colonies, dependencies—				
Hong-Kong ... 53,634		22,950	..	12,207
Australia ... 14,608		4,889	..	..
Canada ... 1,176		4,898	280	7,789
Singapore ... 261	69,679	..	..	..
Japan	371,545	50,530	94,532	2,877
China	108,540	3,332	..	..
Sandwich Islands	19,753	7,174	40	..
Central America	13,799	20,831	..	..
Peru	1,542	..	..	..
Russian Siberia	4,379	..	..	..
Other countries	7,917	8,316	..	8,591
Total	669,629	219,874	94,852	36,283

NOTE.—The domestic trade and goods for immediate transportation are not included in this table.

PORT TOWNSEND.

Mr. Vice-Consul Klöcker reports as follows:—

Trade and commerce.

The commercial record for the year has not been very encouraging for this section of the country, although towards the end of the year, when the excitement in Alaska and in the North-Western Territory broke out, it did somewhat improve, and the indications now are much better than they have been for several years past.

Lumber freights were dull during the whole year, but have improved somewhat, as will be seen from the annexed list of rates:—

Per 1,000 feet.

	Highest.	Lowest.
	£ s. d.	£ s. d.
Sydney, New South Wales	2 0 0	1 10 0
Melbourne, Port Pirie, and Adelaide	2 8 9	1 13 9
Brisbane, Freemantle	2 10 0	1 15 0
China, Shanghai	2 8 0	2 0 0
Africa, Delagoa Bay	3 5 0	2 2 6
West Coast of South America	2 0 0	1 5 0
United Kingdom	3 0 0	2 5 0

The rates as quoted are for sailing ships, steamers having received about 5s. in addition per 1,000 feet.

Several British ships were laid up at this port during the year waiting for the market to improve but found profitable employment at the opening of the wheat season, and were fully repaid for the time spent in waiting. The wheat from up Sound ports has been good, and in consequence it has been almost impossible for lumber merchants to secure vessels for carrying lumber for foreign, as all the old coasting vessels were pressed into the service between Puget Sound and Alaskan ports, carrying lumber, cattle, passengers, and all kinds of merchandise, and are towed between here and Alaska.

The demand for tug-boats is great and all tug-boats on the coast have doubled in value. The Puget Sound Tug-boat Company of this port have acquired three additional tugs to their already extensive fleet and are still in the market for more. It has been impossible for them to supply the demand for tugs.

Shipbuilding. Shipbuilding is going on all round the different mill ports and all kinds of craft are being built, both for private parties as well as the big companies, three are now being built here and it is estimated that over 50 vessels are under construction all over the Sound, all of which are small flat-bottomed crafts intended for the Yukon River or other unexplored rivers in Alaska, in consequence carpenters are in great demand and all find steady employment at good wages.

Steamship lines. Steamship lines for Alaska have been started too numerous to mention and every steamer that can float has been refitted and put into commission, several lines have been started out of this port, all for Alaska, and it is reported that there are now, including sailing vessels, running to Alaska from Puget Sound and British Columbia 100 vessels. About a year ago, before the Klondike excitement, the trade was supplied by three steamers. They now charge a very high rate for freight, and still all boats going north are crowded with freight and passengers eager to pay anything asked to secure passage. There is no question the thing will be before very long overdone, and it is bound to end in great suffering for many people going into Alaska.

Population. The population here has diminished as a number of people have left for the goldfields, and in consequence the excitement in Alaska has rather hurt this place, as we do not here get benefited by the number of people coming to outfit for Alaska, on account of having no railroad communications. All the people coming from the East stop at up Sound ports and depart from there or go to Victoria or Vancouver, British Columbia, to outfit.

Public works. It is reported that the Government intends to rebuild Fort Townsend, 2 miles from this city, and the Government officers are now here inspecting the buildings and intend to build six more barracks with all possible haste and have several companies of troops stationed here.

Fortifications. The fortifications referred to in my last report on Point Wilson, Marrowstone and Admiralty Head have been started, for which there is now 600,000 dol. available, and since the trouble with Spain has arisen the contractors having this work in charge are offered special inducements by the Government to push this work with all possible haste.

The Buffington-Crozier disappearing carriage with 12-inch mortars are the kind of guns to be used, and with the completion of these fortifications the entrance to Puget Sound will be quite effectively protected.

Agriculture and cattle. The agriculture and cattle trade is also looking up. All on account of the Alaska trade, and a great deal of beef is being shipped from here at this place, being the last port in the United States that all steamers clear from for Alaska it is important to get it here to secure it keeping fresh as long as posssible, as the bulk has to be taken up killed. The steamship companies positively refuse to carry cattle alive on account of being able to make much more money out of passengers and other trade.

British merchandise. In regard to British goods I may mention that during the last year a great scarcity has prevailed of Scotch whisky as demand for that kind of goods, in preference to American whisky, is increasing, and time and again I have known it could not be obtained, either on this side or in British Columbia.

Also in regard to cement, there ought to be a good demand as thousands of barrels of cement will be used to build the fortifications now in progress here, besides buildings are again going up in the different Sound ports.

Health. It has been very healthy in the past year, no epidemic of infectious or contagious diseases having occurred either among the people or animals.

The export trade shows a decrease of 107,686*l*., as compared with last year.

The import trade shows an increase of 160,587*l*. This large amount is accounted for by the fact of the great bulk of ore imported from British Columbia and a great increase in imports from Japan and China for eastern cities.

I append the several annexes marked A, B, and C to show the commerce and trade in this district.

Annex A.—RETURN of all Shipping at the Port of Port Townsend during the Year 1897.

ENTERED.

Nationality.	Sailing. Number of Vessels.	Sailing. Tons.	Steam. Number of Vessels.	Steam. Tons.	Total. Number of Vessels.	Total. Tons.
British	39	64,625	11	1,246	50	65,871
American	109	63,638	1,245	671,058	1,354	734,696
German	7	10,914	...	...	7	10,914
Norwegian	6	9,220	1	840	7	10,060
Chilian	6	6,439	...	...	6	6,439
Hawaiian	6	7,398	...	...	6	7,398
Japanese	...	...	2	4,194	2	4,194
Peruvian	1	417	...	...	1	417
Italian	1	1,300	...	...	1	1,300
Total	175	163,951	1,259	677,338	1,434	841,289

CLEARED.

Nationality.	Sailing. Number of Vessels.	Sailing. Tons.	Steam. Number of Vessels.	Steam. Tons.	Total. Number of Vessels.	Total. Tons.
British	38	64,185	13	4,200	51	68,385
American	97	69,076	1,267	682,676	1,364	751,752
Norwegian	6	8,771	...	...	6	8,771
Chilian	6	6,439	...	...	6	6,439
German	5	7,250	...	...	5	7,250
Hawaiian	3	4,598	...	...	3	4,598
Peruvian	1	417	...	...	1	417
Italian	1	1,300	...	...	1	1,300
Total	157	162,036	1,280	686,876	1,437	848,912

PORT TOWNSEND.

Annex B.—RETURN of Principal Articles of Export from Port Townsend during the Years 1897–96.

Articles.	1897. Quantity.	1897. Value.	1896. Quantity.	1896. Value.
		£		£
Wheat	..	66,976	..	..
Flour	..	75,823	..	20,040
Barley and feed	..	18,011	..	..
Coal	..	9,802	..	11,503
Timber .. (feet)	118,239,000	128,252	128,450,135	154,718
Iron, and manufactures of iron	..	96,523	..	55,216
Oils	..	6,601	..	11,203
Furs and hides	..	12,321	..	3,550
Provisions, meats	..	31,302	..	43,531
Cattle	..	27,851	..	19,011
Liquors and wines	..	18,211	..	10,870
Wood, and manufactures of wood	..	6,557	..	46,052
Cotton	..	2,519	..	129,654
Fish	..	60,291	..	32,043
Tinned fruits and vegetables	..	40,161	..	18,927
Chemicals	..	1,161	..	8,125
Wool, and manufactures of wool	..	5,612	..	1,600
Leather	..	2,065	..	5,690
Oil	..	2,119	..	4,560
Paper	..	22,718	..	..
Other articles	..	21,265	..	187,534
Total	..	656,141	..	763,827

PORT TOWNSEND.

RETURN of Principal Articles of Import to Port Townsend during the Years 1897-96.

Articles.	Value. 1897.	Value. 1896.
	£	£
Cement	2,952	2,604
Coal	2,161	2,534
Iron and manufactures of iron	1,426	252
Steel wire rods	..	3,605
Tin-plates	5,619	641
Lead and ore	121,714	8,476
Liquor	6,269	125
Zinc	..	20
Sugar	5,314	3,035
Rice	5,143	697
Tea	6,102	3,554
Raw silk	7,192	42,075
Chemicals	2,061	4,820
Matting	20,169	..
Fish	10,756	826
Household furniture	10,261	..
Wool	19,817	..
Other articles	20,131	13,236
Total	247,087	86,500

PORT TOWNSEND.

Annex C.—TABLE showing Total Value of all Articles Exported from and Imported to Port Townsend to and from Foreign Countries during the Years 1897–96.

Country.	Exports. 1897.	Exports. 1896.	Imports. 1897.	Imports. 1896.
	£	£	£	£
Great Britain	5,126	64,787	3,816	..
British Columbia and Canada	290,163	432,076	107,764	53,411
Australia	72,869	63,901	602	1,059
Germany	5,061	3,990	1,043	6,335
Salvador	8,206	8,957	1,206	..
Japan	46,102	5,169	126,176	672
China	38,064	8,956	2,106	2,900
Africa	70,621	53,149	..	..
Hawaiian Islands	28,104	41,255	562	6,055
Chili	19,952	24,711	..	..
France	19,262	..	362	..
Peru	16,216	18,950	..	..
Mexico	8,204	7,154	..	..
Korea	7,612	..	..	..
New Caledonia	5,534	2,611	..	..
Argentine Republic	4,623	..	..	..
Fiji Islands	2,462	3,188	..	..
Asiatic Russia	1,142	..	..	..
Belgium	..	..	..	3,852
Hong-Kong	1,101	2,570	1,106	8,404
India	..	4,827	261	697
Guatemala	444	3,669	414	..
Samoa	..	1,250	..	..
Other countries	5,273	12,657	1,669	3,115
Total	656,141	763,827	247,087	86,500

NOTE.—The import from British Columbia is mainly ore brought to this side to be smelted.

LONDON:
Printed for Her Majesty's Stationery Office,
By HARRISON AND SONS,
Printers in Ordinary to Her Majesty.
(75 6 | 98—H & S 186)

No. 2147 Annual Series.

DIPLOMATIC AND CONSULAR REPORTS.

UNITED STATES.

REPORT FOR THE YEAR 1897

ON THE

TRADE AND COMMERCE OF BOSTON AND DISTRICT.

REFERENCE TO PREVIOUS REPORT, Annual Series No. 1930.

Presented to both Houses of Parliament by Command of Her Majesty,
JULY, 1898.

LONDON:
PRINTED FOR HER MAJESTY'S STATIONERY OFFICE,
BY HARRISON AND SONS, ST. MARTIN'S LANE,
PRINTERS IN ORDINARY TO HER MAJESTY.

And to be purchased, either directly or through any Bookseller, from
EYRE & SPOTTISWOODE, EAST HARDING STREET, FLEET STREET, E.C., and
32, ABINGDON STREET, WESTMINSTER, S.W.; or
JOHN MENZIES & Co., 12, HANOVER STREET, EDINBURGH, and
90, WEST NILE STREET, GLASGOW; or
HODGES, FIGGIS, & Co., Limited, 104, GRAFTON STREET, DUBLIN.

1898.

[C. 8648—169.] *Price Twopence Halfpenny.*

CONTENTS.

	PAGE
BOSTON—	
General remarks	3
Boston Harbour	3
Pilot stations	3
Elevation and dockage dues	4
Stevedore rates	4
Buildings	5
Railroads	5
Failures	6
Commerce of Boston	7
Imports and exports—	
Cattle	8
Wheat	8
Corn	8
Oats	8
Flour	9
Cotton	9
Hay	9
Provisions	9
Produce trade	9
Butter	9
Cheese	9
Eggs	10
Poultry	10
Fruit	10
Wool	10
Hides and leather	12
Shoes	12
Old materials: rags and metals	13
Fish trade	13
„ salt	14
„ fresh	16
Foreign and maritime trade	17
Money and sterling exchanges	18
Conclusion	19
Annexes—	
A.—Immigrants	20
B, C, D.—Shipping	21
E.—Steamship sailings	24
F.—Freights to Liverpool	25
G.—Exports	26
H.—Value of imports and exports	27
I.—Imports and exports by countries	28
K.—Value of imports by articles	29
L.— „ exports by articles	30
PORTLAND trade report	30

NOTE.—1*l*. has been reckoned as equal to 5 dol. for the purposes of this report.

Principal Authorities Consulted.

Boston Chamber of Commerce Report for 1897; Boston Fish Bureau Report for 1897; United States Fish Commissioners' Report for 1897; Massachussets Railroad Commissioners' Report for 1897; "Commercial Bulletin"; Returns from United States Custom-house, Boston.

No. 2147. Annual Series.

Reference to previous Report, Annual Series No. 1930.

Report on the Trade and Commerce of the Consular District of Boston for the Year 1897

By Sir D. Colnaghi.

(Received at Foreign Office, June 15, 1898.)

General remarks.

The record for the year 1897 presents, in general, much that is of a gratifying nature. While certain sections of this country may not have equally shared in the general improvement, it seems certain that substantial, and, it is to be hoped, permanent gains have been made, that general business has improved and is, at the close of the year, on a sounder and more enduring basis than for several years past.

The Boston Chamber of Commerce, in its yearly report says, "The year has not been free from disturbing influences. The tariff agitation and uncertainty interfered with improvement in many industries during the first six months, and the lingering effects of the silver troubles of 1896, have had a more or less depressing influence throughout the entire year; that these factors in the situation did not interfere more seriously with the upward movement, must be regarded as indicating the substantial character of the improvement." The enhanced prices for many agricultural products, notably in wheat, seem undoubtedly to have been a large factor in the improved business conditions.

A bountiful crop in this country coinciding with a marked shortage abroad, raised the price of wheat to over 4s. a bushel. This rise in price, in a great measure, realised by the western farmers, was followed by a large circulation of money, and has had a far reaching influence on business in general. The West, having been able to cancel much of its indebtedness, the farmers became large purchasers of manufactured products of all descriptions, thus adding their share to the stimulus given during the year, to many industrial centres throughout the Eastern States.

Boston Harbour.

In my report for 1896, I gave a general description of Boston harbour, which is entirely protected and safe at all seasons of the year. The work of dredging the main ship channel has been continued during 1897.

Pilot stations.

There are two pilot stations, an inner and outer. The first is a few miles outside Boston Light, the second off Cape Cod. The

BOSTON.

station boats, as well as the three boats cruising in the bay outside of the station boats are required to show signals by day and by night. The day signal is a white and blue flag, the white being next the mast; by night a white mast head light is shown.

Foreign pilotage is compulsory inward, and for vessels over 350 tons, outward.

Elevation and dockage dues. Vessels loading grain at the port of Boston pay no elevation dues, this charge being borne by the shippers. While discharging or loading, vessels pay no wharfage or dockage dues.

The dockage dues are $\frac{1}{4}d.$ per register ton per diem, but less rates can be obtained for over a certain time.

The commission for obtaining charters is 5 per cent.

Ships of the largest draft and capacity can enter and leave port, and discharge and load at the wharves afloat. The range of tides at the wharves is 9 feet 8 inches. There are four elevators at high tide, two supplied with all modern improvements, of the respective capacity of 3,850,000 bushels, and two local elevators, having each a capacity of 700,000 bushels.

Stevedore rates. The following are the stevedore rates in force at this port :—

		Rates. From £ s. d.	To £ s. d.
DISCHARGING.			
Coal	Per ton of 2,240 lbs.	0 1 0½	..
Iron (according to kind)	Per ton of 2,240 lbs.	0 1 0½	..
Sugar and molasses	Per hogshead	0 0 8	0 0 10
" "	" bag	0 0 1½	0 0 2
Lumber—			
Cypress	Per 1,000 feet	0 2 1	0 2 6
Yellow pine	" "	0 2 1	0 2 6
White "	} " "	0 1 2	0 1 8
Spruce			
Wool	Per bale	0 0 2½	0 0 6
Manilla hemp	"	0 0 2	..
Dry hides	Per 1,000	1 0 10	1 2 1
General cargoes (including sorting)	" cubic foot	0 1 5½	0 1 8
LOADING.			
Lumber	Per 1,000 feet	0 1 8	0 2 1
Petroleum	" barrel	0 0 2½	..
Measurement	" 40 cubic feet	0 1 8	..

BOSTON.

The number and value of new buildings completed in Boston during the Year 1897 were as follows:— *City of Boston. Buildings.*

	Number.	Value.
		£
Class I and II, brick and stone	364	1,626,360
,, III, wood	2,002	1,720,751
Total	..	3,347,111

The twenty-ninth annual report of the Massachusetts Railroad Commissioners for the year ended June 30, 1897, shows that 48 railroad corporations exist, either wholly or in part, in the State; the roads of 34 of the companies were leased to or worked by other companies, 12 companies were engaged in actual railroad operation, while the remaining two were not completed. Five of the 12 companies operated over 97 per cent. of the railroad mileage and conducted about 99 per cent. of the entire passenger and freight traffic; of main and side track, &c., there is a total of 4,294·434 miles. The cost of construction and equipment, per mile, of the standard gauge roads was 87,279 dol. 86 c., showing a decrease of nearly 2,000 dol. per mile over the expenditure of the past year. *Railroads.*

The traffic and revenues of the companies, showed for the year, a falling-off in every particular from those of the fiscal year ended June 30, 1896, but this shrinkage was nearly counterbalanced by strict economy and by a marked reduction in the working expenses. The freight rate reached its lowest average, viz., $1\frac{1}{4}$ c. per ton per mile; the gross working earnings decreased 2,951,700 dol.; the working expenses were reduced by 2,949,100 dol., while the net earnings decreased 2,000 dol. The dividends paid were, however, on a higher scale than before, and this caused a deficit instead of a surplus. The average dividend paid on the total amount of outstanding capital was 5·6 per cent., or an advance of ·11 per cent. A system of long leases and a highly guaranteed dividend rental has, in many cases, become a burthen to the roads leasing, and the acquisition, by exchange or purchase, of the stock of the leased roads is proposed as a measure of relief.

The report states that there has been a marked falling-off during the past four years in the annual number of passengers carried on the railroads in this State, for, whereas, up to 1893, an annual increase of over 500,000 passengers occurred, the decrease, in the last four years, amounted to an average as high as 4,766,000 passengers, or 15·65 per cent., the falling-off occurring in local or short distance travel. This diminution of travel is probably due, in a small measure, to the severe and prolonged commercial depression since 1893, but is, undoubtedly more particularly owing to the remarkable development of the electric railway system, especially during the summer months,

(219)

when the open cars are running and the journey is made more pleasant to the passenger to and from the cities, while dust and cinders are absent.

This is clearly shown by the returns, which state that, in 1893, a total of 156,488,169 passengers were carried to and from Boston on the electric lines, a total which had risen, in 1897, to 205,300,421 passengers, showing an increase of 48,812,252, or over 31 per cent.

From the above it seems probable that in the near future, the railroads may have to adopt electricity as the motive-power, and, indeed, the question has already been mooted, but up to the present time the change is not deemed feasible, as the power cannot be carried for more than 15 to 20 miles from one generating station.

Failures. Bradstreet* regards as business failures only such embarrassment of individuals, firms, and corporations as show liabilities in excess of assets, and no account is taken of financial embarrassments of employés, of those conducting business enterprises, of transportation organisations, or of farmers. According to Bradstreet's excellent report, some interesting features in the year 1897 are clearly brought out:—

"First and foremost, is a heavy falling-off alike in number and in liabilities of those individuals, firms or corporations succumbing to the pressure of unfavourable circumstances, primarily indicating a return of prosperous conditions in general business. In the next place must be mentioned a drop in the percentage of assets to liabilities shown, as compared not only with last year but with 1895 and 1893 of panic memory, indicating thereby a return to more or less normal conditions. Finally there is to be noticed a reduction in the percentage of what might be termed the commercial death-rate, as compared with any year since and including 1893."

The following table shows the business failures of 1897, in the Eastern States, classified as to causes:—

	Number.	Assets.	Liabilities.
		£	£
Incompetence	430	614,335	1,427,756
Inexperience	60	28,310	85,029
Lack of capital	324	195,221	445,000
Unwise credits	87	32,674	83,908
Failures of others	48	268,110	430,164
Extravagance	56	23,108	56,887
Neglect	87	26,210	69,763
Competition	333	125,620	352,988
Disaster	388	576,717	1,134,035
Speculation	28	119,300	323,793
Fraud	242	905,417	1,708,613
Total for Eastern States	2,083	2,905,022	6,115,936
„ United States	13,083	17,311,625	31,739,740

* "Bradstreet," 1897. A record, not a prospectus.

BOSTON.

Both the imports and exports, in 1897, surpass in value all previous records. The imports, the value of which amounted to 17,137,630*l*., showed an increase of 30 per cent., while the exports, which reached the figure of 20,838,338*l*., yielded an increase of about $2\frac{11}{16}$ per cent. These figures clearly prove the magnitude of the traffic passing through this port to foreign countries, but it is only by comparison with other ports, all striving for the control of the foreign trade of the United States, or by the use of percentages, that the success of Boston in competing for the foreign traffic can be shown:—

Commerce of Boston. Imports and exports.

Port.	Per Cent. of Total United States Traffic in—	
	1897.	1896.
New York	47·30	48·33
Boston	10·31	9·81
New Orleans	6·19	6·41
Philadelphia	5·18	4·90
Baltimore	5·95	5·44
San Francisco	4·38	4·51
Galveston	3·35	3·36
All other ports	17·34	17·24
Total	100·00	100·00

The above table shows that with the exception of Baltimore, Boston leads all other ports in an increase of foreign trade, while New York, the largest and most important shipping port in the United States, marks a decrease.

The increase in imports at Boston occurred during the first half of the year, 12,400,000*l*., or 72 per cent. of the total imports being received prior to July, the month in which the new tariff came into effect.

In aggregate value wool still holds the first place, the receipts for the year 1897 amounting in value to 6,654,000*l*., out of a total value for the entire United States of 10,686,000*l*., or over 62 per cent.

Of other principal imports, sugar is set down for 1,575,600*l*., hides and skins, including Morocco, for 1,495,600*l*., vegetable fibres and manufactures for 1,056,800*l*., and cotton and its manufactures for 1,041,600*l*.

In the exports, provisions take a first place, amounting to 10,679,002*l*., as against 9,862,461*l*. in 1896. Breadstuffs amounted to 3,843,312*l*., as against 3,243,702*l*. in the previous year.

In wheat exports were 12,143,204 bushels, as against 12,721,450 bushels in 1896, showing a decrease of 578,246 bushels for the year. Corn showed a marked increase, the exports amounting to 9,464,163 bushels, as against 6,136,603 bushels in 1896, as also oats, 5,471,275 bushels, against 2,147,637 bushels, the export almost doubling. Beef gave 537,290 quarters, as against 493,930 quarters exported during 1896.

Hay, 161,402 bales, as against 50,711 bales; butter, 3,286,337 lbs., as against 3,156,471 lbs. The export of apples markedly decreased, 426,539 barrels, as against 747,106 barrels in 1896.

The "transit" and "transhipment" trade of Boston amounted in value to 2,090,141*l.* as follows:—

	Value. £
From Canada	801,624
Entered at ports on the Canadian frontier and exported to foreign countries viâ Boston	1,288,517
Total	2,090,141

The Boston foreign traffic is, of course, carried mostly in steamers, which in 1888 showed an average tonnage of 3,065 tons, as against an average in 1897 of 4,243 tons per ship, an increase of 38 per cent.

Cattle. The exports of cattle from Boston show a slight decrease as compared with 1896. Nevertheless, this port still holds the first place, the shipments amounting in 1897 to 162,620, out of a total from all United States ports of 397,891 head. The percentage of loss on shipboard from all American ports for the year under review is reported by the Secretary of Agriculture at ·61, while the percentage of loss of cattle shipped on steamers from Boston, which shipped over 40 per cent. of the total exports, is put down at ·14 per cent., being the lowest mortality for shipments of this size on record. The loss on shipments of sheep from Boston was ·61 per cent., as against 1·39 per cent. for all American ports.

Wheat. In 1897 the United States were blessed with an immense crop of wheat, while the harvests of the rest of the world showed a decided decrease. This created an enormous demand in this country, and No. 2 spring wheat cash rose from 2*s.* 7¾*d.*, its lowest point, to 4*s.* 2½*d.* per bushel, the highest price being reached in December.

Corn. The extraordinary crops of 1895 and 1896 were not repeated in 1897, the yield falling 381,000 bushels. In Boston, marked steamer yellow covered a range from 1*s.* 2½*d.* to 1*s.* 8*d.* per bushel, the latter price being reached in September. The year closed with a fair demand and rates steady at 1*s.* 6½*d.*

Oats. The tendency of prices for oats has been upward during the past year. No. 2 clipped white reached 1*s.* 4*d.* per bushel in December, the highest price for the year. In January the price was 1*s.* 1*d.*, in February there was a slight fall to 1*s.* 0½*d.*, since which date the rate rose steadily to the maximum noted above.

Flour. In the early part of the year prices of flour were somewhat depressed, but the last six months were marked by greater strength and buoyancy, with a decided improvement in prices. This was evidently caused by the heavy foreign demand, owing to wheat shortages in France and Russia, while at the same time better grades were in request.

Cotton (American). The cotton crop (August, 1896, to August, 1897) is reported to amount to 8,757,964 bales, being an increase over the crop of the previous year of 1,600,618 bales. The range of rates has, however, been lower, but for this compensation has been found in the statement that no previous crop has been raised at so low a cost, which it is believed has allowed the producer to realise more on last year's crop than on any former one. The highest point reached in prices was a fraction over 4d. per lb., and the lowest 3¾d. per lb. The average commercial value is stated as being 7l. 7s. per bale.

Cotton (Egyptian). The total imports of Egyptian cotton into the United States for the season ended in September, 1897, were 79,385 bales, as against 59,339 bales in 1896. Of these 49,303 bales were entered at the port of Boston.

Hay. The local receipts of hay in 1897 were 17,696 bales, as against 15,605 bales in 1896. The exports amounted to 161,402 bales, more than three times the quantity, 50,711 bales, exported during the previous year. Prices in the early part of the year, owing to the market being overstocked, were uniformly low. They rose during the summer owing to lighter receipts, but increased autumn receipts caused rates again to fall. Prime hay ranged from 2l. 12s. to 3l. 6s. per ton. A surplus of medium and poor grades during the year had a depressing effect on the market.

Provisions. The provision market showed an improvement in both tone and prices over the previous year, the total volume of trade being very satisfactory. The local market gave a better demand and a heavy increase in the exports. The number of hogs packed in Boston in 1897 was 1,648,717, about one-tenth more than in 1896.

Produce trade. Instead of the depression and inactivity shown in the year 1896, with prices all the time at a low ebb, the market has displayed life and energy, and with better prices, in butter especially. While this improvement has not reached large proportions, general conditions have been better, forming grounds for a more hopeful outlook.

Butter. In the local market Western butter brought 10d. per lb., but heavy receipts reduced the price to 7¼d. in May. A strong upward tendency, however, raised the rate to 10½d. in August, and light receipts clearing the market brought the price up to 11¼d. in December. The receipts at Boston were 51,107,033 lbs., as against 50,972,255 lbs. in 1896. The exports also from Boston amounted to 3,286,337 lbs., as compared with 3,156,711 lbs. exported in 1896.

Cheese. In the first part of the year better prices were obtained for cheese than in previous years, but the usual low tide was reached in May, when on the new cheese being put on the market prices were quoted at 3½d. per lb. The rate rose to 4½d. in August, and held through the remainder of the year. Receipts fell off by 40,521 boxes, and the exports were less by 4,729,667 lbs. than in 1896.

The total exports in 1897 were 16,773,781 lbs., of which 13,246,640 lbs. consisted of Canadian cheese shipped viâ Boston.

Eggs. The market for eggs has been unsteady, opening with Western extra at 9d. per dozen. Bad weather conditions, followed by heavy receipts, dropped the price to 5d. in July, when an upward movement took place, and the year closed with Western extra at 11½d. The effects of heat were felt in summer and early autumn, and had a depressing influence on the market. Receipts were heavy, aggregating 912,712 cases, as against 871,059 cases in 1896.

Poultry. Throughout the year the market for poultry may be considered as having been fair. In autumn the thanksgiving holiday receipts were light but arrived in good condition, as was the case with the Christmas arrivals, and although the demand was light the market was easily depleted, good prices generally were realised, and altogether a fairly satisfactory trade was done.

Fruit. The receipts of foreign fruit were the lightest for years, 15 steamers and one barque only arriving from the Mediterranean, whereas as many as 44 steamers and two barques in this trade in former seasons entered Boston in one year.

The demand for apples was poor, which, with the large remaining surplus of apples from 1896, caused low prices to prevail.

The Boston Chamber of Commerce states that owing to the large surplus stock of apples, the average net return of a barrel of apples to the farmer was about the price of one dozen Californian oranges. The exports for the year were 426 barrels.

Florida oranges, while small in the receipts were in good condition, and brought good prices.

The total receipts of lemons were much less than in 1896, but notwithstanding, low prices prevailed, except for lemons from California, which were the largest on record and the best in quality, so that the prices obtained for them were the highest of any year since this fruit has been on the Boston market.

In the banana trade the year has been a decidedly good one, the fruit arriving in good condition, and uniformly good prices being obtained throughout the year. Owing to the Cuban troubles, and the total destruction of the crops in that island, the entire receipts have been from Jamaica, aggregating 1,718,323 bunches as against 1,877,849 bunches in 1896.

Wool. The "Commercial Bulletin" states that the year 1896 was known as the worst on record in the American wool trade. The clip had steadily fallen off and prices as steadily declined. The year

1897 opened with small sales, a large stock, and dull markets generally throughout the world. The new heavy-weight season was inaugurated by the opening of the new goods of the Washington mills at prices 5 to 10 per cent. below the level of 1896, but the volume of early orders was generally so much larger than in the preceding year that the trade felt decidedly encouraged. The following table of quotations is an epitome of the year 1897 :—

Month.	Port Philip 60's Comb Clean.	Ohio XX.	Michigan X.	Territory Fine Delaine Clean.	Kentucky ¼ Blood Clean.
	s. d.	s. d.	s. d.	s. d.	s. d.
January 1	1 10	0 9½	0 8	1 6½	1 4
April 1	1 11¼	0 11	0 9	1 8	1 5½
July 1	2 0	0 11	0 9½	1 9	1 5½
October 1	2 8	1 2½	0 11½	2 2½	1 8
,, 30	2 9½	1 3	1 0½	2 5	1 9½
December 31	2 9½	1 2¾	1 0	? 3½	1 8

A large quantity of foreign wool was purchased by Boston dealers from January to early April, a noted hide-dealer leading in Buenos Ayres wool. It is claimed that in January, February, and March, 1897, Boston sold more wool (95,977,000 lbs.) than any other American market ever sold in a year. The dealing in wool from January till October became actual speculation, and there is no doubt but that many fortunes were both made and lost.

It is further claimed here that Boston is the largest fish market in the world, the largest leather market in the world, and that the dealings in wool during 1897 made it the largest wool market in the world, having at last wrested the standard from London, Boston selling 389,635,000 lbs., against London's 355,871,675 lbs. How much of this was due to speculative sales, &c., cannot be told.

The record of the year is summarised in the following figures :—

The aggregate receipts since January 1, 1897, have been 555,013 bales domestic and 212,927 bales foreign. This is an increase for the year of 110,407 bales domestic and a very slight increase as regards foreign.

The stocks of domestic wool on hand in Boston on December 31, 1897, were 51,606,000 lbs. as against 50,906,900 lbs. a year previously, while the stocks of foreign wool in Boston at the same date, according to the "Commercial Bulletin," were :—

	Quantity.
	Lbs.
Australasian	7,195,000
South American	6,507,000
Cape..	671,000
English and Irish	1,000,000
Coarse and carpet	3,460,000
Scoured and sundries	5,927,000
Total, foreign	24,760,000
„ domestic	51,606,000
„ on hand	76,366,000

Hides and leather.

The tanner, apparently, has not had the easiest of times in 1897; he seems to have been ground between the upper millstone of low-priced leather and the nether one of high cost hides. The shoe manufacturers obtained and kept the advantage, and though finally forced to pay an advance, this was not commensurate with the cost of production. The supply of leather has not been excessive at any time during the year, which opened with light hides strong in tone, gaining fractionally about $\frac{1}{8}$*d.* in January. They continued stronger by another gain of $\frac{1}{8}$*d.* in February, making $\frac{1}{4}$*d.* gain for the first two months, but these prices were lost in March. After this month the market varied till December, when more activity was displayed and a better tone was given which resulted in better prices.

The following table shows the prices quoted between January 1 and December 31, 1897:—

	January 1.		December 31.	
	From—	To—	From—	To—
	s. d.	*s. d.*	*s. d.*	*s. d.*
Rough leather g. d.	0 10	0 10½	0 11½	1 0
„ splits flat	0 6½	0 7	0 7	0 7½
Kip d. K. d. 7 oz. #2	0 5	0 5¼	0 5½	0 6¼
Crimpers #2	0 8	0 9½	0 9	0 10
W. O. gr. 2 7½ oz.	..	0 6½	0 7	0 7¼
Glove B. 4 to 5 oz.	0 5	..	0 5¼	0 5½
Satin B. 4 to 5 oz.	0 5½	0 5¾	0 5½	0 5¾
Russia calf #1	0 10	0 10½	0 11	..
Kang. calf #1	0 8	0 8½	0 8¾	0 9
Sole B. A. p. d.	0 8½	..	0 8¾	..
Union #1	1 2½	1 3	1 2½	..
Buff hides	0 4	0 4⅛	0 4⅞	0 5
B. A.	..	0 9	0 9¾	..

Shoes.

The shoe manufacturers have not been satisfied with last year's business, for, though it was the largest ever known, the profits have not been good. The shipments from Boston to points beyond the New England States reached 4,188,096 cases, an increase of 250,000 cases over the preceding year. The number of pairs of shoes shipped from Boston to foreign ports during 1897 was 299,272.

In such materials as old iron, old metal, and paper stock, the market has been much the same as in previous years, varying only slightly from season to season. The Dingley tariff which came into effect on July 24, seemed to have a hardly perceptible effect on scrap iron, old metals, paper or rubber stock; with woollen rags, however, it was different, as for years no such excitement has been seen, or such abnormal prices made, to be accounted for by the 10 c. per lb. duty on woollen rags, which till then had been on the free list, and by which a thorough revolution in business was effected.

Old materials. Rags and metals.

In previous years the importation of woollen rags was exceedingly heavy, amounting to millions of pounds, but with the imposition of the new duty, imports were absolutely stopped. On examining these imports it is found that they consisted of the very medium or below medium stock ranging from $2\frac{1}{2}d.$ to $7\frac{1}{2}d.$ per lb. Worsted rags were most wanted, as the supply here has been quite limited, and merinos were largely sought after, as also were worsted stockings, but these are now shut out by the high duty. During the first seven months of the year the imports into the United States were about 38,000,000 lbs. of rags, noils, and wool waste, as against 15,503,129 lbs. in 1896.

Cotton rags, old bagging, and rope are still free, but bring low prices, and are, in the main, depressed owing to wood pulp taking their place in making most kinds of paper, only the better qualities now containing rag stock.

Scrap iron and old metals have shown an unusual steadiness in prices, and on the whole the year may be considered to have been a good one for these metals. New England consumers took large quantities, and prices for wrought scrap iron ranged from 1s. 8d. to 1s. $10\frac{1}{2}d.$ per 100 lbs., on a parity with machinery scrap. Large quantities were exported to Canada. Plate iron still met with a good demand, old rails have ranged from 2l. 6s. to 2l. 12s. per ton. These prices run low, when on looking back a few years we find old rails bringing 4l. 8s. and more per ton, but in those times bar iron brought one-third more than it did last year. There was a good foreign demand during the year, chiefly from Italy.

Copper has been in good demand, but has varied only $\frac{1}{2}d.$ per lb. in price, while old lead, owing to the doubling of the duties under the new tariff, has advanced materially, the rise in price amounting to 3s. 4d. per lb.

The Boston Fish Bureau, in its yearly report, shows that the fish trade on the whole has been fairly satisfactory, and that while the demand for salt fish during the year 1897 has been curtailed by a shortage in the receipts of the great staples, salt cod and mackerel, there is a gratifying increase in the receipts of fresh mackerel, being 35,000 as against 22,000 barrels in 1896; while,

Fish.

however, the amount of fresh fish distributed has been large, it has not equalled that of some former years.

In the spring a bill was introduced into the Massachusetts Legislature to abolish fishing by traps and seines, but it met with such strong and unanimous opposition that it was defeated.

The bureau states that the relations with the British North American Provinces have been perfectly free from friction, and where the rights of American fishermen have been involved a spirit of clemency has been shown by the Dominion authorities.

On July 24, 1897, the new tariff became law, establishing an increase of the duties on most kinds of fish.

The duty on salt mackerel and salt salmon was raised from $\frac{3}{4}$ of a cent. to 1 c. ($\frac{1}{2}d.$) per lb. Salt herring remains the same at $\frac{1}{2}$ of a cent. per lb., as also smoked herring at $\frac{3}{4}$ of a cent. The duties on fresh mackerel are increased from $\frac{1}{2}$ to 1 c. per lb. Fresh halibut the same. Fresh salmon and smelt, formerly free, now pay respectively 1 c. and $\frac{3}{4}$ of a cent. per lb. duty.

Salt mackerel. At the opening of the year the visible supply of Irish mackerel was large, while trade was dull, prices ruling low. As the year advanced, however, prices rose on account of the failure of the catch.

'In the third week of June the first new salt mackerel from Nova Scotia arrived, being large 3's, and brought about 2*l.* per barrel, rising during the year to 2*l.* 12*s.* on an average.

Nova Scotia large mackerel sold from 3*l.* 12*s.* to 5*l.* 8*s.* per barrel, and in September Prince Edward's Island mackerel, counting 160 to a barrel, sold at 4*l.* 16*s.*

The first receipts of new Irish mackerel arrived early in September, and prices ruled at about 3*l.* per barrel, each barrel containing 375 fish.

During the year the receipts of salt mackerel at Boston amounted to 30,236 barrels, as under:—

From—	Quantity.
	Barrels.
Ireland	16,956
Nova Scotia	10,865
Norway	264
Domestic ports	2,151
Total	30,236

The catch of salt mackerel on Cape Shore was only 2,454 barrels, as against 16,655 barrels in 1896. The range in price was from 1*l.* 18*s.* to 2*l.* per barrel. The principal arrivals in July and August were from the Georges Shores, where a large body of fish was reported, but they were very wild and hard to catch. Prices ran from 2*l.* 4*s.* to 3*l.* 7*s.* per barrel.

The catch at North Bay was insignificant, but fine fish and bay mackerel sold from the vessel at from 4*l.* to 5*l.* per barrel.

Under the influence of a dull trade prices declined, notwith- Salt codfish.
standing that the stock of codfish in the early part of the year was
small. There also existed an exceedingly light demand for dry
bank fish for export. 4,000 dry bank fish came from Lunenburg,
N.S., in November, which the bureau says took the place of
French codfish, because the duty on the latter is so high as to be
prohibitive.

	Price per Quintal. (100 lbs. avoir.)		Remarks.
	From— £ s.	To— £ s.	
Large pickled bank codfish	0 10	0 17	The catch of salt codfish was 358,479 quintals, as against 342,760 quintals in 1896.
„ dry bank codfish	0 12	0 18	
„ Georges bank codfish	0 15	1 5	
„ shore bank codfish	0 13	1 1	
	Per Cwt.		
	£ s.	£ s.	
Hake	0 8	0 10	
	0 11	0 16	
Haddock	0 8	0 9	
Black salted pollock	0 10	0 13	
Pickled pollock	0 6	0 9	

The amount of fish cured in Boston during the year was
smaller than usual, owing to the dulness of trade.

Smoked herrings, on account of the large supply on hand, Herrings.
brought low prices till September, when the new herrings began to
arrive, and medium scaled sold at from 7d. to 7½d. per box.

There was a good demand for pickled herrings in the autumn,
probably owing to the scarcity of mackerel from Nova Scotia,
split herrings running from 12s. to 1l. per barrel. The demand
for frozen herrings has been fair, ruling from 9s. to 13s. per cwt.
direct from the vessel, the better demand having arisen on account
of the small domestic stock in the refrigerators.

With respect to Scotch herrings, the demand on this market is
very small, the Nova Scotia and Newfoundland fish, although the
quality is inferior, taking precedence over them on account of
their size and lower price. The capacity of a barrel of herring
must be 200 lbs., and this weight is demanded by the market.

Although Boston is not especially a market for herrings, it is
worthy of note that the principal wholesale dealer in cured fish,
&c., states that "the manner in which Scotch herrings are packed,
the uniformity of the goods, the excellence of the package, and
the reliability of the contents is an example worthy of imitation
by the producers of Irish mackerel, and never until it is con-
sistently applied can the best results accrue." Pickled or salted

Salmon. herrings from Scotland are imported to Boston to the amount of 391,170 lbs. of the value of about 2,304*l*.

Salmon. The receipts of northern pickled salmon were large in 1897, and the fish from Labrador showed good quality. Prices for 1's ruled from 3*l*. 12*s*. to 5*l*., and for 2's from 3*l*. 4*s*. to 4*l*. 12*s*. per barrel.

Fresh fish. The demand for fresh haddock, codfish, and hake has been about as good as in former years. The principal supply of these fish came from the fishing fleets which work on the fishing grounds on the New England and Nova Scotia coasts. Fish were plentiful in the spring and low prices ruled until the autumn, when they improved and held up the best for years. Cod and haddock from the vessel reached to 2½*d*. per lb.

Fresh mackerel. Of fresh mackerel 32,700 barrels were received from the northern fisheries, as against 37,237 barrels in 1896; but owing to the increase in the southern catch, the receipts of domestic fresh mackerel were largely augmented and a considerable number of vessels, which habitually salted all their catch, this year landed part of it fresh.

Salmon. The receipts of fresh salmon from Canada in 1897 were the smallest for years, owing to the light catch. In April, when scarce and in good demand, salmon brought 4*s*. per lb., dropping later to 8*d*. and 4*d*. per lb.

Smelts. The supply of smelts comes principally from Canada, 82,306 boxes being received during the year. Prices, on account of the full supply, ruled low, from 1*d*. to 2½*d*. per lb. on common, and 3*d*. to 4*d*. per lb. on extras.

Loss of vessels and life. The following table shows the number of vessels from New England and lives lost in 1897. (Compiled by the Boston Fish Bureau):—

Ports.	Vessels Lost.	Lives Lost.	Value of Vessels.	Insurance.
			£	£
Booth Bay Harbour ..	1	..	400	300
Boston	1	6	700	..
Gloucester	13	63	17,950	..
Harpswell	1	..	200	15,000
Provincetown ..	1	19	1,200	400
Swampscott	1	..	600	..
Total	18	88	21,050	15,700

Cod and lobster spawn. In the latter half of 1895 a new fish hatchery, under the direction of the United States Fish Commissioners, was established at a small place called Ten Pound Island in Massachusetts Bay, and in the autumn of 1897 there were hatched and "planted" in the waters of the bay over 60,000,000 small cod fry. At the end of the year some 30,000,000 eggs were still in process of hatching. The number of eggs successfully hatched is much greater in the early than in the latter half of the season, when only 54 per cent. of the eggs are successfully hatched in proportion to the first half.

Men proficient in stripping a codfish of its spawn are put on board the shore fishing boats, which land their catch at Kittery, Maine, in the proportion of one man to each boat. As the fish are taken alive from the water, they are inspected, and if suitable for the purpose, are stripped of their eggs, which are placed in jars and forwarded by express to Gloucester, Massachusetts.

More or less, the eggs are injured during transit, but it has been, on the whole, advantageous to forward them to Ten Pound Island, where good results in hatching have been obtained. Nature is followed, as far as possible, in the hatching process, the eggs being placed in perforated boxes and sea water direct from the ocean being continuously pumped through the boxes, so that the temperature may be as nearly as possible the same as that of the ocean. As soon as the eggs are hatched, the small fish are planted or released in the waters of Massachusetts Bay and have to rely on themselves, the same as the fry spawned in the open ocean.

Ipswich Bay, Massachusetts, and the contiguous waters appear to be a favourite spawning ground for codfish, and the artificially hatched fry, therefore, mingle with the many others of their kind and take the same chances in the struggle for existence. There is, of course, no data on which to base any calculation as to the percentage of artificially hatched fry which reach maturity, but the officers of the Fish Commission claim that the fish released by them are hardier in proportion, the weaker ones having been sifted and the stronger alone planted. As regards the success of the hatchery, it is proved that since the Fish Commission commenced operations the supply has certainly increased. Some years ago so few codfish were taken by the shore fishermen that the fishery had become unremunerative, but at the present time fish are fairly abundant and the fishery gives employment to a good number of men, who themselves admit that the hatchery operations have been successful.

After the codfish season is over the officials turn their attention to lobster hatching, a work commenced at this station a year ago. The same operations are gone through as with the codfish. It is said that for some occult reason the lobster fishermen regard this work with indifference, and that, although good prices are offered for seed lobsters, they are too often boiled and sold in defiance of the law.

Great interest is taken by pisciculturists in the artificial propagation of the lobster, but it is feared that unless a law similar to that in Nova Scotia, and which provides for a close season, is passed, the work will be useless.

The Boston custom-house returns show that the ocean tonnage, in the foreign trade in 1897, amounted to 1,980,708 tons entered, and 1,656,789 tons cleared, giving a total of 3,637,497 tons, as against 3,457,763 tons in 1896. *Foreign and maritime trade.*

(219)

BOSTON.

The American tonnage entering Boston shows an increase of 16 vessels and 22,599 tons. The foreign tonnage, which in 1896 was the heaviest then recorded, was still heavier in 1897, by about 114,975 tons.

The total number of vessels of all nationalities which entered this port from foreign ports during the year was, according to the custom-house returns, 2,068 of 1,980,708 tons measurement, as against 2,088 vessels of 1,843,134 tons in 1896. Of the above 768 were British steamers of 1,546,503 tons and 936 British sailing vessels of 142,296 tons with cargo, and 8 steamers of 13,482 tons, and 6 sailing vessels of 4,994 tons in ballast. (See Annex B.)

ENTERED.

Nationality.	Number of Vessels.	Tonnage.
British	1,718	1,707,275
American	261	168,875
Other nations	89	104,558
Total	2,068	1,980,708

In 1896 the entries showed a loss of 128 vessels for the year with an increase of 120,045 tons, while the above table, as compared with 1896, shows a further loss in 1897 of 20 vessels entering this port, but with an increase of 137,574 tons. This is accounted for by the increased tonnage of the steamers which are usurping the business formerly carried on in sailing ships.

The number of British vessels from all ports, including those of the United States, entered at this Consulate during the year 1897 was 1,752 vessels of 1,720,086 net tons, as against 1,787 vessels of 1,632,583 net tons in 1896.

The vessels of other foreign nations entering this port show a falling-off in number of 14 vessels, but with an increase in tonnage of 26,615.

The above figures show that British vessels still hold the carrying trade to and from the port of Boston.

Money and sterling exchanges.

In many respects 1897 has been a particularly notable year in the financial world of this country. During its course a Republican President assumed the executive chair, it has witnessed a new tariff and earnest efforts for currency reform, while the high prices obtained for wheat have brought plenty of money into the United States, enabled many of the railroads to earn actual dividends, and supplied the owners of British steamships with good freights and cargoes.

The new year opened with decidedly better prospects than were in view in the beginning of 1896, the gold exports dropping to "nil." Money began and continued easy all through the year and rates receded. Call money was 2 and 3 per cent., whereas in January, 1896, it was sharp 6 per cent. and inclining upwards. In April money was cheap and in excess of the demand, 2 per cent. on call being asked. In this month the failure of five mills in New Bedford caused a dull and heavier feeling which, however, did not last. In June the stock market became buoyant and the money market rich with funds at low rates. The city of Boston borrowed 100,000*l*. at 2·2 per cent. In September a slight depression occurred and again in November, but December, usually a hard month, turned out satisfactory with stocks rising and money still easy.

The Boston Bank clearings of 1897 showed total exchanges of 1,019,123,910*l*. and total balances of 115,918,624*l*. The total sales for the year, at the Boston Stock Exchange, amounted to 7,434,265 listed shares and 3,361,811 unlisted shares of stocks, also 7,900,174*l*. of bonds. These figures show a decided increase over the sales of 1896.

Bankers' sight bills of exchange on London were:—

Month.	Per 1*l*. Sterling.	
	From—	To—
	Dol.	Dol.
In January	4·84	4·86
April	4·86½	4·87½
July	4·86¼	4·87
December	4·82½	4·84

In general, the commercial record for the past year may be considered better than that of any since 1892; a feeling of confidence pervades business which makes, unless unforeseen accidents occur, a favourable outlook for 1898. *Conclusion.*

During the year under review there may have been grumbling over profits in some quarters, but, apart from the cotton goods trade, prosperous conditions appeared, at its close, on every hand.

The iron trade, which is considered to be the barometer of business conditions, displayed a satisfactory state of affairs, prices appeared low but showed profits, the woollen trade was good, the shoe factories were working well and prices hardening, the leather market was improving, and the manufacturing outlook had not been better for some years past. Money was easy and rates exceptionally low compared with the activity of general business; this was a stimulus to enterprise and there seemed to be no cloud looming on the financial horizon. Taking all these factors into consideration it seems more than reasonable to believe that, if no untoward circumstances happen, the improvement shown during the past year will be continued during 1898.

Annex A.—TABLE showing the Arrivals of Immigrants at the Port of Boston, for the last Five Years (prepared by the United States Commissioner of Immigration).

Nationality.	Number.				
	1897.	1896.	1895.	1894.	1893.
Ireland	6,489	8,333	10,995	6,750	10,793
England	3,251	3,246	5,007	3,395	7,430
Scotland	525	741	1,161	686	1,794
Wales	16	31	60	34	57
Germany	128	90	316	959	377
France	50	42	40	31	31
Russia	334	377	2,019	1,158	94
Finland	316	934	479	111	580
Poland	3	15	34	32	72
Switzerland	5	4	4	15	4
Sweden	1,366	2,068	2,061	1,193	3,764
Norway	389	743	676	440	1,376
Denmark	77	48	114	63	137
Holland	3	5	11	10	3
Italy	17	24	32	26	39
Spain	2	9	6	16	7
Portugal	3	10	12	5	551
Hungary	23	6	73	31	12
Austria	56	43	320	149	119
Austria - Hungary, Bohemia, and Moravia	7	..	5	7	..
Austria - Hungary, Galicia-Bukowina	25	10	95	12	..
Australia	3	2	..	..	1
Turkey in Europe	15	22	3	9	5
„ „ Asia	4	..	1	2	..
Greece	3	22	6	65	51
Belgium	5	..	22	26	..
Roumania	6	8	19	2	..
Mexico	..	..	..	1	..
West Indies	27	33	24	18	..
South America	..	2	2	1	..
Japan	4	..	..	1	..
Africa	12	1	..	1	..
All other countries	46	78	40	19	91
Total arrivals at Boston*	13,210	16,947	23,637	15,268	27,393

* In addition, there arrived at the ports of Massachusetts from the Dominion of Canada, by water during 1897, 20,634 aliens, compared with 19,026 in 1896, 20,806 in 1895, 17,893 in 1894, and 26,982 in 1893.

Annex B.—TABLE showing Vessels Entered at the Port of Boston from Foreign Countries during the Year 1897.

BOSTON.

Country.	Steam.					Sailing.					Total.	
	With Cargo.		In Ballast.		With Cargo.		In Ballast.			
	Number of Vessels.	Tons.	Number of Vessels.	Tons.	Number of Vessels.	Tons.	Number of Vessels.	Tons.	Number of Vessels.	Tons.
Great Britain and Dependencies	768	1,546,503	8	13,482	936	142,296	6	4,994	1,718	1,707,275
Austria	1	1,663	...	...	...	...	...	...	1	1,663
Denmark	1	315	...	...	...	...	...	...	1	315
France	12	6,113	...	...	5	724	...	...	17	6,837
Germany	21	50,028	...	...	1	2,678	...	...	22	52,706
Hawaii	...	...	...	...	1	878	...	...	1	878
Italy	...	...	...	...	3	2,897	...	...	3	2,897
Norway	40	33,742	...	...	2	2,477	...	...	42	36,219
Spain	2	3,043	...	...	...	...	...	...	2	3,043
Total foreign	845	1,641,407	8	13,482	948	151,950	6	4,994	1,807	1,811,833
,, United States	63	64,212	8	15,030	188	88,828	2	805	261	168,875
Grand total	908	1,705,619	16	28,512	1,136	240,778	8	5,799	2,068	1,980,708

NOTE.—From returns kindly supplied by the United States Collector of Customs.

Annex C.—TABLE showing Vessels Cleared from the Port of Boston for Foreign Countries during the Year 1897.

BOSTON.

	Steam.				Sailing.				Total.	
	With Cargo.		In Ballast.		With Cargo.		In Ballast.			
Country.	Number of Vessels.	Tons.	Number of Vessels.	Tons.	Number of Vessels.	Tons.	Number of Vessels.	Tons.	Number of Vessels.	Tons.
Great Britain and Dependencies	622	1,316,259	43	48,186	503	65,223	434	56,693	1,602	1,486,361
Denmark	..	..	1	315	..	..	..	..	1	315
France	11	5,071	..	..	5	724	..	..	16	5,795
Hawaii	..	..	..	..	..	..	1	878	1	878
Norway	10	5,021	16	9,805	1	733	2	2,477	29	18,036
Spain	..	..	2	3,043	..	..	..	..	2	3,043
Total foreign	643	1,326,351	62	61,349	509	66,680	437	60,048	1,651	1,514,428
„ United States	54	57,902	7	2,690	71	32,373	153	49,396	285	142,361
Grand total	697	1,384,253	69	64,039	580	99,053	590	109,444	1,936	1,656,789

NOTE.—From returns kindly supplied by the United States Collector of Customs.

BOSTON.

Annex D.—RETURN of British Shipping at the Port of Boston, U.S.A, for the Year 1897.

Direct Trade in British Vessels from and to Great Britain and British Colonies.

Entered.

Total Number of Vessels.			Total Tonnage.			Total Number of Crews.	Total Value of Cargoes.
With Cargoes.	In Ballast.	Total.	With Cargoes.	In Ballast.	Total.		£
1,527	8	1,535	1,456,850	10,618	1,467,468	44,000	...

Cleared.

Total Number of Vessels.			Total Tonnage.			Total Number of Crews.	Total Value of Cargoes.
With Cargoes.	In Ballast.	Total.	With Cargoes.	In Ballast.	Total.		£
1,080	481	1,561	1,365,941	106,014	1,471,955	47,325	...

Indirect or Carrying Trade in British Vessels from and to other Countries.

Entered.

Countries whence Arrived.	Number of Vessels.			Tonnage.			Number of Crews.	Value of Cargoes.
	With Cargoes.	In Ballast.	Total.	With Cargoes.	In Ballast.	Total.		£
Argentine Republic	10	...	10	10,210	...	10,210	175	...
Belgium	30	...	30	56,186	...	56,186	954	...
Chile	2	...	2	2,457	...	2,457	39	...
Dutch Guiana	1	...	1	351	...	351	7	...
Egypt	4	...	4	6,744	...	6,744	102	...
France	1	...	1	1,944	...	1,944	27	...
Germany	27	...	27	45,508	...	45,508	691	...
Hayti	3	...	3	1,612	...	1,612	37	...
Italy	16	...	16	22,807	...	22,807	420	...
Mexico	16	...	16	25,245	...	25,245	383	...
Netherlands and colonies	12	...	12	22,157	...	22,157	332	...
Nicaragua	8	...	8	14,623	...	14,623	237	...
Russia	1	...	1	1,390	...	1,390	22	...
Spain and colonies	59	1	60	33,892	232	34,124	675	...
United States of America	3	22	25	2,016	3,810	5,326	163	...
United States of Colombia	1	...	1	1,934	...	1,934	29	...
Total	194	23	217	249,076	3,542	252,618	4,293	...

Cleared.

Countries to which Departed.	Number of Vessels.			Tonnage.			Number of Crews.	Value of Cargoes.
	With Cargoes.	In Ballast.	Total.	With Cargoes.	In Ballast.	Total.		£
Argentine Republic	9	...	9	8,451	...	8,451	119	...
Belgium	1	...	1	1,193	...	1,193	23	...
Denmark and colonies	...	1	1	...	307	307	18	...
France and colonies	7	...	7	1,087	...	1,087	39	...
Germany	7	...	7	13,680	...	13,680	231	...
Spain and colonies	1	...	1	133	...	133	6	...
United States of America	27	121	148	41,141	175,316	216,457	3,436	...
Uruguay	1	...	1	348	...	348	8	...
Total	53	122	175	66,033	175,623	241,656	3,880	...

Annex E.—TABLE showing Steamship Sailings from Boston to European Ports during the Year 1897 (from the Report of the Boston Chamber of Commerce).

BOSTON.

Month.	To Liverpool.	To London.	To Glasgow.	To Hull.	To Antwerp, via Balto.	To Hamburg, via Balto.	To Bristol.	To Cork, Ireland.	To Stockton-on-Tees.	Total Sailings.
January	17	7	5	2	2	..	..	..	1	34
February	16	8	2	1	3	1	..	1	..	32
March	17	8	2	2	3	..	..	..	..	32
April	16	9	3	3	1	..	..	..	..	32
May	17	8	2	1	3	..	..	..	..	31
June	19	8	2	2	2	1	..	..	..	34
July	17	9	2	2	3	1	..	..	..	34
August	17	7	3	1	2	2	..	..	..	33
September	18	7	2	2	3	2	..	..	..	33
October	18	6	2	2	2	2	..	..	..	32
November	16	6	2	2	2*	2	..	..	..	30
December	15	7	3	2	1	2	1	..	..	31
Total, 1897	203	90	30	22	27	13	1	1	1	388
" 1896	199	82	28	20	23	4	Hull, via New York. 2	Hamburg. 2	Manchester. 1	361

* One sailing to Antwerp direct.

BOSTON.

Annex F.—FREIGHTS from Boston to Liverpool during the Year 1897.

Months.	Grain. Per Bushel.	Flour. Per Ton.	Provisions. Per Ton.	Cotton. Per Lb.	Cattle. Per Head.	Apples. Per Barrel.	Finished Leather. Per Ton.	Sole Leather. Per Ton.	Hay. Per Ton.
	$d.$	$s.\ d.\ s.\ d.$	$s.\ d.\ s.\ d.$	$d.\ \ d.$	$s.\ d.\ s.\ d.$	$s.\ d.$	$s.\ d.\ s.\ d.$	$s.\ d.\ s.\ d.$	$s.\ d.\ s.\ d.$
January	$3\tfrac{1}{2}$ to 4	17 6	11 3 to 15 0	$\tfrac{5}{64}$ to $\tfrac{11}{64}$	30 0	1 6	20 0	25 0	...
February	$2\tfrac{1}{2}$ $3\tfrac{1}{2}$	9 0 to 10 0	12 6 17 6	$\tfrac{9}{64}$	32 6	...	...	20 0 to 30 0	...
March	...	11 3	15 0	...	...	...	25 0	25 0	...
April	$1\tfrac{3}{4}$ $2\tfrac{1}{2}$	17 6	10 0 12 6	...	35 0	1 3	20 0	20 0	...
May	$1\tfrac{1}{4}$ $2\tfrac{3}{4}$	5 0	6 0 11 3	$\tfrac{3}{64}$	35 0 to 40 0	...	15 0 to 20 0	15 0 17 6	...
June	1 $1\tfrac{3}{4}$	6 3	5 6 6 0	$\tfrac{3}{64}$	40 0	...	15 0	12 6 15 0	...
July	1 $2\tfrac{1}{4}$	...	6 0 10 0	$\tfrac{9}{64}$	...	...	17 6	17 6	9 0
August	$\tfrac{3}{4}$ $2\tfrac{1}{2}$	6 0 8 9	10 0 10 0	...	30 0	...	15 0	17 6 20 0	...
September	$2\tfrac{1}{4}$ 3	5 6	10 0 12 6	$\tfrac{5}{64}$ $\tfrac{3}{32}$	...	1 6	...	...	12 6 to 13 6
October	2 $3\tfrac{1}{2}$	8 3 10 0	15 0	$\tfrac{1}{16}$ $\tfrac{9}{64}$	35 0	...	20 0	25 0 30 0	...
November	4	8 9 15 0	...	$\tfrac{3}{32}$	...	...	...	25 0	...
December	$3\tfrac{1}{2}$ 4	13 9	13 9 15 0	$\tfrac{1}{8}$	35 0 40 0	...	...	...	...

25

Annex G.—TABLE showing the Principal Articles of Export from Boston, and the Quantities Exported during the Year ended December 31, 1897, compared with 1896.

Articles.		Quantity 1897.	Quantity 1896.
Flour	Barrels	227,644	289,485
,,	Sacks	1,698,501	1,904,473
Wheat	Bushels	12,143,204	12,721,450
Corn	,,	9,464,163	6,136,603
Oats	,,	5,471,275	2,147,637
Peas	,,	114,299	155,212
Barley	,,	158,050	181,352
Rye	,,	41,837	167,316
Oatmeal	Barrels	52,843	49,773
,,	Sacks	88,851	57,259
Corn meal	Barrels	83,447	66,637
Mill feed	Tons	6,393	4,367
Hay	Bales	161,402	50,711
Cattle	Head	162,620	160,442
Sheep	,,	100,067	120,182
,,	Dressed carcases	1,538	165
Horses	Number	3,826	5,112
Fresh beef	Quarters	537,291	493,930
,,	Lbs.	5,711	3,270
Pork	Barrels	19,396	19,669
,,	Tierces	12,523	11,172
Bacon	Boxes	577,836	429,642
Lard	Lbs.	101,101,090	83,607,417
Hams	Barrels	243	134
,,	Tierces	641	786
Beef	,,	6,457	10,542
,,	Barrels	11,336	11,982
Tallow	,,	6,376	12,111
,,	Tierces	8,306	15,904
Grease	Barrels	7,261	13,426
Oilcake	Sacks	39,523	81,282
Butter	Lbs.	3,286,337	3,156,741
Cheese	,,	16,773,781	21,566,448
Oleo oil	,,	1,883,807	2,279,154
Apples	Barrels	426,539	747,106
Petroleum	Cases	49,446	76,316
,,	Barrels	5,428	5,379
Leather	Rolls	135,238	123,371
,,	Bales	55,730	64,079
,,	Bags	63,046	64,821
,,	Bundles	10,036	18,876
,,	Barrels	814	968
,,	Cases	5,376	5,261
,,	Packages	1,533	1,959
,,	Pieces	797,896	995,855

Annex H.—TABLE showing Total Value of the Imports into the Port of Boston during the Calendar Year 1897.

	Value.
	£
MERCHANDISE.	
Free of duty..	10,988,707
Subject to duty	6,148,923
Total	17,137,630
GOLD AND SILVER COIN AND BULLION IMPORTED.	
American gold coin	200
„ silver coin	..
Gold bullion	19,224
Total	19,424

TABLE showing Total Value of Exports from the Port of Boston during the Calendar Year 1897.

	Value.
	£
MERCHANDISE.	
Domestic	20,600,587
Foreign	237,751
Total	20,838,338
Gold coin	1,620

NOTE.—From returns kindly supplied by the United States Collector of Customs.

Annex I.—TABLE showing the Value of the Exports and Imports at Boston, by Countries, during the Year ended December 31, 1897.

Countries.	Exports (Foreign and Domestic).	Imports.	Total Exports and Imports.
	£	£	£
England..	18,099,643	7,439,886	25,539,529
Germany	339,157	1,164,184	1,503,341
Argentine Republic	92,498	1,129,831	1,222,329
France	4,806	1,173,841	1,178,647
Scotland..	690,492	420,728	1,111,220
British East Indies	1,722	925,750	927,472
Egypt	708	727,769	728,477
Australasia (British)	36,208	564,388	600,596
Belgium	222,777	421,259	644,036
Nova Scotia	326,523	346,251	672,774
Cuba	179	411,780	411,959
Netherlands	242,614	132,647	375,261
Dutch East Indies and Guiana	26,545	408,080	434,625
Philippine Islands	..	307,762	307,762
British Africa and Guiana	234,832	107,872	342,704
Mexico	..	247,785	247,785
Italy	4,746	242,208	246,954
Sweden and Norway	122,209	64,309	186,518
Ireland	81,919	97,377	179,296
British West Indies	11,579	149,007	160,586
Uruguay	17,583	82,536	100,119
Porto Rico	5,516.	84,420	89,936
Russia	60,761	66,540	127,301
Turkey	30,475	78,063	108,538
Denmark	42,690	10,095	52,785
Austria-Hungary	..	44,597	44,597
Quebec, Ontario, &c.	22,708	10,662	33,370
Newfoundland	32,822	22,554	55,376
Miquelon	31,859	33,107	64,966
Spain	..	31,470	31,470
Nicaragua	1,085	25,342	26,427
Colombia	678	25,237	25,915
Chile	..	25,370	25,370
Aden	..	23,970	23,970
French Africa and Guiana	31,202	8,249	39,451
Switzerland	4,446	15,654	20,100
Japan	..	17,544	17,544
China and Hong-Kong	..	19,860	19,860
Hayti	2,371	6,448	8,819
Portugal	506	5,761	6,267
Portuguese Africa	8,038	1,789	9,827
Greece	..	4,701	4,701
Madagascar	..	3,700	3,700
Bermuda	480	2,697	3,177
All other Africa and Asia	..	2,787	2,787
Brazil	2,132	..	2,132
Azores and Madeira	1,050	16	1,066
Hawaii and Fiji Islands	312	28	340
All others	2,467	1,719	4,186
Total	20,838,338	17,137,630	37,975,968

NOTE.—The above figures show that England, Scotland, and Ireland alone took 18,872,054*l.* of the exports, or over 90 per cent. of the whole, and sent 7,957,991*l.* worth of the imports, or 46 per cent. of the whole.

Annex K.—TABLE showing the Value, by Articles, of the Imports at the Port of Boston for the Fiscal Year ended June 30, 1897.

Articles.	Value.
	£
Wool	6,540,167
,, manufactures of	940,198
Sugar and molasses	2,086,225
Vegetable fibres	882,054
,, manufactures of	313,496
Hides and skins	803,423
Cotton	768,290
,, manufactures of	258,224
Leather	714,600
,, manufactures of	75,775
Chemicals, drugs, and dyes	439,685
Wood, and manufactures of	309,999
Iron ,, ,,	336,571
Fish	269,253
Paper-stock	230,505
Fruits	218,050
Earthen, stone, and chinaware	215,967
Indiarubber, crude	146,124
Glass and glassware	111,433
Tobacco, and manufactures of	92,304
Art works	91,880
Oil, vegetable	90,862
Wines	84,306
Cement	80,041
Spirits, distilled	64,225
Silks, and manufactures of	61,448
Grease and tallow	61,374
Coffee	48,223
Cocoa	29,723
Hair, and manufactures of	49,084
Stone ,, ,,	46,655
Books, &c.	46,349
Tea	44,113
Malt liquors	43,191
Tin, in bars, blocks, &c.	43,061
Toys	41,241
Fur and skins	39,802
Vegetables	33,188
Coal	30,310
Metal compositions	29,810
Spices	22,079
Household and personal effects	18,153
Animals	3,578
Clocks, watches, &c.	5,278
Feathers, &c.	15,504
All other articles	1,159,863
Total	18,035,684

Annex L.—TABLE showing the Value, by Articles, of the Exports from the Port of Boston for the Fiscal Year ended June 30, 1897.

Articles.	Value.
	£
Provisions	7,491,686
Live animals	2,788,348
Breadstuffs	3,518,985
Cotton	1,996,996
„ manufactures of	176,579
Leather	1,493,646
„ manufactures of	88,419
Iron, and manufactures of	324,137
Spirits, distilled	224,445
Fruits and nuts	222,246
Lumber	145,232
Wood, and manufactures of	139,289
Tobacco „ „	124,340
Chemicals, dyes, and medicines	76,687
Paper, and manufactures of	73,360
Indiarubber, and manufactures of	46,712
Agricultural implements	42,972
Cycles, and parts of	41,121
Seeds	38,376
Fur and fur-skins	35,406
Glucose	33,391
Books, maps, &c.	33,212
Copper	32,173
Musical instruments	33,381
Wool, and manufactures of	32,822
Grease	23,095
Oils, mineral	24,018
„ all others	2,082
Flax, hemp, and jute, manufactures of	31,719
Oilcake	29,550
Brass, manufactures of	20,521
Builder's hardware	19,440
Hides and skins	12,589
Naval stores	11,487
Fertilisers	11,038
Starch	12,351
Vegetables	6,455
Clocks and watches	5,270
Glass and glassware	2,517
Hops	3,848
Marble and stone	2,557
All other articles	417,824
Total	19,890,322

PORTLAND.

Mr. Vice-Consul Keating reports as follows:—

Review. The commercial depression which for the past three years had been general throughout the State was still in evidence in 1897, although the slight improvement noticeable in the spring continued until the close of the year.

PORTLAND.

Valuation. The total value of property in the city of Portland is placed at 7,848,002*l*., of which 4,319,305*l*. is real estate owned by residents, 896,750*l*. is real estate owned by non-residents, 2,569,860*l*. is personal estate, and 62,087*l*. is owned by banks. The tax rate for the past year was 4*l*. 3*s*. 3*d*. per 200*l*.

New buildings. Over 200,000*l*. has been added to the value of property in Portland and Deering during the past year in the construction of new houses, business blocks, and public buildings.

Harbour. The accommodation for steamers has been greatly improved and further improvements are contemplated in the coming year. Already new wharves have been built and old ones considerably enlarged, new freight sheds constructed and freight yards increased, the harbour dredging continued, and approaches to the wharves dredged so as to permit steamers of 7,000 tons to arrive and depart at almost any season of the tide.

Increase in British tonnage. The tonnage of British vessels which entered this port during the year 1888 from all ports was only 60,349. Last year the total tonnage was 177,159, an increase of 116,810 (64,052 tons represents the amount of increase during the past two years).

Freights. The large crops in Ontario, Michigan, Illinois, and other Western States, and the general demand in Europe being in excess of previous years, the exports greatly increased and the close of the year saw a rise in rates.

Imports and exports. The imports entered at the custom-house during the year 1897 amounted to 1,120,727*l*., and in the year 1896 to 1,070,717*l*.

The exports during the year 1897 amounted to 3,340,430*l*., and in 1896 to 2,557,000*l*.

Grain. The building of the new elevator (which is said to be the largest east of Detroit) has justified its existence, contracts having been made for the export, during the winter months, of 10,000,000 bushels of wheat against 2,000,000 bushels for the same period in 1896. The new elevator is capable of shipping 30,000 bushels of grain hourly, and during the present season at one week's shipment upwards of 700,000 bushels were exported from this port. At the close of the year, in addition to the elevator's capacity being taxed to its utmost, over 1,000 cars were stored in transit awaiting shipment.

Cattle. The improved and new stockyards have enabled a greatly increased number of cattle to be shipped from this port, the total for 1897 being 17,553 head.

Horses. The number of horses shipped from this port last year was 3,026, against 978 for 1896.

Cattle and horse attendants. It is reported by the agents, masters, and shippers that the cattlemen and horsemen shipped at this port are of a superior class. During the past year there has not been a single complaint of any description, as against numerous complaints during the previous years.

Real and personal estate. The total amount of real and personal estate of Maine as returned to the State assessors is 56,375,760*l*., an increase of 703,629*l*. over 1896, 77·13 per cent. being real estate. The 20 cities of the State return a total valuation of 25,982,060*l*., of which 77·23 per cent. is real estate. There are 30 towns with a valuation above 200,000*l*., and a total valuation of 9,419,752*l*., of which 79·57 per cent. is real estate. 318 of the cities, towns, and plantations return a higher valuation of real estate than last year.

Fishing industry.

In my annual report for 1896 I gave some statistical information respecting Maine's deep-sea fishing industry, and the conditions have not, during the past year, materially changed.

Sardine factories.

The whole of the sardine factories have been purchased by a syndicate of American capitalists. It is claimed that competition between factories will be thereby removed, that higher prices and a higher grade of goods will be maintained, and that a stronger market will be secured. It is also claimed, that when the factories were working independently, if any of them were short of herrings there was always a rush to secure the fish, and this enabled the fishermen to take advantage of such a condition and secure fancy prices. The high prices which it is claimed were formerly paid for raw material was one of the causes for "cutting wages," and which induced strikes in some factories, particularly in Washington county. Under the new conditions one price for herrings will prevail at all the factories. Those that handle the fish will naturally lose by this condition, but it is claimed that this loss will be more than offset by the larger and steadier demand for the fish. It is rumoured that some of the factories will be closed in order to centralise the work and reduce the expenses, but it is thought that no hardship will accrue to the men as a consequence because the other factories will be enlarged and improved.

Inland fisheries and game.

There are more than 2,000 inland seas and lakes within the State. From the figures given by the guides to the Fish Commissioners, it would appear that, during the open season of the past year, 10,000 citizens of other States visited the hunting and fishing grounds, and spent therein upwards of 800,000*l*. and killed 8,947 deer, 250 moose, 239 caribou, and 160 bears, and 52 tons of fish (trout and salmon) were caught. In connection with these figures, I would also point out that from the returns made by proprietors of hotels, lodging houses, &c., at the various seaside resorts, at least 1,200,000*l*. were spent at the beaches by non-residents for pleasure. Undoubtedly the stringent protective laws are a necessity and benefit—the question of its legality having been settled by the United States Supreme Court in a decision which reads:—"That the people of a State in their sovereign capacity own the fish and game within its borders, and may say, through its legislature, how, when, and where it may be taken, and what may be done with it after it has been taken; in other words, the legislature may give a qualified property right or ownership to fish or game lawfully taken."

The sum of 5,000*l*. was last year placed at the disposal of

PORTLAND.

the Commission, and the cost of the maintenance and work of the various hatcheries exceeded this amount by about 200*l.*

The guides are required to be registered, and they number 1,316. They usually charge 12*s.* per diem for their services. Last year they received in wages 31,151*l.*, or an average of 23*l.* 13*s.* 5*d.* each.

According to the return made by the taxidermists, at least 10,000*l.* were received by them, during the year, in payment for birds, fish, and game mounted.

In the Commissioners' report for 1897 full detailed accounts are given of the results of the eight hatcheries within the State. This report gives the number of eggs hatched, the cost of feeding, and all the incidental expenses connected with the various hatcheries throughout the State.

I shall have much pleasure in forwarding this report to anyone applying for the same, as the figures are too numerous, and the details too many to enable me to include them in this report.

Last year witnessed a revival of the porgy fishing industry. The porgies are much valued for the oil obtained from them, and for the "chum," as the refuse is termed, which is used in making fertilisers. In appearance they resemble a herring. The process by which the oil is extracted requires the use of costly and heavy operating steam or hydraulic power machinery. The oil is squeezed out of the fish and is of three or four qualities, being largely used in tanning leather. Three tons of the porgy refuse will afford one ton of phosphate. In former years the pressing, &c., was performed in over 40 factories scattered along the coast, when gradually the porgy left these waters and the industry fell off. Last year, however, the fish returned, and a fleet of 12 steamers was employed throughout the season (June to October) in catching this fish. These steamers are of special build and of about 150 tons burden.

Porgy fishing.

The causes of the movements of the porgies are not fully understood, but it is believed that both the temperature of the water and the abundance of the food on which the fish live are factors in determining the direction and extent of the migrations. Those who have made a study of the habits of fish are of the opinion that the long period in which the porgy was a stranger to the Maine coast will be followed by a number of years of abundance.

The manufacture of spools and the sawing and shipping of spool wood in Maine have assumed such proportions that they may be classed among the important industries of the State. The manufacture of spools commenced in the year 1861, and in consequence of the very large area of white birch which extends across the State, the industry has been constantly increasing. Scotland alone last year received 13,550,000 feet of spool bars. The average price paid to the manufacturer was 3*l.* 14*s.* per 1,000 feet.

Spools and spool wood and novelty manufactures.

Besides the above, several millions of feet of spool bars are
(219)

sent to other States to be manufactured into spools. The total amount required for manufacture within the State, and for foreign and domestic shipment, is about 35,000,000 feet of white birch wood annually.

The spool factories turn out annually about 250,000,000 spools consuming 15,250,000 feet.

In addition to the above several millions of feet are required in the spool novelty industry which consists of druggists' boxes, dice boxes, wooden stoppers, toothpicks, children's wagons, step ladders, swings, school desks and chairs, and baby sleighs, &c.

Brickmaking. The season of 1897 has been unusually severe upon the brickmakers of Maine, the effect of the general depression of business of 1893. The weather has been the most unfavourable known in the history of the State. Fifty-eight yards (507 men) equalled an output of 54,550,000 bricks. The price netted 1*l.* per 1,000.

Cotton industry. The cotton industry is in a very unsatisfactory condition, and the outlook not promising for the future. In the 16 cotton mills reported to the Bureau of Industry are 869,473 spindles. The returns of the business of these mills, as tabulated, cover substantially one-half of the business in the State. A comparison of the details of the business with those given by the United States census reports of 1880 and 1890 will show some interesting results. The two main items entering into the production of cotton goods are raw material and labour. Interest on capital invested, wear and tear of machinery, taxes and insurance, repairs of buildings, salaries, breakage, waste, profits, &c., are classed as margin. Taking the value of the products as a basis the following table will show the percentage of the three items, raw material, wages, and margin, at the three periods named:—

Items.	Percentage.		
	1880.	1890.	1897.
Raw material	55	55·2	57·9
Wages	22	28·5	33·1
Margin	23	16·3	9·0
Total	100	100	100

It will be seen that while the percentage of raw material has slightly increased since 1880, the cost of labour entering into the product of a given value of finished goods is over 50 per cent. more in 1897 than in 1880, and the margin which in 1880 was 23 per cent. of the value of the product has now fallen off to 9 per cent.

The following table gives the average annual earnings per employé, including men, women, and children for the periods named:—

PORTLAND.

	Per Employé.		
	1880.	1890.	1897.
	£ s.	£ s.	£. s.
Average annual product	226 10	219 0	174 16
,, ,, earnings	50 0	62 12	58 0

The large falling-off in the average annual product per employé is accounted for in the decline in the price of raw cotton, which, in 1889, had fallen about 8 per cent., and in 1896 about 33 per cent. below the quotations of 1879, and in a similar decline in the selling price of the manufactured goods.

There are 47 woollen mills in the State, and they contain 347 sets of cards. The percentages do not differ materially from those of cotton, while the table of annual product and earnings shows a falling-off in average annual product of 156*l*., and the average annual earnings a gain of only 2*l*. 2*s*. in 17 years:— *Woollen industry.*

Items.	Percentage.		
	1880.	1890.	1897.
Raw material	64·2	65·9	65·4
Wages	15·6	21·7	25·1
Margin	20·2	12·4	9·5
Total	100	100	100

	Per Employé.		
	1880.	1890.	1897.
	£ s.	£ s.	£ s.
Average annual product	434 0	348 0	278 0
,, ,, earnings	67 10	67 10	69 12

The number of children employed in the mills are as follows:—

	1897.			1895.		
	Under 16 Years.	Between 15 and 16.	Under 15 Years.	Under 16 Years.	Between 15 and 16.	Under 15 Years.
Cotton mills	561	331	230	906	469	437
Woollen and worsted mills	113	77	36	53	35	18

A study of the tables of the boot and shoe industry is interesting as compared with the textile industries:— *Boot and shoe industry.*

(219)

Items.	Percentage.		
	1880.	1890.	1897.
Raw material	66·6	56·1	62·5
Wages	22·9	29·8	23·3
Margin	10·5	14·1	14·2
Total	100	100	100

	Per Employé.		
	1880.	1890.	1897.
	£ s.	£ s.	£ s.
Average annual product ..	313 8	297 0	374 0
,, ,, earnings ..	68 0	93 4	87 0

Building of factories, &c.

In 74 towns throughout the State 95 new buildings have been erected during the past year at a total cost of 165,520*l.*, and giving employment to 2,339 hands.

Shipbuilding.

The year 1897 was one of phenomenal depression in wooden ship building, even more pronounced than during the years immediately preceding, and the record is therefore exceptionally low.

In 1896 Bath alone turned out 20 vessels with a total tonnage of 16,242·05 tons, whereas the total number built throughout the State in 1897 was only 41 vessels of a total tonnage of 5,667·83 tons.

The following table is compiled from the records of all the Maine ship yards, and arranged by customs districts:—

District.	Schooners.	Sloops.	Steamers.	Yachts.	Total Number of Vessels.	Tonnage.
Portland	...	1	3	...	4	127·20
Bath	3	3	1	...	7	4,902·04
Wiscasset	...	...	1	...	1	14·69
Waldeboro... ...	4	13	...	2	19	300·95
Castine	...	6	...	...	6	42·95
Machias	1	1	...	...	2	253·45
Passamaquoddy ...	1	...	1	...	2	26·55
Total	9	24	6	2	41	5,667·83

While there has been a falling-off in the shipbuilding industry, shipping in the State shows an increase in valuation, the State assessors returning an increase of 25,000*l.* above the amount returned for 1896.

With reference to this return it may be mentioned that the Portland Board of Trade, assisted by representatives from Bath, Rockland, Thomaston, Bangor, and Belfast, have in hand a bill

PORTLAND.

which will be submitted to Congress for the restoration of American shipping.

Railroads (steam). The number of employés (excluding general officers) employed upon the steam railroads in Maine for the year ended June, 1897, was 5,842, against 5,742 men in 1896, a gain of 100 employés. The amount paid for wages in 1897 was 562,257*l*., against 522,271*l*. in 1896, a gain of 39,986*l*.

Street railroads. There are 16 street railroads in the State, having an invested capital of 700,000*l*. On this investment there was paid in dividends last year 6,350*l*., which is hardly 1 per cent. Out of the 16 railroads only six paid any dividend. The Portland Railroad Company paid 3,600*l*. of the total amount.

Savings, trust and banking companies. From the report of the bank examiner for the State of Maine, it is learned that the number, classes, and assets of the institutions under his supervision are as follows:—

Description.	Number.	Assets.
		£
Savings banks	51	12,565,260
Trust and banking companies	16	1,502,680
Loan and building associations	33	582,592
Total	100	14,650,532

This is a decrease of four in the total number of institutions, but, notwithstanding this, there is an increase of 558,607*l*. in the aggregate amount of assets covered by this report. An equal distribution of these assets would give to each person in the State 22*l*. There are 83 national banks now doing business in Maine, with assets amounting to 8,271,630*l*. This makes the entire number of banking institutions in the State 183, and a total banking capital of 22,922,162*l*., an increase of 1,441,935*l*. during the year. If this total banking capital was divided equally among the inhabitants of the State it would give each individual 35*l*.

The following totals of liabilities and resources show the condition of the savings banks on November 6, 1897, as compared with that of November 7, 1896:—

	Amount.	
	1896.	1897.
	£	£
Total liabilities	10,143,876	12,565,260
„ resources	12,143,875	12,565,260

The following table shows the condition of the savings banks throughout the State:—

	1896.	1897.
Number of depositors	163,115	167,879
„ whose balance is less than 400*l*.	158,855	163,423
Amount deposited	9,325,446*l*.	9,642,815*l*.
Number whose balance is 400*l*. or more	4,260	4,456
Amount deposited	2,169,932*l*.	2,276,854*l*.
Average rate of dividend (approximate)	·0372	·0367
Amount of dividends paid	419,385*l*.	426,473*l*.
Municipal taxes paid	3,502*l*.	3,651*l*.
State tax	76,241*l*.	76,372*l*.

The above statement shows an increase of 4,764 in the number of depositors, and 424,291*l*. in the amount of deposits during the year. This gain is nearly twice that for the preceding year. Out of a total of 167,879 depositors, 129,865 have 100*l*. or less standing to the credit of each. The average amount now standing to the credit of depositors is 71*l*., an increase of 10*s*. 6*d*. over that of 1896. The amount of withdrawals during the year was 2,085,105*l*., and the amount deposited, including dividends credited, 2,510,971*l*. Owing to the general appreciation in the value of securities, the larger amount of investments within the State and in Government bonds, there has been but a slight increase in the amount of taxes paid to the State over that of 1896. The reduction in the premium account is considered highly satisfactory, as the banks paid a premium on a large portion of the securities purchased during the year.

The following table shows the rates and amounts of dividends during the year, as compared with those paid in the year 1896:—

1896.		1897.		
Number of Banks.	Amount of Dividends.	Number of Banks.	Amount of Dividends.	Rate of Dividends Paid.
	£		£	Per cent.
1	76	..		4½
27	314,332	23	305,610	4
2	4,450	2	10,722	3¾
14	76,139	18	88,036	3½
3	10,871	2	7,670	3¼
5	13,517	6	14,436	3
52	419,385	51	426,474	3⅔

This is an increase of 7,089*l*. in the amount of earnings distributed among the depositors over that of last year. The average rate of dividends paid the present year has been 3⅔, while that for 1896 was 3·72.

Deal trade. The deal trade of Bangor, which had been dormant for 20 years, was to some extent revived during the season, about 11,000,000 feet of lumber in that form being shipped to the United Kingdom.

The spool trade at this port was also large, nearly 7,000,000 feet being exported. The shook export to the Mediterranean amounted to 307,164 bundles. Over 5,000 tons of ground wood pulp was sent to England with the first European shipment of paper direct from Bangor; this consignment consisted of 93 tons for a firm in Manchester, England. Imports were very light, only 9,914 bushels of salt from Turk's Island, valued at 139*l*. The leading exports include shooks, deals, spool bars, pulp, paper, and ice, the total value of shipments being 86,716*l*., the greater part, 60,140*l*., being exported to the United Kingdom. The total number of steamers arriving at this port in 1897 was 14.

As these notes refer to the city of Portland, and must be taken as of chiefly local interest, I have thought that they might possibly comprise some points of general interest to British trade, and have, therefore, ventured, to insert them in my report. *General notes on Portland's imported goods.*

From personal observation I learned that the local retail dry-goods and wholesale crockery houses, &c., dealt largely in imported goods. To ascertain how far British goods entered into competition with the goods imported, I addressed a letter to each firm in the city requesting that I might be furnished with a list of the principal goods of British manufacture imported or retailed by them. Also, whether the demand for such goods was on the increase or decrease. Being acquainted with many of the heads of departments, I followed up these letters of inquiry by soliciting suggestions from them which might prove of interest to British manufacturers. I ascertained that white and decorated crockery leads in demand, and that the demand is constantly increasing. The retailers, however, are unanimous in stating that a much larger quantity would be sold if British manufacturers would cease to imitate the American and French ware, and instead manufacture goods that are distinctively English in style and decoration. *Crockery.*

Silk, wool, and black dress goods are in steady demand, and find ready sales at good prices and profit to the retailers. *Silk, wool, and black dress goods.*

Mohair and dress fabrics have a more or less fluctuating demand, but are always sure of a sale. *Mohair and dress fabrics.*

Table damask, napkins, towelling, art embroideries, &c., are in good demand, and when placed in competition, on the counters, with goods of German manufacture, &c., are preferred to all others. *Irish linen, &c.*

Hose of English manufacture is in increasing demand, and needs only pushing to further increase the sales. The recent adoption of the French foot has, I am assured, greatly increased the sales. *Hosiery.*

In fancy and souvenir china the retailers state that British manufacturers have been of late more willing to adopt the suggestions of retailers, and as a consequence the demand in English china has increased. They assure me that our representatives are not yet as accommodating in this respect as the representatives of other manufacturers. *Fancy and souvenir china.*

Nottingham lace goods are in strong demand. *Nottingham laces, &c.*

Tea.

The demand for Ceylon and India teas has greatly increased during the past two years.

The advertising by the Commissioners is regarded by the retailers as an excellent scheme, and the public are fast realising the value of these teas.

Comments.

I was assured by the proprietor of the largest department store in the city that the demand for goods of British manufacture is constantly increasing in proportion to his general business. The senior partner of another large firm suggested to me that the sale of goods to retailers would be much increased if British manufacturers were directly represented by some one selling exclusively British goods. He assured me that our manufacturers often suffered in consequence of salesmen having "side lines" on which they made a larger commission, and for which he was able to give better terms to the retailer. Still another assured me that the system of selling goods by personal solicitation from samples was far from satisfactory to the up-to-date merchant, and he suggested that the British manufacturers should establish headquarters either in New York or Boston, where a "full line" of goods would be displayed. The merchants could view the goods there at a time convenient to them, and thereby be enabled to make quicker, larger, and more satisfactory purchases. The gentleman making the latter suggestion stated that he was aware that the large commission houses would give a different opinion on this subject, as viewed from their standpoint; nevertheless, he was positive that his idea coincided with the oft expressed opinion of his brother merchants. Another informed me that salesmen would frequently approach a merchant in his busiest time and endeavour to push his goods, thereby causing unpleasant feeling which naturally reacts on the manufacturer. The general opinion of the merchants with whom I conversed, was that while great progress has been made by domestic manufacturers during the past few years, the public are naturally dependent on the mother country for many of the most desirable articles of trade, and that goods of British manufacture which can, with the present tariff, enter into competition with domestic goods will readily find purchasers.

The constant and rapid growth of this and other cities throughout the State of Maine, and the now greatly increased facilities offered for shipment by the five lines of steamers plying to and from Great Britain, may make these remarks interesting. In addition to this I would point out that the Grand Trunk Railroad are calling for exclusive steamship service in connection with its line from Portland for a term of years, capacity of steamers to be of 5,000 tons and upwards, with a speed of 14 to 16 knots, and to sail direct between Portland and the various points mentioned, the company to have the option of calling for additional steamers for either of the ports named to be furnished on 60 days' notice, the service to be as follows:—

From—		Number of Steamers.
Portland to Liverpool	Weekly	2
,, Bristol	,,	1
,, London	,,	1
,, Glasgow	Fortnightly	1
,, Hamburg or Antwerp	,,	1

In connection with this subject I would wish, in the interest of steamship owners, to draw their attention to the fact that Portland is especially well equipped for furnishing ship supplies of all descriptions at moderate cost, and that the best goods and lowest prices would be more readily obtained if a system of public contracts or bids were adopted by them.

LONDON:
Printed for Her Majesty's Stationery Office,
By HARRISON AND SONS,
Printers in Ordinary to Her Majesty.
(75 7 | 98—H & S 219)

No. 2152 Annual Series.

DIPLOMATIC AND CONSULAR REPORTS.

UNITED STATES.

REPORT FOR THE YEAR 1897

ON THE

TRADE AND AGRICULTURE OF CALIFORNIA.

REFERENCE TO PREVIOUS REPORT, Annual Series No. 1922.

Presented to both Houses of Parliament by Command of Her Majesty,
JULY, 1898.

LONDON:
PRINTED FOR HER MAJESTY'S STATIONERY OFFICE,
BY HARRISON AND SONS, ST. MARTIN'S LANE,
PRINTERS IN ORDINARY TO HER MAJESTY.

And to be purchased, either directly or through any Bookseller, from
EYRE & SPOTTISWOODE, EAST HARDING STREET, FLEET STREET, E.C., **and**
32, ABINGDON STREET, WESTMINSTER, S.W.; or
JOHN MENZIES & Co., 12, HANOVER STREET, EDINBURGH, and
90, WEST NILE STREET, GLASGOW; or
HODGES, FIGGIS, & Co., Limited, 104, GRAFTON STREET, DUBLIN.

1898.

[C. 8648—174.] *Price Threepence.*

CONTENTS.

	PAGE
SAN FRANCISCO Consulate-General—	
General remarks	5
Shipping and navigation—	
Tables of clearances and entrances of vessels	6
Freights and charters	8
Seamen's wages	9
Scarcity of seamen	9
New steamer lines, &c.	10
Quarantine	10
Shipbuilding	11
Pilotage charges	11
Effects of Klondike excitement on shipping	12
Lightship for the Golden Gate	12
Trade and commerce	12
Table of exports and imports	13
Exports—	
Wheat and flour	13
Barley	13
Salmon	14
Tinned fruit and vegetables	14
Timber	15
Quicksilver, &c.	15
Imports—	
Coal	15
Coke	16
Tin-plates	16
Cement, &c.	16
Value of articles exported and imported, table of	18
Decline of British trade, table showing	18
Woollens	19
Linens	19
Laces	20
China, &c.	20
Cutlery	20
Lack of travellers	20
Electro-plate	21
Trade with the Orient; efforts to increase same	21
Effects of Klondike discoveries on trade	21
Manufactures	22
Bank clearings	22
Enterprise in shoe trade	23

Contents—continued.

	PAGE
SAN FRANCISCO Consulate-General—continued—	
Fire insurance	23
Fire department	23
Mining	23
Production of precious metals	23
Hydraulic mining	24
Quartz mining	25
Modern methods of acquiring mining property	25
British mining investments	26
Population and industry	27
Diseases: tuberculosis, deaths from	28
Inspection of bakeries and laundries	28
Adulteration of food	29
Inspection of cattle	29
Garbage, disposal of	30
Railway construction	30
Electric power in California and Utah	31
Salvation Army colony	32
College of commerce	32
Land frauds	32
Advice to settlers	33
Labour market, &c.	33
Agriculture—	
Wheat	34
Barley	34
Hops, &c.	34
Beet-sugar industry	35
Wine crop	37
Experiment in storing wine	38
Fruit crop	39
Prunes	39
Raisins	40
Hemp	40
Tobacco	40
Plant disease	40
LOS ANGELES Vice-Consulate	41
SAN DIEGO Vice-Consulate	46

NOTE.—All the values in the following report are calculated at the rate of 5 dol. to the 1*l.* sterling.

No. 2152. Annual Series.

Reference to previous Report, Annual Series No. 1922.

Report on the Trade, Commerce, and Agriculture of the Consular District of San Francisco for the Year 1897

By Mr. Acting Consul-General W. Moore.

(Received at Foreign Office, June 20, 1898.)

The year 1897 showed a considerable improvement over that of 1896, which in turn was better than its predecessor. The bank clearances show an increase of over 13,000,000*l.*, and many of our leading products were shipped to the Eastern States in increasing quantities. Exports of merchandise show a slight gain which would have been materially augmented had the shipments of wheat been up to the average. Imports have increased substantially, demonstrating the capacity of the people to buy, and the prices obtained for most of our products were satisfactory.

General remarks.

The wine crop of 1897 was the largest in the history of the State, but prices fell to a point that is unremunerative to the producer.

Sugar beet culture is increasing in California, and is likely to become a leading industry of the State in the near future.

The Klondike gold discoveries have proved of considerable benefit to the shipping and commercial interests of San Francisco.

Attention is directed to the modern method of acquiring mining property, which I have fully described in this report.

The new tariff went into effect in July, 1897, and is likely to interfere seriously with the importation of several lines of goods.

The effect of the war between the United States and Spain has not disturbed business much in this city. Local stocks and bonds declined at the commencement of hostilities, but have since recovered, some of them to their former prices. The outfitting of the expeditions to Manila has proved of some benefit to local merchants, and a number of ships have been chartered or bought by the Government to carry troops and coal.

The outlook for 1898 was exceedingly bright, but unfortunately California suffered from a severe drought during the last winter, and in place of an average rainfall of 18 to 20 inches, in this city, less than 9 inches have fallen. The season has been the driest recorded in 21 years, and the result will be most disastrous to the farming interests. The present indications are that there will only be about sufficient wheat and barley for seeding purposes and the requirements of the domestic market, and very little, if any, for export. Large quantities of maize have been shipped to California from Nebraska, as feed for cattle, and wheat has been sent here overland from Oregon and Washington, a thing that has never happened before. The fruit crop is believed to be seriously damaged through want of moisture, but it is impossible to speak definitely on this point as we have had no very dry winter, until the present, since the fruit interests in California became so important. Mining operations will be restricted in some districts for lack of water to run the mills.

Remarks relating to the various subjects connected with shipping, trade, mining, population, and agriculture will be found in this report under the following heads, viz.:—

Shipping and navigation. The following table shows the number and nationality of vessels which entered and cleared at this port during the past year:—

Annex A.—RETURN of all Shipping at the Port of San Francisco during the Year 1897.

ENTERED.

Nationality.	Sailing. Number of Vessels.	Sailing. Tons.	Steam. Number of Vessels.	Steam. Tons.	Total. Number of Vessels.	Total. Tons.
British	152	280,742	57	112,764	209	393,506
American, from foreign countries	271	205,475	183	338,753	454	544,228
American, from Atlantic ports of Union	24	46,010	...	...	24	46,010
Hawaiian	27	31,307	15	27,418	42	58,725
Norwegian	6	9,077	23	45,466	29	54,543
German	13	22,592	...	...	13	22,592
French	9	13,199	2	2,202	11	15,401
Italian	10	14,584	...	...	10	14,584
Others	6	5,604	3	3,822	9	9,426
Total	518	628,590	283	530,425	801	1,159,015
., for the year preceding	623	783,437	302	602,119	925	1,385,556

SAN FRANCISCO.

CLEARED.

Nationality.	Sailing. Number of Vessels.	Sailing. Tons.	Steam. Number of Vessels.	Steam. Tons.	Total. Number of Vessels.	Total. Tons.
British	193	360,472	56	109,223	249	469,695
American, to foreign countries	257	195,521	186	342,970	443	538,491
American, to Atlantic ports of Union	12	19,851	...	...	12	19,851
Hawaiian	27	29,484	18	29,254	45	58,738
Norwegian	4	5,917	23	45,466	27	51,383
German	15	24,053	...	...	15	24,053
French	9	12,517	1	1,101	10	13,618
Italian	9	13,398	...	...	9	13,398
Others	8	6,756	3	2,820	11	9,576
Total	534	667,969	287	530,834	821	1,198,803
,, for the year preceding	556	668,713	328	608,383	884	1,277,096

NOTE.—The entrances and clearances of American ships do not include the coasting trade, whaling or fishing voyages.

British shipping entered shows a heavy decrease in 1897 as compared with 1896, as will be seen from the following comparison of the two years:—

ENTERED.

Year.	Sailing. Number of Vessels.	Sailing. Tons.	Steam. Number of Vessels.	Steam. Tons.	Total. Number of Vessels.	Total. Tons.
1896	233	443,923	70	158,797	303	602,720
1897	152	280,742	57	112,764	209	393,506
Decrease	81	163,181	13	46,033	94	209,214

CLEARED.

Year.	Sailing. Number of Vessels.	Sailing. Tons.	Steam. Number of Vessels.	Steam. Tons.	Total. Number of Vessels.	Total. Tons.
1896	201	345,092	70	158,982	271	504,074
1897	193	360,472	56	109,223	249	469,695
Decrease	8	...	14	49,759	22	34,379

The decline may be attributed partly to the fact that freights ruled low during the first half of the year, and that few vessels were attracted to this port in consequence. When an active demand for tonnage sprung up it was pretty generally felt all over the world, and ships that would doubtless have come here were chartered for other business. The year 1896 was also an exceptionally large one, and the decrease therefore appears greater than it would if compared with an average season.

(225)

Vessels received much quicker despatch in the autumn of 1897 than in the year preceding, which accounts for the comparatively small decline in the number of vessels cleared.

American vessels trading with foreign countries show a decrease of 36 ships of 34,412 tons entered, and 43 ships of 50,714 tons cleared, as compared with 1896. Those to and from the Atlantic ports of the Union remain about the same.

German shipping shows a decrease of 6 vessels for 7,933 tons entered, and 6 vessels of 8,383 tons cleared. Italian shipping a decrease of 1 vessel of 2,470 tons entered, and 4 vessels of 6,198 tons cleared.

The following countries show increases:—Norwegian, 12 ships of 23,436 tons entered, and 8 ships of 16,242 tons cleared. Hawaiian, 10 ships of 16,031 tons entered, and 12 ships of 14,816 tons cleared. French, 3 ships of 5,166 tons entered, and 3 ships of 4,230 tons cleared.

The increase in French shipping which has taken place at this port in the last few years is attributed to the assistance it receives from the bounty system in vogue in that country.

Freights and charters. Freights ruled very low for the first six months of the year, as will be seen from the following table which is based on prices paid for spot ships to Cork for orders, Havre, Antwerp, or Dunkirk :—

Month.	From— £ s. d.	To— £ s. d.
January	0 16 3	0 16 6
February	0 16 3	0 16 4
March	0 16 3	0 16 3
April	0 17 6	0 17 6
May	1 0 0	1 0 0
June	0 18 0	0 19 10
July	1 1 3	1 3 9
August	1 2 6	1 7 6
September	1 6 3	1 10 0
October	1 7 6	1 11 3
November	1 11 3	1 11 3
December	1 15 0	1 15 0

In July considerable chartering was done from 1*l*. 3*s*. 3*d*. to 1*l*. 3*s*. 9*d*., the latter being the closing figure for the month. Ships which had been offering at 1*l*. 1*s*. 3*d*. and 1*l*. 2*s*. 6*d*. were withdrawn from the market and held for higher figures. At the close two vessels were chartered for Rio de Janeiro at 1*l*. 1*s*. 3*d*.; one for Callao at 15*s*., and three for Cape Town, all to carry wheat. In August a large amount of business was done in tonnage, and freights advanced from 1*l*. 2*s*. 6*d*. to 1*l*. 7*s*. 6*d*. net, closing firm at the latter quotation. Before the end of the month, however, freights came to a standstill and shippers withdrew entirely from the market. During the first part of September there was a large chartering business at from 1*l.* 6*s.* 3*d.* to 1*l.* 10*s.*, the bulk being done at 1*l.* 8*s.* 9*d.* The market was strengthened considerably by Tacoma and Portland taking several ships from here at 1*l.* 15*s.*, inducing owners to withdraw the remaining vessels and hold at 1*l.* 10*s.* to 1*l.* 11*s.* 3*d.* At the close, tonnage rates dropped to 1*l.* 7*s.* 6*d.* The market for freights in October was very active and the rates here advanced from 1*l.* 7*s.* 6*d.* to 1*l.* 11*s.* 3*d.* with but four disengaged ships in port, and near by ships all chartered to arrive at from 1*l.* 8*s.* 9*d.* to 1*l.* 10*s.* The strength of the market came from the north, where the requirements of tonnage were increased, day by day taking more ships from here at full rates, viz., 1*l.* 15*s.* to 1*l.* 17*s.* 6*d.*, and all tonnage to arrive by the end of December was also chartered at 1*l.* 17*s.* 6*d.* At the opening of November freights were firm, and after 1*l.* 11*s.* 3*d.* had been paid a scarcity of tonnage prevented further business. Subsequently a fleet of chartered vessels came in, which provided all shippers with ample tonnage for the time being. At the beginning of December a vessel was taken at 1*l.* 15*s.*, this being the top of the local freight market for the season. Several vessels were announced for December and January arrival at 1*l.* 13*s.* 9*d.* to 1*l.* 15*s.* The market subsequently came to a standstill.

Between 50 and 60 British vessels were laid up here during the spring and summer months, waiting for better freights, many of them being delayed for six months or more. A few of their owners were too eager to accept charters when the market began to rise, but the majority did well by holding off until freights got to a profitable figure.

Seamen's wages opened at 3*l.* per month, and remained at that figure until May. In that month they advanced to 4*l.*, which continued to be the price paid until the end of the year. *Seamen's wages.*

The large number of British vessels that had been laid up here during the spring and summer months, and that had reduced their crews to a minimum, caused a heavy demand for seamen in the autumn, when these vessels commenced to charter rapidly to move the new wheat crop. The men who had been discharged had drifted away to other places in search of employment, and many are supposed to have found their way north on account of the Klondike excitement. A great scarcity of seamen was the result, and fears were entertained that the iniquitous charge of "blood-money" would be imposed by the boarding-house masters before the season was over. Under the old conditions ruling here there is little doubt but that these fears would have been realised, but for the last two or three years a contract system for the supply of seamen for British vessels has been in force at this port. These contracts are made between the shipowners and the shipping agents here, the principal provisions being that no "bonus" or "blood-money" shall be charged; that the wages shall be the lowest obtainable, and that the advance shall not exceed a certain sum. The shipping agents experienced no great difficulty in fulfilling the terms of these contracts until this year, when, on account of *Scarcity of seamen.*

the great scarcity of men, their resources were taxed to the utmost. Fortunately, however, for the reputation of the port they were able to carry out the terms of their agreements, and get the vessels away without any extra expense beyond that entailed by a few days' delay necessitated in getting the requisite number of men together.

Seamen's Institute. The committee of management of the Seamen's Institute finds it difficult to raise funds for the needs of the institute, and it is well worthy of the support of British shipowners. Since it has been established it has been of great benefit to the seamen and apprentices visiting this port.

Fortnightly steamer service between the Pacific Coast and Australia. An arrangement has been entered into between the Oceanic Steamship Company of San Francisco, whose vessels run from here to Sydney, and the Canadian Pacific Company, whose vessels run from Vancouver, British Columbia, to Sydney, which ensures a fortnightly service between the Australian Colonies and this coast. The new schedule came into effect in February, 1898, and will afford much better communication with the colonies than heretofore. Efforts are being made to reduce the time for passage from 21 to 19 days.

New Japanese steamship line. It is reported that an agreement has been entered into between the Toyo Kisen Kwaisha (a Japanese steamship company) and the Pacific Mail and Occidental and Oriental Steamship Companies, under which the former will run a line of steamers between this city and the Orient on an equal footing with the two lines at present engaged in the traffic. The new line will consist of three modern steamers which are now being built in England, and which are expected to be ready for service next September. The addition of these steamers would make a total of 11 vessels in the Oriental trade, and as that is more than can be profitably employed, without a largely-increased volume of business, it is expected that some of the steamers of the existing lines will be taken off.

Proposed steamship line between Valparaiso and San Francisco. The establishment of a steamship line between Valparaiso and San Francisco is being discussed in the newspapers, and the names of the companies interested are said to be the Compañia Sud Americana de Vapores of Chile, and the Pacific Steam Navigation Company of Liverpool, which at present operate only to the South of Panama. The opportunity for invading the Northern Pacific is afforded by the expiration of an agreement with the Pacific Mail Steamship Company by which the business north and south of Panama was divided. One of the advantages to accrue to San Francisco if this line is established will be the opening of a market for mining machinery, a trade which has been almost exclusively enjoyed by eastern manufacturers through shipments to South America, viâ Panama. The line would also compete with the Pacific Mail for business between Mexico and Central America and this port.

Quarantine. The conflict between the Federal and State authorities over the quarantine service at this port, which was referred to in Mr. Warburton's report of last year, is still unsettled. In May, 1897, the President issued an order placing quarantine at San

Francisco entirely under Federal control. When this order came into effect the Federal officer's mode of procedure on visiting an incoming vessel was to visé both bills of health and seal them up in an envelope, which was delivered to the master of the ship with instructions to present it intact to the Collector of Customs, or entry of the vessel would be denied. As several ship masters refused to break the seals to exhibit the documents to the State officer, and proceeded to dock their vessels against his orders he commenced a suit against the master of one of the China steamers for violation of the State quarantine law. The case has recently been tried in one of the police courts of this city, and the judge decided that the passengers and crews of all foreign vessels touching at this port must submit to an inspection by the State quarantine officer and receive his certificate of free pratique before being allowed to land, otherwise the masters of such vessels, together with their pilots, will find themselves subject to arrest by the local police and fine or imprisonment, or both. The case will be appealed to a higher court.

A large new ferry-boat is being built to accommodate the constantly-increasing traffic across the bay to Oakland, Alameda, and Berkeley. The new vessel is designed to be one of the largest and most handsome passenger ferry-steamers in existence, and will be propelled by two screws, one at each end of the vessel attached to the same shaft. This arrangement requires the forward screw to perform an action equivalent to pulling the boat while the rear screw, revolving in the same direction, will help to urge her forward. When the new vessel is completed the service is likely to be increased to three boats hourly during the busy part of the day. *Improved ferry service.*

The new ferry building, which was fully described in last year's report, is rapidly approaching completion. When this building is finished, and the space in front of it cleared of the old wooden structures that obstruct the view, it will prove quite an addition to the large number of handsome buildings that have been erected in this city in the last few years. *Ferry building.*

Shipbuilding was very inactive in 1897, most of the vessels turned out being small schooners or steamers for service on the coast. Owing to the impetus given by the Klondike gold excitement and increased trade with Alaska there will probably be more activity in this line during the present year. *Shipbuilding.*

The catch of the Arctic whaling fleet during the last two years, reported at San Francisco, is as follows:— *Catch of whaling fleet.*

Year.	Quantity.		
	Oil.	Bone.	Ivory.
	Barrels.	Lbs.	Lbs.
1896	7 057	201,997	6,640
1897	5,929	142,326	5,223

Reference was made in last year's report to a Bill *Pilotage charges.*

to reduce pilotage charges, which had been defeated in the last State Legislature. The supporters of this measure claimed that improper methods had been used to defeat the Bill and called the attention of the County Grand Jury to the matter last November. An attempt was made to investigate the books of the pilots, but the expert of the Grand Jury was refused access to them on the ground that the Pilot Commissioners being officers of the State, their appointees, the pilots, were not accountable to that body. I understand that another effort will be made to get these charges reduced when the next State Legislature assembles in 1899.

Effects of the Klondike gold discoveries on shipping.

The news of gold discoveries on the Klondike reached this city last year at a time that was considered unpropitious to make the journey, and only comparatively few extra vessels were put into the trade in addition to the regular liners. Early in 1898, however, the rush commenced in earnest, and by the middle of February there were engaged in the Alaska trade, or coming to this coast for that purpose, 125 steam and sailing vessels ranging from 60 to 2,500 tons register. One of the liners employed in the trade between this port and Honolulu was taken off and chartered for Alaska, and even a wrecking vessel was transformed and pressed into the service. Every available coaster was removed from its regular route and turned into a passenger vessel, with the result that many of the smaller coast ports that are dependent on steam service for communication with the outside world suffered on account of inadequate transportation facilities. It was feared that it would be difficult to obtain tonnage to maintain the coaling stations of Dutch Harbour, Ounalaska, and St. Michael, but traffic fell off materially in March and April and a great many vessels returned to their old lines of travel.

The demand for tonnage resulted in a considerable raising of rates all round for a time with the exception of grain freights, for which service there is little demand at present, owing to the dry season which makes the outlook for the next crop very uncertain.

Lightship for the Golden Gate.

The whistling buoy which has long served to mark the entrance to this harbour has lately been replaced by a lightship which was specially built for the purpose. Powerful electric lights are swung in ball and socket hinges, one at each masthead, 50 feet above the deck of the vessel, and in clear weather will be visible for a distance of 12 to 15 miles. The vessel is also fitted with a fog-horn and a large bell to aid in giving signals in thick weather.

Trade and commerce.

The following table shows the amount and principal articles of export and import for the years 1896-97.

SAN FRANCISCO.

Annex B.—RETURN of Principal Articles of Export from San Francisco during the Years 1897-96.

		1897.		1896.	
Articles.		Quantity.	Value.	Quantity.	Value.
			£		£
Wheat and flour	Centals	11,859,892	3,556,832	15,722,825	3,734,010
Barley	,,	3,164,558	613,924	3,852,455	639,507
Tinned salmon	Cases	612,858	492,702	579,967	483,423
,, fruit and vegetables	,,	332,608	216,904	373,737	247,645
Timber	Feet	25,838,195	94,301	33,576,556	129,872
Wine	Gallons	883,445	79,443	937,874	91,610
Quicksilver	Flasks	5,464	42,073	9,494	63,515
Hops	Lbs.	578,706	13,104	1,350,180	15,276
Brandy	Gallons	8,773	2,086	42,492	8,593
Other articles		...	3,035,872	...	2,673,298
Total merchandise	...	...	8,147,241	...	8,086,749
Treasure	...	...	3,751,267	...	3,102,166
Grand total	...	...	11,898,508	...	11,188,915

RETURN of Principal Articles of Import to San Francisco during the Years 1897-96.

		1897.		1896.	
Articles.		Quantity.	Value.	Quantity.	Value.
			£		£
Raw silk	Lbs.	4,325,560	2,366,659	2,067,379	1,218,007
Sugar	Tons	146,910	1,934,188	163,159	2,432,414
Coal	,,	867,500	1,041,000	898,000	898,000
Coffee	Lbs.	19,212,004	612,278	18,895,057	590,946
Tea	,,	14,172,700	398,202	5,515,385	141,165
Rice	Tons	18,759	252,121	19,441	151,995
Tin-plates	Boxes	277,270	143,181	342,688	169,410
Cement	Barrels	225,168	58,523	343,013	90,943
Pig-iron	Tons	4,006	9,673	8,189	20,720
Other articles		...	1,353,533	...	1,569,372
Total merchandise	...	...	8,169,358	...	7,282,972
Treasure	...	...	2,756,460	...	2,372,885
Grand total	...	...	10,925,818	...	9,655,857

Exports. The exports of merchandise show an increase of 60,492*l*. as compared with 1896, and the exports of treasure an increase of 649,101*l*. on the year preceding.

Wheat and flour. The exports of both wheat and flour are the smallest since 1894, and show a heavy decrease as compared with 1896. Great Britain took 7,454,925 centals of wheat out of a total shipment of 9,250,591 centals. The heaviest shipments of flour were made to China and Central America, but Great Britain took 103,087 barrels. Prices ruled considerably higher than for many years, No. 1 shipping wheat opening at 1 dol. 53¾ c. per cental in January, going up to 1 dol. 56¼ c. in September, and closing at 1 dol. 41¼ c. at the end of the year.

Barley. The exports of barley show a heavy decline as compared with 1896. The crop was a good one and prices were satisfactory to the farmers. The bulk of the exports went to Great Britain.

Tinned salmon.

The exports of salmon show a fair increase over the year 1896. Great Britain took 503,948 cases out of the total shipment of 612,858. The amount sent overland was the heaviest since 1894. The following is an estimate of the total Pacific coast pack prepared by Messrs. Taylor, Young, and Co., of Portland, Oregon:—

	Quantity.
	Cases.*
Columbia River	518,200
Sacramento River	41,000
Rogue River	19,008
Coast rivers and bays	48,655
Willapa and Gray's Harbours	37,500
Puget Sound	491,100
British Columbia	1,034,800
Alaska	907,400
Total	3,097,663

* A case contains 48 1-lb. tins.

Tinned fruit and vegetables.

The exports of fruit and vegetables show a decline as compared with 1896. Prices were very low at the opening of the season and stocks had run down to a minimum. Owing to the general revival of business and a partial failure of the fruit crop in the Eastern States, a heavy demand sprang up suddenly, and in July and August the sales of California canned fruit exceeded those made in any corresponding period. Prices advanced rapidly and were well maintained to the end of the year.

There were 38 canneries in operation in California last year, and the following is an estimate of the pack, prepared by a leading canner:—

Articles.	Quantity.
	Cases.
Tomatoes	348,000
Asparagus	81,500
Peas	30,000
Beans and other vegetables	8,500
Pie fruit	30,000
Jams and jellies	8,000
Table fruits	1,920,000
Total	2,426,000

In the last five or six years the cost of the production of canned fruit has declined about one-third, owing to the fall in the price of most of the commodities used in its manufacture. Except in seasons of great scarcity of fruit these reduced prices are likely to be maintained, and this fact will no doubt be welcome news to the people of Great Britain who have become such large consumers of canned goods.

Timber. The exports of timber show a heavy decrease as compared with 1896. Great Britain was the best customer, taking 10,202,496 feet out of a total shipment of 25,838,195 feet. Prices ruled low during the entire year, the supply exceeding the demand, which was very limited on account of the dulness in the building trades.

Wine. The exports of wine show a decided falling-off as compared with 1896, but the shipments to the Eastern States have increased materially. Prices were extremely unsatisfactory to the producers.

Quicksilver. The exports of quicksilver were little more than one half those of 1896, but the shipments by rail to the Eastern States were considerably heavier. After adding the two together, however, the amount which left the State shows a decrease over the year preceding. Prices showed an advance.

Hops. The exports of hops shrank to less than half those of 1896, but shipments by rail increased in a very satisfactory manner. The amount which left the State was consequently considerably greater than in the year preceding. Prices were eminently satisfactory to the growers.

Brandy. The brandy exports were only about one-fifth of those of 1896, but the overland shipments show a substantial increase. Prices sympathised with those of wine and were unremunerative.

Other articles in regard to wheat, barley, fruit, brandy and wine will be found under the head of agriculture.

Imports. The imports of merchandise show the substantial increase of 886,386*l.* as compared with 1896, and the imports of treasure an increase of 383,575*l.* The increase in the imports of merchandise was largely owing to improved trade relations with Japan and China, and the increase in the treasure is accounted for by the large amount shipped to this port from Australia.

Coal. The imports of foreign coal in 1897 were as follows:—

From—	Quantity.
	Tons.
British Columbia	418,600
Australia	234,400
Great Britain	141,600
Other sources	72,900
Total	867,500

The amount of foreign coal imported was 30,500 tons less than the year preceding. Besides the above we received 518,200 tons from Seattle and Tacoma, bringing out total receipts up to 1,385,700 tons, a considerable increase over 1896.

The highest price paid for British coal based on "spot cargoes" was 7 dol. 25 c. per ton against 6 dol. 75 c. in 1896, and the lowest price was 6 dol. 10 c. against 5 dol. 5 c.

The following remarks are taken from the annual circular of a leading coal broker:—"The fuel consumption of California this year is about 7 per cent. greater than in 1896, which evidences that the outgoing year has been a fairly profitable one for some of our manufacturing branches. Consumers were favoured with low-priced coal the first half of this year but the Dingley tariff went into effect in July, causing an advance on all grades equal to the change of the duty; this change cut a small figure with housekeepers and small consumers, but it is a serious detriment to those industries where fuel is the principal factor in their expense account. Coal freights from Australia and Great Britain have ruled high for several months past, thus aiding to sustain full figures, as our coast colliery managers regulate their scale of prices by the import cost of Colonial and English; hence this year has proved a very profitable one for our northern coalfields. It is a query how the local market will shape itself in 1898; there is no doubt as to the ability of British Columbia and Washington to fully supply us with all the fuel we may need, in case foreign shipments should diminish, but the indications are visible of probable labour troubles when the Klondike exodus commences, and the writer predicts that all grades of labourers will catch the fever. Even if no trouble emanates from that source, there will certainly be a sparsity of vessels for transporting coal, as they will assuredly drift into the more profitable business of carrying freight and passengers towards the Alaskan goldfields. It is true this will last for only a few months, but of sufficient duration to materially affect fuel values within that brief period."

The new tariff, which put a duty on anthracite coal, is likely to seriously interfere with the trade of shipping Welsh anthracite to this market.

Coke. The total imports of coke in 1897 were 30,320 tons, being 5,812 tons less than in 1896. Of this, 2,573 tons came from British Columbia and 1,889 tons from Australia; these are two new sources of supply for this market. I understand that the plant in British Columbia, where some of the above-mentioned coke was manufactured, is being enlarged to double its present capacity, and it is likely that the imports from England and Belgium will be affected by this enterprise as soon as it gets into full running order.

Tin-plates. The imports of tin-plates show a heavy decline as compared with 1896, 65,418 boxes less than that year having been received. These articles are being manufactured in the Eastern States in increasing quantities, and as heavy consignments are shipped to this market they are rapidly superseding the imported plates. It is said that they can be laid down here for 1 dol. per box less than the foreign ones, and it is only a question of time when they will entirely displace them. I understand that the imported article is now principally used in packing goods intended for export, in which case a drawback on the duty is allowed.

Cement. The imports of cement show a decrease of 117,845 barrels as compared with 1896. Belgium supplied the greatest amount as will be seen from the following figures taken from the custom-house records:—

Country.	Quantity.
	Lbs.
Belgium	40,015,610
Great Britain	30,191,656
Germany	17,694,800
France	1,764
Total	87,903,830

The past year cannot be said to have been a very active one, although there was a fairly steady demand for most descriptions during the year. It is expected that the market will take an increasing quantity, but there is always enough on hand to meet any demand that may be made. As will be noticed from the above figures Great Britain has fallen to the second place in supplying this market. This, I am told by importers here, is entirely owing to the course pursued by the producers. It is alleged that after supplying a certain quantity at a price agreed upon they will ask an advance on a further consignment of the same brand. Dealers here have become so disgusted with this method of doing business that they have transferred their orders to Belgian and German firms who can be relied on to supply any quantity of a certain quality at a fixed price. The quality of the British article is said to be quite satisfactory, and the only reason given for its losing ground is the unsatisfactory way it is handled by the British producer.

Pig-iron. The imports of pig-iron were less than one-half those of 1896. The prices were the lowest on record, and it is said that it could only have been laid down here at a loss; 6,015 tons were received from the Eastern States.

Chemicals. Owing to the extended operations of the chemical manufacturers of the Eastern States, and the increase in the duty under the new tariff, the importation of chemicals into this market is likely to fall off materially.

The following table shows the volume of trade with each country:—

| Table of exports and imports. | Annex C.—TABLE showing Total Value of all Articles Exported from and Imported to San Francisco to and from Foreign Countries during the Years 1897-96. |

	Exports.		Imports.	
Country.	1897.	1896.	1897.	1896.
	£	£	£	£
Great Britain	3,488,926	3,194,639	484,789	645,056
Hawaiian Isles	960,854	737,412	1,990,157	2,384,651
China	789,654	655,793	1,471,831	1,067,222
Japan	607,679	495,304	2,001,518	1,097,905
Australasia	513,882	1,028,468	152,131	134,520
Central America	485,238	683,892	539,656	488,837
South Africa	335,898	209,790	..	..
Mexico	269,005	289,722	74,703	62,608
Belgium	163,376	120,740	168,957	132,037
Canada	122,359	86,374	357,937	356,395
South America	96,979	53,443	113,537	113,182
France	96,702	18,621	126,175	153,192
Asiatic Russia	75,485	113,619	22,208	39,988
Pacific Islands	74,642	78,162	73,594	52,462
East Indies	31,215	142,654	339,229	245,888
Germany	4,073	15,427	131,885	213,047
Italy	..	..	29,470	29,616
Other countries	31,274	162,689	91,581	66,366
Total merchandise	8,147,241	8,086,749	8,169,358	7,282,972
Treasure	3,751,267	3,102,166	2,756,460	2,372,885
Grand total	11,898,508	11,188,915	10,925,818	9,655,857

NOTE.—The imports by rail, included in the above totals of merchandise, amounted to 344,876*l.* in 1897, as against 413,725*l.* in 1896.

The exports to Great Britain show an increase of 294,287*l.*, and the imports from Great Britain a decrease of 160,267*l.*; as compared with 1896. The majority of wheat vessels clear for Cork for orders, and the value of their cargoes is included in the exports to Great Britain, although some of them receive orders on arrival there to proceed to Continental ports to discharge. On this account the exports to Great Britain are probably considerably less than the amount that appears in the above table.

Decline of British trade.

As Germany and Belgium are the principal competitors of Great Britain in this market, I have prepared the following table which gives a comparison of the import and export trade of all three countries to and from San Francisco during the last 10 years:—

Year.	Great Britain.		Germany.		Belgium.	
	Imports.	Exports.	Imports.	Exports.	Imports.	Exports.
	£	£	£	£	£	£
1888...	1,169,826	3,682,200	201,709	22,608	184,455	50,362
1889...	926,916	3,845,683	235,953	13,799	118,531	41,234
1890...	937,064	3,329,246	231,201	39,459	145,175	214,716
1891...	1,023,976	3,491,887	273,568	28,279	152,447	370,605
1892...	897,359	3,831,688	170,793	46,576	171,515	76,817
1893...	853,688	3,251,786	149,737	37,615	128,704	20,005
1894...	534,433	1,931,332	123,156	65,700	96,868	788
1895...	774,315	2,907,846	188,362	17,480	124,403	...
1896...	645,056	3,194,639	213,047	15,427	132,037	120,740
1897...	484,789	3,488,926	131,885	4,073	168,957	163,376

Comparing the year 1897 with the year 1888 it will be found that the imports from Great Britain show a loss of 58·56 per cent., German imports a loss of 34·61 per cent., and Belgian imports a loss of 8·40 per cent. In comparing the imports of last year with those of the year 1896 we get the following results:—

British imports show a loss of 24·84 per cent., German imports a loss of 38·09 per cent., while the imports from Belgium show a gain of 27·96 per cent.

It will be noticed that the exports to both Germany and Belgium are insignificant when compared with those to Great Britain.

In making inquiries about various descriptions of merchandise during the past year, the following information that will be of interest to British manufacturers came into my possession:—

Woollens and dress goods. Plain woollen goods for ladies, tailor-made suits, and all kinds of serges are largely imported from the United Kingdom; the latter are also being made in this country. The serges made in England for dress goods are only 46 inches wide; the American-made serges are 52 and 54 inches wide, and on that account command a more ready sale, though the English serges are otherwise preferred.

Underwear. Underwear is almost all of German manufacture in the cheaper grades. The higher-priced is French. Very little comes from the United Kingdom. German goods are said to be more showy for the price. If British manufacturers would only take the trouble to study the requirements of the local market in these matters they would probably be able to compete.

Hosiery and stockings. Importations of hosiery from Great Britain have fallen off a good deal in the past few years, and these articles have been coming from Germany.

Linens. Linens have been coming from Germany for the last three or four years, and they are beginning to monopolise the trade. To hold the business and recover lost ground the British manufacturer must be able to produce a more showy article at a lower price than he does at present. German goods make a better show and command a readier sale, though they do not wear as well as the British article. The British manufacturers will lose the trade in cheap linen goods unless they pay more attention to designs.

(225)

Laces, silk, and cotton.

Very little lace from the United Kingdom comes to this market. British designs are generally inferior to French and Swiss. If the British manufacturers would improve in this respect and sell their goods at the same price as others, they could no doubt gain a share of the local trade.

Curtains and bed covers.

Lace curtains have been coming from England but are being displaced by those from Switzerland. The Swiss makes are very showy and cheaper than the British. Bed covers come from England to a considerable extent, but are now being made in this country.

Gloves.

Gloves were formerly imported principally from Great Britain. The leather gloves are now coming largely from France and the fabric ones from Germany.

China.

A large quantity of French china is now being imported. The prices have been reduced, and as the decoration is very tasteful it meets with ready sale. It is of much lighter make than the English, and this is often preferred. It is thought that if British manufacturers would send a similar class of goods here they would take a greater share of the trade.

Cutlery.

An extensive dealer in cutlery in this city informs me that there are only two brands of English pocket knives that are sold here to any extent. These are the "Rodgers" and "Wostenholms." German pocket knives are extensively sold, particularly the cheaper grades, but under the new tariff it is expected that domestic goods will come more into use. The Germans are said to have captured the razor trade of the United States, and very few English makes are offered for sale here. Most of the table cutlery is of domestic manufacture, said to be on account of the superior designs. American manufacturers are constantly putting new patterns on the market and striving to catch the public taste. Scissors for ladies' use are almost entirely supplied from Germany, and my informant was unable to give a satisfactory reason (except the way their sale was pushed) as he said he had never had the opportunity to compare them with English makes. The large-sized scissors and shears sold here are of domestic manufacture.

Lack of British commercial travellers.

In the course of conversation he informed me that no travellers representing British firms ever visit San Francisco. A traveller from New York representing a German cutlery firm comes here twice a year, and appears to be building up a good business judging from the number of German goods that are offered for sale in the stores. British manufacturers seem quite content to sell their goods through agents in one of the large Eastern cities, and firms desiring to replenish their stocks of British goods have to forward their orders there or purchase by use of a catalogue.

If British cutlery firms that have agencies in the Eastern States would employ one or two active travellers of engaging manners, thoroughly conversant with the American way of doing business, there is no doubt they would find it greatly to their advantage. The field to operate in on the Pacific coast is limited on account of the small population, but they could be kept constantly busy in other parts of the country, and it would only be necessary to visit this coast occasionally.

A reliable firm of silversmiths in San Francisco informs me that the sale of English silver and plate could certainly be increased here were it not for what appears to be the stubbornness of the English manufacturers in ignoring the particular requirements of the American market, and assuming that what suits an English customer should be equally satisfactory to an American. One simple example of this is the custom of stamping the hall mark on the outside of mounts for leather goods. American makers stamp their mark on the inside, where it is not readily discernible. American purchasers consider the hall mark on the outside a disfigurement, especially on plain mounts. German and Austrian makers take pains to avoid these annoyances to their American clients. An alteration in English methods of handling the American market would probably result in largely increased trade. *English silver and electroplate.*

I have noticed the same fault with British cutlery, particularly with table knives, which are frequently stamped with a large trade mark as well as a design containing the maker's name, and much disfigured thereby in the opinion of many buyers.

Judging from the large amount of cotton that arrives here from the Southern States, consigned principally to Japan, the cotton spinners of that country must be extending their operations considerably. The amount of cotton received here from November 1 to December 7, 1897, was 30,550 bales, while the entire shipments for the year ending October 31, 1897, only amounted to 37,000 bales, so that it will be seen that the tonnage handled during the short period above mentioned was entirely out of proportion to the tonnage handled during the previous 12 months. A large quantity of flour continues to be sent to China, where its use is extending among the natives. Every steamer carries a considerable shipment of nails to Japan, some of local manufacture, but more that come from the Eastern States. In the last year or two an innovation has been made by shipping large rolls of paper to Japan, such as is suitable for newspaper printing, and which is said to be displacing paper of European manufacture. *Trade with the Orient.*

At the end of 1896 an effort was made to improve the commercial relations existing between the Pacific Coast and Japan, and with that object in view an agent was sent to Yokohama in the interest of local business men. This gentleman was provided with samples of Californian products, but found it more difficult to extend their sale than had been anticipated, and after a year's residence in Japan he returned to this country. *Efforts to increase the trade in Californian products.*

The Klondike gold discoveries have had a marked effect upon the business of the coast, not so much by means of the treasure brought down as on account of the purchases made by men who left here for the gold fields. Should the good news from *Effect of the Klondike gold discoveries on trade.*

that district continue and Alaska and the north-west territories justify the sanguine hopes that now prevail, the region will remain a tributary one to the Pacific Coast States and British Columbia. It is considered certain that under any conditions Alaska cannot become self-supporting, as the greater part of it is in the latitude of Greenland, where only the hardiest vegetables can be raised. Clothing, food, mining supplies, and almost all the things which a resident finds requisite for his comfort will have to be drawn from this part of the coast, no matter how many people make their homes in the far north. Another advantage which is likely to be felt is the chance for the unemployed to obtain work. For several years past there have been a considerable number of people constantly out of employment in this State, and many of them who are able to raise sufficient funds for the purpose will find their way to Alaska. Last year the bulk of the traffic passed through Seattle and Tacoma, on Puget Sound, and that continues to be the favourite route, although great efforts have been made by the business community of this city to induce emigrants to pass through San Francisco, and make this city their outfitting point. With this object in view an exhibition of suitable articles was opened here during the past winter, and pamphlets have been widely distributed giving advice to travellers to Alaska regarding the goods required for the journey and residence there.

Manufactures.

The manufacturing interests of this coast are not in a very flourishing condition. Although wages have decreased somewhat in the last few years, coal is still very high as compared with the Eastern States, and our manufacturers are severely handicapped on that occount. The Manufacturers and Producers Association has lately drawn attention to the heavy discrimination against Californian producers on account of the much higher rate of freight ruling on goods shipped from here to the Eastern States, as compared with the rates on the same commodities bound to Western terminals. An effort will be made to induce the railroad companies to adjust this difference.

Clearing house.

The report of the manager of the clearing-house gives the bank clearings for the last two years as follows:—

	Amount.
	£
Clearings for 1897	150,157,829
,, 1896	136,645,920
Increase for 1897	13,511,909

The gain is attributed principally to the increase in the value of wheat which occurred in 1897, and to the business depression which prevailed in 1896, in consequence of the agitation for the free coinage of silver, which affected the clearings for that year.

As evidence of business enterprise in this city, I would state that several of the large retail shoe dealers now undertake to clean the shoes of their customers free of expense, and keep an employé in attendance especially for that purpose. A large number of the residents of San Francisco reside in lodgings or boarding houses, but it is not the custom here, as it is in England, to include the cleaning of shoes in their charges. This innovation will consequently prove of some benefit and convenience to such persons, as the usual charge for this service at the street stands is $2\frac{1}{2}d$. One or two of the larger stores also furnish their customers with shoe laces free of cost. *Enterprise in the shoe trade.*

The benefit the insurance companies have derived from the compact formed last year is shown in the reports of California fire business for 1897 made to the State Insurance Commissioner. I have obtained the figures for last year from the preliminary report of that official, and the following table will afford a comparison with the preceding two years. *Fire insurance.*

Year.	Amount Written.	Premiums.	Losses Paid.	Ratio of Losses to Premiums.
	Dollars.	Dollars.	Dollars.	Per cent.
1897	324,254,126	4.767,019	2,637,706	55·3
1896	336,334,238	3,817,315	2,645,595	69·3
1895	358,759,159	4,704,584	2,850,672	60·6

It will be noticed from the above that the premiums received in 1897 exceeded those of either of the two previous years, while the amount written was considerably less. The loss ratio was the lowest since 1894.

In last year's report reference was made to an Act passed at the last session of the State Legislature, which provided for a fully-paid fire department for San Francisco. Under the present system the firemen are employed at various occupations in the neighbourhood of a fire station with the exception of two or three of the principal employés. Time is frequently lost before a full crew can be got together, and it was to abolish this method that the Act referred to was introduced. So far the supervisors have not appropriated funds to put the law into effect, and consequently the insurance companies have not felt able to make the full reduction in rates that they contemplated at the time of its passage. *Fire department.*

Messrs. Wells, Fargo and Co.'s annual statement of the precious metals produced in the States and Territory within the jurisdiction of this Consulate-General for the year 1897 is as follows:— *Mining. Production of precious metals.*

	Gold Dust and Bullion by Express.	Gold Dust and Bullion by other Conveyances.	Silver Bullion by Express.	Ores and Base Metal by Freight.	Total.
	£	£	£	£	£
California	2,509,353	1,015,039	2,590	239,183	3,766,165
Nevada	258,192	268,275	90,292	46,810	663,569
Utah	159,688	172,962	162,750	1,354,088	1,849,488
Arizona	311,175	367,423	28,739	1,739,764	2,447,101
Total	3,238,408	1,823,699	284,371	3,379,845	8,726,323

The fact that attracts the most attention in the abovementioned statement is the corroboration it affords to the estimate made recently by the director of the mint that California had at length been deposed from its proud position as the greatest gold-producing State of the Union. Colorado, hitherto the great silver-producing State, has now become the premier gold producer also. After deducting the silver production of these two States there remains to the credit of Colorado the sum of 4,425,409*l*., and to California the sum of 3,763,575*l*., showing a surplus in favour of the former of 661,834*l*. California shows an increase in the gold production of 1897 over the year preceding of 654,065*l*., but Colorado has increased its output in a much more rapid manner on account of the opening up of the mines in the Cripple Creek District.

The exports of silver from this port for China, Japan, &c., during the past year amounted to 2,231,240*l*., against 1,989,555*l*. in 1896.

Hydraulic mining. The annual report of the California Debris Commission made up to June 30, 1897, shows that since its organisation in March, 1893, the Commission has received 311 applications to mine, and has granted 238 permits. Eight permits have been cancelled, and 28 permits have been at different times suspended, generally on account of the neglect of the owners to comply with instructions concerning the impounding works, or from accidents to those works. The total amount of material mined under permits during the year is estimated at 1,256,910 cubic yards. The available storage provided at present and partially or wholly completed for future operations is estimated at 11,000,000 cubic yards. No dam for impounding detritus in the larger streams has as yet been authorised by the Commission.

Mining dam destroyed. The Big Golden Feather Dam which was erected a few years ago by an English Mining Company on the Feather River, near Oroville in Butte County, California, has been destroyed by order of the owners, as it did not serve the purpose for which it was built. The dam raised the river 37 feet, and backed it up for a distance of two miles, so that it was impossible to work the bed of the stream above the dam. In order that the stream might be lowered it was necessary to blow out this dam, which is said to have been built at a cost of over 20,000*l*. It is reported that the company intends to build one or more dams higher up the river in order to get at the bed of the stream which is said to be rich in gold bearing gravel.

Of late years there has been a gratifying revival in the gold-mining industry. In the short space of five years the production of gold in this State has risen from 2,484,562*l*., where it stood in 1893, to 3,763,575*l.* for 1897, and it is estimated that from 60 to 70 per cent. of this amount is derived from quartz mining. Many old mines long abandoned or worked irregularly have been thoroughly opened and developed, while the exploration of favourable prospects has been vigorously pushed. A very large number of quartz mines are paying well, some of them so well that their returns are kept secret. Improvements in machinery and in the working of ores, the saving of the sulphurets, which in early days were suffered to run to waste, and the use of water power and electricity are among the reasons why mines, once supposed to be worked out or unprofitable, are now operated with satisfactory returns. Nothing but comparatively high grade quartz was worked in early days, while now satisfactory returns are had from ore so poor that at one time it would have been regarded as worthless. Ores are considered low grade in this State when they run from 2½ dol. to 6 or 8 dol. per ton, and high grade from 15 dol. upwards. The average may be put at from 10 to 12 dol. Gold-mining is becoming more of an industry and less of a speculation or gamble year by year, and nothing has conduced to this result more than the modern method of acquiring mining property, which I propose to describe for the benefit of intending British investors.

Quartz mining.

In former times if a mine owner wished to dispose of his property, and was fortunate enough to come into contact with a purchaser commanding capital he simply named his price, and after an examination of the mine, if they came to terms, the money was paid over in a lump sum. This method threw all the risk upon the purchaser, and in the event of the mine not turning out according to his expectations he had no recourse but to enter the investment on his books as a total loss. Attempts are still made to sell mines to inexperienced capitalists under these conditions, but intending purchasers would do well to insist on obtaining more modern terms, that is in securing a bond or option on the property they contemplate acquiring, which would give them ample time to examine it thoroughly, and even work it at the risk of a comparatively small amount of money. In a cases intending purchasers should have full time to examine the property and title, and if there is a mill in the neighbourhood they should be allowed to take out sufficient ore to make a mill test. The intending purchasers should of course put their own men in the mine and mill to extract and treat the ore, and allow no one connected with the owners or their friends to have anything to do with the handling of the ore or in cleaning up the gold from the mill. If after the examination and mill test the intending purchasers are still satisfied with the property, they should be able to secure, if the mine is not a producing one (*i.e.*, if it is still in the form of a prospect) a bond or option for six months, or even a year, before paying 1 c. to the owner. On

Modern methods of acquiring mining property.

the other hand intending purchasers show their good faith by incorporating in the bond an obligation that they shall keep a certain number of men constantly at work on the property for a certain time, and shall do the work in a miner-like fashion. If at the expiration of their bond they have proved the mine to be a valuable one, they can pay the purchase price. If, on the contrary, they are not satisfied with the property they can throw up the bond, and they are only out of pocket the money they have expended in developing the property, while the owner has been benefited to the extent of this development.

If, however, the property is a producer, *i.e.*, if there is a mill on it and the owners have been extracting gold, the conditions of the bond would be somewhat different. The owners in that case would insist on a certain payment down. For instance, suppose the price asked for the mine was 20,000*l*.; the intending purchasers should procure a bond from the owners, prior to making the mill test and examination which should allow them one month for such purpose. If, after this, they are satisfied with the property, and in the meantime the title has been declared valid by the lawyer employed by them to examine same, they would probably have to make a payment to the owners of 1,000*l*. They should then be placed in possession of the property. Three months after acquiring the property they would probably have to pay 2,000*l*., and continue making such payments every three months thereafter until the whole amount was paid. The product of the mine might also have to go to the owners, but in that case it should be credited on account of the purchase price. Should any payments not be made at the time specified the purchasers would forfeit all right and their bond would become null and void. In making a bond the intending buyer should exercise great care not to bind himself to take the property but only to take an option to purchase. This bond can be placed in escrow together with the title deeds, if ready for delivery, in a responsible bank, with a memorandum containing the conditions printed on the envelope, so that the bank's officers will know when the conditions are fulfilled, that is, when the stated amount of money has been paid into the bank to the credit of the owner of the property. When that has been done the bank should hand over to the purchasers the bond and title deeds, which will then place them in full possession of the property. The conditions of many bonds differ somewhat from those described above, but of course in dealing with a mine owner an intending purchaser has to make the best terms possible.

Principal reasons why British mining investments are unfortunate.

The history of the majority of British mining investments in California has been one of misfortune, attributable largely to unbusinesslike methods in acquiring or working the properties, and to other causes, the principal ones of which may be enumerated as follows:—

Investing in mines that are fully developed and on a dividend-paying basis. While such properties are of course very desirable when they can be procured at a reasonable figure and are not worked out, they require a large amount of capital, as the owners are naturally loth to part with them, except at a very high figure, and there is a considerable risk that the mine has seen its best days. Partially developed mines which can be acquired under the bonding system at a small outlay afford a much safer field to operate in, as only sufficient capital is required to open up the property, and if it fails to justify expectations, work can be abandoned at any time at small loss.

In neglecting to have properties thoroughly examined by competent and independent experts before closing the bargain. One instance of this came to my notice where a glib-talker went to England and succeeded in selling a mine to a syndicate of capitalists who took no steps to have it examined on their own behalf. Needless to say that the property turned out to be utterly worthless, and that after sinking considerable money in the concern they threw it up in disgust. In this connection I would say that the first and most important step that can be taken is to have a mine thoroughly examined by independent experts, and that experience has shown the wisdom of depending for advice in mining matters in California upon men who have a practical knowledge of the geological formation of the mineral deposits in the different districts of the State. It has been found safer to trust to their opinions, as conditions here are different from those encountered in other parts of the world, and have frequently misled men of reputation sent here as experts, who would probably be safe and competent authorities in the countries in which they had acquired experience.

In sending out men to manage mining properties who have had no practical experience in the business. Cases have occurred where expensive mills have been erected before a mine has been sufficiently developed to ascertain whether there was sufficient ore in sight to warrant such a course, and mills that have been so erected, and scarcely put to any use, have been sold for less than one quarter of their first cost.

Probably the greatest cause of the disaster to British mining investments is the over-capitalisation of such concerns by London promoters. Only recently attention has been called to an attempt to float a group of California mines in London for 280,000*l.*, which was bonded here by the promoters for less than 20,000*l.* The property had some merit as a low-grade ore proposition, and would have probably proved a profitable investment if capitalised in accordance with its present appearances, and under an honest and capable management. Such schemes as this work incalculable injury to the mining interests of California. Almost all the successful and profitable mines of this State have been worked either by individuals or by close corporations in the same careful spirit of common sense and economy that prevails in a large manufacturing concern.

The health officer's last report, which is made up for the year ending June 30, 1897, classifies the deaths in this city as follows :— *Population and industry.*

Description.	Number of Deaths.
Zymotic diseases	469
Constitutional diseases	1,395
Local diseases	3,287
Developmental diseases	550
Violent deaths	449
Total	6,150

With regard to the mortality tables the Board calls attention to several interesting facts. The total increase in the number of deaths over the fiscal year ending June 30, 1896, is 184. Notwithstanding this increase, the number of deaths resulting from pulmonary tuberculosis has been considerably reduced, there having been during the fiscal year ending June 30, 1896, 1,003 deaths from this disease, while during the last year only 896 deaths were recorded. This shows a decrease of 107, which may be attributed to the following preventive measures:—

Decrease of deaths from pulmonary tuberculosis.

The improved condition of dairy herds in this and the neighbouring counties, the inspection of herds for tuberculosis, the inspection of all milk at the different food stations, the inspection of meat in slaughter-houses and butchers' shops, and the improved sanitary condition of private residences, together with the gradual awakening of the public to the knowledge of the danger always present from association with tubercular patients.

Death rate. The percentage of deaths is given at 17·08 per 1,000 on an estimated population of 360,000.

Marriages and births. The number of marriages registered last year was 3,126, and the number of births recorded was 5,159.

Inspection of bakeries. During the last year an inspector of bakeries was appointed, who, since the commencement of his term of office, has inspected and caused to be placed in a proper sanitary state 257 bakeries. The filthy and disease-breeding surroundings which formerly appertained to many of these bakeshops, are said to have been entirely abated by the exertions of this officer, and his system of daily inspection effectively prevents a relapse into their former deplorable condition.

Inspection of laundries. Two bath and laundry inspectors have also been added to the list of employés. Every laundry in the city, including those conducted by Chinese, has been inspected, and whenever found lacking in sanitation, has been cleansed and renovated. The Chinese laundrymen are in the habit of spraying clothes by means of water emitted from the mouth and an ordinance has been passed forbidding this custom.

Laboratories established. Under an increased appropriation granted to that department, the Board of Health has been enabled to establish and equip two laboratories: one for the examination of food and the other for bacteriological investigation. An official chemist with an assistant has been placed in charge of the chemical laboratory, and is constantly engaged in the analysis of food-stuffs. The chemist renders monthly reports, and where his analysis shows articles purchased to be adulterations, or substitutions, warrants are promptly issued for the arrest of the offending dealers. All brands of condensed milk, catsups, and jellies have been inspected and analysed, and many palpable and startling adulterations have been made known to the public. Out of 31 samples of tomato catsup only two were found to be free from antiseptics, the remainder were found to contain either salicylic acid or boracic acid, and 16 were coloured with aniline dyes. 14 samples of condensed milk and evaporated cream were examined and seven found to be approximately pure condensed milk, representing a standard of about three-parts of pure milk condensed to one part. The remainder seemed to have been made either from skim-milk or milk which was very poor in butter fat. Manufacturers of these goods are now said to be making laudable efforts to bring their products up to a uniform standard. Adulteration of food.

The analytical data regarding fruit jellies, jams, and marmalades shows that in no line of food products has adulteration and substitution been carried to such an alarming extent. Of 87 samples analysed, 28 only had the chance of being called pure, 20 were adulterated and 39 fraudulent substitutes. A majority of those, although passed as pure jellies made from their respective fruits, were not made from choice fruit; some were made from immature fruit, and some from over-ripe fruit that had already passed into a state of incipient putrefaction.

Another important feature in the improvement of the health department has been the appointment of a veterinary surgeon. During the year 152 dairies have been inspected with herds aggregating 8,300 head of cattle. The application of the United States tuberculin tests, officially adopted by this Board, was deferred to the latter part of the year, owing to the earnest plea of interested dairy-men who petitioned the Board of Health to postpone its activity in this direction until legislative measures could be secured providing compensation for cattle destroyed. The Board acceded to this request, but the legislature having taken no action in the premises, it was not deemed advisable to delay longer the enforcement of this important test, and during the last three months the cattle in several of the largest dairies have been subjected to the United States test, and all those found to be in any degree afflicted with tuberculosis were immediately slaughtered. The veterinary surgeon's report shows that out of 8,391 cattle inspected 1,049 showed symptoms of tuberculosis. *Inspection of dairy cattle. Testing cattle for tuberculosis.*

The Board of Health is responsible for the drafting of a number of ordinances adopted by the Board of Supervisors, and now in force, among which are the following:— *New ordinances.*

An ordinance prohibiting expectoration in street cars and public places.

An ordinance requiring food supplies intended for public institutions to pass through food stations for inspection.

Improved method of disposing of garbage and refuse.
San Francisco has recently adopted a method of disposing of its garbage and refuse which is said to place it in the lead of any city in the United States. Up to November, 1897, all the garbage and ashes were removed by scavengers, who were allowed to dump it on vacant lots in the city limits that were designated by the superintendent of streets for that purpose. This created a continuous nuisance, and proved a constant source of complaint and annoyance, besides being an active factor in the death-rate. In November last, a company which had secured a contract to reduce or cremate all refuse matter for the term of 50 years put their works in operation, and scavengers were compelled by a city ordinance to deliver all refuse and garbage at these works. The system adopted by this company is similar to the one in operation at Montreal, Canada, the furnace used being known as The Thackeray Incinerator, named after the inventor, an English engineer of good standing. This incinerator is operated entirely without the aid of fuel, being so constructed that the refuse consumes itself. The cost of operating is therefore limited to the cost of maintenance and labour. Another advantage claimed for this invention is, that it disposes of the garbage in such a manner as to create no odour. The plant erected in this city is about four times as large as the one at Montreal and burns from 300 to 500 tons per day. The cost in January was approximately $14\frac{1}{2}$ c. per ton, but contemplated reduction in the number of men employed will ultimately bring this down to $12\frac{1}{2}$ c. per ton. The residuum from the incinerator has some small commercial value, and it is thought that power can be generated from the burning refuse.

Railway construction.
Owing to the improved condition of business and the return of confidence, the San Francisco and San Joaquin Valley Railway Company has been enabled to make arrangements whereby its entire issue of bonds, amounting to 6,000,000 dol. (1,200,000*l*.), will be taken up by a syndicate of local capitalists. The placing of these bonds enables the company to proceed with the work of construction without hindrance or delay, and the line from Fresno to Bakersfield has been completed. Surveyors have been in the field locating a route between Stockton and Point Richmond, the terminus of the line on the bay of San Francisco, and work has been commenced on this section of line. From Point Richmond a ferry system will be established to make connection with this city. There has been a considerable talk of the Valley Road being connected with a transcontinental line, and as soon as it is completed to San Francisco this matter is likely to receive serious consideration.

The Sierra Pacific Railroad was completed and opened for traffic towards the end of 1897. This line connects with the Southern Pacific Company's system at Oakdale, near Stockton, and runs from there to Jamestown, a distance of 41 miles. The terminus is in a rich mining centre situated on an extensive mineral belt known as the "Mother Lode," and most of the business of the company will consist in carrying supplies and machinery to mines in that neighbourhood.

The development that has taken place in the transmission of electrical power has made the force of the rivers and lakes that formerly went to waste, or laid dormant, available for manufacturing and other purposes, and undertakings have been put in operation or projected in many parts of the State to take advantage of this power which has been so bountifully provided by nature. A part of the great force of the American River at Folsom has been utilised, and the power generated is used at Sacramento for lighting the city and propelling the street cars, &c. The plant has a capacity of 4,000 horse-power, but it is said to be capable of being increased to 20,000. An enterprise of great magnitude is that of the Blue Lakes Water Company whose principal supply of power is derived from the Blue Lakes situated in Alpine County, near the summit of the Sierra Nevada Mountains. The water is conducted by a river and canal for a distance of over 80 miles to the power-house, from which point electric power is furnished to a number of towns and mines in Amador and Calaveras Counties. It is proposed to construct several electric roads from Jamestown, the present terminus of the Sierra Railroad to the principal towns and mines in the neighbourhood, and run them by power furnished by this company. The future development of the plant will depend to some extent upon the growth of the mining industry along the rich mineral belt known as the "Mother Lode." At present it has a capacity of about 10,000 horse-power which it is estimated can be increased to 50,000, at a cost not exceeding 20*l.* per horsepower for the complete undertaking. In the event of the plant being developed to this extent it is very likely that power will be furnished to San Francisco. The North Fork of the San Joaquin River, about 36 miles from Fresno, has been utilised to furnish light and power to that city where it delivers about 1,500 horse-power, and this system has lately been extended to Hanford about 33 miles further away. Bakersfield has a plant of about 1,500 horse-power, and an extensive plant at Clear Lake is projected which will develop 30,000 horse-power for transmission to San Francisco, Oakland, and intermediate cities.

Use of electric power in California.

These are the principal plants that are already in operation or under consideration. They form but a small part of what may be done if the power of the various rivers and lakes of the State is made use of. The manufacturers of California have always been at a great disadvantage on account of the high price of coal and labour as compared with the Eastern States. With plenty of raw material at hand it has had to be sent East to be manufactured, and then returned here at a double expense for transportation. If electric power can be furnished, as it is claimed, for less than half the price of what any fuel would cost, California will be at an advantage as compared with those communities which must depend on coal to generate their power, and employment could be given to thousands of workmen who would make their homes here and contribute to the prosperity of the State.

Electric power in Utah.

An extensive electric plant was put in operation at Ogden in the State of Utah, in May, 1897, which it is claimed is second only in size to that at Niagara. The power is derived from a river, the water of which is conveyed in pipes a distance of 7 miles to the power-house. A pole line for the transmission of 10,000 horse-power to Salt Lake City, 35 miles away, has been constructed, and an electric railway between the two points is projected.

Electric power from coal.

In the report for last year mention was made of the Corral Hollow Coal Mines, near Stockton. The name of the town has recently been changed from Corral Hollow to Tesla, and the company owning the mines has organised a concern with the view of utilising the screenings and waste products at the mines for the generation of electricity and its transmission to Oakland, Alameda, and San Francisco. It is stated that contracts have already been made to dispose of sufficient power to pay interest on the entire investment.

Salvation Army colony.

A colonisation scheme has been started by the Salvation Army which has acquired a tract of land at Soledad in this State for the purpose. The tract comprises about 500 acres, and each family will be allotted 10 acres. All the land has been ploughed and 30 cottages have been erected, 20 families have already been settled on the land and 30 more will be sent down as soon as there are sufficient funds in hand for the purpose. It is estimated that 5,000l. will be enough to establish all the colonists, and of this amount 2,000l. has already been subscribed.

College of commerce to be established.

Some time ago a special committee was appointed by the Board of Regents of the University of California to inquire into the advisability of establishing a college of commerce in connection with the University. This committee reported in favour of the undertaking early this year, and the measure was adopted without a dissenting voice. The President of the University has been directed to make application to the President of the United States to the effect that an engineer officer of the regular army may be detailed to act as instructor in steam engineering and marine transportation. It was the expressed judgment of the regents that the college would expand, and numerous branches be taught, among others that of iron ship-building and the training of students for a Consular career.

Land frauds.

During the session of the State Legislature in the early part of last year a committee, composed of officers of the State Board of Trade, presented a memorial to the Governor calling attention to Mr. Consul-General Warburton's "Report on the distress caused to British Emigrants to California by Fraudulent Land Syndicates and Emigration Agencies" (Miscellaneous Series, 1896, No. 404), which had attracted considerable attention throughout the State and had been extensively quoted in most of the newspapers. In this memorial it was admitted that the strictures contained in that report had for the most part a degree of justification in the facts of the case; that there were now offered in the markets, colony lands in which no intelligent Californian would invest; that they are addressed to foreign ignorance and designed only for the attention and patronage of those whose lack of information makes them easy victims of dishonest immigration schemes. After reviewing the fall in the value of land in California and dwelling on the advantages the State offers for home seekers, the memorialists petitioned the Governor to send a special message to the Legislature setting forth the facts presented in the memorial, and recommending that a Commission of Immigration be created and established whose duty it should be to institute inquiry into the character of all colonisation schemes projected in this State and to commend or condemn according to the merit or demerit of such schemes. In the course of a personal interview the committee had with the Governor he informed the members that the suggestions contained in the memorial met with his hearty approval, and that he would send a special message to the Legislature on the subject. This message was presented to both Houses on February 20, 1897, but no action was taken in the matter.

I attach much importance to the advice that has been given in former reports to intending settlers, not to invest in land before residing for one or two years in this State, as so many of our countrymen have come to grief through ignoring this counsel. With the comparatively low prices of fruit and many kinds of produce now ruling, farming is not the profitable business that it was some years ago, and if a man buys land without knowing what he is about, he will be very apt to regret his bargain before he has been long in the country. There is no difficulty in renting or leasing land in any part of the State and thus ascertaining if the settler has an aptitude for the business before sinking his capital in an undertaking from which he will find it difficult to withdraw. *Advice to intending settlers.*

During the last winter there was not nearly so much distress among the unemployed as in the year preceding, but there are still a number of men here who are willing to work without further remuneration than their board. British subjects continue to come to California under the impression that work is easily obtainable, and neglect to make any inquiries as to the actual state of affairs. On arrival they are generally sadly disappointed and have to take menial work if they can get it or send to their friends for financial assistance. There is no chance for mechanics or labourers to obtain work here and absolutely no opening for clerks, the market being glutted for that kind of labour. *Labour market.*

The real estate market generally was in a very unsatisfactory condition during the whole of 1897. Sales were dull, and prices, already very low for ordinary property, showed lower figures than *Real estate.*

(225)

any previously registered since the dullness began in May, 1891. The only exception to this state of affairs was choice market street property which was in constant demand at good figures. The number of sales for 1897 was 3,215, valued at 2,580,605*l.*, against 3,267 sales in 1896, valued at 2,309,066*l.*

Agriculture. Wheat. — While the crop of wheat was considerably less than that of 1896, the higher prices it commanded made it of equal or more value than that of the former year. It was of excellent quality and the shortage abroad in countries that are usually exporters of grain, caused a very brisk demand. The good prices obtained have in the main benefited the farmers more than the speculators, as the rise took place while much of the crop was in their hands. It has been many years since the Californian agriculturist or fruit grower has realised enough from his crops to enable him to keep out of debt to the banks. Interest became lower, and particularly so during the last three years. Last year the money received was applied to old accounts, and in this way many debts, which involved considerable back interest, were liquidated. All the acreage possible was planted in the winter of 1897 in the firm conviction that with the increasing world's consumption high prices would be maintained. Unfortunately the severe drought experienced has been most disastrous to the growing crops, and reports from many sections of the State show that they are entirely ruined, except on river bottom lands or in certain localities that usually suffer from an excess of moisture.

Barley. — The crop of barley was a good one, and the prices received were considerably higher than in 1896. Next to wheat this is our most important grain crop. The growing crop has been almost entirely lost on account of the drought.

Hops. — The crop of hops for 1897 is estimated at 8,325,000 lbs. For the last few years there has been a gradual but continued increase in the price, and from 12 to 14¾ c. per lb. were realised for the crop.

Honey. — A commercial estimate of the crop of honey for 1897 places it at 3,720 tons.

Wool. — The wool clip of California in 1897, reported in round numbers by a leading authority, was as follows:—

	Quantity.
	Lbs.
Spring	19,163,030
Fall (autumn)	11,175,560
Pulled	2,195,640
Total	32,534,230

The exports were 435,128 lbs. and the overland shipments 29,424,000 lbs. The sales are reported to have been the largest on record, and dealers are said to have done a very profitable business.

The number of head of live-stock in California at present is estimated as follows:— *Live-stock in California.*

	Number of Head.
Horses	550,000
Mules	50,000
Milch cows	300,000
Oxen, &c.	785,000
Sheep	4,700,000
Hogs	400,000

Sugar-beet culture is expected to become one of the leading industries of this State in the near future. Last year there were four large factories in operation, their capacity being given as follows:— *Beet sugar industry.*

Location.	Daily Capacity.
	Tons of Beets.
Alvarado (refined sugar)	800
Watsonville (raw sugar)	1,000
Chino (refined sugar)	800
Alamitos (refined sugar)	350

The following factories are under construction and are expected to commence operations this year:—

Location.	Daily Capacity.
	Tons of Beets.
Salinas	3,000
Crockett	1,000
Hueneme	2,000

The mills at Alvarado and Alamitos are in process of enlargement, and it is stated that a factory will be erected at Carritos, near Alamitos, by those interested in the latter concern. The large amount of money required to build and equip one of these factories has hitherto militated against the increase of the industry, as capitalists were naturally unwilling to invest until assured of success. Now that sugar has received increased protection under the new tariff, and it has been demonstrated that it can be profitably produced on this coast, there is likely to be a considerable increase in the business. From the standpoint of the capitalist the prospect appears alluring, as will be noted from the following estimate taken from one of our local papers which I give for what it is worth. The figures are designed to show the cost and profits in this State of a factory of exactly the same capacity as that at Anklam in Germany, but fitted for turning out refined sugar:—

(225)

	Amount.
	Dollars.
Cost of factory (about double German cost)	350,000
Working capital	50,000
Total capitalisation	400,000

Working Expenses for One Year.

	Amount.
	Dollars.
Cost of 65,767 tons of beets, at 4 dol. per ton	263,068
German working expenses, at 1 dol. 25 c. per ton	82,208
Add 50 per cent. on items of fuel and labour..	33,500
Total expenses	378,776
Product, 7,106 tons (of 2,000 lbs.) of white sugar, at 4 c. per lb.	568,480
Net profit	189,704

In the above estimate sugar is put down at 4 c. per lb., and that is perhaps all the investor should count on. The present price of fine granulated sugar here is fully 1 c. higher, but the bulk of the product would probably have to be shipped to the Eastern States for a market. Even upon the above showing it must not be assumed that the whole of the profit would be available for dividends. The repairs upon a sugar factory are said to be constant and involve very large sums of money, and something would have to be written off for depreciation. In regard to the yield of beets experience seems to show that in the beginning of the industry in a community the average yield will be from 7 to 9 tons to the acre, which will gradually increase to about 12 tons as the farmers learn their business. From 1 dol. 50 c. to 2 dol. per ton is the usual estimate given of the cost of raising beets, exclusive of rent and interest. It is not thought that farmers share equally in the division of the profits with prices as they now are, but without some more effective organisation it does not seem likely that they will be able to improve their position. Under the new tariff sugar has advanced in price, and it is considered that a proportionate increase should be made to the farmers. This has only been done in a few cases, most of the concerns offering no advance on the old price of 4 dol. per ton for beets. There is a difference of opinion as to whether in the long run it is best for the farmer to receive a fixed price per ton for all beets or a varying price based upon the sugar content of the beet. The latter plan seems to be most productive of quarrels and bad feeling. In all contracts the factory owners prescribe stringent regulations for the cultivation of the beets, and this is doubtless necessary for their own protection and is really better for the farmer if he is inclined to be careless. He is compelled to cultivate according to instructions, and is undoubtedly furnished with the directions best fitted for the locality in which he resides. The following extract is taken from the "San Francisco Chronicle" of January 2, 1898:—

"As we have frankly stated, we do not believe that the profits of the business are, or are likely to be, fairly divided since the responsibility of the profitable production of beet sugar rests almost equally upon the farmer and the manufacturer, and the latter gets the lion's share. But he also takes the most risk. The farmer is not at all likely to lose his farm by raising sugar beets, but serious mistakes on the part of the capitalists may cause him to lose his factory. Thus far in this country there have been more factories lost than have succeeded, and, while this is not likely to be so in the future, there is always more risk in manufacturing than in producing. The cost of manufacturing sugar in this State is unknown to the public, and certainly varies somewhat in the different factories and in different years. We have sought to obtain from the factories direct some data upon which, without prying into their private affairs, we could draw some general conclusions. In one case our request was politely evaded, and in the other cases bluntly refused. Our readers must, therefore, make such deductions as they can from the German experience we have given them. Our farmers should master these facts, paying no attention whatever to boom stories, and then in the light of an intelligent public opinion they should make the best terms that they can.

"But without fail they should take up the business and do it promptly, before others get the start of them.

"With whatever drawbacks there may be attending the business, one thing is sure, the communities in which sugar factories are established are to-day, and have been for years, the most prosperous communities in the State and have the most ample assurance for the future. And that settles the question of the profit of the industry."

The president of the sugar beet factory at Alvarado, one of the oldest established factories in the State, caused a count of the farmers to be made who were growing beets under contract for his establishment in 1896. The number was found to be 420, some of whom grew a few acres and some many, the average being 15 acres per farmer. A great deal has been said about the desirability of having more small farms in California, and this industry certainly promises to be a factor in bringing about that result. {Beet culture likely to encourage small farmers.}

The California vintage of 1897, including the sweet wine production, has been the largest in the history of the industry, exceeding the previous record year of 1893 by over 7,000,000 gallons. With less acreage than existed some years ago the vines have been so prolific that the dry wine product is far greater than usual, and has been exceeded in only one or two seasons. The two counties of Sonoma and Santa Clara have surpassed {Wine crop.}

(225)

all former yields, and the quality of the wine promises to be among the best for many years. At the same time the producers and the merchants are confronted with the problem of its disposition. The cessation of the friendly relations which existed during 1895 and 1896 between these two classes adds gravity to the situation. The manager of the California Winemaker's Corporation estimates the vintage of dry wines as follows:—

District.	Quantity.
	Gallons.
Sonoma County	9,000,000
Santa Clara County	7,750,000
Napa County	4,500,000
Miscellaneous	4,500,000
Total	25,750,000

In considering the marketing of the crop the stock left over from former years will have to be taken into account. This will probably amount to 11,000,000 gallons. The demand for the present year (1898) is placed by the manager at 23,000,000 gallons, calculated on a Pacific Coast consumption of 8,000,000 and an export consumption of 15,000,000 gallons. Deducting these 23,000,000 from the 36,750,000 on hand, a surplus of 13,750,000 gallons will remain. Fermentation in 1897 is reported to have been perfect, and it is said to be the judgment of experts that the quality will be much superior to the average. When the above estimate was made (early in December, 1897) the wine was thought to be worth about 17 c. per gallon, including barrel, f.o.b. at San Francisco. At the time of closing this report it was impossible to obtain more than 8 to 10 c. per gallon for the product of 1897, for carload lots.

Sweet wine and brandy. The vintage of sweet wines is estimated at 6,500,000 gallons, and prices have been effected to some extent out of sympathy with the dry wine market. California port and sherry of good quality can be bought in carload lots at from 35 to 40 c. per gallon. This wine is highly recommended by local medical men for invalids, and I should think that it would command a ready sale in England if put on the market at a reasonable figure.

The product of brandy is put down at 2,000,000 gallons.

Experiment in storing wine. An experiment in handling red wine was tried last year at the Italian-Swiss colony's vineyard situated at Asti in this State. The grapes handled by the colony were far in excess of the cooperage facilities it possessed, and some means had to be devised to care for the surplus. Among the different plans suggested was that of building a concrete cistern, and this idea was finally adopted. An excavation was first made in a rocky hillside in the rear of the establishment. Next, walls of concrete two feet in thickness were put in and the floor and top were added in as substantial a manner, the latter being supported by 15 steel girders. Then the entire surface was covered with a lining of pure cement, and finally this was glazed to the impermeability of glass. The whole cistern was buried beneath 3 feet of earth, the object of all these precautions being to preserve the wine at a uniform temperature. This cement tank is 104 feet long, 34 feet wide, and 24 feet high, and is capable of holding 500,000 gallons. The wine was kept in this reservoir for four months or more, and the experiment is said to have been entirely successful. It was then drawn off by gravitation into wooden tanks in which it will be aged previous to being placed in barrels for shipment. There are said to be several advantages derived from treating the wine in this manner. One is that it can be maintained at a cool even temperature; another is the equal blending of such a large quantity of wine at one time; and a third is the great saving in insurance which is expected to repay the cost of the construction of the tank in five years.

Taking the State as a whole, the fruit crop may be said to have been generally large in yield and of good quality, although in several localities certain varieties have suffered from climatic or other causes. A considerable portion of the crop was dried, and there was a good demand from canners. Prices were fairly remunerative. *Fruit crop.*

The following table shows the shipments of fruit and canned goods to the Eastern States by rail for the last three years:— *Shipments of fruit.*

Description.	Quantity.		
	1897.	1896.	1895.
	Lbs.	Lbs.	Lbs.
Canned goods	78,970,000	61,252,000	59,142,000
Dried fruit	130,328,000	84,134,000	102,686,000
Green fruit	147,806,000	105,220,000	119,734,000
Raisins	71,714,000	61,624,000	85,352,000
Total	428,818,000	312,230,000	366,914,000

These shipments do not represent the total movement. Of late years the Southern Pacific Company has declined to make any returns for the two terminals in the Southern section of the State.

The crop of prunes for 1897 is estimated at 82,500,000 lbs., which is a considerable increase over the year preceding. Santa Clara county alone is said to have produced 50,000,000 lbs. The total annual consumption of prunes in the United States is stated to be 70,000,000 lbs., and unless foreign markets can be successfully invaded or something can be done to encourage a more general use of the fruit in this country the outlook for the growers is not very encouraging. *Prunes.*

(225)

40 SAN FRANCISCO.

Raisins. The crop of raisins for 1897 is estimated at 65,000,000 lbs., being about 3,000,000 lbs. less than that of 1896. This does not meet the consumption of the country, and as raisins have received increased protection under the new tariff prices have ruled higher than for some years.

Hemp. Experiments made in growing hemp in this State in 1894 with imported Japanese seed demonstrated the fact that the plant grows to a great height here, and produces a strong fibre much resembling the celebrated Italian product. In 1896 an experienced hemp grower and manufacturer from Illinois was induced to come to this State and set up his mill at Gridley, Butte County, where he planted 200 acres of hemp in the spring of that year. The result was a crop of 2,000 lbs to the acre, but owing to its being worked up very late in the season, when the weather was extremely hot, there was a loss of weight estimated at 25 per cent. arising from the extreme dryness of the tow. The tow sold at 5 c. per lb. f.o.b. the cars at Gridley, and is said to have left a profit to the grower of 80 dol. per acre. Rent of the rich river bottom land along the Feather River, near Gridley, where the hemp is grown without irrigation, is about 9 dol. per acre per annum, and the cost of such land is probably 160 dol. per acre. Alluvial lands where there is sub-irrigation are the most suitable, but wherever a good crop of weeds will grow hemp is said to do well, provided that there is a sufficiency of moisture. There is no doubt plenty of suitable land available in this State from 25 dol. per acre upwards. In 1897 the average at Gridley was increased to 400 acres with equally favourable results. At present about 800 acres are under cultivation there, and more may be planted this year if suitable land can be secured near the two mills in operation.

The attention of capitalists has been drawn to the promising outlook for hemp culture, and efforts are being made to induce them to subscribe sufficient means to erect a factory for the manufacture of twine in this city.

Tobacco. Experiments have been made in growing tobacco in several parts of the State, the most promising results having been achieved in San Diego County. In 1896 about 20 acres were planted there, from which about six tons of tobacco were produced and cured, about one-fourth being made into cigars and smoking tobacco. I have not been able to ascertain the prevailing opinion regarding the former, but the latter is said to have been found satisfactory, except that it is a little too strong for the majority of smokers. About 40 acres were grown in San Diego County in 1897, but none of the product has been offered for sale yet; the industry appears to be of great promise, but is so far entirely in the experimental stage.

Appearance of plant tuberculosis in California. Plant tuberculosis has attacked an olive orchard situated near Merced, and is causing no little alarm at the Agricultural College of the University of California. This is the first hold the dread disease has secured in the State, and every effort will be made to stamp it out. The presence of the bacillus which is causing all the trouble was only discovered this spring, and the entire orchard will be uprooted and burnt, and by this precaution it is hoped the spread of the disease will be effectually checked. The disease is commonly called the olive knot, and has long been the scourge of the orchards of the Mediterranean countries. The symptoms are excrescences on the bark of the limbs of the olive tree and the appearance of small knots on the leaves and twigs. The orchard often over-produces, giving a poor quality of fruit, and finally the trees die from their weakened state. The disease is due to the bacillus oleae, quite similar to the bacillus tuberculosis, and on this account scientific men refer to it as plant tuberculosis.

Los Angeles.

Mr. Vice-Consul Mortimer reports as follows :—

In my report for 1896 I expressed the opinion that a period of great prosperity for this city and district was about to commence. Owing to national and local causes, however, my views have not been justified by events, and business generally here is now less active than for several years. Of the local causes leading to this result the principal is that the rainfall this season has been insufficient, and the crops in consequence will be very light. The oranges and other fruits have been greatly damaged by frost, and the loss on this account may be as much as 20 per cent. of the crop. Local capitalists have great faith in the future of this city, however, and are showing it by expending large sums of money in building operations, more especially in the construction of shops and business houses, costing from 20,000*l.* to 30,000*l.* each. 600,000*l.* had been appropriated by Congress for the construction of a breakwater at San Pedro, the port for this city, and the expenditure of this money and the increase in shipping which will probably follow will have a good effect on this city and district. The following comparative statements will give some idea of the condition of business.

Introductory remarks.

All property is valued annually by the County Assessor for purposes of taxation. These valuations are about one-third to one-half the amount at which owners are willing to sell. The assessed value of all property in the County of Los Angeles for the past two years has been as follows:—

Year.	Value.
	£
1896	20,100,000
1897	18,520,000

The Los Angeles clearing-house (which, however, does not represent all the banks) reports clearings (in round numbers) as follows:—

Year.	Value
	£
1896	11,500,000
1897	11,460,000

Information for British capitalists.

City and County bonds payable in gold, first mortgages on good real property, and the bonds of legitimate enterprises payable in gold are the safest, and, for English investors, the best investments in this district. About 3,500,000*l.* has been invested here on mortgage in 1897. The rate of interest on the best first mortgage security on sums of from 500*l.* to 2,000*l.* has declined in the past 10 years from 10 to 7 per cent. net. Owing to the decline in the rate of interest, City, County, and School bonds are from time to time refunded at lower rates, and absolutely safe City and School bonds can be purchased to pay about 5 per cent. Full information can no doubt be obtained through the London agencies of the banks here. Barclay and Co., Limited, are the London agents for the First National Bank of Los Angeles, a reliable financial institution.

This city is exceptionally well provided with electric tramways, there being upwards of 30 miles of double track electric roads within the city limits. Two of these roads have been extended to the neighbouring cities of Pasadena (10 miles) and Santa Monica (16 miles). Electric tramways are also projected to Redondo (22 miles) and San Pedro (25 miles), and the latter road will, I understand, be built this year. I am informed that negotiations are in progress for the sale to an English syndicate of all the electric tramways in this city and vicinity. The cost of management would be greatly reduced if they were consolidated, and, if they can be purchased at a reasonable price, should prove a remunerative investment. Experiments are being made with a view to changing the motive power from electricity to compressed air.

Advice to emigrants.

I receive many letters from persons who think of settling here, and to answer their queries I wrote at some length on this subject in my report for 1896. Prospective emigrants will find in that report a good deal of information likely to be of use to them.

Sales of land by the Southern Pacific Company.

In the same report I commented on the fact that English people and others had purchased land from the Southern Pacific Railway; that the United States Courts had held that the lands so purchased were not included in the grant to that company, and still belong to the United States; that the railway company would not return the purchase-money, and that some of the purchasers were suing the company. I mention the matter as I find that some of the victims are English people (several of whom have complained to me), and as a warning to emigrants not to buy land, even from a rich corporation, without having the title examined by competent attorneys.

LOS ANGELES.

Full information as to the ports for this city is contained in former reports, to which I beg to refer. The 600,000*l.* appropriated by Congress for a breakwater at San Pedro, and to which reference was made in my report for 1896, is still unexpended. I understand that it is probable that work will commence shortly.

Shipping and navigation.

I am indebted to the Collector of Customs for the following return of shipping:—

Annex A.—RETURN of all Shipping at the Port of Los Angeles, California, during the Year 1897.

ENTERED.

Nationality.	Sailing. Number of Vessels.	Sailing. Tons.	Steam. Number of Vessels.	Steam. Tons.	Total. Number of Vessels.	Total. Tons.
British	3	5,477	...	...	3	5,477
American	1	9	17	20,667	18	20,676
Other countries	1	1,900	20	49,427	21	51,327
Total	5	7,386	37	70,094	42	77,480
,, for the year preceding	11	14,839	35	67,364	46	82,203

CLEARED.

Nationality.	Sailing. Number of Vessels.	Sailing. Tons.	Steam. Number of Vessels.	Steam. Tons.	Total. Number of Vessels.	Total. Tons.
British	3	5,477	...	...	3	5,477
American	1	9	18	20,832	19	20,841
Other countries	1	1,900	20	49,427	21	51,327
Total	5	7,386	38	70,259	43	77,645
,, for the year preceding	11	14,839	35	67,364	46	82,203

The exports and imports are shown in Annexes B and C following. I am indebted to the Collector of Customs for the statistics contained in them:—

Trade and commerce.

Annex B.—RETURN of Principal Articles of Export from Los Angeles, California, during the Years 1896–97.

Articles.		1896. Quantity.	1896. Value.	1897. Quantity.	1897. Value.
			£		£
Wheat	Bushels	...	...	104,701	19,160
Barley	Sacks	40,538	6,077	...	...
Other articles	...	...	...	...	3,373
Total	...	...	6,077	...	22,533

LOS ANGELES.

RETURN of Principal Articles of Import to Los Angeles, California, during the Years 1896-97.

Articles.		1896.		1897.	
		Quantity.	Value.	Quantity.	Value.
			£		£
Coal	Tons	118,833	83,554	106,889	68,453
Pig-iron	,,	...	...	...	...
Cement	Barrels	11,308	3,970	26,992	7,640
Other articles		...	26,300	...	21,464
Total	..	...	113,824	...	97,557

Annex C.—TABLE showing Total Value of all Articles Exported from and Imported to Los Angeles from and to Foreign Countries during the Years 1896-97.

Country.	Exports.		Imports.	
	1896.	1897.	1896.	1897.
	£	£	£	£
Great Britain	6,077	19,160	113,824	78,420
Other countries	..	3,373	..	19,137
Total	6,077	22,533	113,824	97,557

Coals. The imports of coal are from British Columbia, and were imported in Swedish and Hawaiian vessels.

Cement. The cement used here is imported from Germany. The principal importers inform me that the wholesale price here is 13s. per barrel (400 lbs.).

Sugar beets. There are two sugar beet factories in this district, and a third is in course of construction. The manager of the Chino factory writes me as follows: "Our output in 1897 was 15,500,000 lbs. It is difficult to say what 1898 is likely to be, owing to lack of rain. With necessary rainfall we shall probably have a crop which will give us 14,000,000 to 15,000,000 lbs. If rain is short we may not produce over 10,000,000 lbs."

The manager of the Los Alamitos sugar factory writes me as follows: "Our output for the last year was 6,000,000 lbs. of fine granulated sugar. We are now doubling the capacity of our plant, and if we get a reasonable amount of rain we are in hopes of getting double the amount of sugar we had last year, but unless we get, say, about 2 inches of rain our crop will be very light, and the output will not exceed last year."

The manager of the factory now being constructed near Hueneme writes me as follows: "When the factory which we are now building is completed, it will have a capacity of 2,000 tons of beets per day. This will give us a manufactured product of about 400,000 lbs. of sugar every 24 hours. We expect to begin operations not later than August 1. On account of the extreme dryness of the season the tonnage will be very much short of the usual amount."

The official census of 1890 showed the population of this city to be 50,394. In 1897 it was 102,937. The death rate in this city in 1897 was 13 per 1,000. The total number of deaths was 1,412, of which 221 formed the subject of coroner's inquests, and 355 died of affections of the lungs. Many of these persons no doubt came here in search of health. The total number of births was 1,621, of which 59 were stillborn. *Population and industries. Health.*

Mining for gold has received a great impetus in this district in the past two years, and many valuable finds are reported. The mining camp at Randsburg, referred to in my last report, has been connected with the Santa Fé Railway. Some English gold mining companies operating in this district on a small scale are, I am informed, proving very successful. This is due to the fact that they are well managed, and have not been handicapped with promotion money. In this connection I venture to quote the following extract from a San Francisco newspaper: "People who will persist in paying 1,000,000 dol. for a property worth 50,000 dol., cannot expect to make much. . . . Take the best mining investments now offering from California in the London market, and a full 60 per cent. of the capital can be set down as profit for promoters." *Mines.*

Decrees of divorce were granted by the Superior Court of Los Angeles County in the past two years as follows:— *Divorce.*

Year.	Number.
1896	237
1897	299

In my report for 1896 I wrote at some length on orange growing, and on the markets for oranges, lemons, dried fruits, &c. I beg to refer persons interested to that report. It appears from a recent report from the United States Consul at a port in Italy that the price of labour is so low there that the Italian orange growers can pay the increased duties, and successfully compete with California and Florida for the market in the Eastern States. Persons who think of engaging in the business here should carefully consider the question of markets before investing capital. The price of oranges is very low this year for the California product, and this notwithstanding the fact that the frosts in Florida have materially lessened the competition of that State for the Eastern market. *Agriculture. Oranges.*

General farming here is dependent on the rainfall, and it will be seen from the following table supplied to me by the United States Weather Bureau here that the rainfall is very irregular. The amount is given in inches, and the season in each year is from September 1 to August 31 following. The rainfall for the present season will not exceed 6 inches:— *Rainfall.*

Season.	Rainfall.
	Inches.
1890–91	23·33
1891–92	11·86
1892–93	26·27
1893–94	6·74
1894–95	16·10
1895–96	8·54
1896–97	16·83

In this report 2,000 lbs. is taken to be a ton, and dollars have been converted into pounds sterling at the rate of 5 dol. to the 1*l*.

San Diego.

Mr. Vice-Consul Allen reports as follows:—

Trade and commerce. General business.

The expenditure of large sums in the development of the county, and particularly in the construction of the new water system, has contributed towards a better condition than in the few years preceding. The general exodus to the Klondike goldfields will, however, take many people from both town and country. The building of the new water system has been the most important industrial work conducted during 1897—as, when completed, it means the addition of about 100,000 acres of good fruit lands to the county. The business done through the port shows an increase during the year 1897. The imports have increased slightly, the main item being lumber, which exceeds the previous year by 4,185,000 feet, making a total of 19,185,000 feet for 1897. Bullion importations are considerably smaller than during 1896, the difference being 14,777*l*. 8*s*. for 1897, against 25,539*l*. 4*s*. for 1896.

Cement.

Cement imports show a decrease, but have, during the past year, come entirely from the United Kingdom. The exports, however, were far larger than those of the previous year. In 1896 only 463 bushels of wheat and 271,807 bushels of barley were sent from this port. In 1897, 310,501 bushels of wheat and 187,186 bushels of barley. The exports of 1896 amounted to 40,725*l*. 8*s*., and those of 1897 to 88,158*l*. 12*s*. With the exception of about 2,000 bushels, all the wheat was shipped direct to the United Kingdom.

Coal.

Coal shows a slight decrease, the trade from Newcastle, New South Wales, having gradually fallen off since the Santa Fé Railroad has taken to burning crude oil for fuel. The people of San Diego are now working hard for another railroad to connect this town more directly with the East, and should their efforts prove successful, as they must in time, no doubt the coal trade would at once receive a great impetus.

British Columbia coal.

The coal importations from British Columbia amounted to 12,980 tons, valued at 10,383*l*. 4*s*.

SAN DIEGO.

Five cargoes of grain left for the United Kingdom in British vessels during the year, valued at 69,985*l*. 16*s*. — Grain.

Most of the imports, with the exception of coal and cement, and 126*l*. worth of English beer and mineral waters, were received as in previous years, by sail and rail from the East and San Francisco. Were a different method of distribution adopted by English exporters, perhaps, wholesale merchants in Southern California would handle more English goods, of which a considerable amount are used. At present they come through American houses in New York and San Francisco. — Imports.

RETURN of Principal Articles of Import to San Diego, California, U.S.A., during the Years 1896-97.

Articles.		1896.		1897.	
		Quantity.	Value.	Quantity.	Value.
			£ s.		£ s.
Coals	Tons	46,352	23,227 16	44,614	26,768 8
Cement	Cwts.	73,025	14,278 0	34,850	9,462 12
Other articles	...	...	7,161 4		12,580 12
Stock	Number	2,583	4,388 12	3,997	7,849 4
Guano	Tons	1,509	1,387 16	1,937	1,846 8
Bullion	...	...	25,539 4	...	14,777 8
Total	...	...	75,982 12	...	73,284 12
Lumber received from domestic ports	Feet	15,000,000	60,000 0	19,185,000	75,000 0

RETURN of Principal Articles of Export from San Diego, California, U.S.A., during the Years 1896-97.

Articles.		1896.		1897.	
		Quantity.	Value.	Quantity.	Value.
			£ s.		£ s.
Barley	Bushels	271,807	20,841 8	187,186	17,000 0
Wheat	,,	463	...	310,501	52,979 16
Agricultural implements	...	...	360 12	...	860 8
Fruit and nuts	...	...	535 8	...	325 8
Manufactured iron and steel	...	...	4,967 8	...	5,671 12
Wine	...	...	...	...	211 4
Powder and explosives	...	...	...	...	...
Lumber	Feet	...	...	244,000	1,014 0
Lime and cement	...	...	...	...	...
Coals	Tons	...	...	...	...
Other articles	...	...	14,020 12	...	10,096 4
Total	...	...	40,725 8	...	88,158 12

SAN DIEGO.

TABLE showing Total Value of all Articles Exported from and Imported to San Diego from and to Foreign Countries during the Years 1896–97.

Country.	Exports. 1896. £ s.	Exports. 1897. £ s.	Imports. 1896. £ s.	Imports. 1897. £ s.
Great Britain and British possessions	20,841 8	69,985 16	36,709 8	26,377 8
Mexico	19,262 0	16,297 8	35,033 0	30,107 12
Not classified	622 0	1,875 8	4,240 4	16,799 12
Total	40,725 8	88,158 12	75,982 12	73,284 12

CUSTOMS Return for the Port of San Diego, California, for the Year ending June 30, 1897.

Articles.		Quantity.	Value. £ s.
Dutiable imports	..	..	44,101 0
Free imports	..	..	29,183 12
Coal	Tons ..	44,614	26,768 8
Cement	Casks..	34,850	9,462 12
Grain exports	Bushels	497,689	69,985 16

RETURN of all Shipping at the Port of San Diego, California, U.S.A., during the Year 1897.

ENTERED.

Nationality.	Sailing. Number of Vessels.	Sailing. Tons.	Steam. Number of Vessels.	Steam. Tons.	Total. Number of Vessels.	Total. Tons.
British	9	13,068	8	11,429	17	24,497
American	159	21,140	172	163,971	331	185,111
Other countries	2	2,726	74	11,458	76	14,184
Total	170	36,934	254	186,858	424	223,792
,, for the year preceding	134	35,064	233	161,784	367	196,851

SAN DIEGO.

CLEARED.

Nationality.	Sailing. Number of Vessels.	Sailing. Tons.	Steam. Number of Vessels.	Steam. Tons.	Total. Number of Vessels.	Total. Tons.
British	12	18,388	8	11,429	20	29,817
American	158	19,643	171	163,806	329	183,449
Other countries	2	2,726	73	11,354	75	14,080
Total	172	40,757	252	186,589	424	227,346
,, for the year preceding	134	35,064	233	161,784	367	196,851

The total number of vessels arriving was 424, classified as follows:—

Nationality.	Number of Vessels.	Total net Tonnage.
American (U.S.)	331	185,111
British	17	24,497
Nicaraguan	20	2,080
Norwegian and German	3	5,325
Other countries	53	6,779
Total	424	223,792

Shipping and navigation. The number of entries of British vessels shows a decrease of four. One cargo of coal came from Newcastle, N.S.W., in a German vessel. The Norwegian steamer "Peter Gebsen" was recently purchased by parties in San Francisco, and will, in all probability, permanently do the carrying trade in British Columbia coal. This was formerly done entirely by the British steamer "Crown of England."

Seamen's wages. Seamen's wages ruled from 3l. 10s. to 6l. 5s. per month. There is a great scarcity of seamen, owing to the large wages at present paid to men engaged in the Klondike shipping trade. It is consequently hard to get men to go to sea in other vessels. The wages of the ordinary coasting and lumber vessels have advanced to 40 dol. or about 8l. per month from the same cause, which not only keeps seamen on the coast, but is a great incentive to those who come here from foreign ports to desert their vessels.

New steamship line. In the way of ocean commerce, San Diego has added to her facilities during 1897 by the establishment of the Lower California Development Company's Steamship line. This line extends from San Diego on the north to the port of San Benito, State of Chiapas, Mexico, on the south, taking in all the principal ports on the Western Mexican Coast. San Diego is the only Californian port of call.

Proposed line of British steamers. A proposal to run a new line of British steamers on the west coast of North America, between Vancouver and Panama, has for some time been under the consideration of persons of

(225)

commercial importance. The advantages of establishing such a line at the present time would seem very favourable. The following are some of the particulars. The home port of the line to be at Vancouver, B.C., the terminus of the Canadian Pacific Railway, and the western outlet for the commerce of the Dominion. At Vancouver there are great advantages in the matter of a good port and cheap coaling facilities. The proposed line is to operate down the west coast of North America, touching at San Francisco or San Diego and the ports of Mexico, Guatemala, Salvador, Honduras, Nicaragua, Costa Rica, to Panama, where connections can be made with the Pacific Steamship Navigation Company of Liverpool, and viâ the Panama Railroad at Colon, with the Royal Mail Steamship Company, the West India Steamship Company, the Compagnie Générale Transatlantique, and a Spanish line of steamers to Cuba and Barcelona. The line proposes to tap at its several points of call a rich field for Canadian products, as, for example, mining machinery, cotton goods, furniture, flour, &c., and in return would bring north to Vancouver, ores, hard-woods, hides, coffee, and such raw materials as are to be obtained in tropical countries. With such excellent connecting-links at both ends, the Canadian Pacific Railway, and the British steamship lines already established at Panama and Colon, it is expected that a large passenger traffic might be gradually built up, both in the ordinary course of travel and in special arrangements for circular tours out from Europe viâ the West Indies, up the North American coast, and home viâ the Canadian Pacific Railway, or vice versa. It is also hoped that mail and other concessions may be obtained from the Mexican and Central American Governments. In order to economise and successfully meet the competition of the lines partially occupying the field, it is suggested that lascar crews be employed on the steamers.

Population and industries. Railroads. An encouraging feature during the close of the year was the granting of a franchise by the City Council to a committee appointed by the Chamber of Commerce to promote the construction of a direct railroad to the east, and it is hoped that the year 1898 will bring about a definite and feasible plan for forming this connection by a line independent of the Santa Fé Railroad system. The fact that this line does not take a more direct course in reaching the seaboard militates both against the railroad and the port of San Diego. Under the present arrangements of the trans-continental lines connecting with the Santa Fé, passengers can make the journey from San Diego to Chicago in three days, and to or from New York city in four. This is a wonderful decrease in the time necessary only a year ago.

Side walks. Miles of fine cement side-walks have been laid during the past year, for which work Portland cement is used entirely. All the side streets are being improved with the walks also, and there is no indication that graders and cement contractors will be idle for the future. Private residences are being beautified to correspond to the changed conditions, and new ones are being continually added.

SAN DIEGO.

While the amount of money expended in building was not so large as in the previous year, when some very fine business blocks were erected, 1897 has made a very creditable record, the building operations representing an outlay of over 60,000*l*. Up to December 20 the amount shown by the books of the Board of Public Works, which issues permits for the erection of new buildings, was 58,000*l*.; but in many instances the amounts given by intending builders were much less than the actual cost. *Building.*

The water system of the Southern California Water Company, for the irrigation of the southern portion of San Diego County, is one of the largest systems in the State. Work has been prosecuted upon it for several years, especially on the lower Otay dam, which was completed in 1897 to the 130-foot contour line. Since the city voted 300,000*l*. bonds for its new water supply and distributing system, the work of constructing the Morena dam has been pushed with vigour. Morena will supply the city with 1,000 inches of water for the irrigation of an immense tract of land. The city bonds to carry out the contract with the company were voted in June, 1896, and since then the water company has expended on an average about 200*l*. per day for every working day. Morena dam is about half-finished, and a big force is at work putting in rock daily, provision having been made to divert the winter floods in order to permit of steady work. Barrett dam, the third of the system, is well under way, the foundations having been laid and the dam built up to the 35-foot contour line during the past year. Buildings have been erected, roads built, stores laid in, and other preliminary work done, preparatory to active work of construction as soon as the winter flood time is over. The total estimated cost of the entire system is 600,000*l*. *New water system.*

Within the past three years gold mining has been carried on more extensively than at any time since the litigation in 1874-76 between the miners and the owners of the Cuyamaca grant. Operations are conducted on more legitimate mining lines, returns are said to be more certain, and all conditions more satisfactory. New mines have been opened, old ones have resumed operations, and greater depth has been reached. Improved methods of reducing the ores have been inaugurated, the sulphates and other base ores being treated with satisfactory results. *Gold mining.*

The San Diego brewery is the most important manufacturing industry in this portion of the State. It was finished in 1897 at a cost of 35,000*l*., and the first beer was placed on the market in April of last year. The beer was of excellent quality, and at once secured public favour. The total capacity of the brewery is 66,000 barrels per year, with a storage capacity of 25,000 barrels, which will be increased as business demands. *San Diego brewery.*

The mean temperature for the year, 61, was normal; the highest, 88, occurred on April 9; and the lowest, 38, on December 19. During the year there were nine days when the *Meteorological data.*

(225)

Agriculture. Citrons, fruits.

temperature was 80, and three when it was below 40; hence at no time did the temperature reach either 90 or 32. The total rainfall for the year was 10·93 inches, or ·42 above the 26-year normal. The maximum wind velocity was 35 miles per hour on January 13. The character of the weather was as follows: Clear, 259 days; partly cloudy, 39; cloudy, 56; and days on which 0·01 or more rain fell, 41. During the year there were 15 days on which fog occurred.

The citrus output of San Diego County shows material increase over last year. For 1896 the totals were: Lemons, 219 cars; oranges, 162 cars. The figures of the Santa Fé Railroad and of the steamship company for 1897 show: Lemons, 381 cars; oranges, 224 cars, a gain of 60 per cent. It is hardly probable that this ratio of increase will be kept up, although an additional year on 500,000 trees, all young, means much. Prices for the year were fair on oranges, but low on lemons. Until late in the summer foreign importations of the latter were heavy. Then the new tariff resulted, as hoped, in decreasing the imports, and prices would have gone up had not Southern California commenced shipping hundred of cars of half-coloured sour oranges. Altogether, nearly 1,700 cars of new oranges, none of them really ripe and sweet, went forward and had the effect of keeping the market low.

Lemons.

The competition with foreign lemons has been, and is to-day, a great source of discouragement to Californian growers, but this drawback is not so great as the freight rates charged by railroads transporting lemons to Eastern markets. The foreign lemon growers still have a good thing in the eastern part of the United States. The cost of labour with them would be about two-thirds cheaper than here, and they can land their lemons in Chicago for 67½ c. per box, as against 1 dol. 37 c. from this point in the summer months and 1 dol. 5 c. in the winter. Their ocean freight is 12½ c. per box, with railroad freight from New York to Chicago 55 c. From San Diego to Chicago the railroad charge is ordinarily 1 dol. 5 c., and in refrigerator cars during the hot months 1 dol. 37 c. So that Californian growers have no great advantage, notwithstanding the duty of 1 c. per lb. on the foreign fruit.

Fruit-growing industry.

The annual report of the State Board of Agriculture for 1897 affords among other matters a résumé of the fruit-growing industry. The report estimates the total value of the orchard products of the State for 1897 at 4,257,909*l*. This great total is divided as follows:—

Articles.	Value.
	£
Citrus fruits	770,000
Prunes	580,000
Dried fruits other than prunes	520,000
Raisins	457,000
Deciduous fruits	400,000
Nuts	120,000
Canned fruits	1,410,909

This is a good return, but unfortunately the value of the crop is misleading when considered as an index of the profit to the grower. On this point the report says: Comparing the values of California's productions for the past season, it will be observed that the orchard products of this State are second only to wheat. With these values, in some instances much lower than usual, we show a valuable orchard yield, and it is to be regretted that the grower—the one who has taken all the chances of loss up to bearing time, besides having the elements to contend with each season—should receive (excepting for citrus fruits) the smaller portion of the returns, the great bulk of these values going to make good the enormous expense of marketing the product.

In the shipments of deciduous fruits under present methods it is safe to say that refrigeration, transportation, and charges of commission men will average from 75 to 90 per cent. of the entire sales, to say nothing of material and labour in preparing shipments. At present prices for cured fruits, the amount returned from sales thereof pays but little over cost of picking and packing, leaving no returns for investment and time of grower.

The above conclusions of the State Board of Agriculture should be carefully considered by intending English immigrants who may wish to go in for fruit-raising in California. The grower of oranges and perhaps lemons, however, is more fortunately situated. Regarding this branch of the industry the report speaks encouragingly, saying:—

The exception is made in citrus fruits by reason of the growers of this product having organised and perfected a system that controls to a great extent the sale of their crop, and then the failures of the Florida crop have enabled them to establish themselves on a better footing, and we now have what promises to be a permanent market, as the importations of the foreign product are becoming less each year.

The report then goes on to say:—

By references made hereto, we do not intend to convey the idea that our fruit industry is a failure, but only is so far as our marketing methods are concerned. If the grower delegates all his work and financial business to agents, permitting extraordinary charges and non-remunerative sales, he is simply not capable, in a business sense, conducting his affairs, and the sooner he finds it out the better it will be for him.

Wheat and barley. The estimate of the wheat crop, as shown in tables, is 31,449,381 bushels, as against 29,655,174 for 1896. There is not much difference in the yield of barley as compared with that of 1896, and the exports for the year amounted to 3,405,000 centals, or almost 450,000 less than in 1896. The European demand for our best barley still continues, and prices ranged from 90 c. for feed to 1 dol. 15 c. per cental for export.

Wheat estimate for 1898. Regarding the estimate of the crop of 1898 the report says:—

Flour.

While it is quite early to get the exact acreage for 1898, we are safe in saying that there is a very marked increase in the wheat acreage for the coming season, and thus far the condition of plant life is most favourable. With a normal rainfall from this time on, we should have the largest crop since 1889, when the yield for California was 40,000,000 bushels, as all available land in the wheat-growing countries of the State has been seeded.

Exports of flour for the year amounted to 870,000 barrels, against 1,170,000 in 1896, the decrease having been about 200,000 barrels to Australia, and 100,000 to China.

Sheep and wool.

There are in this State only about 3,000,000 sheep. The wool product for 1897 amounted to 32,500,000 lbs., at an average price of about 12 c., equalling nearly 800,000*l*., or 4,000,000 dol. for this output. The prices for spring clip opened up at 7 c., but soon went to 10 and 12 c.; full wools were worth from 12 to 17 c.

Beet sugar.

Four beet sugar factories are now operating in this State, and the output for the year 1897 was 78,000,000 lbs. of sugar, as against 65,000,000 lbs. in 1896 (with one small factory in addition) showing a 20 per cent. increase. California's sugar output is 1·7 per cent. of all kinds of sugar consumed in the United States. There are facilities for extension sufficient to supply at least 50 per cent. of the amount used by the people of this country without encroachment on any of the staple products. Being one of the firm staples, it will always bring a reasonable price. Returns are so quick from the time of planting that not half the year is gone when the land is cleaned of the crop, and the money turned in for it. The sugar product, having the advantage of a protected market, leaves little chance for loss, hence capital is bound to seek investment therein. Within one year it is expected that at least six factories will be in operation in this State, which will equal in number and capacity the entire number in the other States of the Union. The soil and climate are particularly adapted to sugar-beet growing, and the yield per acre is as large as in those foreign countries where the industry thrives most profitably.

Public works. Zuninga jetty.

Up to the end of 1897 there have been employed in the construction of the Zuninga jetty 80,000 tons of rock, 400,000 feet of timber, and 33,000 linear feet of piles. To complete the structure will require a total of 110,000 tons of rock, and 9,000 cubic yards of brush for mattresses. The purpose of the jetty is to concentrate the tide in one channel across the outer bar, and thus deepen the entrance. The work is not under the continuous contract system, and is therefore delayed while Congress is making appropriations to continue it. As the River and Harbour Bill is passed every two years, there is a year lapsing between contracts. An appropriation is expected to be made at the present session, to be available on July 1. The time consumed in preparing specifications, advertising and awarding contracts, will carry the beginning of work probably into next fall. As work can be done here, however, in the winter, little time will actually be lost. The total cost of the jetty is estimated to be between 80,000*l*. and 90,000*l*. It is impossible to gauge the expense accurately, on account of the changing character of the work as the jetty extends seaward. Already, for instance, over 7 acres of land have formed at the base of the jetty. The scouring process at the end, caused by the change of tidal current, is such as to render it impossible to estimate the cost of further work. In round numbers it is believed that about 30,000*l*. more will be required.

Three gun emplacements have been completed during the year on Ballast Point at the harbour's mouth, besides the torpedo casemate. Two of the 10-inch disappearing guns have arrived, and another is on the way. It is estimated that the total cost of the armaments at San Diego will amount to about 300,000*l*.

Harbour defences.

LONDON:
Printed for Her Majesty's Stationery Office,
By HARRISON AND SONS,
Printers in Ordinary to Her Majesty.
(75 7 | 98—H & S 225)

No. 2206 Annual Series.

DIPLOMATIC AND CONSULAR REPORTS.

UNITED STATES.

REPORT FOR THE YEAR 1898

ON THE

TRADE AND COMMERCE OF NEW ORLEANS AND DISTRICT.

REFERENCE TO PREVIOUS REPORT, Annual Series No. 2030.

Presented to both Houses of Parliament by Command of Her Majesty,
FEBRUARY, 1899.

LONDON:
PRINTED FOR HER MAJESTY'S STATIONERY OFFICE,
BY HARRISON AND SONS, ST. MARTIN'S LANE,
PRINTERS IN ORDINARY TO HER MAJESTY.

And to be purchased, either directly or through any Bookseller, from
EYRE & SPOTTISWOODE, EAST HARDING STREET, FLEET STREET, E.C., and
32, ABINGDON STREET, WESTMINSTER, S.W.; or
JOHN MENZIES & Co., 12, HANOVER STREET, EDINBURGH, and
90, WEST NILE STREET, GLASGOW; or
HODGES, FIGGIS, & Co., Limited, 104, GRAFTON STREET, DUBLIN.

1899.

[C. 9044—32.] *Price Twopence.*

CONTENTS.

	PAGE
NEW ORLEANS—	
Review and general remarks	3
Bank clearings	4
Trade of the year	4
Railroad business	5
Total commerce of the port	5
Cotton	6
Grain trade	9
Flour	10
Coffee	11
Rice	12
Lumber	12
Wholesale trade summarised	13
Sugar	13
Shipping	13
Lack of water in South Pass	16
Wharfage	17
Floating and graving dock	17
Sanitary improvements	18
Yellow fever statistics	18
Rank of New Orleans compared with other ports	19
Seamen	19
PENSACOLA report	19
MOBILE report	24

No. 2206. **Annual Series.**

Reference to previous Report, Annual Series No. 2030.

Report on the Trade and Commerce of the Consular District of New Orleans for the Year 1898

By Mr. Consul Vansittart.

(Received at Foreign Office, February 2, 1899.)

New Orleans has enjoyed a larger business during the year 1898 than during the preceding year, and this notwithstanding the yellow fever epidemic and the war with Spain. <small>Review and general remarks.</small>

The bank clearings, commonly accepted as a reliable test of business prosperity, show a gain of a fraction over 6 per cent. compared with the preceding season. It should not be forgotten that there was absolutely no speculation in cotton to swell the clearings, and, although the cotton crop was very large, it sold at such low prices as to make the value of the cotton handled in New Orleans actually less than last year. The increase in clearings, therefore, in reality, represents a better trade than the mere figures indicate.

The value of the exports for the fiscal year ending August 31, 1898, was 20 per cent. in excess of the great commercial year 1892, and 2,069,743*l.* in excess of the year 1897.

One of the most remarkable facts connected with the foreign trade for the fiscal year 1898 has been the decline in the importations in the face of the great purchasing power abroad, conferred upon this country by the volume of agriculture and manufacturing exports. There have, apparently, been two general causes at work which have affected the imports of the past year to a considerable extent. One of these was the large volume of imports of certain classes of dutiable articles during the fiscal year 1897, in anticipation of the Dingley Tariff Law, which took effect on July 24, 1897. The other was the threat of the war with Spain, and its final outbreak.

The expansion of exports was due to the heavy outward movement of grain, and not to the larger volume of cotton handled.

Notwithstanding the small imports of manufactures, it is stated that the New Orleans manufacturers have not only supplied the home markets during the past year, but have been able to increase their exports over those of any preceding year.

(307)

There were several items in which the war actually, immediately, and definitely affected New Orleans. It put an end to the business done with Spain, or through Spanish lines; it suspended the Cuban trade, which was reaching good proportions; and it materially affected the coasting trade by diverting to warlike purposes 15 vessels which went into the United States Government service.

It should, however, be remarked that New Orleans kept up its coasting trade throughout the war, taking all risks and dangers, while Galveston and other Gulf ports suspended business as far as coasting traffic was concerned.

With this diversion of vessels, the coasting tonnage of the port naturally fell off, viz., to 29,344 tons, or less than 6 per cent. from previous year.

The ocean tonnage of the port, compared with last year, shows an improvement of nearly 11 per cent. There was a total improvement in tonnage received and shipped by rail, river, and ocean of 1,265,153 tons, the greatest amount of freight handled and moved during any year in the history of New Orleans.

There was also an increase in the receipts of produce and manufactured goods from the interior of 3,178,087*l*.

The total grain movement was 41,255,642 bushels, against 34,381,956 bushels in 1896–97, a marked improvement.

There was likewise a marked improvement in the provision and breadstuff trade, the exports of flour being three times in bulk and four times in value those of last year. The same is true of bacon, salted meats, and provisions of all kinds. Much of this increase is traceable to the war, and the demands created by it.

Bank clearings.

A comparison of the credit clearings of the associated banks for the 12 months of the commercial year, which many financiers regard as the best indication of the character of trade, results as follows:—

Season.	Bank Clearings.
	£
1897–98	89,394,789
1896–97	86,684,900
Increase	2,709,889

The foreign commerce of the port.

The exact comparison of the foreign commerce of the port is shown by the following figures, giving the value of the merchandise, imported and exported, as taken from the returns of the Collector of the port of New Orleans:—

NEW ORLEANS.

Year.	Imports.	Exports.	Customs Receipts.
	£	£	£
1897–98	1,953,125	22,176,564	282,350
1896–97	3,262,983	20,106,821	589,300
Decrease	1,309,858		306,950
Increase		2,069,743	

The following table shows the business done by the six trunk lines running into New Orleans, in tonnage forwarded from and received at this port, during the year:— *Improvement in railroad business.*

	Quantity.	
	Forwarded.	Received.
	Tons.	Tons.
Southern Pacific..	562,197	562,372
Texas and Pacific	170,722	705,380
Illinois Central ..	263,075	1,076,197
Louisville and Nashville	274,339	379,737
New Orleans and North Eastern	200,231	366,674
Yazoo and Mississippi Valley ..	102,941	734,137
Minor roads	35,000	140,000
Total	1,608,505	3,964,497

The above total, viz., 5,573,002 tons, as compared with the 4,932,212 tons for 1896–97, gives an increase of 640,790 tons in favour of railroad business during 1897–98.

The total commerce of the port of all kinds, received and exported, coastwise and to foreign ports, was:— *Total commerce of the port.*

1897–98.

	Tonnage.	Value.
		£
Receipts from interior by river and rail..	5,101,250	33,491,040
By coasting vessels	524,959	1,265,069
By foreign vessels..	1,595,979	1,951,125
Total receipts	7,222,188	36,707,234
Shipments by rail and river	1,930,662	16,850,881
Exports, coastwise..	481,990	10,106,048
" foreign ..	1,657,929	22,176 564
Total shipments	4,070,581	49,133,493
Grand total of commerce ..	11,292,769	85,840,727

(307)

NEW ORLEANS.

Cotton.

Mr. Hester, Secretary of the New Orleans Cotton Exchange, reports as follows:—

The cotton crop of the United States for the year ending August 31, 1898, amounts to 11,199,994 bales, showing an increase over the crop of 1896–97 of 2,442,030 bales; over that of 1895–96, of 4,042,648 bales; and over that of 1894–95, of 1,298,743 bales. Every State in the cotton belt, except Texas, produced more cotton in 1897–98 than ever before recorded.

Compared with last year, in round figures, 1,615,000 bales of the excess were in the groups known as the "other Gulf" and Atlantic States; Texas (including Indian territory), showing an increase of 827,000 bales; the Gulf States (Arkansas, Louisiana, Mississippi, Tennessee, Missouri, Oklahoma, Utah, Kansas), of 943,000 bales; and the Atlantic States (Alabama, Georgia, Florida, North Carolina, South Carolina, Kentucky, and Virginia), of 672,000 bales. A noticeable feature is the increase of production in Oklahoma and Indian territories (the latter counted statistically as part of Texas), the gain in which has been 264,000 bales.

The year, like its predecessor, has been marked by an absence of speculative influences, and a limited range of fluctuations.

Cotton prices.

The war with Spain was practically without effect upon the price of cotton anywhere. The highest point touched was at the opening of the season, viz., $7\frac{1}{16}$ c. ($3\frac{1}{2}d.$), and the lowest in January, $5\frac{3}{16}$ c. ($2\frac{3}{4}d.$). At or near $2\frac{1}{2}d.$ per lb. for middling seemed to be considered the danger line, and while, in face of the large crop, a constantly timid feeling was manifested by operators for a rise, the low price and past experience deterred short sellers.

The average commercial value of the crop has been $5l.$ $18s.$ $0\frac{1}{2}d.$ per bale, against $7l.$ $11s.$ $7\frac{1}{2}d.$ in 1896–97; $8l.$ $9s.$ $2d.$ in 1895–96; and $6l.$ $3s.$ $9d.$ in 1894–95; and the total value of the crop compares with the previous five years as follows:—

Year.	Quantity.	Value.
	Bales.	£
1897–98	11,199,994	64,110,521
1896–97	8,757,964	64,384,966
1895–96	7,157,346	58,819,069
1894–95	9,901,251	59,407,506
1893–94	7,549,817	56,623,627
1892–93	6,700,365	56,953,102

The commercial crop contains a part of the growths of three seasons, though the quantity of new cotton included for August of this year is smaller than for either of the two previous years.

In considering the actual growth of the current year, Mr. Hester arrives at the following calculation:—

NEW ORLEANS.

	Quantity.
	Bales.
Commercial crop of 1897-98	11,200,000
Less old cotton left over from 1896-97	100,000
	11,100,000
Plus growth 1897-98 marketed in 1896-97	84,000
Growth not marketed in 1897-98	330,000
	11,514,000
Deduct August receipts of new cotton of the growth of 1898-99	29,000
Actual growth of 1897-98	11,485,000

Last year at this time the country was practically bare of cotton, and 100,000 bales was a full, though not excessive allowance for the quantity then remaining on plantations, at counted and uncounted interior towns, and in the hands of southern spinners. As a general rule, from 2½ to 3 per cent. of the crop can be counted as being left over.

TOTAL Exports of the United States.

Year.	Quantity.				Total.
	Great Britain.	France.	Continent and Channel.	Canada, Overland.	
	Bales.	Bales.	Bales.	Bales.	Bales.
1897-98	3,543,330	816,386	3,180,164	118,657	7,658,537
1896-97	3,018,462	702,632	2,250,289	80,617	6,052,000
1895-96	2,299,182	465,870	1,861,116	81,040	4,707,208
1894-95	3,443,574	774,476	2,500,911	99,316	6,818,277

Included under Continent are exports to Mexico, Japan, and China. To Mexico this year there were no exports from New Orleans, 12,050 bales from Galveston, 1,042 bales from Mobile and Pensacola, 16,711 bales from Laredo, 564 bales from El Paso, &c., and 6,335 bales from Eagle Pass—a total of 36,702 bales, against 30,180 bales last year, and 39,298 bales the year before last; to Japan and China, 226,756 bales from San Francisco, Portland, and other ports, against 61,106 bales last year, and 35,578 bales the year before.

The returns of the Southern cotton milling industry for the past season are of a decidedly satisfactory character. Many of the mills have run night and day, and while there have been exceptional complaints of the low price of manufactured goods, the general tone of the reports has been of a cheering nature, and nearly every mill in the South has shared in the increased consumption of cotton.

Cotton consumption of the South. Census of Southern mills.

(307)

NEW ORLEANS.

MILLS.

	Number.
Total number of mills last year	482
Crossed out and merged into other concerns, and burned	20
	462
New and uncompleted mills added to list	29
Total number of cotton mills in the South	491

Last year the number of mills added was 19.

SPINDLES.

	Number.
In the South, total in operation	3,680,741
,, idle	125,160
New, not completed	251,343
Grand total	4,057,244

showing an increase of spindles, old, idle, and not complete, over last year of 205,203, and a gain of spindles at work during more or less of the past year of 261,078.

The total consumption in all the mills (old and new) for the year was 1,231,841 bales, against 1,042,671 bales for the season of 1896–97, and 904,701 bales for that of 1895–96, an increase over last year of 189,170 bales, and over the year before of 327,140 bales.

The increase in the average consumption per spindle in mills in operation has been $15\frac{1}{2}$ lbs.

The following table shows the progress of the industry during the past seven years:—

Year.	Consumption.	Increase.	Decrease.
	Bales.	Bales.	Bales.
1891–92	686,080	81,419	..
1892–93	743,348	57,768	..
1893–94	718,515		25,333
1894–95	862,838	144,323	..
1895–96	904,701	41,863	..
1896–97	1,042,671	137,970	..
1897–98	1,231,841	189,170	..

As a general thing, the weights of bales consumed by the mills have been heavier, the average for all the mills showing $5\frac{42}{100}$ lbs. per bale more than last year.

CONSUMPTION United States. (American Cotton.)

	Quantity.	
	1897-98.	1896-97.
	Bales.	Bales.
Total takings for consumption in United States	3,443,581	2,847,351
Of which—		
Taken by spinners in Southern States	1,231,841	1,042,671
„ Northern spinners	2,211,740	1,804,680

Notwithstanding the low price of the staple, of which the Northern and Eastern mills bought largely, there was little, if any, margin of profit. It is claimed that many mills were run at a loss.

The South, on the contrary, has done well. It has added more spindles, and its increase in the number of bales consumed is greater than has yet been recorded in any one year. The takings of American mills are the heaviest on record.

The importation of foreign cotton during the year has amounted to the equivalent of 97,900 bales in American weight, against an equivalent of 106,000 bales last year. *Importation of foreign cotton.*

This shows a total improvement in tonnage received and shipped by rail, river, and ocean of 1,265,153 tons, as compared with preceding year. This is estimated to be the greatest amount of freight handled and moved during any year in the history of New Orleans.

While New Orleans has not enjoyed as large a proportion of the total grain export trade of the country as the previous season, there has, nevertheless, been a great increase in the aggregate number of bushels shipped. There was a falling-off in the total of corn shipments, but this was more than met by the very large increase in the exports of wheat. *The grain trade.*

A feature of the breadstuff and grain trade is the large number of ports which it has opened to New Orleans, which formerly did nearly its entire business with a few great ports New York, Liverpool, Hamburg, Bremen, and Havre.

The receipts for the year ended August 31, 1898, were:—

	Quantity.
	Bushels.
Wheat	16,310,663
Corn	22,420,841
Oats	2,131,574
Rye	392,564
Total grain	41,255,642

against 33,904,482 bushels of grain in 1896-97, and 22,731,025 in 1895-96, thus nearly doubling in two years.

Flour.

The exports of flour were three times in bulk, and four times in value, those of last year. Much of this increase is directly traceable to the demand created by the war.

It required 470 ships, against 434 the previous year, to carry the grain from this port, and their nationalities were as follows:—

Nationality.	Number of Vessels.
British	395
Spanish	24
German	15
French	9
Norwegian	4
Danish	13
Dutch	2
Austro-Hungarian	3
Greek	2
Belgian	1
Swedish	2

Only two ships appear to have flown the American flag, viz., ss. "Algiers," which carried 11,000 bushels of corn to Havana in January, and ss. "Clio," which carried 80,000 bushels of wheat to Marseilles in February.

The largest cargo of grain was carried by the British steamer "Alberta" to Cork in February, and consisted of 254,000 bushels of corn.

The following statement shows the shipments of grain exported through New Orleans, with the amounts in bushels, from September 1, 1897, to August 31, 1898 :—

NEW ORLEANS.

1897-98.

Destination.	Corn.	Wheat.	Oats.	Rye.
	Bushels.	Bushels.	Bushels.	Bushels.
Liverpool	6,090,559	2,933,019	93,265	..
Rouen	3,002,620	2,642,447	1,652,274	547,480
Hamburg	1,946,997	1,079,092	..	123,890
Copenhagen	1,450,755	91,350	..	24,708
Rotterdam	1,431,548	1,919,245	210,045	20,886
Havre	1,363,030	1,129,519	..	..
Belfast	1,743,141	..	..	..
Hull	882,793	1,251,498	..	..
Dunkirk	687,311	261,345	50,000	..
Antwerp	146,000	1,494,517	..	..
Bremen	384,941	72,000	..	..
Dublin	265,841	68,215	..	..
Marseilles	440,703	413,084	..	..
Bordeaux	167,297	496,556	25,000	..
Manchester	841,753	364,712	..	..
Nantes	..	77,000	40,000	..
London	102,914	156,500	..	..
Bristol	119,000	164,000	..	..
Cork	251,000	121,968	..	..
Newcastle-on-Tyne	68,714	31,680	..	..
Trieste	146,800	..	..	..
Aarhus	104,600	..	..	..
Leith	95,814	..	..	..
Stettin	49,000	..	..	..
Falmouth	482,500	..	..	..
Rochefort	..	288,398	..	..
Genoa	..	26,000	..	..
Havana	28,371	..	..	..
Barcelona	261,571	..	..	..

The following table gives exports of grain, in bushels, from New Orleans for the undernamed years ending August 31:—

Year.	Corn.	Wheat.
	Bushels.	Bushels.
1897-98	22,420,841	16,310,663
1896-97	29,235,895	3,627,105
1895-96	21,031,156	1,642,444

Coffee. During the season of 1897-98 arrivals of Brazilian coffee in New Orleans amounted to 263,000 bags, as against 295,000 in 1896-97, and the receipts of other kinds amounted to 54,300 bags, as against 78,376 in 1896-97. The decline in the mild coffee arrivals was due mainly to the small size of the Mexican crop, which had been damaged by frost, and the increased home consumption, in Mexico due to extremely low prices. During the same period, Baltimore imported 234,365 bags from Brazil, and San Francisco imported 130,000 bags of mild coffee.

Rice.

The history of the rice industry in Louisiana for the season 1897-98 shows improvement over the preceding year. The crop was not heavy, but at the same time it was considerably larger than its predecessor, and its marketing was more satisfactory to producers in every respect. Owing to the fact that the country mills now consume a considerable proportion of the rough rice produced, the receipts at New Orleans no longer represent the entire crop, it being estimated that from 25 to 30 per cent. is handled by country mills.

Reducing the rough rice to clean (three sacks to the barrel) the record of the crops for the past five years is as follows:—

Year.	Total Crop.
	Barrels.
1893-94	313,466
1894-95	264,946
1895-96	442,528
1896-97	150,649
1897-98	229,606

There was a satisfactory range of prices. Average weight for sacks of rough rice, crop 1897-98, was 162 lbs.; average weight for barrels of clean rice, crop 1897-98, 330 lbs.

It is estimated that in Louisiana there are 25 rice mills, representing invested capital not less than 400,000l., employing an average of 30 hands each, making a total of 750 workpeople.

The South-western Louisiana rice production and milling are almost the sole industry, and the entire population is dependent upon it. Some 2,000,000 acres are in cultivation in the rice district, the irrigating plants and canals, in operation, having cost 100,000l. The population dependent upon the rice industry in Louisiana is probably not less than 80,000 people.

The cost of producing rice is estimated to be about 5l. per acre, the average yield about 32 bushels. The tax levied by Congress on imported rice is 2 c., or 1d. per lb.

Lumber.

The production of lumber within the city limits has materially decreased, owing to the keen competition of country mills, and the continued depletion of forests accessible to the city. Exports, on the whole, have steadily increased during the last few years, and had it not been for the war with Spain, the total exports for the year 1897-98 would have been greater than 1896-97 by several millions of feet. Prices are better and steady. Locally the past year will compare very favourably with any year since 1892, while the outlook for the coming year is exceptionally good.

As a general wholesale market in all lines of merchandise, New Orleans is a distributing centre for an immense territory. There has been a decided increase in drugs, chemicals, bananas, lemons, oranges, cocoanuts, and other tropical fruits; also an increase of high wines and fine liqueurs. *Wholesale trade summarised.*

In the tobacco business the enterprising wholesale firms in this city practically secured all the available output, which amounted to some 12,000 bales from Cuba, and several hundreds from Mexico. The improvement shown in high-grade cigars is probably due to the superior quality of tobacco used, and excellence of workmanship. This market distributes large quantities of plug and smoking tobacco, cigarettes, and snuff.

An improvement is also noticeable in the distribution of general hardware, and agricultural implements; stamped tinware; and in the growth of the machine and boiler works, which are following up trade heretofore supplied by other markets.

In the last two years New Orleans has made considerable strides in the manufacture of furniture. These factories are now distributing large quantities of their output throughout a considerable territory.

The bulk of the cheap clothing worn on the plantations in the Southern States is supplied by clothing factories established in the city.

The season of 1897–98 was, on the whole, a prosperous one for the sugar industry of Louisiana. The crop (cane sugar) was very large, viz., 310,447 long tons, and molasses 22,241,510 gallons. *Sugar.*

The season opened with prices at rather a low level, considering the large increase in the import duties under the new tariff law. This was due to the enormous importations prior to the passage of the Dingley Law, which enabled refiners to keep out of the market for raw sugars for a long period; but finally the demand for refined sugar enlarged, and, consequently, the meltings were greater, and the stock was rapidly reduced.

The season closed with a total of about 170,000 barrels more receipts than that of 1896–97.

The number of mills in operation in 1897–98 was a few less than 400. The product of these mills amounted to fully 320,000 short tons, a greater product than was formerly turned out in the 1,000 and more sugar houses of the past.

As has been the case for several years past, there was a further falling-off in the percentage of kettle sugar produced, producers finding that so much better results, both in yield and prices, were secured from centrifugal sugar. The planters, hopeful of the favourable results of a higher tariff, planted a larger acreage last spring. The average price of sugar per lb. during 1897–98 was 2d., as against 1¾d. in 1896–97.

There has been a noticeable increase in the shipping business of the port, and it has been a good season. There were nearly 3,000,000 bales of cotton received at this port from the interior during the season, and most of this was shipped away; over *Shipping.*

NEW ORLEANS.

40,000,000 bushels of grain were shipped from New Orleans, and thousands of tons of general cargo.

On the whole the war with Spain caused no interruption in shipping. Several of the fruit lines gave up their boats to the United States Government, but they chartered others for their business.

The expansion of exports was due to the heavy outward movement of grain, and not to the larger volume of cotton handled.

Coastwise trade.

The coastwise trade shows a moderate falling-off in the number and tonnage of vessels employed, owing to the large drain upon American merchant ships running into this port due to the war. A majority of the ships visiting New Orleans regularly were absorbed either by the Navy or Army for war puposes, and, of course, withdrawn from ordinary traffic.

With the diversion of coasting vessels, the coasting tonnage of the port fell off by some 29,344 tons, or less than 6 per cent. from the previous years.

Ocean tonnage.

The increase of the ocean tonnage of the port, in spite of war, and some derangement of the coasting traffic, was of 126 vessels, and 443,853 tons, entered and cleared, as compared with last year an improvement of 150 vessels and 531,318 tons.

The following table shows the increase in number and tonnage of vessels entered and cleared during the past five years :—

Year.	Cleared. Number of Vessels.	Cleared. Tonnage.	Entered. Number of Vessels.	Entered. Tonnage.
1894	1,165	1,511,227	1,146	1,566,642
1895	1,164	1,606,827	1,193	1,615,640
1896	1,205	1,609,759	1,205	1,665,927
1897	1,285	1,916,360	1,275	1,890,644
1898	1,346	2,119,938	1,340	2,130,919

The following tables, marked Annex A., give various returns in connection with the shipping at the port of New Orleans during the year 1898 :—

NEW ORLEANS.

Annex A.—RETURN of all Shipping at the Port of New Orleans during the Year 1898.

ENTERED.

Nationality.	Steam. Number of Vessels.	Steam. Tons.	Sailing. Number of Vessels.	Sailing. Tons.	Total. Number of Vessels.	Total. Tons.
British	567	1,099,325	...	...	567	1,099,325
American	104	68,443	26	10,102	130	78,545
Austro-Hungarian	2	4,491	...	...	2	4,491
Belgian	1	1,944	...	...	1	1,944
Danish	33	55,517	...	...	33	55,517
Dutch	4	7,795	...	...	4	7,795
French	18	35,070	..	...	18	35,070
German	30	49,322	15	16,056	45	65,378
Greek	3	5,042	...	...	3	5,042
Italian	3	5,625	4	2,559	7	8,184
Mexican	2	190	...	...	2	190
Norwegian	210	88,461	1	470	211	88,931
Portuguese	...	...	26	19,758	26	19,758
Russian	...	...	1	431	1	431
Spanish	31	72,389	5	4,759	36	77,148
Swedish	1	2,247	...	...	1	2,247
Total	1,009	1,495,861	78	54,135	1,087	1,549,996
,, for the year preceding	...	...	...	...	1,049	1,478,911

NOTE.—The above figures do not include American coastwise tonnage, viz., 267 vessels of 512,537 tons, or 33 vessels more than in 1897.

CLEARED.

Nationality.	Steam. Number of Vessels.	Steam. Tons.	Sailing. Number of Vessels.	Sailing. Tons.	Total. Number of Vessels.	Total. Tons.
British	558	1,075,827	...	...	558	1,075,827
American	107	69,069	2	350	109	69,419
Austro-Hungarian	16	33,134	1	594	17	33,728
Belgian	1	1,994	...	...	1	1,994
Danish	35	58,391	...	...	35	58,391
Dutch	4	7,795	...	...	4	7,795
French	15	30,179	...	...	15	30,179
German	36	63,556	17	18,815	53	82,371
Greek	3	5,042	...	...	3	5,042
Italian	4	7,267	5	3,927	9	11,194
Mexican	4	275	...	...	4	275
Norwegian	215	90,431	3	2,324	218	92,755
Portuguese	...	...	24	17,296	24	17,296
Russian	...	...	1	431	1	431
Spanish	32	71,960	5	4,759	37	76,719
Swedish	1	2,247	...	...	1	2,247
Total	1,031	1,517,167	58	48,496	1,089	1,565,663
,, for the year preceding	...	...	...	...	1,052	1,505,467

NOTE.—The above figures do not include American coastwise tonnage, viz., 252 vessels of 465,007 tons, or 37 vessels more than in 1897.

NEW ORLEANS.

TABLE of British Shipping Entered and Cleared at the Port of New Orleans during the Year 1898, compared with 1897.

ENTERED.

Year.	Steam. Number of Vessels.	Tons.	Sailing. Number of Vessels.	Tons.	Total. Number of Vessels.	Tons.
1898	567	1,099,325	...	...	567	1,099,325
1897	466	955,575	...	...	466	955,575

NOTE.—101 more ships entered than last year, 1897.

CLEARED.

Year.	Steam. Number of Vessels.	Tons.	Sailing. Number of Vessels.	Tons.	Total. Number of Vessels.	Tons.
1898	558	1,075,827	...	...	558	1,075,827
1897	470	967,755	...	...	470	967,755

NOTE.—88 more ships cleared than last year, 1897.

CARGOES Carried in British Ships during the Year 1898.

Articles.		Quantity.
Cotton	Bales	1,763,151
Cotton products—		
Cotton seed	Sacks	73,953
,, oil	Barrels	99,950
,, oil-cake	Sacks	501,663
,, meal	,,	1,247,915
,, soap stock	Barrels	14,736
Corn	Bushels	16,903,047
Wheat	,,	10,440,238
Oats	,,	1,494,337
Rye	,,	89,730
Flour	Sacks	267,001
Staves	Pieces	11,218,387
Lumber	Feet	4,443,419
,,	Pieces	2,874,290
Logs	,,	6,349
Tallow	Tierces	35,095
Lard	Packages	11,875
Copper	Tons	31,227
Pig-iron	,,	33,671
Spelter	Plates	84,742
Molasses	Barrels	78,441
Tobacco	Hogsheads	3,234

Lack of water in South Pass. The reputation of the port has suffered of late, on account of vessels stranding in South Pass. There has been a number of cases of vessels ashore there during recent years, and the invariable excuse has been lack of water.

The contract with the Jetty Company calls for a minimum depth of 26 feet, but steamers drawing 25 feet, and even less, have been ashore on various occasions. The attention of Congress has been called to this matter, and a survey was recently held with a view to opening South-West Pass, which, it is stated, would give a channel 30 feet deep during the entire year. Should Congress, however, appropriate the money to open South-West Pass, the work would probably require several years, and it is admitted that something should be done in the meantime to maintain a proper depth of water in South Pass. The regular soundings show that there is plenty of water in the Pass except at one or two points, and it is advocated that two modern dredges could easily maintain 26 feet of water in South Pass, and that a moderate charge upon each vessel entering the port would insure a sufficient sum for working these dredges.

The commerce of the entire Mississippi Valley is involved in the providing of better outlets to the sea, and the demand in reality is not local but national, and some 14 States have shown a direct interest in the matter, and appear to be prepared to support and advocate the improvement of the Pass before Congress. Vessels of 30 feet draft are now numerous, and the port which fails to provide for the entrance and exit of such vessels will certainly no longer be able to maintain itself as a first-class commercial mart.

The South-West Pass Bill, at present before Congress, provides for the construction of sufficient jetties and auxiliary works as are necessary to create and maintain a navigable channel, not less than 30 feet wide and 35 feet deep at mean low water of the Gulf, through South-West Pass, from deep water in the Mississippi River to deep water in the Gulf of Mexico.

The wharfage charge of 6*d*. net on the gross register is heavy, and prevents the majority of vessels from loading at city wharves. The railroads, however, have largely overcome this by building wharves at their terminals, where vessels may load without incurring this expense.

Wharfage.

There are, at present, in addition to city wharves, a number of railroad terminal grain elevators and loading berths on the outskirts of the port, where vessels may load to advantage. Among these are Southport, Westwego, Stuyvesant Docks, and Port Chalmette, all with free wharfage and good accommodation.

After successive acts of legislation, directing investigation and laying the groundwork for action, the United States Congress last session made an appropriation of 40,000*l*. towards the construction of a steel floating and graving dock, to be located at the naval reservation at Algiers, Louisiana, and to be capable of lifting a vessel of 15,000 tons displacement, and 27 feet draft, and accommodating vessels of 500 feet and over; the whole to cost about 170,000*l*.

Floating and graving dock at New Orleans.

The prevalence of yellow fever from the middle of September

Sanitary improvements in the city decided upon.

to the end of October, following as it did the epidemic during the autumn of 1897, has called the serious attention of the city authorities and the public to the absolute necessity of an improved drainage system, a complete system of sewerage, and a liberal supply of filtered water.

New Orleans has many natural advantages as a place of residence, but liberal expenditure will be an absolute necessity if the well-being of citizens is to be properly guarded. A recent vigorous campaign appears, however, to have placed the city on a good sanitary basis, and the drainage system is now in full process of construction, a good portion of the work being already done. The sewage, it is hoped, will be taken in hand in the near future. Ordinances have been passed for the eventual paving of the principal streets and thoroughfares of the city. When these absolutely essential and sanitary improvements have been accomplished, there is reason to hope that yellow fever will be a thing of the past, and that the mortality resulting from the periodical (autumnal) outbreaks of malaria, typhoid fever, &c., will be considerably reduced, and the city would thus lose its bad repute of past times in the matter of health.

Yellow fever statistics.

According to a bulletin issued by the United States Hospital Service on the fever in the South during the autumnal period, there were from July 1 to November 10, 1898, 1,470 cases of yellow fever in Louisiana, and 51 deaths, a mortality of 3·47 per cent., and in Mississippi there were 985 cases and 63 deaths, a mortality of 6·4 per cent. The percentage of mortality for the two States was 4·64.

The cases in the city of New Orleans are put down at 74, with 19 deaths, these figures indicating the large death rate of 25 per cent. As a matter of fact there is every reason to suppose that a considerable number of people were seized with the fever from the middle of September to the end of October, but that owing to the dread disease having lost much of its virulence, the death-rate was exceedingly small. The disease was first officially announced in New Orleans on September 17, but it had probably been in existence some time prior to that date. The figures given out can hardly be taken to express the true prevalence and mortality of the disease.

At Franklin, Louisiana, where there were 607 cases and 9 deaths, the disease was declared to be yellow fever as early as August 11, and despite strenuous efforts it prevailed there until the end of October. The apparent spread from one locality to another in the State of Mississippi was not real, the probability being that a number of places were infected at about the same time from one or more centres of infection. The outbreak was generally considered a recrudescence of the fever of the previous year.

Nineteen successive years of immunity from yellow fever have not been able to dispel the general distrust of the sanitary condition of the city, and it appears to be generally admitted that, until that distrust be dispelled, New Orleans can hardly hope to enjoy any great advance in wealth and population.

NEW ORLEANS.

Total value of imports for immediate consumption and warehousing at the port of New Orleans during the year ended December 31, 1898, was about 1,890,933*l*.

The relative rank of New Orleans as a port of import, compared with other ports of the country for the 10 months ended October 31, 1898, is *sixth*.

Total value of all exports from the port of New Orleans to foreign countries during the year ended December 31, 1898, was 20,271,269*l*.

The relative rank of New Orleans as a port of export, compared with the other ports of the United States for the 10 months ended October 31, 1898, is *fourth*.

Rank of New Orleans compared with other ports in imports and exports.

It is satisfactory to note that the discipline amongst British sailors throughout the year has been remarkably good in comparison with foreign seamen serving on board British vessels.

Seamen.

The prevalent diseases amongst British seamen appear to be malarial fevers and dysentery. These fevers are generally contracted at Central American and Mexican ports, and the men on reaching New Orleans are sent to the hospital. But it is only fair to state that in almost all cases, sailors, firemen, &c., on being summoned to the Consulate to show themselves before leaving the hospital, cheerfully agree to be shipped by first opportunity, either for heavy or light work, according to the discretion of the Consul, who takes their state of health into consideration. This cheerfulness and willingness not to complain unnecessarily is in agreeable contrast to foreign seamen, who are in most cases difficult to deal with.

There have been no suits for wages or libelling the ships in United States Courts on the part of British seamen, but there have been some threats on the part of foreign seamen.

Out of 17,306 men arrived in British ships in this port during the year 1898, 170, who deserted, were British subjects, and 161 foreign subjects. The above showing is distinctly satisfactory in comparison with all former years.

PENSACOLA.

Mr. Vice-Consul Howe reports as follows:—

In view of the trade of Pensacola for the year 1898, this report deals especially with the business of the port as regards British interests.

Trade during 1898.

For many years past shipments of pitch-pine wood, in sawn and hewn timber, as well as in boards, deals, and like manufactures of this excellent species of wood from Pensacola to ports in the United Kingdom and elsewhere have been the principal business of the port, and this trade still continues to employ about the same amount of tonnage as formerly.

Shipments of pitch-pine.

It has been pointed out in former reports that several mercantile houses in the United Kingdom were the agents of the

British mercantile houses employed.

(307)

large timber shipping merchants at Pensacola, and that they were also the sellers of the many shipments of pitch-pine wood, which are made hence to ports in the United Kingdom, the bulk of these cargoes going there. These business relations still fully continue, and the same houses, to a large extent, secure orders for cargoes of this staple of Florida growth and manufacture, for shipment to continental Europe, and to many other parts of the world.

British agencies increased by Pensacola's new export trade.

It may be further stated that business with British firms has been very much added to within the past few years by shipments of grain, cotton, tobacco, pig-iron, phosphate rock, wheat, corn, flour, as well as other articles of western and southern products of this country, large quantities of these articles coming direct to the docks at Pensacola for transportation to Liverpool principally, but also to other ports in the United Kingdom.

Shipments to the Continent.

Many cargoes of the articles above mentioned are now also sent to ports on the Continent, and to places elsewhere.

British shipping largely employed.

In this new export trade, in addition to the long continued timber business of Pensacola, British capital also plays a prominent part. To carry these cargoes, British shipping interests are very largely to the front, as will be shown by the tables annexed to this report.

Direct line to Liverpool.

An organised line of steamers plies at short intervals between Pensacola and Liverpool. Lines of steamers sail at stated periods for ports on the Continent, loaded with various articles of export.

Tonnage of all flags.

Of the total tonnage of foreign bottoms (409 vessels), of 459,155 tons, employed in the carrying trade of Pensacola during the year, 126, of 183,021 tons, were British; and of these, 94 steamers took out slightly over one-half of the value of all foreign exports. Therefore, it may be said that British interests and capital in the shipping, as well as in other lines, are holding their own in the export trade of the port.

Imports.

Imports from the United Kingdom, or from elsewhere abroad, figure very lightly at Pensacola, as the bulk of articles for the supply of establishments in the every day requirements of local and adjacent trade—of places in Florida and Alabama—are imported from the large western and northern markets of this country, the value of which amounts to several millions of dollars yearly.

British goods.

The Consular tables in this office are, of course, always kept carefully supplied with the trade catalogues and similar publications, constantly received from publishers and commercial houses in the United Kingdom, for the purpose of introducing, or making known British products and manufactures under their several heads and values. In the face of the excessive tariff now existing in this country, no direct importation of such goods can be gone into at the present time, at least, in this and adjacent smaller markets. Whatever British products and manufactures come to Pensacola and to the small markets of this part of the country are principally secured from New York merchants and other direct importers in the United States.

PENSACOLA.

Fruits are imported here from the nearest British West India Islands, salt from Liverpool, cement from Germany, iron pyrites from Spain, &c.; but these importations do not amount to very large values in the course of a year. *Articles of import from abroad very few.*

In my last annual report I mentioned that an electric street railroad was being laid down at Pensacola to take the place of the cars run by horses and mules. The road has been finished for some months, and the system is very good, covering a large portion of the town, and will be extended over a larger area. *General remarks.*

The health of Pensacola has been good during the past year, and the welfare and prosperity of the people here has been favourable. *Health.*

The following tables show an increase in exports at Pensacola compared with the year preceding. In fact, in this report it is shown that the year 1898 was the largest business year Pensacola has ever had. *Tables show increase of exports.*

The agricultural pursuits at Pensacola are not of sufficiently important interest to the British public at home and abroad as to warrant a separate report. *Agriculture.*

Kitchen gardens, supplying several varieties of vegetables in their respective seasons, abound at and around Pensacola. Small fruit orchards are also kept up by many families, yielding some of the several species of fruit grown in Florida—principally peaches, pears, plums, strawberries, &c.

There are some farms in the suburbs of Pensacola which are conducted by established gardeners, and they produce quantities of vegetables and fruits, all of these products serving largely toward the general supply of the inhabitants of the town.

The dairies here also supply capital milk, which is sold at 40 c. (about 1s. 8d.) per gallon.

Poultry of all sorts is plentiful at Pensacola and its suburbs for the supply of the town.

Beef, mutton, and other fresh meats are always in good supply at Pensacola, much of it being brought here from the western markets by railroad, and preserved in the cold storage compartments of the ice manufacturing establishments at Pensacola.

All things considered, the routine of domestic life at Pensacola, in its every day provision of the necessary articles of agricultural products, is always of good average quality and supply.

PENSACOLA.

Annex A.—RETURN of Principal Articles of Export from Pensacola during the Years 1898–97.

Articles.		1898.		1897.	
		Quantity.	Value.	Quantity.	Value.
			£		£
Pitch-pine lumber	Super. feet	139,529,357	348,823	158,013,360	395,033
Sawn pitch-pine timber	Cubic feet	9,965,337	249,133	12,011,290	300,283
Hewn ,, ,,	,,	509,366	11,861	339,321	7,774
Cotton	Bales	174,356	1,046,136	91,011	663,622
Tobacco	Hogsheads	7,483	149,660	7,534	116,778
Pig-iron	Tons	36,454	75,945	21,369	44,519
Coal	,,	91,523	76,268	118,011	98,337
Phosphate rock	,,	62,620	65,229	...	...
Wheat	Bushels	543,416	72,454	219,134	41,088
Corn	,,	440,341	40,364	424,767	43,742
Flour	Barrels	64,432	64,432	...	...
,,	Sacks	...	...	17,345	14,454
Rosin	Barrels	46,700	29,187	...	...
Turpentine	,,	10,290	25,725	...	...
Lard	Tierces	3,904	25,376	...	...
Cotton-seed meal	Sacks	76,453	13,060	...	...
Oak staves	...	435,030	4,350	...	...
Other articles	...	...	38,507	...	75,265
Total	...	...	2,336,510	...	1,800,895

NOTE.—Exchange at 4 dol. 80 c. per 1*l*.

PENSACOLA.

Annex B.—TABLE showing Total Value of all Articles Exported from and Imported to Pensacola from and to Foreign Countries during the Years 1898–97.

Country.	Exports. 1898.	Exports. 1897.	Imports. 1898.	Imports. 1897.
	£	£	£	£
United Kingdom	1,122,345	1,071,332	1,638	445
British possessions	4,211	12,798	..	450
Germany	476,195	52,460	8,601	5,261
France and colonies	144,812	73,075	..	..
Italy	140,580	82,991	..	179
Belgium	107,423	34,584	..	604
Netherlands	59,557	77,652	..	..
Brazil	49,211	55,666	..	23
Argentine Republic	22,548	34,434	..	..
Egypt	22,070	16,674	..	..
Portugal	15,491	14,517	..	..
Uruguay	15,382	11,108	..	..
Russia	12,030	2,914	..	..
Japan	9,525	50,370	..	..
Denmark	6,560	2,529	..	..
Austria-Hungary	6,001	8,023	..	..
Spain and colonies	3,726	10,782	2,403	..
Mexico	3,248	93,167	..	94,451
Cuba	1,816	..	..	..
Tunis	1,398	1,627	..	..
Turkey	1,254	..	..	..
Peru	1,027	..	..	..
Venezuela	622	..	..	..
Total to foreign countries	2,227,032	1,706,703	..	..
Total to ports in the United States	109,478	94,192	..	..
Grand total	2,336,510	1,800,895	12,642	101,413

Annex C.—RETURN of all Shipping at the Port of Pensacola during the Year 1898.

ENTERED.

Nationality.	Sailing. Number of Vessels.	Sailing. Tons.	Steam. Number of Vessels.	Steam. Tons.	Total. Number of Vessels.	Total. Tons.
British	33	15,851	98	172,005	131	187,856
American	66	34,676	34	31,770	100	66,446
Swedish and Norwegian	118	114,289	2	3,866	120	118,155
Italian	95	76,781	...	...	95	76,781
Spanish	1	753	19	34,929	20	35,682
Russian	28	22,944	...	...	28	22,944
German	11	10,992	5	7,802	16	18,794
Austro-Hungarian	6	6,314	4	8,154	10	14,468
French	1	509	2	2,251	3	2,760
Greek	...	...	1	1,613	1	1,613
Netherlands	...	...	1	1,153	1	1,153
Danish	1	633	...	...	1	633
Total	360	283,742	166	263,543	526	547,285
,, for the year preceding	334	265,997	178	249,821	512	515,818

PENSACOLA.

CLEARED.

Nationality.	Sailing. Number of Vessels.	Sailing. Tons.	Steam. Number of Vessels.	Steam. Tons.	Total. Number of Vessels.	Total. Tons.
British	32	17,761	94	165,260	126	183,021
American	62	36,280	36	32,925	98	69,205
Swedish and Norwegian	122	115,395	2	3,866	124	119,261
Italian	88	70,017	...	...	88	70,017
Spanish	1	753	17	31,065	18	31,818
Russian	25	20,635	...	...	25	20,635
Austro-Hungarian	4	2,618	6	11,832	10	14,450
German	7	6,526	4	6,475	11	13,001
French	2	1,302	2	2,251	4	3,553
Greek	...	...	1	1,613	1	1,613
Netherlands	...	...	1	1,153	1	1,153
Danish	1	633	...	...	1	633
Total	344	271,920	163	256,440	507	528,360
,, for the year preceding	341	267,197	184	254,659	525	521,856

NOTE.—In the return of entrances and clearances of shipping, it may be stated that as regards steamers of the United States, one steamer, the "Pensacola," of 1,069 tons, arrived 27 times in ballast and cleared 28 times with coal for Texas.

MOBILE, ALABAMA.

(Commercial Year ending August 31, 1898.)

Mr. Vice-Consul Benn reports as follows:—

Notwithstanding the visitation of yellow fever in the autumn of 1897, and the war with Spain, our exports were nearly as large as any other year, and our imports larger than before recorded.

Foreign trade. In view of the disturbing influences mentioned above the foreign trade of the port for the year ending August 31, 1898, makes a satisfactory comparison with the trade of the previous year, the decline being less than 3 per cent., as shown by the following statement:—

	Value. 1896-97. £	Value. 1897-98. £
Exports	2,026,240	1,916,850
Imports	179,625	224,880
Total	2,205,865	2,141,730

Lumber and timber. The following summary of lumber and timber business done in this port shows the result obtained in 1897-98 as compared with 1896-97. The timber is reduced to superficial feet for the sake of comparison:—

MOBILE.

Lumber.

	Quantity.	
	1896–97.	1897–98.
	Super. feet.	Super. feet.
Coastwise and foreign	71,221,574	48,555,709
To railroads	16,025,000	12,000,000
To Ship Island	3,700,000	500,000
Local and rivers	20,000,000	15,000,000
Timber direct—		
Hewn	12,798,336	10,969,728
Sawn	84,843,580	50,807,388
Towed to Ship Island—		
Hewn	250,000	300,000
Sawn	900,000	175,000
Total	209,738,490	138,307,825

Showing a decrease of 71,430,665 super. feet. This decrease is due to the disturbing influences mentioned previously.

Shipments of hardwoods during the past season show a decline as shown by the following statement:— Hardwood shipments.

	Quantity.	
	1896–97.	1897–98.
	Cub. feet.	Cub. feet.
Oak	166,273	82,000
Cedar	2,665	..
Ash	18,200	10,735
Poplar	76,601	12,688
Whitewood	9,504	791
Gum	3,728	13,106
Walnut	13,156	2,711
Cypress	..	14,000
Total	290,127	136,031

There was also exported to foreign ports 2,000 linear feet of piling, 29,500 pickets, 2,500 poles, 97,500 crossties.

Last year's net receipts of cotton were 303,608 bales, average weight per bale 507·35 lbs., average 3½d. per lb., value 2,187,305l. For the season just closed 364,766 bales, average weight per bale 509·10 lbs., average price 2¾d. per lb., value 2,049,985l. Cotton receipts and prices.

MOBILE.

Shipments of cotton.

	Quantity.	
	1897–98.	1896–97.
	Bales.	Bales.
Great Britain	154,401	143,412
Continent	72,582	37,120
Mexico	992	
Total foreign	227,975	180,532
New Orleans	124,263	118,506
North and East	8,068	7,206
Other points	..	460
Total United States	132,331	126,172
„ foreign	227,975	180,532
Grand total	360,306	306,704

Shipments of staves.
Shipments of staves during the past season show a decrease as compared to the amount exported the season previous. 165,900 pieces against 366,425 pieces in 1896–97.

FRUITS.

Fruits.

Year.	Quantity.	
	Bananas.	Cocoanuts.
	Bunches.	Number.
1896–97	2,067,755	3,405,425
1897–98	2,097,113	4,826,469

Shipping. The total number of vessels up and down the channel as reported by the harbour-master is as follows:—

	Number.
Steamships, maximum draft	296
Ships, barques, and brigs	119
Schooners	128
	543
Total	1,086
„ 1896–97	1,156
Decrease	70

Coal. The coal business of this port is in its infancy, but there continues a steady increase in the total handled by local dealers. The increase is due to the demand for bunker coal, and to the efforts being made to build up an export trade with Mexico. There has been exported to Mexico this season, as shown by the books of the Chamber of Commerce, between 8,000 and 9,000 tons, principally in sailing vessels. Owners of foreign steamers, or steamers plying in the Gulf trade, have become satisfied that the best grades of Alabama coals are, for bunker purposes, equal to any mined in the world, and are now content to fill the bunkers of such of their ships as load here with Alabama coal, except in the case of large vessels that draw too much water for our channel.

The receipts in tons this season are 152,010, against 114,895 last season, an increase of 37,115 tons. *Receipts.*

The productive area of the coal fields of Alabama is estimated at 5,350 square miles. The output during the past year amounted to about 6,300,000 tons, being an increase of 10 per cent. over 1897. At the present time the Alabama mines are producing more coal than ever before, and the mines are unable to keep up with the demand. The average price at the mine for the past season has been about 3s. 9d. per ton of 2,000 lbs. There has been no strike of any importance during the year, the miners and operators having in July last agreed on a scale of prices which gave the miner $1\frac{1}{4}d.$ per ton advance on the previous year. The average number of men employed in Alabama in coal mining amounts to about 11,200, and the average number of tons produced per man is about 560 tons per year. The total value of the coal mined in Alabama for 1898 amounted to 1,134,000l. *Coal.*

The output of pig-iron in Alabama is steadily on the increase; the exact figures for 1898 have not been received by the State Geologist, but from the reports which he has, he estimates the output at 1,000,000 tons against 932,918 tons in 1897. It is alleged that in no part of the world can pig-iron be manufactured so cheaply as is done in the Birmingham, Ala., district, for they draw all their materials, fuels, ores, and flux from their own mines and quarries, and can assemble them at any given point within a distance by rail not exceeding an average of 20 miles. The export from the State has risen to 2,000 tons per day. Very little of this, however, is exported as yet through the port of Mobile, only 18,760 tons having been so handled during the past year. One reason of this is that while steamers load in Mobile with light cargo, such as cotton, and need a certain amount of dead weight cargo, they take as little of the latter as they possibly can owing to the fact that the Mobile channel is only 23 feet deep, and vessels like to be as light as possible going down it. The Government, however, has the channel improvement in hand, and the port of Mobile will in the near future be more desirable for vessels than it has been in the past. Some pig-iron, rails, and construction irons, were shipped out of Mobile during the year for Yokohama and Hiogo, but this business, as far as the south is concerned, is in its infancy; it would reach large proportions should the Nicaraguan Canal be built. *Pig-iron.*

MOBILE.

Annex A.—RETURN of all Shipping at the Port of Mobile during the Year 1898.

ENTERED.

Nationality.	Sailing. Number of Vessels.	Sailing. Tons.	Steam. Number of Vessels.	Steam. Tons.	Total. Number of Vessels.	Total. Tons.
British	94	44,069	106	159,783	200	203,852
Norwegian	61	53,105	166	88,379	227	141,484
American	37	12,148	...	...	37	12,148
Russian	21	12,318	...	...	21	12,318
Italian	15	12,006	...	...	15	12,006
Swedish	4	2,927	1	1,325	5	4,252
German	...	...	2	1,691	2	1,691
Dutch	2	1,744	...	...	2	1,744
French	1	432	...	...	1	432
Danish	...	...	2	3,457	2	3,457
Total	235	138,749	277	254,635	512	393,384
Coastwise	...	...	...	...	38	23,540
Grand total	...	...	...	...	550	416,924
„ 1897	...	...	...	...	481	339,605
Increase	...	...	...	...	69	77,319

CLEARED.

Nationality.	Sailing. Number of Vessels.	Sailing. Tons.	Steam. Number of Vessels.	Steam. Tons.	Total. Number of Vessels.	Total. Tons.
British	92	38,123	104	156,951	196	195,074
Norwegian	54	56,383	173	88,725	227	145,108
American	35	8,270	...	...	35	8,270
German	...	...	3	2,249	3	2,249
Italian	13	10,749	...	...	13	10,749
Russian	20	12,328	...	...	20	12,328
Dutch	1	463	...	...	1	463
Swedish	3	2,084	2	1,985	5	4,069
French	1	432	...	...	1	432
Danish	...	...	2	3,457	2	3,457
Total	219	128,832	284	253,367	503	382,199
Coastwise	...	...	...	...	43	21,253
Grand total	...	...	...	...	546	403,452
„ 1897	...	...	...	...	495	354,659
Increase	...	...	...	...	51	48,793

LONDON:
Printed for Her Majesty's Stationery Office,
By HARRISON AND SONS,
Printers in Ordinary to Her Majesty.
(75 2 | 99—H & S 307)

No. 2210 Annual Series.

DIPLOMATIC AND CONSULAR REPORTS.

UNITED STATES.

REPORT FOR THE YEAR 1898

ON THE

TRADE AND COMMERCE OF TEXAS.

REFERENCE TO PREVIOUS REPORT, Annual Series No. 2038.

Presented to both Houses of Parliament by Command of Her Majesty, MARCH, 1899.

LONDON:
PRINTED FOR HER MAJESTY'S STATIONERY OFFICE,
BY HARRISON AND SONS, ST. MARTIN'S LANE,
PRINTERS IN ORDINARY TO HER MAJESTY.

And to be purchased, either directly or through any Bookseller, from
EYRE & SPOTTISWOODE, EAST HARDING STREET, FLEET STREET, E.C.,
32, ABINGDON STREET, WESTMINSTER, S.W.; or
JOHN MENZIES & Co., 12, HANOVER STREET, EDINBURGH, and
90, WEST NILE STREET, GLASGOW; or
HODGES, FIGGIS, & Co., Limited, 104, GRAFTON STREET, DUBLIN.

1899.

[C. 9044—36.]   *Price Twopence Halfpenny.*

CONTENTS.

	PAGE
GALVESTON—	
Prosperous year for Galveston	3
Growth of the Port	3
Increased cotton business	4
Trade with the British Empire	4
Increase of shipping	4
Trade and commerce	5
General domestic trade satisfactory	5
Prosperity of retail trade	5
Increase of bank clearances	5
Total value of foreign trade	6
Percentage for various countries	6
Imports	6
Percentage for various countries	7
Exports	8
Total value of exports	8
Cotton, &c.	8
Cereals	8
Other exports	9
Exports to various countries	9
Remarks on import trade from Great Britain	10
Value of exports to Great Britain	11
Shipping and navigation	12
Freight rates in 1898	14
Cotton fires	14
Proposal to survey vessels on arrival	15
Steam as a means of extinguishing cotton fires	15
Desertions	16
Recent action of the United States immigration inspector	16
Public health	17
Immigration	17
Railways	18
Figures as to Texas railways	18
Decision as to rights of Railway Commissioners	18
Direct line, Chicago-Galveston	18
Acquisition by Southern Pacific Railway of land at Galveston	19
Cotton business, 1897-98	19
„ 1898-99	21
Grain trade	25
Railway and wharf improvements	26
Harbour works	29
SABINE PASS, trade of	36
PORT ARTHUR, trade of	38

NOTE.—Calculations throughout this report are made at 5 dol. to the 1*l.* sterling.

No. 2210. Annual Series.

Reference to previous Report, Annual Series No. 2038.

Report on the Trade and Commerce of Texas for the Year 1898
By Mr. Consul Nugent.

(Received at Foreign Office, February 27, 1899.)

In common with the rest of the Union, the State of Texas experienced a large degree of prosperity during the year 1898. *Prosperous year for Texas.*

Although the price of cotton, the leading product of the State, was exceedingly low, the crop was very large.

Cattle prices ruled very high throughout the year, and the demand was good.

More grain than usual was grown in Texas, and is being sold for export at remunerative rates, whilst a larger diversity of crops has contributed to the general welfare of the farmer and those dependent on him.

Debt collections have been better than anticipated, and commercial failures during the year were few and unimportant, comparatively speaking.

The port of Galveston has shared in the general prosperity, and once more, as was stated in my reports for 1896 and 1897, has it to be recorded that the year just passed has seen the largest volume of business ever known here. *Prosperity at Galveston.*

As 1897 showed a steady gain over 1896, so 1898 shows a large increase over 1897, and this, too, notwithstanding the interruption to business by the Spanish-American War.

Fortunately for this port, the war broke out at a period of the year when business in general, and more especially the export trade in cotton and cotton products, was not particularly affected.

The commercial growth of the port of Galveston will be clearly seen by a glance at the following figures, issued by the custom-house, showing the total shipping, both foreign and domestic, as well as the foreign trade for the years 1892–98 respectively:— *Growth of the Port*

GALVESTON.

TABLE.

Years.	Depth of Water.	Entered: Number of Vessels.	Tonnage.	Cleared. Number of Vessels.	Tonnage.	Foreign Trade. Imports. £	Exports. £
1898	27·28	759	1,214,013	763	1,176,056	459,965	14,748,149
1897	26½	705	1,036,522	705	1,071,258	128,849	12,000,943
1896	25	613	844,426	598	808,411	158,981	11,288,866
1895	20¾	570	627,577	545	631,521	67,422	7,106,425
1894	14¾	543	669,926	515	621,455	135,527	7,232,491
1893	14¼	486	582,515	440	565,939	185,668	6,743,307
1892	13¾	492	559,150	354	518,031	172,796	6,827,520

Increased cotton business. During 1898, the cotton receipts at Galveston have increased enormously, and the end of the year finds this port the leading cotton port of the United States, with a fair prospect of maintaining the position until the end of the season, on August 31 next.

Cotton exports increased during 1898 from 1,374,942 bales to 1,930,250 bales, and the exports of other cotton products show a corresponding gain.

Grain exports. Exports of grain increased from 11,445,655 bushels to 16,055,618 bushels, whilst a large and satisfactory export business has been carried on in lumber, cotton-seed oil, flour, spelter and cattle.

Import trade. The import business, too, whilst still, comparatively speaking, small, shows surprising growth, and was more in value during 1898 than during the three previous years combined.

In short, the business of the year 1898 shows a satisfactory increase all round, and has been handled without any friction to speak of, notwithstanding the immense volume of merchandise poured into Galveston during the comparatively short period of a cotton season.

Trade with British Empire. It is satisfactory to note that the trade of the British Empire with Galveston, which fell off somewhat in 1897, increased during 1898 from 5,793,509*l*. to 6,833,815*l*., although the percentage of the total trade, which belongs to the British Empire, decreased from 47·84 per cent. to about 45 per cent., owing to increased business done between Galveston and the Continent, which formerly was transacted at other United States ports.

Increase of shipping. Increased foreign trade has led to a large increase of shipping, the total tonnage of foreign shipping in 1898 being 1,659,948 tons in and out, as against 1,237,268 tons in 1897.

Here Great Britain is very much to the front, the total tonnage of British vessels entered and cleared during 1898 being 1,372,453 tons, as compared with 1,014,982 tons entered and cleared in 1897, whilst the value of the trade in British vessels rose from 10,268,069*l*. to 12,558,336*l*.

Remarks as to work entailed on the Consul. The vast sum in freight accruing to owners in Great Britain from this large carrying business is too obvious to need pointing out, but the time and attention demanded on the part of British

Consular officers in performing the onerous duties consequent on such a volume of shipping, so as to safeguard the interests of owners, masters, and seamen, and to facilitate in every way a business so remunerative to the British merchant and shipowner, appear to be too often either ignored or forgotten by Chambers of Commerce and other commercial bodies at home in their comparison of British Consular officers with their foreign colleagues, and in their anxiety to have the British Consular corps perform the duties usually assigned to commercial travellers.

Trade and Commerce.

The general domestic trade of Galveston during 1898 was of a satisfactory nature, and a fair increase of business was reported in most lines. <small>General domestic trade satisfactory.</small>

In wholesale groceries there was an increase of some 10 per cent.

Whilst some goods declined in price, others show an advance; but the general average of prices was much the same as in 1897, with increased sales of about 10 per cent.

There was a marked falling-off in the demand for fancy goods, pickles, potted meats, tinned meats, &c., whilst staple products were more largely sold than usual.

This is taken by merchants to indicate a policy on the part of the large farming population of the State to produce as much as possible at home, and to only buy what they cannot produce.

In the wholesale "dry goods" market, the amount of merchandise sold was about the same as in 1897.

This represents an increase of about 10 per cent. in volume, as prices declined about to that extent.

In the wholesale hardware business, prices ruled firm, and were much as last year.

The value of the business done shows an increase of about 8 per cent.

In fruit and vegetable produce there was an increase of about 10 per cent. over 1897, prices keeping about the same as last year.

The establishment of a steamship line from Central America and the West Indies for the carriage of fruit, which is to begin operations early in 1899, tends to make the outlook very favourable for business.

The trade in boots and shoes, hats and caps, and clothing generally, remained about the same as in 1897.

All the factories in the town, including the cotton mill, rope mill, bagging mill, flour mill, brewery, &c., have been running on full time during 1898, and the output of these various factories was about the same as in 1897.

The retail business of the town was very prosperous in 1898, and gave evidence of continuous progress. <small>Prosperity of retail trade.</small>

The increase of business, both domestic and foreign, during <small>Increase of bank clearances.</small>

GALVESTON.

1898, is largely evidenced by the bank clearances, which amounted to 341,473,700 dol., as against 287,068,100 dol. in 1897.

There was an abundance of money, and rates of interest were lower than for years.

Increased deposits in savings banks. The general prosperity of the labouring classes during the year is abundantly evidenced by the deposits in savings banks, which increased 25 per cent. over 1897, and were greater than at any time since 1893.

Taking bank clearances as a guide, Galveston ranked on an average as the eleventh banking centre in the United States.

Total value of foreign trade. The total value of the foreign trade to and from Galveston during the year 1898 amounted to 15,208,154*l.* as against 12,129,794*l.* in 1897.

There was thus an increase of very nearly 25 per cent.

The imports amounted to 459,965*l.*, and the exports to 14,748,189*l.*

The following table sets forth the value of the total trade done by each of the principal countries interested, and the percentage of each country.

It will be noticed that whilst the four or five leading countries have done about the same percentage of trade, there has been a material increase in that done by other countries, notably Mexico and Italy.

TABLE showing Percentage of Total Trade of Galveston, by Countries, during the Years 1897–98.

Country.	1897. Value. £	1897. Percentage.	1898. Value. £	1898. Percentage.
Great Britain and Colonies	5,793,509	47·84	6,833,815	44·94
Germany	2,579,031	21·26	3,059,644	20·12
France	2,088,820	17·22	2,480,233	16·31
Netherlands	658,926	5·43	853,309	5·61
Belgium	506,925	4·18	688,908	4·53
Mexico	109,923	0·90	452,641	2·98
Denmark	160,571	1·32	230,141	1·51
Japan	..	..	171,569	1·13
Italy	113,996	0·94	324,441	2·13
Cuba	75,047	0·60	88,787	0·58
All other countries	43,046	0·31	24,666	0·16
Total	12,129,794	100·00	15,208,154	100·00

Imports.

Total value of foreign imports. The total value of direct foreign imports into Galveston during 1898 was 459,965*l.*

In 1897 it was 128,849*l.* There was thus an increase of 257 per cent.

GALVESTON.

In fact the total imports for 1898 were more in value than the total for the three years 1897, 1896, and 1895.

Increase of imports.

A remarkable feature of the imports during 1898 was the value of merchandise imported in transit for other parts of the United States, which amounted to over 40,000*l.*

This is a new departure here, and is a feature which may be expected to increase, as there is now very good communication between Galveston and the Pacific coast of the United States.

As has often been stated in the reports from this Consulate, the import trade from abroad at Galveston is quite out of proportion to the export trade.

The imports, however, have now begun to increase in value, and it may be expected that this increase will continue from year to year.

Of the total amount of imports 346,825*l.* represented the value of articles free of duty, and 72,941*l.* that of those subject to duty, whilst merchandise to the amount of 40,199*l.* was imported through this port in bond for other parts of the United States.

The principal dutiable articles were asphalte, cement, chemicals, earthenware, manufactures of flax, hemp and jute, sardines, glass, manufactures of iron and steel, malt liquors, rice, salt, and wine; whilst amongst those free of duty were sheep-dip, jute, sisal grass, and mahogany.

Principal imports.

There was a very large increase in the amount of sisal grass imported from Mexico, whilst sheep dip, earthenware, glass, rice, and salt also largely increased.

The chief falling-off was in jute, sugar, and wine.

The following table gives the percentages of the import trade done by the various countries:—

TABLE showing Percentage of Imports at Galveston, by Countries, during the Years 1897-98.

Country.	1897. Value.	1897. Percentage.	1898. Value.	1898. Percentage.
	£		£	
Great Britain and Colonies	53,820	41·77	52,498	11·41
Germany	44,127	34·24	59,666	12·97
France	2,074	1·61	2,823	0·61
Mexico	16,663	12·93	323,667	70·37
Belgium	7,602	5·90	20,478	4·45
All other countries	4,563	3·55	833	0·19
Total	128,849	100·00	459,965	100·00

Besides Great Britain, the import trade of which is alluded to elsewhere, the principal countries from which goods were imported into Galveston were Germany, France, Mexico, and Belgium.

(318)

GALVESTON.

Imports from Germany. The imports from Germany increased from 44,127*l.* in 1897 to 59,666*l.* in 1898.

The principal articles imported were cement, 11,143*l.*; chemicals, 5,162*l.*; earthenware, 1,503*l.*; and rice, 7,182*l.*

Articles to the value of 28,103*l.* were entered in transit for other parts of the United States.

Imports from France. The imports from France rose from 2,074*l.* in 1897 to 2,823*l.* in 1898.

They consisted principally of wine, preserved fruits, and sardines.

Imports from Mexico. There was a very large increase in the imports from Mexico during 1898; the value being 323,667*l.* as against 16,663*l.* in 1897, or 70·37 per cent. as against 12·93 per cent.

This increase was caused by the very heavy importation of sisal grass, value 320,787*l.*

Imports from Belgium. The imports from Belgium also increased from 7,602*l.* in 1897 to 20,478*l.* in 1898.

The principal article imported was cement, value 12,816*l.*, whilst goods to the amount of 6,780*l.* entered in transit.

Exports.

Total value of exports. The total value of the exports from the port of Galveston during 1898 was 14,748,189*l.* as against 12,000,943*l.* in 1897, and 11,288,866*l.* in 1896.

Increased business. There was thus an increase of about 23 per cent. for the year.

As usual, cotton was the leading article of export, and it is probable that more cotton left the port of Galveston during the latter part of 1898 than any other port in the United States.

Cotton. The total amount of cotton leaving the port during the year was 1,956,229 bales, valued at 11,028,316*l.*, as against 1,374,942 bales in 1897, valued at 8,988,313*l.*

It will be thus seen that of the total increase in value of the exports for the year, viz., 2,747,246*l.*, a little over 2,000,000*l.* represented increased exports in cotton.

Cotton seed oilcake and meal. Cotton seed oil. Exports of other cotton products such as cotton-seed meal and cake, cotton-seed oil also increased, the former being 229,085 tons, value 863,388*l.*, as against 164,863 tons, value 650,418*l.* in 1897, and the latter 5,372,124 gallons, value 357,129*l.*, as compared with 4,490,341 gallons, value 236,364*l.* in 1897.

There was also a considerable increase in the amount of grain exported during 1898.

Wheat. The wheat exported was 10,390,586 bushels, value 1,686,255*l.*, compared with 7,372,636 bushels value 1,352,399*l.* in 1897, whilst **Maize.** maize to the amount of 5,365,032 bushels, value 430,897*l.*, was also exported in 1898, as against 4,073,019 bushels, value 260,695*l.*

As remarked elsewhere in this report, the export trade in cereals is becoming a highly important feature at Galveston.

The total gain in value of exports of cereals during 1898 was over 500,000*l.*

Wheat flour. The exports of wheat flour increased from 49,878 barrels, value 40,888*l.* in 1897, to 79,218 barrels, value 68,597*l.* in 1898.

GALVESTON.

Other exports. As regards other exports, which consisted chiefly of lumber, staves, logs, lead, copper, borax, spelter, and cattle, there was rather a slight decrease than otherwise, owing to cargo space being required for more paying freight. The decrease, however, was very slight.

There were no new exports of importance. Turning to the export trade by countries and leaving out Great Britain the export trade to which is dealt with elsewhere, that to Germany rose from 2,534,904*l.* in 1897 to 2,999,978*l.* in 1898, but was only 20·35 per cent. of the total export trade in the latter year, as against 21·13 per cent. in the former year.

Exports to Germany.

The chief items exported were cotton, value 1,907,007*l.*; cotton-seed meal and cake, 588,080*l.*; wheat, 310,937*l.*; maize, 137,674*l.*; cotton-seed oil, 16,485*l.*; and logs, 13,794*l.*

The exports to France were 16·79 per cent. of the total export trade of 1898, as against 17·40 per cent. in 1897, and rose from 2,086,747*l.* to 2,477,410*l.*

Exports to France.

The chief items consisted of cotton, value 2,109,453*l.*; wheat, value 140,777*l.*; cotton-seed oil, value 143,772*l.*; maize, value 61,715*l.*; and cotton-seed oil and cake, value 16,461*l.*

The exports to the Netherlands again increased during 1898, being 853,309*l.*, as against 658,926*l.* in 1897.

Exports to the Netherlands.

The principal articles exported were cotton, value 127,517*l.*; cotton-seed oil and cake, 111,028*l.*; wheat, 450,809*l.*; maize, 51,996*l.*; and cotton-seed oil, 91,982*l.*

The exports to Belgium rose from 499,323*l.* in 1897 to 668,430*l.* in 1898.

Exports to Belgium.

The chief items taken by that country were cotton, value 278,650*l.*; wheat, value 317,057*l.*; wheat flour, value 19,215*l.*; maize, value 13,467*l.*; and cotton-seed oil, value 13,775*l.*

The exports to Denmark increased from 160,571*l.* in 1897 to 230,141*l.* in 1898.

Exports to Denmark.

The principal of these were cotton, value 54,349*l.*; cotton-seed oil meal and cake, 99,896*l.*; wheat, 17,312*l.*; and maize, 50,793*l.*

The exports to Italy show a large gain, being 323,999*l.* in 1898, as against 113,996*l.* for the previous year.

Exports to Italy.

Of these the following were noticeable, cotton, 199,430*l.*; wheat, 44,252*l.*; and cotton-seed oil, 60,282*l.*

The exports to Mexico rose from 93,260*l.* in 1897 to 128,974*l.* in 1898.

Exports to Mexico.

They principally consisted of cotton, 93,462*l.*; and cotton-seed oil, 31,749*l.*

Other noticeable exports during the year were cotton to Japan, value 171,569*l.*; flour, value 29,412*l.*; and cattle, value 55,810*l.* to Cuba; cotton, value 13,488*l.*, to Russia; and flour, value 10,787*l.*, to the West Indies.

Exports to other countries.

The following table shows the standing of the chief countries, as regards exports, during 1897, and 1898, whilst a table showing the exports in detail is annexed:—

Standing of chief countries.

GALVESTON.

TABLE showing Percentage of Exports from Galveston, by Countries, during the Years 1897–98.

Country.	1897. Value. £	1897. Percentage.	1898. Value. £	1898. Percentage.
Great Britain and Colonies	5,739,688	47·83	6,781,317	45·99
Germany	2,534,904	21·13	2,999,978	20·35
France	2,086,747	17·40	2,477,410	16·79
Netherlands	658,926	5·50	853,309	5·79
Denmark	160,571	1·34	230,141	1·56
Belgium	499,323	4·16	668,430	4·54
Russia	18,294	0·15	..	..
Italy	113,996	0·94	323,999	2·19
Mexico	93,260	0·77	128,974	0·87
Japan	..	..	171,569	1·16
Cuba	75,047	0·61	88,787	0·60
All other countries	20,187	0·17	24,275	0·16
Total	12,000,943	100·00	14,748,189	100·00

British Trade with Galveston.

Remarks on import trade from Great Britain.

The remark made above, that the import trade of Galveston is very much out of proportion to the exports, applies to that from Great Britain as well as from other countries.

There is no doubt that there is a large consumption of English goods and manufactures in Galveston, but a very small proportion of these finds its way direct to this port.

New York is the great importing centre of the country, and it is customary for both wholesale and retail dealers to fill their stocks in that city by means of agents, the goods thus purchased arriving here by rail or by coastwise steamer.

There is no doubt a considerable opening for a direct British trade in many lines, but as long as the present conditions continue it is useless to expect a great expansion of imports direct from Great Britain, even should the somewhat prohibitory tariff at present in force be modified.

The direct imports from the British Empire in 1898 decreased from 53,820*l.* in 1897 to 52,498*l.*

List of principal imports.

The following table gives a list of the principal imports for 1897 and 1898.

The greatest falling-off was in jute from India, most of the other articles showing a slight increase.

GALVESTON.

TABLE of Imports from the British Empire during the Years 1897–98.

Articles.	Value 1897.	Value 1898.
	£	£
Bags for grain* (made of burlap)	3,295	..
Paper stock* (old bagging)	1,007	..
Salt*	1,533	2,980
Jute and jute butts*	25,868	14,025
Sheep dip	3,041*	} 8,145*
Chemicals and compounds	2,115	
Earthenware (plain and decorated crockery)	3,625	5,546
Flax, jute, and hemp (manufactures of)	4,461	5,820
Iron and steel (manufactures of)	1,037	1,768
Ale and porter	950	1,938
Rice	..	1,290
All other articles	6,888	5,670
In transit to other United States' districts	..	5,316
Total	53,820	52,498

* Free of duty.

Value of exports to Great Britain. The exports to the British Empire for 1898, increased very nearly 20 per cent. in value, being 6,781,317*l*. in 1898, as against 5,739,368*l*. in 1897.

The largest gain was in cotton which showed an increased value of 1,277,410*l*.

As regards other exports there was a decrease in value to the extent of nearly 250,000*l*.

The export trade, however, to Great Britain was larger in actual quantity than ever before known here.

It was owing to extremely cheap prices that the values, in many instances, show a falling-off.

Table of principal articles exported. The following table sets forth in detail the values of the various exports:—

GALVESTON.

TABLE of Exports to the British Empire during the Years 1897–98.

Articles.	Value. 1897.	Value. 1898.
	£	£
Cotton	4,795,981	6,073,391
Cotton-seed oilcake and meal	76,061	34,146
Maize	89,651	111,109
Wheat	505,653	405,118
,, flour	15,698	3,005
Lumber and staves	9,918	6,132
Cotton-seed oil	6,614	3,906
Logs	1,276	881
Spelter	110,393	65,571
Lead	38,354	..*
Borax	57,045	60,743
Copper and copper-matte	18,816	..*
Cattle	3,780	..
Sundries	10,448	17,315
Total	5,739,688	6,781,317

* Included in "sundries."

Shipping and Navigation.

Increase of shipping in 1898. — There was a marked increase in the tonnage of the shipping at the port of Galveston during the year 1898, the volume being the largest ever recorded.

According to the figures issued by the United States customs authorities the total tonnage entered was 1,151,781 registered tons, as against 979,261 tons entered in 1897, whilst the tonnage cleared was 1,080,724, compared with 1,008,265 in 1897.

Total movement of shipping. — The total movement of shipping in 1898 was the largest known here, viz., 2,232,505 registered tons, but this increase was largely in foreign shipping, the coastwise trade decreasing from 733,787 registered tons in and out in 1897 to 534,516 registered tons in 1898, owing to the interruption to domestic business caused by the Spanish-American War.

Foreign shipping. — The foreign tonnage entered, comprised 466 vessels registering 837,967 tons, and that cleared 458 vessels of 821,989 registered tons.

There were 372 British, 11 Danish, 21 German, 22 Norwegian, and 26 Spanish vessels.

Increase of British shipping. — The increased business in 1898 brought a corresponding increase in British tonnage, which was the heaviest ever recorded here in a year.

In 1898 there were 372 British vessels entered at Galveston, their combined registered tonnage being 697,918 tons as compared with 276 vessels in 1897 of 505,959 tons, thus showing an increase for the year of 96 vessels and 191,959 tons, very nearly 35 per cent. in numbers and 38 per cent. in tonnage.

GALVESTON.

The average tonnage per vessel was very high, being 1,876 tons as against 1,833 tons in 1897.

Only 37 vessels brought full or partial cargoes, and of these but 11 had cargoes for Galveston, the remainder being in transit.

The number of British vessels arriving direct was 196, whilst of the others 31 came from Brazil, 27 from St. Vincent, 22 from Italy, 13 from the Cape Verdes, 17 from other United States ports, and 12 from Cuba.

During 1898, 359 British vessels cleared from Galveston, registered tonnage 674,535, as against 277, registered tonnage 509,023 in 1897.

The increase in numbers and tonnage was almost as great as in the case of those entered.

Of these 359, 122 cleared for Great Britain, 100 for Germany, 56 for France, 38 for the Netherlands, 15 for Belgium, eight for Italy, and the remainder for other countries including three for Japan.

Value of cargoes in British ships.

The total value of the cargoes carried away in 1898 in British vessels was 12,558,336*l.* as against 10,268,069*l.* in 1897, an increase of about 22½ per cent.

The value of this carrying trade can be estimated when it is stated that of the total value exported from Galveston over 80 per cent. was carried in British bottoms.

The following table shows the value of the cargoes shipped in British vessels during 1898 and 1897, and their destination. The general increase will be noted:—

TABLE.

Country.	Value 1897. £	Value 1898. £
Great Britain	4,781,039	5,690,605
Germany	2,158,371	2,632,407
France	2,090,762	2,317,111
Holland	636,152	875,331
Denmark	157,643	90,226
Belgium	375,932	415,746
Italy	48,142	323,520
Mexico	15,278	21,460
Cuba	4,750	13,079
United States of America (transit)	..	7,562
Japan	..	171,289
Total	10,268,069	12,558,336

List of articles exported in British ships.

The following is a list of the principal articles exported in British vessels in 1898 as compared with 1897.

It will be noticed that whilst there is an immense increase in cotton, cotton products and grain, the heavier and cheaper articles, such as spelter, lead, &c., fell off considerably, cargo space being wanted for better paying freight.

Articles.		Quantity.	
		1897.	1898.
Cotton	Bales..	1,175,876	1,657,012
Cotton-seed meal	Sacks..	2,339,035	3,466,849
,, oilcake	,, ..	364,472	205,464
Wheat	Bushels	6,434,742	9,645,865
Maize	,,	3,645,623	4,390,944
Cotton-seed oil	Gallons	3,363,925	5,716,082
Walnut lumber and logs	Pieces	70,365	3,421
Spelter	Plates	220,376	114,304
Borax	Sacks..	37,724	22,444
Copper-matte	,, ..	16,727	19,428
Lead	Bars ..	85,320	71,847
Lumber	Feet ..	399,477	198,400
	Pieces	316,768	454,069
Cedar logs	,, ..	6,589	8,589
Staves	,, ..	4,100,501	1,765,444
Flour	Sacks..	25,773	18,862
Ixtle	Bales..	5,733	3,133
Zacatan	,, ..	4,268	3,414
Canaigre root	,, ..	6,780	..
Rye	Bushels	..	47,695

Freights. Rates in 1898. At the beginning of the year 1898 freight rates continued at the remunerative figures that were obtainable at the end of 1897, viz., $\frac{17}{64}d.$ per lb. for cotton, 3s. 3d. to 3s. 6d. per quarter for grain, and 17s. 6d. to 18s. 6d. per ton for oilcake and meal, according to destination, and so continued until about the end of February.

There was a gradual decline, however, after that, the middle of March seeing cotton rates down to $\frac{1}{4}d.$ per lb., and the end $\frac{15}{64}d.$, with a corresponding reduction for other commodities.

April saw cotton rates down to $\frac{13}{64}d.$, and grain to 3s., and oilcake to 15s.

In May and June, owing to the withdrawal of coastwise boats between Galveston and New York, freight rates by direct boats to Europe advanced somewhat, the former month paying $\frac{1}{4}d.$ for cotton, and 3s. 9d. to 4s. for grain, and the latter $\frac{9}{32}d.$ and 4s. to 5s. respectively.

There was, however, only a limited amount of tonnage here.

The beginning of the cotton season in August and September saw rates phenomenally low owing to the lateness of the crop, and an excessive amount of tonnage, the figures paid being merely nominal.

From October to December they advanced rapidly, and reached as high as $\frac{21}{64}d.$ for cotton, 4s. to 5s. for grain, and 20s. to 23s. for oilcake, the year closing at a little below these figures.

Cotton fires. A few years ago Galveston had a very unenviable name with regard to fires occurring in cargoes of cotton.

During the last year or two, however, such fires have been few and unimportant, and the port was not particularly handicapped in this respect by the insurance writers.

The season of 1898, however, has a different story to tell and fires in cargoes shipped here have been frequent. Numerous fires in 1898.

About four of these fires occurred whilst the vessel was in port, and some eight or 10 whilst on the voyage to Europe.

This, of course, has not been to the credit of the port, and steps have been taken to ascertain the cause of these frequent fires, and to guard if possible against their recurrence.

There seems to be a well-grounded suspicion that many if not most of the cotton fires originate in the coal bunkers.

The insurance underwriters have recently issued a circular strongly recommending that steamers be thoroughly surveyed on arrival, to ascertain if there be anything defective, and, if so, to have such defect remedied. Proposal to survey vessel on arrival.

The surveyors would ascertain if the coal in the bunkers is in good condition, whether or not it was on fire, to see that no matches were stuck to the skin of the vessel, that there was no waste or other material liable to ignite spontaneously; in short, to see that the holds were clean and the vessel fit to receive a cotton cargo.

This course is followed in the case of grain cargoes, and the underwriters see no reason why it should not be done in the case of cotton and other merchandise.

The matter is one of the greatest importance to the port of Galveston, which is one of the two largest cotton shipping ports in the country, and it is to be hoped suitable means of prevention will be found.

Of course, with the immense quantity of cotton handled here in October, November, and December, accidents will occur, especially as vessels are loaded at the very highest possible rate of speed, but these very misfortunes should lead to increased caution in every way when loading such inflammable material as cotton.

Of fires in presses and warehouses in Galveston there have been none in 1898, notwithstanding that in the latter, cotton has been piled bale upon bale to the roof, so that it is evident that the origin of the fires must be sought for either in improper loading or some such cause as fire from the bunker coal.

That the latter is at least likely is borne out by the fact that the majority of cotton fires start in the hold nearest the bunkers.

With regard to the fires that did occur in port it is worthy of note that in several instances steam was used in the first place in extinguishing the fire instead of water. Steam as a means of extinguishing cotton fires.

This course is now always recommended by the port association here, and apparently rightly so, for in the cases in which it was used the damage was confined to the bales actually burnt or scorched, whereas when water alone was used and the hold flooded, much more cotton in proportion was damaged, especially by water.

As an example of this the two following cases may be cited:—

The ss. "Birchfield" (where steam was used) total number of bales damaged 179, of which 53 by water.

The ss. "Burton" (where water was used) total number of bales damaged 1,026, of which 726 by water.

Desertions. One of the chief difficulties with which British shipmasters have to contend with in United States ports is desertion of seamen.

This port had formerly a very unenviable name in this respect, and prior to the Treaty of 1892 with the United States, regarding merchant seamen deserters, it was practically impossible for a master to count on retaining a large proportion of his crew.

Improvement in this respect. Of late years, however, much improvement has taken place, and the proportion of desertions has steadily decreased.

In 1894, the proportion of deserters from British vessels was as high as one man out of every 24 entering the port.

The following year, 1895, it fell to one out of every 53, owing to a very short cotton crop, and consequent reduction in number of vessels, whilst very little work, as long shoremen, &c., was to be obtained by deserting sailors.

In 1896, the proportion rose to one out of every 31, but since that time has steadily decreased, being one out of 35 in 1897, and one out of 43 in 1898.

That is to say, with 372 vessels entered in 1898, with combined crews of 10,632 men, there were but 240 desertions, or under 2½ per cent., as against nearly 5 per cent. in 1894.

This decrease is probably due to the deterrent effect of the Treaty of 1892.

Owing to the appointment of a United States Commissioner, who specially devotes himself to such business, British shipmasters can now receive all the assistance they require in Galveston, either with regard to desertions or unruly and insubordinate seamen.

Vexatious suits, too, regarding wages, are no longer so frequent as they once were, a seaman being required to clearly show his American citizenship before any such suit is entertained by the Commissioner.

Many masters have availed themselves of the Treaty to arrest deserters.

During the last four months, when this port is at its busiest, 51 applications for arrest were made, and of these about 50 per cent. were successful.

The fees payable to the United States Commissioner are about 12s. 6d. per man if the deserter is not found, and about 2l. 5s. if he is found and returned to the ship.

Recent action of the United States Immigration Inspector. Quite recently, by order of the United States Immigration Inspector, some 25 men who had deserted British vessels, and who did not attempt to ship, but loafed about for weeks, were arrested.

Under the Alien Immigration Act, the agents of the vessels these men deserted have been notified to ship them out of the country under a penalty of 300 dol. fine, the men being held to be without visible means of support, and liable to become charges on this country.

This action on the part of the United States authorities will probably tend to further check desertions at Galveston.

The Health Officer of Galveston reports as follows:—

Public health. "In 1898, owing to the warm winter, the fever germs appear to have lain dormant in Louisiana, and made their appearance on September 9 in Franklin, Louisiana. A strict and vigorous quarantine was put in operation at once, which seemed to inspire confidence, and, instead of a panic, every city seemed to have perfect confidence in our State quarantine, and with their united and hearty support, together with that of the railway officials, in the enforcement of the State quarantine laws, the fever was kept out of the State, notwithstanding the fact that we were surrounded on every side with yellow fever; on the east, with half-a-dozen railroads running out of infected districts into our State, and on the south and west, from Mexico and Cuba.

"A heavy travel and traffic had to be intercepted and inspected.

"I am glad to report that not a single case of yellow fever was imported, and but one case developed in the State.

"This was found in the barracks at Galveston, having come from the effects of a soldier from Cuba.

"We should be thankful for the success with which our efforts have been crowned, and more thoroughly satisfied with our present effective system of quarantine, as there is nothing more convincing than success."

Mortality of Galveston. Although there was a good deal of sickness in Galveston during 1898, such as influenza, dengue fever, &c., the mortality was very low, being only about 10½ per 1,000, based on an estimated population of 60,000 inhabitants.

Immigration. According to the statement of Mr. Levy, United States Immigration Inspector at Galveston, from July, 1897, to December 31, 1898, nearly 2,000 immigrants arrived here, and of this number some 700 entered the port in the last five months of 1898.

Previous to 1896 there had been no immigration since 1888.

As regular steamship lines now ply between Galveston and European ports, immigration is expected rather to increase than otherwise.

General remarks. In view of the great extent of still undeveloped territory in Texas and the neighbouring States, the possibilities for immigration through Galveston are great, but the best chance appears to await agricultural labourers and small farmers. There is no demand for clerks, book-keepers, &c., the supply being ample.

The climate appears too warm for British-born farm labourers, and the conditions, which, for the first few years, require the most rigid economy, not to say deprivation, are not such as they have been accustomed to.

The more frugal Germans and Bohemians seem to do well, and although here and there an Englishman succeeds, it is the exception rather than the rule.

Galveston.

The greatest caution should be exercised by persons coming here, and on no account should a man at first be accompanied by his family.

Railways.

Figures as to Texas railways.

According to the figures issued by the Railway Commissioners of Texas for the year ending June 30, 1898, there were 72 railways in operation during the year in the State, as against 68 in 1897.

The total length of main line used in 1898 was 9,540 miles, as against 9,484 in 1897, thus showing an increase of 56 miles for the year.

This does not include sidings, yard lines, &c., in which there was an increase of 125 miles.

Since the date of the report, some 140 miles of new line of all kinds have been built, making a total of about 11,200 miles altogether now in use in Texas.

The aggregate earnings of these lines in Texas amounted to 41,102,587 dol. (8,220,517*l.*) in 1897–98.

This shows an increase of 752,472*l.* over 1896–97, or a little over 10 per cent. gain.

The percentage of working expenses to gross incomes was 73·70 per cent., as compared with 78·12 in 1896–97.

The amount of freight carried showed a considerable gain, being 18,590,046 tons for the year 1897–98, as against 16,342,302 in the previous year.

The result of the business done was favourable, there being an increase of net earnings of about 50,000*l.*, or 32 per cent. over the previous year.

Decision as to rights of Railway Commissioners.

Towards the end of 1898, a very important question, viz., the right of the Railway Commissioners to lay down obligatory rates for the carriage of merchandise by Texas railways, came before the Courts, and was decided in favour of the railway companies.

The decision of the Court not only permits the railroads to restore the tariffs in force in Texas in 1894, but it removes one order of the Commission equally obnoxious to the railroads and the shippers.

The Commission required that all cotton in progress of transportation should be stopped for compressing at the first place possessing such facilities reached on its way to its destination.

The result of the order was an added expense to the railroad and delay to the shippers, and the large compresses in Houston and Galveston were consequently deprived of much business that otherwise would have gone there.

This order, like the others of the Commission, is now swept aside, and the railroads will no longer be obliged to stop en route for compressing, whilst the shippers may use their right of selection in this respect.

About the same time two other matters of great importance to Galveston in regard to railway affairs took place.

Direct line, Chicago-Galveston.

The first was the arrangement by which direct connection

between Chicago and Galveston is secured by a through line as follows:—

	Miles.
Chicago to St. Louis (Chicago and Alton Railroad)	280·70
St. Louis to Denison, Texas (Missouri, Kansas, and Texas Railroad)	633·75
Denison to Houston (Missouri, Kansas, and Texas Railroad)	442·97
Houston to Galveston (Galveston, Houston, and Henderson Railroad)	50
Total	1,407·42

This line will undoubtedly largely augment the grain shipments through Galveston at the probable expense of the eastern ports, not to speak of bringing into this port other produce for export.

It is a striking instance of the growing appreciation of the Gulf route for grain.

Acquisition by Southern Pacific Railway of land at Galveston.

The second was the probable acquisition here by the Southern Pacific Railroad Company of some 230 acres of land with 3,600 feet of channel front, for the purpose of building railway terminals and berths for steamers.

Hitherto this Company has transacted most of its business through New Orleans, and, in consequence, although it has brought cotton and other freight to Houston, 50 miles away from Galveston, it has then diverted it by means of its own line to New Orleans.

This diversion of much produce that would naturally be expected to come to Galveston for shipment will now probably cease, for although the New Orleans' service will be continued, the bulk of the heavy frieght will pass through this port.

Consequently Galveston should prove a gainer and New Orleans a loser if this arrangement is brought to a positive conclusion, and the volume of business here should materially increase.

Cotton.

United States crop of 1897–98.

The cotton crop of the United States for the year ended August 31, 1898, amounted to 11,199,994 bales, valued at 320,552,606 dol., as compared with 8,757,964 bales, value 321,924,834 dol. for the year ending August 31, 1897.

The total increase of the crop was 2,442,030 bales and of this increase 1,615,000 bales were produced outside of Texas, the increase in this State, which is taken to include Indian territory, being 827,000 bales.

Every cotton-growing State except Texas produced more cotton in 1897–98 than ever before known, but whilst the crop in Texas was much larger than in 1896–97, it yet fell short of that grown in 1894–95 by over 200,000 bales.

Prices.

Prices throughout the year were limited in range and there was a marked absence of speculation.

(318)

GALVESTON.

They varied from $7\frac{1}{16}$ c. per lb. early in the season to $5\frac{3}{16}$ c., which latter figure was reached in January, the average being $5\frac{64}{100}$ c. per lb., as against $7\frac{32}{100}$ c. for the crop of 1896–97.

From the end of October to the close of February the extreme variation was only $\frac{1}{2}$ c. per lb.

The average commercial value of the crop was only 28 dol. 62 c. per bale, as against 36 dol. 76 c. in 1896–97, and 41 dol. 9 c. in 1895–96.

Texas crop. The following table shows the details of the Texas crop, which includes cotton grown in the Indian territory.

The latter crop increased wonderfully, being 274,001 bales in 1897–98, as against 86,128 bales in 1896–97.

	Quantity.	
	1897–98.	1896–97.
	Bales.	Bales.
Receipts at Texas seaboard	1,950,667	1,430,602
Shipped inland to Mexico and points west of Mississippi River	164,660	94,167
Shipped by rail viâ St. Louis and Cairo..	306,916	172,727
Receipts at New Orleans (exclusive of Galveston)	599,880	538,210
„ points on Mississippi River, &c., north of St. Louis, bound eastward, &c.	52,688	11,848
Total	3,074,811	2,247,554

Percentage of production The proportion of the crop produced by the various groups of the cotton-growing States during the last two seasons was as follows:—

	Quantity.	
	1897–98.	1896–97.
	Bales.	Bales.
Texas	3,075,000	2,248,000
Other Gulf	3,774,000	2,831,000
Atlantic	4,351,000	3,679,000
Total	11,200,000	8,758,000

Receipts and exports of cotton at various United States ports. The net receipts of cotton in bales at the different United States ports, and the detailed exports from these ports, during the season of 1897–98 and 1896–97 are shown in the following tables.

The gain at Galveston will be noticed, even though the Texas crop was not so heavy as that grown elsewhere.

The proportion of the Texas crop received at Galveston was about 63 per cent., as against 61 per cent. in 1896–97, whilst New Orleans, Galveston, and Savannah were the only three ports to handle over 1,000,000 bales of cotton.

GALVESTON.

Net Receipts of Cotton at United States Ports.

Ports.	Quantity 1897–98.	1896–97.
	Bales.	Bales.
New Orleans	2,690,256	2,128,315
Galveston	1,939,308	1,430,602
Mobile and Pensacola	478,086	371,222
Savannah	1,192,028	845,353
Charleston	472,567	402,317
Wilmington	323,273	234,664
Norfolk	609,454	738,286
Baltimore	74,404	61,255
New York	161,613	107,885
Boston	225,647	162,429
Philadelphia	88,284	53,097
West Point	..	50
Newport News	15,699	9,707
Brunswick	244,587	121,475
Port Royal	65,972	70,971
El Paso, Texas	..	100
Laredo, Texas	16,711	13,759
Eagle Pass, Texas	6,335	10,131
San Francisco, &c.	165,136	67,482
Total	8,769,360	6,829,100

Table showing Exports of Cotton from United States Ports for 1897–98.

From—	Great Britain.	France.	Continent and Channel.	Total.	Total, 1896–97.
	Bales.	Bales.	Bales.	Bales.	Bales.
New Orleans	1,141,958	422,754	819,288	2,384,000	1,984,169
Galveston	775,752	299,362	439,866	1,514,980	1,230,842
Mobile and Pensacola	228,289	...	113,006	341,295	252,501
Savannah	73,740	32,547	627,659	733,946	436,140
Charleston	84,740	...	236,597	321,337	270,228
Wilmington	117,719	...	180,367	298,086	206,794
Norfolk	68,139	...	41,867	110,006	200,275
Baltimore	96,350	4,393	123,058	223,801	173,043
New York	377,914	57,130	328,622	763,666	681,468
Boston	312,461	...	...	312,461	235,688
Philadelphia	17,950	...	1,650	19,600	12,802
Newport News	13,704	200	6,613	20,517	9,707
Brunswick	157,249	...	89,778	247,027	125,161
Port Royal	57,972	...	8,000	65,972	71,529
El Paso, &c.	...	...	564	564	100
Laredo	...	...	16,711	16,711	13,759
Eagle Pass	...	...	6,335	6,335	10,131
San Francisco, &c.	19,393	...	140,183	159,576	57,046
Total	3,543,330	816,386	3,180,164	7,539,880	5,971,383
Last year (1896–97)	3,018,462	702,632	2,250,289	5,971,383	...

Cotton business, 1898–99.
Heavy crop.

As was the case in 1897, early in the cotton season a very heavy crop was predicted, and whilst the estimates now are not so large as they were a few months ago, yet the prediction has been verified in large measure.

At first, a crop equal to that of last season, namely, 11,200,000 bales was confidently looked for, but recently there have been good reasons to modify this estimate and now a moderate calculation puts the crop at about 10,750,000 bales.

Big crop in Texas.

Of this amount Texas is looked upon as being likely to produce from 3,250,000 to 3,500,000 bales, as against 3,075,000 last season.

In distinction to the crop of 1897–98, when Texas produced relatively less cotton than "Atlantic" and "other Gulf" States, this State appears this season to have increased her production, whilst the others have fallen-off.

Very low prices.

This succession of two exceedingly heavy crops has naturally had a depressing effect on prices, notwithstanding increased demand by spinners. In fact, prices have been the lowest ever recorded.

The price for spot middling cotton in Galveston on September 1, 1898, was $5\frac{7}{16}$ c., and during the latter part of October and the whole of November fluctuated between 5 and $4\frac{7}{8}$ c. per lb.

A little later the idea got about that the crop had been over-estimated and the price rose to $5\frac{7}{16}$ c., the same as at the corresponding date in 1897.

Shortly after the New Year prices began to rise and at the end of January there was a sharp upward movement, middling cotton selling at over 6 c., the price to-day (February 1) being $6\frac{1}{16}$ c., as against $5\frac{1}{2}$ c. this day last year.

As far as this port is concerned the striking feature of this season has been the heavy receipts of cotton here.

First cotton port in the United States.

Galveston has, at length, attained her ambition and is, to-day, the first cotton port in the United States, whilst her gain has been the loss of other ports.

Comparison with other ports.

From the following table giving the receipts thus far this season and to the same date last season at Galveston, New Orleans, Savannah, and Charleston, together with the percentage of increase or decrease, the gain at this port will be clearly seen, she alone of the four having increased receipts this season:—

	Galveston.	New Orleans.	Savannah.	Charleston.
	Bales.	Bales.	Bales.	Bales.
Receipts to February 1, 1899	2,008,713	1,660,649	928,288	334,112
" " 1898	1,613,403	1,986,044	968,590	402,848
Percentage of increase or decrease	+ 24·50	− 16·38	− 4·16	− 17·06

The following table gives the receipts at Galveston during the last five seasons up to February 1:—

GALVESTON.

Year.	Receipts to Date.	Receipts for the Season.	Texas Crop.
	Bales.	Bales.	Bales.
1894–95	1,433,288	1,659,999	3,275,938
1895–96	758,372	1,001,075	1,989,582
1896–97	1,162,799	1,376,355	2,247,554
1897–98	1,606,577	1,950,667	3,074,811
1898–99	2,008,713	..	..

The following table gives the receipts, foreign and coastwise, exports, and stocks from September 1 to February 1 in each of the last five seasons at Galveston :— *Receipts and exports at Galveston.*

Year.	Receipts Net.	Exports. Foreign.	Exports. Coastwise.	Stock, February 1.
	Bales.	Bales.	Bales.	Bales.
1894–95	1,433,288	1,081,262	179,334	162,731
1895–96	758,372	489,051	155,326	113,448
1896–97	1,159,765	990,271	140,371	107,323
1897–98	1,606,577	1,129,835	274,746	214,072
1898–99	2,008,713	1,654,984	164,032	217,717

The standing of Galveston up to February 1 this season, as compared with other United States cotton exporting ports, is shown in the following table, as also the exports of cotton to date in detail.

The great increase in foreign exports will be noticed, especially those to Great Britain, whilst the coastwise exports will be seen to have largely decreased.

GALVESTON.

Ports.	Quantity. 1898-99.	1897-98.
	Bales.	Bales.
Galveston	2,008,713	1,613,403
New Orleans	1,660,649	1,986,044
Mobile	223,665	290,311
Savannah	928,288	968,590
Charleston	334,112	402,848
Wilmington	282,261	286,965
Norfolk	496,294	472,253
Baltimore	23,697	47,616
New York	90,131	94,797
Boston	228,358	135,885
Philadelphia	29,496	52,364
Newport News	14,128	7,120
Brunswick	226,957	156,923
Pensacola	138,240	..
Port Royal	20,865	45,038
Port Arthur	19,585	..
Other ports	..	77,847
Total	6,725,439	6,638,004
Difference	87,435	

TABLE of Receipts and Exports at Galveston, 1898-99, up to February 1, 1899.

RECEIPTS.

	Quantity. 1898-99.	1897-98.
	Bales.	Bales.
Net	2,008,713	1,613,403
Other ports	94	174
Gross total	2,008,807	1,613,577

EXPORTS—FOREIGN.

Destination.	Quantity. 1898-99.	1897-98.
	Bales.	Bales.
Great Britain	918,969	601,901
France	320,187	242,817
Continent	404,924	284,794
Channel	10,904	8,500
Total	1,654,984	1,138,012

GALVESTON.

EXPORTS—COASTWISE.

Destination.	Quantity.	
	1898–99.	1897–98.
	Bales.	Bales.
New York	103,365	231,608
Other domestic ports	60,613	43,129
North, by rail	54	9
Total	164,032	274,746

Grain Trade.

The export trade in grain at Galveston, which is of rather recent growth, again shows an increase for 1898 over 1897, and may now be said to be second only in importance to the export trade in cotton at this port. Increasing importance of grain trade.

The possibilities are great, and there is but little doubt that now that Texas has entered the field as a grain producing State the amount shipped at Galveston will year by year increase.

When it is recalled that the greater portion of the surplus of cereals grown in the United States is produced west of the Mississippi, and that year by year these States produced more and more grain, and the Eastern States less and less, it may not appear visionary to say that Galveston's chances for becoming a very important grain exporting point are most favourable, owing to her close proximity to much of this surplus grain producing area.

The facilities here, as has been before pointed out in the reports from this Consulate, are excellent, and ample for a business of 50,000,000 bushels a year or more.

During 1898 Galveston was visited by one or two associations of grain dealers in a body, and by various persons interested in the trade as individuals.

The universal opinion was that the port was both from situation and from facilities able and destined to do an immense grain shipping business.

Apparently little fault has been found with cargoes of grain shipped from here. In fact some consigners have requested further shipments through Galveston, owing to the good condition of the grain on its arrival at its destination.

There was an increase of some 430,000 bushels storage capacity during the year, and the total is now 2,750,000 bushels, whilst another elevator of 1,000,000 bushels capacity will probably be built shortly.

As showing the good facilities and rapid loading work at this port, the following instance may be given:— Good facilities and rapid loading.

On the last day of November, 1898, four vessels took in 238,740 bushels of grain in 15½ hours, which included about five hours necessary to shift these four vessels.

GALVESTON.

Total amount of grain shipped.

Only one elevator was employed, yet one vessel took 96,000 bushels in a little over four hours.

The total amount of grain shipped in 1898 was 16,055,618 bushels, as against 11,445,655 bushels in 1897.

There were 10,690,586 bushels of wheat and 5,365,032 bushels of maize, as compared with 7,372,636 bushels of wheat and 4,073,019 bushels of maize in 1897.

A small quantity of rye was also shipped.

The increased value of the grain exported was about 500,000*l*.

Grain-laden British vessels. Table of grain exports.

There were 201 full or partial cargoes of grain shipped in British vessels during 1898, as against 149 in 1897.

The following table shows the amount of grain shipped in 1898 and its destination.

There is at present, February 1, 1899, a stock of 1,259,000 bushels of wheat and 345,882 bushels of maize in Galveston.

From July 1, the beginning of the grain season, up to February 1 there had been received here 14,698 cars of wheat and 3,887 cars of maize, as against 11,717 cars of wheat and 2,835 cars of maize in the corresponding period last year.

Destination.	Quantity.	
	Maize.	Wheat.
	Bushels.	Bushels.
Great Britain	1,369,775	2,426,769
Germany	1,723,147	2,190,214
Holland	649,305	2,900,657
France	765,738	806,442
Italy	51,785	233,000
Belgium	178,988	2,013,504
Denmark	626,294	120,000
Total	5,365,032	10,690,586

Public Works.

Railway and wharf improvements.

It would have been out of the question to have handled the greatly increased business of Galveston had not the terminal and wharf facilities of the port been largely developed and augmented during the past few years.

Even during 1897, in spite of much that had been done in this direction, some friction was experienced, and blockades of railway cars were not infrequent.

It speaks exceedingly well for the improvements effected during 1898, which were more extensive than those of any other year, that the business of this last season, which was far in advance of that of any other season, has been carried on without the least friction.

The prime mover in these great improvements has been the Galveston Wharf Company, a large corporation owning, with some few exceptions, practically the whole front of the port, with its wharves, grain elevators, storage sheds, &c.

The efforts of the Wharf Company have, moreover, been ably seconded by the various railway companies running into Galveston.

It is interesting to pass in review the improvements during the last eight or 10 years, which exhibit very strikingly American energy and resource.

They may be said to have really started about 1890, when Congress voted the sum of 6,500,000 dol. for the purpose of improving the entrance to the harbour of Galveston.

The contrast between the state of affairs as regards shipping facilities then and now is most striking.

To-day the actual berth room for vessels is more than double what it was in 1890, and as the ships are much larger in capacity than formerly, and now obtain much quicker despatch, the facilities for shipping may be said to be quadrupled what they were eight years ago. *Increased berth room for vessels.*

In 1890 there were no grain elevators here, except a small one at the flour mills, used for purely local business. *Increased grain facilities.*

To-day there are three large elevators for export trade, as well as two smaller ones, with an aggregate capacity of 2,750,000 bushels, and able to do a business of over 50,000,000 bushels a year.

In 1890 there were 17 blocks of straight wharf frontage, some 5,000 feet in length. None of the wharves were quayed, and there were no slips for small craft. *Increased wharfage.*

Since that time four large quayed wharves have been built, one on the west end of the wharf front, and three on the east, whilst another of similar character is in course of construction at the west end.

These new wharves are capable of accommodating as many vessels as all the rest of the wharf frontage combined, and the sidings and general arrangements are such as to reduce the time and expense of loading vessels to a minimum.

In 1890 the storage facilities on the wharf front were few and unsatisfactory. *Increased storage facilities.*

With the exception of the piers used by the coastwise lines, all the wharves were open, and the storage of freight under tarpaulins both dangerous and troublesome.

To-day every pier is covered in with sheds, which are substantially built and fitted with water hydrants in case of fire.

Freight from ship to car and from car to ship need never now come in contact with mud or water whilst there is accommodation for over 1,000,000 bales of cotton at one time.

One of the most striking improvements effected was the change of the system of trackage, which was accomplished by the Wharf Company during 1898. *New system of trackage.*

Without this, the expansion of wharfage would have been useless, and its value is readily appreciated by the railway and shipping interests of Galveston.

The old system of sidings on the wharf was not laid with any definite plan, but was put down from time to time as necessity demanded.

Whenever a new wharf was built, new sidings were laid to it, and tacked on without much regard to their relation to other lines and sidings.

The result was a most heterogeneous system of lines, which was found wanting when the business of the port suddenly increased in 1896.

To add to the difficulties there were then on the wharf-front numerous little wooden buildings, such as warehouses, stores, saloons, fish packers, &c., which interfered greatly with the handling of freight.

The general railway station for passengers also stood on the wharf, and fully 50 per cent. of goods trains had to pass along the line leading to it.

The passenger trains, moreover, had of course right of way, and as there were some 50 of such trains daily, the handling of cars with freight or empty was seriously interrupted.

Within the past two years all this has been changed. A new railway station has been built, reached by separate lines, which entirely relieves the freight lines and yards of any interference on the part of passenger traffic.

The old patchwork of lines and sidings owned by the wharf company was entirely torn up in 1898 and a new system built, superior in every way, whilst all the small buildings above alluded to have been removed.

There are now 35 miles of line in the wharf yards, more than double the previous mileage.

These lines and sidings have been laid on the most approved modern system with 70 lb. steel rails, automatic points, &c.

The wharf front has been divided into sections, each of which has a number of independent leads, and under the new order of things five or six trains can be seen running within the limits of 200 yards in different directions without delay or interference.

The wharf-yard is now worked under the joint management of the wharf company, and the several railroads and the result of this joint supervision has been exceedingly satisfactory to all concerned.

The motive power used has also been much improved during the last year or so.

Modern 55-ton engines have supplanted the small engines formerly used with the result that the trains now handled here are said to be the largest in the country.

It is not uncommon to see a train of 90 or 100 cars, each car averaging over 30 feet in length, brought from the railway companies' yards to the wharf companies' east end yards, a distance of 6 miles, without stop or interference.

The long trains are made up in order of piers, the cars being dropped as their destination is reached.

Nor have the various railway companies been backward in doing their share towards the general improvement of shipping facilities.

Within the last 18 months they have added over 40 miles of line to their storage yards, being twice the previous amount.

These additions have been constructed upon the most modern principles, and are specially adapted for the rapid handling of business.

All of the improvements, both of the wharf company and of the railways have been planned for years to come, and with an eye to future expansion, and it may be taken for granted that there will be no further patchwork.

General results of improvements.

The results of these great improvements will be seen when it is stated that the wharf company handled, during the year ended December 1, 1898, 91,577 cars, as against 74,629 cars in the year ended December 1, 1897, being an increase of 16,948 cars, and this, too, without any appreciable friction or delay.

As many as 804 loaded cars and as many empties were handled in one day in November, whilst it is believed that 1,000 loaded cars would be as easily taken care of.

Prior to the late improvements, the greatest number ever handled in one day was 408 in 1896, and that with difficulty.

Harbour works. Jetties completed.

The gigantic jetties built under the supervision of the United States Government were practically completed at the beginning of 1898, and no work on them to speak of was done during the year.

Dredging.

A certain amount of dredging, however, was done in 1898 by the Government dredge-boat, for the purpose of keeping the channel free from lumps and other obstructions formed by the action of the water.

The amount thus removed was some 240,000 cubic yards.

Depth of water.

There has been an increase of about 6 inches in the depth of the channel during 1898, owing chiefly to the natural action of the tides and winds.

The recorded depths, which are taken daily, show as high as 29 feet at mean low tide, but the average is from 27 to 28 feet.

The deepest draught vessel that left during the year was the "Loch Tay" in August last, drawing 25 feet 9 inches, so it is evident that there is water enough and to spare.

IMPORTS at Galveston for the Year 1898, Free of Duty.

Commodities.	Value.									Total Value, 1898.	Total Value, 1897.
	Great Britain.	Germany.	France.	Mexico.	Porto Rico.	Italy.	British West Indies.	British East Indies.	Belgium.	All other Countries.		
	£	£	£	£	£	£	£	£	£	£	£	£
American manufactures (re-imported)	42	352	...	422	...	...	...	...	5	...	821	2,614
Books and printed matter	2	7	6	...	...	...	...	...	...	...	15	66
Chemicals (all kinds)	8,143	...	...	15	...	...	2	...	...	...	8,160	3,041
Fibres (jute and jute butts)	...	...	...	...	...	...	...	14,025	...	...	14,025	25,868
,, (sisal grass)	...	...	...	320,787	...	...	...	...	...	...	320,787	12,635
Fruits and nuts	...	...	...	31	8	...	...	...	...	...	39	...
Household and personal effects	44	115	78	...	...	...	...	...	30	...	267	146
Wood (unmanufactured)	...	...	...	2,168	...	...	...	...	...	...	2,168	3,998
Miscellaneous articles	26	387	...	15	...	6	...	...	12	97	543	10,243
Total value of free imports for 1898	8,257	861	84	323,438	8	6	2	14,025	47	97	346,825	...
,, ,, 1897	9,080	3,685	39	16,618	2,881	...	...	26,155	60	63	...	58,611

GALVESTON.

Imports at Galveston for the Year 1898, Paying Duty.

Value.

Commodities.	Great Britain.	Germany.	France.	Mexico.	Porto Rico.	Italy.	British West Indies.	British East Indies.	Belgium.	All other Countries.	Total Value, 1898.	Total Value, 1897.
	£	£	£	£	£	£	£	£	£	£	£	£
Asphaltum	...	...	...	...	...	...	1,400	...	...	...	1,400	778
Books and printed matter	58	2	2	...	...	...	...	...	...	...	62	77
Breadstuffs	55	...	...	...	...	121	...	...	...	...	176	93
Cement (Portland in barrels)	681	11,143	...	...	...	...	...	...	12,816	...	24,640	24,033
Coal and coke (bituminous)	781	91	...	...	36	...	...	...	...	...	908	755
Chemicals and compounds	635	5,162	...	...	...	4	...	...	167	...	5,968	7,735
Cotton manufactures	203	615	...	...	...	...	...	...	1	...	819	673
Earthenware (plain and decorated)	5,546	1,503	...	...	...	7	...	...	...	...	7,056	4,116
Fibres (manufactures of flax, hemp, and jute)	5,820	30	...	18	...	...	...	...	...	...	5,850	4,475
Fruits and nuts (preserved and prepared)	27	...	438	...	...	26	...	...	...	...	509	117
Fish (sardines and others)	480	385	530	...	...	10	...	...	...	...	1,020	441
Glass (all kinds)	28	422	394	...	...	...	...	...	539	129	1,475	396
Iron and steel (manufactures of)	1,768	81	8	...	...	8	...	...	...	...	2,190	1,767
Metals (manufactures of)	9	5	...	...	...	...	...	...	...	...	98	451
Malt liquors (ale, porter, and beer)	1,938	...	268	...	...	124	...	...	...	...	1,951	959
Oils (olive or salad)	...	5	...	...	...	50	...	...	...	...	392	34
Provisions (dairy products and meats)	2	...	...	...	...	3	...	...	1	...	58	95
Rice and rice meal	1,290	7,182	...	9	...	...	...	...	...	...	8,472	3,247
Sugar (beet above 16 D.S.)	...	350	167	...	...	11	...	...	...	...	359	13,125
Spirits (distilled)	53	65	...	...	...	53	...	...	93	...	288	50
Salt	2,980	16	...	...	...	...	...	...	4	...	2,980	466
Vegetables (preserved and prepared)	284	281	756	...	...	...	...	...	...	121	404	556
Wines (still and sparkling)	263	117	4	...	...	12	...	...	...	...	1,215	1,878
Wool (manufactures of)	3	64	...	120	...	7	...	...	30	...	384	410
Wood	593	3,183	172	82	...	...	1	...	...	...	199	11
Miscellaneous articles											4,068	3,500
Subject to duty for 1898	23,497	30,702	2,739	229	36	436	1,401	...	13,651	250	72,941	70,238
Free of duty for 1898	8,257	861	84	323,438	8	6	2	14,025	47	97	346,825	58,611
In transit to other districts	5,316	28,103	...	...	...	...	...	6,780	...	...	40,199	...
Total imports for 1898	37,070	59,666	2,823	323,667	44	442	1,403	14,025	20,478	347	459,965	...
,, ,, 1897	26,885	44,127	2,074	16,663	3,473	...	...	26,155	7,602	1,870	128,849	...

Exports from Galveston for the Year 1898.

Destination.	Cotton. Quantity.	Cotton. Value.	Cotton-seed Meal and Cake. Quantity.	Cotton-seed Meal and Cake. Value.	Wheat. Quantity.	Wheat. Value.	Corn (Maize). Quantity.	Corn (Maize). Value.	Wheat Flour. Quantity.	Wheat Flour. Value.	Lumber. Quantity.	Lumber. Value.
	Bales.	£	Tons.	£	Bushels.	£	Bushels.	£	Barrels.	£	1,000 ft.	£
Great Britain and Colonies	1,079,904	6,073,391	9,046	34,146	2,426,769	405,118	1,369,775	111,109	3,351	3,005	749	3,282
Germany	336,637	1,907,007	156,027	588,030	2,190,214	310,937	1,723,147	137,674	972	814	1,859	5,298
France	374,696	2,109,453	4,441	16,461	806,442	140,770	765,738	61,715	..	..	323	746
Netherlands	22,392	127,517	29,289	111,028	2,900,657	450,809	649,305	51,996	3,114	3,159	1,547	3,613
Belgium	50,393	278,650	3,630	13,775	2,013,504	317,057	178,988	13,467	23,025	19,215	2,691	6,675
Italy	28,718	199,430	..	..	233,060	44,252	51,785	4,143	..	..	5	17
Denmark	9,574	54,349	26,651	99,896	120,000	17,312	626,294	50,793	3,086	2,205	219	1,234
Mexico	15,880	93,462	..	..	..	..	..	..	..	..	320	362
Japan	25,979	171,569	..	2	..	..	..	..	..	..	..	..
Cuba	..	..	1	..	..	..	..	..	33,546	29,412	29	69
West Indies	..	..	..	..	..	..	..	..	12,121	10,787	..	..
Russia	2,056	13,488	..	..	..	..	..	..	..	..	..	..
Total for 1898	1,956,229	11,028,316	229,085	863,388	10,690,586	1,686,255	5,365,032	430,897	79,218	68,597	7,742	21,296
,, 1897	1,374,942	8,988,313	164,863	650,418	7,372,636	1,352,399	4,073,019	260,695	49,878	40,888	..	26,924

GALVESTON.

EXPORTS from Galveston for the Year 1898—continued.

Destination.	Cotton-seed Oil. Quantity. Gallons.	Cotton-seed Oil. Value. £	Staves. Value. £	Lead. Value. £	Logs. Value. £	Borax. Value. £	Spelter. Value. £	Cattle. Value. £	Sundries. Value. £	Total, 1898. £	Total, 1897. £
Great Britain and Colonies	97,500	3,906	2,850	..	881	60,743	65,571	..	17,315	6,781,317	5,739,688
Germany	312,455	16,485	9,546	..	13,794	..	..	..	10,343	2,999,978	2,534,904
France	927,305	143,772	427	..	1,041	..	1,120	..	1,905	2,477,410	2,036,747
Netherlands	1,850,289	91,982	5,997	..	2,440	..	4,723	..	45	853,309	658,926
Belgium	108,846	4,618	7,349	..	4,759	..	2,235	..	630	668,430	499,323
Italy	1,085,349	60,282	..	..	136	..	..	..	15,739	323,999	113,996
Denmark	74,510	4,335	..	..	..	..	..	..	17	230,141	160,571
Mexico	915,870	31,749	..	..	..	..	..	..	3,401	128,974	93,260
Japan	..	..	..	..	..	..	..	..	..	171,569	..
Cuba	..	..	26	..	..	..	..	55,810	3,468	88,787	75,047
West Indies	..	..	..	..	..	..	..	..	..	10,787	6,606
Russia	..	..	..	..	..	..	..	..	..	13,488	18,294
Total for 1898	5,372,124	357,129	26,195	45,124	23,051	60,743	73,649	55,810	52,863	14,748,189	..
,, 1897	4,490,341	236,364	106,906	..	23,274	57,045	112,394	62,882	36,140	..	12,000,943

GALVESTON.

TABLE of Shipping engaged in the Foreign Trade at Galveston during the Year 1898.

ENTERED.

Nationality.	In Ballast.		With Cargo.		Total.	
	Number of Vessels.	Tons.	Number of Vessels.	Tons.	Number of Vessels.	Tons.
American	2	981	3	1,365	5	2,346
Austro-Hungarian	1	2,179	...	...	1	2,179
British	335	629,587	37	68,331	372	697,918
Danish	11	22,085	...	...	11	22,085
Dutch	3	4,930	...	...	3	4,930
French	...	...	...	...	...	...
German	...	...	21	40,777	21	40,777
Italian	2	1,249	...	...	2	1,249
Mexican	...	...	3	201	3	201
Norwegian	18	14,679	4	3,722	22	18,401
Spanish	24	44,356	2	3,518	26	47,874
Total	396	720,046	70	117,914	466	837,960

CLEARED.

Nationality.	In Ballast.		With Cargo.		Total.	
	Number of Vessels.	Tons.	Number of Vessels.	Tons.	Number of Vessels.	Tons.
American	1	80	4	7,034	5	7,114
Austro-Hungarian	...	...	1	2,179	1	2,179
British	...	...	359	672,535	359	672,535
Danish	...	...	10	20,495	10	20,495
Dutch	...	...	3	4,930	3	4,930
French	...	...	1	1,592	1	1,592
German	1	1,368	19	37,107	20	38,475
Italian	...	...	1	679	1	679
Mexican	...	...	2	160	2	160
Norwegian	1	979	26	19,828	27	20,807
Spanish	...	...	29	53,021	29	53,021
Total	3	2,427	455	819,560	458	821,987

GALVESTON.

RETURN of British Shipping at the Port of Galveston in the Year 1898.

Direct Trade in British Vessels from and to Great Britain and British Colonies.

Entered.

Total Number of Vessels.			Total Tonnage.			Total Number of Crews.	Total Value of Cargoes.
With Cargoes.	In Ballast.	Total.	With Cargoes.	In Ballast.	Total.		£
11	185	196	20,208	366,251	386,459	5,814	...

Cleared.

Total Number of Vessels.			Total Tonnage.			Total Number of Crews.	Total Value of Cargoes.
With Cargoes.	In Ballast.	Total.	With Cargoes.	In Ballast.	Total.		£
122	...	122	245,328	...	245,328	3,945	5,690,605

Indirect or Carrying Trade in British Vessels from and to other Countries.

Entered.

Countries whence Arrived.	Number of Vessels.			Tonnage.			Number of Crews.	Value of Cargoes.
	With Cargoes.	In Ballast.	Total.	With Cargoes.	In Ballast.	Total.		£
Brazil	...	31	31	...	55,024	55,024	866	...
Portugal and colonies	...	27	27	...	44,316	44,316	654	...
Italy	...	22	22	...	38,616	38,616	542	...
United States of America	10	7	17	16,737	14,955	31,692	567	...
Cuba	7	5	12	14,792	7,182	21,974	386	...
Spain and colonies	...	13	13	...	21,946	21,946	347	...
Argentine Republic	...	9	9	...	17,662	17,662	229	...
Belgium	2	5	7	3,698	9,762	13,460	190	...
Mexico	...	8	8	...	12,508	12,508	184	...
Germany	1	5	6	2,141	9,833	11,974	168	...
France and colonies	...	7	7	...	11,185	11,185	161	...
United States of Colombia	3	1	4	5,423	1,965	7,388	140	...
Danish West Indies	...	4	4	...	6,758	6,758	105	...
Netherlands	...	3	3	...	5,721	5,721	85	...
Guatemala	3	...	3	5,332	...	5,332	116	...
Other countries	...	3	3	...	5,903	5,903	78	...
Total	26	150	176	48,123	263,336	311,459	4,818	...

Cleared.

Countries to which Departed.	Number of Vessels.			Tonnage.			Number of Crews.	Value of Cargoes.
	With Cargoes.	In Ballast.	Total.	With Cargoes.	In Ballast.	Total.		£
Germany	100	...	100	181,411	...	181,411	2,596	2,632,407
France	56	...	56	103,366	...	103,366	1,567	2,317,111
Netherlands	38	...	38	70,002	...	70,002	1,049	875,331
Belgium	15	...	15	26,646	...	26,646	382	415,746
Italy	8	...	8	14,735	...	14,735	201	323,520
Denmark	6	...	6	10,154	...	10,154	146	90,226
United States of America	1	3	4	1,451	6,167	7,618	133	7,562
Mexico	5	...	5	6,320	...	6,320	116	21,460
Japan	3	...	3	6,279	...	6,279	85	171,289
Cuba	2	...	2	2,676	...	2,676	59	13,079
Total	234	3	237	423,040	6,167	429,207	6,334	6,867,731

SABINE PASS.

Trade and commerce.

Mr. Vice-Consul Roland reports as follows:—

The increase of the shipping this year over 1897, in spite of the war with Spain, has been something marvellous. As will be seen by my annual report the increase of shipping in British vessels to Great Britain and other countries is over 700 per cent. The total number of feet of lumber shipped to foreign countries in 1897 was in round numbers 60,000,000, and in 1898, 75,000,000 feet, or an increase of 15,000,000 feet. Value of imports, foreign, for 1898, as against none in 1897, 1,500,000 dol. The total value of business done in 1897 was 698,598 dol., in 1898, 8,085,414 dol., or an increase in 1898 of 7,386,816 dol.

A regular line of steamers ran from New York to this port during the months of October and November. This business would come under the head of coasting business, and amounted to over 4,000,000 dol. On account of the scarcity of tonnage this line was discontinued, but arrangements have been made to resume operations permanently early in the spring.

There is now a regular line of steamers running from here to Mexican ports.

It is a well-known fact that the Trans-Mississippi district is a large consumer of imports of all kinds, and that it would be extremely advantageous to importers to consider sending their shipments viâ Sabine Pass in the vessels which handle export business already established, as favourable rates could be obtained on all freight commodities in which time is not the particularly essential element. Investigation will disclose the fact that it is cheaper to ship goods from English ports to Gulf ports when the destinations of such goods are points in the interior west of the Mississippi River, and particularly favourable opportunities exist for importing houses at Sabine Pass, inasmuch as this business is in its infancy, and in the upbuilding of this industry the greatest opportunity exists.

Industries.

A dredging company has a number of suction and clam-shell dredges, and carry on business here and in this vicinity, having their office and headquarters at this place. The same company has established a coal yard, which bids fair to develop into a coaling station for steamers, on account of the convenient location and ease of access.

The oyster and fishing business here is rapidly expanding and assuming large proportions. Two firms have started, and are now extensively engaged in shipping oysters to the interior towns and cities, as well as supplying the local markets.

Numerous store buildings and dwelling houses have been erected, as well as two churches and a fine hotel, at a cost of 25,000,000 dol. Two weekly newspapers have been published here during the year. A large freight and passenger station has been erected at a cost of 3,000 dol.

The Mexican Consul and a new ship agent have opened offices here. Large general merchandise stores are well established, and are in a position to fit out vessels of all description with everything necessary in the ship chandlering line. The truck gardening business is carried on extensively all the year around. The soil and climate may be said to be particularly adapted to the melon business, and in seasons past hundreds of car loads of all kinds of melons have been shipped to the northern markets.

The harbour improvements at Sabine Pass for the year 1898 have been many, and of a very substantial character. The most important is the work done by the Government in the construction of the jetties and the placing of large iron buoys which mark the channel from the harbour to the deep waters of the Gulf.

<small>Harbour improvements.</small>

An appropriation of 400,000 dol. was made for the work this year. The West Jetty has been extended 17,000 feet, and the East Jetty 22,000 feet. An appropriation of 300,000 dol. has been recommended by the Government engineers as sufficient to finish the work next year, which will make the total length of each jetty 24,000 feet. All doubts are now removed regarding a sufficient depth of water to allow deep draught ocean vessels to enter, as has been fully demonstrated this year, steamers of over 2,500 tons net register having entered and cleared through this port with full cargoes both in and out, drawing $23\frac{1}{2}$ feet of water. This was accomplished without the use of tug-boats, vessels using their own steam both in and out. An appropriation of 100,000 dol. has been made by the Government to build a dredge boat for the harbour of Sabine Pass, and a Bill has passed the House for an appropriation of 18,000 dol. for a lighthouse on Sabine Banks, 15 miles out from the bar. Efforts are being made to obtain a lightship, with fog signal, to be placed on these banks for the guidance and help of vessels bound for this port until the lighthouse is erected, and there is every reason to believe that this will be granted.

Clusters of piling have been driven along the bank of the harbour for vessels loading in the stream to moor and lie against. Two large and commodious slips have been constructed at a cost of 150,000 dol., one 700 feet long, 185 feet wide, the other 1,000 feet long and 200 feet wide, both 24 feet deep on the sides and 30 feet in the centre. The third slip, 800 feet long, 200 feet wide at the bottom, and 250 feet wide at the water-line, is partially constructed.

Over 3 acres of substantial sheds have been built for the handling of cotton and general merchandise, and some 7 or 8 miles of tracks for terminal and yard facilities have been constructed.

A new quarantine station has been erected near the jetties at a cost of about 3,000 dol. Two large forts have been constructed at a cost of about 30,000 dol. In connection with this the Government is negotiating for a tract of 300 acres on which it is contemplated to erect a system of modern fortifications in addition to the two forts already mentioned.

The present population of Sabine Pass is estimated at from 2,000 to 2,500. Sabine Pass is considered one of the healthiest places in the south on account of its close proximity to the Gulf, and the even temperature which exists here all the year around. Malaria, typhoid, and fevers of all kinds are unknown here.

<small>Health and population.</small>

PORT ARTHUR.

Items of interest concerning improvements now under construction at this place, viz.:—

Trade and commerce. As stated in my report of the previous year, all exports, as well as imports, must be lightered to vessels lying at Sabine Pass, and vice versâ, a distance of 8 miles, until the completion of the canal. The exports from Port Arthur consist chiefly of grain, flour, cotton, oils, lumber, and farming implements. Imports consist mainly of sisal grass, transported by a line of steamers plying between Mexican ports and Sabine Pass.

Industries. A company has erected a plant for the manufacture of fish oil and fertilizer. The fish used is manhaden, large shoals of which abound in the Gulf. By a new process this company has been able to eliminate all odours, usually a disagreeable feature of such an establishment.

A large elevator, with a capacity of 500,000 bushels, is now completed. It is so arranged that its receiving and discharging capacity is one of the greatest of any on the coast.

Harbour improvements. The Port Arthur Ship Canal is an artificial waterway, which, when completed, will bring 25 feet of water to the Port Arthur docks. The canal is 37,600 feet long, or a little over 7 miles. It is 75 feet wide at the bottom, and 175 feet wide at the water-line, and sloping 2 in 1.

The country it runs through is low, level, and marshy; the average elevation being less than 2 feet above mean low tide. The work of this canal is done by means of hydraulic dredges. They cut up the ground by means of an improved rotary cutter. The material thus loosened is carried through a large suction pipe and forced by a centrifugal pump to a great distance. 9,000 cubic yards per day can be disposed of. The material dredged is all deposited between earth levees or pile revetments, and thus forms a bank which protects the canal from injury from the waters of the adjoining lake.

Work on the canal commenced in May, 1897. On January 1, 1898, the amount dredged out of the canal was 945,000 cubic yards. From January 1, 1898, to January 1, 1899, 1,300,000 cubic yards, or a total since the work began of 2,245,000 cubic yards; to complete the entire canal to 25 feet of water will require 5,000,000 cubic yards. It is, however, safe to predict that this will be accomplished in the next twelve months.

A large basin near the head of the canal in which vessels may turn is nearing its completion. One slip is practically completed, 1,000 feet long, 250 feet wide with a depth of 25 feet.

Health and population. Regarding the health of Port Arthur there are no natural causes for sickness more than that since its existence. The town is practically free from malaria or diseases of that nature. The present population is estimated at 1,800 people. Common labourers receive from 1 dol. 25 c. to 1 dol. 75 c. per day. Longshoremen 30 to 40 c. per hour. Mechanics 2 dol. 50 c. to 3 dol per day.

SABINE PASS.

RETURN of British Shipping at the Port of Sabine Pass, Texas, during the Year 1898.

Direct Trade in British Vessels from and to Great Britain and British Colonies.

Entered.

| Total Number of Vessels. ||| Total Tonnage. ||| Total Number of Crews. | Total Value of Cargoes. |
With Cargoes.	In Ballast.	Total.	With Cargoes.	In Ballast.	Total.		
...	8	8	...	16,860	16,860	220	£ ...

Cleared.

| Total Number of Vessels. ||| Total Tonnage. ||| Total Number of Crews. | Total Value of Cargoes. |
With Cargoes.	In Ballast.	Total.	With Cargoes.	In Ballast.	Total.		
8	...	8	16,860	...	16,860	223	£ 293,298

Indirect or Carrying Trade in British Vessels from and to other Countries.

Entered.

| Countries whence Arrived. | Number of Vessels. ||| Tonnage. ||| Number of Crews. | Value of Cargoes. |
	With Cargoes.	In Ballast.	Total.	With Cargoes.	In Ballast.	Total.		
Mexico	...	3	3	...	3,218	3,218	45	£ ...
Central America	...	1	1	...	1,389	1,389	18	...
Total	...	4	4	...	4,607	4,607	63	...

Cleared.

| Countries to which Departed. | Number of Vessels. ||| Tonnage. ||| Number of Crews. | Value of Cargoes. |
	With Cargoes.	In Ballast.	Total.	With Cargoes.	In Ballast.	Total.		
West Indies	1	...	1	270	...	270	7	£ 422
Holland	2	...	2	2,952	...	2,952	40	48,836
Belgium	1	...	1	1,385	...	1,385	17	22,015
Total	4	...	4	4,607	...	4,607	64	71,273

No. 2220 Annual Series.

DIPLOMATIC AND CONSULAR REPORTS.

UNITED STATES.

REPORT FOR THE YEAR 1898

ON THE

TRADE OF CHARLESTON AND DISTRICT.

REFERENCE TO PREVIOUS REPORT, Annual Series No. 2031.

Presented to both Houses of Parliament by Command of Her Majesty.
APRIL, 1899.

LONDON:
PRINTED FOR HER MAJESTY'S STATIONERY OFFICE,
BY HARRISON AND SONS, ST. MARTIN'S LANE.
PRINTERS IN ORDINARY TO HER MAJESTY.

And to be purchased, either directly or through any Bookseller, from
EYRE & SPOTTISWOODE, East Harding Street, Fleet Street, E.C., and
32, Abingdon Street, Westminster, S.W.; or
JOHN MENZIES & Co., 12, Hanover Street, Edinburgh, and
90, West Nile Street, Glasgow; or
HODGES, FIGGIS, & Co., Limited, 104, Grafton Street, Dublin.

1899.

[C. 9044—46.] *Price Twopence.*

CONTENTS.

	PAGE
CHARLESTON—	
General trade conditions	3
Cotton	6
Phosphates and fertilisers	11
Rice	14
Lumber and naval stores	16
Shipping and navigation	17
Freights	18
Fruits and vegetables	20
Cotton mills	20
Miscellaneous	22
Public health and quarantine	24
SAVANNAH trade report	25
BRUNSWICK trade report	30
DARIEN trade report	31

No. 2220.   Annual Series.

Reference to previous Report, Annual Series No. 2031.

Report on the Trade and Commerce of the Consular District of Charleston for the Year 1898

By Mr. Consul Coëtlogon.

(Received at Foreign Office, March 20, 1899.)

At the close of the last commercial year, September 1, 1898, Charleston was well prepared for the transaction of what appeared to be a slowly increasing business, but the great depression that prevailed throughout the country since the panic of 1893 was again reflected in the commercial and financial operations of this port. In addition to the low prices for cotton, and the natural conservatism with which capital generally moves, the volume of trade here was also somewhat unfavourably affected by the conditions of war that prevailed during the middle part of the year; buyers were careful in their purchases and sellers were not disposed to take large risks, in the early part of the season especially, owing to the uncertainty that marked the earlier phases of the Spanish-American dispute. *General trade conditions.*

The total trade of Charleston during the commercial year ending September 1, 1898, amounted to 76,304,785 dol., as compared with 75,254,581 dol. during the previous year, showing an increase in the value of last season's trade of 1,050,204 dol.; but it may be remarked this does not account for the relatively greater increase in the volume of business done here in several leading branches, as for example the total receipts of cotton which last year were nearly 70,000 bales in excess of the receipts of the year before, and yet the value of the cotton trade of Charleston during the year ending August 31, 1898, was more than 2,000,000 dol. less than that of the previous season. Had the higher prices of the previous year prevailed the value of last year's trade would have been more than 2,000,000 dol. in excess of the year before. *Total trade.*

There was also a decrease of about 11,000 dol. in the value of the rice trade, of 26,000 dol. in the turpentine business, of 50,000 dol. in rosin, of 166,336 dol. in the liquor business of the State dispensaries, and of about 140,000 dol. in lumber and railway crosstie (sleepers) trade. On the other hand, there was an increase of 751,728 dol. in fertiliser business; 830,324 dol. in cotton goods; 88,617 dol. in fruits, vegetables, &c.; 380,500 dol. in wholesale *Decrease in values.*

Increase.

and retail trade; 1,154,750 dol. in manufactured products; and 250,000 dol. in dry goods.

Tax exemption. Under an act of the legislature of the State of South Carolina, manufacturing industries established in this city are exempted from municipal taxation for a period of five years, and this fact should encourage the establishment of many new industries. In addition to this, manufacturers here have an abundance of trustworthy labour, cheap raw material, nearness to home and foreign markets, and low freight rates.

Advantages.

Jetties. During the past year little was done for the further improvement of the jetties, but the work already done appears to have been so satisfactory that the harbour entrances are reported to be gradually improving; which fact was made manifest during the recent war with Spain when ships drawing over 23 feet of water came directly to the wharves of the city to be loaded with troops for Cuba and Puerto Rico; and about the middle of last September one of the largest troopships in the Government service passed through the Charleston jetties under her own steam drawing fully 24 feet. It is also evident that this port is regarded as one of considerable importance, as is shown by the large expenditure last year for the improvement of the defences of the harbour on Sullivan's Island and Fort Sumter, and it is to be hoped that future appropriations of money by Congress will be adequate for further needed improvements to the harbour and its approaches.

Charleston export line. The Charleston Export Line, running direct steamers to Europe, did a fairly good business, having cleared 38 vessels with full cargoes for foreign ports during the year ending September last, including a moderately increased quantity of western grain, compared with the previous year when grain shipments were made for the first time from this port.

Fertilisers. Charleston held its position as the principal centre for the manufacture of phosphate fertilisers in this country and most of the mills did well, and should continue to do so next year, with better prospective railway facilities and freight rates. There has recently been a general combination of the fertiliser manufacturing industries so as to make them practically under one management for the future, thus securing greater concentration of capital and increased economy in working expenses.

Cotton mill industry. One of the most important features in the manufacturing line in this State is the cotton-mill industry which has been established largely in Upper South Carolina, but to a lesser extent through other parts of the State.

A large amount of Charleston capital is invested in cotton mills, particularly those of Upper Carolina, and these enterprises have proved quite profitable, dividends as a rule being much larger than in the New England mills. The competition of Southern mills has caused a number of New England companies to establish branches in the South, where the abundance of cheap labour, advantages of climate, and raw material lying conveniently at hand would appear to assure continued success for the Southern industries.

During last year there was an increase reported in the cotton goods trade of Charleston of more than 800,000 dol., and it would seem to be reasonable and practicable that, with direct steamships between this port and foreign countries, the business men and investors of this town should be able to divert a large part of the output of the Carolina mills through this port, controlling, as they do, so large an interest in the cotton mills of the State. And yet, up to the present time, none of the Carolina mills appear to have selling agents at Charleston; nearly all of the goods manufactured in the State, out of raw material produced within her borders, being sold through agencies in New York, Baltimore, Boston, and Philadelphia.

Figures. On September 1 last there were 94 cotton mills in South Carolina employing 18,614,000 dol. with about 38,500 looms and 1,300,000 spindles, five new mills having been added to the list last year. These mills manufacture almost everything that can be produced from cotton, including lace curtains, print cloths, and heavy duck weighing 8 ozs. a yard; the idea formerly entertained that fine cotton fabrics could not be manufactured in the South is an exploded fallacy.

Imports and exports. The clearances at the custom-house show that there was an increase in the import business during the year of 70,000 dol., or about 5 per cent. over the previous season; and in the exports the increase was 908,013 dol., or about 8 per cent. over the year before. The principal exports were cotton, grain, pig-iron and phosphate rock to foreign markets, and fertilisers, lumber, rice and cotton to home markets and ports in the United States. The imports consist mostly of kainit, sulphur ore (pyrites), sulphur, muriate of potash, and nitrate, these articles being used largely in the manufacture of phosphate fertilisers.

Largest cotton crop on record. The production of another large cotton crop in the United States—the largest on record—produced a naturally unfavourable effect on prices for this staple and also on the value of the business of this port; the total quantity of cotton received being greater than that of the previous year, while the comparative value of the same was much less. An important factor now affecting the American crop is the annual production of about 3,000,000 bales of cotton which the State of Texas alone is adding to the cotton product of the country. The total yield has also been further augmented of recent years by different methods of cultivation adopted by a smaller class of planters, whose aggregate product has been large enough to materially affect the crop and market prices.

Seashore railway. A review of the affairs of Charleston would hardly be complete which did not make some mention of what is regarded as one of the most important and valuable local enterprises organised and put into operation during the year; namely the extensive plant of the Charleston and Seashore Railway Company, including the new Sea Island resort, 10 miles from the city, which is the property of the company, the terminus of its line and the objective point of its present operations. The system includes covered wharves, and a commodious steamer of the ferry boat class, connecting the city with the shore at Mount Pleasant, on the opposite side of the harbour. From this point 7 miles of electric railway, well constructed and equipped, carry passengers over trestle work to Sullivan's Island, up the length of which it crosses Breach Inlet over to Long Island and thence northward to the Isle of Palms, about a mile and a half distant, where there is an excellent beach and well constructed buildings for the convenience and comfort of health and pleasure seekers. The object of the promoters has been to establish a resort suitable for both summer and winter visitors. The wharves, cars, boats, and buildings are all brilliantly lighted by electricity. Visitors from this or other towns can reach the shelters at the seaside, without exposure to rain at any point on the way, the swift electric cars halting at the steps of the main pavilion and within a few yards of the ocean surf. A fine beach extends for miles, fringed with a line of sand hills and backed with a forest of oaks and palms.

The military advantages also of this railway system should not be overlooked, connecting as it does Sullivan's Island with the mainland and Long Island both by railway bridges and by bridges for foot passengers and vehicles. In times of war, storms or emergencies, this would enable forces to be promptly thrown into or withdrawn from the island. The importance of this is apparent as Sullivan's Island is the principal fortified post guarding Charleston Harbour, having three batteries and a considerable garrison now established there.

tton. During the last cotton season of 1897–98 which ends August 31, 1898, Charleston received 462,408 bales of upland cotton, which in comparison with the previous season, showed an increase of 69,218 bales; the highest price paid in this market during the year being 6⅞ c. per lb. for medium, and the lowest 5 c. for the same grade of cotton. While the acreage planted throughout the cotton territory did not materially differ from the season before, the prospects for receipts were not so good for Charleston in the section from which she draws most of her cotton as they were a year ago, owing to the continued wet weather which retarded the picking and shipping and also tended to reduce the yield. Foreign and coastwise freight facilities were fairly satisfactory at the opening of the new cotton season last September, but the outlook for higher prices for spot cotton were not encouraging.

Comparative exports. Comparative exports of upland cotton from this port during the year ending August 31, 1898, and for the same period of the previous year were, as follows:—

CHARLESTON.

EXPORTS, FOREIGN.

Exported to—	Quantity.	
	1897-98.	1896-97.
	Bales.	Bales.
Liverpool	77,658	71,423
Continental ports	235,155	191,889
Total foreign	312,813	263,312

EXPORTS, COASTWISE.

Exported to—	Quantity.	
	1897-98.	1896-97.
	Bales.	Bales.
New York	48,778	107,225
Boston	95,379	28,822
Interior points, by railway	200	11,483
Total coastwise	144,357	147,530

GRAND TOTAL.

	Quantity.	
	1897-98.	1896-97.
	Bales.	Bales.
Grand total, foreign and coastwise	457,170	410,842

Receipts, exports and consumption by city cotton mill, together with the stock of uplands on hand August 31, 1898, were as follows:— *Receipts.*

	Quantity.
	Bales.
Stock on hand, September 1, 1897	569
Received during the year	462,408
Total	462,977

Carolina Sea Island cotton opened about the middle of October, 1897, at 18 c. per lb. for medium fine quality and gradually declined to 15 c. Extra fine qualities, however, which were sold *Sea Island cotton.*

CHARLESTON.

Prices.

early in the season, brought moderately fair prices, but later sales showed a heavy decline.

A considerably quantity of the crop was of inferior colour, and sold as low as 10 c. per lb.

Georgia Sea Island cotton opened at $12\frac{1}{2}$ c. for extra choice, declined to 12 c., and later advanced to $12\frac{1}{2}$ to 13 c. per lb.

Florida Sea Islands of the better and poorer grades were in fair demand, but there was only a limited demand for extra choice and fancy East Floridas, and about 1,500 bales remained unsold at the close of the season.

Crop conditions.

Accounts as to the condition of the crop for the new season of 1898–99 were bad, and indications pointed to a smaller crop than during last season. Rains were of almost daily occurrence for several weeks in last August and September, threatening further damage to the new crop.

Receipts and exports.

The receipts, exports, and stock of South Carolina, Georgia, and Florida Sea Island cotton, during the year ending August 31, 1898, at Charleston, as compared with the same period in the previous year, were :—

RECEIPTS.

	Quantity.	
	1897–98.	1896–97.
	Bales.	Bales.
Carolina	10,164	10,700
Georgia and Florida		367
Texas	10	97
Stock on hand, Sept. 1, 1897	927	572
Total	11,101	11,736

Exports.

Comparative exports of Sea Island cotton from Charleston, from September 1, 1897, to August 31, 1898, and for the same period of the previous season, were as follows :—

EXPORTS, FOREIGN.

Exports to—	Quantity.	
	1897–98.	1896–97.
	Bales.	Bales.
Liverpool	5,968	7,092
Havre	1,378	1,563
Bremen and Continental ports	64	..
Total foreign	7,410	8,655

CHARLESTON.

Exports, Coastwise.

Exports to—	Quantity.	
	1897-98.	1896-97.
	Bales.	Bales.
New York	2,462	2,085
Savannah	..	69
Total coastwise	2,462	2,154

Grand Total.

	Quantity.	
	1897-98.	1896-97.
	Bales.	Bales.
Grand total, foreign and coastwise	9,872	10,809

The following comparative statement shows the total amount of the Sea Island crop of 1897-98, and that of the previous season of 1896-97, also the total exports and their destination, as well as the stock on hand at Charleston and Savannah— *Total crop.*

South Carolina.

Receipts at—	Quantity.	
	1897-98.	1896-97.
	Bales.	Bales.
Charleston	10,164	10,631
Savannah	37	69
Total	10,201	10,700

Georgia and Florida.

Receipts at—	Quantity.	
	1897-98.	1896-97.
	Bales.	Bales.
Charleston	..	367
Savannah	59,202	83,931
Fernandina	..	260
Jacksonville	5,565	4,917
Brunswick	1,805	1,795
Total	66,572	91,270

Total crop of South Carolina, Georgia, and Florida received during season of 1897-98 were 76,783 bales, compared with 102,067 bales in the previous season of 1896-97, these figures including 10 bales last year and 97 bales for the year before of the Texas crop which came to this port.

Exports. The total exports of Sea Islands cotton from Charleston last year were 9,872 bales, of which 5,968 bales went to Great Britain, 1,442 bales to European continental ports, and 2,462 bales to American ports.

The stock remaining on hand at Charleston on August 31, 1898, was 1,229 bales.

In comparison with the Charleston exports, the following are the exports from the principal neighbouring seaports during the past season, namely: from Savannah, the total Sea Island shipments were 59,567 bales; from Brunswick, 1,805 bales; and from Jacksonville, 5,565 bales.

Additional figures. In addition to the foregoing figures the following shows the receipts of cotton, and the exports from Charleston from September 1 to December 31, 1898, this period forming the first four months of the new cotton season of 1898-99, which will also be included in the next annual trade report.

Decreased receipts. The total receipts of all classes of cotton at Charleston, from September 1 to December 31, 1898, were 305,925 bales, as compared with 350,620 bales for the corresponding time of the preceding year, showing a falling-off in receipts for the former period of the past year of 44,695 bales.

The total exports from September 1 to December 31, 1898, were 264,307 bales, as compared with 310,356 bales for the same time during the previous year; thus showing a falling-off in exports last year of 46,049 bales.

The stock on hand and on shipboard on the last day of the year 1898 was 44,014 bales, in comparison with 39,359 bales on hand the same date in 1897.

Closing prices. The closing prices for medium cotton, posted at the Cotton Exchange at Charleston, on the last day of December, 1898, were $5\frac{1}{8}$ c. per lb., with the tone of the market very quiet and no sales reported for the closing day of the year.

Sea Islands. The Sea Island market was steady during the last week of December, 1898, with sales of 38 bags and quotations per lb. as follows: for medium fine, 18 c. per lb.; fully fine, 22 to 25 c.; extra fine, 40 to 50 c.

Receipts. The total receipts from September 1 to December 31, 1898, were 4,497 bags, compared with 8,405 bags for the corresponding time of the year before.

Exports. The total exports from September 1 to December 31, 1898, were 2,056 bags, compared with 3,070 bags for the corresponding period of the preceding year, leaving a stock on hand and shipboard at the close of the year of 3,670 bags, compared with 6,262 bags, for the corresponding day of the year before.

Of the Sea Island exports during the last four months of the past year 735 bags were shipped to foreign countries, Great Britain taking 684 bags and 51 going to Continental ports.

The shipments during the same time to ports of the United States were 1,321 bags, of which 1,229 bags went to New York and 92 to Boston, making the grand total of all shipments, both foreign and domestic, amount to 2,056 bags for the last four months of the past year.

Phosphate deposits are known to exist in quantities sufficient to be commercially important, and are now mined for home consumption and export in the following countries, namely: Algiers, Tunis, Mexico, Hayti, British West Indies, Dutch West Indies, Canada, Spain, England, France, Belgium, Germany, Norway, Russia, and in the United States. In this country phosphate mining is carried on in South Carolina, North Carolina, Tennessee, Florida, Pennsylvania and Virginia. According to a statement made by Messrs. Wm. Stubbs and Co., of Bristol, Western Europe consumed, during the period from 1840 to 1895, the following quantities:— *Phosphates and fertilisers.*

Year.	Quantity.
	Tons.
1840	3,000
1850	15,000
1860	50,000
1870	75,000
1880	250,000
1890–91	200,000
1893	1,500,000
1895	1,865,000

The American export trade in phosphate is worth 5,000,000 dol. a year; shipments to Germany amounting in value to 2,000,000 dol., and shipments to Great Britain to 1,000,000 dol.; Canada, Japan, Australia, and the West Indies are also good customers.

There were a great many changes in ownership of the mining properties in this section during the past year; the Magnolia mines, the Horseshoe mines, the Farmers' Phosphate Mining Company, and the St. Helena Mining Company all changed hands.

There were also many changes in the control of the fertiliser companies, and most of the establishments manufacturing phosphate fertilisers around Charleston are now practically under one management, or will be as soon as they can wind up the affairs of their separate organisations.

During the early part of 1897 great stagnation prevailed in all branches of the business; many of the mining companies made but little profit, and although there were a few exceptions the changes made in ownership of these properties will greatly affect the business of river mining during the present year. But it is impossible as yet to say what the effect will be on the land mining companies, as the latter conduct their operations altogether on

Decreased royalties.

land, and it is possible for them to control their output better than the river mining companies.

The State of South Carolina lost heavily in royalties last year on account of decreased mining operations of the river companies.

During the year 1890 the State received on account of phosphate royalties, 237,000 dol.; in 1891, 170,000 dol.; in 1892, 192,000 dol.; and in 1893, 257,000 dol.; the aggregate income which the State has derived from this source having amounted to about 3,000,000 dol.

Product and consumption.

It is estimated that the South Carolina mines are able to supply at least 600,000 tons of phosphate rock annually; the relative consumption in this and other States is as follows:— South Carolina uses phosphates to the value of 2,792,958 dol.; North Carolina, 2,811,435 dol.; Pennsylvania, 3,750,000 dol.; Virginia, 4,034,944 dol.; New York, 4,691,500 dol.; and Georgia, 4,691,652 dol.

During the past year the Virginia and Carolina Chemical Company purchased the Southern Fertiliser Company, embracing works at Rome (Georgia), Atlanta, Savannah and Cordele (Georgia), at a cost of 750,000 dol. Other changes also occurred many of the Charleston local companies having undergone new ownership; including the Ashley, Stono and Wando companies, the Wappoo Mills and the Wilcox and Gibbes Company.

New business fields.

It is believed that one result of the late Spanish-American war will be to open up a new and growing field for phosphate business in the newly-acquired territories of Cuba, Manila, and Hawaii.

Shipments.

The total shipments of fertilisers from Charleston during the business year of 1897–98 amounted to 437,128 tons, compared with 374,494 tons for the previous year of 1896–97.

During last year shipments from Savannah were 110,000 tons, and Port Royal 36,000 tons, and for the previous season Savannah's shipments were 120,000 tons and Port Royal 35,000 tons.

Chemical imports.

The imports of chemicals used in the manufacture of fertilisers at Charleston last year were as follows:—

Articles.	Quantity.	Value.
	Tons.	Dollars.
Kainit	41,667	267,246
Muriate potash	6,473	213,319
Pyrites	37,601	57,968
Manure salt	3,355	40,628
Nitrate soda	3,399	96,482
Sulphate potash	84	3,117
Sulphur	23,941	74,096
Dried blood	127	3,696
Brimstone	4,730	83,836
Total	121,377	840,388

Comparative increase.

The total quantity and valuation of the above-mentioned

chemical imports here during the year 1897 were 107,828 tons, valued at 810,941 dol.; these figures showing that, in comparison with last season's imports, there was an increase in 1898 of 13,549 tons, valued at 29,447 dol.

Phosphate rock is found along the margins and in the beds of the Carolina navigable streams, much of it being very conveniently situated for conveyance to railways; it can be mined quickly and delivered alongside steamers and sailing vessels for shipment abroad and can be cheaply loaded on cars for inland use. *South Carolina phosphate rock.*

Up to the present time no great amount of phosphate has been mined in North Carolina, the total shipments last year having amounted to only 12,500 tons, almost all of which was shipped to places within that State. It is expected, however, that the extent of phosphate mining will increase, and that in future it will become an article of export. *North Carolina rock.*

Tennessee rock, which has now become a recognised branch of the phosphate industry of the country, is of good quality and can be mined easily and cheaply; it is also found in considerable quantities, and some of the deposits are accessible to railway lines, but the principal disadvantage is in its remote situation from the ocean, compared with the Carolina and Florida rock. Pensacola, on the Gulf coast of Florida, is the nearest available port of foreign shipment for this product, although there seems to be an impression that with better and improved railway connections, Newport News, Virginia, will likely become in future the principal point for shipment of Tennessee phosphate to foreign countries. *Tennessee phosphate.*

The growth of this business so far has been rapid and appears to be increasing; the output last year was over 250,000 tons, it having grown to this volume from almost nothing four or five years ago.

There were no foreign shipments of phosphate rock in its crude state from Charleston last year, and the total shipments to home ports and interior places together with the quantity consumed here were 323,121 tons, of which 170,000 tons were consumed by the local fertiliser companies; compared with the previous year's total shipments of 322,272 tons, of which 1,300 tons were exported, 145,000 tons consumed here, and the remainder shipped to home ports. *Shipments Carolina crude rock.*

Shipments of South Carolina rock from Beaufort were, during last year, 86,460 tons, of which 49,463 tons went to foreign countries, 16,000 tons were consumed locally, and the rest shipped to home ports and interior places in this country; compared with shipments the previous year of 111,846 tons, of which 75,108 tons went to foreign countries, 17,000 tons were consumed locally, and the rest shipped to home ports and places. *Beaufort shipments.*

Prices quoted for Carolina phosphates September 1, 1898, were as follows:—For Charleston crude rock, at mines, 3 dol. per ton; Charleston hot air dried, Ashley River, 3 dol. 25 c. per ton; Charleston hot air dried at City, 3 dol. 50 c. per ton; Charleston ground rock in bulk, 5 dol. 50 c. per ton. *Prices.*

The newly discovered phosphate deposits in Juanita County, *New phosphate deposits.*

CHARLESTON.

Pennsylvania, between the Oriskany sandstones and the Owandaga limestones, are said to be poor both in phosphate and lime.

The discoveries reported in Arkansas have so far attracted but little attention.

Phosphate deposits discovered in Decatur County, Georgia, owing to their nearness to Florida, have not been developed to any extent up to this time.

Phosphates found in the "Bad Lands" of Dakota have amounted to nothing commercially.

Later figures. Later phosphate figures covering the period from September 1 to December 31, 1898, at Charleston were as follows:—Total exports of crude rock were 39,466 tons, all of which was shipped to home ports and places, compared with 29,950 tons shipped during the corresponding period of 1897.

Closing prices. Closing prices at Charleston on December 31, 1898, were for crude rock at mines, 3 dol. per ton; hot air dried, 3 dol. 25 c.; f.o.b. vessels in Ashley River, 3 dol. 45 c.; f.o.b. city ground rock in bulk, 5 dol. 50 c., with the general tone of the closing market firmer on the last day of the year.

Rice. The rice season of 1897–98 commenced on September 1, 1897, but harvesting of the new crop was begun on August 25; a few planters began cutting a little earlier, the weather throughout that season being generally favourable, no disastrous gales or freshets interrupting its progress. The crop, however, matured later than usual, and there were no arrivals of new rice until September. A small cargo of rough rice was received at Bennett's mill, in this city, on September 1, but it was not put on the market until the 4th, when it sold at $5\frac{1}{4}$ c. per lb. One day before this 50 barrels of rice, which had been milled at the Waverly Mills, in Georgetown County, South Carolina, were received here and sold at $5\frac{1}{2}$ c. per lb. For the following 10 days the prevailing winds were easterly, preventing the arrival of vessels from the South, and the only receipts were about 150 barrels from the Waverly Mills.

Early crop conditions.

Prices, &c. The market did not fully open until September 15, 1897, but after that date receipts became more regular, and prices during the remainder of the month ranged from $4\frac{1}{2}$ c. per lb. for fair qualities, to $5\frac{1}{4}$ c. per lb. for good rice. In October prices became easier, and there was a decline of $\frac{1}{4}$ to $\frac{3}{8}$ c. From this time on through the winter of 1897–98 the market continued steady with a good demand, all rice offerings being freely taken, thus preventing any accumulation of stock in first hands.

Prices hardened again during February and March, good grades advancing to 5 to $5\frac{1}{4}$ c. In April, 1898, this advance was well maintained, and the better grades sold for $5\frac{1}{4}$ to 6 c. a lb. By May the crop was practically sold, and the mills having no more rough rice commenced necessary repairs for the ensuing season's work.

Receipts. Receipts of rough rice during the past season at South Carolina mills were 976,084 bushels, in comparison with 1,007,908 during the preceding year, showing a decline of 31,824 bushels last year.

The rice crop of the Atlantic coast States, which is principally raised in Georgia and Florida, amounted last year to 1,401,084 bushels, compared with the previous year's crop of 1,407,908 bushels, a decrease last season of 6,824 bushels. *Atlantic coast crop.*

The relative extent of the Carolina crop as compared with the Louisiana crop is shown by the following figures: for last year, 3,511,980 bushels, and for the year before, 2,558,292 bushels. *Louisiana crop.*

The above-named figures for Carolina, Georgia, and Louisiana rice comprise practically the rice crop of the United States for the years mentioned.

Harvesting for the new season of 1898–99 was unfavourable for rice interests up to nearly the middle of September last; frequent rains fell for many days in August, and the few planters whose early rice was ready for cutting about the middle of August were compelled to delay harvesting until the 25th of that month, when the work began on many plantations. But with the exception of a few days of fair weather, there were almost constant rains up to September 17, 1898. A storm of considerable severity came up the Atlantic coast from Florida, striking the shore in the neighbourhood of the Savannah River on August 30, doing much damage to plantations in that section, and also on river rice fields between Savannah and Charleston. Banks were broken, fields flooded, rice in many cases submerged, causing large quantities of the grain to rot away. The extent of the loss, however, was considerably less on plantations adjacent to Charleston than was the case at Savannah, owing to the greater force and destructiveness of the storm at the last-named place, which was also visited by a second storm of considerable force about October 1 last. Cooper River, at Charleston, and the rivers to the northward, felt very little the effects of the storms, and the plantations along these streams were not damaged to any extent, but none of the new crop, however, came to market before September 17 last. *New crop conditions. Autumn*

The South Carolina crop of milled rice during the season of 1897–98 amounted to 88,735 barrels of 300 lbs. net weight, of which 64,726 barrels were milled at Charleston and 24,009 barrels at Georgetown. *Total crop Carolina milled rice.*

The amount milled at Savannah during the same year was 31,818 barrels. *Georgia crop.*

The North Carolina crop was 6,500 barrels, which was milled at Wilmington, Washington, and Newbern, in that State. These figures showing that the total crop of the Atlantic coast rice growing States last year was 127,053 barrels, which compared with the total Louisiana crop of 292,665 barrels, shows an increase of 165,612 barrels of milled rice in favour of the Louisiana product. *North Carolina crop.*

The total exports of rice from Charleston for the year ending August 31, 1898, were 58,774 barrels, compared with 56,577 barrels during the previous year, all of which during both years were shipped to American ports and interior places, there being no exports to foreign countries. *Exports, &c.*

CHARLESTON.

City consumption. The quantity of rice consumed in Charleston last year was 15,952 barrels, compared with 19,083 barrels for the year before, leaving no stock remaining on hand on September 1, 1898.

Later figures. The total receipts of rice from September 1 to December 31, 1898, were 23,402 barrels, in comparison with 23,992 barrels during the corresponding period of the previous year.

Expor The total exports from September 1 to December 31, 1898, were 13,784 barrels, compared with 23,992 barrels during the last four months of the preceding year; and the stock on hand and on shipboard December 31, 1898, was 7,094 barrels, against 6,986 barrels on the last day of the year before.

All the above-mentioned exports were to American ports and places; there being no foreign exports during the periods stated.

Closing prices. The closing prices for rice in the Charleston market, on the last of December, 1898, were :—for choice qualities, $5\frac{1}{2}$ to $5\frac{3}{4}$ c. per lb.; good, 5 to $5\frac{1}{4}$ c.; fair, $4\frac{1}{2}$ to $4\frac{3}{4}$ c.; the tone of the market being steady with fairly good sales.

Lumber and naval stores. The lumber business underwent little change during the past year, and prices continued low with but small margins for profits. There was a falling-off in shipments, but the demand for local business was somewhat better.

Charleston now has good facilities for handling lumber, and shippers here are in a position to compete in prices with any other Southern port. Lumber can be shipped by water from many of the interior mills direct to this market.

Crossties (railway sleepers) arriving by railway are discharged from the cars on the wharves, directly alongside the vessels. When the new season opened on September 1 last the indications were for a fairly good business for the next season both in the demand for home consumption and in orders from ports north of Charleston, which it was expected would result from the general revival of business throughout the country.

Exports of lumber. Exports of lumber, timber, and crossties from Charleston from September 1, 1897, to August 31, 1898, were :—54,296,940 feet, of which the shipments to foreign countries were, 749,090 feet, the remainder going to New York, Baltimore, Boston, Philadelphia, and other American ports. In comparison with these figures the exports for the preceding year ending August 31, 1897, were 63,109,946 feet, of which 1,475,000 went to foreign and the balance to various American ports.

The largest shipments of lumber from this port on record were 77,297,779 feet, which were exported during the season of 1895-96.

Later exports. The exports of lumber from Charleston from September 1 to December 31, 1898, were 7,349,626 feet, of which only 75,000 feet went to foreign ports. In comparison with this the exports for the corresponding last four months of 1897 were 15,803,919 feet, of which 275,000 feet were shipped to foreign countries; these figures showing that there was a decrease last year, during the period mentioned, of more than 50 per cent. in the total shipments compared with the previous year.

There was a light demand for well manufactured stock at the close of 1898, with a fair export trade; closing quotations for lumber being as follows:—for merchantable lumber, 14 to 16 dol. per 1,000 feet; city sawn, 12 to 14 dol.; railway lumber, square and sound, 9 to 13 dol.; raft lumber, 8 to 11 dol.; dock timber, 4 dol. 50 c. to 6 dol. 50 c.; shipping timber, 8 dol. 50 c. to 10 dol. 50 c.; shingles were quoted at 4 to 7 dol. per 1,000 in shipping quantities. *Closing quotations.*

The resin and turpentine market ruled steady last season, with a gradually increasing demand for turpentine, which opened at 23½ c. per gallon at the beginning of the business year, and advanced to 27 c. by September 17, 1898. *Resin and turpentine.*

Receipts both of resin and turpentine were small, but the business that was done proved satisfactory both to producers and merchants. *Small receipts.*

The following comparative statement shows the receipts of naval stores at Charleston for the year ending September 1, 1898, and for the previous year, namely: last year, 3,808 casks of turpentine and 31,740 barrels of resin; and for year before, 5,850 casks of turpentine and 63,946 barrels resin; these figures including the stock on hand for both the above years.

The total exports during the year ending September 1, 1898, of naval stores from Charleston were, 3,709 casks of turpentine and 31,352 barrels resin, of which there were 18,708 barrels of resin shipped to foreign countries, but no turpentine exports In comparison with the previous year's exports of 5,717 casks, turpentine, and 59,607 barrels resin, the foreign exports were: 315 casks turpentine and 27,444 barrels resin. *Exports.*

Of the total foreign shipments of resin and turpentine last year, about half went to Great Britain, and the rest to continental ports of Europe.

From April 1 to December 31, 1898, the total receipts were of turpentine, 2,931 casks, and resin 20,490 barrels in comparison with receipts the previous year of 3,484 casks turpentine and 23,522 barrels of resin. During the same time the total exports were 2,906 casks of turpentine and 20,924 barrels resin, in comparison with 3,336 casks turpentine and 30,969 barrels resin for the corresponding period of the year before. *Later figures.*

Of the exports, 14,191 barrels of resin went to foreign ports last year, and 15,346 the year before; there being no foreign shipments of turpentine.

The closing quotations for resin and turpentine, on the last day of December, 1898, were 40 c. per gallon for turpentine, with the market firm, and resin quotations for the leading grades as follows: for B. resin, 90 c. per barrel; F., 1 dol.; I., 1 dol. 30 c.; N., 1 dol. 50 c.; W.G., 1 dol. 95 c.; W.W., 2 dol. 20 c. *Closing prices.*

The total amount of tonnage arriving at this port during the commercial year ending August 31, 1898, was 989,220 tons, compared with 924,560 tons net register for the year before; the total number of vessels of all classes and nationalities were 842 for the past season and 742 for the previous year. These figures show an increase for the last commercial year, and may *Shipping and navigation.*

(329)

Arrivals.

be compared with the shipping of the port for the year ending December 31, 1898, which was as follows:—

Total arrivals of shipping of all nationalities at Charleston from January 1 to December 31, 1898, were 784 vessels, of 923,069 tons, their nationalities being as follows:—American, 685 vessels, of 802,062 tons; British, 65 vessels, of 94,629 tons; Norwegian, 17 vessels, of 7,335 tons; German, 9 vessels, of 12,776 tons; Spanish, 5 vessels, of 3,491 tons; French, 2 vessels, of 2,229 tons; and Swedish, 1 vessel, of 547 tons.

The shipping arrivals during the preceding year of 1897 were 804 vessels, with a total tonnage of 1,021,826 tons, of which 72 vessels were British, with a tonnage of 119,118 tons. Full particulars of the British carrying trade at this port, during 1898, will be found in the return on the next page.

Freights.

During last season foreign freights were fairly steady for the first few months, when there was some pressure on the part of exporters to get shipments away promptly. In addition to cotton there were considerable shipments of grain, flour, pig-iron, and other general cargo, which latter items are somewhat new features in Charleston's exports, but, notwithstanding this fact, rates for this class of freight have ruled on a full equality with those of northern ports of America.

Coastwise freights early in the year were nominal, but for a short time during the Spanish-American war rates advanced to very high figures, lumber paying as much as 6 dol. per 1,000 feet to New York, and phosphate rock, 3 dol. to Elizabethport, N.J., and 2 dol. 50 c. to Baltimore. Since the cessation of hostilities, however, rates fell somewhat, but at the opening of the new season in September last, they were still above the rates prevailing at the beginning of the year. The ruling rates on September 1, 1898, were for phosphate rock to Philadelphia, 1 dol. 80 c.; to Town Creek, 2 dol. and towage; to Baltimore, 1 dol. 65 c.; fertilisers, to Norfolk and Baltimore, 1 dol. 75 c. to 1 dol. 80 c.; lumber, to New York, 4 dol. 37 c.

In comparison with the foregoing the following were the ruling freight rates at close of the past year. Cotton, by steamers, to Liverpool, per 100 lbs. net, 42 c.; Havre, viâ New York and Bremen, 42 c.; Barcelona, 62 c. By sailing vessels for Mediterranean ports, resin and turpentine, and cork for orders, firm at 2s. 6d. for resin and 3s. 9d. for turpentine; for Genoa, 2s. 3d.; Trieste, 2s. 6d. Timber and phosphate freights were quiet. Coastwise lumber rates were firmer, as they were favourably affected by a better demand, quotations for lumber being, to New York, 6 dol. to 6 dol. 50 c. Wet ties (sleepers), to Perth Amboy, N.J., 15 c. each; to Fall River, Massachusetts, 4 dol. 50 c. Phosphate rock, to Baltimore, 2 dol. 50 c.; to Philadelphia, 2 dol. 50 c.; to New York, 2 dol. 50 c.; to Elizabethport, 3 dol.; to Norfolk, 2 dol.; and to Richmond, 2 dol. 10 c.

CHARLESTON.

RETURN of British Shipping at the Port of Charleston, S.C., in the Year 1898.

Direct Trade in British Vessels from and to Great Britain and British Colonies.

Entered.

Total Number of Vessels.			Total Tonnage.			Total Number of Crews.	Total Value of Cargoes.
With Cargoes.	In Ballast.	Total.	With Cargoes.	In Ballast.	Total.		
5	17	22	5,518	28,633	31,157	566	£ 24,985

Cleared.

Total Number of Vessels.			Total Tonnage.			Total Number of Crews.	Total Value of Cargoes.
With Cargoes.	In Ballast.	Total.	With Cargoes.	In Ballast.	Total.		
17	2	19	27,519	1,820	29,339	459	£ 563,755

Indirect or Carrying Trade in British Vessels from and to other Countries.

Entered.

Countries whence Arrived.	Number of Vessels.			Tonnage.			Number of Crews.	Value of Cargoes.
	With Cargoes.	In Ballast.	Total.	With Cargoes.	In Ballast.	Total.		
Chile	3	...	3	2,238	...	2,238	45	£ 12,800
France	...	2	2	...	2,823	2,823	42	...
Germany	11	...	11	17,661	...	17,661	177	55,000
Italy	2	...	2	2,763	...	2,763	47	22,000
Portugal	5	...	5	5,683	...	5,683	84	11,000
United States	...	5	5	...	7,595	7,595	115	...
Spain	15	...	15	21,709	...	21,709	336	14,000
Total	36	7	43	50,054	10,418	60,472	846	114,800

Cleared.

Countries to which Departed.	Number of Vessels.			Tonnage.			Number of Crews.	Value of Cargoes.
	With Cargoes.	In Ballast.	Total.	With Cargoes.	In Ballast.	Total.		
Germany	17	...	17	30,503	...	30,503	517	£ 550,000
Italy	1	...	1	1,200	...	1,200	14	32,000
Spain	5	...	5	7,404	...	7,404	99	27,707
United States	...	21	21	...	27,700	27,700	492	...
Total	23	21	44	39,107	27,700	66,807	1,122	609,707

Fruits and vegetables.

The early fruit and vegetable industry, known here as truck farming, for the season ending July 31, 1898, was one of the worst on record as regards yield. For the first six months of the year there was little or no rain, and there was the additional misfortune of a late frost in April, so that, between frost and drought, there was a poor chance for crops. The frost nipped most of the vegetation in April, and with insufficient moisture, the crops had no opportunity to recover. The result was a small yield and poor quality. The crop was far below a good average one.

The acreage in Irish potatoes was the largest ever planted, but shipments were small. The yield of cabbage was little more than three-fourths of a crop, and in addition prices were very low and many growers preferred to let their cabbage stand in the fields rather than accept the low prices offered in the markets. Owing to the late frost the cucumber crop also was reduced to about 10 per cent. of a full yield. Many farmers who had planted largely in this vegetable suffered heavily.

Short crops.

Shipments.

The total amount and value of the strawberry shipments last spring were 981,204 quarts of berries, valued at 83,332 dol.; cabbage shipments, 140,960 crates, worth 120,409 dol.; Irish potatoes, 102,401 barrels, worth 300,826 dol.; and the aggregate total value of the shipments of lettuce, beans, beets, asparagus, melons, tomatoes, okra, corn, and sweet potatoes, amounted to 677,183 dol.

Cotton mills.

South Carolina is now the leading cotton manufacturing State in the South, and she is rapidly becoming one of the principal manufacturers of textiles in the American Union. For several years she has ceased to be an exclusively agricultural State, as was formerly the case. The conditions of climate and labour, particularly in the central plateau lying between the mountains of Upper Carolina and the pine belt of the coast, are very favourable to the cotton manufacturing industry. During the past year great disadvantages were encountered by cotton manufacturers all over the United States, but notwithstanding this there was a steady growth in South Carolina of cotton manufacturing, where the capital now invested in cotton mills is 18,614,000 dol.

The comparative importance of the South Carolina industry compared with cotton manufacturing in the other Southern States is shown from the following official figures, published at the end of last season on September 1, 1898.

In the States of Arkansas, Alabama, Georgia, Kentucky, Louisiana, Mississippi, Missouri, North Carolina, South Carolina, Tennessee, Texas, and Virginia, there are 491 cotton mills, having 3,680,741 spindles and 103,305 looms in operation.

Next to South Carolina in cotton manufacturing are—

	Number of Spindles.	Number of Looms.
North Carolina	1,018,303	23,351
Georgia	765,142	18,109
Alabama	380,886	7,084
Tennessee	158,990	3,937
Virginia	150,993	5,079
Mississippi	71,770	2,002
Kentucky	68,936	2,106
Louisiana	61,792	1,545
Texas	46,396	1,093

the remainder being distributed in the other Southern States of Missouri and Arkansas, which have about 12,000 spindles and 300 looms a-piece.

The total cotton consumption of all the Southern mills during the past year was 1,231,841 bales, as compared with 1,042,671 for the year before, an increase of 189,170 bales. Of last year's consumption :— *Mill consumption.*

	Quantity.
	Bales.
South Carolina used	378,154
North Carolina	332,801
Georgia	258,617
Alabama	101,162
Kentucky	26,156
Virginia	41,848
Tennessee	36,651
Mississippi	20,080
Louisiana	16,049
Texas	14,694
Missouri	3,735

As the total cotton crop produced in the United States during the year 1897–98 was 11,199,994 bales, it will be seen from the foregoing figures that Southern cotton mills now consume about one-tenth of the yearly product, when the yield is at its highest point; last year's crop having been the largest on record. In further comparison with the Southern cotton mill consumption of 1,231,841 bales last season, it may be stated that the takings of American spinners in the Northern States during the same period were 2,211,740 bales, thus making the total quantity of cotton consumed by American mills, both Northern and Southern, amount to 3,443,581 bales.

These figures are significant and indicate the progress that has been made in the cotton spinning industry in the United States during the last few years. They also furnish a fair index of the changes which have taken place in this business, and bring into prominence the question whether the spinning capacity of the country has not been over-reached, in view of its present outlets for manufactured products. *Figures significant.*

The question is perhaps rather too large for anything like full discussion in this report, but it may be proper to allude to it as much attention is now being given in some quarters to this matter. The increase of spindles for the entire country during the past eight years was nearly 33 per cent.; and during the same time the consumption of cotton increased nearly 37 per cent. A fair estimate of the increase of population of the United States, since the last census in 1890, based on the Treasury Department's calculations, is about 11,500,000, or say about 18 per cent. Even when, in addition to this, due allowance is made for the greater purchasing power per head, owing to the increased wealth and general prosperity of the country, the question still remains is there room sufficient for the absorption of the quantity of cotton goods now manufactured?

At all events, facts show that this industry in the Northern States is apparently passing through a crisis which it would seem can scarcely be weathered without radical changes from past and present methods.

Miscellaneous. Charleston's geographical position appears to be so advantageous that it is a matter of wonder that her importance as a railway centre is not far greater than is the case. The Atlantic Ocean lies but seven miles from the wharves of the city; there is now a sufficient depth of water in the harbour to accommodate the larger and better class of vessels, and, all things considered, the port appears to afford every requirement necessary for making it one of the principal points on the South Atlantic coast for handling a large foreign and home commerce.

There are three railways owning wharf properties here, and the water frontage they control is sufficient to enable them to deal with a large volume of business.

But there is only one of these railways at present that uses its Charleston water terminals; the South Carolina and Georgia Railway is the only one at whose wharves any activity is shown at any time of the year in shipping business. The Atlantic Coast Line Railway Company owns a splendid wharf property, but makes comparatively little use of it, beyond an occasional schooner taking a load of lumber. The same may be said of the Louisville and Nashville Railway which also owns much terminal property here, practically unused. The last named railway does not, as yet, reach Charleston with its main line, and for this reason it could hardly be expected to utilise its terminal facilities at this port which are capable of handling a very large business. It is hoped that in time the Louisville and Nashville rails will reach Charleston, and that eventually this railway will be able to make use of its facilities now lying idle.

The principal railway feeder to the commerce of Charleston is The South Carolina and Georgia Railway. The management of the line has been unremitting in its efforts to bring its freight and passenger business to such a condition as will ensure an independent position. It has continued the work of improving and maintaining its terminals, which were commenced three years ago; and on its Cooper River water frontage, a fourth wharf is now being built to handle its growing business; its grain elevator, a first rate and well equipped structure, built two years ago, has enabled Charleston to be added to the list of grain exporting ports.

The Charleston Hardwood Manufacturing Company was started on a small scale in April, 1897, for the manufacture of shuttle blocks, for use in cotton mills. The factory is now a thoroughly well equipped establishment, and is furnished with the latest improvements; it is run by the largest electric motor in the city, and has been pronounced by experts to be one of the best factories of its kind in the country. The first shipment made from this mill was a sample order of 8,000 shuttle blocks shipped to Liverpool, which were reported by the consignee to be the best blocks he had received from America. *Hardwood manufacture.*

The dogwood and persimmon trees which grow freely in the Southern forests, supply a close and finely grained article for making these shuttles, and it is stated that there are orders enough now in hand to keep the factory going for five years. Although the capital of the company is quite moderate, it gives employment to numbers of hands engaged all over the lower country in cutting dogwood and persimmon trees. The labour employed at the factory in the city consists of expert hands, brought here for the purpose. As the work requires great nicety and skill, it is long before the ordinary hand can learn the business. None of the blocks made here have been sold in America, the orders having come entirely from abroad. Eight different sizes of blocks have been shipped, so far, varying from $12\frac{1}{2}$ to 23 inches in length.

The wood is brought here in the rough state, in sizes of about cord wood dimensions, 2, 4, and 8 feet in length, and not less at the small end than 5 inches in diameter. It must be freed from knots and other blemishes, as the inspection is very strict.

The refuse wood from the manufactured articles makes excellent fuel for use in stoves or grates. Many persons in Charleston discarded coal last year, and used in its place this rejected wood, as it is very clean, making a hot fire with little ash.

There is also a factory for making shuttles at Westminster, South Carolina, which started with a capital of about 1,500 dol., and is reported to have been quite successful. *Westminster shuttle factory.*

These two factories are small, but being without competitors in the State, their establishment and growth are being watched with interest, on account of the benefits likely to arise from their possible future development.

The Charleston knitting mill employs 100 hands, and daily turns out several hundred pairs of hose and half-hose, which find sale in the country; some shipments even going as far as the Pacific coast. This mill has adopted the most improved machinery and methods, and it was expected that the output would be greatly increased with the ending of the Spanish- *Knitting mill.*

(329)

Public health.

American war. The capital stock is 25,000 dol., all owned in Charleston, and the annual product amounts to 75,000 dol.

The last annual report of the Health Officer speaks well for the general health of Charleston. The Board of Health has been alive to the needs of the community, and everything has been done to protect the public health.

The report says that although this city was dangerously threatened with yellow fever during the autumn of 1897, nevertheless remarkably good health was enjoyed. There was no epidemic of any character whatever, severe or mild, and, although it was feared at one time that there might be a serious outbreak of scarlet fever, the cases that occurred were generally mild. There were only five white and one coloured deaths from that disease during the entire year; and there was not a single death from diphtheria, either white or black, in 1897. There was the same number of deaths from typhoid fever among the whites as occurred in 1896, and among the coloured race the deaths from typhoid were four less than during 1896.

Total deaths.

The total number of deaths among the whites in 1897 was 447, and 521 in 1896, a decrease for 1897 of 74 deaths.

Among the coloured people there were 1,143 deaths in 1897, compared with 1,348 in 1896, a decrease of 205 in 1897. This is the lowest death record in 10 years with the single exception of 1888, when the number of white deaths was 419. It was the lowest ratio of the total mortality of whites and blacks together that has been recorded in 29 years; the rate per 1,000 of white deaths in 1897 was 15·52, and of blacks, 31·49.

A noteworthy fact in connection with the death-rate among the coloured people is that there were 158 deaths among them in 1897 from consumption, and in 1896, 243 from the same disease; this is somewhat remarkable, as during the slavery period consumption was almost unknown among the negro race here.

Sanitary needs.

The Health Officer's report also calls attention to two important needs of this port, namely, a more adequate water supply and some efficient system of food inspection. For several years the necessity for more water and a better food supply have been urgently needed, and it is hoped that the authorities will soon be able to devise some means of providing for these important sanitary needs of the community.

Quarantine.

There were no arrivals of contagious or infectious disease at the Charleston quarantine station during 1897, which has been maintained in an efficient manner. The Maritime Sanitation Committee, who have charge of this matter, have been assiduous in their efforts to keep the plant in good order and readiness for work. During the past year a new quarantine naphtha launch has been bought, longer and broader than the one in use for the previous seven years. The new launch is a commodious and useful adjunct to the quarantine equipment of the port, and is much appreciated by those having quarantine business.

The total number of arrivals at the quarantine station during the year above mentioned was 127, most of which were foreign vessels. Comparatively few American vessels having arrived from infected or suspected ports, with the exception of the Government warships and transports, which have from time to time within the past six months passed to and fro between Charleston, Cuba, and Porto Rican ports.

Savannah.

Mr. Vice-Consul Harkness reports as follows:—

The trade year of 1897-98 at Savannah opened in a good deal of doubt and uncertainty owing to the dark and threatening war-clouds then hovering over Cuba, causing trade and commerce to be somewhat restricted during the earlier part of the season.   *Trade conditions.*

After the war storm had broken and passed away and the transactions of the year were reviewed, the gratifying fact was shown that Savannah's trade was not hurt by the war disturbances, but, on the contrary, had made considerable gains in several leading departments. In cotton receipts, for instance, the high-water mark was passed, the total receipts for last season having been 1,192,057 bales, or 345,466 bales more than for the year before. In the lumber business, also, there was an increase of substantial proportions, and in naval stores (resin, turpentine, &c.) dealers had reason to be well satisfied with their transactions.   *Increased business.*

In shipping there was a larger number of arrivals than for many years, and the aggregate tonnage of the craft was larger than for any previous year on record. During the year ending August 31, 1898, the arrivals at this port were 1,005 vessels, in comparison with 944 for the season before, and the aggregate tonnage was, for last year, 1,187,692 tons, compared with 1,090,799 tons for the year before. A number of last year's arrivals were vessels drawing from 23 to a little over 24 feet, and several were from 450 to 480 feet in length.   *Shipping increase.*

Bank clearances for the past year were larger than ever, and amounted to 131,329,494 dol., in comparison with 125,137,827 dol. for the year before.   *Bank clearances.*

This increase is partly attributable to the unusually large cotton crop and the largely increased receipts at the port, which undoubtedly helped, but was by no means the sole cause of the bank's increase in business; Savannah's business men are steadily extending their volume of trade; they are constantly opening up new ground, and this is materially helping the banks.

The total value of Savannah's trade during the past commercial year ending August 31, 1898, was in round numbers 135,800,000 dol., and for the previous year 127,600,000 dol., showing an increase of 8,200,000 dol. The increase in naval stores alone was about 2,000,000 dol., but in cotton, however, although there was a largely increased movement of the staple   *Total year's trade.*

SAVANNAH.

to this port, being 350,000 bales more than for the previous year, low prices greatly reduced the relative increase in value of this department of trade.

Few failures. There were comparatively few failures reported last season, and business houses and institutions generally were, at the end of the year, in sound condition, the business done was satisfactory in character, having been safely conducted, with very little risk.

Lumber shipments were larger than ever before, and prices were fairly good at the opening of the season, but towards the close, however, they declined. The increase in the total value of lumber for the year was 750,000 dol.

Phosphates and fertilisers. There was a decrease in the phosphate rock business, but a slight increase in shipments of fertilisers to interior points; prices, however, were low, and there was a material decrease in the value of the total product compared with the season before.

Fruits and vegetables. There was a considerable increase in shipments of early fruits and vegetables to Northern and Western markets, which added to the total trade and increased its value by about 500,000 dol.

In several other departments of regular business there was a substantial increase, the gain in groceries, liquors, tobacco and provisions being estimated at 100,000 dol.; the retail trade held its own very well throughout the business year, and was unusually good during the last four months of 1898, owing to the presence of about 30,000 American troops who were encamped here for different periods before departing for Cuba.

Causes of increased business. Much of the increase in last year's trade at this port has been due in a great measure to the commodious and excellent docks built by the Central Railway and the Savannah, Florida, and Western Railway Companies, which have given the trade here distinct advantages over competitors, not only in handling cotton, naval stores, and lumber, but also by other kinds of merchandise finding its way through this port as an outlet to other countries.

Great efforts have also been made to give more care to the handling of cotton than formerly, and as only 55 bales were destroyed during the season from fire, &c., these efforts would appear to have been fairly successful, in view of the alarming frequency of cotton fires, which occurred here a few years ago

Terminal improvements. During the past three or four months steps were taken by the Georgia and Alabama Railway Company to greatly improve their terminal facilities at this port. They have purchased large tracts of land extending along the Hutchinson's Island River front on the opposite side of the river at Savannah.

An extensive system of docks is to be built at an early day, with commodious warehouses, buildings, and every equipment necessary for the accommodation of the company's large and increasing business. This line expects to deal with large quantities of Western products for foreign export, and as its rails afford a direct outlet from the coalfields and iron mines of Alabama, as well as the grain and provisions from the Western States, the construction of the proposed terminal improvements will add greatly to Savannah's present facilities for the berthing of shipping and handling of merchandise. The United States Congress has recently passed a Bill, giving the Railway Company authority to construct a bridge across the Savannah River, just above the present Central Railway wharves, which will be utilised to connect the Georgia and Alabama Railway from Montgomery direct, to the Hutchinson's Island docks, &c., when the latter are finished. Efforts are being made to have the work well under way and partly completed by the opening of next autumn's business season.

The following figures will give some idea of Savannah's general trade in its principal branches from September 1 to December 31, 1898, which four months form the first third of the new business year of 1898–99. *Later figures.*

The total cotton receipts from September 1 to December 31, 1898, were 816,814 bales, compared with 855,234 bales for the corresponding time during the previous year. The exports for the last four months of the past year were 654,787 bales, compared with 709,516 bales for the same period the year before. Of last year's exports, 49,520 bales went to Great Britain, 27,999 bales to France, 345,014 bales to the Continent of Europe, and the remainder, 232,254 bales, was shipped coastwise to American ports, mostly New York, Boston, Philadelphia, and Baltimore. *Cotton*

The closing prices for cotton posted on the Savannah Cotton Exchange, December 31, 1898, were, for middling uplands, $5\frac{1}{16}$ c. per lb., with the tone of the market quiet and easy. For Sea Island cotton the market was firm and quiet with closing quotations as follows:—Choice to fancy Floridas, 12 to $14\frac{1}{4}$ c. per lb.; choice to fancy Georgias, $10\frac{1}{2}$ to 13 c. The total receipts of Sea Islands at Savannah from September 1 to December 31, 1898, were 41,357 bales, compared with 45,667 bales for the corresponding time of the year before. The total exports for the same time last year were 29,624 bales, in comparison with 25,192 bales for the year before, and the stock on hand and on shipboard, December 31, 1898, was 17,776 bales, and for the year before, on the same date, 26,892 bales. *Closing prices. Sea Islands.*

The receipts of naval stores at this port, from April 1 to December 31, 1898, were (including stock on hand) as follows:— Resin, 1,032,700 barrels; and spirits of turpentine, 314,684 casks; compared with 1,105,785 barrels resin, and 297,653 casks turpentine for the previous year. *Naval stores.*

The exports during the same time last year were: 807,115 barrels resin, and 299,794 casks of turpentine, compared with 910,464 barrels resin, and 252,729 casks turpentine during the previous year.

The closing price at the end of last year for spirits of turpentine was $43\frac{1}{2}$ c. per gallon, with the market very firm and an advancing tendency. The demand for resin was firm, at prices ranging from 1 dol. to 1 dol. 75 c. per barrel for "A" to "N" grades, and 2 dol. 5 c. to 2 dol. 30 c. for "W.W." (water white) and "W.G." (window glass) grades of resin respectively. *Prices.*

SAVANNAH.

Of last year's exports, 477,576 barrels of resin and 209,469 casks of turpentine were shipped to foreign countries, the remainder going to coastwise American ports and interior points by railway.

Ocean freights. Ocean freights at the end of the year were steady with a downward tendency; the rate on cotton per 100 lbs. to Liverpool was 52 c.; to Bremen, 55 c.; Genoa, 65 c.; Reval, 70 c.; Hamburg, 57 c.; Havre, 65 c.; and Barcelona, 65 c. The coastwise cotton rates were 1 dol. per bale to Baltimore, Philadelphia, and New York, and 1 dol. 25 c. to Boston.

Soon after the close of the last year, freights declined rapidly from these figures, and carrying business became very dull, paying cargoes being hard to obtain.

British shipping. British shipping did a good business here from September 1, 1898, to the end of the year, rates were remunerative, and cargoes were promptly supplied, there being few complaints or claims for demurrage during this period; later on, however, cotton receipts fell off, and too much tonnage came to the port, charterers had much difficulty in supplying cargoes within time allowed by charter limits, and several instances of demurrage claims had to be adjusted in January.

The proportion of Savannah's carrying trade done in British vessels during last year will be found in the following return:—

SAVANNAH.

RETURN of British Shipping at the Port of Savannah, Ga., in the Year 1898.

Direct Trade in British Vessels from and to Great Britain and British Colonies.

Entered.

Total Number of Vessels.			Total Tonnage.			Total Number of Crews.	Total Value of Cargoes.
With Cargoes.	In Ballast.	Total.	With Cargoes.	In Ballast.	Total.		
3	57	60	1,704	82,399	84,103	1,340	£3,103

Cleared.

Total Number of Vessels.			Total Tonnage.			Total Number of Crews.	Total Value of Cargoes.
With Cargoes.	In Ballast.	Total.	With Cargoes.	In Ballast.	Total.		
20	...	20	25,404	...	25,404	422	£473,480

Indirect or Carrying Trade in British Vessels from and to other Countries.

Entered.

Countries whence Arrived.	Number of Vessels.			Tonnage.			Number of Crews.	Value of Cargoes.
	With Cargoes.	In Ballast.	Total.	With Cargoes.	In Ballast.	Total.		
Brazil	...	4	4	...	4,385	4,385	72	£ ...
Belgium	...	2	2	...	3,137	3,137	50	...
Denmark	...	1	1	...	147	147	6	...
France	...	5	5	...	6,569	6,569	109	...
Holland	1	1	2	1,033	2,318	3,351	42	500
Italy	...	8	8	...	11,740	11,740	186	...
Spain	...	10	10	...	14,407	14,407	228	...
United States	...	24	24	...	38,775	38,775	573	...
Portugal	5	...	5	6,786	...	6,786	105	15,520
Total	6	55	61	7,819	81,478	89,297	1,371	16,020

Cleared.

Countries to which Departed.	Number of Vessels.			Tonnage.			Number of Crews.	Value of Cargoes.
	With Cargoes.	In Ballast.	Total.	With Cargoes.	In Ballast.	Total.		
Argentine Republic	1	...	1	914	...	914	16	£3,200
Brazil	4	...	4	3,886	...	3,886	59	5,119
Belgium	1	...	1	772	...	772	20	600
France	2	...	2	3,543	...	3,543	48	79,000
Germany	52	...	52	88,675	...	88,675	1,322	2,157,000
Holland	1	...	1	1,008	...	1,008	17	3,000
Italy	10	...	10	13,936	...	13,936	298	477,000
Russia	5	...	5	8,015	...	8,015	123	157,000
Spain	11	...	11	12,094	...	12,094	282	299,000
Sweden	2	...	2	2,560	...	2,560	43	83,000
Portugal	2	...	2	1,804	...	1,804	33	38,000
United States	...	4	4	...	4,161	4,161	74	...
Total	91	4	95	137,207	4,161	141,368	2,335	3,301,919

BRUNSWICK.

Mr. Vice-Consul Torras reports as follows:—

The increase in the trade of Brunswick for the year 1898 compared with the previous year is in every respect a source of great satisfaction.

Despite the retarding influences of the past year, viz., the war with Spain and the disastrous equinoctial hurricane causing great damage and delay to shipping, Brunswick has forged ahead and her relative advancement will compare favourably with that of any other port in the country.

Population. Brunswick has increased in population fully 25 per cent. since the year 1897, and present conditions appear to indicate a still greater proportionate increase for the present year.

Immigration. The year 1898 has witnessed the immigration into Glynn and adjoining counties of a colony of Shakers from Union Village, Ohio. They are a thrifty and industrious people, materially assisting in the agricultural and commercial development of the districts they occupy.

Improvements. Two rich railway companies, the Plant System Company and the Southern Railway Company, anticipating the future growth of Brunswick, have greatly improved and are still improving their terminal facilities, trackage, and water frontage. They have constructed commodious wharves and erected substantial and spacious warehouses and magnificent offices.

The Plant System Railway Company have two dredgers at work deepening their one-mile water frontage, which will add considerably to the existing facilities for loading any heavy draught vessel that may pass over the ocean bar. This work, it is asserted, will continue for about three years, and the estimated expenditure will aggregate over 1,000,000 dol.

Transportation facilities. The well-known steamships, the Churchill Line, of which Captain A. F. Churchill of this city is president, has been steadily increasing year after year its volume of business through this port. There have been shipped on steamers of this line during the past year many valuable cargoes of cotton, pig-iron, phosphate rock, hardwoods, &c., the same being loaded from the Plant System Company's docks.

The Johnston Blue Cross Steamship Line, well-known throughout Europe and this country, are also exporting numerous cargoes of cotton and other products over the Southern Railway Company's wharves. This steamship company is credited with a good percentage of the remarkable growth of the business of this port.

For coasting trade the Mallory Steamship Company have two steamers plying regularly between New York and Brunswick, and at times vessels have to be supplied by the company to satisfy the increasing demand for transport.

Real estate. A firm of real estate agents recorded about 200,000 dol. in real estate deals, a gain of 46 per cent. over their sales for the year 1897. Another real estate agent of Brunswick effected a great number of important sales the past year. His records are not accessible, but he has done a very extensive business.

These sales of real estate, and the many improvements already completed, with those now in course of completion, proclaim the confidence of the people of Brunswick in regard to their city's future growth.

In 1897 there were shipped from this port 132,110,000 feet of lumber and timber, crossties and shingles. In 1898 the number of feet of lumber exported was 138,000,000, or an increase of nearly 6,000,000 feet over the former year. *Exports.*

The increase in the exports of cotton also deserves special notice. During the years 1884–85 the shipments of cotton through Brunswick amounted to 4,000 bales. In 1898 the records show an output of 325,764 bales, the amazing increase of 321,764 bales of this staple exported in the last 13 years.

The shipments of flour have also rapidly advanced from a total of 1,624 barrels for the year 1892 to 1,073,543 barrels for 1898.

The total value of the exports from Brunswick for 1898 was over 21,000,000 dol., revealing a gain of no less than 15,908,271 dol. for the past five years from 1893 to 1898 inclusive.

Articles under the heading of imports have slightly advanced in the past few years; but it is not believed that this branch of trade will disclose any very pronounced improvement for some time to come, owing to the reason that most of the articles needed from other countries are imported here through New York. *Imports.*

The greatest boon to shipping, which is the principal factor in Brunswick's onward march to progress, has been the deepening of the ocean bar. The last Government survey on this bar reported a depth of 24 feet, and the contractor is confident of being awarded a depth of 25 feet at mean high water, by the survey now in progress. According to a recent statement the work of deepening the bar will be energetically pushed until a depth of 30 feet is secured. *Shipping.*

With these natural advantages as well as those of being in close proximity to the great farming districts of the west, having excellent transport facilities and being within easy access to the sea, thus affording a splendid opportunity for the export of products to the newly-acquired territory in the West Indies, Brunswick has, indeed, a very bright future.

DARIEN.

Mr. Vice-Consul Manson reports as follows:—

The total shipments from the port of Darien during the year 1898 were 106,000,000 feet of pitch pine timber and deals, valued at about 1,100,000 dol. (equal to, say, 240,000*l.*). Most of this timber is shipped from Sapelo, a few miles from Darien, where the anchorages and loading berths for timber *Timber shipments.*

vessels are situated, but being within the jurisdiction of the Darien custom-house, where Sapelo-loaded vessels enter and clear. Sapelo and Darien have now become places of great importance, owing to the increasing demand for pitch-pine timber throughout the world.

Shipping, &c.
For last year's shipments of timber 18 British vessels were employed, with a tonnage of 27,696 net tons. The total number of vessels of all nationalities arriving last year was 151, having a net tonnage of 126,496 tons.

The timber shipments in British vessels were altogether 25,584,000 superficial feet; there being no other exports but pitch-pine timber from this port.

Harbour facilities.
Sapelo harbour is well sheltered, being almost land locked, and vessels load at docks having every necessary facility for giving quick dispatch. The harbour is also well buoyed, but badly lighted, and with a view to remedying this drawback there is a project now on foot to build a lighthouse on the south end of St. Catherine's Island, which would enable ships to enter or depart at night.

Ill effects of war and storms.
During the past summer the Spanish–American war interfered greatly with timber shipments from this port, and much injury also resulted from the disastrous tidal wave and storm of October 2, 1898, which carried away about 12,000,000 feet of timber.

Prospective improvements.
An appropriation of 70,000 dol. has recently been made by the United States Government for the purpose of deepening the water on Doboy Bar at the entrance to Doboy Sound to 24 feet. Doboy is situated within 12 miles of Darien, but at present is used only for light draught vessels owing to insufficient water on the bar. In the event of the expected depth of 24 feet being obtained at Doboy, it would have the effect of taking the greater part of the lumber shipments away from St. Simons, near Brunswick; most of which shipments, however, even at present pass through Darien, either as round or manufactured timber on its way to St. Simons for shipment abroad.

The authorities of the National Quarantine Station, at Sapelo Island, are now constructing a telephone line which will connect that point with the Western Union Telegraph Company's Office at Darien, and hereafter, vessels arriving or departing from Sapelo can be promptly reported to all parts.

LONDON:
Printed for Her Majesty's Stationery Office,
By HARRISON AND SONS,
Printers in Ordinary to Her Majesty.
(75 4 | 99—H & S 329)

No. 2237 Annual Series.

DIPLOMATIC AND CONSULAR REPORTS.

UNITED STATES.

REPORT FOR THE YEAR 1898

ON THE

TRADE, COMMERCE, AND NAVIGATION OF THE CONSULAR DISTRICT OF BALTIMORE.

REFERENCE TO PREVIOUS REPORT, Annual Series No. 2082.

Presented to both Houses of Parliament by Command of Her Majesty,
MAY, 1899.

LONDON:
PRINTED FOR HER MAJESTY'S STATIONERY OFFICE,
BY HARRISON AND SONS, ST. MARTIN'S LANE,
PRINTERS IN ORDINARY TO HER MAJESTY.

And to be purchased, either directly or through any Bookseller, from
EYRE & SPOTTISWOODE, EAST HARDING STREET, FLEET STREET, E.C., and
32, ABINGDON STREET, WESTMINSTER, S.W.; or
JOHN MENZIES & Co., 12, HANOVER STREET, EDINBURGH, and
90, WEST NILE STREET, GLASGOW; or
HODGES, FIGGIS, & Co., Limited, 104, GRAFTON STREET, DUBLIN.

1899.

[C. 9044—63.] *Price Twopence Halfpenny.*

CONTENTS.

	PAGE
BALTIMORE—	
General remarks	5
Exports	5
Large exportation of steel rails	5
Imports	6
Custom receipts	6
Bank clearances	7
Grain trade	7
Wholesale dry goods	8
„ clothing	8
Boots, shoes, and leather trade	8
Canning industry	8
Coal	9
Tobacco	9
Coffee	9
Lumber	10
Cotton	11
Drugs and chemicals	11
Cattle, sheep, and horses	11
Bicycles	12
Oysters	12
Fish	13
Terrapin	13
Fruit evaporating factory	13
Cement factory	13
Electrical matters	14
Public buildings	14
Tax rate	14
Licenses	14
Marriage and divorce	14
Commercial enterprises	14
Friendly Inn Association	15
New law affecting foreign companies	15
Immigration	15
Vital statistics	16
Shipping and navigation—	
Continued increase in British shipping	17
Desertion from British ships	18
War revenue tax on charter-parties	18
Shipbuilding	18
Baltimore Channel	18

(352)

4

Railways—
- Re-organisation of Baltimore and Ohio ... 18
- Pennsylvania Railway ... 18
- Application of oil to permanent way ... 19
- Street railways ... 19

Annexes—
- Return of principal articles of export for 1897–98 ... 20
- ,, ,, import ,, ... 21
- Statement of values of exports and imports from 1887–98 ... 22
- Articles exported or imported to and from foreign countries during 1898 ... 22
- Table of receipts and exports of grain for 1896–98 ... 23
- Statement of prices of wheat, maize, oats, and rye for 1898 ... 24
- ,, ,, flour for 1898 ... 25
- Return of all shipping for 1898 ... 25
- Table of ocean freights ... 26
- ,, immigration ... 27

NORFOLK, VIRGINIA—
- General remarks ... 27
- Manufactories ... 27
- Railways ... 28
- Channel ... 28
- Coal ... 28
- Oysters ... 28
- Fruit and vegetables ... 29
- Population ... 29

Annexes—
- Table of principal articles exported and imported during 1898 ... 29
- ,, all shipping for 1898 ... 30

NEWPORT NEWS, VIRGINIA—
- Trade report ... 31
- Shipping ... 34
- Ocean freights ... 34
- Exports ... 36
- Agricultural statistics ... 37

No. 2237. Annual Series.

Reference to previous Report, Annual Series No. 2082.

Report on the Trade, Commerce, and Navigation of the Consular District of Baltimore for the Year 1898

By Mr. Consul Frazer.

(Received at Foreign Office, April 10, 1899.)

General remarks.

The expectation that the very flourishing business conditions which existed at the end of the previous year would continue in 1898 was fully realised. There being no prominent political matters to interfere with trade, it went on in a very prosperous manner until the outbreak of hostilities with Spain.

Although for some time previous to the actual declaration of war there naturally existed an uncertainty as to the outcome of affairs, which had a baneful influence on trade. But when war actually began every kind of business would seem to have come to a standstill.

The manufacturers of duck and canvas, of which there are several large ones in Baltimore, and who received extensive orders from the United States Government, as did also packers of canned goods, were perhaps the only persons whose businesses were benefited by the existence of war.

However, when the news of the success of the United States troops was received, business immediately began to revive, and became more and more extensive, until at the termination of the year it not only retrieved lost ground, but exceeded in point of volume any previous year in the history of Baltimore.

There has been a wonderful rise in the prices of local securities, and several trust companies with large capital have been added to the financial institutions of the city.

Exports.

Again the exports from Baltimore have assumed enormous proportions, and have even exceeded last year, which was a phenomenal one. Wheat, by an increase of about 3,200,000 bushels, or a total export of 18,542,000 bushels, heads the list, and is followed proportionately by maize, oats, rye, and flour. The other principal articles of export were tobacco, copper, lard, petroleum, and lumber.

Large exportation of steel rails.

The exportation of steel rails continued, the quantity amounting in the aggregate to 58,219 tons of the value of about 226,391*l*. This was an increase compared with 1897 of almost 50,000 tons.

(352)

The greater quantity was shipped to Vladivostock for the construction of the Trans-Siberian Railway. It is given as 18,913 tons, valued at 364,560 dol. About half the quantity, 3,039 tons, was sent to Calcutta that was shipped in 1897. 6,925 tons, valued at 138,460 dol., was exported to Melbourne, and also 360 tons of fittings, valued at 11,880 dol. To Bombay was forwarded 3,000 tons. of the value of 76,000 dol., and 50 tons of fittings, the price of which was 1,650 dol.

Rails shipped to Dublin.
There was shipped to Dublin for the use of the Great Southern and Western Railway of Ireland, 2,500 tons of standard steel rails, which was the first shipment of the kind ever sent to that country from the United States. An exportation of 1,500 tons of steel rails and fittings was made to Barbadoes. They were of light weight—about 45 lbs. to the yard, and 10 yards long.

Shipment of steel plates to Belfast.
A shipment of steel plates to Belfast, Ireland, said to be the first of this nature ever shipped from this country, was made last year from Baltimore. They were made at Pittsburg, Pennsylvania, and comprised over 600 tons. The dimensions of the plates are given as 28 by 5 feet, and their weight between 4,000 and 5,000 lbs.

Annex No. 1 is a statement of the principal articles of export from Baltimore during the years 1898-97.

Imports.
Great decrease in imports.
There was a distinct decrease in 1898 in the quantity and value of almost every article imported into Baltimore. The whole imports amounted in value to only 8,193,848 dol., a decrease of over 2,000,000 dol. as compared with 1897, and the smallest since 1885. The quantity of tinplate imported fell from 1,343,921 lbs. in 1897 to 614,467 lbs., coffee from 28,015,641 lbs. to 22,682,240 lbs., sugar from 37,243,697 lbs. to 12,517,120 lbs. The only articles that showed an increase worth noting were cement, by over 14,000,000 lbs.; muriate of potash, over 3,500,000 lbs; and liquorice root and chloride of lime, each about 2,000,000 lbs.

The war with Spain is given as one of the causes for the great decrease, but no doubt the principal reason is that a greater quantity of certain articles was imported during 1897 in anticipation of the higher duties imposed by the Dingley Tariff.

Importation of fruit from West Indies.
The importation, however, of foreign fruits is doubtless increasing, and it promises to develop into a large business. It is difficult to obtain the exact value of the bananas and cocoanuts imported from the West Indies, as they are not dutiable, and no reliable statistics of the quantity are kept, but the value of the former is given for 1898 as 500,000 dol., and of the latter 50,000 dol. Pineapples are imported principally from the Bahamas, and the value of them upon which duty was paid was 119,988 dol.

Annex No. 2 is a statement of the principal articles of import into Baltimore during the years 1898-97.

Customs receipts, great decrease in.
With the decline in imports for 1898, the customs receipts showed a sympathetic falling-off. The sum of only 1,869,321 dol. was received, which, compared with 1897, was a decrease of

419,790 dol. Of the sum collected, 1,765,291 dol. were received as duties.

The sum of over 143,000,000 dol. was the increase last year over 1897 in bank clearances. The amount for the latter year was 795,688,363 dol., whereas in 1898 it was 939,059,328 dol., and an increase of 250,000,000 dol. over the year 1889.

Bank clearances, great increase in.

The year 1898 showed a still greater improvement in the export of grain, and exceeded the previous year, which was a phenomenal one, and heretofore the largest in the history of the port by 6,267,165 bushels. Although flour has not yet risen to the position it occupied in 1896, still there has been last year the very substantial gain in its exportation of 487,363 barrels. In all kinds of grain there was a decided gain in exportation, with the single exception of oats, which fell 410,410 bushels, the light weight of the crop causing this in a great measure.

Grain trade. Immense increase in shipments.

In the receipts of all varieties of cereals there was an increase of 2,313,308 bushels of wheat, 3,012,968 bushels of maize, and 1,073,328 bushels of rye. The recovery in price which the constant and large demand would seem to warrant was set aside by the throwing on the market of large quantities of wheat in consequence of the collapse of the Leiter deal in Chicago. It is predicted that the consumption is not likely to decrease in the coming year at home and abroad, for the reason that the conditions do not appear to have changed to any extent.

Large increase in receipts.

A very important matter, and one of vital importance to Baltimore, is the almost total abolition of the differential rail rates in her favour in the carriage of grain from the West. In consequence of her position being so much nearer the great grain centres than the other large grain exporting ports, she would seem to be entitled to lower rates. The remedy would appear to be a uniform rate of so much per ton per mile.

Differential rail rate.

In 1898 cargoes of grain were shipped for the first time from Baltimore to Egypt and to Portugal, and the first steamer with a full grain cargo was sent out to Naples.

Grain shipped to certain ports in Europe for the first time.

The following are the rates for the inspection of grain at Baltimore, and at the other centres of the trade:—

Rates for inspection.

	Per Car (700 Bushels).	Per 1,000 Bushels Outward.
	Cents.	Cents.
Baltimore	21	20
New York	25	25
Philadelphia	30	40
Chicago	25	50
Toledo	30	40
St. Louis	30	45

Annex 5 gives a detailed statement of the receipts and exports of grain for the years 1896, 1897, and 1898, and Annexes 6 and 7 the prices of grain and flour respectively for 1898.

BALTIMORE.

Wholesale dry goods.

The disturbing influences which preceded and culminated in the war with Spain had an injurious effect on the wholesale dry goods trade. In the month of July a somewhat better condition of affairs was brought about by the purchase of army supplies for the use of the troops under arms. Again in the autumn Chinese and Japanese purchasers bought a large quantity of Southern-made coarse yarns, and this tended to still more improve the trade. The immense cotton crop kept the manufactured article at a low price. The manufacture of woollens was very unsatisfactory, produced no doubt by the immense importations of these goods to escape the higher tariff of the McKinley Bill. As a whole, however, the trade for the year is said to be fairly remunerative, and 5 to 10 per cent. is given as the increase in its volume.

In my last report I called attention to the almost entire disappearance of British hosiery from the Baltimore market. No steps have yet been taken, so far as I have been able to ascertain, to recover the superior position formerly held by British manufacturers in that branch of trade.

Wholesale clothing.

It is somewhat difficult to ascertain the exact condition of the wholesale clothing trade during the past year, but it perhaps may be safely said that the output was somewhat greater than in 1897. The Southern trade has again suffered in consequence of the very low price of cotton, but a greater demand in the West and South-Western States off-set that depression. The clothing is as a rule made at the homes of the workers in Baltimore and in the adjoining villages, although some of the larger manufacturers have factories. The sweater's shop is unknown. The estimated value of the output for 1898 is given as about 20,000,000 dol.

Boots, shoes, and leather.

Again as in other branches of trade in Baltimore the low price of cotton in the south had a depressing effect on the boot and shoe business. The trade extends through a large section of the southern part of the country. In the southern and western States it was excellent, and counterbalanced the bad trade in the extreme south. It is reported that taken as a whole the trade was good, and there was an increase of from 5 to 10 per cent. in the volume of business as compared with 1897. Manufacturers of shoes and dealers in leather complain that the tariff on hides has had a baneful influence on this great industry of Baltimore, and it is stated that they will petition Congress to remove it.

Leather trade.

In the leather trade the increase of business is stated to be about 10 per cent. in 1898 over 1897. The prices were, No. 1, scoured oak backs ranged from 30 to 34 c.; belting butts were from 31 to 36 c.; packer hides ranged from $7\frac{3}{4}$ to $11\frac{3}{4}$ c. The stock in hand is much smaller than at the close of 1897.

Canning industry.

The canning industry was very much benefited by the outbreak of the war with Spain. In anticipation of a great demand for the use of the armies in the field prices went up very rapidly, and those who held large stocks were able to sell out at considerable profit. Prices were maintained until the new crop came into the market in September. Tomatoes, corn, and peas were the principal articles in which were the greater activity. 1898 was far more prosperous than any year for some time past, and it is expected that the trade will not fall back, for at least several months to come, into its former unsatisfactory state. Corn was packed to a far greater extent than last year. Tomatoes have not been packed as much as in 1897, owing to the unsuitable weather, but it is thought that sufficient has been put up to meet the demand and at fairly good prices. The pack of peaches was small, owing to the crop in the district being practically a failure, and prices have ruled high, and it is expected they will continue to advance. Apples were scarce and dear, both canned and green. Peas were packed to a less extent than in 1897, and they were soon sold off. The standard and sifted grades were very short, and indeed, it was extremely difficult to find peas of any kind in the packers' hands.

Coal. The total production of bituminous coal in the coal region of Maryland in 1898 was 4,400,000 tons, an increase over the previous year of over 99,025 tons.

The output in West Virginia was 14,000,000 tons of coal, 3,000,000 tons of which was used in making coke. The increase compared with 1897 in the coal production was 500,000 tons.

The increase of the output of coal in Virginia was 150,000; the quantity for 1898 being 1,600,000 tons.

3,600,000 tons of coal were mined in Kentucky during 1898, an increase of 316,238 compared with the previous year.

The price per ton at the mines in Virginia and in West Virginia was 60 c.; in Maryland, 70 c.; and in Kentucky, 75 c. The product of the mines in all these States averaged 1 dol. 75 c. f.o.b. at tide water.

Tobacco. The tobacco crop in 1898 was most excellent both as to character and quantity. The hogsheads received of Maryland tobacco were 36,288, a gain over the previous year of 1,415, and the prices ranged from 2 to 13 c. a pound. The ground-leaf crop was the largest for some years past and amounted to 3,500 hogsheads, and the prices realised were from 2 to $8\frac{1}{2}$ c.

The French Government contracted for 73,000 hogsheads more than in 1897, and purchased 15,100 hogsheads of Maryland tobacco and 3,200 hogsheads of the Ohio crop.

The stock in hand on January 1, 1898, was 16,844 hogsheads, of which 8,851 were Maryland, 7,987 were Ohio, and six Virginia tobacco. The receipts in 1898 were 36,288 hogsheads of Maryland and 5,970 hogsheads Ohio, making with the stock in hand a total for the year of 59,102 hogsheads. The shipments were 46,571 hogsheads.

Coffee. A large falling-off took place in 1898 in the importation of coffee, showing a decrease of 30,280 bags from the number imported in 1897. The number for the latter year was 203,066 bags, and the past year 172,786 bags. These figures do not, however, show the quantity of coffee received at Baltimore, as a considerable amount is received viâ New York. The prices ranged from 5½ to 7 c. per lb., and the year was one of depression in the trade.

Lumber. Previous to the commencement of the hostilities with Spain the lumber business for the year had been most encouraging, but then matters assumed a different phase, sales suddenly ceased, and the business at the end of 1898 was still in a very unsatisfactory state. At the close of December, however, the Government made considerable purchases for shipment to Cuba, which produced a firmness in prices. It is stated that the volume of business has not materially changed from other years and the profits have been smaller.

It is difficult to ascertain the exact amount of capital employed in the wholesale industry in Baltimore, but it is given as about 6,000,000 dol. It is estimated that the value of the business done amounted to 5,150,000 dol.

The total number of feet of lumber received at Baltimore during 1898 was 262,000,000 feet. The quantity of lumber and logs exported was 61,728,000, and beadings and staves numbered 2,652,062. From the latest statistics obtainable it appears that there is invested in mills in the United States 750,000,000 dol., giving direct employment to 600,000 persons, and that there are 3,000,000 people dependent on the industry. The total annual value of wood products would therefore seem to be 10 times the value of the output of the gold and silver and three times the value of wheat.

In connection with this subject it may be of interest to state what products are now obtained from the distillation of the pine tree besides tar and turpentine, and which even are more valuable than these. These are: spiritine oil, wood creosote oil, tar oil, pyroligneous acid, wood naphtha, wood spirit, and fine balsam. Parts of these products are used in preserving wood and iron. Other parts are used in aniline colour-works and paint and varnish-works. Still others are used in the drug trade and for disinfecting purposes. The roots and stumps of the pine, which were formerly considered useless, are now considered as valuable as any other part of the tree.

The following is a statement of the quantity, value, and destination of the lumber exported:—

BALTIMORE.

Destination.	Timber, Logs, &c. Quantity.	Timber, Logs, &c. Value.	Boards, Planks, Scantlings, &c. Quantity.	Boards, Planks, Scantlings, &c. Value.	Staves and Beadings. Quantity.	Staves and Beadings. Value.	Sundry Wood Products partly Manufactured.
	Feet.	Dollars.	Feet.	Dollars.	Number.	Dollars.	Dollars.
England	4,044,000	153,605	26,404,000	784,420	456,260	24,575	100,725
Scotland	1,289,000	45,956	6,310,000	196,846	251,344	9,695	41,570
Ireland	117,000	4,151	648,000	25,566	...	...	39,646
Germany	3,851,000	191,803	2,546,000	90,632	114,720	5,375	60,456
Belgium	731,000	25,576	4,346,000	111,153	221,486	9,378	5,865
Netherlands	1,410,000	44,140	4,903,000	145,777	1,580,252	81,095	38,931
France	376,000	16,519	2,297,000	59,762	28,000	1,400	22,141
British West Indies	...	...	449,000	7,283	...	...	7,313
Colombia	...	...	74,000	1,584	...	...	1,305
Denmark	4,000	190	136,000	5,359	...	...	...
Mexico	...	...	472,000	11,265	...	...	...
Danish West Indies	...	...	80,000	1,360	...	...	...
Argentine Republic	...	...	1,241,000	17,500	...	...	...
Total	11,822,000	481,940	49,906,000	1,458,507	2,652,062	131,518	317,952

	Quantity. Lumber. Feet.	Quantity. Staves. Number.	Value. Dollars.
Total exports from December 1, 1897, to November 30, 1898	61,728,000	2,652,062	2,389,917

Cotton on Nov. 5, 1898, reached the very low price of $2\frac{1}{2}d.$ *Cotton.* per pound, and it is said that on the great cotton exchanges bonâ fide sales were made at even a less figure. The highest price of $3d.$ a pound was reached on June 1. Notwithstanding these low prices, there was considerable activity, and the total receipts showed a great increase over 1897. In that year 278,777 bales were received against 421,878 bales last year. The exports were 338,556 bales, an increase of 93,233 bales over 1897. In the manufacture of duck and canvas the local mills consumed 75,000 bales. Twenty years ago the cotton crop sold for $10d.$ a pound; now it fetches a fourth of that sum. It costs a planter in the South $3d.$ to $3\frac{1}{2}d.$ a pound to raise, and at present prices he receives less than $2d.$ a pound.

It is reported that the wholesale drug trade was better in 1898 than it has been for the past 10 years, and the manufacture and sale of chemicals have increased about 25 per cent. Baltimore is the second city in the United States—Philadelphia being the first—for the manufacture of drugs and chemicals. It is also engaged to a great extent in the sale of crude drugs. Although manufacturing has been very flourishing, the retail sale of drugs has been most unsatisfactory, doubtless owing to the existence of too many retailers. It is said that the sale of patent medicines has nearly fallen off 25 per cent., because of the cutting of prices which leaves no profit to the druggist. *Drugs and chemicals.*

The receipts at, and exportation from, Baltimore, of live stock, *Cattle, sheep, and horses.*

show a considerable decrease from 1897. The number of cattle exported in 1898 was 49,856, and the number in the previous year exceeded it by 8,147. A decrease is also shown in the number of sheep of 18,201, the number exported being 31,178, while 49,379 was the number in 1897. March would appear to be the month when the greater quantity of live-stock is exported, and 5,508 cattle and 8,208 sheep were shipped. The export of horses had a great decrease, namely, from 861 in 1897, to 220 in the past year, and it would seem that they were almost entirely shipped from New York. The value of these exportations will be found in Annex I.

The following table shows the receipts of live-stock at the Union Stockyards, Baltimore, during 1897 and 1898, and which are somewhat less for the former year:—

Nature of Stock.	Receipts. 1897.	Receipts. 1898.
Cattle	161,078	156,982
Sheep	156,982	372,156
Hogs	823,061	862,700
Calves	..	12,194
Horses	..	8,930
Mules	..	1,901
Total	1,141,121	1,414,863

Bicycles. It may be truthfully said that the bicycle fad has ceased to exist, and that the days of high prices and great demand have passed. But the business will, without doubt, settle down to a proper basis, and be carried on in a similar manner to other trades. The past year was a most unsatisfactory one for those engaged in the trade, and the low prices, great competition, and radical methods in the manner of doing business operated most disastrously, especially for those who dealt in second-hand machines.

New machines were sold for what old ones brought a year or two ago, and the latter had to be disposed of, if at all, at a great loss. With the low prices the instalment plan has almost ended, and the taking of second-hand machines in part-payment of new ones is discontinued to a great extent. It is roughly estimated that the number of new machines sold in Baltimore last year was 4,000.

Oysters. The past season was rather an unsatisfactory one for the oyster trade. At the opening of the season, in September, the weather was extremely hot throughout that month and also during October It was impossible to ship oysters to market quick enough to prevent them from being spoiled in transit, and besides there was no demand for them. Then came a period of extremely cold weather when it was impossible to carry on the fisheries. The quantity handled in Baltimore was therefore reduced about 2 per cent. The number of bushels were 4,561,973, against 4,726,250, in 1897. The prices were about the same as last year, 75 to 80 c. a bushel for extras and 40 to 60 c. for second quality. It is said that the quantity of oysters packed has fallen below the previous year, but the prices have been somewhat higher.

Mackerel and herring. The supply of mackerel and herring appears to be decreasing year by year, the former especially. The catch of mackerel some years ago was estimated to be about from 300,000 to 400,000 a season, and the prices per barrel were 3 dol. to 8 dol., the latter obtained only for very fine fish. A notable decrease in the number of mackerel was first observed in 1886, and it has steadily gone down until the present time, when the catch is said to be only about 50,000 a year. The prices now range from 20 to 25 dol. a barrel. No reason can be given for the scarcity other than the use of the seine when the fish were plentiful.

A very marked decline in the quantity of herring taken at the local fisheries took place last season, with the exception of the Susquehanna where the catch was fair. The fish never fail to put in an appearance in those waters from April 10 to 15, and the fisheries are stated to be the most reliable on the whole coast. Herring were in great demand and sold at from 3 dol. 50 c. to 4 dol. a barrel.

Terrapin. In my last report I called attention to the danger of the terrapin becoming extinct. It would seem that the efforts made to raise them in other States have been most successful and it is incomprehensible, seeing that they are easily produced and bring such high prices, that the States or private individuals along the Chesapeake Bay do not engage in farming them. Terrapin are brought up on shrimp and crabs, of which thousands can easily be found along the shores of the bay. It is really a question, however, whether, if they are placed in about six inches of mud, terrapin need food at all. Certainly the young do not, for they seem to flourish better on what they get in the water. It is impossible to kill a terrapin with cold, and they have been known to have been frozen in a block of ice without any apparent harm, but the young must be carefully protected from cold.

Fruit evaporating factory. A new industry for the evaporation of fruit and vegetables has been begun in Beltimore. The system differs from other methods in that the article to be evaporated is not subjected to the steam process which is believed to take away much of the original flavour.

Cement factory established. In February of 1898 a cement company began operations in Baltimore. The slag from the furnaces of the Maryland Steel Company is used, and about fifty men are at present employed. This mill is said to be the third of the kind in the United States and the only one in Maryland. The Company makes its own barrels.

Electrical matters.

The syndicate that purchased the whole of the Baltimore street railways has, it is reported, purchased the property of the three electric lighting companies. It is announced that the consolidation of these two organisations—the street railways and electric lighting—will result in mutual benefit to the public and the syndicate in consequence of expenses being reduced by the concentration of the production of electricity for traction and lighting purposes. Although Baltimore may be said to be fairly well lighted at present with electricity, it is reported to be far behind other large cities in its use for private lighting and for power.

Post office orders paid through banks.

On June 1, 1898, there went into operation at the Baltimore post office a system under which holders of money-orders can deposit them in bank and pass them through the clearing-house just as an ordinary cheque. The system is not extended as yet to the branch offices, and applies only to orders payable at the principal office.

Public buildings.

The new court-house is almost completed. It is a splendid marble structure, and a fine addition to the public buildings of the city. Without doubt it is one of the finest edifices of the kind in the country.

The large addition to the Maryland Penitentiary in Baltimore is also approaching completion.

Tax rate.

The taxes in Baltimore on property continue to steadily increase. The rate in 1888 was 1 dol. 90 c. per 100 of the estimated value, and it has gradually risen from year to year, until in 1898 it rose to 2 dol. 25 c.

Licenses.

In all, 17,825 licenses were taken out in Baltimore in the year 1898, for which the sum of 142,222*l*. was received. There was a falling-off from the previous year in traders' licenses of 178, and in marriage licenses of 282, the numbers being respectively 9,337 and 4,541. The sum received for liquor licenses in 1898 was 113,033*l*., an increase of over 3,000*l*. from the previous year. The State as its proportion received one-fourth of this sum, the city obtaining the other three-quarters.

Marriage and divorce.

Of the 4,541 marriages which took place in Baltimore in 1898, 481 occurred in the month of April, and the least number in July, with 264.

There were 479 divorces applied for in the two circuit courts during the year, of which 158 were granted, 31 dismissed, and 290 pending. This is an increase compared with 1897 of 37 applications, a decrease of four in the number dismissed, and 25 in the cases pending.

Commercial enterprises.

There were registered in Baltimore in 1898 111 corporations for trade and manufacturing purposes, with a capital stock of 12,559,800 dol., and 30, with a capital stock of 40,869,800 dol., were for building, land, and loan associations. This is a decrease in number, compared with 1897, of 22 in the former, but an increase in capital of over 7,000,000 dol. Three more of the latter were registered, and the capital was, however, over 3,000,000 dol. less.

BALTIMORE.

Friendly Inn Association of Baltimore.

The object of the Friendly Inn Association is to provide a shelter or home for friendless men, who may secure food, bath, and lodging in exchange for work of from one to four hours a day, and is founded wholly on the principle that food and lodging are given for work only. Any able-bodied man will be admitted to either of the homes of the Association, which have together accommodation for 300 men, without money or any formality, and given a good meal in return for sawing and splitting four sticks of wood about 5 feet long by 8 inches in diameter. For sawing and splitting 10 pieces he will receive a good meal and a night's lodging. On admission a lodger must take a tepid bath and consent to his clothes being fumigated. In the autumn of 1893 the police stations, as lodging houses, were closed to able-bodied men, and this class since that time have been referred to the Association for relief. The city pays 4d. for each man received by the Association from station houses, the total sum paid in a year not to exceed 200l. The Association has been of great service in numerous ways. It has without doubt reduced vagrancy, and also the danger of contagion to which these unfortunate people were subjected when huddled together on the floors of police stations. During the year 1898, 48,578 meals were worked out, 28,459 lodgings were earned, the baths given were 18,774, 11,617 lodgers were received from station houses, and 1,213 cords of wood were sold. The average yearly expenditure for the past six years, exclusive of the cost of the buildings, was 2,000l., and the receipts, including the sale of wood, bequests, &c., have been about 2,500l. a year.

Law affecting foreign corporations in Baltimore.

There came into operation on July 1, 1898, a law requiring foreign corporations doing business, or which shall desire to do business in the State, either through an agent or otherwise, to file, in the office of the Secretary of State, accompanied by a fee of 25 dol., a certified copy of the company's charter, a sworn statement by its president of the amount of its capital stock, the amount of stock actually issued, the amount of its assets and liabilities, the character of the business to be transacted, with the name of the place where its principal office is to be situated, and the name, or names, of its agents who reside in the State on whom legal process may be served. The penalty for non-compliance with the law is 100 dol. a day, and no corporation shall maintain an action-at-law until it shall have complied with it.

It is believed that the law is unconstitutional, and it is intended to bring the matter into the courts should an attempt be made to enforce it, which does not appear to have been done. It will be observed that the registration and payment of the fee is required only once. What is most objected to is the filing of a statement of assets and liabilities, which corporations look upon as somewhat inquisitorial.

Immigration.

There was an increase in the number of immigrants landed at Baltimore during 1898 of 4,320 over the previous year, the greater number being Austrians. The State Bureau of Immigration reports that no new colonies have been founded, although large additions have been made to the colonies of Hollanders, in

Wilhelmina and Caroline counties, and to the German in Preston and Westover counties. The Secretary of the Bureau went to Holland, where he delivered a number of lectures on the advantages of Maryland and its climate, with the object of inducing the people of that country to emigrate to the State.

A company has been organised, called the Maryland Land and Immigration Company, having a capital of 50,000 dol., for the purpose of assisting the Secretary of the Bureau in providing suitable places in the State on which such settlers from Holland as he may induce to emigrate may be located. This is the first occasion in Maryland in which a company has been formed to assist immigration in conjunction with the State authorities. Annex No. 10 is a table showing the number, nationality, &c., of the immigrants who arrived at Baltimore in 1898.

Vital statistics.

Pneumonia was in 1898 the cause of an unusual number of deaths, and was to a great extent responsible for the high death-rate. It usually followed an attack of influenza, which was epidemic in Baltimore. It ranked next to consumption, from which 1,061 persons died. This disease continues to be the cause of the greater number of deaths. There were numerous cases of diphtheria, and antitoxin was constantly used, both to treat the disease and to immunize children. 2,077 cases were treated in 1898, and 1,610 in the previous year. The number of deaths in the latter year was 362, against 412 in the former. Two cases of small-pox, which came by steamer from Europe, were treated at the quarantine hospital, but the last case of the disease in the city was in 1886. The use of glycerinated virus in vaccination was brought into use, as it is said to produce less inflammation and fever than the ordinary virus points. Typhoid fever prevails to a great extent, and 200 people die of it annually, no doubt caused by the want of a proper system of sewerage. There are 80,000 cesspools in Baltimore, and the water-supply is quite unprotected.

The total deaths from all causes in Baltimore in 1898 was 10,385, of which 7,918 were white and 2,467 coloured. Estimating the population at 541,000, this is a death-rate of 19·19 per 1,000. Exactly 300 more white males than females died, and of the coloured population the contrary was the case, and 35 more females died than males. The death-rate per 1,000 of the white population is 17·10 and of the coloured 31·62. The number of births of whites reported during the year was 7,227, being a decrease of 155 from 1887; 1,566 births of coloured children were reported, a gain of 148. The male births reported were 4,571 and females 4,219, a total of 8,793, a falling-off from 1887 of 7. The birth-rate per 1,000 of the whites is 15·60 and of the coloured people 20·07. 748 still-births were reported, an increase of 42 compared with 1897.

The Health Commissioner calls special attention to the necessity of a regular sewage system for Baltimore, of which it is very much in need, and urges that ashes and garbage be collected separately and disposed of at different places.

BALTIMORE.

The following is a list of the principal diseases which caused death in 1897 and 1898, with the number of deaths from each:—

Diseases.	1897.	1898.
Measles	16	48
Scarlet fever	53	46
Diphtheria	362	412
Croup	13	..
Whooping cough	42	64
Typhoid fever	189	189
Typho-malarial fever	20	12
Diarrhœa	99	97
Dysentery	57	82
Cholera infantum	401	386
„ morbus	14	12
Consumption	1,047	1,061
Pneumonia	759	889
Bronchitis	243	110
Influenza	88	25
Bright's disease	203	454
Cancer	316	331
Diseases of the heart	478	498
Sun and heat stroke	11	54
Appendicitis	33	34
Accident	87	78
Child birth	10	23
Abortion	6	1
Pernicious anæmia	12	5
Cerebro-spinal fever	22	3
Illuminating gas	9	9

Shipping and navigation. Continued increase in British shipping.

The British shipping at Baltimore for the first six months of 1898 exceeded any previous year for the same period by 71 vessels and 138,521 tons. Unfortunately, shortly afterwards, the existence of the war with Spain and the depression in the freight market caused inactivity in shipping, and it was not until the beginning of October that it recovered. Notwithstanding this, the number of British vessels that arrived during the year was 712, and their total tonnage 1,389,277, being an increase of 102,001 tons over 1897, which hitherto had the largest volume of British shipping ever at Baltimore.

The total number of British shipping which entered in the Consular district of Baltimore in 1898 was 1,623, of a tonnage aggregating 3,012,078 tons, an increase compared with the preceding year of 43 vessels and 108,552 tons, and which exceeded in number and tonnage any previous year. The average tonnage of ships was greater than in former years.

Vessels under the German flag again ranked next to the British in tonnage. They consisted of 95 vessels with an aggregate tonnage of 444,115 tons gross. This is a decrease of 11 vessels but an increase of 26,906 tons.

No British line of steamers has yet thought it well to engage in the passenger trade between Europe and Baltimore which is still solely in the hands of the North German Lloyd and Hamburg American lines. They together landed at the port 815 cabin passengers and 12,043 immigrants, a decrease from last year in the number of the former of 152 and an increase in the latter of 4,472.

Desertion from British ships. Desertion from British ships was of frequent occurrence during the past year in consequence of the demand for seamen for the United States navy, and wages accordingly rose. It was necessary in many cases to pay as high as 5l. advance to A.B.'s for the passage in steamers across the Atlantic.

War revenue tax on charter-parties. On July 1, 1898, under the war revenue measure, a tax of 3 dol. on vessels not exceeding 300 tons, of over 300 tons and not exceeding 600 tons, 5 dol., and over 600 tons, 10 dol., was imposed on every charter-party, memorandum, contract, or agreement, for the charter of a vessel or the renewal thereof. Marine insurance policies, by the same measure, were taxed ½ c. on each dollar or fraction thereof of the amount of the premium charged.

Shipbuilding. Shipbuilding was quite active in Baltimore during 1898, and 42 vessels of various types aggregating 9,185 tons and valued at 689,385 dol. were constructed. Steel tug-boats were the principal craft built. It would seem that the torpedo-boat "McKee" was the only vessel built for the United States Government. Contracts have, however, been made for the construction of another torpedo-boat, three torpedo-boat destroyers, and a floating dry dock, all for the Government. It is claimed by the shipbuilders in Baltimore that they have more work than they can possibly do during the present year.

Deeper and larger channel necessary. In consequence of the constantly increasing size of the vessels coming into Baltimore it is urgently necessary that the channel should be enlarged and deepened. A uniform width of 600 feet and a depth of 30 feet are required to make the port what it should be.

Railways. Re-organisation of the Baltimore and Ohio Railroad. The plan for the reorganisation of the Baltimore and Ohio Railroad which promises to place the system on a fresh and sounder basis was undoubtedly one of the most interesting railroad occurrences of the past year. It is intended that Western capitalists will take charge of it, and with the facilities already at their disposal it is hoped that traffic will be increased, and in that way still further improve Baltimore commerce.

Pennsylvania Railroad 50 years in existence. In 1898 the Pennsylvania Railroad completed the fiftieth year of its existence. Organised in 1846, it completed in 1852 its first line from Philadelphia to Pittsburg. It has now under its control 9,000 miles of line and represents a combination of corporations which have a capital of 834,000,000 dol. In the first year of its operations it carried 70,000 tons of goods, now it transports as much every day. Last year it carried over 75,000,000 passengers, while at its start the number conveyed was about 500,000 annually. The number of locomotives have increased from 50 to 3,500, and its cars from 1,000 to 141,000. The amount paid in wages to persons in its employ was last year over 40,000,000 dol., or over 100,000 dol. per day.

Application of oil to permanent way as a dust preventative.

Experiments have been made on the line of the Baltimore and Potomac Railroad between Baltimore and Washington, to keep down the dust by spraying the track with oil of a very high fire test and of low gravity. It is said that these experiments have been most satisfactory and have been proved excellent for the purpose, especially where the tracks are ballasted with gravel. The non-existence of dust reduces the wear and tear on the rolling stock, preserves the upholstery of the carriages, besides making travel much more comfortable and enjoyable. The oil is said to sink into the ballast on the first application to a depth of 4 inches; destroys vegetation in it, and remains effective in every way for about a year. A second or third application penetrates below the cross-ties, and subsequent treatment is unnecessary unless a fresh ballasting is used. A specially constructed car for sprinkling purposes is made use of and is connected by a rubber hose with an ordinary tank car in which the oil is carried. The cost of oil per mile of single track is from 6*l*. to 9*l*., depending on point of delivery, and the quantity used is about 2,000 gallons. This is for the first application, and 1*l*. to 1*l*. 10*s*. annually will be a sufficient expenditure for oil in subsequent treatment. About 1,000 miles of track in the United States have been treated with it.

Street railways.

A consolidation of the whole city tramway-system has been accomplished. The railways merged are the City Passenger with about 100 miles; the Baltimore and Northern, 35 miles; Baltimore, Middle River, and Sparrows Point, 15 miles; and the Consolidated with about 200 miles. The management of the property will be in the hands of a Board of Directors of seven members, as this small number is considered more workable. It is believed that if the whole system is worked from a large central electric-power station a very great saving will be made in the motive power. An improvement on the road bed has been made by bringing in close contact the ends of the rails and placing them in very heavy fish-plates. Any irregularities at the ends of the rails after they were in position were ground down by an emery wheel driven by a motor, its power being derived from the electric wire used to propel the cars. It was feared that buckling of the rails would result from the very extreme heat and cold in Baltimore, but after a very hot summer and unusually cold winter no movement whatever of the road-bed is observable. The jar noticeable when a car passes over the rail ends has by this means been entirely removed, and there is no doubt but the wear and tear is less.

Liabilities of street railway companies.

By the charter granted to the street railways by the city they are compelled to keep the streets between the rails and on 2 feet on each side of them in good repair. By a recent decision of the Courts the companies have been declared liable for any accident that may occur by reason of their failure to do so.

BALTIMORE.

Annex 1.—RETURN of Principal Articles of Export from Baltimore during the Years 1898-97.

		1898.			1897.		
			Value.			Value.	
Articles.		Quantity.	Currency.	Sterling.	Quantity.	Currency.	Sterling.
			Dollars.	£		Dollars.	£
Agricultural implements	...	...	295,408	59,081	...	277,663	55,532
Animal foods	Tons	15,073	227,724	45,545	22,325	336,412	67,282
Bacon and hams	,,	38,539	6,361,230	1,272,246	21,592	3,426,454	685,290
Bark, and extract of for tanning	...	...	109,979	21,996	...	95,272	19,054
Beef—							
Fresh	Tons	6,475	1,097,845	219,569	4,651	713,755	142,751
Canned	,,	5,220	946,647	189,329	3,113	663,554	132,710
Cured and salted	,,	1,629	234,945	46,989	1,954	269,676	53,935
Barley	Bushels	19,910	8,971	1,794	14,231	6,397	1,279
Books, maps, &c.	...	...	31,128	6,225	...	56,735	11,347
Casings for sausages	...	...	720,282	144,056	...	488,659	97,731
Carriages and parts thereof	...	...	26,414	5,282	...	21,680	4,336
Cattle live	Number	49,856	4,666,756	933,351	58,003	5,800,300	1,160,060
Chemicals	...	...	141,253	28,250	...	161,470	32,294
Copper, ingots, bars, &c.	Tons	38,852	10,130,826	2,026,165	39,460	9,830,604	1,966,120
Cotton—							
Raw	,,	56,795	7,389,404	1,477,881	38,926	5,697,675	1,139,535
Cloths	Yards	964,575	132,957	26,591	707,999	106,124	21,224
Cycles and parts	...	...	33,336	6,667	...	14,625	2,925
Drugs and patent medicines	...	...	6,690	1,338	...	4,915	983
Flour	Barrels	2,813,166	12,090,121	2,418,024	2,325,803	9,937,253	1,987,450
Fruit	...	...	378,387	75,677	...	303,295	60,659
Furs and hides	...	...	5,298	1,059	...	22,564	4,512
Glucose	Tons	19,793	689,523	137,904	8,795	369,071	73,814
Hair	...	...	204,738	40,947	...	145,736	29,147
Hardware	...	...	1,854	371	...	1,076	215
Horses	Number	220	27,505	5,501	861	132,922	26,584
Indian corn	Bushels	45,096,477	16,799,244	3,359,848	43,048,008	13,287,413	2,657,482
Iron and steel, and manufactures of	...	...	1,328,067	265,613	...	842,366	168,473
Lard	Tons	59,780	8,390,686	1,678,137	44,470	6,423,455	1,284,691
Lead	,,	...	...	...	557	35,253	7,050
Leather	...	...	15,671	3,134	...	28,098	5,619
Machinery	...	...	116,484	23,297	...	99,132	19,826
Oats	Bushels	4,859,686	1,587,646	317,529	5,270,096	1,308,778	261,755
Oil—							
Illuminating	Gallons	45,278,795	2,728,019	545,604	65,263,498	3,715,922	743,184
Lubricating	,,	989,568	121,538	24,307	872,431	109,418	21,883
Cotton-seed	,,	1,482,321	360,378	72,075	526,636	140,141	28,028
Oilcake and meal	Tons	61,440	1,448,995	289,799	64,445	1,417,861	283,572
Oleomargarine oil	,,	20,298	2,727,380	545,476	11,488	2,377,748	475,549
Paper	...	...	94,771	18,954	...	28,577	5,715
Paraffin and paraffin wax	Tons	3,918	365,733	73,146	2,711	243,021	48,604
Pork	,,	7,164	926,494	185,298	2,889	455,612	91,122
Rye	Bushels	4,581,406	2,606,976	521,395	3,195,974	1,501,299	300,259
Sewing machines	Number	...	39	7	...	3,088	617
Sheep	,,	31,178	215,110	43,022	49,379	387,644	77,528
Starch	...	...	496,465	99,293	...	524,449	104,889
Steel rails	Tons	58,219	1,131,956	226,391	8,700	163,800	32,760
Tallow	...	6,510	577,735	115,547	2,208	187,398	37,479
Timber	...	...	480,689	96,137	...	550,443	110,088
Tobacco—							
Leaf	Tons	32,982	5,459,490	1,091,898	36,261	5,873,132	1,174,626
Stems	,,	3,176	184,799	36,959	2,996	125,755	25,151
Wheat	Bushels	18,542,034	16,143,528	3,228,705	15,304,039	14,439,276	2,887,855
Lumber and manufactures of	...	...	1,892,410	378,482	...	2,382,156	476,431
Coal	Tons	120,785	251,354	50,271	...	...	...

BALTIMORE.

Annex 2.—RETURN of Principal Articles of Import into Baltimore during the Years 1898-97.

		1898.			1897.		
Articles.		Quantity.	Value.		Quantity.	Value.	
			Currency.	Sterling.		Currency.	Sterling.
			Dollars.	£		Dollars.	£
FREE.							
Art works	...	...	75	15	...	7,652	1,530
Books	...	...	14,490	2,898	...	19,993	3,998
Chemicals	...	...	745,760	149,152	...	655,283	131,056
Coffee	Tons	10,126	1,275,787	255,157	12,507	2,070,811	414,162
Fruits	...	...	482,184	96,437	...	513,815	102,763
Liquorice root	Tons	5,066	190,845	38,169	4,104	145,863	29,172
Soda, nitrate of	,,	6,576	129,299	25,859	7,092	227,650	45,530
Tea	,,	9	2,082	416	59	19,633	3,926
Tin, bars and pigs	,,	1,190	366,296	73,259	1,452	434,469	86,893
Wool (unmanufactured)	,,	...	...	...	1,311	513,966	102,793
DUTIABLE.							
Art works	...	...	4,865	973	...	...	...
Burlaps	...	...	229,617	45,923	...	...	...
Cement	...	...	309,654	61,931	...	250,493	50,098
Cheese	Tons	32	8,404	1,681	83	25,706	5,141
Chemicals	...	...	268,472	53,694	...	373,176	74,635
China	...	...	490,837	98,167	...	613,886	122,777
Dry goods—							
Cotton (manufactured)	...	...	146,121	29,224	...	227,848	45,569
Silk (manufactured)	...	...	48,460	9,692	...	36,995	7,399
Wool (manufactured)	...	...	76,687	15,337	...	285,883	57,176
Fish	...	...	24,117	4,823	...	19,288	3,857
Flax	...	...	...	...	...	357,858	71,571
Fruits	...	...	165,296	33,059	...	301,380	60,276
Glass	...	...	26,735	5,347	...	44,750	8,950
Iron ore	Tons	140,815	177,764	35,553	292,613	369,483	73,896
Iron in pigs	,,	8,466	264,598	52,919	4,567	130,336	26,067
Iron and steel (manufactured)	...	...	91,050	18,210	...	158,787	31,757
Matting	...	...	220,679	44,136	...	216,752	43,350
Metals	...	...	27,666	5,533	...	21,360	4,272
Paper	...	...	32,948	6,589	...	33,452	6,690
Rice	Tons	4,111	142,657	28,531	4,611	175,697	35,139
Salt	,,	4,670	11,068	2,213	2,939	8,323	1,664
Sugar	,,	5,588	299,821	59,964	16,627	891,937	178,387
Tea	,,	74	29,001	5,800	...	...	...
Tin-plates	,,	274	15,326	3,065	599	33,288	6,657
Tobacco leaf	...	...	56,198	11,239	...	36,943	7,388
Wines and spirits	...	...	40,764	8,152	...	83,243	16,648

BALTIMORE.

Annex 3.—STATEMENT showing the Export and Import Values at Baltimore for the past 12 Years, also the Monthly Export and Import Values during the Year 1898.

Year.	Value. Exports.	Value. Imports.	Months during 1898.	Value. Exports.	Value. Imports.
	Dollars.	Dollars.		Dollars.	Dollars.
1887	49,545,970	13,055,880	January	11,461,850	890,436
1888	45,099,334	12,098,629	February	7,910,373	371,877
1889	62,077,610	15,409,234	March	10,738,009	769,825
1890	72,120,053	15,339,312	April	9,779,667	866,502
1891	79,475,125	18,270,000	May	12,487,748	875,645
1892	93,126,389	14,258,570	June	8,603,116	792,462
1893	73,153,487	14,858,621	July	7,086,418	620,516
1894	63,961,279	11,749,927	August	8,061,375	590,766
1895	60,171,591	19,934,369	September	8,005,660	455,131
1896	81,508,836	10,208,741	October	8,781,985	700,712
1897	98,560,604	11,126,556	November	10,439,198	624,976
1898	115,820,274	8,206,764	December	12,524,874	587,916

Annex 4.—TABLE showing Total Value of all Articles Exported from or Imported into Baltimore during the Year 1898.

Country.	Value Exports.	Value Imports.
	Dollars.	Dollars.
Great Britain	48,660,594	1,703,864
Belgium	6,775,875	91,912
Brazil	1,144,723	1,205,682
Spain and Cuba	76,669	817,476
France	10,712,499	61,520
Germany	21,640,883	1,730,233
Netherlands	19,836,867	244,431
Mexico	273,231	10,543
Italy	113,960	365,414
Other countries	6,585,473	2,177,589
Total	115,820,274	8,206,764

Annex 5.—TABLE of the Receipts and Exports of Grain for the Years 1896-98.

RECEIPTS.

Articles.		1896.	1897.	1898.
Wheat	Bushels	7,592,041	17,896,008	20,209,316
Maize	,,	27,724,535	44,514,388	47,527,356
Oats	,,	10,428,850	7,685,950	7,874,361
Rye	,,	1,381,485	3,661,709	4,735,037
Barley and malt	,,	772,267	807,234	791,058
Total		47,899,178	74,565,289	81,137,128
Flour {	Bushels	..	..	17,279,492
	Barrels	4,104,896	3,398,333	3,828,776

EXPORTS.

Articles.		1896.	1897.	1898.
Wheat	Bushels	6,589,856	15,304,039	18,542,034
Maize	,,	26,382,182	43,048,008	45,096,477
Oats	,,	6,919,518	5,270,096	4,859,686
Rye	,,	1,028,745	3,195,974	4,581,406
Barley and malt	,,	64,352	14,231	19,910
Total		40,984,653	66,832,348	73,099,513
Flour {	Bushels	..	..	12,659,247
	Barrels	3,065,845	2,325,803	2,815,166

Annex 6.—STATEMENT showing the Prices of Wheat, Maize, Oats, and Rye, in the Baltimore Market during the Year 1898.

Month.	Southern Wheat. By Sample.		Southern Wheat. On Grade.		Western Wheat.		Southern White Corn.		Southern Yellow Corn.		Two White Oats.		Two Mixed Oats.		Two Rye.	
	Cents.	Cents.	Cents.	Cents.	Cents.	Cents.	Cents.	Cents.	Cents.	Cents.	Cents.	Cents.	Cents.	Cents.	Cents.	Cents.
January	90 to	101½	90¾ to	101¼	96 to	101½	29 to	35¾	28 to	34½	29½ to	·30	27½ to	28	52¼ to	54½
February	93	104	94½	103¾	97⅝	102¼	32	36	32	36	29½	35	28	33	53½	57
March	94	103	93¼	102½	101¾	102	32½	35	32½	34¾	33	35	30	32½	55	56
April	95	115	95½	114½	98¾	114	34	42	33	43	33	38	30	35	55½	64¾
May	110	146½	110	146	114	148	36¾	42½	37	45	35½	40	33	36	51	75½
June	60	116½	73½	116	80½	111½	35½	37½	35¼	37½	30½	36	27½	33	45½	54
July	62	87	68	86	70	83¾	35	42	36½	42	29½	34	26½	32	46½	51½
August	60	71	65	80½	69½	77	33	41	34	41	27	34	24	33	46	49½
September	60	73¼	61½	72¾	65⅞	72¼	34	36½	35	37	26	28½	24	26	48	51
October	63	77½	63¼	77	67½	75½	34	38	35½	38½	28	30	25½	28	48½	55½
November	65	74	65¾	73½	70	73	32	39	33	39	29	33	27½	32	53¼	56⅝
December	62	77	67½	76½	70	76⅜	36	43½	34	43½	32	34½	31½	32½	56½	59
Range ..	60	146½	61½	146	65⅞	148	29	43½	28	45	26	40	24	36	45¾	75½

Annex 7.—STATEMENT showing the Average Prices of Flour in the Baltimore Market during the Year 1898.

Month.	Per Barrel.										
	Family.				Extra.				Super.			
	Dol.	c.		Dol.	c.	Dol.	c.		Dol.	c.		Dol.	c.
January	4	35	to	4	70	3	35	to	4	10	2	70	to	3	20
February	4	40		4	70	3	45		4	10	2	80		3	20
March	4	25		4	70	3	35		4	10	2	70		3	20
April	4	25		5	30	3	85		4	75	2	70		3	50
May	5	0		6	60	4	0		5	50	3	25		4	25
June	4	0		5	90	3	25		5	0	2	90		4	0
July	3	90		4	40	3	15		3	75	2	80		3	15
August	3	50		4	30	2	90		3	65	2	50		3	05
September	3	25		4	0	2	60		3	25	2	25		2	75
October	3	25		3	80	2	50		3	25	2	15		2	80
November	3	25		3	70	2	55		3	10	2	15		2	70
December	3	25		3	60	2	55		3	15	2	15		2	60
Range	3	25		6	60	2	50		5	50	2	15		4	25

Annex 8.—RETURN of all Shipping at the Port of Baltimore during the Year 1898.

ENTERED.

Nationality.	Sailing.		Steam.		Total.	
	Number of Vessels.	Tons.	Number of Vessels.	Tons.	Number of Vessels.	Tons.
British	36	14,101	676	1,375,176	712	1,389,277
American (foreign)	97	38,621	8	5,272	105	43,893
German	...	...	95	444,115	95	444,115
Norwegian	...	...	117	105,474	117	105,474
Danish	...	...	35	37,568	35	37,568
Italian	11	7,500	...	...	11	7,500
Total	144	60,222	931	1,967,605	1,075	2,027,827
American (coastwise)	52	43,126	1,301	1,631,695	1,353	1,674,821

CLEARED.

Nationality.	Sailing.		Steam.		Total.	
	Number of Vessels.	Tons.	Number of Vessels.	Tons.	Number of Vessels.	Tons.
British	36	14,101	674	1,366,831	710	1,380,932
American (foreign)	106	47,489	9	6,855	115	54,344
German	...	...	95	444,115	95	444,115
Norwegian	...	...	118	104,559	118	104,559
Danish	...	...	35	37,568	35	37,568
Italian	11	7,500	...	...	11	7,500
Total	153	69,090	931	1,959,928	1,084	2,029,018
American (coastwise)	146	65,931	1,534	1,942,111	1,980	2,008,042

Annex 9.—Table of Ocean Freights from Baltimore for the Year 1898.

Month.	Steam. Grain per Bushel. To Liverpool.		Steam. Grain per Quarter. To London.		To Glasgow.		To Cork for Orders.		To Rotterdam.		To Antwerp.	
	d.	d.	s. d.	s. d.	s. d.	s. d.	s. d.	s. d.	s. d.	s. d.	s. d.	s. d.
January	3½ to	4	2 7½ to	3 0	3 0 to	3 3	3 0 to	3 7½	2 9 to	3 0	3 0	3 3
February	3⅜	3⅝	2 4½	2 7½	2 9	3 0	3 0	3 6	2 6	2 10½	2 9	3 3
March	3¼	3½	2 3	2 6	2 7½	3 0	3 4½	3 10½	2 10½	3 0	3 0	3 3
April	3¼	5	2 3	4 0	2 4½	3 9	3 3	4 6	2 10½	4 0	3 0	4 0
May	4	5	2 0	4 0	3 0	3 10½	3 3	4 7½	2 9	4 0	2 9	4 0
June	2	4	2 0	2 3	2 3	3 0	3 0	3 6	2 3	2 9	1 9	2 9
July	1¼	2¼	1 9	2 3	1 9	2 9	2 9	3 1½	2 4½	2 9	2 6	2 9
August	1⅜	2½	1 9	2 3	0 6	2 6	2 0	3 3	2 0	3 3	2 0	2 6
September	2¼	4	2 0	3 3	2 6	3 3	2 7½	4 0	2 6	3 6	2 6	3 9
October	4	6	3 3	3 9	3 3	3 9	4 0	4 6	3 6	3 9	3 9	4 3
November	4¼	5	3 9	4 0	3 4½	3 6	4 0	4 7½	3 3	3 9	3 7½	4 3
December	4	4¼	3 3	3 9	3 3	3 4½	3 6	4 3	3 3	3 6	3 6	3 7½
Range	1¼	6	1 9	4 0	0 6	3 10½	2 0	4 7½	2 0	4 0	1 9	4 3

Annex 10.—TABLE showing the Nationality, &c., of the Immigrants Arriving at Baltimore during the Years 1898-97.

Country.	1898. Males.	1898. Females.	1898. Total.	1897. Total.
England	25	3	28	35
Scotland	4	..	4	4
Ireland	10	..	10	6
Bohemia	197	171	368	376
Hungary	1,492	744	2,236	1,303
Austria	1,828	772	2,600	1,131
Denmark	1	..	1	7
France	2	1	3	2
Germany	1,059	1,181	2,240	2,292
Italy	5	2	7	1
Netherlands	2	..	2	..
Norway	1	..	1	2
Roumania	17	15	32	47
Russia	2,643	1,840	4,483	2,320
Spain	1	..	1	..
Sweden	1	1	2	..
Switzerland	3	3	6	6
Malta	1	..	1	..
British West Indies	7	5	12	24
Danish West Indies	2	..	2	1
Cuba	1	..	1	4
Argentine Republic	1	..	1	..
Australia	1	..	1	..
Japan	1	..	1	..
Other countries	..	..	..	10
Total	7,305	4,738	12,043	7,571

NORFOLK.

Mr. Vice-Consul Myers reports as follows:—

General remarks. Few cities in this country offer such advantages as Norfolk for manufacturing establishments of every description, combining facilities for transportation by nine railroads and 12 steamship lines; these reach all points on the coast and interior, north, south, and west, affording competitive freight rates to every point of importance. New York has equal facilities for freight rates, but labour can be had here at much lower prices, and the hours of work are longer.

Manufactories. The following is a partial list of some of the manufacturing plants in successful operation here:—Six six-set knitting mills, employing about 1,200 people; a large brewery, two grain mills, two creosoting plants, five peanut cleaning establishments, two paper-box factories, two book-binderies, several factories for making barrels, boxes and crates for garden vegetables and fruits, three ice plants, two cotton compresses, 10 fertiliser factories, carriage and harness factories, agricultural implement foundries, machine shops, ship-yards, marine railways, cigar and candy factories, grain elevators, 18 saw and planing mills, and a silver-plating factory, the last-named having moved here from Bridgeport, Connecticut, about a year since. The Norfolk Silk Company has recently been organised and promises to be a most important addition to the manufacturing interests of the place. The climate and industrial conditions of Norfolk are particularly favourable to silk manufacturing, and it was these facts which attracted the attention of some northern capitalists interested in silk mills in New York and New Jersey, and induced them to organise a company to put in operation a similar plant at Norfolk. The capital stock of the company is divided into two classes, preferred and common stock, there being 100,000 dol. of the first, which is guaranteed an annual dividend of 8 per cent., and 400,000 dol. of common stock. The business for which the company was formed is the weaving, printing, dyeing and cleaning of silk, cotton and other fabrics, and the preparation, manufacture, and sale of the same.

Railways. The Belt Line referred to in my last report as being under construction, has been completed and is in operation. This line connects the various lines centering here, and enables a prompt interchange of business.

The Chesapeake and Ohio and the New York, Philadelphia, and Norfolk Railroad Companies have been making extensive improvements and additions to their terminal facilities.

Channel. During the last six months the Government has deepened the channel from Hampton Roads to the Navy Yard, giving a depth at low water of 28 feet and a width of 400 feet.

Coal. The shipments of Pocahontas coal are steadily increasing, and are reaching new territory every year. During the past 12 months initial shipments have been made to the Argentine Republic, Brazil, and South Africa, with such satisfactory results that increased business is assured for the future. The Toms Creek Coal and Coke Company have within the past two years opened offices in Norfolk and secured a large amount of the local business. Recently they have been seeking a share of the export and bunker business, and are meeting with sufficient success to justify the belief that they will eventually become sharp competitors of the Pocahontas Coal Company. Their coal is brought from the same section of the State, and by many is claimed to possess superior steam-producing qualities.

Oysters. The packing and shipping of oysters continues to occupy a conspicuous place among the industries of Norfolk. During the eight months of the season, from September 1 to May 1, thousands of people find employment in the 23 large oyster-packing establishments here, which are estimated to handle during the season 2,500 bushels of oysters valued at 2,000,000 dol. Comparatively few oysters are shipped in the shell, but are opened and put in barrels or tubs, iced, and sent to almost every State east of the Mississippi River. The Lynhaven oysters, famed for their size and flavour, are taken from Lynhaven Bay, near Cape Henry. These command the highest prices obtained for any oysters sent from this district, the price being 4 to 6 dol. per barrel in the shell; the annual business is about 9,000 barrels.

"Trucking," as the raising of early vegetables and fruits for the Northern market is called, continues to hold its own, though the competition of the more Southern States, due to increased transportation facilities, has made the business less profitable. From this source between 3,500,000 dol. and 7,000,000 dol. are returned annually, according to the size of the crops raised and prices obtained. As practically all this money is spent in Norfolk, the trucking interest has been a most important factor in building up and developing the place. *Fruit and vegetable raising.*

The increase in population since 1880 has been rapid, as will be seen from the following figures:—1880, population 21,960; 1890, 34,871; 1896, 54,842; 1898, 65,813. The population has nearly doubled in the last 10 years, and if the same ratio of increase continues, the beginning of the next century will find Norfolk with a population of nearly 100,000. *Population.*

Annex 1.—TABLE showing Principal Articles of Export and Import at the Port of Norfolk during the past Year.

EXPORTS.

Articles.		Quantity.	Value.
			Dollars.
Cattle	Head	264	19,800
Corn	Bushels	9,436,323	3,530,925
Wheat	,,	600,791	476,489
Flour	Barrels	57,226	155,788
Other breadstuffs			25,700
Coal (bituminous)	Tons	238,460	529,732
,, for ships' use			298,932
Coke	Tons	42,702	139,846
Copper	Lbs.	5,406,220	585,314
Cotton	Bales	93,619	2,578,432
Pig-iron	Tons	23,398	255,241
Oil	Gallons	8,700	5,867
Logs and lumber			1,176,775
Lard	Lbs.	33,631,411	1,987,511
Tobacco	,,	2,704,891	173,734
Staves		3,692,496	179,859
Soap			8,518
Miscellaneous			888,404
Alcohol	Gallons	43,538	3,483
Cotton-seed oil	,,	908,780	218,226
Nuts			11,807
Headings			9,864
Cotton waste	Lbs.	3,438,403	91,519
Bark			18,575
Grease			19,082
Pea-nuts			674
Coal (anthracite)			51,977
Phosphate			65,590
Tallow	Lbs.	740,973	21,534
Hams	,,	69,325	8,319
Steel	Tons	4,053	81,060
Iron rails	,,	2,554	51,080
Total			13,669,657

NORFOLK.

IMPORTS.

Articles.	Value.
	Dollars.
Land plaster	1,767
Sulphate of ammonia	16,278
Nitrate of potash	37,187
Sulphate of potash	8,926
Manure salt	42,711
Kainit	31,869
Wines	569
Miscellaneous articles	7,249
Total	146,556

Annex 2.—RETURN of all Shipping at the Port of Norfolk during the Year 1898.

ENTERED.

Nationality.	Sailing. Number of Vessels.	Sailing. Tons.	Steam. Number of Vessels.	Steam. Tons.	Total. Number of Vessels.	Total. Tons.
British	19	20,502	428	736,930	447	757,432
American	62	45,118	...	...	62	45,118
Norwegian	...	...	22	36,988	22	36,988
German	2	3,095	15	20,862	17	23,957
Italian	11	6,435	4	7,267	15	13,702
Spanish	...	...	9	17,533	9	17,533
Danish	...	...	6	12,901	6	12,901
Swedish	...	...	3	6,515	3	6,515
All others	1	588	3	6,039	4	6,627
Total	95	75,738	490	815,035	585	920,773

CLEARED.

Nationality.	Sailing. Number of Vessels.	Sailing. Tons.	Steam. Number of Vessels.	Steam. Tons.	Total. Number of Vessels.	Total. Tons.
British	18	18,365	422	753,058	440	771,423
American	71	55,251	...	...	71	55,251
Norwegian	...	...	22	36,988	22	36,988
German	2	3,095	15	20,862	17	23,957
Italian	11	6,434	4	7,267	15	13,701
Spanish	...	...	10	19,585	10	19,585
Danish	...	...	6	12,901	6	12,901
Swedish	...	...	2	4,598	2	4,598
All others	2	961	3	6,039	5	7,000
Total	104	84,106	484	861,298	588	945,404

NEWPORT NEWS.

Mr. Vice-Consul Haughton reports as follows:—

This Vice-Consulate was re-established on January 10, 1898.

During the cessation (a period of nine years) Newport News has experienced a phenomenal development; the population has grown from 4,500 to between 17,500 and 20,000; the wealth and industries in larger ratio.

The town is lighted by electricity, and electric cars run through the streets and suburbs, with a through line to Fortress Monroe, on Hampton Roads.

Trade and commerce. The Chesapeake and Ohio Railway, organised July 1, 1878, under the general laws of the States of Virginia and West Virginia, is the most potent factor in the development of the port. During 1897 the freight traffic movement over this road, excluding company's material is shown in Annex No. 1.

The facilities for coastwise shipping between here and New York, Boston, Philadelphia, Baltimore, Norfolk, &c., are excellent; daily sailings and low rates are available.

This port is perhaps the finest on the Atlantic coast. It contains one of the most complete shipbuilding yards in the world—the largest in America. The dry dock is 610 feet long by 130 feet broad, and 26 feet over the sill. There are six slipways (two 400 feet, two 500 feet, and two 600 feet long). The yard covers over 10 acres, and contains, besides the shipbuilding yard, joiners, machine, boilers, and fitting shops, an electric cantiliver crane, which is capable of lifting about 15 tons, and shears to lift 150 tons. The improvements now under way will give Newport News the largest private dry dock in the United States, the dimensions of which are to be as follows:—

Clear length inside caisson, 806 feet; breadth on bottom, 80 feet; breadth at top, 162 feet; depth of water over the sill, 30 feet at mean high-water; mean average of the tide, 2 feet 6 inches.

There are at present 5,000 employés, and the work on hand will aggregate 125,000 tons displacement.

The company state that contracts for two 12,000 ton steam ships for the Pacific Mail Company have been secured, and that the work of building them will shortly be begun. The price of these two steamers, which are to be the largest ever built in the United States, is said to be 3,500,000 dol.

A recently established industry, which promises considerable development, is the importation of bananas and other tropical fruits from Jamaica. Two Norwegian steamers have been put on a line from Newport News to Kingston, and other out ports of Jamaica, taking out, when obtainable, coal, &c., returning with fruit. This line is affording the United States an excellent opportunity to capture West Indian coal markets; low coal rates can be quoted, as the fruit cargoes brought back yield large returns. This venture, it is generally understood, has the financial backing of the Chesapeake and Ohio Railway.

Another important industry—an iron and brass foundry of large capacity, employing between 150 to 200 men—is now in full operation.

Good facilities exist here for the rapid coaling of vessels. Coal supplied is known as New River, the quality of which is undoubted, and is well known to British steamship owners. It is contracted, trimmed in bunkers, at 3 dol. 35 c. per ton of 2,240 lbs. The coastwise and foreign business take about 125,000 tons per month. The recent Welsh strike may be credited with this coal getting into foreign markets, hitherto exclusively British. As this is being written, we note the charter of a British steamer at 14s. from Virginia to St. Michaels, and a British bark from same place to Genoa or Savona with coal. A British steamer is now loading a full cargo of this coal to Montevideo for orders, and a couple of steamers have cleared for other South American ports during the past month.

As a port of call Hampton Roads (for which Newport News is the port of entry) cannot be excelled.

The port charges are light: custom-house entry, 2 dol.; custom-house clearance, 2 dol. 70 c.; harbour master's fee, 5 dol.; quarantine officer's fee, 7 dol.; towage, when required by master, 1 c. per net register ton per shift; wharfage 1 c. per net register ton per 24 hours; pilotage, as per scale, 2 dol. 50 c. per foot upwards, 4 dol 50 c. per foot on vessels over 16 feet, in and out.

Stevedoring is now being done by the agencies of the various lines operating from this port.

Rates rule about 35 c. per ton over all commodities, and screwed cotton at 35 c. per bale.

The total exports of cattle for 1898 amounted to 24,172 head.

NEWPORT NEWS.

Annex 1.—Freight Traffic Movement for the Year 1897.
(Company's Material excluded.)

Commodity.	Freight Originating on this Road.	Freight Received from Connecting Roads and other Carriers.	Total Freight Tonnage.	Per Cent.
	Whole tons.	Whole tons.	Whole tons.	
Products of agriculture—				
Grain	55,703	508,730	564,436	8·70
Flour	23,217	193,030	216,247	3·33
Other mill products	10,896	40,118	51,014	·79
Hay and hemp	9,465	33,463	42,928	·66
Tobacco	33,466	12,582	46,048	·70
Cotton	481	2,802	3,283	·05
Other articles	13,859	27,348	41,207	·63
Products of animals—				
Live stock	25,137	23,635	48,772	·75
Packing-house products	4,724	58,357	63,081	·97
Wool	693	4,406	5,099	·08
Other articles	2,265	5,330	7,595	·12
Products of mines—				
Anthracite coal		36,312	36,312	·56
Bituminous coal	2,608,174	27,416	2,635,590	40·60
Coke	365,981	8,637	374,618	5·77
Ores	244,428	7,127	251,555	3·87
Stone, sand, and other like articles	288,806	4,321	293,127	4·53
Products of forest—				
Lumber	185,077	58,416	243,493	3·75
Other articles	257,470	76,724	334,194	5·15
Manufactures—				
Petroleum and other oils	7,986	63,750	71,736	1·10
Sugar	1,471	30,175	31,646	·49
Iron, pig and bloom	202,890	69,726	272,616	4·20
", manufactured	48,229	63,333	111,562	1·72
Cement, brick and lime	57,468	29,967	87,435	1·35
Agricultural implements and machinery	7,258	4,274	11,532	·18
Wines, liquors, and beers	6,940	11,163	18,103	·28
Household goods and furniture	1,829	523	2,352	·03
Salt	8,947	11,514	20,461	·31
Merchandise	158,664	161,740	320,404	4·94
Miscellaneous—				
Other commodities not mentioned above	102,464	182,387	284,851	4·39
Total tonnage, entire line	4,733,991	1,757,306	6,491,297	100

Annex 2.—SUMMARY of British and Foreign Shipping at Newport News for Year ending December 31, 1898.

ENTERED.

Nationality.	Sailing. Number of Vessels.	Sailing. Tons.	Steam. Number of Vessels.	Steam. Tons.	Total. Number of Vessels.	Total. Tons.
British	3	2,807	461	862,562	464	865,369
German	6	10,544	52	100,085	58	110,629
Danish	..	...	10	17,161	10	17,161
Spanish	3	2,584	5	10,475	8	13,059
Norwegian	1	490	30	42,133	31	42,623
Austrian	...	...	18	37,451	18	37,451
American	3	3,533	1	863	4	4,396
Other countries	4	2,572	4	6,596	8	9,168
Total	20	22,530	581	1,077,326	601	1,099,856

CLEARED.

Nationality.	Sailing. Number of Vessels.	Sailing. Tons.	Steam. Number of Vessels.	Steam. Tons.	Total. Number of Vessels.	Total. Tons.
British	4	2,953	462	864,610	466	867,563
German	6	10,544	52	100,085	58	110,629
Danish	..	...	10	17,161	10	17,161
Spanish	3	2,584	5	10,475	8	13,059
Norwegian	1	490	30	42,133	31	42,623
Austrian	...	...	18	37,451	18	37,451
American	20	14,349	...	...	20	14,349
Other countries	4	2,572	4	6,596	8	9,168
Total	38	33,492	581	1,078,511	619	1,112,003

Annex 3.—OCEAN Freights from Newport News.

GRAIN.

Monthly Average.	Steam. Per Bushel. To Liverpool.	To London.	To Glasgow.	To Bristol.	To Leith.	To Hull.	To Antwerp.	To Cork for Orders.
	d.	d.	d.	d.	d.	d.	d.	s. d.
January	$2\frac{15}{16}$	$3\frac{1}{4}$	$3\frac{3}{4}$	$3\frac{15}{16}$	$4\frac{1}{8}$	$3\frac{7}{16}$	3	3 $3\frac{3}{4}$
February	$2\frac{5}{8}$	$3\frac{3}{8}$	$2\frac{5}{8}$	$3\frac{3}{8}$	$4\frac{3}{16}$	$3\frac{9}{16}$	$3\frac{1}{4}$	3 $1\frac{1}{4}$
March	$2\frac{5}{8}$	$3\frac{3}{8}$	$2\frac{11}{16}$	$3\frac{3}{8}$	$4\frac{3}{16}$	$3\frac{9}{16}$	$3\frac{1}{4}$	3 $1\frac{1}{4}$
April	$2\frac{7}{16}$	$3\frac{1}{16}$	$2\frac{5}{8}$	$2\frac{7}{8}$	$3\frac{3}{8}$	$3\frac{13}{16}$	$2\frac{7}{16}$	2 $10\frac{1}{2}$
May	$1\frac{11}{16}$	$2\frac{9}{16}$	$2\frac{7}{16}$	$3\frac{1}{16}$	$3\frac{5}{8}$	3	$2\frac{15}{16}$	2 $8\frac{1}{4}$
June	$1\frac{7}{8}$	$2\frac{1}{2}$	$2\frac{3}{16}$	$2\frac{13}{16}$	3	$2\frac{15}{16}$	3	2 $6\frac{1}{2}$
July	$2\frac{15}{16}$	$3\frac{1}{8}$	$2\frac{5}{8}$	$3\frac{3}{8}$	$3\frac{1}{2}$	$3\frac{1}{2}$	4	3 $1\frac{1}{2}$
August	$3\frac{5}{16}$	3	$2\frac{9}{16}$	$3\frac{1}{2}$	$3\frac{15}{16}$	$4\frac{1}{8}$	$4\frac{3}{8}$	3 4
September	$3\frac{3}{4}$	$3\frac{3}{8}$	$3\frac{1}{4}$	4	$4\frac{1}{8}$	$4\frac{3}{16}$	4	3 $6\frac{1}{4}$
October	$4\frac{1}{2}$	$4\frac{7}{16}$	$4\frac{5}{8}$	$4\frac{3}{4}$	5	$4\frac{7}{8}$	$4\frac{3}{4}$	3 9
November	$4\frac{5}{8}$	$4\frac{13}{16}$	$4\frac{3}{4}$	$4\frac{15}{16}$	$5\frac{1}{4}$	$5\frac{1}{16}$	5	4 1
December	4	$4\frac{11}{16}$	$4\frac{11}{16}$	$4\frac{15}{16}$	$5\frac{1}{4}$	5	$4\frac{11}{16}$	3 9

NEWPORT NEWS.

FLOUR.

Monthly Average.	Sacks per Ton.			
	To Liverpool.	To London.	To Glasgow.	To Bristol.
	s. d.	s. d.	s. d.	s. d.
January	10 0	12 6	10 7½	14 0¾
February	10 0	14 0¾	10 0	12 6
March	10 0	13 6	9 9	12 6
April	10 0	10 10½	8 5¼	12 6
May	8 2½	10 0½	8 1¼	10 10¾
June	7 8½	9 7½	8 0	10 7½
July	9 3	10 9	8 1¾	10 7½
August	10 0	10 7½	8 9	12 6
September	12 3	11 10½	10 7½	13 9
October	15 0	15 0	15 3	14 9
November	16 3	19 0¼	16 10½	17 2¼
December	17 0	19 0	17 6	17 0

BEEF.

Monthly Average.	Steam. Per Tierce.				
	To Liverpool.	To London.	To Glasgow.	To Bristol.	To Antwerp.
	s. d.	s. d.	s. d.	s. d.	s. d.
January	3 0	3 4¼	4 0	4 6	4 1½
February	3 0	3 6	3 9	4 0	4 0
March	3 0	3 8½	4 0	4 0	4 0
April	2 10½	3 6	3 9	4 0	3 7½
May	2 1¼	3 0½	3 1¼	4 0	3 6
June	2 0	2 9	3 0	3 6	3 6
July	2 2	2 11¼	3 0	3 6	3 9½
August	2 6	3 0	3 0	3 6	4 0
September	2 10½	3 0	3 6	3 6	4 0
October	3 4¾	3 4¼	4 0	3 10¾	4 6
November	4 0	4 1½	4 3	4 3	4 6
December	3 8½	4 4¼	4 6	4 6	4 6

PORK.

Monthly Average.	Steam. Per Barrel.					
	To Liverpool.	To London.	To Glasgow.	To Bristol.	To Antwerp.	To Hamburg.
	s. d.	s. d.	s. d.	s. d.	s. d.	M. pf.
January	2 1½	2 5¼	3 0	3 6	3 0	3 50
February	2 0	2 7	2 11¼	3 0	3 0	3 50
March	2 0	2 6	2 9	3 0	3 0	3 50
April	2 0	2 6	2 6	3 0	2 9¼	3 50
May	1 7½	2 0½	2 1¼	3 0	2 8¼	3 0
June	1 6	2 0	2 0	2 9	2 6	3 0
July	1 7	2 0	2 0	2 9	2 9½	3 13
August	1 9	2 0	2 0	2 9	3 0	3 50
September	1 11¼	2 0	2 6	2 9	2 0	3 62½
October	2 2¼	2 2¼	3 0	2 11¼	3 6	3 55
November	2 9	2 11¼	3 3	3 4¼	3 6	3 50
December	2 7¼	3 2½	3 6	3 6	3 6	3 50

PROVISIONS.

Monthly Average.	Steam. Per Ton.					Steam. Per 100 Lbs.
	To Liverpool.	To London.	To Glasgow.	To Bristol.	To Antwerp.	To Hamburg.
	£ s. d.	£ s. d.	£ s. d.	£ s. d.	£ s. d.	M. pf.
January	0 15 0	0 15 0	1 0 0	1 2 6	1 0 7½	1 0
February	0 15 0	0 16 10½	0 18 9	1 0 0	1 0 0	1 0
March	0 15 0	0 17 6	1 0 0	1 0 0	1 0 0	1 0
April	0 14 4½	0 17 6	0 19 4½	1 0 0	0 18 1½	0 97½
May...	0 10 6	0 15 6	0 15 6	0 19 0	0 17 6	0 75
June	0 10 0	0 12 6	0 15 0	0 17 6	0 17 6	0 75
July	0 11 0	0 13 0	0 15 0	0 17 6	0 19 0	0 80
August	0 12 6	0 15 0	0 15 0	0 17 6	1 0 0	0 90
September... ...	0 14 4½	0 14 7	0 17 6	0 17 6	1 0 0	0 97½
October	0 18 3	0 17 1	1 0 0	0 19 6	1 2 6	1 5
November	1 0 7½	1 0 7½	1 1 3	1 1 3	1 2 6	1 5
December	0 18 6	1 2 0	1 2 6	1 2 6	1 2 6	1 5

OIL-CAKE.

Monthly Average.	Steam. Per Ton.					Steam. Per 100 Lbs.
	To Liverpool.	To London.	To Glasgow.	To Bristol.	To Antwerp.	To Hamburg.
	s. d.	s. d.	s. d.	s. d.	s. d.	Cents.
January	10 11¼	12 6	10 7½	13 9	13 1½	18½
February	10 0	13 9	10 0	12 6	14 4½	18
March	9 6	12 6	9 6	10 7½	12 6	18
April	9 0	11 10½	8 4½	10 0	10 0	18
May...	7 10¼	12 3	8 1¼	10 4½	10 0	$16\frac{7}{16}$
June	7 6	9 0	7 9	10 0	10 0	15
July	9 6	10 10¾	8 5¼	11 0	14 0	16⅝
August	10 0	10 4½	8 9	12 6	15 0	18
September... ...	11 3	10 11¼	10 7½	11 3	15 7½	18
October	15 0	15 0	15 0	14 9½	17 6	$18\frac{7}{16}$
November	16 3	18 9	16 3	17 1½	17 6	19
December	17 0	19 0	17 6	17 0	17 6	19

Annex 4.—RETURN of Exports during the Year 1898.

	Quantity.			Value.
	To Great Britain.	To Other Countries.	Total.	
	Tons.	Tons.	Tons.	Dollars.
In British vessels ..	513,571	180,713	694,284	..
In foreign vessels ..	30,815	165,248	196,063	..
Total	544,386	345,961	890,347	32,018,000

Annex 5.—GRAIN Crop of the State of Virginia as per Reports of the United States Agricultural Department.

Articles.		Quantity.					
			1892.	1893.	1894.	1895.	1896.	1897.
Wheat	Bushels	7,591,000	8,681,086	6,995,249	6,505,583	5,724,913	8,451,864
Corn	,,	...	31,234,046	32,195,858	32,607,158	38,067,986	31,552,164
Oats	,,	5,472,000	8,378,440	5,400,504	8,125,061	8,492,296	5,233,092
Rye	,,	...	...	...	...	...	138,702
Buckwheat	,,	...	...	...	...	...	67,298
Potatoes	,,	...	...	...	...	...	2,120,116
Hay	Tons	...	...	...	...	...	592,114
Cotton	Bales*	...	...	...	...	...	11,539

* Commercial bales.

Annex 6.—AVERAGE Yield per Acre of the Principal Farm Crops of the State of Virginia.

		Average Yield per Acre.				
		1893.	1894.	1895.	1896.	1897.
Corn	Bushels	18·9	19·1	18·6	21·5	18
Wheat	,,	11·2	9·5	9·3	9·3	12
Oats	,,	17·5	12	17·7	18·5	12
Hay	Tons	1·11	·72	1·13	1·08	1·03
Cotton	Bales	...	·21	·18	·24	·24

AVERAGE Value per Acre of the Principal Farm Crops of the State of Virginia.

	Average Value per Acre.				
	1893.	1894.	1895.	1896.	1897.
	Dol. c.	Dol. c.	Dol. c.	Dol. c.	Dol. c.
Corn	8 69	8 98	6 88	6 88	6 84
Wheat	7 6	3 32	6 5	7 44	11 4
Oats	6 13	4 44	5 31	4 81	3 48
Hay	14 53	8 56	12 92	11 3	11 7
Cotton	..	5 94	7 31	8 7	..

PRICES of Principal Agricultural Products on the Farm, December 1, 1893–97, in the State of Virginia.

		Price.				
		1893.	1894.	1895.	1896.	1897.
		Dol. c.	Dol. c.	Dol. c.	Dol. c.	Dol. c.
Corn	Per bushel	0 46	0 47	0 37	0 32	0 38
Wheat	,,	0 63	0 56	0 65	0 80	0 92
Oats	,,	0 35	0 37	0 30	0 26	0 29
Hay	Per ton	13 09	11 89	11 43	10 21	10 25
Cotton	Per lb.	0 071	0 05	0 078	0 071	0 069

(75 5 | 99—H & S 352)

No. 2239 Annual Series.

DIPLOMATIC AND CONSULAR REPORTS.

UNITED STATES.

REPORT FOR THE YEAR 1898

ON THE

TRADE, &c., OF CHICAGO.

REFERENCE TO PREVIOUS REPORT, Annual Series No. 2085.

Presented to both Houses of Parliament by Command of Her Majesty,
MAY, 1899.

LONDON:
PRINTED FOR HER MAJESTY'S STATIONERY OFFICE,
BY HARRISON AND SONS, ST. MARTIN'S LANE,
PRINTERS IN ORDINARY TO HER MAJESTY.

And to be purchased, either directly or through any Bookseller, from
EYRE & SPOTTISWOODE, East Harding Street, Fleet Street, E.C., and
32, Abingdon Street, Westminster, S.W.; or
JOHN MENZIES & Co., 12, Hanover Street, Edinburgh, and
90, West Nile Street, Glasgow; or
HODGES, FIGGIS, & Co., Limited, 104, Grafton Street, Dublin.

1899.

[C. 9044—65.] *Price Twopence Halfpenny.*

CONTENTS.

	PAGE
CHICAGO—	
Chicago as a commercial centre	3
Population	3
Clearing-house	3
Shipping	4
Railways	4
General remarks	4
Imports to United Kingdom from United States	6
Exports from „ to „	7
Corn and wheat	8
Provisions: beef, sheep, &c.	8
Hogs	8
Stock-yards	9
Furniture	9
Iron and steel	9
Trusts	9
Coal	10
Oleomargarine	10
ST. LOUIS trade report	10
DENVER „	22
ST. PAUL „	29
OMAHA „	30

No. 2239. **Annual Series.**

Reference to previous Report, Annual Series No. 2085.

Report on the Trade, &c., of Chicago for the Year 1898
By Mr. CONSUL WYNDHAM.

(Received at Foreign Office, April 6, 1899.

It would perhaps be as well to consider Chicago as it now is before entering into a report on its commerce and progress during the past year. For a long time after this great city, situated at the foot of Lake Michigan, had acquired a position among the commercial cities of the United States, she remained comparatively stationary, owing to the distance from the coast, and the fact that its principal products for shipment abroad were derived from the extensive western farm lands and cattle ranches. {Chicago as a commercial centre.}

Among other things, the World's Fair in 1893 brought it to the front, and to-day Chicago and the State of Illinois are to be ranked among the manufacturing, as well as coal and agricultural, districts of the United States.

Next to New York, Chicago, with over 2,000,000 residents, is the second city in the United States in respect to the number of its inhabitants, and, after a long struggle with Boston for the second place in its bankers' clearing, Chicago at last follows New York, and heads all other cities with a total clearing house account of 1,114,916,700*l.* during 1898. In bank clearances Chicago must be content with the second place, as New York will, by its geographical position, be the leading place of imports and exports in the United States, and also the financial centre, a position from which it can hardly be driven. {Population. Clearing House.}

Clearances in 1898 at the following places amounted to:—

At—	Value.
	£
New York	8,302,794,600
Chicago	1,114,916,700
Boston	1,094,621,300
Philadelphia	767,880,900
St. Louis	295,665,600
Baltimore	185,034,700
San Francisco	169,908,600
New Orleans	92,725,500
Galveston	34,660,084

CHICAGO.

From the above figures it will be seen that, if clearances are a proof of commercial prosperity, Chicago has in the past year, been the second city in the United States in the extent of its transactions.

Shipping.

As regards the shipping arriving and leaving the two ports of North and South Chicago, the following comparisons with other American ports will probably astonish many persons, who think of this place as removed from the bustle of shipping, wharves, &c. :—

VESSELS Entered and Cleared, with Tonnage, to June 30, 1898.

Ports.	Entrances. Number of Vessels.	Tonnage	Clearances. Number of Vessels.	Tonnage.
Chicago	9,575	7,831,757	9,617	7,818,116
New York	7,305	7,771,412	7,140	7,576,630
Boston	2,846	1,969,756	2,947	1,661,872
Baltimore	2,603	1,554,361	3,167	1,824,973
Philadelphia	1,731	1,636,149	1,926	1,592,596
New Orleans	1,354	1,598,557	1,363	1,642,962
San Francisco	1,056	1,096,279	1,453	1,119,559

Thus it will be seen that Chicago is not only the largest shipping port in the United States, but that, roughly calculating, three vessels enter Chicago to one in Boston or Baltimore, five to one at Philadelphia, seven to one in New Orleans, and nine to one in San Francisco.

Railways.

Thirty-eight railway lines, from all points of the compass, centre in Chicago, and have terminal stations there, and it is by the lines running to the coast that a great portion of the grain, cattle, and manufactured goods are conveyed for shipment. These statements will, in a small way, convey the idea of the importance of Chicago as a commercial centre.

General remarks.

During the past year, although the United States were for a time engaged in war with Spain, business was brisk, and Chicago prospered not only through large orders placed by the Government purchasing agents, but also from the increased demand from the industrial classes, whose prosperity caused a constant and increased demand for all kinds of goods.

With the growth of population, business, and capital, there has been a corresponding growth of culture and refinement in these parts, which not long ago were regarded as the Far West. This should be borne in mind by merchants abroad who think that the Eastern States are the only places where trade should be sought, and that as long as they are in touch with them they need not look further for fresh markets. There could not be a greater mistake made. Many of the Western cities deal with their foreign customers independently of the coast towns, and there is as large a field for the sale of artistic wares in the cities of Chicago, St. Louis, &c., as at the coast cities. Chicago especially, as the great distributing centre of the largest part of the Western States, should be carefully cherished as a base for European trade.

Nearly all the leading British banks and insurance companies, and many of the large firms of London, Manchester, Liverpool, Sheffield, Bradford, &c., have either branches or agencies here, and I am glad to say commercial travellers are numerous; still there is plenty of room for further effort, and above all there is much to be studied in not only what is required and can be sold, but also in what is being done in the way of competition in all classes of goods. When it is known that the American manufacturer is creeping into markets formerly held by British manufacturers, the time has come not only for increased activity in soliciting trade, but also for the commercial traveller to open his eyes as he travels, and see in what way his competitors are beating him. He should find out why steel rails, engines, and locomotives enter so much into competition with British productions, and why in the smallest detail, from a golf stick to a machine, ground is being lost. In 1889 we exported 37,397,261*l*. worth of goods to the United States, as compared with 21,117,003*l*. in 1898, whilst on the other hand our imports during the same period from the United States increased from 87,764,815*l*. to 112,214,373*l*., of which at least a large part was an increase in manufactured goods ordered abroad, as a consequence of the strikes at home, and trade thus lost is hard to recover.

It is practically impossible to obtain any statistics of the actual foreign commerce of Chicago, and although the Secretary of the Chamber of Commerce has been most obliging in placing his statistics at my disposal, and has given every assistance in his power, no actual data as to either the imports or exports of Chicago can be obtained.

The local custom-house, it is true, shows the statistics of what has arrived from abroad in bond, but it can give no idea of the vast trade that is cleared at the Atlantic seaports, and which necessarily figures in the tables of imports and exports of those ports, and it is consequently only possible to give the figures of the import and export trade with the United Kingdom.

Before closing these remarks, I may mention that at the Pencoyd ironworks, in a neighbouring State, a seven-span bridge, of a total length of 1,100 feet, has been completed, and is already shipped, and an erecting gang is about to proceed and construct the bridge across the Atbara River in the Soudan, near Khartoum. The order was placed with the Pencoyd ironworks, the Company agreeing to build the structure within seven weeks, though it was actually completed within six weeks, whilst British builders stated that it would require seven months to complete.

CHICAGO.

Imported by the United Kingdom from the United States.

Articles.		Quantity (12 Months ending Dec. 31)— 1897.	1898.	Value (12 Months ending Dec. 31)— 1897. £	1898. £
Animals living (for food)—					
Cattle	Number	416,299	369,478	7,230,854	6,238,984
Sheep and lambs	,,	186,755	147,021	272,421	219,706
Corn—					
Wheat—					
On the Atlantic	Cwts.	24,969,800	30,460,300	9,620,110	12,281,135
On the Pacific	,,	9,633,400	7,344,000	3,484,660	2,991,453
Meal and flour	,,	14,062,970	17,445,890	7,089,094	9,470,433
Oats	,,	8,082,300	8,435,820	1,913,478	2,294,021
Indian corn or maize	,,	39,645,100	37,466,100	6,623,230	7,314,935
Bacon	,,	3,592,635	4,087,389	5,353,624	6,438,239
Beef—					
Salted	,,	171,970	203,645	212,184	266,660
Fresh	,,	2,242,063	2,301,956	4,609,130	4,677,341
Hams	,,	1,603,533	1,851,520	3,411,559	3,651,414
Meat, salted or fresh	,,	76,102	90,412	126,714	156,736
Pork, salted (not hams)	,,	141,428	175,000	167,500	224,534
Butter	,,	154,196	66,712	633,549	285,309
Cheese	,,	631,616	485,995	1,413,079	1,006,588
Fish, cured or salted	,,	271,825	272,113	606,250	515,949
Hops	,,	84,905	191,535	280,453	838,074
Lard	,,	1,685,119	2,044,726	1,927,162	2,796,281
Sugar, refined and candy	,,	13,861	7,780	14,205	8,459
Copper—					
Ore	Tons	1,860	1,146	31,666	23,421
Regulus and precipitate	,,	11,863	9,626	353,125	292,500
Unwrought or part unwrought	,,	29,545	39,211	1,474,578	2,058,820
Lead, pig and sheet	,,	29,988	31,079	356,331	399,257
Cotton, raw	Cwts.	12,323,090	16,119,227	24,557,513	27,513,032
Tallow and stearine	,,	271,533	571,959	240,617	538.243
Wood and timber—					
Hewn	Loads	178,923	140,475	777,571	656.975
Sawn or split, planed or dressed	,,	639,390	527,092	1,721,202	1,421,037
Clocks, and parts of	...	...	...	86,257	91,466
Leather	Cwts.	515,728	572,540	2,606,406	3,036,811
Horses	Number	26,520	25,328	793,565	779,059
Flaxseed or linseed	Quarters	104,758	37,292	159,761	65,138

CHICAGO.

Exported from the United Kingdom to the United States.

Articles.		Quantity (12 Months ending Dec. 31)—		Value (12 Months ending Dec. 31)—	
		1897.	1898.	1897.	1898.
				£	£
Beer and ale	Barrels	32,940	32,592	159,796	146,113
Salt, rock and white	Tons	92,678	79,213	94,405	81,146
Spirits, British and Irish	Gallons (proof)	831,605	338,119	160,242	145,941
Wool, sheep and lambs'	Lbs.	33,735,900	5,090,400	1,238,285	128,503
Cotton manufactures—					
Piece-goods, grey or unbleached	Yards	4,302,800	2,594,700	84,010	44,703
Piece-goods, bleached	,,	12,272,400	11,694,800	228,547	246,935
,, printed	,,	4,191,200	2,634,300	86,355	59,015
,, dyed or manufactured of dyed yarn	,,	41,708,900	34,759,300	1,109,334	897,203
Total piece-goods of all kinds of cotton	,,	62,475,300	51,683,100	1,508,246	1,247,856
Jute yarn	Lbs.	376,800	359,300	3,941	3,782
Jute manufactures—					
Piece-goods of all kinds of jute	Yards	151,013,000	104,796,700	1,253,494	840,198
Linen yarn	Lbs.	1,000,100	1,330,500	38,625	39,053
Linen manufactures—					
Piece-goods of all kinds linen	Yards	103,081,300	86,992,700	1,925,861	1,634,288
Silk—					
Thrown, twist, and yarn	10-lbs.	406,100	830,156	104,564	174,570
Manufactures—					
Wholly of silk—					
Broad stuffs of silk or satin	Yards	206,000	334,674	23,823	32,126
Lace	...	...	...	64,879	44,643
Other articles of silk only	...	...	...	11,941	14,189
Of silk and other materials	...	...	...	56,453	71,763
Woollen yarn	Lbs.	57,800	6,900	4,412	473
Worsted ,,	,,	687,400	118,600	67,623	13,475
Woollen and worsted manufactures					
Woollen tissues	Yards	8,071,900	1,614,600	868,574	276,501
Worsted ,,	,,	41,943,400	13,993,700	2,431,221	764,761
Carpets, not being rugs	Yards	260,800	203,900	53,970	43,699
Metals and articles manufactured therefrom, except machinery—					
Hardware and cutlery unenumerated	...	...	...	154,463*	85,891
Iron and steel—					
Iron, pig	Tons	13,772	20,061	72,709	124,549
Bar, angle, bolt, and rod	,,	1,758	2,540	27,865	39,577
Railroad of all sorts	,,	...	259	...	1,692
Wire of iron or steel, and manufactures of (except telegraph wires)	,,	2,221	2,021	42,974	40,184
Hoops, sheets, and boiler and armour plates	,,	253	197	2,444	1,993
Tin plates and sheets	,,	85,472	65,337	927,751	683,913
Cast and wrought iron, and all other manufactures unenumerated (except ordnance)	,,	1,449	1,431	32,250	37,486
Old, for re-manufacture	,,	29	367	112	1,270
Steel, unwrought	,,	13,046	12,089	265,643	250,802
Black plates for tinning (iron and steel)	,,	731	678	7,072	6,543
Manufactures of steel, or of steel and iron combined	,,	800	530	86,053	84,967
Lead—					
Pig and manufactures of	,,	154	80	2,237	1,178
Tin, unwrought	,,	2,724	1,657	8,942	5,944
Machinery and millwork, or parts thereof—					
Steam engines—					
Locomotives	...	...	...	597	610
Agricultural	...	...	...	15	243
Other descriptions	...	...	...	6,085	6,925
Not steam engines—					
Agricultural	...	...	...	360	3,354
Mining	...	...	...	70	875
Textile	...	...	...	224,083	286,998
Other descriptions	...	...	...	46,517	56,157

* Hardware unenumerated only.

CHICAGO.

EXPORTED from the United Kingdom to the United States—continued.

Articles.		Quantity (12 months ending Dec. 31)— 1897.	1898.	Value (12 months ending Dec. 31)— 1897.	1898.
				£	£
Apparel and articles of personal use—					
Apparel and slops	...	...	...	54,380	46,462
Haberdashery and millinery, including embroidery and needlework	...	...	...	34,554	30,539
Chemicals, and chemical and medicinal preparations—					
Alkali	Cwts.	1,925,400	855,393	439,706	169,221
Bleaching materials or preparations	,,	754,300	738,016	236,886	194,309
All other articles—					
Bags and sacks, empty, for packing merchandise	Dozen	82,800	14,397	9,499	2,261
Cement	Tons	65,720	46,547	107,177	87,875
Earthenware, chinaware, parian and porcelain	...	...	...	643,323	534,209
Paper—					
Writing or printing or envelopes	Cwts.	10,143	8,221	24,121	15,704
All other descriptions	,,	9,815	8,736	34,830	31,581
Saddlery and harness	...	...	...	36,260	38,557
Skins and furs of all sorts	...	...	...	654,561	706,454
Stationery other than paper	...	...	...	59,734	63,766

Of which Chicago imported in bond to the local customhouse—

	Value.
	£
Imports free	443,556
,, dutiable	1,667,188
Total	2,110,744

Total imports registered in bond from abroad to the local customs, Chicago, in 1898, 2,110,744*l.*

The following general statement of trade in various articles, may also be useful as showing the trade of Chicago:—

Corn and wheat. During the year 1898 it is estimated that the importing countries of Europe took breadstuffs equivalent to 300,000,000 bushels, of which America supplied 218,000,000 bushels. The world's shipment of corn was estimated for the year at 260,000,000 bushels, of which 200,000,000 bushels, or over 75 per cent. were shipped by America.

The gross clearances of breadstuffs, corn and oats, for 1898 amounted to 469,000,000 bushels, as compared to 408,000,000 bushels in 1897.

Provisions. Beef, sheep, &c. The exports of provisions amounted in 1898 to 1,600,000,000 lbs., as compared to 1,385,681,000 lbs. in 1897.

Hogs. The number of hogs slaughtered at Chicago in 1898 was 9,380,000, as against 8,366,000 in 1897.

Stockyards. The volume of business at the Chicago stockyards was never so large as during 1898. Receipts of all kinds of live-stock aggregated 15,700,000 head, being 1,000,000 head more than ever arrived before, and the valuation the largest in about five years. Receipts of hogs were about 800,000 larger than the previous record year, while the number of cattle was the smallest since 1887. Sheep were within a few thousand of the record, and the year's total of horses about 8,000 larger than ever before.

Furniture. Of the cities of the United States, Chicago leads in the value of the output of furniture, exceeding the sum of 4,166,660*l*. Chicago is the chief manufacturing centre for parlour and upholstered furniture, chairs, woven wire mattresses, and metal bedsteads. Grand Rapids probably comes next, with an output, it is claimed, of 1,333,333*l*., principally of chamber suites, sideboards, fancy furniture, chiffoniers, &c.; St. Louis, it is admitted by many, occupies third position, with an estimated output of 1,020,083*l*.; the other principal centres possessing more than a dozen factories, and producing goods in amounts from 200,000*l*. upwards, are in this order of importance: Cincinnati, Philadelphia, Sheboygan, Rockford, Evansville, Indianapolis, Jamestown, Gardner, Massachusetts, Detroit, Baltimore, Williamsport, High Point, North Carolina. The cities of New York and Boston, while they still manufacture considerably, have, however, become more jobbing than manufacturing centres in this class of goods.

Iron and steel. In two respects the Western iron and steel markets for 1898 have been especially notable. The volume of trade was large beyond precedent, but prices throughout the year were low and remarkably uniform. The conjunction of these hitherto contradictory conditions marks a revolutionary change in the great industrial metals. Throughout the year there was enough demand to have sent prices upwards during any ordinary year. But orders were filled as fast as crowded and overworked mills and furnaces could turn out the products. The secret of these conditions was the birth of a new industrial era, the adjustment of levels between home and foreign markets, the recognised entrance of American iron and steel into the markets of the world. American energy and invention, vast mineral resources, and legislation had at length made possible the production of iron and steel in this country as cheaply as abroad. Improved facilities had increased production beyond the measure of home requirements.

The foreign shipments of iron and steel from Chicago increased from about 120,000 tons in 1897 to 150,000 tons in 1898, much of the product going to Canada.

The production of pig-iron in the State of Illinois in 1897 amounted to 1,117,239 tons.

Trusts. The year gone by has been remarkable for the formation of large trusts, small corporations amalgamating with large ones until there are many industries controlled by trusts with enormous capital. Whether this is for the general good is a very open question, but it seems to portend a coming clash between capital and labour of a more serious nature than has yet occurred, a contest in which the consumer will side with the workmen against the producers and the monopolies they are creating.

Coal. The output of bituminous coal in the State of Illinois amounted to 17,922,105 tons in 1897, the latest year for which statistics are published.

Oleo-margarine. The production of oleomargarine in the State of Illinois during the year 1898 amounted to 20,835,316 lbs., valued at over 88,000*l*. This is the largest amount produced in any State of the Union, Kansas being second with 13,331,614 lbs., and Ohio third with 8,795,891 lbs.

ST. LOUIS.

Mr. Vice-Consul Western Bascome reports as follows:—

Review. The year just closed has left a fair record of work accomplished and new enterprises begun.

Few realise that St. Louis has the largest railroad station, hardware store, drug store, woodenware establishment, tobacco factories, lead works, brick yards, and stove and range factories in the world.

The year that has just passed will go down into history as a conspicuous one in the affairs of the nation, and in the history of St. Louis. It marks the accomplishment of several noteworthy events and the beginning of several others.

As an example of work completed may be mentioned the new City Hall, the construction of which had dragged on for years. It was completed early in 1898, and the beginning of 1899 finds the city government located in one of the finest municipal buildings in the United States. As an example of work begun may be mentioned the burial of the electric wires, a large proportion of which have been put underground during the past year. Others will follow as rapidly as possible. The beginning of the end, when all electric wires, both telephonic, telegraphic, electric lighting, and street railway, will be underground, has certainly been made.

The year in St. Louis will be remembered, as elsewhere, because of the war. In response to the nation's call for volunteers St. Louis furnished more than her full quota of soldiers, part of whom are still in the service in Cuba.

The war, too, brought benefits to St. Louis in more ways than one. First, it aroused the patriotism of the people; brought them to see more clearly the needs of the national guard, and increased the trade of the city in every line of business, estimated at from 10 to 25 per cent. over 1897.

Financial matters. Banking business and stock transactions. St. Louis made great strides in a financial way during 1898, and the year was by far the largest for bank clearances in the history of the city. The total bank clearings have been about 290,000,000*l*. in round figures, as against 273,340,000*l*. for 1897,

ST. LOUIS.

or an increase of about 17,000,000*l.* With 20 banks capitalised at 293,000,000*l.*, and several big trust companies, it is estimated that the financial deals of 1898 through the clearing house and over the bank counters aggregated 600,000,000*l.* *Finances and banking.*

In stock and bond transactions 1898 has been a record year for St. Louis. It was characterised by gigantic financial deals involving millions upon millions of dollars. Stocks, bonds, and other securities are generally higher than at the close of 1897, and besides this a number of big street railway and industrial deals are pending which will cause a further advance in local securities. *Stocks and bonds.*

Brokers declare that 1898 has been very prosperous for them, and that the outlook for 1899 promises even a greater volume of business. The presence of so much outside capital in the local market has given a decided impetus to the stocks and bond trade, and the tendency seems to be generally upward.

The annual output of the breweries of St. Louis is truly wonderful. The statement that millions of barrels of beer are brewed annually in this city sounds rather big, but the facts and figures prove the assertion. *Beer.*

The output of the largest brewery in St. Louis for the year 1898 was the largest in the brewery's history. Over 800,000 barrels is the record for 1898, an increase of 10 per cent. over the year 1897. While this brewery's output has increased during the past year, the general consumption of beer throughout the whole country has decreased.

The revenue collected in the first district office of Missouri by the sale of stamps for beer is as follows:—

Old tax, 2 dol. per hogshead, 1 dol. per barrel, 50 c. per half barrel, 25 c. per keg, 12½ c. per one-eighth barrel. The tax was doubled on January 14, 1898.

With 7½ per cent. discount on face value, this amounted, for January 1 to June 13, inclusive, to 176,493*l.* net, and from then to December 28, 1898, inclusive, 424,628*l.* net.

The business in agricultural implements and vehicles was prosperous in 1898, especially in the territory tributary to St. Louis. Prices, however, were low. As compared with last year the gain amounted to about 10 per cent., bringing the total sales up to 1,870,700*l.* In this estimate the agricultural implements, vehicles, and all kinds of binder twine are included. *Agricultural implements and vehicles.*

Figures show the extent of increase in the boot, shoe, and slipper trade of St. Louis for the past 12 months, better than anything else. A comparison of sales and shipments, receipts and purchases shows that St. Louis shoe merchants have enjoyed an exceedingly prosperous year. *Boots and shoes.*

As during the year 1897, St. Louis ran far ahead of her competitors in shoe sales. Boston is the main shipping point of the shoe trade, and St. Louis is the main distributing point. There were shipped to St. Louis for distribution over 600,000 cases of boots and shoes, New York coming next with over 340,000 cases, Chicago with over 300,000, and Philadelphia 174,000 cases. During the past year St. Louis receipts from the same source reached a figure nearly 10 per cent. higher, showing a wonderful increase in trade.

Total receipts to date have been over 1,000,000 cases. These shoes have been distributed to all parts of the South-West, Central-West and South. When the Spanish-American war created a big demand for footwear, St. Louis manufacturers and dealers sold nearly 50,000 pairs of shoes to the United States Army.

Buildings. In 1898, 861 brick buildings and 786 frame buildings were erected, at a total expenditure of 1,566,779*l.*

Property in St. Louis is usually assessed at about 60 per cent. of its real value, the assessments for 1898 being 72,123,332*l.*, against 68,949,800*l.* in 1897.

Population. The estimated population for 1898 is 651,821, against 638,577 in 1897.

Coffee. The coffee trade with South America fell off in 1898, there being only 274,228 bags imported, against 320,005 bags in 1897.

Clothing. There has been an enormous demand for clothing this year. The large clothing establishments in St. Louis, which are among the largest in the West, have done a most magnificent business during the past year. The trade has been a gratifying increase over that of 1897, although an estimate of the trade in figures cannot be obtained. It is safe in stating, however, that there will be a decided increase over last year. In 1897 the amount of the clothing trade amounted to 500,000*l.*, as shown by the Merchants' Exchange Report.

Coal. The year 1898 was a pretty good one for the coal industry of St. Louis. According to carefully compiled statistics, the amount of coal handled in St. Louis in 1896 was 3,226,379 tons. In 1897 it was only 3,105,648 tons, while for 1898, up to and including December 27, the amount was 3,600,291 tons.

It will be noticed that during the year 1897 there was a slight decrease. This is accounted for by the fact that the Illinois miners were on strike, which for a time interfered greatly with the coal output.

The recent strikes in Illinois, which for a time became quite alarming, did not materially affect St. Louis, except to make a slight change in the price. The fluctuation of price, however, did not continue long, becoming settled before the coal season began.

Cotton trade. Heavy crops of cotton kept prices down, but volume increased.

By January 1, 1898, it was clearly seen that the cotton crop of 1897–98 would be a record breaker. Prices steadily declined until middling was quoted at $5\frac{3}{8}$ c. to $5\frac{7}{16}$ c. in St. Louis market the latter part of December and throughout January. Early in February a reaction set in, and prices steadily advanced until 6 c. was reached in May, and extended into June. Prices then began again to decline, and touched the low figure of $4\frac{15}{16}$ c. on November 1 in St. Louis.

The low figures of the fall stimulated the foreign demand to such an extent that the stock in Liverpool on December 23 showed 1,158,000 bales of American cotton against 620,000 bales for the same date in 1897, the Continental stocks showing 570,000 bales American, against 511,000 bales for same date in 1897. This export demand also very rapidly absorbed the bulk of the cotton of good grade and staple in this crop, the heavy rains of the fall having reduced the average grade and quality to the lowest we have seen in several years. This, coupled with the fact that much of the cotton would not be gathered on account of the very low prices, served somewhat to stimulate the market, and from November 13 to December 10 the local market advanced from $4\frac{15}{16}$ c. to $5\frac{3}{8}$ c., with a good active demand.

The crop of 1897–98 reached the grand total of 11,200,000 bales; we are now leading that crop by 400,000 bales, but many are inclined to the belief that this lead will be wiped out for the causes above given.

The movement to and through St. Louis thus far this season has been 548,523 bales, against 511,494 bales to the same date last year.

Dry goods. Dry goods dealers do not hesitate to say that trade during the past twelve months has shown a steady increase.

It is generally known that the market for woollens was poor at the beginning of the year. This brightened considerably. The demand for cottons, especially prints, has been good throughout the year, and prices on standard prints have held steadily to the regular figure. In dress goods plaids have been in great demand. Half-wool novelties have fallen as the year progressed, probably because the over-supply became a factor in reducing prices. Velvets have improved. Always an article of luxury, these goods are bought in larger quantities as times improve. Taffetas have been in such demand that dealers are said to be oversold. Fancy hosiery is in better demand, and accessories to the dress are also higher.

A leading St. Louis trade journal says:—"The magnitude of last year's business has made possible many changes and improvements; it has insured the carrying of larger and more varied stocks, been instrumental in obtaining railway concessions which heretofore seemed impossible, simplified and facilitated the quick, sure and speedy delivery of goods from department to shipping room, and from the shipping room to station. In short, it has been pregnant with result everywhere, and hastened the correction of any defect apparent in the system of buying, selling, or rapid delivery of merchandise. There is to-day no market in the country, taken as a whole, that is better prepared to meet and satisfy the demand which its tributary trade will make than the market of St. Louis."

Drugs, wholesale. St. Louis has several wholesale drug establishments whose annual business amounts to over 400,000*l*. One of them handles everything from a box of chewing-gum and a can of paint to the most expensive and rare drugs known, and has manufactories of perfumery articles connected with it. A manufactory of

Listerine and also one of Antekamenia do a world-wide business.

The increase in the trade over 1897 is reported as 200,000*l.*

Furniture. St. Louis furniture dealers had the biggest year in the history of the trade during the past 12 months.

Reports show shipments heavier and receipts of manufacturing materials consequently larger.

Department houses helped to swell trade, and make the jobber's profits larger. Retailers in many instances enlarged their stores.

Groceries. There are 27 exclusively wholesale grocery firms in the city, and five more which sell both wholesale and retail. Altogether they represent about 1,680,000*l.* of actual capital invested, and annual sales amounting to 13,000,000*l.* These latter figures are considered low by some wholesale grocers. The sales of retail establishments are not included, because they have nothing to do with the wholesale firms, save that they purchase from the latter.

The wholesale trade of St. Louis extends as far west as California, north to Canada, encroaching on territory which ought to belong to Chicago, and south to the Gulf, including the southern part of Illinois, some of Kentucky, Mississippi and even Alabama. This extensive territory, including the city of St. Louis, is traversed by fully 200 salesmen

The increase in trade, notwithstanding the war, amounts to about 15 per cent. over the year 1897, or nearly 1,800,000*l.*

Foreign grain trade. Exports. The exports of cereals did not assume the proportions that had been expected, in view of the large demand for breadstuffs from abroad. The total exports from the United States for the year shows a large increase over the previous year, being 148,053,394 bushels of wheat, as against 109,909,328 bushels for 1897, and 205,394,289 bushels of corn, as against 189,127,570 bushels for 1897.

St. Louis handled a large amount of grain for export, only a portion of which passed through the city, a large proportion, estimated at about 35,000,000 bushels, being shipped direct from points west of the Missouri River by rail to New Orleans, Galveston, and Port Arthur, and also the Atlantic seaboard.

The low railway rates of freight precluded shipment viâ St. Louis and the Mississippi River, thus diverting shipments which, under normal conditions, would seek the water route.

St. Louis standards of grain are well known and established in foreign markets, and, did freight conditions permit, the river route would do a large share of the business.

The amount forwarded from St. Louis during 1898 was 6,600,707 bushels, including wheat, corn, oats, and rye. In addition to this amount 342,260 bushels were taken viâ rail through Cairo and Belmont to New Orleans. In addition to the amount shipped viâ New Orleans nearly 17,000,000 bushels, principally corn and wheat, was exported by Atlantic seaports, making the total amount handled direct from St. Louis 23,942,967 bushels. Added to this, 35,000,000 bushels handled by St. Louis exporters from outside points makes the grain export trade from St. Louis during 1898 58,942,967 bushels.

Shipments were mainly to Great Britain, France, Germany and Holland.

STATEMENT of Bulk Grain Exported from New Orleans during 1898 and Comparisons to Previous Years.

To—	Quantity.			
	Wheat.	Corn.	Oats.	Rye.
	Bushels.	Bushels.	Bushels.	Bushels.
Great Britain	3,437,040	7,032,974	78,325	..
Ireland	84,215	2,138,181	..	17,500
France	3,746,433	4,319,963	1,531,859	143,666
Holland	2,261,945	1,860,263	..	..
Germany	1,374,339	3,151,843	..	96,809
Belgium	978,179	206,114	..	..
Denmark	127,970	1,150,946	..	24,708
Austria	800,000	..	..	..
Spain	72,535	83,000	..	..
Italy	26,000	..	..	..
Cuba	..	28,371	..	..
Total, 1898	12,908,656	19,971,655	1,610,184	282,683
,, 1897	10,195,693	27,239,639	1,365,063	240,242

The gross receipts for cotton during 1898 reached 899,229 bales, the largest amount ever received. The local receipts were 127,517 bales, to which should be added 23,318 bales, round bales cotton shipped on through bills of lading but actually sold in this market. In addition there were about 400,000 bales compressed at interior points, which were sold through this market by samples sent here and classified, the cotton itself being shipped from the compressor to the consumer. The receipts show an increase in nearly every State. From Arkansas 508,636 bales, Indian Territory 40,661 bales, against 3,964 bales the previous year. The shipments show 371,005 bales, of which 72,000 went to Canada, 11,803 to Japan, and 50 to China, 538,772 went to points in the United, States and the balance to European ports. The crop of 1897–98 is given at 11,199,994 bales, the largest ever grown.

Grain.

		Quantity.	
		Receipts.	Shipments.
Grain—			
Wheat	Bushels	14,240,252	11,026,765
Corn	,,	26,733,962	27,869,091
Oats	,,	10,725,380	5,975,364
Rye	,,	571,707	670,122
Barley	,,	2,001,911	52,933
Flour	Barrels	1,358,088	1,584,112

Cotton exports.

EXPORTS of Cotton.

Country.	Quantity.	
	1898.	1897.
	Bales.	Bales.
England	221,832	119,288
Germany	11,798	4,791
France	1,934	800
Belgium	500	176
Russia	670	..
Italy	9,104	25
Scotland	691	257
China	50	..
Sweden	500	..
Nova Scotia	..	793
Japan	11,803	668
Canada	72,123	22,643
Total	331,005	149,441

Average weight of cotton received at St. Louis 506 lbs., 5*l*. 15*s* per bale, or more than 64,000,000*l.* for the crop of 1897–98.

Fifteen corporations, firms, and companies in St. Louis are engaged in handling wholesale or in manufacturing hardware and implements. Not one of these failed in the year 1898 to increase its sales over 1897.

Hardware. Hardware men are of the opinion that the increase in their business altogether for the year will amount to 200,000*l.* In 1897 the sales in iron and heavy hardware alone amounted to 1,400,000*l.* Last year that figure was exceeded by 40,000*l.*

Ironwork. It is estimated that 5,000 men are directly engaged in this city in turning out structural ironwork. There are 20 corporations, firms, and companies in the city which make a speciality of this industry, and they represent investments of many million dollars. They turn out railings, roofs, ceilings, fences, columns, pillars, shutters, piping, beams, flooring, fittings, ornamental work, including cornices and corrugated ironwork. Some of the plants are very extensive, covering in one case two blocks, and generally a block. Of course, most of them have other outputs beside structural ironwork, but the men so employed are not included, nor is the value of the outputs.

Nearly all the ironwork on buildings which were put up in 1898 came from St. Louis. Each year since 1890 has recorded an increase in the demand for home-made material. This is due to the fact that all foundries make a speciality of structural ironwork, and can turn out an article equal, if not superior, to that of any other city. One or two buildings put up since 1890 have ironwork which came from other cities, but this was due to the fact that the contractors were outsiders who had contracts with outside corporations.

The war did not interfere with the structural ironwork industry. There was an increase in the demand, but how much it is impossible to estimate. The entire west and south-west depends upon St. Louis for its structural ironwork. The opening of new railroads has brought new territory to the front, which was quickly appropriated.

Bridge-building materials are included under this heading, and the demand for them was very good. Thousands of beams, columns, rods, and bolts were turned out and used on trestle work and railroad bridges in the south-west. One firm has a contract for 1899 to furnish a railroad with the material for eight iron bridges of various lengths.

Leather and hides. The demand for leather has increased with the larger shoe sales during the latter part of the past year, the feeling grew better, and as a consequence, comparison of receipts and shipments show interesting results.

During the year 1897 there were sold on the local market for shipment 78,781 rolls. During 1898 the city shipped 123,000 rolls, an increase of 44,219. This shows a gain in shipments of about 56 per cent.

Hides also show an increase, but not to such an extent as leather. Shipments from the local market for 1897 were 85,758,900, while for 1898 they were 70,345,355. Receipts were: 1897, 56,691,470; 1898, 67,355,205.

Paints and oils. While the figures are not yet known, St. Louis' trade in paints and oils has been the best during 1898 for many years. St. Louis is naturally for these articles the distributing point of the west, south, and north, and the demand is large. The sales of paints and paint oils for 1897 were, in round figures, 1,000,000*l*. For 1898 it is estimated that the sales will exceed those of the previous year by fully 15 per cent. One of the largest firms in St. Louis states that their business has been exceptionally large this year, and it is safe to say the same regarding other large firms in St. Louis, prices having materially advanced.

Growth of the Postal Service. The business in the St. Louis post-office has increased the past year about 11 per cent. over the year previous. St. Louis ranks fifth in gross receipts. The gross receipts of the five largest offices for the last fiscal year are as follows:—

	Amount.
	£
New York	1,684,829
Chicago	1,128,373
Philadelphia	593,910
Boston	578,329
St. Louis	339,321

Stoves.

Gasoline, gas, coal and wood stoves are turned out in St. Louis at an astonishing rate. Eleven corporations, firms, and companies, with a total capital of 1,400,000*l.*, are engaged in this industry, and employ about 3,000 men. One plant covers two blocks, and another a large block. The larger turns out everything in the heating and cooking line, from a grate to the old-fashioned crane, to a range large enough to cook the food for a regiment of soldiers. The other makes a speciality of ranges, and sells them all over the country. One firm, which makes a speciality of gas and gasoline stoves, manufactured and sold 3,000 more in 1898 than it did in 1897.

In 1897 the output of stoves and ranges was valued at 300,000*l.*, in 1898 it comes close to 360,000*l.*

Tobacco.

As a tobacco centre, St. Louis leads the country. It is located in the centre of the tobacco-producing States, and, therefore, has natural advantages which, combined with the activity and enterprise of the men engaged in the industry, have served to keep the city at the head of the tobacco markets. Millions of dollars are invested in warehouses and manufacturing plants, and thousands of men and women are employed.

The deal during the year, by which several large plants passed into the possession of a syndicate, had its advantage from the fact that it caused thousands of dollars to be expended in needed improvements, creating a demand for building materials of all kinds and new machinery. In this way thousands of citizens were benefited.

Not one of the acquired plants running when purchased has been shut down. For the coming year the largest of the purchased plants will have many more improvements made to it, and the money which formerly went for dividends will reach mechanics.

Within its boundaries St. Louis has one of the largest plug tobacco plants in the world, free from all combination. It alone furnishes employment, directly and indirectly, to 2,000 men and women, and has spent close upon 1,000,000 dol. since the cyclone in improvements.

This firm alone for the year 1898 turned out about 27,500,000 lbs. of plug tobacco. The other large plant, which was absorbed by the syndicate, put out, in round numbers, about 22,000,000 plugs. Then follow three other fair-sized plants, and some smaller ones, which put on the market about 15,000,000 lbs. At wholesale rates, the combined output of tobacco from St. Louis this year is valued at 5,400,000*l*. These figures are exclusive of the cigarette manufacturing industry, which has during the past few years furnished employment for hundreds, and investment for thousands of dollars. Neither is cigar-making or the smoking tobacco industry included. These three swell the output of manufactured tobacco close on to 10,000,000*l*.

In every line in the tobacco industry there has been an increase over the year 1897. It was especially marked in the manufacture of chewing tobacco, the leading factories recording an increase of about 10 per cent., and the others being not far behind.

The following statistics from the internal revenue show the exact amount of business in smoking and plug tobacco for the year. The revenue tax was doubled from June 13, 1898. Grand total collected by United States Internal Revenue Collector, First District, Missouri, for stamps for smoking and plug tobacco, from January 1, 1898, to and including December, 1898. Recapitulation, January to June 13, 34,901,512 lbs.; June 14, to December 27, 29,512,135 lbs.,; total, 64,413,647 lbs.

It will be noticed that from January 1 to June 13, while the tax was 6 c. per lb. this market sold 34,901,512 lbs. of smoking and plug tobacco, the period being five and a half months, and the Government revenues therefore amounting to 418,814*l*. But during a period of six and a half months, under the war revenue, this market sold only 29,512,135 lbs. or 5,389,377 lbs. less than the preceding five and a half months. However, the extra tax on the six and a half months made the total Government revenue run up to 708,291*l*. which was 289,477*l*. in excess of the first five and a half months of the year.

St. Louis is to-day the largest centre in the manufacture of smoking and plug tobacco in the world.

St. Louis is the extensive wooden and willow-ware centre, and has several large factories and wholesale houses devoted to this line. The year 1897 made strides in this industry and the year 1898 was still better, the increase ranging from 7 to 12 per cent. *Woodenware.*

Last year the output in this line amounted to about 1,400,000*l*. This year it is close to 1,600,000*l*.

The annual report of the State Mine Inspector reports both lead and zinc ores wonderfully increased for the year ending June 30, 1898, the increase in lead being 6,283 tons, and of zinc ore 46,520 tons. The prices for lead ore have been better than for the former year, but they did not reach the proportion increased in the prices on zinc, especially during the latter part of the year. *Mining industries of Missouri. Lead and zinc.*

The output of lead was 73,687 tons and sold for 622,211*l*. The output of zinc ore reached 139,668 tons and sold for 585,464*l*. The total value of the metals was 1,207,675*l*., an increase over the former year of 66 per cent. There has also been a large increase in the output of tripoli and barytes.

The receipts of rice were 127,275 packages against 95,801 *Rice.*

(348)

packages in 1897, showing an increase of 31,474 packages over 1897.

Sugar. The receipts of sugar in 1898 were 223,314,100 lbs., showing a falling-off of 2,224,125 lbs. from 1897.

Wool. The total receipts of wool in 1898 were 23,710,715 lbs., showing a falling-off of 7,154,695 lbs. from 1897.

Lumber. The total receipts by river of lumber of all kinds amounted to 46,395,100 feet in 1898, as against 57,322,780 feet in 1897, showing a falling-off of 10,927,680 feet. The total receipts of lumber and logs by river and railroad amounted to 964,468,100 feet in 1898, against 818,998,922 feet in 1897.

Live-stock. The receipts of cattle in 1898 were 795,611 head, showing a falling-off of 165,152 head from 1897.

The receipts of sheep were 477,091 head, and showed a falling-off of 183,289 head from 1897.

The receipts of hogs were 2,136,328 head, which showed an increase of 1,298,045 head over 1897.

The receipts of horses and mules were 128,342 head in 1898, showing an increase of 22,972 head over 1897.

Potatoes. The receipts of potatoes in 1898 were 3,108,676 bushels, against 2,566,055 bushels in 1897, an increase of 542,621 bushels over 1897.

ST. LOUIS.

CUSTOM-HOUSE Transactions.—Condensed Classification of Commodities Imported into St. Louis during the Year ending December 31, 1898, showing Foreign Value and Duty Paid.

Commodities.	Value.	Duty.
	£	£ s. d.
Ale and stout	3,480	1,442 0 0
Anvils	2,538	722 5 0
Art work	545	108 19 0
Books and printing matter	1,494	375 7 0
Brushes and brooms	1,499	599 12 0
Bone and horn, manufactured	855	256 9 0
Cloth, oil	1,642	512 6 0
Cement	1,740	372 7 6
Chemicals and drugs	26,871	7,335 6 0
China and earthenware	22,789	13,525 11 6
Corks, manufactured	9,292	2,337 1 6
Cutlery	9,927	6,372 19 6
Diamonds and precious stones	3,871	396 6 6
Dolls and toys	3,054	1,070 17 0
Fish	10,285	1,451 13 6
Free goods	49,454	..
Glass and glassware	1,651	832 3 0
Guns and firearms	9,135	3,943 2 6
Marble	4,333	2,447 6 0
Manufactured cotton	88,948	59,674 15 10
,, linen	6,408	3,702 15 0
,, leather	289	84 6 0
,, metal	6,212	2,786 17 6
,, paper	6,206	1,921 17 0
,, silk	9,927	5,486 5 0
,, wood	2,510	736 3 3
,, wool	5,646	5,399 15 10
Paints, colours, and oils	2,165	561 15 2
Rice, granulated	33,251	5,046 2 6
Wire, steel	16,877	6,911 11 5
Spirituous liquors	1,915	2,268 5 0
Tobacco and cigars	11,675	13,384 7 0
Wines, sparkling	13,214	6,295 4 0
Window-glass	73,543	33,312 16 8
Woollen fabrics	74,632	35,435 10 6
Straw matting	12,512	5,606 10 0
Miscellaneous	9,765	5,993 13 6
Collections from all other sources	..	4,593 8 0
Total	540,150	243,303 11 8

(348)

ST. LOUIS.

Comparative Business in Leading Articles at St. Louis during the Years 1897–98.

Articles.		Quantity. 1897.	Quantity. 1898.
Flour, amount manufactured	Barrels	1,080,916	1,054,875
Wheat, total receipts	Bushels	12,057,735	14,240,252
Corn "	"	31,077,440	26,733,962
Oats "	"	12,147,225	10,725,380
Rye "	"	712,428	571,707
Barley "	"	1,605,811	2,001,911
All grain received (including flour)	"	63,581,364	60,384,608
Cotton, receipts	Bales	734,819	986,193
Bagging, manufactured	Yards	9,000,000	..
Hay, receipts	Tons	178,516	127,263
Tobacco, receipts	Hogsheads	53,850	48,618
Lead, receipts in pigs of 80 lbs.	Pigs	2,280,548	2,830,012
Hog product, total shipments	Lbs.	391,676,519	305,746,800
Cattle, receipts	Head	960,763	795,611
Sheep "	"	660,380	477,091
Hogs "	"	2,065,283	2,136,328
Horses and mules, receipts	"	105,570	128,542
Lumber and logs "	Feet	818,998,972	964,468,110
Shingles, receipts	Pieces	67,789,000	90,375,000
Laths "	"	9,667,350	9,547,350
Wool, total receipts	Lbs.	30,865,410	23,710,715
Hides "	"	59,372,110	58,716,130
Sugar, received	"	225,538,650	223,514,100
Molasses (including glucose), received	Gallons	4,486,970	3,838,830
Coffee, received	Bags	320,005	274,228
Rice, receipts	Packages	95,801	127,275
Coal "	Bushels	85,730,980	83,562,450
Nails "	Kegs	681,930	572,847
Potatoes, receipts	Bushels	2,566,055	3,108,696
Salt, receipts	Barrels	351,635	383,120
" "	Sacks	33,045	48,280
" (in bulk)	Bushels	419,450	451,540
Butter	Lbs.	15,253,165	14,905,745
Freight of all kinds received and shipped	Tons	19,104,579	20,948,337

DENVER.

Mr. Vice-Consul Pearce reports as follows:—

Review. The conditions of trade and commerce of the city of Denver and State of Colorado for the year 1898 were generally favourable, and in nearly all departments of business a decided improvement is shown.

New buildings. The total cost of buildings erected in Denver during the year was 346,400*l.*, an increase over 1897 of 96,180*l.* The number of building permits issued show an increase of 194. Building operations were largely confined to dwelling-houses.

The United States Government is erecting a building in Denver to be used as a coinage mint, the cost of which will be 100,000*l.*

Real estate. It is impossible to obtain a correct report of the transactions in real estate for the year, but prominent dealers state that there was a considerable increase in the value of the property transferred over that of the previous year. A slight advance in prices is reported.

Clearing-house. The records of the bank clearing-house of Denver show a total of 30,271,169*l.*, an increase of 5,388,320*l.* over 1897.

Banks. The condition of the four national banks in the clearing-house at the close of the year is given as follows:—

	Amount.
	£
Deposits	5,775,171
Loans and discounts	2,537,986
Resources	6,563,932

As compared with 1897 this shows an increase as follows:—

	Amount.
	£
Deposits	1,049,520
Loans and discounts	325,628
Resources	1,231,479

Custom-house. The values of imports passing through the custom-house for the year were as follows:—Lead ore, 42,900*l.*, decrease from 1897 of 25,100*l.* Merchandise, 30,600*l.*, increase of 6,362*l.*

Post office. The gross receipts at the Denver post office for the year were 84,306*l.*, an increase of 5,640*l.* over 1897.

Manufacturing. The following is a summary of the manufacturing industry of Denver, including the product of the smelting companies for the years 1897–98:—

Year.	Number of Men.	Amount of Wages Paid.	Value of Product.
		£	£
1897	16,669	2,198,156	8,690,340
1898	13,276	1,484,748	9,476,747

Taxable property. The total assessed valuation of taxable property in the State for the year was 38,448,616*l.*, a decrease of 1,008,686*l.* from 1897.

Agriculture. Agricultural conditions in the State show very little change from those given in my last report. The acreage under cultivation was practically the same, but the harvest was not as large as in 1897, owing to a partial shortage of water and to unfavourable weather in many localities.

The estimated value of the agricultural products for the year is as follows:—

	Value.
	£
Wheat	840,000
Alfalfa	1,200,000
Clover and timothy	180,000
Natural grasses	400,000
Corn, oats, barley, and other grains	800,000
Potatoes	350,000
Garden products	800,000
Dairy products	1,455,447
Poultry	15,457
Wool	170,000
Hides	90,000
Honey	12,600
Total	6,313,504

This shows a falling-off from 1897 of 287,096*l.*

Fruit. Reports to the Secretary of the State Board of Horticulture show the orchard-bearing area of the six leading fruit-growing counties in the State to be 29,633 acres; planted, but not yet bearing, 35,736 acres; number of trees planted in 1898, 716,000.

The value of all the horticultural products for 1898 is estimated at 800,000*l.*, a falling-off from 1897 of 200,000*l.* During the year there was an increased demand for Colorado fruit from many Eastern States, owing to its excellent quality.

Live-stock. The live-stock industry of the State for 1898 shows a marked improvement over that of 1897, due principally to the increased receipts of cattle and sheep from other States, and the general advance in prices.

Following is the estimated number and value of live-stock in Colorado:—

	Number.	Value.
		£
Cattle	1,075,850	5,207,134
Milch cows	96,440	665,436
Sheep	1,784,365	902,888
Hogs	29,600	29,896
Horses	156,000	799,884
Mules	8,590	82,402
Total	3,150,845	7,687,640

Increase in value over 1897, 2,373,000*l.*

DENVER.

The future of Denver as a live-stock market is apparently assured on account of its central position, and the Denver Stockyards Company were compelled during the year to make very extensive improvements to provide additional capacity for the largely increased receipts.

The estimated value of live-stock received at the stock-yards in 1898 compared with 1897 is given as follows:—

Year.	Value.			
	Cattle.	Sheep.	Hogs.	Horses.
	£	£	£	£
1898	2,030,532	199,472	121,129	27,780
1897	1,939,319	125,183	118,437	13,476
Increase	91,213	74,289	2,692	14,304

The value of the products of the dairy farms in the State for the year shows a large increase over the previous year, being 1,455,447l. against 500,000l. in 1897. Considerably less butter was imported into the State than in 1897.

Dairy products and poultry.

The estimated value of the poultry and egg supply of the State for the year is 404,960l., which is more than double that of 1897.

During the year 38 miles of new railroad have been added to the 4,770 miles of railway already existing, making a total of 4,808 miles. The business done for the year has been generally satisfactory.

Railroads.

The iron and steel industry of the State for the year shows a large increased production over that of 1897 as indicated by the following table:—

Iron and steel.

Articles.	Quantity.	
	1897.	1898.
	Lbs.	Lbs.
Pig-iron	14,743,290	197,136,440
Spiegel	..	5,643,310
Steel rails	..	164,893,279
Merchant iron	38,194,536	43,515,653
Castings	1,643,810	13,787,226
Spikes, bolts, nuts	7,790,731	11,918,242
Iron ore	47,927,300	447,794,600

The value of this product is 906,449l. an increase over the previous year of 733,038l.

During the year 40,000 tons of manganese iron-ore were shipped from the Leadville district to Chicago, for use in the manufacture of steel.

DENVER.

Coal. The production of coal for the year was the largest in the history of the State, amounting to over 4,000,000 tons, the value of which amounts in round numbers to 1,400,000*l*. The prolonged strike in the northern coalfields, in the spring and summer, caused the production of that portion of the State to fall off, but the difference was made up by the increased output of the mines of Southern Colorado. At the close of the year all mines were in active operation and 7,500 men given steady employment.

TABLE showing Output of Coal by Counties during the Years 1897-98.

Counties.	Quantity. 1897. Tons of 2,000 lbs.	Quantity. 1898. Tons of 2,000 lbs.
Arapahoe	413	514
Boulder	607,890	491,503
El Paso	27,906	48,388
Fremont	319,641	437,086
Gunnison	319,116	361,113
Garfield	237,277	240,981
Huerfano	361,702	553,196
Jefferson	7,650	11,925
Las Animas	1,406,455	1,684,183
La Plata	74,805	107,705
Larimer	6,000	2,843
Mesa	27,611	19,167
Pitkin	147,461	182,927
Weld	21,733	22,506
Small mines, estimated	..	10,000
Total	3,565,660	4,174,037

Coke. The production of coke for the year was 445,925 tons, an increase of 144,963 tons over 1897.

Oil. The oil production for the year is estimated at 730,000 barrels valued at 146,000*l*., which is practically the same as in 1897.

Stone. The several quarries of the State produced during the year building and all other classes of stone and marble, to the estimated value of 400,000*l*., an increase over 1897 of 302,000*l*.

TABLE showing Value of the Output of the Mines in Colorado during the Year 1898.

	Value.
	£
Gold	4,635,452
Silver	2,891,314
Lead	878,983
Copper	366,300
Total	8,772,049

This shows an increase in value over 1897 of 1,861,445*l*.

The average price of silver for the year was 58 c. per oz., as against $59\frac{7}{10}$ c. in 1897.

The State Bureau of Mines gives the average number of men employed in metalliferous mining during the whole year as 30,231.

The increase in yield of gold, as shown in the above statement, is largely due to Cripple Creek's increased production. In my report for 1897 I stated that a very conservative estimate showed a yield of gold for that year from Cripple Creek of about 500,000 oz., or a value of 2,000,000*l*. I have made some careful enquiries in reference to the output for 1898, and the following figures will represent the tons of ore mined, together with the value of the output: 100,000 tons high grade ore sent to smelters, contained 375,000 ozs. of gold, 225,000 tons of lower grade ore, sold to the various chlorination and cyanide mills, contained 332,500 ozs. of gold, or a total of 707,500 ozs., showing a gross value of 2,830,000*l*.

It may be of interest to know that the Cripple Creek district continues to show, as a result of further developments from year to year, very marked indications of permanency. The veins or zones of ore have been in many cases explored to the depth of from 900 to 1,000 feet, at which point they continue to yield the usual quantity and quality of ore.

I have to report that there have been no fresh mining discoveries of importance made in Colorado during the year.

DENVER.

STATEMENT of Values of Imports from Great Britain Entered at the Port of Denver during the Year 1898.

Articles.	Value.
	£ s.
Indiarubber..	60 8
Iron and steel	188 0
Jewellery	102 0
Wood, manufactures of	126 0
Earthenware	1,894 0
Cotton goods	290 8
Wool goods..	902 16
Tobacco and pipes..	112 0
Spirits	328 0
Wine	58 0
Tea..	823 8
Effects	1,160 0
Toys..	130 0
Seeds	64 0
Books	112 0
Plants	28 0
Silk goods	90 0
Glassware	227 0
Live rabbits	20 0
Leather goods	84 0
Silver ware	168 0
Bamboo	12 0
Total	6,980 0

RECORD of Imports from Great Britain for the Past 10 Years.

Year.	Value.
	£ s.
1889	17,585 7
1890	32,512 4
1891	26,008 16
1892	9,357 4
1893	6,603 16
1894	4,984 4
1895	6,481 4
1896	7,366 12
1897	4,275 8
1898	6,980 0

During the year 20,000,000 lbs. of lead ore, valued at 80,000*l*., passed through the custom-house here in bond, from British Columbia. This ore was treated by the Colorado smelters, and the lead shipped by way of Galveston to Liverpool and Havre.

ST. PAUL.

Mr. Vice-Consul Morphy reports as follows:—

During the past few years the State of Minnesota has passed through the fiery furnace of depression. It has come out all right; business of all kinds and industries of all kinds have felt the revival, and things are now in a very promising condition. *Condition of business.*

The general distribution of wealth is shown by the existence of over 500 financial institutions with total resources aggregating 30,000,000*l*. *Wealth.*

The assessed value of the State is over 120,000,000*l*. *Assessed value.*

The population is 1,600,000. *Population.*

There are 600 miles of railway worked by 32 different companies. *Street railways.*

The area sown in wheat in 1898 was 3,101,000 acres yielding 53,957,000 bushels. The oat acreage last year was 1,849,000, yielding 58,244,000 bushels. *Area of wheat sown.*

Fully one-half of the flax raised in the United States grows in Minnesota. *Flax.*

Regarding the deposits of ore, when the census of 1880 was taken, Minnesota did not appear in the list of iron-producing States, yet to-day she stands fourth in the Union. In 1884 the first shipments of ore were made amounting to 64,000 tons. The shipment in 1898 exceeded 3,000,000 tons. *Product of iron.*

Copper and silver have been found along the north shore of Lake Superior, and free-milling gold-bearing rock is found along Rainy Lake and River, and 20 or more stamp mills are at work at or near the Ontario boundary line. *Silver and copper.*

The city of St. Paul has an area of 35,482 acres or 55 square s, and a population of 175,000. *St. Paul city and population.*

According to the official returns the banks have a capital and surplus of over 1,400,000*l*., with deposits of over 4,000,000*l*., and loans amounting to over 3,000,000*l*. *Banks.*

There are railways radiating from St. Paul with a mileage of 34,811. There are seven lines of railway from St. Paul to Chicago and the east, four to Lake Superior, five to the Canadian province of Manitoba, four to the Pacific coast, three to the south-west, and four to the south. *Railways.*

The city is the distributing point of the west as far as the Pacific Ocean, and to the north-west as far as the International boundary. *St. Paul distributing point.*

The amount of business done by the wholesale houses during the past year was over 32,000,000*l*. *Wholesale business.*

There are 579 manufacturing concerns in the city employing over 15,000 people. The manufactures are as follows:—Boots and shoes, saddlery, clothing, paints, fur goods, cigars, baking powder, brass foundings, furniture, stoves, ranges, agricultural implements, and fire engines. The amount of manufacturing done during the past year is 15,000,000*l*. *Manufacturing.*

Business in all branches during the past year has been good.

ST. PAUL.

The wholesale houses did a greater volume of business than ever before in the history of the city.

Real estate is improving in value throughout the State, there being a keen demand for good farms by actual settlers.

Real estate in the city is improving in value, although there is not the same demand for city property as there is for farm lands.

It is anticipated that the following year will show a great improvement in all branches of business over 1898.

OMAHA.

Mr. Vice-Consul Hall reports as follows:—

The city of Omaha is located on the western bank of the Missouri River and has a population of about 150,000, which is constantly growing. The locality is said to be one of the healthiest in the United States, and the death-rate of the city is relatively less than in any other city of its size. This is in part attributed to its excellent drinking water, and to its splendid drainage and sewerage system. Though the population in 1898 increased in that year the death-rate was less than that of the previous year.

The past year has been a most prosperous one, and has been marked by progress and development in nearly every line of business, so that there has not been for a long time such a confident feeling concerning future prosperity as exists here to-day.

Business generally. Retailers, manufacturers and dealers generally report a most encouraging state of affairs, which is all the more appreciated because of the low condition which existed here for a number of years, owing to failure of crops throughout the country, low prices for products, and scarcity of money.

Trans-Mississippi and International Exposition. Omaha was particularly fortunate during the year 1898 in its Trans-Mississippi and International Exposition which opened on June 1 and continued to November 1, and which was in many respects the most successful of the kind ever held. Over 450,000*l.* were spent in its construction and maintenance, and upwards of 3,000,000 of visitors passed within its gates, the record day being that on which President McKinley honoured it with his presence, when he was greeted by 100,000 persons.

Some idea of the successful management of the Exposition may be had from the fact that within five days after its gates closed 75 per cent. of the paid up stock was returned by the management to the stockholders.

Canadian exhibit. The Canadian Government and some Canadian exhibitors made very creditable displays, from which they doubtless received great benefit. The manufacturers from the United Kingdom were, however, conspicuous by their absence.

Greater American Exposition. The beautiful buildings and grounds will not be destroyed

OMAHA.

at once, as was the case with those of the World's Fair in Chicago, as already preparations on a large scale are being made to hold another Exposition in 1899 in the same place, commencing July 1, and lasting for four months. Prospective exhibitors, concessionnaires and others can secure full information by addressing the Secretary of the Greater America Exposition, Omaha, Nebraska, U.S.A. Certainly no better means can be found to introduce British goods into this western country if the attendance of visitors be anywhere near that of the one held during the past year.

Public schools. The Omaha public schools are among the best in the land and are conducted on the most improved modern methods. The 40 buildings with surrounding grounds are valued at 320,140l., and each year some additions are made to keep pace with the constantly increasing attendance.

Real estate. The transfers of real estate for 1898 amounted to 1,246,573l., being an increase over 1897 of over 100,000l. Among brokers and dealers it is confidently expected that 1899 will show still greater activity and results.

Bank clearings. The clearings through the banks were nearly 64,000,000l., being an increase over 1897 of 31 per cent., though the average increase through the United States as a whole was only 20 per cent.

Post office. At the Post-office the total receipts were 71,535l., as against 57,171l. the previous year.

Imports. At the custom-house the duties collected on imports amounted to 193,566l. as against 159,259l. the previous year, being an increase of over 20 per cent.

Imports from United Kingdom. Of goods received from foreign countries the following were from the United Kingdom.

Articles.	Value. 1897.	Value. 1898.
	£	£
Crockery and chinaware	800	952
Ginger ale and bottled beer	1,280	1,280
Linen canvas	375	96
Horn combs	51	50
Pickles	..	500
Laces	..	308
Farm and garden seeds	..	46
Olive oil	105	..
Furs	..	145
Burlap	454	..
Salt	611	73
Cotton cloth	26	21

OMAHA.

IMPORTS FROM CANADA.

Articles.	Value.	
	1897.	1898.
	£	£
Maple sugar	706	1,975
Silver ore	133,400	90,321
Lead ore..	62,040	50,844

Smelting works. — In this connection it may not be amiss to state that the biggest smelter in the country is located here, which accounts for the large amount of ore which came from British Columbia.

Of course a vast amount of imports received here and distributed through the West is entered at other ports, notably New York.

Cement. — Dealers in English cement report a few thousand barrels sold in 1898, but the price of this compared with cement of German and American make is so high as to practically preclude its use in this country.

Jobbers and manufacturers. — It is estimated that there has been an increase of 25 per cent. in the jobbing and manufacturing trade over 1897, and the volume of business done, including the meat packing-houses at South Omaha, amounted to about 35,000,000*l*. It took 575 travelling salesmen, 1,229 office clerks, and 12,766 factory and warehouse hands to deal with the output, and they were paid 1,560,656*l*. in salaries and wages. One implement dealer received 30 car loads in one shipment containing 1,000 buggies valued at 10,000*l*., which indicates the magnitude of the business done.

City bonds. — The credit of the City of Omaha has always been high, but it was thought that no western city could sell 4 per cent. bonds above par, yet in 1898 the city sold over 60,000*l*. of such bonds at a good premium.

Railways. — In railway circles the changed conditions for the better have been felt in a marked degree. Two new lines of railway have entered the city in the past year, so that now 14 systems centre here, and, with their numerous branches threading Nebraska and the surrounding States, make this city the great distributing centre for the West. This fact is being recognised more and more, and it is said that two, if not more, other large systems are contemplating having Omaha on their time-tables in the near future. A magnificent new brick and stone depôt has just been erected by the B. & M. R. R. at a cost of 70,000*l*., and opposite it the Union Depôt is now being erected, which will cost about the same sum. There has been a noticeable improvement in road beds and in rolling-stock generally, and altogether the past year has been prosperous for the railway companies.

Stockyards. — In South Omaha, the adjoining municipality, are located the immense stockyards and packing-houses which constitute the

OMAHA.

third greatest packing centre in the word. In the past year one company alone completed an entire new plant at an outlay of 400,000l., and many additions and improvements were made by the other companies, so that now over 100 acres are covered by buildings, pens, yards, sheds, &c. The following comparative statement of receipts and shipments of live-stock will indicate the magnitude of the business transacted.

	Receipts.		Shipments.	
	1897.	1898.	1897.	1898.
Cattle	822,447	824,096	355,175	322,194
Hogs	1,651,317	2,150,282	83,061	172,024
Sheep	640,128	1,104,390	205,617	483,171
Total	3,113,892	4,078,768	643,853	977,389

Packing-houses. The packing-houses have a daily killing capacity of 7,850 cattle, 25,500 hogs, and 13,000 sheep, and in 1898 over 40,000 car loads of finished products were shipped away, as against 33,000 car loads in 1897, showing a gain of about 21 per cent. In addition to the meat packing industry, large quantities of soap, tallow, caustic, glycerine, lard, and other by-products are manufactured and shipped abroad.

Exports. A large percentage of the meat products, chiefly hams, bacon, lard, and canned meats, are exported to Great Britain, one company alone in 1898 reporting sales of 400,000l.

Horses and mules. The stockyards at South Omaha have also developed into an extensive market for the sale of horses and mules, 9,797 being received in 1897, and 12,468 in 1898.

Acreage. Nebraska contains nearly 50,000,000 acres of land, of which 10,000,000 acres are yet owned by the Government. About one-third is under cultivation, so there is plenty of room for growth.

Crops. Corn continues to be the staple crop, but all kinds of grain and seeds are raised.

The following comparative table will indicate the results for the last year—

	1898.			1897.	
	Area	Quantity.	Number of Bushels Per Acre.	Area.	Quantity.
	Acres.	Bushels.		Acres.	Bushels.
Corn...	7,560,000	160,000.000	21	9,043,000	185,000,000
Wheat	2,115,000	35,000,000	16½	2,126,000	42,510,000
Oats...	1,753,000	56,250,032	32	2,843,000	85,000,000
Barley	...	...	...	119,000	3,550,000
Rye ...	...	...	...	41,000	803,000
Flax...	...	...	...	99,000	...
Millet	...	...	...	15,000	...
Potatoes	...	...	...	...	7,000

(348)

Fruit. Fruit of all kinds is grown in abundance, there being shipped in one year over 2,000,000 bushels of apples, 850 tons of grapes, and 5,000,000 boxes of small fruits.

Sugar beets. Two large beet sugar factories are in operation and two more are projected for 1899, as it has been found that the manufacture of beet sugar is a very profitable industry. The farmer likewise reaps good results by growing beets, as is shown from the fact that from 10 to 12 tons to the acre have been raised at a cost of 5*l*. per acre when the selling price was 1*l*. 6*s*. per ton thus showing a profit of from 7*l*. to 9*l*. to the acre. Some 50,000 tons were grown in 1898 and ground into sugar at the factories.

Hemp. About 5,000 acres were planted in hemp, which yielded about 23,000 tons at 1*l*. 12*s*. per ton.

Flax. Many thousands of acres have in recent years been devoted to flax, the seed finding a ready market at Omaha, where one of the largest mills in the west is located.

Chicory. About 3,000 acres were devoted to chicory in 1898, and the crop yield was from 6 to 10 tons per acre, worth at the factories about 1*l*. 8*s*. per ton. A large plant has been erected at Omaha to prepare the raw material for the market and this is supplemented by two large factories in the State, so that the industry is likely to become prominent and permanent.

Cattle. But the feeding and raising of cattle in Nebraska in 1898 received more attention than did any other industry, particularly of the western and northern parts of the State where millions of acres are available for ranches, less than 20 per cent. of these portions being under cultivation, and the comparatively mild winters enable the cattle to flourish without being housed. In December last one shipment of 30 cars of wire fencing was received, sufficient to construct a fence over 400 miles in length, as the ranches are being gradually enclosed by the farmers and ranchers, thereby enabling them to keep better trace of the cattle. In the past year 490,000 were shipped to the Omaha stockyards.

Sheep. Sheep feeding has also developed extensively, over 1,000,000 being prepared for the market in the past year.

Hogs. While the fear of cholera has deterred many from breeding hogs, yet there has been a notable increase in the supply, particularly of thoroughbred animals.

South Dakota. Gold mining. The great feature of this State is the gold-mining in the Black Hills in the western part. There are located the great wealth-producing mines which yielded 1,160,000*l*. in 1898, as against 1,060,000*l*. in 1897. Seven of the leading mines have paid since their operation the enormous sum of 2,400,000*l*. in dividends.

Hot springs. In the Black Hills are likewise located the famous hot springs, being more than 75 in number, which have a temperature of from 85 to 95 degrees Fahrenheit, and which are possessed of wonderful medicinal qualities.

Agriculture. The eastern part of the State is devoted largely to agricultural pursuits, and it is said that the past year showed a gain over previous years, both in acreage cultivated and in the crop yield.

Cattle. Much attention is being given to raising cattle for the Omaha market and likewise for dairy purposes, over 100 creameries having been erected in the past two years.

To sum up the situation in these two States, we are safe in saying that never before in their history have they been in such a flourishing condition, and whoever invests his money either in the lands or mines or manufacturing and business industries, and looks after it with a reasonable degree of care and caution has the almost certain assurance that he will receive a fairly good income from his investment.

LONDON :
Printed for Her Majesty's Stationery Office,
By HARRISON AND SONS,
Printers in Ordinary to Her Majesty.
(75 5 | 99--H & S 348)

No. 2256 Annual Series.

DIPLOMATIC AND CONSULAR REPORTS.

UNITED STATES.

REPORT FOR THE YEAR 1898

ON THE

TRADE AND COMMERCE OF THE CONSULAR DISTRICT OF NEW YORK.

REFERENCE TO PREVIOUS REPORT, Annual Series No. 2081.

Presented to both Houses of Parliament by Command of Her Majesty,
MAY, 1899.

LONDON:
PRINTED FOR HER MAJESTY'S STATIONERY OFFICE,
BY HARRISON AND SONS, ST. MARTIN'S LANE,
PRINTERS IN ORDINARY TO HER MAJESTY.

And to be purchased, either directly or through any Bookseller, from
EYRE & SPOTTISWOODE, EAST HARDING STREET, FLEET STREET, E.C., and
32, ABINGDON STREET, WESTMINSTER, S.W.; or
JOHN MENZIES & Co., 12, HANOVER STREET, EDINBURGH, and
90, WEST NILE STREET, GLASGOW; or
HODGES, FIGGIS, & Co., Limited, 104, GRAFTON STREET, DUBLIN.

1899.

[C. 9044—82.] *Price Twopence Halfpenny.*

CONTENTS.

	PAGE
NEW YORK—	
General remarks	5
Treasury gold reserve	5
Agricultural products	5
Mining—	
Gold	6
Silver	6
Copper	6
Lead	6
Spelter	6
Production of pig-iron	6
Railways	7
Exports and imports	7
New York money market	8
„ banks	9
„ clearing-house returns	9
Clearing outside New York	10
New York Stock Exchange	10
„ produce exchange	10
„ cotton exchange	10
Sterling exchange in London	10
Failures	11
State banks of deposit and discount	14
Debt of State of New York	16
New York City debt	16
Freights	17
Time charters	18
Shipping at New York	19
New lines	19
Public works—	
Canals	19
Ship canals	21

(368)

Contents—continued.

	Page
NEW YORK—continued—	
Public works—continued—	
Proposed improvement of water front	21
Improvement of harbour	21
Railroad goods traffic	22
Vital statistics	22
Immigration	23
Labour conditions	24
Effect of immigration	25
Report of factory inspector	26
Strikes	27
Comparative prices of staple commodities	27
Trade and commerce—	
Anthracite coal	28
Bituminous coal	28
Iron and steel	28
Dry goods—	
Cotton	29
Silk	30
Woollen	31
Flax and hemp	31
Leather	31
Hides	31
Cattle	32
Cheese	32
Scotch herrings	32
Sugar	32
Tables of exports and imports	32
Return of principal articles of export	34
„ „ import	35
Value of imports and exports by countries	37
Grain shipments	37
Return of shipping	38
„ number of seamen engaged, &c.	40
PROVIDENCE, RHODE ISLAND, trade report	41

No. 2256.

Annual Series.

Reference to previous Report, Annual Series No. 2081.

Report on the Trade and Commerce of the Consular District of New York for the Year 1898

By Mr. Consul-General Sanderson.

(Received at Foreign Office, April 20, 1899.)

General remarks. Following the improvement noted in 1897, the year 1898 has been one of extraordinary activity and prosperity from both the industrial and the financial point of view. In the beginning of the year progress was checked to a certain extent by the unsatisfactory conditions in Cuba and the prospect of war with Spain, but the war, when it came, was of short duration, American victories were unattended by anything in the shape of a reverse, and the effect was rather in the nature of a stimulus to trade than otherwise. In the autumn, again, there was a short period of uncertainty as the time for the elections to Congress approached, and the silver question came once more into notice; fears on this head, however, proved to be groundless, the elections showed that the silver party had lost ground even in the West, and the Republicans maintained control of the Lower House of Congress, in addition to obtaining a majority in the Senate, as it would be composed after March 4, 1899. The treaty of peace with Spain was signed on December 10, and the year closed with most branches of business at their best. Iron production reached its highest point in December, the cotton industry, which had been suffering from depression showed signs of recovery, the bank clearings were the largest on record for any month, and the gold reserve in the United States Treasury on December 31 amounted to 246,973,027 dol., which is higher than had ever been reached before.

Treasury gold reserve. The gold reserve in the United States Treasury was high throughout the year, due in some measure to the bond issue of 200,000,000 dol. in July, and also to the very large export trade.

Agricultural products. The crops were again very large, that of wheat, 675,000,000 bushels, being the largest ever produced in the United States, and about 145,000,000 bushels more than in 1897. The price of wheat was maintained at a high figure during the early part of the year by the dealings of a speculator on a very large scale, but

(368)

the operations closed somewhat disastrously in the month of June, and the average price received by farmers throughout the year, as estimated by the Agricultural Department, was lower than in 1897. On the other hand, the prices of Indian corn, oats, rye, and barley, were all somewhat higher. The price of cotton has again ruled extremely low, falling to 5¾ cents in October, and although there was some improvement at the close of the year, the price on January 1, 1899, was quoted at 5⅞ cents, or about $2\frac{15}{16}d.$ per lb.

The following table shows the average prices received by farmers and planters all over the country during the last six years as reported by the Agricultural Department.

AVERAGE Prices received by Farmers and Planters.

Articles.		1898.	1897.	1896.	1895.	1894.	1893.
		Cents.	Cents.	Cents.	Cents.	Cents.	Cents.
Wheat	Per bushel	58·2	80·8	72·6	50·9	49·1	53·8
Rye	,,	46·3	44·7	40·9	44·0	50·1	51·3
Oats	,,	25·5	21·2	18·7	19·6	32·4	29·4
Barley	,,	41·4	37·7	32·3	33·7	44·2	40·6
Indian corn	,,	28·7	26·3	21·5	26·4	45·7	36·5
Cotton	Per lb.	...	5·0	6·6	7·59	4·6	6·99

For purposes of rough calculation, the cent may be taken as equal to a half-penny.

The cotton crop of 1897–98 reached 11,180,000 bales; it was the largest on record, and followed large crops in former years. Very favourable conditions attended the planting of the crop of 1898–99, and this was estimated at between 11,750,000 and 12,000,000 bales.

Mining. Gold. The gold production of the United States continues to increase, the estimate for 1898 being 3,182,242 ounces, valued at about 13,156,000*l*., as compared with 2,774,935 ounces in 1897 and 2,568,132 ounces in 1896. The largest increase is from the gold mines of Colorado for the last two years, while the tendency has been towards a diminution in the yield from California, owing to the severe and prolonged drought interfering with placer mining.

Silver. The production of silver is estimated at 60,000,000 ounces, as compared with 53,860,000 in 1897 and 58,835,000 ounces in 1896.

Copper. The production of copper was estimated at about 235,000 tons. The figures in 1897 were production about 215,000 tons, and exports about 130,000 tons.

Lead. Spelter. The production of lead is estimated at a little over 200,000 tons, which was the amount in 1897; and that of spelter at 115,400 short tons (2,000 lbs. each), being an increase of about 15 per cent. as compared with 1897.

Production of pig-iron. The total production of pig-iron in the United States is returned at 11,773,934 tons in 1898, as compared with 9,652,680 tons in 1897, and 8,623,127 tons in 1896. This is the largest production on record, showing an increase of about 22 per cent. over 1897, when the output was the largest of any calendar year up to that date. The rate of production seems to have been tolerably even throughout the year in spite of declining prices during the earlier months, the first half year showing 5,869,703 tons and the second, when there was some slight advance in values, 5,904,231 tons. Prices throughout the year ruled low, but the consumption and export exceeded the production, large as it was. The stock at the close of the year was estimated at a little over 415,000 tons, as against 875,000 tons at the end of 1897; the import is estimated at about 150,000 tons, and the total consumed and exported at 12,383,579 tons, as compared with 9,783,178 tons in 1897, and 8,547,073 in 1896. In 1895, however, the consumption and export amounted to close on 10,000,000 tons.

Railways. The improvement in the earnings of the railways, which commenced in the latter part of 1897, was continued through 1898, and the gain during the year has been very large. Both the cotton traffic in the South and the grain traffic in the West and East increased largely; the crops were abundant and, although wheat was on the whole lower than in 1897, prices were good, and farmers were thus in a position to obtain large supplies. These circumstances and reviving trade, with increased shipments of merchandise and general freight, all tended to swell the revenues of the railroads. The transport of United States troops contributed in the same direction while there was comparative freedom from adverse influences. It is estimated that about 3,000 miles of new railroad were constructed in the United States in 1898, bringing the total up to about 187,500 miles in operation at the end of the year, and that the gross revenues, which had been increased by between 70,000,000 to 75,000,000 dol. in 1897, were further augmented by about 90,000,000 dol. or 18,000,000l., in 1898; the improvement continued throughout the year, but the larger part of the increase occurred during the first six months.

Exports and imports. The value of the total exports of merchandise from the United States during 1898 amounted to over 1,255,000,000 dol. (251,000,000l.), showing an increase of 156,000,000 dol., or upwards of 31,000,000l., over those of 1897, and of 249,000,000 dol. or nearly 50,000,000l. over those of 1896, each of which years had in turn surpassed all previous records in this respect. Taking the leading products, the shipments of cotton amounted to 8,146,617 bales as compared with 6,455,319 bales in 1897, and with 6,030,535 bales in 1896, but the fall in prices has reduced the values to 232,626,000 dol. in 1898 as against 212,745,576 dol. in 1897, and 233,412,777 dol. in 1896; breadstuffs valued at 317,755,833 dol. show an increase of about 25,000,000 dol. over 1897; provisions, &c., 174,735,106 dol., an increase of 29,000,000 dol.; cattle, sheep, and hogs, 34,365,884 dol., show a decrease of 6,500,000 dol., and there was also a decrease in the value of petroleum, 53,415,627 dol., as against 60,007,425 dol. in 1897. The total value of these articles

(368)

of export amounted in 1898 to 812,898,856 dol. (162,579,771*l*.), in 1897 to 711,424,284 dol. (142,284,857*l*.), and in 1896 to 653,369,675 dol. (130,673,935*l*.), showing an increase from year to year, and the same is the case with the remaining articles of export, including manufactures and miscellaneous goods, the figures being 442,026,313 dol. (88,405,263*l*.) in 1898, 388,284,761 dol. (77,656,952*l*.) in 1897, and 352,467,566 dol. (70,493,513*l*.) in 1896. On the other hand the value of the imports in 1898 amounted to only 634,958,229 dol. (126,991,646*l*.) as compared with 742,595,229 dol. (148,519,046*l*.) in 1897, and 681,579,556 dol. (136,315,911*l*.) in 1896. This is the smallest total since 1885. The comparison with 1897 is affected by the large imports which took place at the beginning of that year in anticipation of higher duties under the new tariff, and the war with Spain tended to check imports while it lasted, but irrespective of these facts the general tendency seems to be towards a diminution of imports. The values most affected were wool, unmanufactured, of which there was a decrease in quantity of about 255,000,000 lbs. and in value of about 8,400,000*l*. or nearly 80 per cent.; manufactures of wool which showed a decrease in value of over 5,000,000*l*. or about 63 per cent.; cotton, unmanufactured a decrease in quantity of about 9,000,000 lbs. and in value of 350,000*l*. equal to about 27 per cent.; manufactures of cotton, a decrease in value of about 750,000*l*. or somewhat less than 10 per cent.; wood, unmanufactured, where the decrease has been about 800,000*l*. or nearly 25 per cent.; and fibres, manufactured, a decrease of about 800,000*l*. or 24 per cent. There are also decreases in manufactures of iron and steel, and of leather, in tin-plate, sugar, tea, and a decrease of over 4,000,000*l*. in the value of coffee, the quantity imported remaining, however, much the same, namely somewhat over 800,000,000 lbs. On the other hand there has been an increase in the importation of copper and tin in bars, blocks, and ingots, in fibres, unmanufactured, hides, and crude indiarubber. The value of the exports of merchandise has been nearly double that of the imports, and the difference amounts to about 124,000,000*l*.

The import of gold ore, bullion, and coin on balance amounted to 141,956,898 dol., about 28,400,000*l*.; in the year 1897 there was an export balance of about 51,000*l*.

In silver there was an export balance of 24,670,848 dol. (4,935,000*l*.), showing a decrease as compared with 1897 of about 200,000*l*.

New York money market. Early in January the Re-organisation Committee of the Union Pacific Railroad made the final payment to the Treasury on account of the Government interest which had been purchased, and shortly afterwards rates which had reached 6 per cent. began to recede in view of the heavy payments made by the Treasury in this month. At the end of February a fall on the Stock Exchange and withdrawals of currency for the interior due to the fear of war with Spain led to a sharp advance, but large imports of gold in March and April caused a reaction, and in May rates had again been reduced to a very low point. In August payments into the United States Treasury on account of the loan of 200,000,000 dol. issued in July began to produce their effect, and these, combined with greater animation on the Stock Exchange and a prospective increase in the mercantile demand, led to a temporary hardening of rates; at the end of September there was, however, a downward tendency, and with the exception of a temporary rise at the end of December, the market was easy during the remainder of the year.

The rate for call money was 4 per cent. at the banks and 6 per cent. on the Stock Exchange at the beginning of January; in February, 1½ to 2 per cent.; March, 2 to 3 per cent.; April, 2 to 4½ per cent.; May, 4 per cent.; dropping to 1½ to 2 per cent. till September, when it fluctuated between 2 and 6 per cent.; and from that time till the close of the year it remained at 2 to 2½ per cent., with the exception of a few days in December, when as much as 6 per cent. was obtained.

The rate for choice 60 to 90 day commercial bills with two signatures was from 3 to 3½ and 4 in January and February, in March and April it gradually rose from 4 to 6, and in May declined gradually to 3½, and in December to 3.

The following table shows the position of the New York clearing-house banks at different periods of the year, the rate of conversion being 5 dol. to the 1l. :—

New York banks.

Week ending—	Loans.	Deposits.	Specie.	Legal Tender.	Reserve to Deposits.	Surplus Reserve.
	£	£	£	£	Per Cent.	£
January 8	121,955,400	137,118,500	21,317,700	17,614,840	28·24	4,452,900
February 5	126,771,960	146,765,500	22,817,640	20,830,060	29·73	6,956,320
March 5	125,657,280	141,204,080	24,025,180	15,840,540	27·94	4,164,700
April 2	119,170,240	136,447,360	28,311,240	12,944,760	30·21	7,144,160
May 7	114,217,040	131,922,380	31,958,300	9,805,840	31·65	8,783,280
June 4	120,323,660	141,883,920	35,100,420	10,820,500	32·35	10,449,940
July 2	124,196,760	150,014,920	37,214,040	12,692,400	33·26	12,402,700
August 6	129,899,960	151,410,320	33,797,600	12,033,580	30·26	7,978,600
September 3	134,434,780	150,477,960	29,677,660	10,942,040	27·00	2,998,200
October 1	127,114,560	140,425,640	27,262,880	10,908,960	27·17	3,065,420
November 5	135,769,020	153,817,280	31,485,760	10,773,220	27·46	3,804,600
December 3	139,549,480	157,905,160	31,692,460	11,203,420	27·13	3,419,580
,, 31	143,661,740	164,607,540	33,951,260	11,036,820	27·32	3,836,180

The surplus reserve represents the excess over 25 per cent. of the deposits, and the returns give the average of each week, not the actual figures for the day mentioned.

The maximum and minimum of deposits were:—maximum, 164,600,000l. on December 31, as compared with 115,000,000l. on December 11, 1897; and minimum, 131,700,000l. on April 30, as compared with 106,000,000l. on January 2, 1897; the maximum and minimum of reserve, 12,440,000l. on June 25, and 850,000l. on September 17, 1898, compared with 11,830,000l. on January 30, and 2,300,000l. on December 24, 1897.

The New York clearing-house returns show an increase of 25 per cent. over those of 1897, the figures being 41,971,782,437 dol. or about 8,394,356,500l., and 33,427,027,471 dol. or about 6,685,405,000l. respectively.

New York clearing-house returns.

NEW YORK.

Clearings outside New York.
The clearings outside New York amounted to 26,912,136,143 dol., an increase of 12½ per cent. over those of the previous year. The total clearings show an increase of over 20 per cent., the greater part of which occurred during the first and last quarters of the year. In the whole list of places furnishing clearing-house returns there were only four which showed a diminution during the year, namely, Providence and Fall River, in the New England district, where for a part of the year cotton goods, woollen goods and leather were very much depressed, and Macon and Augusta in Georgia, where the low price of cotton had an adverse influence. At the close of the year there was a general improvement, and the clearings in December were very large.

New York Stock Exchange.
The number of shares sold on the New York Stock Exchange was 112,700,000 as compared with 77,324,000 in 1897, and the approximate values are given at about 1,640,000,000l. in 1898 and 1,000,000,000l. in 1897. The number falls somewhat below that for the years 1881 and 1882, but the transactions in December, amounting to 15,250,000 million shares, is larger than has ever been reached in any previous month.

Produce exchange.
On the produce exchange the sales were only 994,000,000 bushels in 1898, as compared with 1,477,000,000 bushels in 1897. Wheat and flour show a remarkable diminution, caused in all probability by the Leiter speculations. There was an increase in the sales of Indian corn and rye, but a decrease in those of oats, barley, and malt.

Cotton exchange.
On the cotton exchange dealings are said to have been much restricted, but there is difficulty in ascertaining the volume of transactions, as the report of sales was discontinued in July.

Sterling exchange on London.
Sterling exchange on London has ruled lower than in 1897 or the previous five years. The following table gives the posted rates, highest and lowest, for each month in the year; these are fractionally higher as a rule than those for actual business.

NEW YORK.

TABLE showing the Posted Rates of Sterling Exchange on London for the Year 1898.

Month.		At 60 Days.	At Sight.
		Dollars.	Dollars.
January	highest	4·84	4·86
	lowest	4·82½	4·85½
February	highest	4·84	4·87
	lowest	4·82½	4·85½
March	highest	4·83	4·85½
	lowest	4·81½	4·84½
April	highest	4·82	4·86
	lowest	4·80½	4·84
May	highest	4·85	4·88
	lowest	4·81½	4·85
June	highest	4·85½	4·88
	lowest	4·81½	4·86
July	highest	4·85½	4·87
	lowest	4·84½	4·86
August	highest	4·85	4·86½
	lowest	4·84	4·86
September	highest	4·84½	4·86
	lowest	4·82	4·84½
October	highest	4·83½	4·87
	lowest	4·82	4·85
November	highest	4·83½	4·87
	lowest	4·82	4·85
December	highest	4·82½	4·86
	lowest	4·82	4·85½

Under ordinary circumstances the rate for bills payable on demand which admits of the export of gold from New York to London is about 4 dol. 88 c. for bars and 4 dol. 89 c. for coin, and the rate at which gold coin can be imported without loss is about 4·835 dol. per 1l.

The rate of exchange adopted in this report is the London Stock Exchange rate of 5 dol. to the 1l. As the true value of the 1l. at par is 4·8665 dol. the Stock Exchange valuation is about 2¾ per cent. below par, and accordingly the quotations of American securities are about 2¾ per cent. higher than in New York, a bond worth 100 in New York being quoted 102¾ in London.

The following, taken from the tables prepared by Messrs. R. G. Dun and Co., shows the number of commercial failures in the Consular district as well as those in the whole of the United States in 1898, as compared with 1897:— *Failures.*

	Number of Failures.		Amount of Liabilities.	
	1898.	1897.	1898.	1897.
			£	£
New York	1,333	1,871	4,447,106	6,196,047
Connecticut	339	350	489,135	483,806
New Jersey	196	132	445,325	382,178
Rhode Island	180	109	605,575	318,332
Delaware	25	47	28,890	42,260
Whole of the United States	12,186	13,351	26,132,580	30,866,414

The figures for the whole of the United States show a decrease in the number of failures of about 8¾ per cent. and in the liabilities of about 15 per cent. as compared with 1897, and they are the lowest figures in each case since 1892. In the State of New York there is a diminution in the number of failures of 28 per cent. and in the liabilities of about the same amount, there is also a diminution in Connecticut and Delaware as compared with 1897, but both New Jersey and Rhode Island show an increase. In the year 1897 the number of failures in the United States was 13,351, and the average liabilities for each failure 11,559 dol., or about 2,312*l.*, in 1898 the number was 12,186 and the average liabilities for each failure 10,722 dol., or about 2,145*l.*; as in 1897 the larger number of failures occurred in the first six months of the year, in 1898 however the average liabilities were larger in the latter part of the year.

In the tables published by Messrs. R. G. Dun and Co., showing the insolvencies, by branches of trade, among the manufacturers there is a large increase in the business of machinery and tools, 216 failures with liabilities amounting to 1,457,278*l.*, as compared with 177 and liabilities 942,864*l.* in 1897; in woollens, carpets, and knitted goods 46 failures with liabilities of 1,285,740*l.*, against 39 failures with liabilities of 298,372*l.* in 1897; and in chemicals, drugs, and paints, 66 failures with liabilities 566,671*l.*, against 78 failures with liabilities 164,000*l.* in 1897. On the other hand, in the business of iron, foundries, and nails the failures were only 55 with liabilities of 421,240*l.*, as compared with 108 and 1,189,167*l.* in 1897; and in cottons, lace, and hosiery 26 with liabilities of 403,315*l.*, against 59 and 1,960,143*l.* in 1897. There was also a considerable decrease in the number of failures and the amount of liabilities under the heads of printing and engraving, milling and bakers, and liquors and tobacco. The failures amongst traders show an increase under the heads groceries, meats and fish, and hats, furs and gloves, but a decrease under all other heads, and notably those of dry goods and carpets, and hardware, stoves and tools.

The figures published by Bradstreets differ slightly from the above as regards the totals. They classify the failures according to their primary causes under 11 heads. Eight of these imply faults of those failing, namely, incompetence, irrespective of other causes; inexperience without other incompetence; lack of capital, including trying to do too much business for the capital employed; granting of unwise credit; speculation outside of regular business; neglect of business due to doubtful habits; personal extravagance; fraudulent disposition of property. The remaining three heads refer to failures not due to the faults of those failing, namely, specific conditions (flood, fire, failure of crops, commercial crisis); failure of others, apparently solvent debtors; special or undue competition. The following summaries are taken from these tables:—

NEW YORK.

Number of Failures in the United States, with Amount of Liabilities and Percentage of Total.

	1898.			1897.			1896.			1892.		
	Number.	Liabilities.	Per Cent.	Number.	Liabilities.	Per Cent.	Number.	Liabilities.	Per Cent.	Number.	Liabilities.	Per Cent.
		£			£			£			£	
Incompetence ...	1,581	2,546,318	13·6	1,610	3,261,154	10·3	1,892	6,867,114	13·6	1,781	3,104,309	9·8
Inexperience ...	578	358,115	5·0	734	465,065	1·7	688	767,905	1·6	518	556,382	1·7
Lack of capital ...	3,968	7,570,076	34·1	4,108	7,489,597	23·6	4,609	10,194,538	20·7	4,305	8,424,695	26·1
Unwise credit ...	347	2,616,153	3·0	456	1,684,305	5·3	653	1,905,452	3·5	603	1,637,407	5·1
Speculation ...	117	962,673	1·0	106	1,614,421	5·1	182	2,118,435	4·3	146	1,203,064	3·7
Neglect	263	317,383	2·3	311	320,659	1·1	345	435,255	0·9	333	430,556	1·3
Extravagance ...	109	377,681	1·0	159	226,584	0·7	140	539,616	1·1	128	425,108	1·6
Fraud	1,195	2,236,525	10·3	1,338	3,724,960	11·6	1,395	2,769,028	5·7	1,154	2,105,998	6·9
Specific conditions	2,592	7,789,609	22·3	3,312	10,072,005	31·7	4,153	18,444,749	37·4	3,229	10,677,113	33·6
Failure of others	230	2,778,224	2·0	266	1,962,437	6·1	397	4,499,445	9·2	299	2,569,468	8·1
Competition ...	635	769,525	5·4	683	918,557	2·8	550	842,266	2·0	462	611,438	2·0
Total	11,615	28,322,282	...	13,083	31,739,744	...	15,094	49,383,803	...	12,968	31,745,538	...

The totals for 1898 as compared with those for 1897 show a decrease of 11·2 per cent. in number and of 10·8 per cent. as regards the amount of liabilities, and the figures are the lowest since 1892. Taken under the separate heads the only case in which the numbers show an increase is that of "Speculation," 117 as against 106; as regards the liabilities there is a considerable increase under the heads of "Unwise credit" and "Failure of others," but a large decrease under "Incompetence," "Fraud," and "Specific Conditions." The number of business firms is given at 1,093,373 in 1898 and the number of failures 11,615 represents a trifle over 1 per cent.; if Canada be included the number of firms reported as carrying on business is given as 1,182,093 and the failures as 13,085, a slightly-increased percentage, but still only about 1·1 per cent. Of these 11,888, or 91 per cent., were trading with a capital not exceeding 1,000*l.*; 788, or 6 per cent., with a capital of between 1,000*l.* and 4,000*l.*; 263, or 2 per cent., with a capital of from 4,000*l.* to 10,000*l.*; 80 with a capital of between 10,000*l.* and 20,000*l.*; 58 with 20,000*l.* to 100,000*l.*; and 10 with a capital of over 100,000*l.* There were two failures where the capital was 200,000*l.* and over. These figures compare on the whole favourably with those of 1897; but, as regards the amount of liabilities of the firms which failed, the percentage is higher of those which failed for the larger sums, while the proportion of assets to liabilities is slightly lower in 1898 than it was in the former year. The influence of the conditions prevailing in general business in different parts of the country may be traced in the detailed statistics of failure and the number of business firms in the different sections. The best reports as to trade in 1898 came from the sections of the United States west and south of what are known as the Eastern and Middle States, and large increases in the number of firms accompanied by great proportionate decrease in the number of failures are reported from the North Western and Pacific States, while decreases in numbers and increases in failures are reported from the Middle and Eastern States.

State banks of deposit and discount. Number. The report of the Superintendent of Banks for the State of New York for the fiscal year ended September 30, 1898, shows that at that date the number of State banks of deposit and discount transacting business was 208, being a decrease of four since the same date in 1897. There were no failures during the year, but one bank, whose capital had never been fully paid up, was dissolved in consequence of judicial proceedings; two went into voluntary liquidation; three were converted into National banks, and one into a trust company; three new banks were formed during this period. The total amount of capital of these 208 banks was about 6,000,000*l.*, showing a reduction of about 140,000*l.*; and the assets and liabilities amounted to 64,300,000*l.*, as compared with about 65,850,000*l.* in 1897.

Resources. The total resources of all the institutions under the supervision of the department are given as follows:—

	Date.	Amount (about).
		£
Banks of deposit and discount	September 29, 1898	64.301,600
Savings bank	July 1, 1898	177,850,000
Trust companies	July 1, 1898	105,417,000
Safe deposit companies	July 1, 1898	1,043,200
Foreign mortgage companies	January 1, 1898	3,980,200
Building and loan association	January 1, 1898	12,117,000
Total		364,710,000

The increase as compared with 1897 is about 25,150,000*l*.

The securities and cash held by the Superintendent in trust for the protection of depositors amounted to about 946,000*l*., an increase of about 140,000*l*.

In addition to the State banks there were on September 20, 1898, 325 National banks carrying on business in New York with an aggregate capital of about 16,000,000*l*.

Amendments to Banking Law. Several amendments were made to the Banking Law during 1898; amongst them a new article was added providing for the incorporation of Building and Lot Associations, to accumulate funds for the purchase of, and to aid members in acquiring and dealing with building lots, adding to the list of securities in which savings banks may legally invest their deposits up to 20 per cent. of the total; railroad bonds based on a first mortgage issued by a New York corporation, having the principal part of its railroad in the State, and having paid not less than 4 per cent. annual dividends regularlarly during the preceding five years; allowing a bank situated in a city of more than 1,000,000 inhabitants to open one or more branch offices in that city.

Recommendations. The Superintendent refers with satisfaction to recent legal decisions exempting the surplus of a savings bank from taxation, and also the individual depositors in savings banks as far as their deposits are concerned. He recommends that the law be amended, however, so as to restrict the payment of interest on any deposit exceeding 3,000 dol. (600*l*.), or to any individual having more than one account in any one bank. He also recommends that the sections giving a preference to savings banks as creditors of any bank which may fail up to the legal limit of their deposit, viz., 25 per cent. of the capital and surplus of that bank, be amended so as to make it clear whether the preference extends to any nominal surplus that may have been reported, and that if the preference be not allowed to this extent that the savings bank be restricted from depositing more than an amount equal to 25 per cent. of the capital alone; that provision should be made for annual meetings to be held on uniform dates; that the boards of directors be compelled to examine the assets and liabilities of the banks with which they are connected at least once in every six months; that corporations for lending money on personal property should be brought under the supervision of the Superintendent of

Debt of the State of New York.

Banks, who should have authority to compel a reduction of the interest charged when profits in excess of 10 per cent. per annum are being realised; that building, mutual, loan, and accumulating fund associations should be brought under the same supervision as savings banks; and that the banking law be carefully and thoroughly revised.

The debt of the State of New York amounted on September 30, 1898, to 9,340,660 dol., equivalent to about 1,870,000*l*. as compared with about 1,153,000*l*. at the same date in 1897. Almost the whole of this sum is represented by the bonds issued for the purpose of improving the Erie, Champlain, and Oswego Canals. The tax rate for the purpose of State Government is 2·08 per 1,000 dol., as compared with 2 dol. 67 c. in 1897–98, and 2 dol. 69 c., in 1896–97. The purpose to which the funds are applied being the canals, State schools, and maintenance of the insane.

New York City debt.

The debt statement of the city of New York is complicated by the consolidation of the various municipalities into "Greater New York," under the provisions of the law passed in 1897. The indebtedness has been scrutinised with a view to establishing its legality and the means of payment at maturity, and only such bonds and stocks as have stood this test are included in the statement given below:—

FUNDED Debt of the City of New York.

	Amount.		
	Currency.		Sterling.
	Dollars.	Dollars.	£
Debt of Greater New York, contracted in 1898	..	30,164,907	6,033,000
Debt of New York City, as constituted prior to January 1, 1898	221,916,334		
Brooklyn and County of King's	80,500,868		
Borough of Queen's	7,550,221		
,, Richmond	3,136,798		
		313,104,221	62,621,000
Total funded debt	..	343,269,128	68,654,000
Sinking funds—			
City of New York	92,085,546		
,, Brooklyn	6,970,746		
		99,056,292	19,811,300
	..	244,212,836	48,842,700

The valuations for the year 1898 for the city of New York, as constituted prior to January 1, 1898, were: real estate, 1,856,467,923 dol.; personal estate, belonging to residents, 325,892,478 dol.; belonging to non-residents, 108,105,545 dol.; shareholders of banks, 75,024,426 dol., making a total of 2,365,490,372 dol., or about 473,100,000*l.* as compared with 433,727,000*l.* in 1897. All these items show an increase, except that of shareholders of banks. The rate of taxation was 2·01 per cent. upon the assessed valuation of real and personal estate, as compared with 2·10 per cent. in 1897, and that upon the assessed valuation of the personal estate of such corporations, &c., as are not subject to local taxation for State purposes was 1·7558 per cent. as compared with 1·834 per cent. in 1897. The total taxes for this part of the city were 47,356,863 dol. (about 9,471,400*l.*), as compared with 45,332,402 dol. (9,066,500*l.*) in 1897. As regards appropriations, State taxes, and common schools for the State, 1,142,000*l.*; city debt interest, 1,205,360*l.*; redemption of debt, 870,000*l.*; public works, 749,100*l.*; public charities, 273,000*l.*; police, 1,410,300*l.*; fire department, 522,000*l.*; Board of Education, 1,392,500*l.*; judiciary, 391,600*l.*; asylums, reformatories, and charitable institutions, 315,700*l.*, all show an increase as compared with the former year.

Freights. With very slight and only temporary interruptions, the carrying trade from the United States has been active throughout the year, and rates have been maintained at a point yielding satisfactory returns to shipowners.

Grain freight. The export of grain has been very large; there was a brisk demand from Italy and from France, where the import duty on wheat was temporarily suspended, and there was but little competition from other countries. Freights advanced gradually, till, towards the end of March, a speculator in Chicago practically obtained control of all the stocks of wheat in the West, and was thus enabled to influence the freight market so far as the active demand in Europe would admit of this being done. The breaking out of hostilities with Spain, and the uncertain political prospect produced a very heavy demand towards the end of April, and a consequent advance in freights which reached 5*s.* a quarter for Cork for orders and 4*s.* 4½*d.* to 4*s.* 6*d.* for large vessels to special ports. At this time the additional advantage of a proportion of light grain could not be obtained as it had been earlier in the year. Towards the end of May shipments on account of the speculation in Chicago were suspended, and rates gradually fell to 3*s.* 4½*d.* to Cork, and on the collapse of the speculative dealings in wheat about the middle of June rates remained low till well into September, when 4*s.* was obtained for direct ports and 4*s.* 6*d.* for Cork for orders. In December there was a lower tendency, and rates for business in January were about 10½*d.* lower for both medium and large-sized boats. During the time of greatest activity several large sailing vessels were chartered at about 9*d.* per quarter under the current rates for steamers. As in former years, New York freight business was most active during the period of the year when the canals were open; more southerly ports, including those of Virginia, maintained their advantage, due to cheaper railway transportation during the season when the canals were closed.

Cotton freights. The shipments of cotton of the 1897-98 crop were maintained well into the spring months at about the same rates that ruled during the autumn and winter of 1897. Rates for the 1898-99 crop opened somewhat higher, and an advance to 2*l*. 15*s*. from Gulf ports and 2*l*. 5*s*. from Atlantic ports took place in November, which was generally maintained through December. The enquiry, however, declined rapidly at the close of the year, partly in consequence of the exhaustion of the stock of the particular class of cotton required, and partly in consequence of speculation for an advance notwithstanding the magnitude of the crop as estimated; cotton shipments appear to have come to an unusually sudden termination at the close of the year, and it seemed doubtful if much would be shipped during the spring.

Petroleum freights. In shipping petroleum to the Far East the Standard Oil Company has adopted the same methods as during 1897, shipping almost entirely by sailing vessels; where steam vessels have been employed the rates have been comparatively low. Exportation to Europe was mainly carried on by means of the Company's tank steamers, and shipments in this direction by sailing vessels continue to diminish.

Timber and deal freights. Timber and deal freights were favourably affected by the large demand for steam tonnage to carry grain, and rates for deals advanced to 2*l*. 15*s*. per standard, which is higher than had been paid for some time. In mid-summer the decline in freights for grain brought about a corresponding reduction in those for deals, which ranged about 10*s*. lower during the remainder of the season.

Sugar freights. Immediately previous to the opening of hostilities with Spain there was a very brisk movement in chartering for sugar from Cuba and Porto Rico, and such stocks as were held there were for the most part shipped to the United States; and, in consequence of the duty imposed on bounty-fed sugar, there was an unusually large importation at one time from Java, Mauritius, and other sugar-producing countries in the East. A large number of steamers and sailing vessels were employed in this trade, and freights were well maintained. Shipments of beet sugar were resumed at the end of the year, but these came almost entirely by vessels of the regular lines.

Cattle freights. Cattle shipments were made, as in 1897, exclusively by steamers of the regular lines, and owing to large mortality during the preceding winter, and consequent advance in prices in this country, the number was smaller and the rate of freight lower.

General cargo. Shipments of locomotives, bridge and railway material continued, and trade with China and Japan was active throughout the year, with Japan more particularly owing to an approaching increase in the tariff.

Time charters. A large business has been done in time charters, for which, owing to circumstances connected with the war, unusually high rates were made. A number of the larger boats trading with the West Indies under the United States flag were either bought or hired by the Government for transports, the prices paid admitted of charters being made on liberal terms for vessels to replace them, and, owing to the coasting trade being restricted to vessels under the United States flag, foreign tonnage could not profit by the temporary interruption of this trade at the commencement of the year.

Shipping at New York. The return of shipping at New York shows a decrease of 40 in the number of vessels entered, the number being 4,284 in 1898, and 4,324 in 1897; there is, however, an increase of about 200,000 tons, the tonnage being returned at 7,716,879 tons in 1898, as compared with 7,518,351 tons in 1897. The clearances show 4,153 vessels of 7,471,133 tons in 1898, and 4,664 vessels of 7,334,647 tons in 1897, which also represent a decrease in the number of vessels accompanied by an increase in the tonnage, brought about in each instance by a falling-off in the number of sailing vessels and a slight increase in the number of steamers.

British tonnage shows an increase in the entries of 283 vessels and nearly 500,000 tons, the figures being 2,389 vessels of 4,254,490 tons in 1898, as compared with 2,156 of 3,771,463 tons in 1897. United States tonnage, 715,079 tons, is about 370,000 tons less than in 1897, owing to the war with Spain; German, 1,436,611 tons, shows an increase of about 115,000 tons; Dutch, 359,000 tons, an increase of 35,000 tons; French, 256,538 tons, a decrease of 39,000 tons; Norwegian, 246,000 tons, remains the same; and Belgian, 182,313 tons, shows a decrease of 11,500 tons.

New lines of steamers. A new line of steamers is now running to the Levant, calling at Constantinople, Smyrna, and Alexandria, and returning thence to New York. The American and Australian steamship line sends vessels at regular intervals to Australia, New Zealand, and Tasmania, and the United States and Australasia Steamship Company despatches vessels for New Zealand ports, issuing through bill of lading. The United Steamship Company of Copenhagen has begun to run steamers between Russian Baltic ports and Boston and New York. The Wilson and Leyland Furness line, formed in 1897, has been absorbed by the Atlantic Transport line.

Public works. Canals. The report of the Superintendent of Public Works of the State of New York shows that 3,360,063 tons (of 2,000 lbs. each) of freight were carried on the canals of the State during the year 1898, being nearly 258,000 tons less than in 1897, and the smallest tonnage on record since 1858.

The amounts carried by the different canals were as follows:—

	Quantity.
	Tons.
Erie Canal	2,338,020
Champlain Canal	804,076
Oswego Canal	47,662
Black River Canal	69,963
Cayuga and Seneca Canal	100,342

The total east-bound tonnage was 2,314,050 tons, of which 1,111,699 tons were through freight and 1,202,351 tons way

(368)

freight. The westward tonnage amounted to 1,046,013 tons, of which 461,528 tons were through freight, and 584,485 tons way freight.

The goods carried are classified as follows:—

	Quantity.
	Tons.
Products of the forest	820,668
„ agriculture	707,855
Manufactures	175,632
Merchandise	220,107
All other articles	1,435,801

As compared with 1897 there is a decrease in the traffic of every one of the canals, and a decrease under each of the headings with the exception of manufactures.

The report states that the canals were officially opened for navigation for the season of 1898 on May 8, but that a series of leaks and breaks at and around structures caused many vexatious delays to boatmen generally, and the Superintendent expresses his belief that no succeeding season will prove satisfactory until existing conditions are materially changed. He points out that while the canals, if maintained in proper condition, will furnish an outlet for the productions of the West through the State to the seaboard in the City of New York, they have to compete for this traffic with railways which transport grain from Duluth to New York at 6 c. per bushel. If the price be fixed at 5½ c. per bushel for transport by canal, that amount would have to be divided as follows:—Duluth to Buffalo, 2c.; elevator charges at Buffalo, 1 c.; leaving for the canal rate from Buffalo, only 2½ c. This is too low a rate to be profitable under the present conditions of the canals and the existing provisions for transport. While the improvements contemplated and partially carried out with the 9,000,000 dol. already voted will, when completed, furnish a sufficient waterway, it will be necessary to have a better class of boats of greater carrying capacity and with a more modern motive power than the present mule traction. To this end the Superintendent repeats the recommendation made in former years, that the law should be amended which restricts to 50,000 dol. the capital of transportation companies formed to do business on the State canals, and expresses himself in favour of the State encouraging the formation of financially strong companies for canal and lake transport, with fleets of canal boats, elevators, tugs, and lake-freight vessels, so that the shipper of grain in the West can make contracts for through shipments of grain, including all incidental charges, with such companies as safely as with a railroad corporation, and with the same certainty that such a contract can be enforced. Under such conditions he is of opinion that grain may be profitably transported from Duluth to New York by way of the lakes and the Erie Canal at a rate which would result in a loss by all rail transport.

As regards the vote of 9,000,000 dol. above alluded to, the proposition to issue bonds of the State up to that amount was submitted to the popular vote at the election held in November, 1895, the purpose to which the money was to be applied being the enlarging and improving of the Erie, Oswego, and Champlain Canals. The proposition was adopted, a law framed in consequence was passed in 1896, and contracts were made for the execution of the work, which was carried on till the spring of the past year, when it had to be suspended, as it was apparent that the funds would not be sufficient to cover the expense. The report shows that the work was stopped suddenly just as navigation was about to be resumed, and that structures, walls, and embankments are left in a partly completed condition, rendering them liable to rapid disintegration and destruction from the weather and the effects of the navigation, so that it appears absolutely necessary that there should be a further appropriation to admit of the work being completed.

Surveys were made, for the purposes of a ship-canal, of a route leaving the Niagara River at Tonawanda, passing a short distance west of Lockport and reaching Lake Ontario at Olcott; also of another route leaving the Niagara River at La Salle, five miles below Tonawanda and entering the Niagara River near Lewiston, below the falls and rapids. These surveys were completed in the course of the year with the exception of diamond borings and small surveys at the mouth of the Niagara River and at Olcott harbour. The surveys have also been nearly completed of the portions of the proposed waterway between deep water in Lake Ontario in front of Oswego and the mouth of the Mohawk River at West Troy, and between deep water in the Saint Lawrence River below the outlet of Lake Ontario and deep water in the Hudson River below Albany. *Ship canal.*

Complaints have been made of the diversion of trade and decline of the commerce of the city of New York, and an inquiry into the subject has been made by a State Commission. In connection with this inquiry recommendations were submitted that the improvement of the water front of the North River should be carried above the point where new piers are now in course of construction, and plans were submitted providing for piers which will accommodate the largest vessels now building or whose construction is contemplated. This would involve the expropriation of a large amount of private property, and the original cost would fall on the city, but it is calculated that several years must elapse before the work can be completed, and confidence is expressed that there will be a full demand for leases of the improved water front when piers of this description have been completed. *New York proposed improvement of water front.*

In the course of this inquiry it was pointed out that the size of vessels and their draught of water has constantly increased of late years. In 1871 the draught of the largest vessels running to and from New York was 21 feet; in 1888 it was 27 feet; the draught has now increased to a ruling depth of 29 feet, with vessels occasionally drawing $30\frac{1}{2}$ feet, and some are building *Improvement of New York harbour.*

NEW YORK.

which will draw 32 feet, and possibly 34 feet. In the same period freights have fallen from 8 dol. 40 c. to 2 dol. 40 c. per ton on flour, from 6 dol. 32 c. to 1 dol. 92 c. on wheat, and from 9 dol. 60 c. to 3 dol. on provisions. The importance of deepening and widening the channel was brought into prominent notice, and as this work falls within the province of the general Government representations were made to Congress on the subject. Surveys and estimates were made by the engineer corps, and their report was submitted recommending that a channel 35 feet deep and 2,000 feet wide should be provided, that the east channel should be selected, and that ultimately the channel should be deepened to 40 feet.

Other improvements suggested are, that the present Bay Ridge and Red Hook channel along the Brooklyn shore, from the Narrows to Governor's Island, be widened and deepened so as to afford passage for the deepest draught sea-going vessels from the Narrows into the East River.

Railroads. Goods traffic.

During the year 1898 the total tonnage of all classes of merchandise sent westward from New York City by railroad consigned to or beyond Buffalo, Salamanca, Pittsburg, Bellavie, &c., was 1,463,902 tons of 2,000 lbs.; that arriving in New York City from the places above noted, or from points west of them amounted to 7,473,908 tons. The railroads which carried these goods are the New York Central and Hudson River; Erie; Pennsylvania; Baltimore and Ohio; West Shore; Delaware, Lackawanna and Western; Chesapeake and Ohio (10 months) and Central of New Jersey. The amounts show an increase of 80,000 tons in goods sent westward, and of about 727,000 tons in goods received from the west as compared with 1897.

Vital statistics.

The vital statistics of the City of New York for the past two years are given as follows:—

	New York City, as constituted prior to January 1, 1898.		Present City of New York.
	1897.	1898.	1898.
Births	54,089	53,359	78,928
Still-births	3,574	3,465	5,638
Marriages	20,365	20,769	28,885
Deaths	38,877	40,438	66,294

Of the deaths reported from the old city 15,590 were of children under five years of age, which compares with 15,394 in 1897. In the present city there were 25,498.

NEW YORK.

	New York City, as constituted prior to January 1, 1898.		Present City of New York.
	1897.	1898.	1898.
Small-pox	24	1	1
Measles	391	446	651
Scarlet fever	500	523	703
Diphtheria	1,376	788	1,459
Croup	214	135	319
Whooping-cough	308	442	716
Typhoid fever	299	376	676
Diarrhœal diseases	2,515	2,802	4,821
Puerperal fever	169	157	230
Cancer	1,217	1,260	2,006
Phthisis	4,843	4,957	7,724
Other tuberculous diseases	848	944	1,541
Congenital debility	2,460	2,524	4,159
Diseases of nervous system	3,344	3,155	5,820
Heart disease	2,346	2,379	4,093
Bronchitis	1,089	1,127	1,923
Pneumonia	4,621	5,301	8,094
Diseases of digestive organs	3,059	3,384	5,998
Bright's disease	2,059	2,426	3,847
Acute nephritis	440	535	839
Accident	1,782	1,860	2,861
Homicide	65	93	121
Suicide	436	463	695

The cases of contagious diseases reported in the greater city were diphtheria, 10,576; croup, 612; measles, 15,058; scarlet fever, 9,239; typhoid fever, 2,217; small-pox, 16.

The population of the former city was estimated on July 1, 1898, at 2,048,830, and the death rate for the year is given as 19·74 per 1,000 as compared with 19·53 in 1897. The population of the present city was estimated on January 1, 1898, at 3,438,899, and the death rate 19·28.

There is some difficulty in comparing the immigration returns at the port of New York for the calendar year 1898 with those of the previous year, owing to the fact that during the second half of the year, the return is made out by races instead of nationalities, but the following table is approximately correct :— *Immigration.*

NEW YORK.

	1898.			1897.
	Male.	Female.	Total.	Total.
	Number.	Number.	Number.	Number.
Great Britain	4,438	2,295	6,733	7,000
Ireland	7,426	11,271	18,697	18,417
Austria-Hungary	13,291	9,262	22,553	25,037
Belgium and Netherlands	780	442	1,222	1,375
Denmark, Norway, and Sweden	7,569	6,629	14,198	16,337
France	1,123	789	1,912	1,975
Germany	8,426	7,098	15,524	14,665
Greece	2,111	109	2,220	1,486
Hebrews	7,206	6,569	13,775	..
Italy	46,726	22,045	68,771	56,808
Portugal	680	609	1,289	1,555
Roumania	275	155	430	629
Russia and Poland	6,535	5,620	12,155	20,511
Spain	163	24	187	258
Switzerland	417	126	543	1,365
Turkey in Europe	58	6	64	116
Turkey in Asia	873	520	1,393	..
Other countries	110	30	140	4,890
Not specified	..	..	19,102	..
Total	108,207	73,599	200,908	174,931

In addition to the above, 3,568 persons were rejected on the following grounds;—2,863 as paupers or likely to become a public charge, 462 as contract labourers, 224 on account of disease, 12 as insane, 1 as an idiot, and 6 as convicts; 156 returned within one year after landing.

The total is higher than in 1897, but the numbers from Great Britain and Ireland remain much the same.

As regards the destination of these 200,908 immigrants 95,500 were for New York, 25,200 for Pennsylvania, 12,000 for Massachusetts, 11,400 for New Jersey, 10,000 for Illinois, and 7,200 for Connecticut, while 3,151 were in transit.

Labour conditions. From the report of the Commissioner of the Bureau of Labour Statistics of the State of New York it appears that on September 30, 1898, there were 1087 labour organisations in the State with a membership of 171,067, of whom 7,505 or about 4½ per cent. were women. These figures compare with 1,009 unions and 168,454 members, of whom 5,764 or about 3½ per cent. were women, at the same date in 1897. The number of the unions shows a progressive increase since the commencement of 1897, when there were only 927, and the same holds true both of the number and of the proportion to the whole of the female members of these unions; but the total number of members was at its highest on March 31, 1898, with 179,955 members; it had fallen to 172,340 on June 30, chiefly in consequence of the dissolution of one union with about 8,000 members, and in the following quarter a decline of 1,835 in the membership of another union accounts for the further reduction in the total membership to 171,067. The inference seems to be that the decrease in membership is due to exceptional circumstances of local interest and is probably only of a temporary nature. Of the 1,087 unions 280 were in the building trades, showing an increase of 31; in the iron and steel trade the number was 137, an increase of 22; railroads 131; printing, binding, &c. 68; clothing 62, an increase of 15; cigars, cigarettes and tobacco 54. As regards the employment of women 80 per cent. on an average were employed in the cigar and clothing trades and the remainder chiefly in the printing, textile, and theatrical trades. The report states that there are no statistics giving the number of persons in the States who could be classed as "wage workers," but that making an estimate from the statistics of occupations in the State in the eleventh census of the United States and allowing for the increase of population since 1890, it appears probable that the proportion of working people organised is about 10 per cent. As regards want of employment the number of members unemployed on the last day of the quarter shows an increase in the second quarter of 1898 but decreases in the first and third quarters, while the number unemployed during the whole of any quarter shows a decrease throughout. The average number of days of employment were: for men 62 days in the first quarter, 61 in the second, and 65 in the third, the general average being 63 days, as compared with 65 in the same three quarters of 1897; for women, the average was: 61 days in the first quarter, 58 in the second, and 64 in the third, with a general average of 61 days, as compared with 62 in 1897. The average earnings were: for men 163 dol. 61 c. (32*l.* 15*s.*) during the first quarter, 168 dol. 5 c. (33*l.* 13*s.*) during the second quarter, and 175 dol. 41 c. (35*l.* 2*s.*) during the third quarter, showing an increase of about 5½ per cent. during the first two quarters and a fractional increase in the third quarter when compared with the earnings in 1897. The earnings for women, 75 dol. 6 c. (15*l.*) in the first quarter, 76 dol. 88 c. (15*l.* 8*s.*) in the second quarter, and 81 dol. 63 c. (16*l.* 7*s.*) in the third quarter, show a reduction in each case of about 10 per cent. The figures above quoted refer to 23 different industries and over 150 different trades.

The second part of the Commissioner's report deals with immigration and its effect on organised workers. It is estimated that from 1783 to 1819 the number of immigrants to the United States was 250,000, and from 1820 to June 30, 1898, there were upwards of 18,800,000 arrivals. Of the latter 4,970,000 came from Germany, 3,800,000 from Ireland, 2,600,000 from England and Wales, nearly 1,200,000 from Norway and Sweden, and about 1,050,000 from British North America. Nearly 13,000,000 of these landed at New York. During the last five years 24·6 per cent. of the immigrants claimed to be skilled mechanics, 12·1 per cent. farmers, 36·6 per cent. labourers, and 18 per cent. servants. In view of numerous complaints made by labour organisations as to the adverse effect of immigration on the trades

Effect of immigration.

in the State of New York questions on the subject were sent out to every trade union in the State. Answers were received from 1,039 organisations with a membership of 175,959. Of these 774 unions with 105,889 members replied that they were not affected, while 265 with a membership of 70,000, or about 39·8 per cent. of the whole, stated that they were detrimentally affected by immigration. Of these 265 unions 120 with 34,304 members state that the rate of wages was reduced. It is said that the competition was felt in 85 trades (or 45 per cent. of the 189 covered by the enquiry), and that its influence was observed to some extent in every general industry except that of glass working. In the building trade the workers most affected seem to have been bricklayers, stonemasons, carpenters, and painters. The secretary of one bricklayer's union stated: "The English mechanic sends his washing home to England every week, and he goes home in the winter to spend our good American dollars, and comes back in the spring." In the steel and iron trades the workers most affected were blacksmiths, stationary engineers, iron moulders, and machinists. Other trades reporting that they were adversely affected were cigar makers, clothing trades, bakers, leather workers, stonecutters, and coopers, and the complaints are of members being displaced by immigrants, of opportunities for employment being diminished and of decreased earnings and reductions in wages. Among the common labourers employed on contract work the greater part are said to be Italian aliens, and this is particularly the case in work on the canals.

Report of factory inspector.

The report of the Factory Inspector shows that during the year there were inspected 28,920 factories, employing 472,784 males and 208,145 females; 3,836 bakeries, employing 14,812 males and 2,020 females; and 156 mines, employing 4,674 men. Among these 702,435 persons the total number of accidents during the year was 1,110 of which 34 were fatal, 133 serious, and 943 slight, and 50 per cent. of these are returned as due directly to want of thought or carelessness on the part of the persons injured. It is remarked in this connection that while it is impossible to place guards on some machines, the inspectors have insisted on guards being placed on others against the protests of those employed, and that on more than one occasion it has been necessary to threaten the workman with arrest unless he used the guard provided, which did not really interfere in any way with his work. The Factory Inspector recommends that the law should be amended so as to forbid any person under 16 years of age being employed on or about dangerous machinery; that the working hours of all women should be restricted to 10 hours per day, or 60 hours per week; that engineers and firemen in charge of engines and boilers in connection with factories should be required to have a licence or other valid evidence of their fitness; and that the compulsory inspection which is now provided for boilers used in mines should be extended to boilers used in factories. Mention is also made of the meeting of the International Association of Factory Inspectors, where resolutions were passed for extension of factory inspection

NEW YORK.

departments, for uniformity of factory laws, and for restricted immigration.

Strikes. The report of the State Board of Mediation and Arbitration shows that during the year ended October 31, 1898, information had been given of 271 strikes and lockouts, as compared with 243 in 1897. Of these 29 were among the tailors in New York, and 26 among canal labourers in different parts of the State.

The most serious of these strikes was that of the brick-makers, near Haverstraw, where more than 2,000 men were idle for over two months. The demands of the men were for a reduction in the number of bricks to constitute a day's work, and of an enhanced rate of wages. They finally returned to work towards the close of the season on the understanding that wages would be increased at the opening of business next season.

The tailors' strikes recur every year. In the case of the ladies' tailors strike, the chief cause was that the slack season covers about six months of the year, and that while the wages for the six busy months are good on the whole for certain classes of workmen, the average earnings for the year are extremely meagre. The organisation of a co-operative shop was proposed, and measures were being taken for the establishment of such a shop at the end of the year.

Comparative prices of staple commodities. The prices of leading staple commodities, as shown by Bradstreet's Index of 107 staple articles, indicated a steady advance throughout the year with the exception of a check in the month of March growing out of the uncertainty ruling just previous to the outbreak of war. The index number shows an advance in values at the close of the year of 5 per cent. as compared with January 1,1898, of 12 per cent. as compared the the same date in 1897, and 10 per cent. as compared with 1896. The index numbers are given as follows:—

Date.	Index Number.		
	1898.	1897.	1896.
January 1	74,184	69,364	70,576
April 1	73,586	68,760	66,191
July 1	75,570	66,937	65,952
October 1	76,562	73,277	66,803

On January 1, 1899, the number was 77,819.

Comparing prices on January 1, 1899, with those on the same date in 1898, it is found that out of 107 staple articles 58 have increased in price, 36 have decreased and 13 have remained stationary. There has been an advance in prices of live-stock with the exception of sheep, cereals with the exception of wheat, of provisions, coffee, tea, wool, hemp, jute, silk, flax, print cloths, iron-ore, and pig-iron, steel billets and beams, copper, lead, and tin, petroleum, timber, rubber, and paper; a decline in wheat and flour, sheep, milk butter, sugar, fruit, cotton, and sheetings,

28 NEW YORK.

Trade and commerce. Anthracite coal.

wool, steel rails, anthracite coal, and oils; bread, hides, ginghams, and coke have remained stationary.

The amount of anthracite coal brought to market in 1898 is returned at 41,900,000 tons, as compared with 41,638,000 tons in 1897, with 43,177,000 tons in 1896, and 46,511,000 tons in 1895. Reviving trade did not seem to affect this branch of the coal business, there was no active demand and prices were not maintained. The amount mined is returned at 47,145,166 tons.

Bituminous coal.

The amount of bituminous or soft coal mined in the United States during 1898 is estimated at close on 159,000,000 short tons of 2,000 lbs., being an increase of about 11,500,000 tons as compared with 1897.

Iron and steel.

The prices of iron and steel advanced somewhat in 1898, but the average for the year was still decidedly low, and the recovery only took place in the last few months. Pig-iron at the close of the year was quoted at 10 dol. 75 c. per ton, as against 10 dol. at the beginning; gray forge, 9 dol. 50 c., against 9 dol.; and steel billets, 16 dol. 25 c., against 15 dol. The average prices for the year were: for Bessemer pig-iron, 10 dol. 33 c., as against 10 dol. 13 c. in 1897; steel rails, 17 dol. 62 c., against 18 dol. 75 c.; and steel billets, 15 dol. 31 c., against 15 dol. 8 c. The production of pig-iron in 1898 exceeded that of 1897 by a little over 2,000,000 tons and amounted to close on 11,800,000 tons; the consumption for the year is estimated at over 12,250,000 tons. The statistics compiled by the American Iron and Steel Association show that the production of Bessemer steel ingots in 1898 was 6,609,017 tons, as compared with 5,475,315 tons in 1897, and of steel rails, 1,955,427 tons, against 1,614,399 tons in 1897, showing an increase in each case of somewhat over 20 per cent. The export of steel rails from the United States was 291,038 tons in 1898, or more than double that of 1897 (142,808 tons), and of this the largest amount, 107,669 tons, was sent to Canada; Japan and Mexico came next with 45,131 and 37,781 tons respectively, and in each case there was a large increase compared with the former year.

At the close of the year there were said to be enquiries in the market for upwards of 250,000 tons of steel rails required for Japan, China, Australia, Russia, and South Africa.

There was also a considerable increase in the export of steel in sheets and plates, in iron and steel wire, and in pipes and fittings.

Attention has been directed to the South American market for galvanised sheet-iron, and it is not unlikely that United States mills will enter into competition in this field. It was pointed out at the end of the year that the rate of freight from New York to Buenos Ayres was only about 6 dol. per ton and 10 per cent. primage, while freights from England were fully 10 per cent. higher.

The number of locomotives exported from the United States was 580 in 1898, an increase of 132 over the export of 1897.

The total import of tin-plate diminished by about 20 per cent. to about 67,000 tons, and the import at New York fell off in about the

NEW YORK.

same proportion from 58,349 tons, valued at 532,000*l.*, to 46,724 tons, valued at 457,000*l.* The tendency towards combination, which has been manifested in the case of most industries in the United States, has of late been very marked in all business connected with iron and steel industries; combinations have been formed with vast capitals, and others still larger are spoken of.

Dry goods. The import of dry goods at New York under the heads of cotton, silk, and woollen manufactures is returned at a total value of about 11,444,000*l.* in 1898, as compared with 15,230,000*l.* in 1897, and 14,494,000*l.* in 1896. The decrease in cotton goods is about 300,000*l.*, or 6 per cent.; in silk 55,000*l.*, or nearly 1¼ per cent.; but in woollens 3,430,000*l.*, or nearly 60 per cent. as compared with 1897; the figures being 5,783,000*l.* in 1897, and 2,353,000*l.* in 1898.

Cotton goods. The year 1898 opened with large stocks of cotton goods on hand and with strained relations between employers and their workpeople in New England owing to reductions in wages. While reductions were accepted, as a rule, some mills were closed during the first three months of the year; this, however, seemed to have little effect on the market and the general tendency of prices was downwards. When the war with Spain broke out a special demand was created for a variety of heavy cotton goods, some of the machinery was diverted to their production, and the decline in prices was checked so far as this class of goods was concerned; the general market remained however in the same depressed condition, and at the end of the summer the general range of prices was lower than it had ever been before. Prices of print cloths reached their lowest point in May, brown sheetings and drills, coarse coloured cottons and printed fabrics in July, bleached cottons late in the autumn. A change occurred in October with an unusually active demand for export to China, Africa, and India; very large orders were placed, prices rose, and for the remainder of the year there was a distinct improvement in business.

The stock of print cloths at the beginning of the year was estimated at 2,500,000 pieces, while at the close only about 500,000 pieces were said to remain unsold. Prices were weak at the opening at about 2¼ cents. and gradually declined till the lowest point 1⅞ cent. was reached in May; the recovery was to 2⅜ cent. at the close with an upward tendency, brought about largely by curtailing production and entrusting sales to a committee with a view to avoiding competition by individual manufacturers. A number of mills entered into an agreement to close for four weeks during the three months, during which the plan was to be tried, or to pay a fine for not doing so, and to sell the goods on hand, and those that might be manufactured through two trustees and through them only, the operations of these trustees being governed by an advisory committee of five. The result is said to have been that in less than a month and a half 1,500,000 pieces which had accumulated were disposed of in addition to the current output of the mills, and prices were advanced ½ c. per yard. The total number of spindles in the country is given at 17,570,290 as compared with 17,356,537, and the increase is entirely in the south, where the number has risen from 3,011,196 in 1896 to 3,455,537 in 1897 and to 3,670,200 in 1898, while in the north there has only been an increase from 13,800,000 in 1896 to 13,900,000 in 1897 and 1898. The total exports of cotton cloths from the United States amounted to about 330,000,000 yards in 1898 as compared with 285,700,000 in 1897; to the United Kingdom 11,269,000, an increase of nearly 2,000,000 yards as compared with 1897, but about the same amount as in 1896; to Canada 18,200,000, an increase of nearly 4,000,000 yards as compared with 1897 but 17,000,000 yards less than in 1896; China 156,300,000 yards, an increase of 22,800,000 yards; British East Indies 7,900,000 yards, a decrease of nearly 10,000,000 yards. The exports from New York amounted to 248,000,000 yards as compared with 197,000,000 in 1897. The total import of cotton manufactured goods into the United States from Great Britain in 1898 was returned at a value of 2,040,000*l.* as compared with 2,740,000*l.* in 1897, showing a reduction of about 25 per cent.; the importation of cotton cloth increased slightly, but in other manufactures of cotton there was a decrease from about 2,000,000*l.* to 1,350,000*l.*, nearly equivalent to the total diminution in the importation of this class of goods into the United States during the year.

Silk. The demand for silk fabrics was good at the commencement of the year, and although this market was, like others, affected by the fear of war with Spain, there was at first a fair consumption, and prices were maintained. Later in the year there was an accumulation of fancy silks which led to the production of this class of goods being materially curtailed. Early in the autumn reduced supply and advanced prices for raw material brought about an improvement which was maintained up to the close. There are now in the United States 27,000 power looms for broad silk weaving, and 6,000 power looms for ribbon weaving; during the year a number of plants have been established by foreign firms. From the returns of the Silk Association of America it appears that the imports of silk manufactures were much the same in 1898 as in 1897, the values being given at about 4,680,000*l.* in 1898 and 4,633,000*l.* in the former year; silk piece-goods valued at about 2,514,000*l.* as against 2,568,000*l.* show a reduction of about 2 per cent., in velvets, 223,500*l.*, there was a falling-off of about 30 per cent., and in laces 515,800*l.*, there was a reduction of nearly 10 per cent.; on the other hand ribbons, 462,000*l.*, show an increase of over 65 per cent., and there were also increases in thread and yarns and braids and bindings. The imports of raw materials, viz., raw silk, cocoons, waste, and noils amounted to 9,979,482 lbs. valued at 5,647,000*l.*, as compared with 11,854,347 lbs., valued at 6,244,500*l.* in 1897, and 5,661,630 lbs. valued at 2,970,000*l.* in 1896. The same association gives the number of towns in the United States in which the silk industry has a pronounced foothold as 228, and the number of mills in those towns as 861; of these, 43 towns with 228 mills are situated in the State of New York; 41 with 257 mills in New Jersey; 28 with 66 mills in Connecticut, and 9 with 26 mills in Rhode Island.

Woollen goods. In the woollen market the highest prices obtained at the close of 1897 were maintained at the commencement of the year, and there was an expectation of a further advance as the price of raw wool continued to rise. About the middle of February, however, raw wool declined in price, and this was followed immediately by the cancelling of many orders for woollen goods which had been previously placed, showing that much of the business had been of a speculative character. From that time till the close of the year the market was continuously overstocked with domestic and foreign merchandise in fabrics for men's wear and dress goods. The mills were not kept fully occupied, and notwithstanding large orders from the United States Government for kerseys, flannels, &c., for army and navy purposes, prices as a rule receded to about 10 per cent. below those of 1897, the exception being in dress goods, all wool, which closed at an advance. In carpets the weakness was even greater than in clothing fabrics, and large auction sales had to be resorted to in order to lighten stocks. The importation of woollen goods at New York decreased from a value of 5,782,675$l.$ in 1897 to 2,353,618$l.$ in 1898, a falling-off of nearly 60 per cent., almost entirely in cloth and dress goods. The importation of manufactured wool decreased in the same proportion, namely from 49,900 tons valued at 2,246,000$l.$ in 1897, to 20,658 tons valued at 865,473$l.$ in 1898.

Flax and hemp. The importation of manufactures of flax and hemp at New York decreased from a value of 3,196,000$l.$ in 1897 to about 2,012,000$l.$ in 1898.

Leather. The export of leather and manufactures of leather from New York increased slightly in 1898 from a value of 1,391,000$l.$ in 1897 to about 1,529,000$l.$ in 1898 in the case of leather, and from 314,000$l.$ to 351,000$l.$ in the case of manufactures. The total exports from the United States amounted to 4,383,500$l.$, as compared with 3,845,400$l.$ in 1897; of this export 3,733,200$l.$ was represented by leather, the British import of which was valued at upwards of 2,800,000$l.$ In a paper prepared for the "Shoe and Leather Reporter," of New York, by the Philadelphia Commercial Museum, mention is made of the increasingly profitable trade carried on by American shoe and leather manufacturers with Queensland and New South Wales, and it is suggested that more attention should be paid to New Zealand. The practical observations of a New Zealand trader to British makers as to the necessity for different lasts, and his recommendation as to the class of work to be put into boots and shoes for that market are quoted, and rates of freight from New York are shown to be such as to place the American exporter in an admirable position to underbid the English and Continental maker.

Hides. The total imports of hides and skins, other than fur skins, into the United States increased from a value of about 6,650,000$l.$ to about 8,000,000$l.$; those from the United Kingdom were valued at about 1,434,000$l.$, as compared with about 1,073,200$l.$ in 1897.

NEW YORK.

Cattle. The export of cattle from New York decreased from 135,200 to 127,000; the total export from the United States was about 343,000, a decrease of over 50,000.

Cheese. There was a considerable decrease in the export of both butter and cheese from New York and also a decrease in the import of cheese.

Scotch herrings. The trade in Scotch herrings at New York remains about the same as last year, the sales amounting to 25,000 barrels and 8,000 half barrels. The demand during the year was said to be sufficient to absorb all arrivals, but the market requires the size to run very even and the fish to be soft cured.

Sugar. The total consumption of sugar in the United States is returned at 2,047,344 tons in 1898, as compared with 2,071,413 tons in 1897, showing a decrease of 24,069 tons, equal to a little over 1 per cent. The consumption of 1898 was made up as follows, 317,447 tons of domestic cane sugar, 33,960 tons of domestic beet sugar, 5,000 tons maple, 300 tons sorghum, and 1,700 tons molasses, making a total of 358,407 tons of domestic production, 1,432,847 tons of foreign cane sugar, 179,465 tons of foreign raw beet sugar, and 26,625 tons of foreign refined, a total of 1,638,937 tons of foreign production. The amount of refined sugar which went into consumption in 1898 was 1,855,533 tons, of which only 26,625 tons, or about 1·4 per cent. were manufactured by foreign refiners; in 1897 the figures were, total refined sugar 1,958,343 tons, of which 77,288 tons, or 3·95 per cent. were refined abroad. The amounts refined by beet sugar factories in the United States were 27,960 tons in 1898, and 28,051 tons in 1897. The difference in price between raw and refined sugar averaged about $\frac{3}{8}d.$ per lb. The importation of sugar from Europe fell from 637,426 tons in 1897 to 206,087 tons in 1898, chiefly in consequence of the countervailing duties placed on bounty-fed beet sugar.

The manufacture of beet sugar is assuming large proportions in the United States. In the State of New York the factory at Rome has again had a successful year, and a new factory at Binghamton is said to be doing well; a number of factories are being built in Michigan, one in Illinois, which is likely to be followed by a second, and others are being built or are in contemplation in Iowa, South Dakota, Kansas, Nebraska, Wyoming, Montana, and Idaho. These, with existing sugar mills, notably those in California, are expected to produce 200,000 tons of beet sugar in 1899.

Tables of exports and imports. Tables are annexed of the principal articles of export and import at New York, and as regards the latter, a distinction has been maintained between articles entering free and those subject to duty. There is a large increase in the exports to Great Britain and Ireland, to British possessions and to most European countries, and an increase of about 10 per cent. in those to China and Japan. The exports from New York to British Africa are returned at a value of 1,916,100*l.*, as compared with 1,845,000*l.* in 1897, and 1,980,000*l.* in 1896. The imports from Great Britain show a diminution of about 3,580,000*l.*, those from British possessions an increase of about 1,000,000*l.*. Imports from France show an increase of about 1,200,000*l.*, those from Italy an increase of about 500,000*l.*; imports from Spain and Russia increased slightly, but those from most other countries show a reduction. The total exportation of merchandise from New York was valued at nearly 94,000,000*l.*, or about 37½ per cent. of the total from the United States, the importation at about 84,000,000*l.*, or about 66 per cent. of the total ; the two combined represent over 47 per cent. of the export and import trade of the United States.

NEW YORK.

RETURN of Principal Articles of Export from New York during the Years 1898–97.

Articles.		1898. Quantity.	1898. Value. £	1897. Quantity.	1897. Value. £
Agricultural implements	...	...	1,368,530	...	801,205
Bacon and hams	Tons	158,551	5,444,412	137,619	4,555,640
Barley	Bushels	2,451,271	220,172	8,916,452	629,967
Beans and peas	,,	729,478	202,972	709,365	187,303
Beef—					
Fresh	Tons	55,605	2,085,507	68,713	2,257,746
Canned	,,	7,331	278,067	10,058	364,708
Cured	,,	14,451	348,088	13,101	299,228
Bread stuffs for table food	...	...	219,291	...	78,500
Books and maps	...	...	259,064	...	292,199
Butter	Tons	4,424	304,772	8,577	539,368
Carriages	...	...	287,626	...	298,504
Casings	...	...	190,568	...	209,843
Cattle	Number	126,937	2,413,854	135,217	2,674,948
Cheese	Tons	10,305	393,574	17,509	711,376
Clocks and watches	...	...	251,058	...	208,642
Clover-seed	Tons	7,989	213,672	4,458	132,104
Copper	,,	84,443	4,180,454	81,708	3,908,535
Corn (Indian)	Bushels	39,623,273	3,087,237	33,226,359	2,200,446
Cotton—					
Raw	Tons	182,797	5,106,600	156,319	5,165,244
Cloths	Yards	248,178,023	2,473,586	197,222,076	2,055,752
Cycles	...	...	1,170,072	...	1,105,296
Drugs	...	...	496,316	...	659,236
Flax-seeds	Bushels	1,627,364	331,128	878,938	157,084
Flour	Barrels	4,737,214	4,101,478	4,717,867	3,947,533
Fruit	...	...	877,090	...	869,520
Furniture	...	...	406,045	...	482,929
Furs	...	...	463,148	...	524,679
Glucose	Tons	41,428	254,440	43,491	257,229
Grease, &c.	...	...	309,927	...	301,933
Hardware	...	...	724,213	...	678,275
Hops	Tons	8,822	657,785	4,086	295,164
Horses	Number	32,551	922,246	30,442	841,624
Indiarubber, manufactures of	...	...	155,164	...	163,600
Instruments, scientific	...	...	492,897	...	467,788
Iron and steel, manufactures of	...	...	1,742,464	...	1,567,277
Lard	Tons	153,989	3,945,064	124,787	2,890,724
,, compounds	,,	9,046	220,543	6,813	138,080
Leather	...	...	1,528,751	...	1,391,202
,, manufactures of	...	...	351,203	...	313,473
Machinery	...	...	3,215,900	...	2,644,563
Meat produce	...	...	314,021	...	367,053
Medicines	...	...	354,643	...	332,748
Nickel	...	...	273,572	...	199,054
Oats	Bushels	23,765,046	1,532,958	34,714,008	1,851,148
Oatmeal	Tons	16,797	158,745	12,898	117,754
Oils—					
Illuminant	Gallons	498,513,494	5,294,247	497,237,227	5,237,468
Lubricating	,,	49,816,219	1,239,160	41,629,492	1,115,592
Cotton-seed	,,	20,084,759	1,179,049	16,325,231	889,500
Oilcakes and meal	Tons	80,972	409,378	92,976	421,744
Paper	...	...	574,058	...	497,176
Paraffin, &c.	...	57,284	1,021,174	45,468	836,395
Pipes, &c.	...	...	571,440	...	166,247
Pork	Tons	23,730	681,838	18,871	435,857
Pumps	...	...	372,290	...	149,941
Railway cars	...	...	275,071	...	124,075
Roofing slates	...	...	202,137	...	158,169
Rye	Bushels	8,307,854	994,595	5,797,516	557,347
Sewing machines	...	...	543,016	...	570,857
Steam engines	Number	308	507,810	228	355,920
Tallow	Tons	18,903	434,680	13,869	236,232
The oil	,,	34,200	976,152	33,371	838,179
Timber	...	...	388,299	...	425,198
Tobacco	...	...	3,266,727	...	2,937,616
Tools	...	...	385,511	...	387,408
Typewriters	...	...	309,814	...	291,190
Wheat	Bushels	49,293,158	9,550,283	25,105,887	4,587,983
Wood, manufactures of	...	...	265,426	...	286,690
Specie	...	...	11,654,738	...	15,031,311

NEW YORK.

RETURN of Principal Articles of Import during the Years 1898-97.

FREE.

Articles.	1898.		1897.	
	Quantity.	Value.	Quantity.	Value.
	Tons.	£	Tons.	£
Books	..	279,382	..	255,151
Chemicals	..	1,947,004	..	2,100,231
Cocoa	12,068	778,566	10,831	521,344
Coffee	321,810	9,416,872	316,476	13,017,693
Copper pigs	7,010	309,367	4,834	197,766
Corkwood or bark ..	..	204,375	..	233,840
Cotton, unmanufactured	4,524	187,085	7,328	356,895
Diamonds, rough ..	..	502,678	..	273,998
Jute, manila, and sisal	136,114	1,726,204	110,019	964,250
Fruits	..	384,747	..	347,778
Fur skins, undressed ..	..	720,703	..	..
Hair	..	209,004	..	..
Gums	..	4,839,867	..	1,232,398
Iron bars	22,285	1,396,394	..	..
Indiarubber, crude ..	18,785	4,944,674	17,573	4,067,382
Liquorice root	30,581	219,560	20,357	152,529
Oils	..	419,543	..	500,693
Skins	..	3,711,255	..	4,666,397
Silk, raw	1,085	1,731,536	1,403	1,916,604
Spices	10,619	396,373	14,825	445,962
Sugar	87,681	1,430,254	71,505	938,228
Tea	6,751	428,202	27,756	1,483,303

(368)

NEW YORK.

DUTIABLE.

Articles.	1898. Quantity.	1898. Value.	1897. Quantity.	1897. Value.
	Tons.	£	Tons.	£
Argols	10,238	371,942	..	..
Artworks	..	311,708	..	..
Books	..	214,247	..	..
Bristles	604	214,552	..	..
Burlaps	..	278,921	..	..
Chemicals	..	780,389	..	769,455
China	..	705,267	..	904,756
Coal tar colours	..	658,538	..	670,421
Cheese	4,088	246,175	4,741	253,540
Dry goods—				
Cottons	..	4,622,428	..	4,925,240
Silk	..	4,467,865	..	4,522,112
Wool	..	2,353,618	..	5,782,675
Feathers—				
Crude	..	358,399	..	
Artificial	..	308,071	..	..
Fish	..	473,514	..	479,237
Flax, manufactured	..	2,011,761	..	3,196,376
Fruit	..	1,621,802	..	1,622,566
Furs	..	442,381	..	606,939
Glass	..	327,245	..	644,321
Gloves and leather manufactures	..	1,350,855	..	1,546,367
Hat materials	..	313,225	..	..
Hides	42,270	2,132,574	..	..
Jewellery and precious stones	..	1,505,763	..	1,084,618
Matting	..	234,710	..	..
Metals	..	614,493	..	545,276
Paper	..	363,480	..	443,983
Rice and rice flour	47,394	433,794	..	..
Sugar	..	7,826,075	..	7,822,892
Tea	10,760	643,002	..	..
Tin-plates	46,724	457,150	58,349	532,219
Tobacco	..	1,568,501	..	1,313,065
Toys	..	281,991	..	..
Wines and spirits	..	1,364,385	..	1,275,243
Wool, unmanufactured	20,658	865,473	49,909	2,456,000
Specie and bullion	..	22,176,181	..	5,615,860

NEW YORK.

TABLE showing Total Value of all Articles Exported from and Imported to New York to and from Foreign Countries during the Year 1898.

Country.	Exports. Value. £	Imports. Value. £
Great Britain and Ireland	35,232,400	14,400,042
British possessions	8,642,432	7,072,318
Germany	12,025,556	11,308,289
France and possessions	6,752,975	9,584,545
Belgium	5,980,874	1,170,188
Spain and possessions	1,962,797	3,474,188
Netherlands	5,786,142	2,166,022
United States of Colombia	496,571	819,500
Central American States	405,684	781,652
Italy	2,524,221	3,801,673
Brazil	2,150,090	10,032,572
China	1,739,130	1,662,081
Denmark and possessions	962,297	109,827
Venezuela	545,205	1,319,080
Portugal	840,585	474,738
Argentine Republic	1,323,120	626,241
Mexico	1,005,400	2,084,525
Hayti	507,400	118,651
Sweden and Norway	1,139,860	302,966
Japan	1,277,676	1,217,307
Chile	385,610	454,934
San Domingo	212,625	557,752
Uruguay	218,037	234,576
Austria-Hungary	927,406	814,805
Russia	977,703	562,037
Peru	235,434	166,624
Other countries	622,625	8,581,285
Total	93,979,855	83,898,418

TABLE showing Shipments of Grain from the Port of New York to Great Britain and the Continent of Europe, with the Nationality of the Vessels, for the Years 1898–97.

Nationality of Vessels.	Steam.	Sail.	1898. Total Number of Vessels.	1898. Total Number of Bushels.	1897. Total Number of Vessels.	1897. Total Number of Bushels.
Great Britain	950	9	959	92,412,322	853	83,563,448
Belgium	37	...	37	3,249,365	34	3,542,718
Netherlands	59	...	59	3,493,100	78	3,894,280
Germany	155	2	157	17,678,808	169	15,307,409
France	36	...	36	1,321,140	37	1,671,796
Portugal	27	...	27	1,890,423	19	1,473,265
Denmark	42	1	43	2,068,569	26	1,066,699
Italy	1	...	1	135,972	1	85,237
Spain	1	...	1	32,822	3	421,379
Norway	38	1	39	4,149,327	37	3,121,055
America	1	...	1	42,761	17	1,138,158
Austria-Hungary	7	...	7	387,128	5	290,206
Russia	1	...	1	38,449	...	...
Brazil	1	...	1	12,200	...	...
Total	1,356	13	1,369	126,912,386	1,279	115,575,650

NEW YORK.

The grain shipments by steam and sail for 1898 were as follows:—

Name of Grain.	Total Quantity. 1898.	1897.
	Bushels.	Bushels.
Wheat	54,462,336	33,624,005
Maize	36,790,873	30,982,268
Rye	7,875,615	5,405,672
Oats	23,373,570	34,409,704
Barley	2,320,166	8,539,013
Buckwheat	1,224,727	1,694,410
Flax seed	865,099	920,572
Total	126,912,386	115,575,644

RETURN of all Shipping at the Port of New York during the Year 1898.

ENTERED.

Country.	Number of Vessels.			Tonnage.		
	Steam.	Sailing.	Total.	Steam.	Sailing.	Total.
Great Britain and colonies	1,789	600	2,389	3,892,477	362,013	4,254,490
United States	212	430	642	498,851	216,228	715,079
Austria-Hungary	24	...	24	49,202	...	49,202
Belgium	55	...	55	182,313	...	182,313
Brazil	1	1	2	230	834	1,064
Netherlands	136	5	141	352,470	6,576	359,046
Denmark	50	7	57	84,680	3,717	88,397
France	90	2	92	255,985	553	256,538
Germany	465	50	515	1,370,063	66,548	1,436,611
Hayti	...	2	2	...	371	371
Hawaii	...	2	2	...	2,495	2,495
Italy	3	54	57	5,880	41,522	47,402
Norway	226	30	256	219,715	26,203	245,918
Portugal	25	1	26	46,031	773	46,804
Spain	19	...	19	25,991	...	25,991
Sweden	1	1	2	1,918	575	2,493
Other countries	1	2	3	1,214	1,451	2,665
Total	3,097	1,187	4,284	6,987,020	729,859	7,716,879

NEW YORK.

Cleared.

Country.	Number of Vessels.			Tonnage.		
	Steam.	Sailing.	Total.	Steam.	Sailing.	Total.
Great Britain and colonies	1,692	723	2,415	3,722,246	418,464	4,140,710
United States	216	286	502	493,525	152,379	645,904
Austria-Hungary	9	...	9	19,332	...	19,332
Belgium	58	...	58	190,298	...	190,298
Brazil	...	...	...	...	...	...
Denmark	53	3	56	87,858	1,128	88,986
France	92	2	94	261,681	585	262,266
Germany	464	52	516	1,354,210	73,887	1,428,097
Hayti	...	4	4	...	740	740
Hawaii	...	3	3	...	3,673	3,673
Italy	2	48	50	4,300	35,466	39,766
Netherlands	130	11	141	334,417	14,752	349,169
Portugal	25	...	25	48,200	...	48,200
Spain	23	...	23	34,992	...	34,992
Sweden and Norway	219	31	250	188,532	27,013	215,545
Other countries	3	4	7	1,684	1,771	3,455
Total	2,986	1,167	4,153	6,741,275	729,858	7,471,133

RETURN of the Number of Seamen who have been Engaged, Discharged, Left Behind, Reported Dead, or Deserted, or who have been Relieved at the British Consulate-General, New York, and the Total Number of British and Foreign Sailors who were Engaged, Discharged, &c., from British Ships, with the Amount of Wages paid at the Consulate to Seamen on Discharge from their Ships, and from Hospital or Jail; and also the Number of New Agreements entered into during the Year 1898.

NEW YORK.

Seamen.											Nationality.			Wages.			Agreements.
Engaged.	Discharged.	Left Behind.			Dead.			Deserted.	Relieved.		British.	Foreign.	Total Number of Seamen.	Paid on Discharge from Vessel.	Paid on Discharge from Hospital or Jail.	Total Wages Paid.	Number Opened
		In Hospital.	In Jail.	Total.	At Sea.	On Shore.	Total.										
10,750	10,164	223	22	245	46	31	77	2,295	295		12,120	11,629	23,826	Dol. c. 384,785 54	Dol. c. 3,319 52	Dol. c. 388,105 06	174

Providence, R.I.

Mr. Vice-Consul Stockwell reports as follows:—

As in other parts of the country, the war with Spain interfered generally with business operations here. There was, however, a quick recovery, a return to former conditions and confidence when hostilities terminated.

New territory. During the year 1898 a part of the town of Johnston, adjoining the city on the west, has been added to the city proper, increasing the population by 15,000, and adding 1·38 square miles, making total population of the city of Providence about 167,000, with an area of 18·286 square miles. The density of population in Providence is over 9,000 per square mile.

Public improvements. During the year the new railway station of the consolidated railways was completed and occupied. This, or matters pertaining to it, has been before the people for 15 years. The old station, the largest in the country when it was erected (1848) and the most picturesque, perhaps, has been removed and the space occupied by it (in front of the new station) has been added to the public square. Trains approach the new station on raised viaducts and thus grade crossings are avoided.

The new State house in process of construction may be completed by January, 1900. To erect this marble building 2,300,000 dol. has been appropriated, and it is estimated that the total cost will be 3,000,000 dol. The structure stands on an eminence north of the railway station. The new Normal School building near the State House has been completed during the year, and is now occupied. The cost of this building was about 500,000 dol.

The city needs a new post-office building, and a site for it has been presented to the Federal Government. The Bill providing for a new post-office building (to be used also by the United States court, custom-house, and revenue office) has passed the United States Senate, and only action on the part of the House of Representatives is needed.

A movement has been started to revive the shipping interest at this port by improving the docks and harbour. The United States Government has continued its work of dredging the ship channel from the city to the mouth of the bay to a depth of 25 feet at mean low water. Providence has the best harbour on the Atlantic coast, and if the commercial world knew and appreciated it, ships of all nations would ride at anchor in it.

Education. During the year, in addition to the erection of the new Normal School, the school facilities have been further increased by a new High School building on the east side of the city, and by two grammar school buildings. The population of the city in 10 years has increased about 35 per cent., while the expenditure for schools in the same period has increased 104 per cent. The outlay for schools in 1898 was 23·3 per cent. of the total income of the city, which was 2,463,188 dol. 22 c.

Jewellery. The jewellery trade and manufacture in this city has 200 establishments, and 100 other establishments dependent upon them. About 12,000,000 dol. is invested in the general jewellery plant in Providence. Business in 1898 was much better that in 1897, and during the last six months better than for five or six years previous. All help obtainable has been employed, and some establishments have been enlarged to meet the increased demand. The workers in gold average 14 to 16 dol. per week, and the workers on plate average 7 to 9 dol. per week. Collections have been good and easy, and failures have been rare. Some jewellery is exported, but the best market in the latter part of the year was found in the Western States. The "boom" there was due to "dollar wheat" and "flush times" generally. The first exhibition of prosperity on the part of the labouring class, especially the foreign element, after human wants have been supplied, is made in the wearing of jewellery.

Cotton manufacturing. The business of cotton manufacturing was very slack in the early part of the year, but improved towards the close. There have been no strikes and no demonstrative dissatisfaction with wages, which have not changed. Spinners receive, average, 9 dol. per week, weavers the same, and carders 7 dol. per week.

Woollen manufacturing. The manufacture of woollens was comparatively active at the beginning of the year, but diminished in volume and energy in the latter part. There have been no strikes and no change in wages. Spinners receive 10 to 11 dol. per week, carders 7 dol., and weavers 10 to 11 dol.

Building trades. The building trades have kept all workmen busy nine months of the year. Carpenters receive 2 dol. 50 c. per day, painters 2 dol. 25 c., and masons 3 dol.

Prints. In the dyeing, bleaching and printing industry unusual activity has prevailed. Print cloths were as low as $2\frac{1}{8}$ c. per yard: this unusual price led printers to buy largely and convert into prints or calicoes.

Machinery. The manufacture of mill machinery has been active, with a good demand for reliable labour. Tool machine shops have run full and overtime, the average in one establishment, employing 1,200 hands, being 10 to 12 dol. per week. The demand for locomotive and stationary engines has not been up to the average. One engine shop, employing 1,000 hands, has been closed during the year.

Money. Money has been plentiful; too plentiful from the point of view of the capitalist who has money to lend. Loans on prime paper have been made as low as $2\frac{1}{2}$ to $3\frac{1}{2}$ per cent. Before the flush times in the West, much Eastern capital was invested there at high rates of interest, and some of the investors did not see interest or capital again. Hence money seeks investment at home and finds it.

The valuation of Providence real estate in 1898 was 142,430,200 dol.; personal, 39,127,920 dol.; total, 181,558,120 dol. The rate of taxation was 1 dol. 65 c. per 100 dol. The valuation of the whole State of Rhode Island was: real estate, 308,967,317 dol.; personal, 81,945,263 dol.; total, 390,912,580 dol. The town

PROVIDENCE.

and city debt was 28,725,795 dol.; State debt, 1,500,000 dol.; total, 30,225,795 dol.

Annex A.—RETURN of Shipping at the Port of Providence during the Year 1898.

ENTERED.

Nationality.	Sailing. Number of Vessels.	Tonnage.
British	49	6,445
American	11	3,614
Italian	3	1,629
Haytian	2	370
Total	65	12,058
„ 1897	98	13,651

CLEARED.

Nationality.	Sailing. Number of Vessels.	Tonnage.
British	39	4,460
American	4	1,387
Total	43	5,847
„ 1897	82	9,895

Annex B.—RETURN of Principal Articles of Export from Providence during the Years 1898-97.

Articles.	1898. Quantity.	Value.	1897. Quantity.	Value.
	Lbs.	£	Lbs.	£
Iron and steel	..	..	..	848
Miscellaneous	..	..	..	20
Scrap-iron	268,470	297	..	..
Total	..	297	..	868

PROVIDENCE.

RETURN of Principal Articles of Import into Providence during the Years 1898–97.

Articles.	1898. Quantity.	1898. Value.	1897. Quantity.	1897. Value.
		£		£
Dry goods	..	29,316	..	44,632
Chemicals	..	16,949	..	16,081
Metals, and manufactures of	..	16,899	..	16,330
Wool	..	..	..	27,961
Lumber	..	..	..	14,135
Liquors	..	4,705	..	3,290
Precious stones	..	51,339	..	39,864
Wood, and manufactures of	..	4,276	..	..
All others	..	26,974	..	26,982
Total	..	150,458	..	189,275

Annex C.—TABLE showing Total Value of all Articles Exported from and Imported into Providence to and from all Countries during the Years 1898–97.

Country.	Imports. 1898.	Imports. 1897.	Exports. 1898.	Exports. 1897.
	£	£	£	£
Austria-Hungary	..	..	9,598	6,927
Belgium	..	..	225	440
British West Indies	..	..	3,904	4,952
Canada	297	868	4,843	15,688
Cuba	..	..	1,225	1,576
England	..	..	32,756	74,154
France	..	..	61,239	45,021
Germany	..	..	16,762	16,136
Hayti	..	..	1,115	..
Ireland	..	..	362	5,586
Italy	..	..	712	2,785
Netherlands	..	..	1,247	592
Portugal	..	..	109	112
Russia	..	..	5,404	4,005
Scotland	..	..	1,506	2,342
Sweden and Norway	..	..	1,302	112
Switzerland	..	..	3,656	3,358
Turkey in Asia	..	..	4,450	5,055
All others	..	..	43	434
Total	297	868	150,458	189,275

(75 5 | 99—H & S 368)

No. 2257 Annual Series.

DIPLOMATIC AND CONSULAR REPORTS.

UNITED STATES.

REPORT ON THE

FOREIGN TRADE OF GALVESTON FOR THE FIRST QUARTER OF 1899.

REFERENCE TO PREVIOUS REPORT, Annual Series No. 2210.

Presented to both Houses of Parliament by Command of Her Majesty,
MAY, 1899.

LONDON:
PRINTED FOR HER MAJESTY'S STATIONERY OFFICE,
BY HARRISON AND SONS, ST. MARTIN'S LANE,
PRINTERS IN ORDINARY TO HER MAJESTY.

And to be purchased, either directly or through any Bookseller, from
EYRE & SPOTTISWOODE, East Harding Street, Fleet Street, E.C., and
32, Abingdon Street, Westminster, S.W.; or
JOHN MENZIES & Co., 12, Hanover Street, Edinburgh, and
90, West Nile Street, Glasgow; or
HODGES, FIGGIS, & Co., Limited, 104, Grafton Street, Dublin.

1899

[C. 9044—83.]   *Price One Penny.*

No. 2257.   Annual Series.

Reference to previous Report, Annual Series No. 2210.

Report on the Foreign Trade of Galveston for the First Quarter of
1899
By Mr. Consul Nugent.

(Received at Foreign Office, April 24, 1899.)

As has frequently been stated in reports from this Consulate **Exports.** the foreign trade of Galveston is chiefly an export trade, the imports from abroad mostly arriving here indirectly, *i.e.* by rail or sea from New York, the great importing centre of the country.

The principal export is cotton, Galveston having received more of this commodity during the present season of 1898–99 than any other port in the United States.

To cotton may be added cotton-seed products, such as cotton-seed meal and cake and cotton-seed oil, and cereals, chiefly wheat and maize.

The heavy exporting business is, in consequence, limited to the months during which these products, and especially cotton, are marketed, *i.e.* from September 1, when the cotton season is officially stated to begin, up to March or April, the length of the shipping season, depending on the size of the crop, the rapidity with which it is brought forward for export, the available tonnage, &c.

November is usually the heaviest exporting month here.

In November, 1898, upwards of 500,000 bales of cotton, valued at about 3,000,000*l.* left Galveston, besides large quantities of other cotton products and grain.

Of late years, however, the season has extended, and whilst the months of January, February, and March cannot in any way compare in value of exports with the three months preceding them, yet so large a business is done as to merit a short summary for the information of shipping firms and merchants at home, who otherwise might not receive such information until the publication of the next annual report from the Consulate.

Figures covering the first quarter of 1899 have been issued by the United States Customs authorities here, and from them I have drawn up the following tables:—

(370)

GALVESTON.

TABLE of Exports from Galveston by Countries for the First Three Months of 1899.

Country.	January.	February.	March.	Total.
	£	£	£	£
Austria-Hungary	33,053	..	15,011	48,064
Belgium	76,999	148,116	31,873	256,988
Cuba	9,249	10,441	24,276	43,966
Denmark	18,599	41,938	43,657	104,194
France	236,793	207,608	98,659	543,060
Germany	613,730	343,445	239,693	1,196,868
Great Britain	762,709	451,488	245,362	1,459,559
Italy	70,975	..	..	70,975
Japan	88,194	..		88,194
Mexico	33,316	9,782	23,600	66,698
Netherlands	125,145	132,426	140,830	398,401
British West Indies	1,278	..	..	1,278
Canary Islands	..	1,235	..	1,235
Colombia	436	638	990	2,064
Total	2,070,476	1,347,117	863,951	4,281,544
,, 1898	1,289,689	1,428,428	1,372,603	4,090,720
,, 1897	1,384,800	863,771	686,335	2,934,906
,, 1896	1,059,149	892,837	591,000	2,542,986
,, 1895	1,684,767	511,574	418,377	2,614,718

GALVESTON.

TABLE showing Principal Exports of Domestic Origin from the Port of Galveston for the First Three Months of the Year 1899.

Destination.	Cotton. Quantity. Bales.	Cotton. Value. £	Cotton-seed, Meal, and Cake. Value. £	Cotton-seed Oil. Quantity. Gallons.	Cotton-seed Oil. Value. £	Wheat. Quantity. Bushels.	Wheat. Value. £	Corn (Maize). Quantity. Bushels.	Corn (Maize). Value. £	Wheat Flour. Quantity. Barrels.	Wheat Flour. Value. £	Cattle. Value. £	Logs. Value. £	Staves. Value. £	Spelter. Value. £	Lumber. Value. £	Sundries. Value. £
Austria-Hungary	...	...	...	...	...	329,264	47,968	...	...	...	...	...	...	...	...	...	...
Belgium	15,669	98,282	1,932	26,000	1,400	920,005	132,217	109,742	8,215	13,285	9,708	...	2,093	...	2,265	604	...
Cuba	...	...	27	...	...	...	...	18,083	1,367	18,925	13,783	13,320	...	...	...	8,485	4,773
Denmark	4,895	32,347	47,084	52,785	3,028	...	...	250,885	19,285	3,072	1,577	...	...	...	...	502	...
France	75,157	471,033	1,541	426,560	22,554	40,000	6,000	325,168	25,881	...	...	...	...	...	9,021	416	2,923
Germany	131,047	797,496	181,372	94,250	4,899	1,064,200	152,820	582,346	44,096	534	389	...	1,948	5,889	...	3,919	...
Great Britain and colonies	200,204	1,259,361	30,794	34,860	1,618	678,641	99,049	387,968	30,541	6,862	4,867	...	369	1,996	25,012	4,202	2,650
Italy	7,000	44,189	...	...	...	129,200	18,605	...	...	...	...	...	...	...	...	...	...
Japan	13,882	88,194	...	...	...	...	...	...	...	...	...	...	...	...	...	...	...
Mexico	6,451	40,920	...	259,415	8,041	...	...	...	...	...	...	...	...	...	...	9,668	1,580
Netherlands	4,184	25,231	53,801	1,482,627	69,775	1,600,166	230,534	78,903	5,879	4,151	2,908	...	145	2,283	...	6,903	736
Other countries	...	...	...	...	...	...	...	93	9	156	114	...	...	...	...	1,483	2
Total	458,489	2,857,003	316,551	2,376,497	111,315	4,761,476	687,193	1,753,188	135,273	46,985	33,346	13,320	4,555	10,168	36,298	36,182	12,664

On examining these figures it will be noticed that the quarter shows a gain of nearly 200,000*l.* in value, or about 5 per cent. over the corresponding three months last year.

This gain was, however, all made in the month of January, both February and March falling behind the corresponding months in 1898.

This was due to an unusually rapid shipment of the cotton brought here for export. It will be noticed that whilst there is a steady gain year by year for the quarter, yet in previous years the exports for the quarter were more evenly divided on the three months.

On examining the exports by countries, the smaller countries are found to have gained more in proportion than Great Britain, Germany, or France.

Thus Belgium, the total exports to which were in 1898 668,430*l.*, took in three months this year 256,988*l.*, or more than one-third of the total for ast year.

Denmark took 104,194*l.* in the quarter as compared with 230,141*l.* for the whole of 1898, and Holland 398,401*l.*, as against 853,309*l.* for the whole of 1898.

Of course, in all these cases the actual shipping period in the year is only about seven months, yet even allowing for this there seems a gain, as far as these countries are concerned, for the quarter.

As was naturally to be expected, the export trade to Cuba shows great expansion, being 43,966*l.* for the three months, as against 88,787*l.* for the whole of 1898, and this, too, with a more or less all the year round trade.

There is no doubt Galveston, from its proximity and the nature of its trade, is destined to do a large business with Cuba ere long.

The exports to Great Britain, Germany, and France, all show decreasing value, month by month, for January, February, and March, which is to be, of course, expected.

Germany really makes the best show, as, with the exception of cotton, in which Great Britain leads, she has taken more grain, cotton-seed, meal, &c., than any other country during the quarter.

There has been evidently more demand there for such products than in Great Britain.

The carrying of these exports has been, as usual, chiefly in British vessels.

It is satisfactory to note that the values of cargoes of British vessels during the first three months in 1899 increased from 2,976,510*l.* for the first quarter of 1898 to 3,312,695*l.*, and were 78 per cent. of the total value of exports from the port of Galveston.

British shipping evidently holds its own here.

Imports.

From figures recently issued by the United States customhouse authorities here, it appears that the total Foreign Imports into Galveston for the months of January, February, and March amounted to 118,790*l.*, as against 50,162*l.* for the same period in 1898; thus showing an increase of 127 per cent.

GALVESTON.

The following table gives the foreign imports for the three months, including imports in transit, and imports for re-exportation.

As regards the imports in transit, nearly all were destined for the Californian coast; only a small quantity going to other interior points.

GRAND Total of Foreign Imports at Galveston for the First Quarter of 1899.

	Value.			Total.
	January.	February.	March.	
	£	£	£	£
Imports for Galveston	23,554	24,785	62,049	110,388
„ in transit	2,319	3,712	763	6,794
„ for re-exportation	667	941	..	1,608
Total, 1899	26,540	29,438	62,812	118,790
„ 1898	18,630	2,177	29,355	50,162
„ 1897	12,747	12,990	12,273	38,010

The following table gives the total imports directly arriving from the various countries named:—

TABLE showing Foreign Imports at Galveston by Countries during the First Quarter of 1899.

Country.	Imports.		Total.
	Free of Duty.	Paying Duty.	
	£	£	£
Austria-Hungary	..	10	10
Belgium	..	6,486	6,486
Brazil	10,577	..	10,577
France	..	1,357	1,357
Germany	60	11,967	12,027
Great Britain	10	4,674	4,684
Mexico	69,022	315	69,337
Netherlands	..	321	321
Porto Rico	507	..	507
Portugal	..	168	168
United States of Colombia	3,195	1,763	4,958
Total	83,371	27,061	110,432

It will be seen that Mexico heads the list, as far as imports are concerned.

This is owing to a heavy business in sisal grass, for use in the mills here, of which 3,087 tons, value 69,000*l.*, were imported during the period under consideration.

Next comes Germany, with importation of cement, value some 9,600*l.*, and sugar 1,136*l.*, miscellaneous articles making up the remainder.

Owing to the fact that the North German Lloyds run a boat here regularly every month, direct German imports into Galveston have steadily increased, and are the heaviest from any European country.

The imports from Belgium consisted chiefly of cement, value some 6,000*l.*

Importations of coffee into Galveston have again begun after a lapse of some years.

There was a total importation of 11,652*l.*, of which 10,557*l.* was from Brazil, 578*l.* from Mexico, and 517*l.* from Porto Rico.

There seems every chance for British coffee exporting firms in Brazil to do business with Galveston, as there are many vessels arriving thence every year in ballast, which might just as well bring coffee, for which there is good demand here.

The imports from Great Britain during the quarter were mostly of a miscellaneous character, all in small quantities, such as cotton goods, caustic soda, cotton bagging (1,640*l.*), salt (1.237*l.*), rice, pickles, sauces, &c.

As has been often mentioned in reports from this Consulate, whilst there is no doubt a good consumption of articles from Great Britain in Texas, yet the major portion arrives here indirectly, being imported by way of New York.

The imports from Colombia were all bananas, Galveston being the distributing point of a large fruit importing company.

Shipping. According to the figures issued by the United States custom-house authorities, 101 foreign vessels, registered tonnage 183,480, entered Galveston during the months of January, February, and March, 1899, as against 118, tonnage 203,596, in the corresponding period last year; the decrease being due to the earlier shipment of the cotton crop.

135 foreign vessels cleared, registered tonnage 246,917, compared with 124 vessels, registered tonnage 220,195.

Here there is an increase due to the same cause.

British shipping. During the first quarter of 1899, 76 British vessels entered, registered tonnage 151,706 tons, compared with 89 vessels, registered tonnage 163,507 tons in the same period last year.

There cleared 94 British vessels, registered tonnage 184,834 tons, as against 95 vessels, registered tonnage 174,026, during the first three months last year.

The value of the cargoes shipped in British vessels during the quarter was 3,312,695*l.*, as against 2,976,510*l.* for the corresponding period in 1898, whilst the principal items composing the cargoes were as follows:—

GALVESTON.

Articles.		Quantity.
Cotton	Bales..	361,753
Cotton-seed oilcake	Sacks..	78,142
" meal	" ..	1,010,507
Wheat	Bushels	3,725,851
Maize	"	1,292,924

General remarks.

From a comparison instituted with other ports in the United States regarding the export trade of 1898, based on figures recently issued by the federal authorities, it has been ascertained that Galveston's share of the total export trade of the country rose from 5·54 per cent. in 1897 to 6·11 per cent. in 1898.

During the past 10 years this port has made steady progress.

In 1888 Galveston did 2·09 per cent. of the entire export business of the country, whilst last year she did 6·11 per cent.

Ten years ago she was in the eighth place with a total of 2,899,332*l*. exported, at the close of 1898 she was fifth with an export business of 15,357,647*l*.; New Orleans occupying fourth place with a total of 19,020,060*l*.

Ten years ago San Francisco occupied the place now held by Galveston, whilst New Orleans was second. Not that New Orleans has fallen off in total quantity of business, but other ports have made greater progress during the last 10 years.

New York, Boston, and Baltimore have more than doubled their business in the past 10 years, and the trade of Galveston has increased more than five-fold.

LONDON:
Printed for Her Majesty's Stationery Office,
By HARRISON AND SONS,
Printers in Ordinary to Her Majesty.
(75 5 | 99—H & S 370)

No. 2295 Annual Series.

DIPLOMATIC AND CONSULAR REPORTS.

UNITED STATES.

REPORT FOR THE YEAR 1898

ON THE

TRADE, COMMERCE, AND AGRICULTURE OF PORTLAND AND DISTRICT.

REFERENCE TO PREVIOUS REPORT, Annual Series No. 2115.

Presented to both Houses of Parliament by Command of Her Majesty,
JUNE, 1899.

LONDON:
PRINTED FOR HER MAJESTY'S STATIONERY OFFICE,
BY HARRISON AND SONS, ST. MARTIN'S LANE,
PRINTERS IN ORDINARY TO HER MAJESTY.

And to be purchased, either directly or through any Bookseller, from
EYRE & SPOTTISWOODE, East Harding Street, Fleet Street, E.C., and
32, Abingdon Street, Westminster, S.W.; or
JOHN MENZIES & Co., 12, Hanover Street, Edinburgh, and
90, West Nile Street, Glasgow; or
HODGES, FIGGIS, & Co., Limited, 104, Grafton Street, Dublin.

1899.

[C. 9044—121.] *Price Twopence Halfpenny.*

CONTENTS.

	PAGE
PORTLAND—	
Introductory	3
Exports; newspaper, wheat	3
Flour, barley, oats	4
Fruit trade	4
Hop trade	5
Wool trade	5
Timber trade	6
Fish trade; salmon	6
Chittim bark	7
Horse meat	7
Imports; general remarks	7
Imports from different countries compared	7
British trade and competition	8
Coal trade	10
Finance	10
Exchange	10
Insurance	11
Shipping and navigation	11
British shipping	11
Freights	12
Sailors and crimps	12
Oregon law respecting crimps	13
Seamen's Institute	15
Wrecks and casualties	15
Port and harbour	15
Lights, buoys, &c.	15
Pilotage	16
Shipbuilding	16
Population, industries, and health	16
Mining; precious metals	16
Copper, &c.	17
Coal mines	17
Manufactures	17
Fishing industry	18
Flour milling	18
Woollen mills	18
Paper and pulp	18
Beet sugar	18
Other manufactures	18
Labour; clerks, &c.	19
Births, deaths, and health	19
Public works	19
Railways	20
Agriculture	20
Lands in Oregon and Idaho	20
Cereals	20
Orchards	21
Prunes; cost of orchard	21
Flax seed	23
Stock farming	23
Angora goats; mohair	24
General remarks; dry dock needed	24
Assessment and taxation	24
City government and finances	24
Real estate	24
Statistical tables	25
ASTORIA report	27
TACOMA AND SEATTLE report	32
PORT TOWNSEND report	41

No. 2295.   Annual Series.

Reference to previous Report, Annual Series No. 2115.

Report on the Trade, Commerce, and Agriculture of the Consular District of Portland, Oregon, for the Year 1898

By Mr. Consul Laidlaw.

(Received at Foreign Office, June 5, 1899.)

Introductory. The statistics in this report, which have as usual been carefully drawn up from the records of the custom-house, and from the most reliable sources of information, show a very satisfactory state of trade throughout this district, a continuous improvement having been going on for the last two years. For the first time in its history, the exports of wheat from this port have been not only in excess of those from California, but almost equal to the shipments from all other parts on the coast. This was consequent upon a practical failure of the Californian crop. Being a producing, and not to any extent a manufacturing district, the healthiness of trade depends upon good markets for agricultural products and mining, which during the year 1898 have brought an abundance of money into the country, and much produce has been carried over by farmers who were unwilling to sell at ruling prices and could afford to hold.

Annex A gives returns of all vessels entered and cleared, showing a very large increase; Annex B shows all exports and imports at this port, giving the principal articles in detail; and Annex C shows the value of trade with different foreign countries compared with the year 1897.

All calculations throughout the report are made on the basis of 5 dol. to the 1*l.* sterling.

Exports. Exports increased 50 per cent. The exports from Portland, as will be seen from Annex B, show an increase of 886,927*l.* as compared with 1897, which is more than 50 per cent. This increase is principally in wheat and flour to the United Kingdom, and flour to China and Japan, but there has also been an increase (nearly 600 per cent.) in exports of paper to Japan, and in timber and provisions to Siberia. **Paper.** Exports coastwise have also been much greater. The cotton and much of the iron goods were not products of this district, but were brought by rail from the Eastern States.

Wheat. A very large crop of wheat of good quality was harvested, and during most of the year the export was brisk. Market prices however, were lower than last year, the average being 1*l.* 4*s.* per quarter f.o.b. for Walla Walla, against 1*l.* 6*s.* 8*d.* in 1897. Valley, which is a soft white wheat, and also blue stem, commands 1*s.* per quarter more than Walla Walla. In addition to the quantity shown in Annex B, there were 163,326 quarters shipped to San Francisco, valued at 206,454*l.* During the year the exports of wheat to foreign countries from this Consular district reached 2,361,252 quarters, of which 83 per cent. was to Great Britain, 9 per cent. to South Africa, and 6 per cent. to Cape de Verdes for orders.

Flour. The increase of flour shipments was very great, exports to foreign ports and California reaching 774,304 sacks, valued at 759,240*l.* The destination of shipments to foreign countries was as under:—

To—	Sacks of 280 Lbs.	
	1898.	1897.
Great Britain	163,347	125,863
Hong-Kong and Chinese ports	227,186	105,683
Japanese ports	98,439	41,666
South African ports	48,774	35,630
Siberia	35,866	..
Other countries	831	3,183
Total	574,443	312,025

The total shipments of flour from this Consular district were 1,315,742 sacks of 280 lbs. Prices were highest from April to June, the average for the year being 1*l.* 2*s.* per sack for roller extras, and 13*s.* 6*d.* for superfine.

Other cereals. Barley. Oats. Shipments of barley and oats during the year were as under:—

Country.	Barley.		Oats.	
	Bushels of 46 Lbs.	Value.	Bushels of 36 Lbs.	Value.
		£		£
To United Kingdom	232,452	26,539	..	..
Siberia	..	..	100,430	8,404
Other countries	..	..	2,023	154
Coastwise	1,247,024	118,231	1,115,814	81,508
Total	1,479,476	144,770	1,218,267	90,066

Market prices of good malting barley averaged 4*s.* 6*d.* per 100 lbs., and feed, 4*s.* 1*d.* Average price of oats was about 4*s.* 3*d.* per 100 lbs.

Fruit trade. Large quantities of fruit, both green and dried, have been exported to Europe by rail to New York, and thence by steamer. The tendency of the trade in fresh fruits is to decrease.

PORTLAND.

Green fruit. During the months of November and December apples were shipped in boxes weighing 50 lbs. net, each apple wrapped in paper.

To—	Quantity.
	Boxes.
London	36,000
Liverpool	38,400
Glasgow	5,900

Apples sold at 3s. to 4s. per box in carload lots here. According to reports, which should be fairly correct, about 900 carloads (24,000 lbs. each) of apples, pears, plums, strawberries, and cherries were sent out of the State.

Dried fruit. It is reported that about 700 carloads of dried prunes and 88 carloads of dried apples were shipped during the year. The average price of dried prunes was $3\frac{1}{2}$ c. ($1\frac{3}{4}d.$) per lb., $2d.$ to $2\frac{1}{2}d.$ being paid for larger sizes. Dried apples averaged 6 c. ($3d.$) per lb. The cost of railway carriage to New York is 4s. for apples, 6s. for other fresh fruits, and 4s. for dried fruit per 100 lbs.

The fruit produced in Oregon, Washington, and Idaho is wonderfully fine; but formerly was neither well dried nor attractively packed. There has been a great improvement in this respect. The production of dried fruit increases yearly, as there is more profit than in the green fruit, which owing to its juicy nature is more likely to arrive in bad condition.

Hop trade. At the beginning of the year there were about 8,000 bales of old hops on hand, and the new crop, which was of generally fine quality, was about 70,000 bales of 180 lbs. Many early contracts were made at an average of $4\frac{1}{4}d.$, but prices advanced, and the larger proportion of the hops were sold at $6\frac{1}{4}d.$ up to $7\frac{1}{2}d.$ towards the close of the year. The carry-over stock was small. These prices are quite profitable, but there is always a tendency to overproduction. Shipments are made by rail to Eastern seaboard, and thence by steamer to Europe. Through rates were made by rail and steamer to England as low as $1\frac{1}{4}d.$ per lb. The product of Washington was about 30,000 bales.

Wool trade. The wool market was not equal to the expectations of growers or dealers, and opened at from $6d.$ (12 c.) to $7d.$ (14 c.) for Eastern Oregon and similar wools, and $7d.$ to $8d.$ for valley combing wools. Demand was sluggish, and at the close of the year prices had fallen at least $1\frac{1}{2}d.$ per lb., with stocks in warehouses of probably 10,000,000 lbs.

The condition of the wools was average, shrinking about 70 per cent.

Oregon produced more wool than any other State in the Union, and its clip was about 20,591,000 lbs. in Eastern Oregon, and 700,000 lbs. in the Umpqua and Willamette valleys. Washington clip was 6,173,000 lbs., and that of Idaho, 11,617,000 lbs.

PORTLAND.

Timber trade.

A small but increasing quantity of mohair is clipped annually. Consumption of the woollen mills in Oregon was not less than 2,000,000 lbs. of wool.

The timber trade with foreign ports was small, and confined to the following markets:—Japan, 3,543*l.*; China, 6,234*l.*; Siberia, 7,212*l.*; at an average price of 1*l.* 15*s.* 6*d.* per 1,000 feet of sawn fir, commonly known as Oregon pine. There is no reliable record of the coastwise trade. The "Lumberman" gives the shipments by rail from Portland as 90,138,109 feet, and the local consumption as 28,985,702 feet. A reference to the reports of the Vice-Consuls at Tacoma, Port Townsend, and Astoria will show the trade at other points in this Consular district.

Fish trade. Salmon, tinned.

The tinned salmon trade of Oregon is of less interest to the British public than it was a few years ago when most of the product was shipped to Great Britain. It is generally conceded that the Chinook salmon of the Columbia River is the richest in flavour of all the species, but it is not so red as the British Columbia and Alaska salmon, nor can it be packed as cheaply. The latter have taken the British market, to which very little Columbia is now sent, and the consumption is largely confined to the middle Western and Eastern States. The pack was somewhat smaller than in 1897 and prices rather higher, flat 1 lb. tins averaged about 4*s.* 8*d.*, ovals 7*s.* 2*d.*, talls 4*s.* 2*d.*, and flat ½ lbs. 2*s.* 11*d.* per dozen.

The following summary of this business throughout this Consular district is taken from the reports of the Oregon and Washington Fish Commissioners and other authorities.

	Quantity.	Value.
	Cases.	£
Columbia River (spring), Oregon	309,780	281,900
,, ,, Washington	90,915	82,460
,, (fall), Oregon	66,639	43,802
,, ,, Washington	14,127	9,386
Other rivers and bays in Oregon	85,309	56,079
Puget Sound (spring), Washington	272,400	217,920
,, (fall) ,,	152,600	106,820
Grays Harbour, Washington	12,100	8,712
Willapa Harbour, ,,	21,420	15,402
Total	1,025,290	822,481

Fresh and salt fish.

The business of shipping fresh fish in refrigerator cars to the Eastern States is quite large. The principal fish shipped is salmon, sturgeon, and halibut. Reports show a heavy decrease, and I fear the sturgeon is being exterminated. I give below a comparison of the shipments of the last two years:—

	1898.		1897.	
	Quantity.	Value.	Quantity.	Value.
	Lbs.	£	Lbs.	£
Salmon, fresh	4,157,789	49,893	5,060,000	4°,056
„ salt	708,227	5,666	930,300	9,303
Sturgeon, fresh.. ..	285,418	2,854	995,400	9,954
Halibut „	400,000	4,800	950,000	9,506
Total	..	63,213	..	76,819

Chittim bark is shipped to some extent, generally going to San Francisco, from which it is usually sent to the London market. 12*l.* per ton is paid for the bark. — *Chittim bark.*

A large business has been done in pickled horse meat. Large numbers of range horses have been brought here and butchered within the last two or three years, and the meat is pickled and shipped overland to European ports. Some has also been tinned as an experiment. Details are kept very quiet. — *Salt horse-meat.*

I have given more details in Annex B than the importance of the import trade would seem to warrant, but they may be of some interest to the British manufacturers; the return does not give any idea of the trade in woollen, cotton, or linen goods which usually pass through the custom-houses on the Atlantic seaboard and come here by rail. It is not practicable to give the amount of this trade. All the larger firms have buyers in New York, where assortments can be found of such articles as are required for their trade, and where they can meet the agents of British and other manufacturers. The Japanese trade is of the highest value, consisting principally of raw and waste silk, 98,189*l.*; tea, 10,727*l.*; rice, 8,223*l.*; matting, 4,110*l.*; and sulphur, 10,118*l.*, the latter being extensively used by the paper and pulp makers. All of the sugar came from Hong-Kong, and amongst other imports from Hong-Kong and China were, rice, 9,125*l.*; tea, 2,554*l.*; Manila fibre, 12,043*l.*; coffee, 957*l.*; and raw silk, 5,311*l.* From Calcutta jute bags and bagging were received to the value of 38,448*l.*, but in addition, there were even larger imports viâ San Francisco, where duties were paid, and the value does not appear in these returns. — *Imports. Imports compared. Japan. Hong-Kong and China. India.*

From the East Indies were received: coffee, 4,608*l.*; manufactures of jute, &c., 4,563*l.*; and spices, 1,671*l.* — *East Indies.*

Raw hemp and fibre to the value of 6,578*l.* came from the Philippines. — *Philippines.*

Amongst European countries Great Britain takes first place, showing an increase, the principal articles being earthenware, 9,360*l.*; salt, 3,483*l.*; cement, 1,035*l.*; flax netting twine, 3,418*l.*; fire-bricks, 596*l.*; cutlery, 275*l.*; malt liquors, 2,926*l.*; spirits, 334*l.*; and knitted goods, 208*l.* — *Great Britain.*

(414)

Belgium. Belgium is next with cement, 5,800*l*.; window-glass, 4,077*l*.; spices, 205*l*.; spirits, 1,725*l*.; cured fish, 608*l*.; earthenware, 91*l*.

Italy. From Italy was received a cargo of sulphur valued at 7,857*l*.

Germany. Direct imports from Germany show a decrease of over one-third, due to there having been no German cement received. Principal articles were earthenware, 1,811*l*.; glass, 156*l*.; toys, 1,157*l*.; cutlery, 324*l*.; knitted goods, 657*l*.

British trade and competition. A few remarks on the principal articles of British trade and the competition of other countries would not be inappropriate.

Tin-plates. As anticipated in my last Report (Annual Series No. 2115) the large trade in tin-plate is now monopolised by American makers, who, protected by the duty, supplied the trade at 3 dol. 10 c. (12*s*. 5*d*.) per 100 lbs., and contracts were made for delivery up to June, 1899. A "trust" has been formed controlling the trade and prices have been advanced 50 per cent. At present price, 4 dol. 62½ c. (18*s*. 6*d*.), it is believed British mills can compete as foreign tin received the benefit of drawback when manufactured and exported, and as the consumption in this district exceeded 100,000 boxes in 1898, I expect a renewal of this trade in 1899.

Cement. Of the cement imported only 15 per cent. was British, the rest being Belgian. I am told that the Belgian and German makers are so full of orders that more British is likely to be imported in 1899, especially as some of the British makers have at last begun to grind as fine as their Continental competitors.

The trade was satisfactory, prices averaging 12*s*. per cask.

Window glass. Of the window-glass, which shows an increase, 4 per cent. was entered from Quebec and the rest from Belgium. Dealers tell me that more than twice as much American glass was brought here which, of course, does not appear in custom-house statistics.

Jute bags and bagging. India has a practical monopoly of the trade in jute bags and bagging. The consumption of this district was fully 17,000,000 bags, and of hop-cloth 500,000 yards. The Washington Penitentiary Mill furnished a small percentage of the supply of bags. The average price paid for standard size wheat bags was low, not over 19*s*. per 100. In consequence of a failure in Californian crops large quantities were thrown on this market and sold below normal value.

Salt. Owing to the competition of the Utah Salt Works, which put a well granulated salt on the market nicely packed, English salt is in less demand and the trade is likely to diminish very much.

Earthenware. The trade in earthenware was much larger than last year, but the proportion of British trade was 10 per cent. less, that from Germany being being about the same, Japan, China, and Belgium having increased a little. Dealers have complained that there is too much delay in filling orders, but I do not think that is the fault of the manufacturers generally as the opportunities for shipment are less numerous than at one time.

In caustic soda and soda ash there is now a strong competition with American, and the trade is falling-off. For fire bricks there has been a good demand, with a tendency to increase. In flax twine for nets there has been a fair trade, but a combination of manufacturers has resulted in the checking of imports, the trade being largely supplied by British manufacturers owning factories in the Eastern States.

<small>Other articles.</small>

Practically all the hardware used is of American manufacture, and anvils, formerly imported to a large extent, are being supplanted by the American make. In cutlery there will always be a small demand for high grade knives of British make; medium and low grade have been imported from Germany, but are being superseded by American. In razors Germany holds the trade, and sheep shears are of British manufacture. Toys of German and Belgian make are imported to some extent. Imports of malt liquors have increased and all the entries are from England. Of the spirits imported, 1,725*l*. are credited to Belgium, and I have learned that this is American whisky which was exported largely from this country years ago to avoid payment of duty and held in Bremen and elsewhere and is now being returned.

Bradford holds its trade for such goods as crepons and mohair fancy goods. Moreen cannot now be imported on account of high duty. High-grade worsteds are imported, but there is competition with very fine goods made in Connecticut Mills, which produce admirable designs in fine worsted trouserings. The suggestion has been repeatedly made that trade in these fine goods could be increased if they were put up in shorter lengths. Some fine broadcloths and dress goods came from Germany, and lucene of German make is gaining ground. The finer grades of tweeds are nearly all imported from Scotland and England, but lower grade pure woollen goods of very fair quality are produced by the Oregon and Eastern Mills, and with these, owing to the enormous duty, the British manufacturer cannot compete. Nor can he do so in blankets or any heavy woollen goods with few exceptions.

<small>Woollens.</small>

In cheap to medium grades of underwear the American makers are rapidly getting control, and the Germans have also a strong hold on the market, producing a good and showy article cheaper than the British, but the finest grades are either British or French.

There is a good trade in canvas padding.

All hats are American except the trimmings and bindings. Hosiery, except fancy, is nearly all German and American. The British manufacturer is still able to hold the trade in all the finer qualities of linen damasks, sheetings, &c., but the German is pushing the trade and improving his goods, and there is danger in the makers relying too much on the superior quality and allowing their competitors, who are willing to cater to the demand for showy and cheaper articles, gradually to absorb the trade. This has happened in other branches, notably the hosiery which was, not long ago, controlled in England. I have had enquiries as to the trade in oakum, and find that no English has been imported for some time back, that the American is preferred, because it is lighter and spins better. I am told that even the British ships here prefer the American in most cases.

Coal trade.

The trade in foreign coal was very small during 1898, and the great bulk of the trade was in domestic coals. The following are the receipts during the year as nearly as can be ascertained:—

From—	Quantity.
	Tons.
Australia	4,327
Great Britain	2,933
British Columbia	720
Japan and China	397
Atlantic Coast	5,459
Coast mines, by sea	20,000
,, ,, rail	44,280
Total	78,116

The coal from Great Britain was mostly anthracite, and that from Atlantic States, anthracite and blacksmiths. The rest was bituminous.

Australian sold at an average of 21s. per ton.

Financial matters.

There has been a very easy money market during the year, particularly after harvest, and the country banks have loaned freely on wheat in warehouses. The banking facilities remain very much the same as last year, and the clearing-house returns were as follows:—

Clearing-house returns.

	Amount.		
	1898.	1897.	1896.
	£	£	£
Clearances	18,744,324	14,859,050	12,481,779
Balances	3,740,566	3,027,757	2,723,965

Exchange.

Exchange was low but steady throughout the year, the average for commercial bills at 60 days having been 4 dol. 80 c. from January to June; during June, July, and August, rates were nominal, but opened rather higher in September, averaging 4 dol. 81 c. per 1l. From the end of September to the close of the year the average was 4 dol. 80 c. Bank exchange generally sold about two points higher.

Failures.

The commercial failures in the entire district during the last two years are given by Dun's Commercial Agency as under:—

States.	1898.		1897.	
	Number of Failures.	Liabilities.	Number of Failures.	Liabilities.
		£		£
Oregon	138	122,648	169	131,388
Washington	163	201,975	136	106,047
Idaho	61	81,770	75	72,440
Total	362	406,393	380	309,875

The State Insurance Commissioner makes the following statement of the insurance business in the State of Oregon during 1898:—

Insurance.

	Premiums.		Losses Paid.	Net Premiums.	
	Gross.	Returned.		1898.	1897.
	£	£	£	£	£
Fire insurance companies..	240,601	46,215	85,029	109,357	89,964
Life and accident	145,715	8,254	69,210	68,251	44,277
Marine and miscellaneous..	33,385	586	6,001	26,798	3,376

The law of Oregon requires that all foreign fire and marine insurance companies shall, before doing business in the State, deposit with the State Treasurer for the security of policy holders, either in interest-bearing bonds of the United States or of the State of Oregon, or Municipal, School District, or County bonds issued by authority of law in the State of Oregon, or bonds or notes secured by first mortgage upon real estate within the State of Oregon to the extent of 50,000 dol., or an investment may be made in real estate in Oregon to the value of not less than 65,000 dol. The State is held responsible for such deposits.

Annex A shows the number and nationality of all vessels which entered and cleared at the port during the past year. There has been a very heavy increase, and the individual tonnage of the vessels has been larger. 121 British ships, of 219,046 tons register, entered, as against 84 ships, of 146,453 tons register, in 1897, but the proportion of British vessels to those under other flags is slowly decreasing. 79 per cent. of the total tonnage in the foreign trade was British, 13 per cent. German, and 8 per cent. other nationalities. The proportion of British tonnage in 1897 was 81 per cent., and 88 per cent. in 1896. Many of the foreign vessels were formerly under the British flag. All of the regular liners in the China trade, both for Tacoma and this port, were transferred during the year to the United States flag, and several British sailing ships to the Hawaiian flag. There has been some complaint of an insufficiency of steamers, and it might be

Shipping and navigation.
British shipping.

Freights.

well for some of the British lines to look into the trade and see whether there is not an opening for business.

The average rate of all vessels loading grain for orders to the United Kingdom, Havre, Antwerp, or Dunkirk was 34s., and to South African ports 38s. 10d. The greater proportion of the charters were made to arrive, the highest rate to the United Kingdom being 41s. 3d., and the lowest 24s. 9d. At the opening of the year rates were about 37s. 6d., dropping during March and April to 28s. 9d., advancing during May and June to the highest point, and gradually falling away till the close of the year, when there was little demand.

The following is a comparison of the engagements of tonnage, exclusive of coasting voyages, during the last four years:—

Tonnage engagements.

Cargoes.	Tons Register.			
	1898.	1897.	1896.	1895.
Grain and flour	223,129	140,117	131,381	138,356
Timber	12,936	17,596	14,976	8,419
Miscellaneous	4,706	3,175	3,516	843
Total	240,771	160,888	149,873	147,618

Coasting trade.

There was a fair amount of coasting traffic, but no such rush to the Klondike goldfields during 1898 as there was the previous year; many large steamers, both American and foreign, were bought or chartered by the Government for troopships or colliers.

Crimps and sailors.

I think it necessary to point out to shipowners that they should take into account, in chartering for this port, the outrageous extortion practised by the crimps here in the matter of furnishing crews, and for which there seems to be at present no remedy. I estimate the allowance for this to be not under 2s. per ton.

The Federal Law recently passed rendering it illegal to allot more than one month's wages on long voyages, and smaller amounts on shorter ones, came into effect on February 20, 1899, but is already (May, 1899) evaded on all sides. It is good as far as it goes, but enacts no penalty against crimps, who demand and receive remuneration from masters for providing seamen, and it will have no good effect so long as sailors voluntarily place themselves in the power of the crimps. The result has so far been at this port that masters requiring a crew have been compelled to pay from 55 to 112 dol. per man as a bonus, and wages have been reduced from 5l. to 4l., but no advance is taken. In view of the unenviable reputation this port has acquired with respect to the desertion of seamen and crimping generally, I give below the text of the Oregon Law of 1889, which is still in force, and was very effective for a time, but for some years past it has practically become a dead letter, and the crimps have met with no restraint. This is partly due to the fact that there is only one set of boarding-house keepers here, and that foreign ship-masters are so afraid of delay in obtaining crews, that they will make no stand for their rights under the law, and there is therefore a practical impossibility of procuring evidence sufficient to convict. There is, however, a strong public sentiment springing up which may have the effect of causing an enforcement of the laws, and a change for the better in this respect. I have repeatedly and strongly advised the masters of British ships to take advantage of the treaty for return of deserting seamen, and to make complaints of infringement of local laws, but they are generally averse to doing so, fearing they will not get the deserters, and will meet with delay in procuring men from the crimps to fill up their complement. Only nine applications for arrest of deserters were made during the year 1898. The cost is 4s. if an arrest is made, and 2l. 12s. if successful, with jail fees of 2s. 6d. a day if held in custody. It must also be remembered that American citizens cannot be arrested here for desertion. An attempt was made at the last session of the Oregon Legislature to amend the law, and create a commission which would have drastic power to license boarding-houses, make rules for the conduct of the business, and see that masters and seamen were not imposed upon. The Bill was endorsed by the best portion of this community, and would have been effective, but was defeated by the crimps, who seem to have acquired some political influence.

The following is the Oregon Law as it now stands:—

"An Act passed February 21, 1889, *for the Prevention of, and* Oregon law.
Punishment for, Enticing and Harbouring Seamen from Ships, Steamers, and other Vessels at the Ports of Portland and Astoria, Oregon, U.S.A.

"Be it enacted by the Legislative Assemby of the State of Oregon:—

"Section 1. That Section 1952 of the General Laws of Oregon, as annotated by William Lair Hill, be amended to read as follows:—

"Sec. 1952. That if any person or persons shall entice, persuade, or by any means attempt to persuade any seaman to desert from, or, without permission of the officer then in command thereof, to leave or depart from, either temporarily or otherwise, any ship or steamer or other vessel, while such ship, steamer, or other vessel is within the waters under the jurisdiction of this State, or within the waters of concurrent jurisdiction of this State and the territory of Washington, such person or persons shall, upon conviction thereof before any justice of the peace, or before a circuit court of this State, be punished by imprisonment in a county jail for not less than one nor more than six months, or by a fine not less than fifty nor more than two hundred dollars, or by both such fine and imprisonment.

"Section 2. That Section 1953 of the General Laws of the State of Oregon, as annotated by William Lair Hill, be amended to read as follows:—

"Sec. 1953. If any person shall knowingly, and with manifest intention to deprive the owner or master of any ship or vessel of the service of any seaman, harbour or secrete, or by any means aid in harbouring or secreting, with the intention aforesaid, any seaman mentioned in this Act, such person or persons shall, upon conviction thereof before a justice of the peace or circuit court, be punished by imprisonment in the county jail not less than sixty days nor more than six months, or by a fine of not less than fifty dollars nor more than two hundred and fifty dollars.

"Section 3. If any person or persons shall demand or receive, either directly or indirectly, from any seaman or apprentice, or from any person seeking employment as a seaman or apprentice, or from any person on his behalf, any remuneration whatever for providing him with employment on board a sea-going vessel, he shall for every such offence, on conviction thereof before any justice of the peace or circuit court of this State, be punished by imprisonment in a county jail for a period not less than ten nor more than one hundred days, or by a fine not less than twenty nor more than two hundred dollars.

"Section 4. If any person or persons shall demand or receive, either directly or indirectly, from any owner or master, or agent of owner or master of a sea-going vessel, any remuneration whatever, other than a fee of ten dollars per man, for supplying any seaman or apprentice to be entered on board such sea-going vessel, he shall for every offence, on conviction thereof before a justice of the peace or circuit court, be punished by imprisonment in a county jail for a period not less than ten nor more than one hundred days, or by a fine not less than twenty nor more than two hundred dollars.

"Section 5. If any person, not acting in an official capacity, shall board or attempt to board any ship or vessel on the Willamette or Columbia River, not engaged in the carrying of passengers for hire, without the consent first obtained of the captain, master, or other officer in command thereof at the time, such person, on conviction thereof before any justice of the peace or circuit court, shall be fined not less than twenty nor more than one hundred dollars, or be imprisoned in a county jail not less than ten nor more than one hundred days, or both.

"Section 6. No officer or seaman of a sea-going vessel or ship shall be arrested or imprisoned for debt; and any officer executing a process of arrest for debt upon such officer or seaman shall, upon conviction thereof before any justice of the peace or circuit court be fined in a sum not less than twenty nor more than one hundred dollars.

"Section 7. It is hereby made the duty of the mayor and common council of the cities of Portland and Astoria, in this State, severally to appoint or designate a person or officer, whose duty it shall be to see that this Act is not violated, and that the

PORTLAND.

provisions thereof are enforced; and such person or officer so appointed or designated shall have all the authority and powers of a peace officer, and may make arrests for violations of the provisions of this Act, and shall perform such other duties as to the enforcement of this Act as may be enjoined upon him by the common council of said cities respectively, and shall receive such compensation for his services as said common council may by ordinance provide."

The number and changes in crews of British vessels during the year were as under:—

	Number.
Total number of crews	3,534
Deserted	693
Discharged	124
Engaged	878
Deaths reported	4
Sent to hospital	33

The percentage of desertions to numbers of crews was 8 per cent. in 1896, $15\frac{1}{2}$ per cent. in 1897, and $19\frac{3}{10}$ per cent. in 1898, so that the ratio is increasing. Desertions from steamers are rare.

Seaman's institute. It seem to me that if the work of an institute for seamen were taken in hand by the Missions to Seamen's Society it would have a good effect on the morals of the seamen visiting here, the majority of whom are British; the work of the local society is somewhat feeble.

Wrecks. Casualties. The only serious casualty which took place in the district was the total loss of the British ship "Atalanta" off Alseya Bay, Oregon, whereby the master and 23 of the crew lost their lives.

Port and harbour. During the year dredging has been carried on in the Columbia and Willamette Rivers below Portland, both by the United States Engineers and Port of Portland Commission, and a low water draft of 23 feet has been maintained, with the exception of a few weeks in the autumn. A new suction dredger was built; the Columbia River bar was surveyed in July, showing that the channel had moved a little further to the north and that there was a minimum depth on the bar at low water of 29 feet which is one foot less than in 1897 (caused by the severe storms of the winter and the consequent large movement of sand from the top of Clatsop Spit).

Lights, buoys, and fog signals. There were some slight changes in the lights and buoyage of the district but those affecting deep sea sailing were as follows:—

Cape Disappointment Light permanently changed to a fourth order red and white flash on February 17, 1898.

North Head Light described in my last report (Annual Series, No. 2115) went into commission on May 16, 1898.

Umatilla Reef Light Vessel No. 67, described in same report,

PORTLAND.

went on its station May 22, 1898, and Whistling Bay was discontinued.

Grays Harbour Light was established June 30, 1898. It is a light of the third order, flashing red and white alternatively, with intervals between flashes of 5 seconds, situated in a tower on a low sand dune on Point Chehalis, and is fully described in the United States List of Lights, corrected to February 1, 1899.

Grays Harbour fog signal. On or about March, 1899, a first-class steam siren will be established on the seaward side of Point Chehalis, southerly side of the entrance to Grays Harbour, to sound, during thick foggy weather, blasts of 5 seconds duration separated by alternate silent intervals of 5 and 75 seconds.

Point Adams Light has been discontinued since the close of the year.

Clatsop Spit Buoy No. 8, a first-class nun, was changed November 18, 1898, and is now moored in 45 feet of water to mark the north edge of Clatsop Spit, its bearings being:—Fort Stevens wharf port light, E.S.E. 5/8 E.; Cape Disappointment (Lighthouse), N.W. by W.; McGowans wharf (outer end), E.N.E.

On November 26, 1898, the position of the wreck of the Great Republic black bell buoy was changed and it is now moored in 33 feet of water:—North Head Lighthouse, bearing N.W. 3/8 W.; Cape Disappointment Lighthouse, N.W. by N.; Point Adams Lighthouse, S.E. by E. 1/4 E.

Pilotage. An Act of the last legislature abolished compulsory pilotage on the Columbia and Willamette Rivers, but bar pilotage remains as hitherto.

Shipbuilding. Two torpedo boats were finished during the year, both of which attained a higher speed than the contract rate of 22 knots. A destroyer is now in process of construction, and will be launched about July. The vessel is contracted to have a speed of 30 knots.

Population, industries, and health. Population. It is said there has been a large immigration to Oregon and Washington during 1898 and so far in 1899, but the methods of estimating the population are not to be relied upon. The census will be taken in 1900.

Agriculture, mining, fisheries, lumber, and flour-milling are still the principal industries in this State, and in fact of the entire district. Pulp and paper mills show increased development, but the woollen mills did a smaller business, owing to the lessened demand for the Klondike. The mines increased their production, and a beet sugar factory has been in operation, though it did only a small business during the year. Another large one is being built in Spokane County, Washington.

Mining. Precious metals. According to Wells, Fargo and Co.'s annual report the value of the precious metals produced in the States of Idaho, Oregon, and Washington during the year 1898 was as follows:—

States.	Gold.	Silver.	Ores and Base Bullion.	Total.
	£	£	£	£
Idaho	497,400	744,733	1,087,520	2,329,653
Oregon	434,474	7,747	803	443,024
Washington	64,119	10,400	17,000	91,519
Total	995,993	762,880	1,105,323	2,864,196

The following reports by the superintendents of the United States Assay Offices at Boise City in respect of Idaho's product and at Helena in respect of that of Oregon differ very considerably from the foregoing, but do not agree with other estimates, which exceed those of Wells, Fargo, and Co. :—

Product.		Idaho. Quantity.	Idaho. Value.	Oregon. Quantity.	Oregon. Value.
			£		£
Gold	Fine ozs.	110,000	454,740	58,856	243,334
Silver	„	6,000,000	1,548,000	128,326	33,183
Lead	Lbs.	141,467,260	1,075,151	..	..
Total		..	3,077,891	..	276,517

Copper. A great development in the production of copper in this district may be looked for in the near future, particularly in the Seven Devils District of Idaho, to which a railway is being built and where the deposits of copper are rich and extensive.

Lead. The production of lead was largely increased, as the metal has appreciated very much.

Iron. The Oregon iron furnaces have not been in blast for two years past, but there has been some production in Washington.

Coal. The product of the Washington coal mines was 1,775,257 tons and the number of men employed 3,337. The Oregon mines produced 56,782 tons. Average value of coal at tidewater about 12s. per ton. There were nine fatal accidents and 75 injuries reported by the mine inspector of Washington during the year 1898.

Manufactures. Oregon and Washington have great potentialities in the way of manufactures, producing raw material in abundance and having good water power at many points; but there has not been as yet any great development in this respect, which is probably due to the competition of eastern goods manufactured by cheaper labour and landed under favour of railroad tariffs which are lower from east to west than from west to east, and also, of course, to the larger capital of the eastern manufacturers. There has been a continued improvement in the minor industries during the year, and I hear few of the complaints of want of employment which have been so common of late years.

Fishing industry. The report of the Fish and Game Protector of the State of Oregon states that there were 26 firms in the State engaged in salmon fishing and that these employed 3,265 fishermen and 2,104 other hands; 1,435 boats were employed and 1,547 gill nets in addition to traps and seines. 34,970,293 lbs. of salmon were taken from the waters of the Columbia and its tributaries, 2d. per lb. was paid for Chinook, 1d. per lb. for steel heads, 1½d. for blue backs, and ⅞d. for silver sides.

On the Washington side of the river there were seven firms employing 1,970 hands.

Flour milling. As will be noted under another heading in this report the production of flour has largely increased. The Portland Flour Mills have a daily capacity of 2,000 barrels, and there are large mills at Oregon City, Salem, Albany, and Pendleton, besides numerous smaller mills throughout the State. At Tacoma, Seattle, Spokane, and Walla Walla in Washington there are also large export mills. Prospects are for a large increase in this industry.

Saw mills. The saw mills generally run full time during the year, employing a great many hands.

Woollen mills. The woollen mills were generally run to their full capacity during 1898. These mills find a ready market for their blankets and heavy goods in which they excel, and their flannels, tweeds, cashmeres, and worsteds are steadily improving. As an example of what they are doing I send with this report small samples of their best grades of suitings and trouserings.*

Paper and pulp. There are many mills in this State which manufacture paper-pulp from straw, cottonwood, spruce, and white fir. Two mills at Oregon City, it is stated, turn out 80 tons of paper per day, principally for newspapers, of which, as noted in Annex B, over 2,500 tons were shipped during the year to China and Japan.

Beet sugar. The sugar factory at La Grande, although fully equipped to use 350 tons of beets per day, found itself hampered last year by the inexperience of farmers, and only received 8,147 tons of beets, which enabled the mill to run only 28 days, and from which was manufactured 1,830,000 lbs. of sugar. The quality was satisfactory, but the quantity was not what had been expected, owing to lack of culture. Strong efforts were made to pass a Bill granting a bounty of 1 dol. (4s.) per ton of 2,000 lbs., but they were unsuccessful. The State of Washington passed a Bounty Bill in 1896 granting ½ c. (¼d.) per lb. of refined sugar for five years, with the provision that it should not exceed 50,000 dol. (10,000l.) in any one year. Another large factory is being constructed at Waverley, in Spokane County, Washington, and will probably be in operation during the season of 1899.

Other manufactures. Meat packing is carried on on a fair scale with a most complete plant under Government inspection. Rope and cordage is supplied from a well-equipped factory here, and there is a linseed

* Sent to the Association of Chambers of Commerce.

oil mill with a capacity of 450,000 bushels per annum, but the production of the State does not at present supply more than one-third of the seed required. Foundry and repair shops were fairly busy during the year, and furniture factories were better employed than for years past. The home manufacture of clothing is increasing.

Labour. There is still room for improvement in skilled labour, but the building trade has advanced considerably. The demand has exceeded the supply for unskilled labour on railways, and also for farm hands.

Clerks, &c. I must, however, repeat my annual warning that the services of clerks and salesmen are not always in demand, and the movement towards the concentration of business in the form of trusts does not tend to improve matters in this respect.

Births and deaths. Health. The number of births registered in this city during the year was 867, 20 per cent. less than in 1897, and the deaths were 842, somewhat larger than in 1897. Estimating the city's population at 89,000, this gives a mortality rate of 9·46; but the Health Department takes the population as 92,500, excludes the deaths of persons brought here for treatment, and brings out the death-rate as 8·17. There is a plumbing inspector employed by the city who has done systematic work, and strong efforts are made to have a special officer appointed to inspect milk and meats. There has been a remarkable decrease in the number of cases of diphtheria and measles, and an increase in scarlet and typhoid fevers. Deaths from tuberculosis, pneumonia, and bronchitis were more numerous. All garbage is cremated.

Public works. River and harbour works. Oregon. From the annual report of Major W. L. Fisk and Captain Charles L. Potter, of the United States Engineers, I extract the following information as to work under their charge:—

At Coos Bay, a harbour of some importance in Southern Oregon, the entrance is being improved by the jetty system, and during the fiscal year ending June 30, 1898, a considerable quantity of rock was dumped on the jetty, bringing 4,528 feet of it up to a high tide level. The results have so far been satisfactory. The original estimate of cost was 493,282*l.*

The work done on the Willamette and Columbia Rivers is mentioned in another part of this report. Works of improvement are also being carried on at Coquille, Siuslaw, Tillamook Bay, and Yaquina, and on several inland rivers, but these are only of local importance.

Washington. Gray's Harbour, Washington, is under the charge of Captain Taylor, and from his annual report the information is derived.

Work was begun on the 3½-mile jetty; a receiving wharf was built, and a trestle 7,000 feet long was constructed to the jetty proper. The work will cost 200,000*l.*, and should be completed in 1900. 570,000 tons of rock will be required on the work, and the engineers expect to obtain a depth of 24 feet at mean low water across the bar. This harbour has a foreign trade in lumber. During the last half of the year some progress was made with the work.

(414)

PORTLAND.

Railways. There has been some movement in railway construction in the district during the year, principally in subsidiary lines to the Oregon Railway and Navigation Company and the Northern Pacific. The following mileage has been added to the existing works: Biggs to Moro, Oregon, 30 miles, with ultimate destination Prineville; Wallula to Grange City, Washington, 66 miles; Dayton to Covello, Washington, 13 miles; Fairfield to Waverley, Washington, five miles; Juliaetta to Lewiston, Idaho, 25 miles; being 139 miles in all, and other extensions are projected, notably a line from Lewiston up the Clearwater, 101 miles, to Mount Idaho.

The North-West Railway Company is constructing a line from Huntington along the Snake River to Ballards, tapping the Seven Devils copper district.

Agriculture. Agricultural conditions were extremely favourable during the year, and, with the exception of potatoes, the yield of all crops was large and the quality and condition excellent. And, as the Section Director of the United States Department of Agriculture puts it, "There is not a single adverse condition, weather or crops, for the season of 1898 to chronicle in the State of Oregon." Equally favourable reports were made by the Section Directors of the States of Washington and Idaho. The losses of animals on the ranges were rather above the average.

Lands: Oregon. In his last report the Oregon State Land Agent says: "As respects land sales by the State of Oregon, I can say they are well-nigh closed." This refers to school lands, but in every county of the State there is more or less Government land open for entry, and also railroad lands which may be purchased on reasonable terms, though most of the land within reach of transportation facilities is taken. Improved land can be bought at from 2l. to 20l. per acre, according to location and amount and quality of improvements. The Land Receiver at Oregon City makes the following statement of Government land in Oregon:—

	Acres.
Total area of land surface	61,626,218
Area appropriated	19,829,172
„ unappropriated	35,892,318
„ reserved	5,904,728

In Idaho. The Idaho State Board of Horticulture gives the area of the State as 55,228,160 acres, classified as 16,000,000 acres of agricultural land, of which about two-thirds require irrigation, 25,000,000 acres grass-growing lands, and the rest mineral lands.

The minimum price of selected school lands belonging to the State is 2l. per acre, which is a very high price for raw uncultivated land, but these lands are very productive, and a large quantity of wheat is exported through the parts of the district.

Cereals. No reliable returns are at hand of the cereal harvests, but that of wheat in the entire Consular district was undoubtedly about 40,000,000 bushels, and it is believed the yield of oats and barley was considerably in excess of 1897. Wheat was a profitable crop, though prices were lower than in 1897, and this is also true of oats and barley. Statistics are given under the head of exports. Acreage under wheat in Oregon is given as 1,060,000.

Much attention is now paid to orchards and the cultivation of fruits, and constant supervision is exercised over this rapidly increasing business by the State Board of Horticulture which this year issued a very handsomely illustrated report. This Board is composed of experienced growers, and under the system of district inspectors there is less chance than formerly of the spread of disease; although prices were comparatively low, growers generally made money, and are improving the quality of their dried fruit. There is, of course, some danger of over-stocking the markets.

Orchards.

In order to show the increase in the production of prunes alone I give the following comparison of the product of 8,921 acres in six counties:—

Prunes.

DRIED PRUNES.

Year.	Quantity.
	Lbs.
1895	1,454,000
1898	5,950,000
Increase in 3 years	4,496,000

The following estimate of cost of an orchard of 10 acres of prunes in Polk County, the trees planted 20 feet apart, may be interesting. It does not include the value of the land:—

EXPENDITURE.

	Amount.
	Dollars.
1,100 yearling trees (110 per acre), at 6 c.	66
Ploughing and cultivation	20
Planting trees, 1,100, at 1 c.	11
Cultivation and care, 1st and 2nd years, more than offset by potato or bean crop	..
Cultivation, 3rd year	30
,, 4th, 5th, 6th, and 7th years	120
Total	247
	£ s.
Equiv. in sterling	49 8

(414)

PORTLAND.

RECEIPTS.

	Amount.
	Dollars.
4th year, ⅓ bushel of prunes per tree, at 60 c. per bushel	220
5th year, ½ bushel per tree, at 60 c.	330
6th year, allow for a failure of crops	..
7th year, 1 bushel of dried prunes per tree, at 1 dol.	1,100
Total	1,650
	£
Equiv. in sterling	330

Profit on prunes.

In connection with the above a farmer from the same county gives the following as the result of his work on 25 acres planted with 300 trees to the acre:—

EXPENDITURE.

	Amount.
	Dollars.
One man's wages, 12 months, at 26 dol.	312
,, ,, 3 months, at 26 dol.	78
Horse and feed, &c.	200
Picking fruit	300
50 days' drying, 12 hands, at 15 dol. 50 c. per day	775
Lye and repairs	20
Sacks	96
Cartage of fruit	10
Fertilisers	75
Paid for 1,500 bushels of prunes, at 30 c.	450
Total	2,316
	£ s.
Equiv. in sterling	463 4

RECEIPTS.

	Amount.
	Dol. c.
Petites, 16 tons	505 0
Italians, 52½ tons	3,709 75
,, 900 lbs., at 2 c.	18 0
,, 4 tons	160 0
Silvers, 3 tons	240 0
Total	4,632 75
	£ s.
Equiv. in sterling	926 11

This prune grower has 2,000*l*. invested in his property. I have, however, heard very different accounts from individuals, some of them British, who say they cannot make anything in fruit farming, and I would therefore advise no one to be led away by published figures, but to make personal examination before going into this or any other business.

According to the Idaho State Board, there are 30,686 acres planted in fruit in that State.

Flax seed and fibre. Farmers are being encouraged to raise flax both for the seed and the fibre. A Belgian expert in fibre recently made the remark that he was astonished at the excellence of the flax fibre cultivated for the seed alone, and said it compared favourably with straw grown for fibre only. The cost of growing flax for the seed only is said by good authorities to be 1*l*. 14*s*. 5*d*. per acre, and the average product is 19½ bushels, valued at 3*l*. 18*s*. So far growers have not utilized the fibre, but experiments have been made on a scale large enough to demonstrate its superior quality. Experiments are also being made in the cultivation of hemp, ramie, and American jute.

Hops. Hops have been a profitable crop during the year, which will tend to a larger acreage being planted in 1899.

Sugar beets. As mentioned under the head of sugar, farmers were not particularly successful in growing sugar beets, but a large quantity will be grown next year for which the factories contract at 16*s*. per ton. 3,200 acres are planted in Union County alone.

Potatoes. The crop of potatoes was below the average, and prices ran up very high at the close of the year, when good potatoes retailed at 4*s*. per 100 lbs.

Stock farming. Although winter losses of stock and sheep were rather above normal, these losses were more than made up in value by the continued advance of prices. Large numbers of cattle and sheep were sold at higher prices to Eastern buyers and there is no doubt that ranching was highly profitable. A careful canvass of the State at the close of the year produced the following result, but statistics in this State are not as a rule very reliable:—

	Number.	Average Value.	Value.
		£ s.	£
Horses	217,535	5 0	1,087,675
Cattle	459,034	4 10	2,065,653
Sheep	1,807,928	0 10	903,964
Swine	87,532	1 12	140,051

At the beginning of 1898 the number of sheep in this Consular district was given on reliable authority as 2,580,833 in Oregon; 726,302 in Washington; and 1,548,960 in Idaho. The average market value on the ranges for cattle was, yearlings 3*l*. 15*s*., two-year-olds 4*l*. 17*s*., and three-year-olds 6*l*. Sheep averaged, after shearing, 8*s*. for lambs, 10*s*. 8*d*. for two-year-olds, and 9*s*. 7*d*. for ewes.

Angora goats.

The flocks of Angora goats are increasing and there is a good demand for the mohair, which sold readily at about 1s. 4d. per lb. They thrive on rough, partially cleared brushy land, require little care, and are profitable.

General remarks. Dry dock needed.

In my last report (Annual Series No. 2115) I referred to the need of a dry dock here. Both the port of Portland Commission and a private firm had the matter under consideration, but so far no practical steps have been taken in the matter. I am inclined to believe British capitalists would find this a fair investment, and might even find a disposition on the part of residents here to assist in the enterprise.

Assessment and taxation.

The valuation of all property within the State of Oregon liable to taxation during 1898 was 26,706,715l., and within this city 7,679,324l. Rate of taxation for State, county, and road purposes 1·85 per cent.; school purposes 0·40 per cent.; port of Portland 0·15 per cent.; and city tax 0·80 per cent.

City government and finances.

A new city charter passed through the Legislature which increased the power and responsibility of the mayor, provided for a board of public works, and limited the indebtedness of the city. Under its provision the floating debt was funded and 30-year 5 per cent. bonds to the extent of 86,000l. were sold. These were sold at a premium of 24·83 The bonded debt of the city of Portland at the close of the year was 1,084,850l. Interest charges are promptly met and the credit of the city is good. The total general revenue of Portland was 106,299l., and expenditure 113,184l. This does not include either street and sewer assessments or water commission revenues.

Real estate.

There has been a decided improvement in values of real estate both in town and country, and more property is changing hands than for a long time back.

Mr Vice-Consul Alexander's report annexed gives much favourable information regarding the Washington section of this district, and reports from the Vice-Consuls at Astoria and Port Townsend are also annexed.

Annex A.—RETURN of all Shipping at the Port of Portland, Oregon, during the Year 1898.

ENTERED.

Nationality.	Sailing. Number of Vessels.	Sailing. Tons.	Steam. Number of Vessels.	Steam. Tons.	Total. Number of Vessels.	Total. Tons.
British	102	178,690	19	40,356	121	219,046
American, from Atlantic ports	1	1,931	1	428	2	2,359
American coasting	18	8,443	133	169,493	151	177,936
German	20	35,444	2	2,130	22	37,574
Norwegian	1	1,567	2	2,886	3	4,453
French	3	4,395	...	...	3	4,395
Danish	2	3,347	...	...	2	3,347
Japanese	2	2,346	...	...	2	2,346
Austro-Hungarian	...	...	1	1,974	1	1,974
Russian	1	1,325	...	...	1	1,325
Total	150	237,488	158	217,267	308	454,755
,, for the year preceding	115	141,520	165	193,724	280	335,244

CLEARED.

Nationality.	Sailing. Number of Vessels.	Sailing. Tons.	Steam. Number of Vessels.	Steam. Tons.	Total. Number of Vessels.	Total. Tons.
British	105	181,222	20	43,372	125	224,594
American, to foreign countries	...	...	1	1,689	1	1,689
American coasting	16	4,986	136	160,060	152	165,046
German	19	33,028	2	2,130	21	35,158
French	5	7,836	...	...	5	7,836
Norwegian	...	...	2	2,886	2	2,886
Japanese	2	2,346	...	...	2	2,346
Austro-Hungarian	...	...	1	1,974	1	1,974
Danish	1	1,640	...	...	1	1,640
Russian	1	1,325	...	...	1	1,325
Total	149	232,383	162	212,111	311	444,494
,, for the year preceding	126	146,665	162	186,562	288	333,227

PORTLAND.

Annex B.—RETURN of Principal Articles of Export from Portland, Oregon, during the Years 1898-97.

Articles.		1898. Quantity.	1898. Value. £	1897. Quantity.	1897. Value. £
Wheat	Quarters	1,539,084	1,860,424	907,774	1,254,144
,, flour	Sacks	574,443	579,086	312,025	350,997
Timber	Feet	9,618,000	16,989	13,129,273	20,358
Barley	Bushels	232,452	26,539	2,726	206
Oats	,,	102,453	8,558	...	...
Paper	Lbs.	5,675,443	24,312	...	4,486
Tinned salmon	,,	38,500	385	62,400	975
Raw cotton, in transit	,,	1,867,500	21,560	1,518,500	17,919
Beef	Barrels	1,050	2,074	...	...
Bottled beer	Dozen	5,027	1,303	...	...
Boilers, engines, and machinery	...	...	5,829	...	...
Railway iron and material	Tons	...	4,128	984	3,438
Tools, hardware, and other manufactures of iron and steel	...	...	2,764	...	...
Wire nails	...	...	...	...	10,625
Bar- and sheet-iron and steel	Tons	142	1,139	...	...
Other articles	...	...	4,243	...	9,258
Total	...	...	2,559,333	...	1,672,406

RETURN of Principal Articles of Import to Portland, Oregon, during the Years 1898-97.

Articles.		1898. Quantity.	1898. Value. £	1897. Quantity.	1897. Value. £
Raw and waste silk	Lbs.	209,922	103,500	142,696	86,771
Jute bags and bagging	...	...	38,448	...	14,721
Hemp, manilla, and jute	Tons	942	19,353	1,506	19,045
Sulphur	,,	3,703	18,107	1,157	4,340
Rice	Lbs.	4,195,919	17,348	3,993,119	12,415
Sugar	,,	1,943,759	10,620	2,500,297	13,029
Tea	,,	506,766	13,375	861,025	25,140
Earthenware and chinaware	...	...	13,559	...	8,845
Raw clothing wools	Lbs.	65,875	1,529	...	...
Coffee	,,	239,415	5,565	135,500	4,256
Matting	Sq. yards	239,590	4,240	...	37,537
Salt	Lbs.	5,162,400	3,483	6,136,600	2,357
Cement	Casks	23,702	6,835	51,086	12,230
Window glass	Lbs.	1,092,166	4,409	857,954	3,281
Coal	Tons	8,377	3,845	25,879	10,449
Tin and terne plate	Lbs.	2,094	11	599,715	2,717
Spirits	Gallons	18,955	2,812	18,482	2,330
Malt liquor	,,	14,643	2,926	2,843	594
Caustic soda	Lbs.	391,846	1,256	345,304	1,168
Soda ash	,,	507,454	615	334,350	528
Chloride of lime	,,	19,276	72	7,895	35
Soda	,,	116,547	153	152,186	226
Fire-bricks	Tons	747	596	...	...
Oils	...	...	1,721	...	1,545
Paints	...	...	294	...	1,150
Flax, twine, and manufactures of flax and hemp	...	...	7,954	...	4,326
Pig-tin	Lbs.	22,482	605	...	...
Spices	,,	126,829	2,576	89,211	1,242
Toys	...	...	1,427	...	...
Cutlery	...	...	619	...	806
Pig- and bar-iron	Tons	150	631	...	...
Knit goods	...	...	865	...	...
All other articles	...	...	18,471	...	24,650
Total	...	...	307,820	...	295,733
Transit entries—					
Tea	Lbs.	1,967,213	53,241	1,104,934	33,585
Matting	...	...	17,521	...	36,728
Silk	...	...	7,403	...	131,056
Rice	Lbs.	1,567,550	7,425	...	...
Other articles	...	...	21,351	...	34,612
Grand total	...	...	414,761	...	531,714

ASTORIA.

Annex C.—TABLE showing Total Value of all Articles Exported from and Imported to Portland, Oregon, to and from Foreign Countries during the Years 1898–97.

Country.	Exports. 1898.	Exports. 1897.	Imports. 1898.	Imports. 1897.
	£	£	£	£
Great Britain	1,756,362	1,154,333	31,724	30,490
South Africa	198,471	65,281	25	..
British India and East Indies	113	..	51,087	21,243
British India and East Indies transit	..	..	1,896	240
Australia	..	..	1,553	7,425
British Columbia	..	1,052	3,671	4,239
Canada by rail	..	..	174	..
Hong-Kong	242,392 ⎫		45,631 ⎫	
China	9,232 ⎬	184,615	2,304 ⎬	203,929
Japan	128,982 ⎭		133,833 ⎭	
China and Japan in transit	21,560	31,983	105,045	235,741
Cape de Verdes for orders	101,353	105,122	..	..
Asiatic Russia	57,160	4,642	..	..
Korea	..	3,729	..	..
Germany	..	..	5,505	7,761
Belgium	12,000	..	15,733	13,725
France	28,620	114,167	106	331
Italy	..	..	7,857	..
Philippine Islands	944	..	6,578	3,931
Hawaiian Islands	1,958	7,057	163	67
Cuba	..	..	1,353	..
Other countries	186	425	523	2,592
Total	2,559,333	1,672,406	414,761	531,714

ASTORIA.

Mr. Vice-Consul Cherry reports as follows:—

At the commencement of the year business in Astoria was very dull. Canned salmon was quoted at a very low figure and the prospects for the coming summer season were very gloomy. Shortly after the opening of the fishing season, however, prices advanced materially, which enabled the canners to pay a higher price for the raw article. This, with the completion of the long-looked-for railroad connecting the town with the interior of the State, gave rise to a more hopeful feeling, which was upheld by the steady fishing in the autumn. Real estate business has shown no improvement, one reason being, in my opinion, the enormous indebtedness, amounting to 80,000*l.*, in a population of 8,000. In the country there has been a fair demand for timber lands, and more has changed hands in the past six months than for several years previously, while prospects are good for further sales at still better prices.

General remarks.

Imports.

Owing to the almost total loss of the British tin-plate trade, the total value of imports into Astoria has fallen off greatly. Items other than tin-plates show a slight increase.

Exports.

But little salmon is now exported, nearly all of the pack being consumed in the markets of the United States.

Products of the district.

Owing to geographical features the district of Astoria is divided into four parts, the products of which are the same, viz.:— Forest products, fisheries, and agriculture, the last being principally confined to dairying. In the north, forest productions have the greatest proportion; in the south, agriculture; and in the mid-section, fisheries. As there is but little intercourse between these sections, I find it very difficult to obtain statistics.

The following table shows the value of the products sent away from the different divisions:—

	Value.			
	Gray's Harbour.	Willapa Harbour.	Columbia River.	Tillamook Bay.
	£	£	£	£
Forest products	300,000	40,000	140,000	24,800
Fisheries	15,000	35,000	394,000	15,900
Agriculture	14,900	12,000	56,000	40,000

A comparatively small amount of the above went to foreign markets, merely a few cargoes of lumber and a few thousand cases of canned salmon.

Mining.

Although it is known that there are beds of coal of fair quality in this district, nothing has been done to develop them on account of their inaccessibility. No other minerals have yet been discovered in the district.

Logging.

Owing to the increased demand logging has been engaged in to a greater extent than formerly, most of the logs, at least in the Columbia River section, having gone out of the district. Prices have ranged from 1*l*. to 1*l*. 4*s*. per 1,000 feet. Two large rafts of piling were towed from Astoria to San Francisco, one of them meeting with disaster, resulting in the loss of over one-third of the raft.

Lumber.

The anticipated increase in the lumber business has not been realised. The mills have devoted themselves to the making of boxes for canned salmon for the local demand, and for canned fruit in the parts of this State and in California. In the Gray's Harbour section the lumber trade shows an increase.

Fisheries.

Prices of canned salmon went up early in the season, and thus canners were able to pay fishermen the full price of 2½*d*. per lb. for the raw fish. The autumn fishing was conducted on a larger scale than ever before, giving fishermen a longer season to keep at work in.

Sturgeon-fishing on the lower Columbia River seems to be a lost industry.

ASTORIA.

Salmon canning. The total salmon pack for this Vice-Consular district amounts to 460,450 cases, both spring and fall pack as follows:—

	Quantity.
	Cases.
Columbia River, spring catch	325,000
,, ,, fall catch	75,200
Coast north of Columbia River	33,100
,, south of ,, ,,	27,150
Total	460,450

This shows a considerable falling off in the pack of spring salmon on the lower Columbia River. Prices were good and the pack was sold off promptly. A great effort was made to consolidate the canneries on the Columbia River into an association with the ostensible purpose of curtailing expenses and avoiding injurious competition. Less than half of the canneries, however, have joined the combination. This association is known as the Columbia River Canneries Company.

Can making. The can factory has all that it can do during the season to keep up with its orders. In this connection it may be well to mention the fact that American tin-plates in 100 lb. boxes are quoted at 4 dol. in Astoria, equal to 16s. 8d. Block-tin has risen in price fully 75 per cent. since the beginning of last year.

Tanning. I understand that the local tannery is steadily increasing its business, confining itself to the making of saddle and harness leather, which is sold in Chicago.

Frozen fresh fish. The completion of the railroad at once made it possible to operate cold storage plants, and two were installed in old buildings. More than 200,000 fresh salmon, exceeding 6,000,000 lbs in weight, were shipped by rail to the principal cities in the Mississippi Valley and on the Atlantic Coast. One of the cold storage concerns is now completing a building with the latest improved machinery, and promises to double the shipments from Astoria during the coming season. At least half of this increased output is intended for the German market.

Shipping and navigation. There has been a decided increase in the number and tonnage of vessels entering the Columbia River in the foreign trade. The proportion of British vessels, while smaller in numbers, is slightly greater in tonnage.

Disasters. I am glad to report that no disasters to shipping of any account have occurred in the district last year.

Pilot service. The new pilot schooner "Joseph Pulitzer" arrived from New York in July, just in time for the new shipping season. Shortly after her arrival the Washington State pilot-boat was condemned, and a number of her pilots joined the Oregon boats. The Oregon pilots now have two schooners, but are considerably hampered in that they are compelled to rely on the tug-boats to get back to the schooners after having piloted vessels in.

ASTORIA.

Tug-boat service.
The tug-boat service at the bar was anything but what it should have been, and there was much detention to shipping. A new tug is now building for the service, and it is hoped that with this boat under a more efficient management, there will be an improvement.

Harbour improvements required.
Further improvement of the harbour by the continuation of the present jetty at the mouth of the river is greatly needed, for at the present time shipping is exposed to the sweep of the sea for 2 miles before the shallowest place is reached. This has been the means of preventing vessels from getting to sea when the depth of water was quite sufficient.

Marine ways:
Marine ways, I am sure, would pay dividends if constructed at this port, but they should be built to accommodate vessels of at least 1,800 tons register. At present there is nothing to serve a ship between San Francisco and Esquimalt.

New lighthouse.
The first-class light on North Head, mentioned in my last report as being under construction, was completed, and the light has been continually exhibited since March 1 last. It is considered by both shipmasters and pilots a very satisfactory aid to the navigation of the approach to the river.

Public works. Fortifications.
The work commenced in 1897 on the fortifications at Fort Stevens, to the south of the entrance, and on Chinook Point, a few miles in on the north side, is still progressing. When these fortifications are completed, the works at Cape Disappointment will, no doubt, receive attention.

Railway.
The completion of the long-looked-for railroad connecting Astoria with the great railway systems of the United States was not effected until May 17, 1898, only two weeks within the contract time.

Bridge.
A much-needed bridge over Young's River to the south of Astoria is now under construction, and, when finished, will be of great benefit to the thriving farming community adjacent as well as to the town.

Buildings.
Building in the town proper has been confined to a few business establishments, which, with the new railroad wharf and warehouse and a fish-freezing factory, are all the improvements made in the town during the year.

ASTORIA.

Annex A.—RETURN of all Shipping at the Port of Astoria during the Year 1898.

ENTERED.

Nationality.	Sailing. Number of Vessels.	Sailing. Tons.	Steam. Number of Vessels.	Steam. Tons.	Total. Number of Vessels.	Total. Tons.
British	95	168,524	19	40,081	114	208,605
American coasting	69	22,379	391	360,020	460	382,399
,, foreign	2	1,164	24	22,427	26	23,591
Danish	1	1,651	...	...	1	1,651
French	4	5,477	...	...	4	5,477
German	18	31,832	1	1,065	19	32,897
Austro-Hungarian	...	...	1	1,974	1	1,974
Japanese	2	2,296	...	...	2	2,296
Norwegian	1	1,568	3	3,722	4	5,290
Russian	1	1,365	...	...	1	1,365
Total	193	236,256	439	429,289	632	665,545
,, for the year preceding	163	166,437	380	343,151	576	509,588

CLEARED.

Nationality.	Sailing. Number of Vessels.	Sailing. Tons.	Steam. Number of Vessels.	Steam. Tons.	Total. Number of Vessels.	Total. Tons.
British	10	21,018	11	25,596	21	46,614
American coasting	62	17,602	343	349,928	405	367,530
,, foreign	2	1,226	11	9,051	13	10,277
Danish	...	...	...	...	...	...
German	1	2,708	...	...	1	2,708
Norwegian	1	1,002	...	...	1	1,002
Total	76	43,556	365	384,575	441	428,131
,, for the year preceding	124	54,217	309	310,125	433	364,342

Annex B.—RETURN of Principal Articles of Export from Astoria during the Years 1898-97.

Articles.		1898. Quantity.	1898. Value.	1897. Quantity.	1897. Value.
			£		£
Salmon	Cases	13,668	12,850	13,457	13,855
Wheat	Bushels	145,382	23,242	170,252	28,664
Flour	Barrels	850	511	..	..
Lumber	1,000 feet	1,817	3,003	5,533	9,594
Sundries	..	..	523	..	1,989
Total	..	..	40,129	..	54,102

ASTORIA.

RETURN of Principal Articles of Import from Astoria during the Years 1898–97.

Articles.		1898.		1897.	
		Quantity.	Value.	Quantity.	Value.
			£		£
Tin-plates	Boxes	3,000	1,388	56,935	26,835
Salt	Lbs.	67,200	60	..	..
Coal	Tons	3,562	1,825	3,202	1,599
Cement	Barrels	7,000	1,946	6,500	1,684
Sundries	..	240	240	..	143
Total	..	..	5,459	..	30,261

Annex C.—TABLE showing Total Value of all Articles Exported from and Imported to Astoria, Oregon, to and from Foreign Countries during the Years 1898–97.

Country.	Exports.		Imports.	
	1898.	1897.	1898.	1897.
	£	£	£	£
Great Britain	20,552	18,800	1,688	26,605
British colonies	3,314	9,509	1,825	2,500
All other countries	16,263	25,793	1,946	1,156
Total	40,129	54,102	5,459	30,261

TACOMA AND SEATTLE.

Mr. Vice-Consul Alexander reports as follows:—

General remarks relative to the State of Washington. The past year has been more prosperous in the State of Washington than that preceding it. In addition to the finding of gold in the North-West Territory of Canada and the acquisition of the Sandwich Islands, the events following the Hispano-American war have contributed largely to this result. The drought in California has created a market for Washington products, and has brought them more widely to public attention. The exportation of flour and timber goes on without abatement between here and the Orient, but imports thence seem to have diminished to some extent lately.

Health. The general state of health has been good, no epidemic diseases of a serious nature having occurred. The winter was very severe on stock, the loss on the ranges having been heavy, where no provision was made. The State Veterinarian reports that during the past two years his office has examined 452 horses, 691 cattle, and 15,500 sheep—16,643 animals in all. Of this number 108 horses and seven cattle were found to be diseased; black leg in calves and distemper and influenza in horses have also prevailed to some extent. The lack of adequate appropriations by the Legislature for the State Veterinarian's office prevented proper attention being paid to requests received for examination of stock, and in consequence not a few centres of infection have been left, from which the different diseases have spread, causing more or less loss to the stock industry.

Industries.

The railway shipments from the State to Eastern points viâ the Great Nothern, Northern Pacific, and Canadian Pacific Railways amounted during the year to 157,202,000 feet of timber and 2,869,510,000 shingles, as compared with 122,736,000 feet of timber and 2,806,400,000 shingles in the preceding year. The cargo shipments from the State were 127,686,000 feet of timber, valued at 218,014*l*., and 22,041,000 shingles, valued at 6,699*l*. These cargo figures are exclusive of the domestic trade. The total timber and shingle shipments for the year are estimated by the local authorities at 575,388,000 feet of timber, and 2,900,551,000 shingles.

Mining.

There has been a general increase in activity in the coal-mining business, a few more mines being developed. The output of coal for the year is estimated by the State Coal Mine Inspector at 1,715,515 tons, valued at 857,758*l*., making an average of 10*s*. per ton. Statistics of the two smelters in the State show a total output of 58,083 ozs. of gold, valued at 240,115*l*.; 1,891,350 ozs. of silver, valued at 219,397*l*.; 1,642,000 lbs. of copper, valued at 39,408*l*.; and 17,847,167 lbs. of lead, valued at 122,100*l*.; making a total value of 621,020*l*.

Fisheries.

In 1898, 1,889 fishing licenses were issued, as compared with 2,692 in the preceding year. The run of salmon was one of the smallest ever known, particularly of the "sockeye" variety, the total pack amounting to 603,000 cases as against 620,277 cases in 1897. The value of the canned salmon is given as 439,099*l*.; that of fresh, salted, and smoked fish of all kinds, as 5,192*l*.; oysters, 38,200*l*.; clams and crabs, 7,278*l*. The State invested 4,240*l*. in four salmon hatcheries during the year, from which over 17,000,000 young salmon were produced. One or two more new hatcheries are in contemplation, for which appropriations have been made and the sites are being selected. There are now 820 acres of cultivated oyster beds in the waters of Puget Sound, and 2,200 acres in Willapa Harbour.

Agriculture.

Crop statistics for the State are estimated for the year as follows:—Wheat, acreage 1,250,000, yielding 19,000,000 bushels, of which a very considerable portion is held by farmers at the present time; oats, acreage 42,500, yielding 600,000 bushels, valued at 185,000*l*.; barley, acreage 15,000, yielding 600,000 bushels. In addition to this, about 100,000 bushels of maize are credited to the State. The price of oats and barley has been high in 1898—4*l*. to 4*l*. 8*s*. per ton—while an average price ruled for wheat. Farmers harvested their crops in good condition, and the yield, on the whole, was very good. The prices obtained

(414)

for oats and barley have been profitable to producers, and wheat has sold for a price that leaves a fair return on the investment, after paying expenses, to the farmer; generally speaking, agriculturists have made money. Although the potato crop was very good some disease has appeared, which made the supply very short, and has increased the price per ton far above that of 1897 The sheep and wool industry of the State shows an improvement, being valued at 402,660*l*.

Dairying. In spite of the fact that the dairy industry has shown considerable increase during the year, the home products are still far from adequate to the demand, and much butter and cheese is shipped from the Eastern States. The acreage of forage crops in the State is estimated at 210,851 acres, and that of grazing lands at 7,234,684 acres; of these lands, 2,942,198 acres are "improved," and support 62,597 milch cows. The total number of cattle is given as 229,395, valued at 614,466*l*. The value of dairy products manufactured by the various creameries in the State during the year is estimated at 118,000*l*., an increase of nearly 20,000*l*. over the year 1897. Some progress has been made by the Washington dairymen in improving the quality of their stock; during the last half of the year there has been a demand for dairy cattle generally, and prospects for the growth of this industry are good. The Sandwich Islands, China, Japan, and the Philippines offer good fields for expansion, but careful, intelligent methods are necessary to insure success, and to these insufficient attention has been paid in the past. The price of creamery butter has ranged from 10*d*. to 15*d*. per lb.

Horticulture. Fruit-growing continues to hold a foremost place among the industries of the State, and very large numbers of fruit trees of the several varieties have been planted. The value of the 1898 crop is placed by the State Commissioner of Horticulture at about 175,000*l*. The farmers still have to contend with the difficulty of finding markets for their products, but a good market for apples has been found in the eastern part of the country. Market-gardening, as an adjunct of horticulture, has grown steadily, the growth of celery in the Puyallup Valley having been especially heavy and of fine quality. On the islands of the San Juan group bulb-growing has been taken up and shows good promise specimens having gained first prizes at the Trans-Mississippi Exhibition in Omaha.

Hops. More hop-yards were cultivated than in the preceding year, and the yield increased to 37,500 bales, valued at 200,000*l*., of which 25,000 bales were grown in Western Washington and 12,500 bales in the Yakima country. The average yield per acre for the State was 1,250 lbs., and prices were profitable, ranging from 7½*d*. to 9*d*. per lb. The growers feel considerably encouraged after their unfortunate experiences in 1897.

Agricultural statistics. The following figures are taken from the returns of the State Board of Equalisation for 1898 for the State of Washington:—Total number of acres of land under assessment, 15,687,192; acres "improved," 2,679,247; assessment valuation, 15,151,272*l*.;

improvements, 1,453,537*l*.; town lots, 12,462,854*l*.; improvements on same, 5,116,546*l*.; railways assessed: 2,744 miles main tracks, 384 miles side tracks, total valuation 4,054,935*l*.; rolling-stock, &c., 554,320*l*.; other rail and tram-car lines, 81,794*l*.; telegraph and telephone lines, 124,351*l*.; steam and sailing craft, 163,320*l*.; live-stock: 171,985 horses, valued at 400,299*l*.; 229,395 cattle, valued at 494,982*l*.; 503,324 sheep, valued at 100,665*l*.; 56,853 pigs, valued at 17,056*l*. The United States Department of Agriculture places the following average prices per head on Washington animals: Horses, 4*l*. 16*s*.; cattle, 5*l*. 5*s*.; sheep, 9*s*.; and swine, 19*s*.

Commercial relations. China and Japan. The trade with China and Japan has made some little advance over that of 1897, especially in exports. Incident to the war with Spain, the Northern Pacific Steamship Company has made many changes in its vessels, those engaged in the regular service up to the present time having assumed American register. One ship passed entirely out of the hands of the Company, being afterwards sold to the United States Government as a transport ship, which has necessitated the chartering of another large ocean carrier. The duty on tea has made a marked change in the quantity received at this port, as well as in matting and other articles formerly admitted duty free. There has been a noticeable increase in exports of machinery and other manufactures of iron, while the exports of manufactured tobacco have greatly fallen off. The increase of exports to ports in Russian Siberia has been very perceptible, especially in flour, timber, and manufactures of iron.

Japan. The Nippon Yusen Kaisha (Japan Mail Steamship Company) has taken away large cargoes from the port of Seattle, principally to Japan and Korea, the latter country receiving a very large number of steel rails. The bulk of the cotton going to the Orient has been carried by this line from Seattle.

Sandwich Islands. The acquisition of the Sandwich Islands has created a demand for United States products, which have found their way to the islands from Puget Sound ports, where formerly San Francisco held the greater part of the trade. This may be accounted for by the fact that the drought in California diminished the supply of staple products, and it is very possible that that State may regain this trade next season. Large shipments of machinery for sugar refineries and other works have recently been made to these islands, as well as exports of coal for the Government coaling stations. At present little or no return trade seems to be found.

South Africa. Several cargoes of wheat and timber have gone to the British possessions in South Africa, showing that this trade is increasing very largely, but whether it will be permanent or not is hard to say.

Alaska. The Alaska business in the early part of the year was enormous, almost every available craft being brought into requisition. It is thought that during the month of March there must have been about 70 vessels in this business, the majority

(414)

leaving the port of Seattle. As the season advanced, however, the number materially decreased, some having been chartered by the Government as transports, others being lost in northern waters, and still others withdrawing from the trade on account of the lull in the gold excitement, until, at the present time, not more than 15 are in this service. Preparations are being made to meet the demand for traffic to Alaska during the coming year, especially with a view to carrying up supplies; for which purpose vessels of light draught, with refrigerating appliances and cold storage departments, are under construction. During the past season a railway has been built and is in operation over the mountain pass, thus considerably decreasing the time consumed and hardships to be undergone in the overland journey to the interior.

Other industries. One of the most notable features is the acquisition by the Great Northern Railway Company in Seattle of large terminal grounds on the northern part of Elliott Bay, which are expected to greatly increase the export trade of that port. Large warehouses, repair shops, and other conveniences for shipping are in course of construction, with waterways and docks accessible at all stages of the tide. Similar improvements on a small scale are also going on towards the centre of the town for the benefit of the home trade.

Freights. Grain freights from ports in the Puget Sound district to Europe have ranged from 25s. to 36s. 9d. per ton of 2,240 lbs., the average being 32s. 6d. To South Africa, 30s. to 36s. 3d., average 33s. 9d. To Rio de Janeiro, 31s. 3d.

Timber freights to Europe, 55s. to 65s., average 60s. To the west coast of South America, 42s. 6d. to 55s., average 47s. 6d. To Australia, 42s. 6d. to 65s., average 50s. To South Africa, 57s. 6d. to 65s., average 60s.

Exports and imports. The total business at the port of Tacoma during the year is estimated by the local authorities at 3,829,550*l*., of which the exports may be summed up as follows:—Foreign, 1,868,311*l*.; domestic, 875,921*l*. The imports were 1,085,318*l*., and indicate a great falling-off, but there was a small augmentation of the export trade.

For the port of Seattle during the same period, the business amounted to 1,264,237*l*., of which 782,283*l*. were exports and 481,954*l*. imports, as compared with 668,375*l*. exports and 126,654*l*. imports during the year 1897; showing a considerable increase in the imports. These figures, however, do not include the very large domestic business—probably over 2,000,000*l*. sterling—and the rail shipments, of which no statistics are available.

Bank clearings. The bank clearings at Tacoma during 1898 amounted to 8,716,756*l*., while those at Seattle reached the sum of 13,261,246*l*. as compared with 6,658,383*l*. in the year preceding.

TACOMA AND SEATTLE.

The following table shows the number and nationalities of vessels which entered and cleared the port of Tacoma during 1898:—

Annex A.—RETURN of all Shipping at the Port of Tacoma during the Year 1898.

ENTERED.

Nationality.	Sailing. Number of Vessels.	Sailing. Tons.	Steam. Number of Vessels.	Steam. Tons.	Total. Number of Vessels.	Total. Tons.
British	33	62,791	35	48,621	68	111,412
American	8	2,990	10	8,293	18	11,283
German	1	2,527	...	...	1	2,527
Norwegian	1	1,258	...	...	1	1,258
Japanese	...	...	1	1,666	1	1,666
French	1	1,397	...	...	1	1,397
Total	44	70,963	46	58,580	90	129,543
,, for the year preceding	42	67,915	46	58,169	88	126,084

CLEARED.

Nationality.	Sailing. Number of Vessels.	Sailing. Tons.	Steam. Number of Vessels.	Steam. Tons.	Total. Number of Vessels.	Total. Tons.
British	46	86,464	29	41,340	75	127,804
American	26	19,835	9	19,192	35	39,027
Hawaiian	3	3,047	...	...	3	3,047
German	2	3,805	...	...	2	3,805
Chilean	2	1,492	...	...	2	1,492
Norwegian	1	1,258	2	3,937	3	5,195
French	1	1,397	...	...	1	1,397
Total	81	117,298	40	64,469	121	181,767
,, for the year preceding	58	92,610	36	52,676	94	145,286

NOTE.—The entrances and clearances of American vessels do not include the domestic trade.

The following tables show the exports and imports for the past two years:—

Annex B.—RETURN of Principal Articles of Export from Tacoma during the Years 1898–97.

Articles.		1898. Quantity.	1898. Value.	1897. Quantity.	1897. Value.
			£		£
Wheat	Bushels	5,105,418	747,053	3,976,419	681,637
Flour	Barrels	284,899	214,963	321,594	246,957
Cotton	Lbs.	11,051,000	154,579	6,901,000	86,447
Tobacco	...	...	141,814	...	20,582
Textiles	...	...	80,336	...	150,254
Steel rails	Tons	15,737	72,892	...	...
Timber	Feet	25,320,000	42,993	29,508,000	51,905
Iron and manufactures	...	...	38,419	...	34,678
Liquors	...	...	19,817	...	...
Electrical supplies	...	...	8,973	...	11,610
Coal	Tons	8,060	4,308	...	...
Paper	...	...	2,874	...	...
Milk, condensed	Lbs.	56,950	968	556,300	9,132
Other articles	...	...	68,534	...	40,367
Total	...	...	1,598,523	...	1,333,569

TACOMA AND SEATTLE.

RETURN of Principal Articles of Import to Tacoma during the Years 1898-97.

		1898.		1897.	
Articles.		Quantity.	Value.	Quantity.	Value.
			£		£
Free—					
Silk, raw	Lbs.	787,800	319,805	1,857,300	642,162
Ore	...	...	14,771	...	22,615
Tea	Lbs.	531,053	14,631	200,000	2,838
Other articles	...	...	2,275	...	79,795
Total	...	...	351,482	...	747,410
Dutiable—					
Tea	Lbs.	1,708,351	51,109	...	...
Sugar	,,	748,000	3,912	1,830,000	9,386
Ore	...	...	2,977	...	5,926
Matting	...	...	2,427	...	...
Tin-plates	Lbs.	518,600	2,272	...	...
Liquors	...	...	1,989	...	2,320
Cement	Barrels	2,500	694	...	...
Rice	Lbs.	122,000	610	247,400	896
Other articles	...	...	5,041	...	13,472
Total	...	...	71,031	...	32,000
,, free and dutiable	...	...	422,513	...	779,410

Annex C.—TABLE showing Total Value of all Articles Exported from and Imported to Tacoma to and from Foreign Countries during the Years 1898-97.

Country.	Exports.		Imports.	
	1898.	1897.	1898.	1897.
	£	£	£	£
Great Britain	15,120	66,762	5,128	1,442
British colonies and dependencies—				
	£			
Hong-Kong	160,169	148,248	29,090	24,509
Africa	132,567	23,828	..	..
Australia	22,249	14,969	..	..
Canada	1,480	3,754	20,438	31,263
Straits Settlements	357	..	..	..
Other countries	40	27	210	3,189
	316,862	..	..	..
Queenstown and St. Vincent for orders	630,894	625,349	..	..
Japan	466,865	218,554	341,467	472,305
China	117,672	162,875	25,326	246,321
South America—				
	£			
Brazil	16,600			
Peru	15,200			
	31,800	5,438	..	..
Sandwich Islands	12,795	5,589	19	..
Africa, Portuguese	3,234	12,384	..	..
France	2,180	43,000	35	..
Other countries	1,101	2,792	800	381
Total	1,598,523	1,333,569	422,513	779,410

NOTE.—The domestic trade is not included in this table.

The following table shows the number and nationalities of vessels which entered and cleared the port of Seattle during the last year:—

Annex A.—RETURN of all Shipping at the Port of Seattle during the Year 1898.

ENTERED.

| Nationality. | Sailing. || Steam. || Total. ||
	Number of Vessels.	Tons.	Number of Vessels.	Tons.	Number of Vessels.	Tons.
British	9	16,202	18	6,500	27	22,702
American	15	8,601	129	83,454	144	92,055
Japanese	...	...	14	34,183	14	34,183
Norwegian	...	...	2	2,971	2	2,971
Danish	...	...	2	2,574	2	2,574
Total	24	24,803	165	129,682	189	154,485
,, for the year preceding	7	10,087	30	41,915	37	52,002

CLEARED.

| Nationality. | Sailing. || Steam. || Total. ||
	Number of Vessels.	Tons.	Number of Vessels.	Tons.	Number of Vessels.	Tons.
British	12	19,148	24	10,790	36	29,938
American	41	26,845	110	33,080	151	59,925
Japanese	...	...	15	35,849	15	35,849
Norwegian	1	993	1	1,002	2	1,995
Italian	1	1,200	...	...	1	1,200
Danish	...	...	1	1,287	1	1,287
Sandwich Islands	1	926	...	...	1	926
Chilian	1	914	...	...	1	914
Total	57	50,026	151	82,008	208	132,034
,, for the year preceding	26	26,570	33	42,720	59	69,290

The following tables show the exports and imports for the past two years:—

Annex B.—RETURN of Principal Articles of Export from Seattle during the Years 1898–97.

| Articles. | | 1898. || 1897. ||
		Quantity.	Value.	Quantity.	Value.
			£		£
Wheat	Bushels	1,187,891	178,628	444,346	69,106
Flour	Barrels	214,222	159,229	89,744	61,420
Timber	1,000 feet	16,635	29,933	21,258	43,467
Cotton	1,000 lbs.	30,093	254,982	108,057	275,335
Iron manufactures	...	...	29,400	...	61,245
Tobacco	...	...	12,001	...	6,337
Lead	...	...	12,726	...	...
Iron rails	Tons	1,648	7,833	...	...
Tinned salmon	...	...	2,906	...	...
Electrical supplies	...	...	2,273	...	11,157
Alcohol	...	...	6,728	...	...
Textile manufactures	...	...	630	...	91,264
Condensed milk	...	...	195	...	...
Other articles	...	...	64,165	...	50,298
Total	...	...	761,629	...	669,629

(414)

RETURN of the Principal Articles of Import to Seattle during the Years 1898-97.

		1898.		1897.	
Articles.		Quantity.	Value.	Quantity.	Value.
			£		£
Free—					
Silk	Bales	3,795	316,059	...	...
Tea	Lbs.	19,031	448	...	...
Other articles		...	13,000	...	...
Total		...	329,507	...	79,873
Dutiable—					
Sugar	Lbs.	1,230,000	6,633	...	...
Rice	,,	1,300,000	4,700	...	...
Coal	Tons	12,000	6,700	...	...
Liquors		...	3,398	...	...
Matting	Yards	112,256	2,524	...	...
Jute	Bales	400	592	...	...
Other articles		...	14,900	...	...
Total		...	39,447	...	14,979
,, free and dutiable		...	368,954	...	94,852
Goods for immediate transportation		...	159,533	...	...
Grand total		...	528,487	...	...

Annex C.—TABLE showing Total Value of all Articles Exported from and Imported to Seattle from and to Foreign Countries during the Years 1898-97.

Country.	Exports.		Imports.	
	1898.	1897.	1898.	1897.
	£	£	£	£
Great Britain	..	11,989	3,420	..
Colonies, dependencies— £				
Hong-Kong 121,399		53,634	12,774	..
Africa 13,000		..	..	..
Australia 11,014		14,608	..	..
Canada 1,700		1,176	25,000	280
India 223		261	592	..
Other countries 2,045		..	..	..
	149,381			
Queenstown or Falmouth for orders	181,228	60,486	..	..
Japan	346,901	371,545	473,000	94,532
Sandwich Islands	23,267	19,753	..	40
China	20,909	108,540	7,674	..
Russian Siberia	17,190	4,879	..	..
South America— £				
Peru 1,641		1,542	..	..
Chile 1,133		..	..	..
	2,774			
Portuguese South Africa	2,105	..	..	..
Belgium	..	..	4,122	..
Germany	..	..	1,600	..
Other countries	17,874	21,716	305	..
Total	761,629	669,629	528,487	94,852

NOTE.—The domestic trade is not included in this table.

PORT TOWNSEND.

Mr. Vice-Consul Klocher reports as follows:—

Trade and commerce. The trade and shipping for this district for the past year has been generally speaking satisfactory. The general tone of the country has been that of steady advancement. The lumber shipments were a little short of the previous year as shown in Annex B, but taking into consideration the lumber shipped to Alaska, I think the output will equal that of 1897.

I can get no record of lumber shipments for Alaska owing to the fact that vessels going to Alaska are treated as coasting between two United States ports, hence no records kept in this custom-house; besides this there has been an increased demand for railway lumber and car material much of which is shipped east by rail.

The shipments by rail of lumber and shingles for 1898 show a large percentage of gain over any former year, and there seems to be a steady and increased demand. Logs everywhere are of good value, and the prices obtained now are higher than they have been for many years past. Wages in logging camps are good and promise to remain so, unless there should be an unexpected influx of labour from Eastern States.

Shipping and freight. Lumber freights were not particularly good during the year, but improved considerably towards the last, and rates are at present better than they have been for several years, as will be seen from the annexed list. During the Klondyke excitement a number of steamers were brought round from the eastern coast with the intention of entering into the Alaska trade, but most of them arrived here too late. This would have entailed a great financial loss to the promoters if it had not been for the American-Spanish war breaking out, as these steamers were readily chartered at fancy prices to the United States Government to carry troops and stores to the Philippines. The scarcity of steamers was so great that the Government were obliged to charter a number of foreign steamers, several of which were British, granting them United States papers with readiness so as to allow them to be chartered by the Government.

| | Per 1,000 Feet. ||
	Highest.	Lowest.
	£ s. d.	£ s. d.
Sydney, New South Wales	2 3 9	1 17 6
Melbourne, Port Pirie, and Adelaide	2 11 10	1 15 6
Brisbane, Freemantle	3 2 6	2 10 0
China, Shanghai	2 15 0	2 5 0
Africa, Delagoa Bay	3 7 6	3 0 0
West Coast of South America	2 7 6	2 0 0
United Kingdom	3 5 0	2 15 0
Buenos Ayres	2 17 6	2 10 0
China, Haifhong	3 5 0	2 15 0
Calcutta	3 0 0	2 17 6
Russia, Vladivostock	2 8 9	2 5 0

Alaska and the Klondyke. The rush to the Klondyke at the commencement of 1898 was something enormous, and for a few months although over 100 steamers and sailing vessels were engaged in the Alaska trade they were inadequate to handle the business; it suddenly stopped however and large amounts of money were lost by nearly all new companies, the old lines still holding the trade which has now settled down to a good and steady basis. Later in the season good diggings were discovered in the Atlin district which resulted in another rush this winter. This has however been materially checked owing to the passing of a law of British Columbia, which excludes all but British subjects from holding claims; this law undoubtedly has worked a great detriment to Puget Sound outfitters and steamship companies.

Ship-building. During the past year this State holds in shipbuilding the record of the Union, 147 vessels of all kinds with a total tonnage of 28,774 tons having been built; the demand for vessels last year was caused principally by the rush to the Yukon gold fields, and as a result Puget Sound was brought into the field as the most available place for building with rapidity as all material for building purposes could be found there.

Steamship lines. The steamers running out of Puget Sound to the Orient seem to do a profitable business, particularly those leaving here, as they have continually to refuse cargo. The trade with the Orient is steadily increasing which will be seen by the following table:—

Year.	Imports. Dollars.	Exports. Dollars.
1890	71,355	313,845
1891	125,300	316,050
1892	118,025	555,055
1893	282,200	680,020
1894	699,895	1,131,730
1895	999,097	1,188,435
1896	2,503,450	4,160,020
1897	971,117	6,077,650
1898	3,555,970	7,176,746

It seems now an assured fact that the North German Lloyds Steamship Company will this year commence a line of passenger steamers between here and the Orient; it is also rumoured, on good authority, that this company have an arrangement with the Russian Siberian Railroad Company to do all the carrying for that company between here and Vladivostock, and the prospects of a big trade with that port seem indeed very promising this year, as large orders for railroad ties, lumber, steel rails, railroad material, machinery, and flour are now on the market; there are also large lumber orders for China. A number of sailing vessels have already been chartered at good rates to go to Vladivostock, and I know of several agents leaving

Puget Sound for that place to push American trade at this important point. Two new steamship lines have been started to the Hawaiian Islands, and there is also some talk about extending these lines to the Philippines. The prospects for a remunerative trade for steamships is very bright.

Pilotage. A law has again this year been pending before the State legislature to make pilotage compulsory, but as usual it will meet such strong opposition from shippers, mill owners, and shipping men in general, that it is certain to be defeated.

Fortifications. The fortifications on Point Wilson, Marrowstone and Admiralty Head have been all the year pushed with great energy and are now nearing their completion and are about ready to receive ordnance. The Government have maintained strict exclusion from the works, but it is well known that when ready they will be quite formidable.

Cement. A great deal of cement has been used for the building of the fortifications, and there are also several more cargoes coming, all of which however have been imported from Antwerp.

Fur sealing. The Canadian catch of sealskins for last year amounted to 28,898 skins. The Americans have been obliged to give up the business by order of the Government, and nearly all of the American sealing fleet have left these parts for the new possessions, Hawaiian Islands and the Philippines, there either to dispose of their vessels or to engage in the coasting trade, and they complain bitterly of being driven out of the business without compensation.

Disasters. There have been no wrecks reported of British ships in this district, but the ships "Celtic Bard" and "Carradoc" both bound here from Japan are now such a long time overdue that they are unquestionably lost.

British shipping. The total import and export trade for the whole Puget Sound custom-house district last year was:—

	Value.
	Dollars.
Total import trade..	4,969,566
Out of this the amount carried was—	
In British sailing vessels	100,199
„ steam „	2,014,022
Total	2,114,221
Total export trade..	15,599,012
Of this the amount carried was—	
In British sailing vessels	4,517,151
„ steam „	3,786,306
Total	8,303,457

which clearly goes to prove that the British flag is still the most prominent factor in the carrying trade of this district. I may also

PORT TOWNSEND.

Fish.

mention that the carrying trade between here and the Orient was (outside of the Japanese Steamship Line running here) nearly exclusively carried on in British steamers.

The salmon industry last year fell short of the catch of 1897, but still the season was a profitable one to the canneries. This year the leading canneries have been bought up by a big eastern combine, and they expect to do an increased business the coming year. Last year trial shipments of dried and smoked fish were sent to China and Japan which proved a success, and it is reported that orders have been placed with the shippers here to be forwarded this season as these countries can practically use an unlimited supply of this article.

Health.

The general health of this district has been excellent, no epidemic or other diseases having occurred.

The export trade shows an increase of 60,304*l.* over last year.

The import trade shows an increase of 47,076*l.*

I append the several annexes marked A, B and C to show the commerce and trade in this district.

Annex A.—RETURN of all Shipping at Port Townsend during the Year 1898.

ENTERED.

Nationality.	Sailing. Number of Vessels.	Sailing. Tons.	Steam. Number of Vessels.	Steam. Tons.	Total. Number of Vessels.	Total. Tons.
British	28	47,816	2	1,871	30	49,687
American	101	66,225	1,058	625,707	1,159	691,932
Chilian	14	16,854	...	...	14	16,854
German	5	9,613	...	...	5	9,613
Hawaiian	4	5,377	...	...	4	5,377
Italian	2	2,553	...	...	2	2,553
French	...	...	2	2,424	2	2,424
Norwegian	1	2,653	1	1,967	2	4,620
Dutch	1	1,391	...	...	1	1,391
Argentine Republic	1	921	...	...	1	921
Peruvian	1	750	...	...	1	750
Mexican	1	99	...	...	1	99
Total	159	154,252	1,063	631,969	1,222	786,221

PORT TOWNSEND.

CLEARED.

Nationality.	Sailing. Number of Vessels.	Sailing. Tons.	Steam. Number of Vessels.	Steam. Tons.	Total. Number of Vessels.	Total. Tons.
British	16	25,348	2	1,871	18	27,219
American	127	101,542	1,151	697,026	1,278	798,568
Chilian	11	10,893	...	...	11	10,893
Hawaiian	3	6,064	...	...	3	6,064
German	2	4,422	...	...	2	4,422
French	...	...	2	2,424	2	2,424
Norwegian	1	1,660	...	...	1	1,660
Italian	1	1,353	...	...	1	1,353
Danish	...	...	1	1,287	1	1,287
Dutch	1	1,391	...	...	1	1,391
Argentine Republic	1	921	...	...	1	921
Peruvian	1	750	...	...	1	750
Mexican	1	99	...	...	1	99
Total	165	154,443	1,156	702,608	1,321	857,051

PORT TOWNSEND.

Annex B.—RETURN of Principal Articles of Export from Port Townsend during the Years 1898–97.

Articles.	Value. 1898.	Value. 1897.
	£	£
Wheat	5,875	66,976
Flour	19,132	75,823
Barley and feed	30,302	18,011
Coal	4,062	9,802
Timber	123,367	128,252
Wood, and manufactures of wood	16,982	6,557
Furniture	18,822	..
Iron, and manufactures of iron	97,882	96,523
Oils	10,820	6,601
Furs and hides	939	12,321
Provisions, meats	26,943	31,302
Cattle	31,332	27,851
Liquors and wines	21,117	18,211
Cotton	16,164	2,519
Fish	40,717	60,291
Tinned fruits and vegetables	9,891	40,161
Chemicals	17,159	1,161
Wool, and manufactures of wool	3,922	5,612
Leather	14,241	2,065
Oil	..	2,119
Paper	67,669	22,718
Books and printed matter	6,410	..
Hay	10,702	..
Coffee	2,641	..
Fibres and grasses	6,480	..
Fruits and nuts	15,026	..
Cycles and carriages	16,795	..
Indiarubber, and manufactures of rubber	6,923	..
Electric instruments	1,092	..
Lime	2,700	..
Dairy products	10,163	..
Musical instruments	3,062	..
Tobacco, and manufactures of tobacco	17,153	..
Tin, and manufactures of tin	4,520	..
Lead, and manufactures of lead	1,702	..
Gunpowder	4,200	..
Eggs	7,060	..
Sugar	3,593	..
Soap	2,302	..
Salt	592	..
Other articles	15,991	21,265
Total	716,445	656,141

PORT TOWNSEND.

RETURN of Principal Articles of Import to Port Townsend during the Years 1898–97.

Articles.	Value. 1898.	Value. 1897.
	£	£
Cement	14,550	2,952
Coal	5,126	2,161
Iron and manufactures of iron	1,063	1,426
Tin-plates	6,302	5,619
Lead and ore	94,422	121,714
Liquor	10,574	6,269
Sugar	2,915	5,314
Rice	2,097	5,143
Tea	942	6,102
Raw silk	..	7,192
Chemicals	2,043	2,061
Matting	192	20,169
Fish	1,103	10,756
Household furniture	10,220	10,261
Wool	910	19,817
Chinaware	2,223	..
Hides	2,311	..
Copper ore	80,130	..
Coffee	972	..
Opium	350	..
Paper	1,344	..
Furs	5,323	..
Wood	3,383	..
Vegetables	1,181	..
Salt	943	..
Cocoa	962	..
Cattle	1,530	..
Hops	1,000	..
Other articles	40,052	20,131
Total	294,163	247,087

PORT TOWNSEND.

Annex C.—TABLE showing Total Value of all Articles Exported from and Imported to Port Townsend to and from Foreign Countries during the Years 1898-97.

Country.	Exports. 1898.	Exports. 1897.	Imports. 1898.	Imports. 1897.
	£	£	£	£
Great Britain	1,716	5,126	3,672	3,816
British Columbia and Canada	352,815	290,163	209,746	107,764
Australia	80,419	72,869	47	602
Germany	..	5,061	1,755	1,043
France	..	19,262	171	362
Belgium	..	..	8,536	..
Japan	29,508	46,102	24,099	126,176
China	24,897	38,064	42,287	2,106
Asiatic Russia	31,205	1,142	..	..
Hong-Kong	7,671	1,101	349	1,106
Korea	4,126	7,612	..	..
Dutch India	440	..	..	..
British ,,	1,038	..	441	261
Philippine Islands	279	..	..	..
Hawaiian ,,	57,082	28,104	1,148	562
Portuguese Africa	43,510	70,621	..	..
British ,,	4,482	..	..	..
Argentine Republic	10,464	4,623	..	..
Brazil	16,600	..	..	..
Peru	17,157	16,216	..	..
Chile	9,542	19,952	..	..
Mexico	11,927	8,204	1,912	..
Ecuador	5,623	..	..	..
Salvador	..	8,206	..	1,206
Guatemala	2,964	444	..	414
New Caledonia	..	5,534	..	..
Fiji Islands	1,177	2,462	..	..
Samoa	1,774	..	..	..
Other countries	29	5,273	..	1,669
Total	716,445	656,141	294,163	247,087

LONDON:
Printed for Her Majesty's Stationery Office,
By HARRISON AND SONS,
Printers in Ordinary to Her Majesty.
(75 6 | 99—H & S 414)

No. 2314 Annual Series.

DIPLOMATIC AND CONSULAR REPORTS.

UNITED STATES.

REPORT FOR THE YEAR 1898

ON THE

TRADE AND COMMERCE OF BOSTON AND DISTRICT.

REFERENCE TO PREVIOUS REPORT, Annual Series No. 2147.

Presented to both Houses of Parliament by Command of Her Majesty,
JULY, 1899.

LONDON:
PRINTED FOR HER MAJESTY'S STATIONERY OFFICE,
BY HARRISON AND SONS, ST. MARTIN'S LANE,
PRINTERS IN ORDINARY TO HER MAJESTY.

And to be purchased, either directly or through any Bookseller, from
EYRE & SPOTTISWOODE, East Harding Street, Fleet Street, E.C., and
32, Abingdon Street, Westminster, S.W.; or
JOHN MENZIES & Co., 12, Hanover Street, Edinburgh, and
90, West Nile Street, Glasgow; or
HODGES, FIGGIS, & Co., Limited, 104, Grafton Street, Dublin.

1899.

[C. 9044—140.] *Price Twopence Halfpenny.*

CONTENTS.

	PAGE
BOSTON—	
General review	3
Pilots and stevedore rates	4
Rates of pilotage	5
Commerce of Boston	6
Failures	8
Imports and exports—	
Wheat	9
Corn, oats, flour, &c.	9
Provisions	10
Produce	10
Fish	11
Shipping	12
Money and sterling exchange	13
Conclusion	14
Annexes—	
A.—Immigrants	15
B, C, D.—Shipping	16
E.—Steamship sailings	19
F.—Freights to Liverpool	20
G.—Exports	21
H.—Value of imports and exports	22
I.—Exports and imports by countries	23
J.—Value of imports by articles	24
PORTLAND trade report	25

NOTE.—1*l*. has been reckoned as equal to 5 dol. for the purposes of this report.

No. 2314. Annual Series.

Reference to previous Report, Annual Series No. 2147.

Report on the Trade and Commerce of the Consular District of Boston for the Year 1898

BY MR. ACTING-CONSUL STUART.

(Received at Foreign Office, June 22, 1899.)

The year 1897 closed with every hope and belief that the coming year would be prosperous in almost every respect; and the commercial and industrial record of this country for the year 1898 has certainly proved the belief to have been well founded, and noticeably in the amount and character of foreign trade, not only in agricultural products, but also in the exports of manufactures, in which the element of labour enters largely. <small>General review.</small>

This also has increased domestic consumption, due to the larger purchasing power of the people.

While this is true for the whole country, however, the Eastern States, more especially the New England States, have not enjoyed a fair and general share of the general movement.

The iron trade has had a most successful year, while the textile and boot and shoe trades, with which the prosperity of the New England States is so closely identified, have not been so favoured as other branches of industrial activity; as also other trades not so New England in character, but having a market in those States.

The harbour of Boston is entirely protected and safe at all seasons. <small>Port charges and disbursements. Boston.</small>

Vessels loading grain pay no dues for the use of elevators, this charge being paid by the shippers. Vessels pay no wharfage or dockage while discharging or loading.

Dockage, $\frac{6}{25}$ of $1d.$ per register ton per day, but berths can be obtained at lower rates where vessels are to lay any length of time.

Commission for procuring charters, 5 per cent. Coal and iron (coastwise), $2\frac{1}{2}$ per cent. The harbour is well lighted and buoyed, and throughout the winter months is free from ice. Ships of the largest capacity and draft can enter and leave the port, and discharge and load at the wharves afloat.

There are four elevators at tide water, two with all modern improvements, capacity, 3,850,000 bushels; and one local elevator,

BOSTON.

Pilots and pilotage.

capacity, 200,000 bushels. Total storage capacity of the port, 4,050,000 bushels.

There are two pilot stations, an inner station near the entrance of the harbour, a few miles outside Boston Light, and an outer station off Cape Cod, "from where Race Point bears south, to where the Highland Light bears west-north-west," the land in fair weather to be kept "in sight from boat's deck." The station boats must show signals by day and night, and are by law required to keep the stations until relieved. Also, three boats cruising in bay outside of station boats.

Pilotage is compulsory inward, and for over 350 tons outward.

The average width of the main ship channel is about 2,000 feet, and its average depth about 25 feet at mean low water. Its least width at the "Narrows" is 625 feet, and at the "Lower and Upper Middles," 850 feet, with a least depth at both places of 23 feet at mean low water, or 32 feet 8 inches at mean high water. The built-up wharfage front below the bridges is 7 miles long, above the bridges, about 12 miles, as measured by following the Commissioners' line of solid filling, and not including the indentations of the piers.

The range of tides at the wharves is 9 feet 8 inches, and at the entrance to the outer harbour 9 feet 4 inches.

Stevedore rates.

The following are the stevedore rates in force at this port:—

		Rates. From— £ s. d.	Rates. To— £ s. d.
Discharging.			
Coal	Per ton of 2,240 lbs.	..	0 1 0½
Iron (according to kind)	Per ton of 2,240 lbs.	..	0 1 0½
Sugar and molasses	Per hogshead	0 0 8	0 0 10
" "	" bag	0 0 1½	0 0 2
Lumber—			
Cypress	Per 1,000 feet	0 2 1	0 2 6
Yellow pine	" "	0 2 1	0 2 6
White "	} " "	0 1 2	0 1 8
Spruce			
Wool	Per bale	0 0 2½	0 0 6
Manilla hemp	"	..	0 0 2
Dry hides	Per 1,000	1 0 10	1 2 1
General cargoes (including sorting)	Per cubic foot	0 1 5½	0 1 8
Loading.			
Lumber	Per 1,000 feet	0 1 8	0 2 1
Petroleum	" barrel	..	0 0 2½
Measurement	" 40 cub. ft.	..	0 1 8

BOSTON.

Rates of Pilotage for Boston Harbour. Act of May 13, 1873.

Over 25 feet the rates are the same inward and outward, with the addition of distance money inward from November 1 to April 30, 20 per cent.

Outward Rates.

Draft Water.	Amount.
Feet.	Dol. c.
7	11 55
8	13 28
9	15 03
10	17 0
11	19 14
12	21 36
13	26 0
14	28 0
15	31 50
16	36 0
17	42 50
18	49 50
19	57 0
20	65 0
21	73 50
22	82 50
23	92 0
24	102 0
25	125 0
25½	132 38
26	139 75
26½	147 50
27	155 25
27½	163 37
28	177 50
28½	180 0
29	188 50

BOSTON.

INWARD RATES.

Draft Water.	Amount.	Amount, including Distance Money.*
Feet.	Dol. c.	Dol. c.
7	18 48	22 18
8	21 52	25 82
9	24 57	29 48
10	27 70	33 24
11	30 80	36 96
12	34 20	41 04
13	38 35	46 02
14	48 30	57 96
15	52 50	63 0
16	56 80	68 16
17	63 75	76 50
18	68 40	82 08
19	76 0	91 20
20	85 0	102 0
21	94 50	113 0
22	99 0	118 80
23	115 0	138 40
24	120 0	144 0
25	125 0	150 0

* Distance money, from November 1 to April 30, inclusive, eastward on a line drawn from Manomet Land, Plymouth, to Thatcher's Island, Cape Ann.

The pilot signal by day is a white and blue flag, *white next the mast;* and in the night a white masthead light. Pilotage rates the same all the year round.

Towage inward, according to agreement, varying with size of vessel and distance, from 15 to 50 dol. Quarantine fees, payable from June 1 to November 1: ships and barques, 8 dol.; brigs, 5 dol. No wharfage or special port charges.

Tonnage dues levied by National Government in all American ports:—
From West Indies, 3 c. per ton, net register.
From other foreign ports, 6 c. per ton, net register.

Two cargo manifests and provision lists required by custom-house.

Commerce of Boston. The exports were by far the largest on record, amounting to 24,972,957*l.*, an increase over the preceding year of 20 per cent. The significance of these figures is made clear by the statement that the exports for 1898 were greater than the combined exports and imports in 1888. The imports were 9,762,984*l.*, as against 17,137,630*l.* in 1897, showing a falling-off of 7,374,646*l.*

It should be borne in mind, however, that the figures for 1898 were abnormally large, owing principally to the heavy imports of wool and other merchandise during the first six months of the year.

As compared with the showing of the other ports, also, it must be remembered that the increase in imports at Boston in 1897 over 1896 was very much larger relatively than the increase at any other port. Consequently a general decrease in the imports of the country, as a whole, would show itself with the greatest emphasis at Boston.

Notwithstanding this falling-off in imports of nearly one-half, however, the port continues to hold by a substantial margin its position as the second port in the United States in the value of both its imports and exports, and as regards the latter, shows a gain during 1898 greater proportionately than any other Atlantic port. The percentages and figures for the principal ports of the United States are given in the following table:—

Ports.	Exports and Imports.	Per Cent. of Total Trade of United States.
	Dollars.	
New York	889,587,491	47·06
Boston	173,679,708	9·19
Baltimore	124,072,069	6·56
New Orleans	108,464,959	5·74
Philadelphia	97,026,025	5·13
Galveston	78,886,693	4·17
San Francisco	68,056,763	3·60
All other	350,678,879	18·55
Total	1,890,452,587	100

Among exports, provisions occupy a commanding position, the shipments being 11,686,213*l*., or 47 per cent. of the total exports. The figures for 1897 were 10,679,002. Breadstuffs amounted to 5,308,171*l*., against 3,843,312*l*. the previous year. The wheat shipments were 13,000,000 bushels, against 12,000,000 bushels in 1897; corn, 12,000,000 bushels, against 9,500,000 bushels; oats, 8,700,000 bushels, against 5,500,000 bushels.

Owing largely to the establishment of a direct line of steamers between Galveston and Boston, a substantial increase has occurred in receipts at this port of cotton, both that destined for export and that for consumption by New England mills. The exports amounted to 382,626 bales, an increase of 67 per cent., while the receipts for domestic consumption aggregated 508,000 bales, an increase of 51,000 bales.

The transit trade of the port of Boston amounted to 1,986,905*l*., and was made up as follows:—

Entered at Boston for transhipment to foreign countries, principally Canada, 987,466*l*.; entered at ports on the Canadian frontier and exported to foreign countries viâ Boston 999,439*l*.

Probably owing to an unsatisfactory state of the foreign market, the exports of cattle from the United States show a marked falling-off from the previous year, a corresponding decrease appearing in the figures for Boston.

The number exported from this port was 134,838 as against 162,620 in 1897, being practically the same as the shipments from New York, which port shares with Boston the control of this trade.

The mortality on shipboard again strikingly illustrates the superior facilities possessed by the steamship lines (British) running from Boston for carrying this class of freight. While the figures of the United States as a whole are given by the United States Bureau of Animal Industry as ·23 per cent., the losses on shipments viâ this port were only ·10 per cent., or less than one-half the average for all ports. The loss of the "Londonian," which was abandoned at sea with 655 cattle on board, is not of course included in either the figures for Boston or the United States.

The ocean tonnage entering and leaving the port of Boston in the foreign trade during 1898 exceeded all previous records, aggregating 3,663,831 tons. The arrivals of vessels engaged in the coasting trade numbered 9,671, being, with the exception of 1896, which exceeded it by 13, the largest on record. There were 204 sailings to the single port of Liverpool, and a total of 409 sailings to all European ports, as against 388 in 1897. Two new lines have been established during the past year, one to Manchester, England, and one to Copenhagen and other Baltic ports. Besides these two lines, the European service now includes lines to Liverpool, London, Glasgow, Hull, Bristol, Antwerp, and Hamburg.

Two new southern lines have also been added to the service, one to Galveston and one to Charleston and Brunswick. These with the lines to New York, Philadelphia, Baltimore, Savannah, Charleston and Jacksonville, comprise the coastwise service to the south.

Lines are also established between this port and Point Antonio, Ja., Nicaragua and Progreso, Mex.

Bradstreet says in his report of business failures for the year 1895, that embarrassments in that year were the smallest in number and in liabilities involved since 1892. The total number of failures reported for 1898 is 11,615, with aggregated liabilities of 28,322,283*l*., fewer in number by 11·2 per cent. than in 1897, and, therefore, less than in any previous year since 1892, smaller as regards liabilities by 9·5 per cent. than in 1897, and making fully as favourable a comparison with every year since that just preceding the year of panic memory, 1893. It is further to be noted that, with the exception of 1892, the liabilities of failing traders in 1898 were the smallest there is any record of since 1890, the percentage of liabilities to assets being only 52·1 per cent., against 54·4 per cent. in 1890, 65 per cent. in 1893, and 50 per cent. in 1892, pointing to a return to the normal in most of the conditions affecting business life.

Incompetence, the third great cause of business embarrassment, was most fatal in the Eastern States, but not so great as specific conditions.

The following table shows the business failures of 1898 in the Eastern States, classified as to causes:—

	Number.	Assets.	Liabilities.
		£	£
Incompetence	462	616,344	1,219,210
Inexperience	40	9,195	26,229
Lack of capital	382	347,787	761,713
Unwise credits	70	27,248	75,985
Failures of others..	51	338,478	658,031
Extravagance	26	21,107	53,787
Neglect	48	9,460	29,938
Competition	365	140,700	404,475
Specific conditions	461	1,422,990	2,735,101
Speculation	29	42,620	194,890
Fraud	268	106,418	518,000
Total for Eastern States	2,202	3,082,347	6,677,359
,, United States	11,615	14,632,266	28,322,282

Wheat. An extraordinary crop of wheat was harvested in the United States in 1898 which, according to the Government figures, amounted to 675,000,000 bushels. Prices, evidently forced by a combination, reached early in the year to above 7s. 5d. a bushel, but dropped in October to 2s. 7d. per bushel.

The receipts of wheat at Boston shows an increase of 30 per cent., aggregating 13,568,460 bushels; the exports were 13,021,229 bushels, an increase of 878,025 bushels over the exports of the year before.

Corn. In the Boston market imported yellow corn sold at 1s. 6½d. in the early part of the year, rising to 1s. 10¾d. in May—the year closing with 2s. 0¼d. The receipts at Boston were 13,110,262 bushels, against 11,817,529 bushels in 1897, and the exports 11,799,265 bushels, as against 9,464,163 bushels in 1897.

Oats. A higher level of prices has obtained in the oat market throughout the year than for several years past, "No. 2 clipped white" fluctuated between 1s. 3d. and 1s. 8d. There was a good increase in the local trade as also a heavy advance in the export movement, the receipts being 14,063,484 bushels, against 10,849,665 bushels in 1897; and the exports being 8,720,931 bushels, as against 5,471,275 bushels in 1897.

Flour. Wide fluctuation in price and an uneven demand has prevailed in the flour market, but a foreign demand helped the export trade. Standard patents ran from 16s. to 32s., the extreme being coincident in point of time with the extremes in wheat.

The year closed with a good foreign demand, but was unsupported by an equally good domestic market, causing prices to suffer. The receipts of flour at Boston were 2,556,245 barrels, against 2,270,430 barrels in 1897, and the exports were 1,635,867 barrels, as against 1,416,595 barrels in 1897.

Hay. It is generally conceded that the hay crop for the year 1898 was the best ever secured, but that the prices realised by the farmer were about the worst, the value being about 1l. 4s. per ton. Prices in the local market have also been low, running from 2*l.* 8*s.* to 3*l.* per ton for prime hay in large bales. The local demand for outside hay was small owing to the unusually fine crop raised in Massachusetts. The local conditions were reflected by the figures of receipts and exports.

The receipts were 14,441 cars, against 17,696 cars in 1897, and the exports 245,338 bales, against 161,402 bales in 1897.

Provisions. The market or trade in provisions showed nothing unusual during the year.

The demand for meats was certainly stimulated during the period of the war, but the general effect was slight and only temporary. The receipts far exceeded the heavy totals of 1897, as also the receipts of lard which were nearly double and also the exports.

Dressed hogs showed an increase from 9,600 to over 70,000 carcases, and the number of hogs packed in Boston was the largest for several years, amounting to 1,725,919.

Produce trade. The local market on the whole has been one of mixed conditions, for while the butter trade has been most unfortunate, causing general loss, the egg market has been one of the best for years, a good and profitable business having been done throughout the year, and on the other hand the trade in cheese has been normal with no special features.

The year opened with a quiet trade in butter, and Western Creamery Extra (in assorted sizes) was quoted at $11\frac{1}{4}d.$ per lb.; unfavourable reports soon brought a sharp cut in prices, which, owing to accumulations of stock and a falling-off in demand, continued till $8\frac{1}{2}d.$ per lb. was quoted. In July hot weather caused a rise, the year closing with Western Creamery at $10\frac{1}{2}d.$ per lb.

In the cheese market a lower general average of prices prevailed than for many years, 5*d.* per lb. being the highest quoted. The receipts were 324,443 boxes, against 436,005 boxes in 1897, and the exports show a decrease of 5,882,934 lbs. or 33 per cent.

This decrease is wholly in the exports of the Canadian product, and is probably due to the improved facilities for shipping Canadian product viâ lines running from their home ports.

In all 108,890,797 lbs. of cheese were exported from Boston, of which above 67 per cent. was Canadian.

The egg market during the year has been unusually steady in movement, Western fresh bringing $11\frac{1}{2}d.$ a dozen, with a slight decline—when in July, hot weather causing receipts of good stock to fall-off, took prices up to 1*s.* $0\frac{1}{2}d.$ The receipts were 889,000 cases, a slight falling-off from the previous year.

The local fruit trade has enjoyed a fairly satisfactory year. Foreign fruit imports have been lighter than usual, and the receipts were confined to the better grades, the heavy tariff making it impossible to import profitably the inferior qualities. California supplied the bulk of the oranges for this market, but the Jamaicas are finding a ready sale, and the imports are assuming large proportions. Owing to more careful picking and packing the condition of Jamaicas was much improved over that of previous years, and if the handlers of oranges in Jamaica are careful and send good fruit, carefully picked and packed, a ready market with good prices can be assured, as the Jamaica fruit is liked.

The banana trade has been satisfactory, the receipts were 1,640,880 bunches, and owing to the troubles in Cuba, were entirely from Jamaica, which trade can probably be kept up, as the fruit was generally good.

The local trade in apples has also been satisfactory. Prices have ranged too high to permit of a free movement in certain quarters, but the demand has been good enough to keep prices firm and yet permit of clearing up stocks. The receipts were 447,093 barrels, against 712,144 barrels in 1897; the exports were 222,254 barrels, as against 426,539 barrels in 1897.

The Boston Fish Bureau, in their review of trade and fishing for the year 1898, state that both prices and demand have been better, and the autumn trade in salt-fish unusually good. *Fish.*

The receipts of both salt and fresh mackerel at Boston were 55,445 barrels, against 62,836 barrels in 1897, the decrease being in fresh mackerel. While the production of salt mackerel in the world was 11 per cent. less than in the year 1897, the trade at Boston has shown an increase, 31,329 barrels of salt mackerel being received as against 30,136 barrels in 1897. *Mackerel.*

The chief catch by countries is ascertained to be as follows:—

Country.	Quantity. 1897.	1898.
	Barrels.	Barrels.
Ireland	48,352	35,000
Canada	20,000	23,000
United States	13,154	14,286
Norway	9,000	7,000

The first receipts of salt mackerel (spring Irish) were received in Boston on May 23 and sold at 2*l.* 12*s.* per barrel, and the first autumn Irish mackerel arrived September 14 and sold at 3*l.* per barrel, while Nova Scotia mackerel arriving in May brought 2*l.* 8*s.* per barrel, but Prince Edward Island mackerel arriving August 5 brought from 2*l.* 18*s.* to 3*l.* 2*s.* per barrel. During the autumn large bodies of very small mackerel, thought to be of 1898 year's spawn, were seen all along the New England coast, and if they return to the grounds in 1899 they will be a good-sized fish.

With respect to salt mackerel received from Newfoundland, it is stated that the barrels should contain 200 lbs. of fish, but they have been very irregular in weight, running 15 lbs., and sometimes more, short. This has caused great dissatisfaction, complaint, and distrust.

The export of salt cod, hake, haddock, &c., is largely to South America and the West Indies, and in recent years this trade has *Salt cod, hake, haddock, &c.*

been chiefly from Canada, Newfoundland, and Norway, but in view of recent events it is expected that more attention will be given in New England to the development of this trade and some of the trade diverted to this country.

The year closes with light stocks of codfish, &c., the receipts being 47,857 cwts., as against 56,423 cwts. in 1897. The fish arrivals in June from the Banks were sold at 10s. per cwt. for large and 8s. per cwt. for small.

Fresh cod, &c. The catching of fresh codfish, haddock, hake, cusk, pollack, and halibut, is a fishery of great promise in the New England States. When the market is overstocked with fresh fish they are sold for splitting and also for smoking, and a large portion of the salt fish now sold are the product of the "fresh fish fleet."

During the past year 223 vessels, mostly engaged in this fishery, and hailing from New England ports, came to the Boston market, and prices for fresh haddock in December rose to 5d. per lb.

Salt and smoked herring. The shore catch of salt herring has been extremely poor, and foreign receipts light, but still prices have ruled about the same as last year.

The price of Norwegian, Scotch, and Dutch herring is about 4s. per barrel higher than in 1897. Smoked herring receipts have equalled those of 1897, and sold from 5d. to 7½d. per box.

Canned fish. The pack of canned lobsters has been light, and while the pack was good at some points, at many places it was poor. There has been an increase in factories, and 1 lb. cans have sold from 9s. 7d. to 10s. per dozen for talls and 10s. 5d. to 10s. 10d. for flats.

The pack of sardines has been large, selling from 12s. 7d. down to 8s. 10d. per case.

The year's losses. The number of vessels lost during the year 1898 was 36, seven of which were lost with all on board. The great gale of November 27 will long be remembered on account of the large number of vessels lost and damaged:—

Ports.	Vessels Lost.	Lives Lost.	Value of Vessels.	Insurance.
			Dollars.	Dollars.
Boothbay Harbour	1	..	600	..
Boston	5	2	13,800	7,000
Gloucester	24	142	113,200	77,768
Bucksport	2	..	8,000	6,000
Provincetown	3	..	2,500	1,500
Rockland	1	..	500	..
Total	36	144	138,600	92,268
			£	£
Equiv. in sterling	..	..	27,720	18,453

Shipping. The returns from the Boston custom-house show that the ocean tonnage in the foreign trade in 1898 amounted to 1,948,536 tons entered and 1,715,295 tons cleared, giving a total, entered and cleared, of 3,663,831 tons, as against 3,637,497 tons in 1897.

BOSTON.

The American tonnage entering Boston shows a decrease of 103 vessels and 79,368 tons, but in all probability this was caused by the war with Spain, which caused British bottoms to be used in preference.

The total number of vessels of all nationalities which entered this port from foreign ports during the year was, according to the custom-house returns, 1,797 vessels of 1,948,536 tons measurement, as against 2,068 vessels of 1,980,708 tons in 1897.

Of the above 792 were British steamers of 1,636,912 tons and 774 British sailing vessels of 119,739 tons with cargo and ballast:—

ENTERED.

Nationality.	Number of Vessels.	Tonnage.
British	1,566	1,756,651
American	158	89,507
Other nations	73	102,378
Total	1,797	1,948,536

Money and sterling exchange.

The good feeling in the money market that closed the year 1897 was continued. 1898 opened auspiciously, and business men generally had great confidence in the future.

Money was abundant at low rates, Boston actually lending New York upwards of 1,000,000*l*. Money on call was 2½ to 3 per cent., and time money 3 to 3½ per cent. for four to six months. The State of Massachusetts sold in January 400,000*l*. 40-year 3½ per cent. gold bonds at 113–126, a 3 per cent. basis. From February to May depressing times, owing to the war scare, were experienced, stocks dropping heavily and money going from 4 to 6 per cent., but with the success of the American forces in Manila and Cuba, confidence was regained and stocks advanced while money became plentiful and obtainable at easy rates. This continued, and the year ended with an abundance of money unparalleled, low rates and stocks booming.

The year 1898 in Boston, the great home of copper stocks, showed the highest prices for copper ever experienced. The Boston Bank clearings of 1898 showed total exchanges of 1,085,129,434*l*., and total balances of 122,731,216*l*.; the total sales for the year at the Boston Stock Exchange amounted to 8,797,024 listed shares and 4,259,896 unlisted shares of stocks, also of 6,349,556*l*. worth of bonds.

Bankers' sight bills of exchange on London were:—

| | Per 1*l*. Sterling. ||
Month.	From—	To—
	Dol. c.	Dol. c.
In January	4 82½	4 84
April	4 80½	4 82
July	4 84½	4 85½
October	4 82	4 83½
December	4 85½	4 86

Conclusion. In reviewing the business conditions that have prevailed during the year 1898, the Boston Chamber of Commerce says that the exhilarating experiences of the Central and Western States have not been shared by Boston and the New England portion of the country, but that the prosperity enjoyed by the Western farmers has set in motion the industrial energies that are already and will be felt in greater or lesser degree in all sections of the country.

The increased purchasing power of all classes of people who have benefited in direct and indirect ways through the growing, transporting, and marketing of the crops of the country, has acted as a general stimulus to trade, resulting in the absorption of large quantities of surplus stocks that have for a long time exercised a depressing influence upon the manufacturing industry. This cannot fail to be of distinct and increasing benefit to the producers of this Eastern manufacturing section.

The country as a whole is enjoying a season of real and substantial prosperity; the volume of exports was never so large nor of such an encouraging character; the ability of manufacturers to successfully meet competition has never before been so firmly established, and with these conditions the belief is that the year 1899 will fulfil in a reasonable measure the hopeful anticipations that very generally prevail among business men.

BOSTON.

Annex A.—TABLE showing the Arrivals of Immigrants at the Port of Boston, for the last Five Years (prepared by Colonel George H. Billings, Commissioner of Immigration at Boston).

Nationality.	Number.				
	1898.	1897.	1896.	1895.	1894.
Ireland	5,863	6,489	8,333	10,995	6,750
England	3,159	3,251	3,246	5,007	3,395
Scotland	556	525	741	1,161	686
Wales	31	16	31	60	34
Germany	177	128	90	316	959
France	67	50	42	40	31
Russia	695	334	377	2,019	1,158
Finland	454	316	934	479	111
Poland	243	3	15	34	32
Switzerland	5	5	4	4	15
Sweden	1,751	1,366	2,068	2,061	1,193
Norway	333	389	748	676	440
Denmark	198	77	48	114	63
Holland	18	3	5	11	10
Italy	11	17	24	32	26
Spain	11	2	9	6	16
Portugal	1	3	10	12	5
Hungary	16	23	6	73	31
Austria	60	56	43	320	149
Austria - Hungary, Bohemia, and Moravia	..	7	..	5	7
Austria - Hungary, Galicia-Bukowina	98	25	10	95	12
Australia	5	3	2	..	..
Turkey in Europe	1	15	22	3	9
,, ,, Asia	12	4	..	1	2
Greece	1	3	22	6	65
Belgium	12	5	..	22	26
Roumania	1	6	8	19	2
Mexico	..	..	..	..	1
West Indies	83	27	33	24	18
South America	2	..	2	2	1
Japan	1	4	..	..	1
Africa	1	12	1	..	1
All other countries	154	46	78	40	19
Total arrivals at Boston*	14,020	13,210	16,947	23,637	15,268

* In addition, there arrived at the ports of Massachusetts from the Dominion of Canada, by water during 1893, 18,113 aliens, compared with 20,634 in 1897, 19,026 in 1896, 20,806 in 1895, and 17,893 in 1894.

Annex B.—TABLE showing Vessels Entered from Foreign Countries at the Port of Boston during the Calendar Year 1898.

BOSTON.

Nationality.	Sailing. With Cargo. Number of Vessels.	Sailing. With Cargo. Tons.	Sailing. In Ballast. Number of Vessels.	Sailing. In Ballast. Tons.	Steam. With Cargo. Number of Vessels.	Steam. With Cargo. Tons.	Steam. In Ballast. Number of Vessels.	Steam. In Ballast. Tons.	Total. Number of Vessels.	Total. Tons.
American	121	52,018	2	776	26	28,328	9	8,385	158	89,507
Argentine	1	596	1	499	..	..	..	..	2	1,095
Austro-Hungarian	..	..	..	..	2	4,210	..	..	2	4,210
British	771	115,852	3	3,887	775	1,591,110	17	45,802	1,566	1,756,651
Danish	..	..	..	..	2	2,044	..	..	2	2,044
Dutch	4	7,341	..	..	..	..	..	..	4	7,341
French	2	279	..	..	11	5,071	..	..	13	5,350
German	1	1,737	..	..	24	54,987	..	..	25	56,724
Italian	2	1,697	..	..	..	..	..	..	2	1,697
Norwegian	1	1,438	..	..	22	22,479	..	..	23	23,917
Total	903	180,958	6	5,162	862	1,708,229	26	54,187	1,797	1,948,536

Annex C.—TABLE showing Vessels Cleared for Foreign Countries at the Port of Boston during the Calendar Year 1898.

BOSTON.

| Nationality. | Sailing. |||| Steam. |||| Total. ||
| | With Cargo. || In Ballast. || With Cargo. || In Ballast. || ||
	Number of Vessels.	Tons.	Number of Vessels.	Tons.	Number of Vessels.	Tons.	Number of Vessels.	Tons.	Number of Vessels.	Tons.
American	53	24,150	144	47,513	27	28,553	5	1,199	229	101,415
Argentine	1	596	..	..	..	..	..	..	1	596
British	364	57,571	398	46,549	685	1,450,377	28	22,971	1,475	1,577,468
French	4	444	..	..	11	5,071	..	..	15	5,515
German	..	..	..	..	11	21,169	..	..	11	21,169
Italian	..	..	1	874	..	..	..	..	1	874
Norwegian	..	..	..	..	6	3,439	8	4,308	14	7,747
Portuguese	1	511	..	..	..	..	..	..	1	511
Total	423	83,272	543	94,936	740	1,508,609	41	28,478	1747	1,715,295

Annex D.—RETURN of British Shipping at the Port of Boston, Massachusetts, in the Year 1898.

Direct Trade in British Vessels from and to Great Britain and British Colonies.

Entered.

Total Number of Vessels.			Total Tonnage.			Total Number of Crews.	Total Value of Cargoes.
With Cargoes.	In Ballast.	Total.	With Cargoes.	In Ballast.	Total.		£
1,424	13	1,437	1,547,054	29,068	1,576,122	47,961	...

Cleared.

Total Number of Vessels.			Total Tonnage.			Total Number of Crews.	Total Value of Cargoes.
With Cargoes.	In Ballast.	Total.	With Cargoes.	In Ballast.	Total.		£
1,007	432	1,439	1,472,383	68,935	1,541,318	48,290	...

Indirect or Carrying Trade in British Vessels from and to other Countries.

Entered.

Countries whence Arrived.	Number of Vessels.			Tonnage.			Number of Crews.	Value of Cargoes.
	With Cargoes.	In Ballast.	Total.	With Cargoes.	In Ballast.	Total.		£
Argentine Republic	15	...	15	8,979	...	8,979	160	...
Belgium	25	...	25	54,377	...	54,377	864	...
Brazil	2	...	2	1,309	...	1,309	23	...
Chile	2	...	2	3,550	...	3,550	53	...
Danish colonies	3	...	3	554	...	554	22	...
Egypt	5	...	5	8,493	...	8,493	122	...
France	4	...	4	7,505	...	7,505	108	...
Germany	1	1	2	2,678	2,611	5,289	60	...
Hayti	2	...	2	1,334	...	1,334	40	...
Italy	8	...	8	9,895	...	9,895	177	...
Mexico	8	...	8	13,189	...	13,189	205	...
Netherlands and colonies	11	...	11	19,684	...	19,684	269	...
Nicaragua	9	...	9	16,533	...	16,533	251	...
Russia	1	...	1	1,540	...	1,540	23	...
San Domingo	1	...	1	609	...	609	9	...
Spain and colonies	39	1	40	15,701	1,937	17,638	400	...
United States of America and possessions	4	11	15	4,546	3,842	8,388	175	...
Total	140	13	153	170,476	8,390	178,866	2,961	...

Cleared.

Countries whence Departed.	Number of Vessels.			Tonnage.			Number of Crews.	Value of Cargoes.
	With Cargoes.	In Ballast.	Total.	With Cargoes.	In Ballast.	Total.		£
Argentine Republic	15	...	15	14,820	...	14,820	214	...
Belgium	2	...	2	4,127	...	4,127	65	...
French possessions	1	...	1	117	...	117	6	...
Germany	1	...	1	1,725	...	1,725	24	...
Netherlands and colonies	1	...	1	199	...	199	7	...
Portuguese possessions	1	...	1	271	...	271	8	...
United States of America	36	82	118	67,705	103,313	171,018	2,679	...
Uruguay	3	...	3	2,241	...	2,241	39	...
Total	60	82	142	91,205	103,313	194,518	3,042	...

BOSTON.

Annex E.—TABLE showing Steamship Sailings from Boston to European Ports during the Year 1898.

Month.	To Liverpool.	To London.	To Glasgow.	To Hull.	To Bristol.	To Antwerp, and Antwerp viâ Baltimore.	To Hamburg.	To Hamburg, viâ Portland, &c.	To Manchester.	To Cork.	To Stettin.	To Copenhagen, viâ New York.	To Stockton.	Total Sailings.
January	16	7	2	2	3	2	...	3	...	...	...	...	...	35
February	14	7	2	2	2	4	...	2	...	...	1	...	...	34
March	16	9	2	1	3	2	...	2	...	...	...	...	...	35
April	17	6	2	1	2	3	...	1	...	...	...	...	...	32
May	16	8	3	3	2	2	2	...	...	...	...	...	...	36
June	19	7	2	2	2	2	2	...	...	...	...	...	...	36
July	15	6	2	1	2	2	2	...	...	...	...	...	...	30
August	17	8	2	2*	1	1	1	1	...	...	...	...	...	33
September	17	6	3	3	2	2	1	1	...	...	...	...	...	35
October	16	6	2	1	1	1	1	1	...	...	...	...	...	29
November	17	8	2	2	3	3	1	1	...	...	...	...	...	37
December	24	6	2	1	1	1	...	...	1	...	...	1	...	37
Total	204	84	26	21	24	25†	10	12	1	...	1	1	...	409
„ 1897	203	90	30	22	1	27	...	13	...	1	...	...	1	388

* Viâ New York. † Three sailings to Antwerp direct.

Annex F.—FREIGHTS from Boston to Liverpool during the Year 1898.

Months.	Grain.	Flour.	Provisions.	Cotton.	Cattle.	Apples.	Hay.	Finished Leather.	Sole Leather.
	Per Bushel.	Per Ton.	Per Ton.	Per Lb.	Per Head.	Per Barrel.	Per Ton.	Per Ton.	Per Ton.
	d. d.	s. d. s. d.	s. d. s. d.	d. d.	s. d. s. d.	s. d. s. d.	s. d. s. d.	s. d. s. d.	s. d. s. d.
January	3 to 3½	12 6 to 15 0	12 6 to 15 0	$\frac{1}{8}$ to $\frac{9}{64}$	35 0	1 3 to 1 6	...	20 0	20 0 to 30 0
February	2¼ 3	10 0 13 9	11 3 13 9	$\frac{1}{8}$ $\frac{9}{64}$	35 0	1 6	...	20 0	...
March	2¼ 3	10 0 11 3	11 3 17 6	$\frac{5}{64}$ $\frac{9}{64}$	35 0	1 3 1 6	17 6 to 20 0	20 0	25 0 30 0
April	2¼ 3	9 0 11 3	11 3 13 9	$\frac{5}{64}$ $\frac{9}{64}$	35 0	1 6	15 0 17 6	20 0	25 0
May	1¼ 2¾	10 0 11 3	15 0 25 0	$\frac{3}{64}$	35 0	...	17 6	25 0 to 30 0	25 0 30 0
June	1½ 4	10 0 12 6	10 0 17 6	$\frac{1}{16}$ $\frac{9}{64}$	25 0	...	...	17 6 20 0	25 0
July	1 1¾	6 8 7 0	10 0 11 3	$\frac{3}{64}$ $\frac{1}{8}$	25 0 to 30 0	...	10 0 17 6	15 0	17 6
August	⅞ 1½	6 8 7 0	10 0	$\frac{3}{64}$	25 0 30 0	1 6	8 7 10 0	15 0	17 6
September	1 1⅞	6 0 8 0	10 0	$\frac{3}{64}$ $\frac{5}{64}$	25 0	1 6	10 0	15 0	17 6
October	2½ 3⅜	7 0 10 0	10 0 17 6	$\frac{1}{8}$ $\frac{9}{64}$	25 0	1 6 2 0	10 0	15 0 25 0	17 6 30 0
November	2½ 4½	7 6 12 6	17 6 25 0	$\frac{7}{64}$ $\frac{5}{32}$	25 0 30 0	1 6 2 6	...	25 0 to 30 0	30 0 35 0
December	3¾ 4	9 3 17 6	20 0 25 0	$\frac{1}{8}$ $\frac{5}{32}$	30 0	1 6 2 0	15 0	20 0 25 0	25 0

BOSTON.

Annex G.—TABLE showing the Principal Articles of Export from Boston, and the Quantities Exported during the Year ended December 31, 1898, compared with 1897.

Articles.		Quantity 1898.	Quantity 1897.
Butter	Lbs.	1,574,682	3,286,337
Cheese	,,	10,890,797	16,773,781
Oleo oil	,,	3,483,281	1,883,807
Apples	Barrels	222,254	426,539
Petroleum	,,	5,866	5,428
,,	Cases	51,457	49,446
Leather	Rolls	144,842	135,238
,,	Bales	61,620	55,730
,,	Bags	57,201	63,046
,,	Bundles	8,383	10,036
,,	Barrels	554	814
,,	Cases	7,242	5,376
,,	Packages	1,416	1,533
Staves	Pieces	483,685	797,896
Flour	Barrels	149,026	227,644
,,	Sacks	2,124,059	1,698,501
Wheat	Bushels	13,021,229	12,143,204
Corn	,,	11,799,265	9,464,163
Oats	,,	8,720,931	5,471,275
Peas	,,	86,780	114,299
Barley	,,	64,968	158,050
Rye	,,	266,925	41,837
Buckwheat	,,	18,462	..
Oatmeal	Barrels	53,633	52,843
,,	Sacks	137,398	88,851
Corn meal	Barrels	54,734	83,447
Mill feed	Tons	2,542	6,393
Hay	Bales	245,338	161,402
Cattle	Head	134,838	162,620
Sheep	,,	75,569	100,067
,,	Carcases	1,335	1,538
Horses	Number	3,173	3,826
Fresh beef	Quarters	599,647	537,291
,,	Rounds	7,418	5,711
Pork	Barrels	19,239	19,396
,,	Tierces	14,366	12,523
Bacon	Boxes	600,637	577,836
Lard	Lbs.	121,448,593	101,101,090
Hams	Barrels	1,556	243
,,	Tierces	1,446	641
Dressed hogs	Carcases	70,640	9,602
Beef	Barrels	4,845	11,336
,,	Tierces	7,374	6,457
Tallow	Barrels	14,735	6,376
,,	Tierces	34,425	8,306
Grease	Barrels	12,137	7,261
,,	Tierces	1,389	..
Oilcake	Sacks	63,487	39,523
Glucose	Barrels	25,068	..
Grape sugar	Bags	89,440	..
Wool	Lbs.	2,161,294	..

(433)

Annex H.—TABLE showing Values of Imports Received at the Port of Boston, from Foreign Countries, during the Calendar Year 1898.

	Value.
	£
MERCHANDISE.	
Free of duty	3,306,181
Subject to duty	6,456,803
Total	9,762,984
GOLD AND SILVER COIN AND BULLION IMPORTED.	
American gold coin	96,784
British gold coin	4,866
Gold bullion	26,579
Total	128,229

TABLE showing Values of Exports Shipped at the Port of Boston to Foreign Countries, during the Calendar Year 1898.

	Value.
	£
MERCHANDISE.	
Domestic	24,686,866
Foreign	286,091
Total	24,972,957
GOLD AND SILVER COIN AND BULLION EXPORTED.	
American silver coin	1,600
Gold ore	1
Total	1,601

BOSTON.

Annex I.—TABLE showing the Value of the Exports and Imports at Boston, by Countries, during the Year ended December 31, 1898.

Countries.	Exports.	Imports.	Total Imports and Exports.
	£	£	£
England	21,543,138	2,902,385	24,445,523
Germany	693,397	711,106	1,404,503
Scotland	770,233	301,963	1,072,196
Egypt	1,135	755,663	756,798
British East Indies	19,864	686,261	706,125
Dutch East Indies and Guiana	2,712	599,811	602,523
Nova Scotia	329,897	258,599	588,496
Belgium	325,608	222,878	548,486
Argentine Republic	76,220	457,012	533,232
Australasia	29,282	470,758	500,040
France	12,012	345,464	357,476
Cuba	986	351,736	352,722
Netherlands	233,358	114,793	348,151
British Africa	251,556	53,879	305,435
Sweden and Norway	181,003	91,770	272,773
Ireland	109,010	113,830	222,840
Mexico	1,600	217,952	219,552
Russia	87,643	118,360	206,003
Italy	11,373	177,592	188,965
British West Indies	19,561	126,522	146,083
Turkey	54,360	73,090	127,450
Philippines	..	93,143	93,143
Puerto Rico	641	72,668	73,309
Quebec, &c.	55,549	14,431	69,980
Uruguay	10,161	55,518	65,679
Switzerland	5,874	59,082	64,956
Denmark	50,758	5,692	56,450
Miquelon, &c.	38,695	13,157	51,852
Nicaragua	119	47,181	47,300
Austria-Hungary	761	44,046	44,807
Spain	..	41,290	41,290
China and Hong-Hong	..	28,258	28,258
Colombia	..	27,902	27,902
Japan	659	20,473	21,132
Newfoundland	16,204	3,316	19,520
Aden	..	15,512	15,512
French Africa	14,130	571	14,701
Chile	..	12,328	12,328
Hayti	6,367	5,361	11,728
Other African and Asian not specially mentioned	..	11,537	11,537
Brazil	1,718	8,498	10,216
Malta, &c.	9,741	..	9,741
Peru	..	9,123	9,123
St. Domingo	..	9,027	9,027
Portuguese Africa	4,297	2,924	7,221
Portugal	374	3,347	3,721
Greece	..	3,030	3,030
Gibraltar	2,883	..	2,883
All others	78	4,145	4,223
Total	24,972,957	9,762,984	34,735,941

(433)

BOSTON.

Annex J.—TABLE showing the Value of Articles of the Imports at the Port of Boston for the Fiscal Year ended June 30, 1898

Articles.	Value.
	£
Wool	1,918,060
„ manufactures of	174,605
Sugar and molasses	1,119,797
Hides and skins	987,877
Chemicals, drugs, and dyes	820,493
Cotton	743,621
„ manufactures of	171,984
Leather	658,754
„ manufactures of	70,513
Vegetable fibres	571,233
„ manufactures of	167,355
Iron, and manufactures of	330,847
Fish	278,518
Paper stock	224,752
Fruits and nuts	217,346
Indiarubber, crude	210,115
„ manufactures of	12,949
Wood, and manufactures of	184,244
Earthen, stone, and chinaware	141,582
Glass and glassware	90,059
Oils, vegetable	73,752
„ animal and mineral	10,265
Wines	70,569
Silk, and manufactures of	62,600
Tin, in blocks, bars, &c.	54,637
Hair, and manufactures of	52,521
Clays	52,018
Art works	44,191
Tobacco, and manufactures of	39,897
Books, &c.	39,257
Articles returned free	36,657
Stone, and manufactures of	36,100
Cement	34,070
Metal compositions	32,830
Vegetables	31,468
Malt liquors	29,837
Spirits, distilled	29,481
Grease and tallow	29,317
Bristles	27,909
Toys	25,619
Coffee	24,480
Cocoa	22,586
Paper, and manufactures of	22,137
Rice and rice flour	20,185
Fur and fur skins	19,245
Household and personal effects	16,251
Breadstuffs, and preparations of	15,117
Salt	13,800
Clocks, watches, &c.	13,282
Coal	13,073
Tea	13,017
Zinc, and manufactures of	12,922
Jewellery	12,852
Feathers, &c.	12,765
Paints	11,532
Fertiliser	10,641
For religious and educational institutions	9,872
Bones, horns, &c.	9,207

TABLE showing the Value of Articles of the Imports at the Port of Boston for the Fiscal Year ended June 30, 1898—continued.

Articles.	Value.
	£
Musical instruments	8,853
Coal-tar	8,356
Emery	8,271
Spices	7,761
Plants, orchids, &c.	6,663
Seeds	6,441
Ivory, and manufactures of	5,492
Soap	5,133
Hats, bonnets, &c.	4,633
Mica	4,142
Beverages, not spirituous	3,815
Chocolate	3,527
Plaster of Paris	2,948
Shades, manufactures of	2,906
Pipes, &c.	2,695
Ores, chrome and sulphur	2,612
Cork	2,388
Lead, and manufactures of	2,369
Wax beans	2,251
Perfumes and cosmetics	2,181
Chalk	2,171
Platinum, and manufactures of	1,980
Carbon	1,905
Copper, and manufactures of	1,719
Starch	1,568
Felt, adhesive	1,387
Moss, seaweed, &c.	1,126
Matting and mats	1,194
Gunpowder and explosives	1,074
Antimony	843
Asphaltum	619
Brass, and manufactures of	458
All other articles	4,895
Total	10,295,039

PORTLAND, MAINE.

Mr. Vice-Consul John B. Keating reports as follows:—

Introductory remarks. Before entering into a brief detail of the trade and commerce in this district for the year ended December 31, 1898, it may be interesting to dwell briefly upon the numerous attractions which Maine offers the tourist and sportsman.

Along the coast are established successful steamship lines (starting out from New York and travelling to Eastport), and these companies carry tourists in and about the shores of Maine; shores which are deeply indented with a succession of excellent harbours, fringed with numberless islands, and having, in this State alone, an actual sea-coast of 2,500 miles. The scenery along the coast of Maine is beautiful and varied, being a combination of mountains, lakes, forests, shore, brooks, rushing rivers, and the Atlantic Ocean.

The rapid and constant expansion of Maine as a summer resort is certainly remarkable. A few years back, only a limited number of localities received any noticeable patronage, now the visitors spread all over the State and along the shores, from Piscataqua to Passamaquoddy Bay, and they reach back into the interior.

To meet the demand of this rapid growth, new hotels are constantly being erected, and the many thousand cottages already occupied are annually increased. Some of these "cottages" ought, more correctly speaking, to be classed as "summer mansions," and especially so is this evident at Bar Harbour, where the mountains, the sea, and the various wooded islands unite in forming the most enchanting and beautiful scenery, and combining to make one of the most delightful summer resorts possible to find on this Continent.

The Rangeley Lakes also receive a large share of patronage, particularly since the completion of the broad gauge railroad. To accommodate visitors numerous camps and hotels are erected.

Poland Springs, another famous resort, also receives a liberal share of patronage, and so much so that it is often difficult for tourists to find accommodation.

The accommodation furnished by the various railroads and steamship companies is considered very good.

The roads throughout the State are fair and projected improvements annually receive the attention of the Legislature.

The sanitary condition of the towns is excellent.

The propagation and preservation of fish and game ensures to the sportsman almost unlimited resources in the pleasures of angling and shooting.

General review. The conditions of labour have apparently during the past year been generally encouraging. In most branches of industry employment at fair wages has been continuous and abundant, and the relations between employers and employés undisturbed. The principal exception was in the cotton mills, where in several cases, extensive strikes occurred in the early part of the year, involving several thousand workmen and lasting several weeks. These strikes were the result of reductions in wages, made necessary, as was claimed by the mill-owners, by the small margin of profit in the manufacture of cotton goods. Estimates based on its investigation and reliable information place the losses in wages at about 40,000*l*. In March of the present year wages were generally restored in nearly all the factories and cotton mills, the average advance in all industries being apparently over 10 per cent.

British shipping. The total number of British ships entered at the various ports in this district was 1,138, with a total of 367,641 tons, of which number 236 entered at Portland, with a total tonnage of 257,384 tons.

A better idea of the increase of tonnage is shown in the following figures:—In 1888 the net tonnage entered was 60,349; in 1897 it was 177,159, an increase of 116,810 tons; and last year the increase amounted to 190,482 tons.

By these figures it will be seen that the commerce in British ships has increased to an important extent, and with the establishment in 1899 of a summer line of steamers direct to the United Kingdom, it would seem that at last exporters have recognised the advantages of this port, and I feel that British exporters would also find it to their advantage to study the local and natural facilities of Portland. Goods can be received here and transhipped with the least possible delay, and the serious and disastrous detention complained of by shippers while in the custom-house would naturally be avoided.

There will be six steamers engaged in the summer line from this port to London during the summer of 1899. Considerable interest has always been manifested in trying to make Portland an all-the-year-round port, and the efforts of the Thomson line will be watched with considerable interest. If they are successful, I am assured that other lines will next year follow their example, and a regular all-the-year-round communication will be established between Portland, London, Liverpool, Bristol, and Glasgow. And it is thought that with their influence and through their energetic and persistent co-operation, the experiment of running steamers to Portland in the summer will undoubtedly be a financial success.

Protection of harbour. While the regulations adopted by the United States Government for the protection of harbours during the war with Spain was somewhat rigid, no delay or hardship to British shipping resulted therefrom. The local authorities kindly assisted in every possible way to insure an uninterrupted and safe service by the various steamship lines. Shipmasters cheerfully and cautiously obeyed the regulations with the exception of one schooner which arrived at this port from Puerto Rico. The master, being unacquainted with the regulations which closed the harbour during certain hours of the night, attempted to enter, but was compelled to anchor by the troops at Portland Head, without, however, any serious injury to crew or vessel.

Sailors. Sailors at the commencement of the war were very scarce, and their services were at a high premium; consequently rigid regulations had to be adopted to guard against desertion from the ships in port, as it was impossible to obtain substitutes. Some of the men who did desert managed to secrete themselves until after their vessel had sailed, and were found to have registered their names for examination prior to entering the United States Navy.

These men were promptly arrested and returned to the United Kingdom in other ships. This precaution was sufficient to deter others from following their example, and the ships were secured from any serious loss or delay.

Crimping. Until recently there was not, in this district, any law, either State or Federal, under which "crimps" could be punished for enticing

28 PORTLAND.

seamen to desert. Recently, however, the following law has been passed:—

"An Act for the Better Protection of Ship Masters and Seamen.

"Section 1. Whoever entices or persuades, or attempts to entice or persuade, or aids, assists, or attempts to aid or assist, a member of the crew of any vessel arriving in or about to sail from a port in this State to leave or desert such vessel before the expiration of his term of service therein, shall forfeit a sum not exceeding 100 dol. for each offence, and be punished by imprisonment for not more than six months nor less than 30 days at the discretion of the court.

"Section 2. Municipal courts and trial justices shall have original jurisdiction in all cases arising under this Act."

It will be noticed that this law is especially useful by the fact that Trial Justices and Municipal Courts are empowered to take jurisdiction in these cases.

New buildings. In the city of Portland there were issued in 1898, by the Building Inspector, 29 permits for the erection of brick buildings.

Portland's commerce. The reports of the commercial houses and factories state that all kinds of trade are in a good and prosperous condition, and that at no previous period was trade more promising than at present. New firms and factories are coming into existence, and many of the old-established industries are enlarging their facilities to meet the increased trade.

Export, domestic. During the winter season of 1897–98 (from returns furnished by the Board of Trade) there were exported from this port:—

PORTLAND.

Articles.		Quantity.	Value.
			£ s.
Wheat	Bushels	113,110	26,600 0
Corn	,,	576,875	39,564 8
Oats	,,	1,067,670	65,089 0
Malt	,,	11,287	1,506 8
Wheat-flour	Barrels	135,142	119,180 0
Corn-meal	,,	30	12 0
Oatmeal	Lbs.	201,600	843 8
Oilcake	,,	2,116,110	4,415 0
Butter	,,	236,265	8,638 0
Beef product	,,	2,856,186	47,695 12
Cheese	,,	232,936	6,173 0
Pork product	,,	28,713,880	465,114 8
Tallow	,,	1,847,169	11,943 4
Olive oil	,,	706,121	8,473 4
Cottelene	,,	100,494	1,108 8
Brown sugar	,,	112,000	896 0
Wood-pulp	,,	4,611,300	9,381 8
Deal boards, &c.	1,000 feet	3,742	12,309 8
Manufactured wood			33,678 12
Cattle		10,619	116,247 4
Horses		548	11,360 0
Sheep		2,252	2,754 4
Oils			97 0
Liquors			200 16
Apples	Barrels	1,576	1,231 4
Hay	Bales	111	238 16
Cotton	,,	7,581	48,615 8
Clover seed			6,600 0
Manufactures			2,312 0
Sundries			17,505 0

At a banquet given by the Board of Trade of Portland to Mr. Hays, the General Manager of the Grand Trunk Railway, that gentleman stated that the transhipments from this port during the season of 1896–97 showed an increase of 100 per cent., in 1897–98 the increase was 60 per cent. over that of the previous year, and during the present season of 1898–99 he expected to increase the volume of exports 500 per cent. *Increase of exports.*

To meet the requirements of the rapid and healthy growth of the export trade at this port, the harbour has been dredged so that at the wharves vessels can load in a depth of water not less than 29 feet at mean low tide. New sheds have been constructed, and the wharves are now about to be lengthened to at least 600 feet.

The present elevators can load six steamers, and deliver on board from 12,000 to 15,000 bushels per hour. The largest elevator has a capacity of 1,250,000 bushels, and the smaller one 160,000 bushels, and it is reported that further facilities are to be given by the erection in the near future of another large elevator. *Elevator capacity.*

Considerably increased despatch has this winter been given the steamers by the completion of an extensive track-yard capable of *Freight track yards.*

Lines of steamers.

holding 1,500 loaded cars, and this and the other yard-room gives capacity for 2,000 cars.

The lines of vessels sailing from Portland include two weekly lines to Liverpool, one weekly line to London, and a fortnightly line to Glasgow, Bristol, and Hamburg.

Cereals.

The cereal production of Maine for the year 1897 was as follows:—

Articles.	Quantity.
	Bushels.
Wheat	24,651
Corn	366,411
Oats	4,139,740
Rye	12,270
Barley	305,775
Total	4,848,847

The number of acres devoted to the growth of wheat was 1,494; of corn, 9,903; of oats, 133,540; of rye, 983; of barley, 12,231 acres. A total acreage of 158,151 devoted to grain.

Food supplies.

From a table of the average retail prices of the necessaries of life in the matter of provisions, fuel, &c., it is found from the returns of the cities and towns that in 1894 the prices averaged 4·3 per cent. lower. In 1897, 0·3 per cent. higher; and in 1898, 1·7 per cent. higher than in 1893. The articles showing the most downward tendency of prices were beans, coffee, lard, eggs, and butter. Cheese shows a constant though slight decline, but beef, lard, and mutton show higher prices than in 1893. Coal with a small fluctuation shows a slight downward tendency. The average prices of wood, as a whole, though influenced by constantly changing local prices, are not much different now from 1893—hard wood being a little lower and soft wood a little higher. Kerosene is somewhat higher, and soap, vinegar, and some minor articles lower than in 1893.

Adulteration of flour.

The Secretary of the State Board of Agriculture during the past year issued a circular notice for the information of the public, cautioning them against an adulteration termed "mineraline," which the manufacturers claimed was being extensively used in high and medium-grade flour, also in bread and feed-meal. Chemical analysis proved "mineraline" to be ground soapstone. The manufacturers in urging its adoption and sale, claimed that when mixed with flour the latter became whiter, &c., and by this adulteration an increased profit to the retailer was assured.

Potatoes.

From Aroostook County potatoes are exported to all parts of the Union. In 1897 the Maine crop was limited, and suffered by competition with the Western crop. Last year the conditions were reversed. The prices varied, but at all times the farmer was able to sell at a fair profit, the average price being 100 per cent. higher than in 1897.

The corn pack last year has been the largest ever harvested in this State. Prices for high-grade corn ruled high and remained firm, and it is reported that at one period the sale of canned corn was so heavy that the packers found it difficult to supply the demand.

Corn.

957,976 acres were devoted to growing hay, resulting in a crop of 1,053,774 tons, valued at 2,054,859*l*.

Hay.

In view of the reported purchase of the sardine factories by capitalists, a short history of the sardine industry may be interesting. The first factory was opened about the year 1867, and at the start did not succeed, owing to the difficulty experienced in extracting the oil from the fish, which gave it an unpleasant taste. This and other difficulties were not overcome until 1875. After that date the industry rapidly increased, and machinery took the place of former primitive modes for drying the fish, &c.

Sardines.

In 1886 there were 20 factories in Eastport and numerous others at Lubec, Jonesport, Bar Harbour, South-West Harbour, &c. Prices have declined from 12 dol. a case to 3 dol. and less.

Last year the Legislature passed an Act providing for the packing of a higher grade of fish, and the shortening of the packing season by about 40 days, that is from May 10 to November 30. It also provided for a rigid system of inspection of the fish and of the oils used, and limited the size and number of fish packed in each tin, and imposed penalties for violation. The Act also regulated the labelling of tins, it being stated that under the former condition it was impossible for the purchaser when buying to know whether he was purchasing domestic or foreign fish. The fact that this industry has not been a profitable one is accounted for by the statement that all packers have been in sharp competition with each other, but this state of affairs will, it is thought, be remedied by the joint ownership of a syndicate.

From the Fish Commissioners' report I learn that upwards of 250 men are employed in catching lobsters in Cumberland County alone. The fishermen reside on the shores of the Casco Bay. In the month of September 378,194 lobsters were landed at Portland. Of this number 95,533 were boat lobsters caught in Casco Bay. The total caught in October, it was thought, exceeded this number. These figures will, however, suffice to give an idea of the importance of this industry, which is constantly increasing. Portland merchants now supply the markets of St. Louis, Chicago, Minneapolis, and other cities further west. It is estimated that there are about 900,000 lobsters in "pounds" along the coast of Maine. The fishermen get an annual average of 5*d*. a lb. for lobsters, and when not engaged in lobster fishing they are employed in catching smelts, for which they receive an average of 4*d*. a lb.

Lobsters.

Steamers are employed in the lobster fishing. At this port

PORTLAND.

there are seven of them, making each two or three trips a week with lobsters. Very few lobsters are imported from the Nova Scotia coast.

At one time the canning of lobsters was a prosperous industry, but this business, since the enactment of the Short Lobster Law, has been removed to Nova Scotia.

Short Lobster Law.

The fishermen are trying to get the Short Lobster Law repealed, as they claim that the law as it now stands is injuring the industry, and acting in an opposite manner to what the framers of the Short Lobster Law intended or expected.

Cultivation of lobsters.

An interesting experiment in lobsters is about to be undertaken by two men who are reported to have made a study of the lobster problem, and one of whom has already established a successful clam farm, which he works profitably. The new "lobster farm" is situated in a cove, enclosed with a wire fence stretched from headland to headland, and time will prove whether lobsters can be successfully farmed. In raising lobsters artificially these farmers state that they will avail themselves of the expert knowledge possessed by the United States Fish Commission, and as far as possible will adopt the methods which the Commission has found to result so successfully at Woods Holland, Gloucester, Mass., where the Government hatcheries are located, and where the experiments are confined to hatching.

There are not any hatcheries in Maine, but during the past two seasons the lobster fishermen have been permitted to collect egg-bearing lobsters, and to deliver them to the United States authorities on board the schooner "Grampus," they agreeing to return the lobsters, and to distribute the fry from the eggs in Maine waters. The amount of lobster fry thus set free in 1896 and 1897 was about 21,000,000, all of which was placed in the bays and shoals selected by the Maine Commission. How many of these fry will mature no one can properly tell, but according to Commissioner Nickerson about 95 per cent. of the eggs were hatched and returned to Maine in fry.

Mackerel fishing.

At one time mackerel fishing was a most important industry, upwards of 100 schooners being employed in the trade. The average value of these schooners was 800*l*., and each vessel was manned by a crew of from 15 to 17 men. The average value of each catch was between 1,200*l*. to 3,000*l*. Nearly all the outfits and supplies, &c., were purchased in Portland. Many theories have been advanced for the cause of the disappearance of the mackerel, and I understand that the most generally accepted cause is that seining has destroyed or at least driven the mackerel away, but others assert that it is because the mackerel do not show on the surface of the water as formerly, and again others account for their scarcity as due to their destruction by other fish, and they do not breed fast enough to counteract the slaughter.

Porgies.

Last year I gave some particulars relating to the return to these waters of the porgies. This year the industry has continued good, several steamers being engaged as formerly in the fishing.

PORTLAND.

In Maine upwards of 2,500 hands are employed in the fish canneries industry, as against 800 employed in Massachusetts; the industry is of considerable importance, and steadily increasing.

In the annual report made by the Commissioner of Industry and Labour, complete returns were received in 1898 from 10 of the 16 cotton mills located in the State, eight of which were identical with those received last year. These returns were tabulated, and the aggregate of the 10 factories makes the following showing: capital invested, 2,511,700*l.*; cost of material used, 781,150*l.*; value of product, 1,491,079*l.*; number of weeks in operation, 47·2; average number of hands employed, 9,588, of which 3,938 were men, 5,025 women, and 625 children.

The average weekly wages for men was 1*l.* 10*s.*, for women 1*l.* 2*s.* 4*d.*, and for children under 16 years 11*s.*

In the following table of figures a comparison is made with those of former years, taking the value of the product as a basis:—

Item.	Percentage.			
	1880.	1890.	1897.	1898.
Raw material	55·0	55·2	57·9	52·4
Wages	22·0	28·5	33·1	34·8
Margin	23·0	16·3	9·0	12·8
Total	100	100	100	100

It will be noted by this table that the percentage of raw material fell off 5·5 per cent. during the past year, and the percentage of wages shows a steady increase. The percentage of margin, which fell off from 23 per cent. in 1880 to 9 per cent. in 1897, has recovered 3·8 per cent. during the past year.

The following table shows the average annual earnings per head, including men, women, and children for the years named:—

	1890.	1897.	1898.
	£ s.	£ s.	£ s.
Annual product	219 0	174 16	155 10
,, earnings	62 10	57 16	54 4

The average annual product per head shows a constant decrease, but it is explained that the large decrease during the last year may be accounted for through certain unfortunate conditions. The average running time of the mills in 1897 was 48·1 weeks, while for 1898 it was 47·2 weeks, an average shortening of nine-tenths of a week. The shortening of time occurred among the largest mills, brought about principally by a strike early in the year.

The falling-off in annual earnings from 1890 to 1898 is considered a normal decrease.

Comparisons are made between the returns of eight mills received in 1897 and the same in 1898. The showing is:—Increase in capital, 94,000*l.*; decrease in cost of material, 8,454*l.* 4*s.*; decrease in total wages paid, 21,554*l.*; decrease in value of product, 69,206*l.* 8*s.*; decrease in average weekly wages of men, 7*d.*; decrease in average weekly wages of women, 9*d.*; increase in average weekly wages of children, ½*d.*; decrease in number of men employed, 38; increase of women employed, 275; increase of children, 37; decrease in average number of weeks in operation 3·9.

Woollen mills. Returns were received from 22 woollen mills, from which the following figures are taken:—Capital invested, 564,159*l.*; cost of material used, 491,909*l.* 8*s.*; value of product, 978,964*l.* 16*s.*; number of weeks in operation, 49·7; average number of hands employed 2,555, of whom 1,710 were men, 823 women, and 22 children under 16 years. Average weekly wages for men, 1*l.* 12*s.*; for women, 1*l.* 4*s.* 1*d.*; for children, 15*s.* 7*d.*; total wages paid, 191,726*l.* 8*s.* Similar tables are deduced and comparisons made as in the cotton industry.

On the basis of the value of the product the following shows the percentage of raw material, wages and margin at different periods:—

Item.	Percentage.			
	1880.	1890.	1897.	1898.
Raw material	64·2	65·9	65·4	60·1
Wages	15·6	21·7	25·1	23·4
Margin	20·2	12·4	9·5	16·5
Total	100	100	100	100

The above figures show that up to 1897 while in the percentage of raw material little change is indicated, the percentage of wages steadily increased, and that of margin decreased to a figure which would warrant no profit in the business. In fact the industry was evidently much demoralised, but the percentage for the past year shows the business to be in a much better condition than for several years past.

The average annual product and earnings per head are shown as follows for the different periods named:—

PORTLAND.

	1890.	1897.	1898.
	£ s. d.	£ s. d.	£ s. d.
Annual product	347 19 9	278 8 0	320 1 7
„ earnings	75 8 0½	69 15 2	75 0 10

In the basis of 21 woollen mills, from which returns were received both in 1897 and 1898, the following is obtained:— Increase in capital invested, 68,399*l*.; increase in cost of material, 67,585*l*.; increase in total wages paid, 29,599*l*. 4*s*.; increase in value of product, 164,702*l*. 8*s*.; decrease in average weekly wages of men, 1*s*. 0½*d*.; decrease in average weekly wages of women, 11½*d*.; increase in average weekly wages of children, 6½*d*.; increase in men employed, 184; increase in women, 53; decrease of children, 4; increase in average number of hands, 233; increase in average weeks in operation, 4·4.

New buildings. In response to inquiries regarding factories, mills, and shops built and enlarged during the year 1898, the returns from the various counties (65) show that 72 new buildings were erected at a total cost of 135,020*l*., giving employment to 2,024 new hands. These numbers are the smallest in eight years, with the exception of 1894, when but 55 factories, &c., were constructed at a cost of 132,740*l*.

Farm animals. According to returns furnished to the State Bureau of Industries from the counties in the State of Maine, there were in this State in 1898 59,208 horses, 327,255 meat cattle, 649,261 sheep, and 17,386 swine.

Poultry. According to statistics furnished last year the number of fowls in the State was 1,577,252; value of poultry produced 101,094*l*., value of eggs produced 273,262*l*. The estimated average production of poultry and eggs in the State is per hen, 4*s*. 9*d*.; turkey, 11*s*. 8½*d*.; duck, 10*s*. 4*d*.; goose, 8*s*. 6½*d*. The lowest average production per hen was in Aroostook county, 3*s*. 1½*d*., the greatest was in Washington county, 5*s*. 2½*d*.

Maine horses. Maine has always had a stock of fine horses. It is supposed that there is something in the natural advantages of the State particularly favourable to supplying to the horses strength, endurance and speed. Throughout the State there are many establishments devoted exclusively to the breeding of driving horses and trotters.

Machine shops and foundries. Various new industries have come into existence and old industries enlarged and improved, notably shipyards, lumber mills, cotton and woollen mills. Of the 170 foundries and machine shops established in the State of Maine, Portland has 27, which give employment to 974 persons. The capital invested is 200,000*l*. The largest foundry and machine shop in Eastern Maine is the Union Iron Works at Bangor. The combined capital invested in foundries and machine shops in the State, exclusive of the railroad shops, pulp, paper, cotton, woollen and other mills in the State amounts to about 700,000*l*., and the number of men employed is about 4,500. The average wages earned in foundries and machine shops throughout the State is a little over 8s. per day per man.

Steam and street railroads.

The number of men employed on the railways for the year ending June 30, 1897, was 5,842, receiving 562,257*l*. 10s. in wages; in 1898 there were 5,852, receiving 566,510*l*. 3s. 6*d*. On the street railroads there were 725 people employed in 1898, an increase of 125, and the wages paid was 65,000*l*., an increase of 5,000*l*. The steam railroads employ 3,010 men, and there were dependent on this number 38,000 persons. One new railroad has been opened, viz., the Washington County Railroad, connecting Bangor with Eastport.

Lumber industry.

The lumber industry for the past year has been most unsatisfactory, especially for those engaged in sawing for the home market. At Bangor, when the river opened for navigation last spring, there was a good stock of logs on hand at the mills, and the indications were that the season would be a good one. The war with Spain, however, demoralised the market, and as a result trade was smaller last year, with prices lower than for 20 years past. Some of the Penobscot mills have not started at all this year, owing to the stagnation, whilst others have been worked only a part of the time. The amount of lumber sawn last winter was much less than in 1897.

The logs cut last winter are estimated at 140,000,000 feet, or 20,000,000 feet less than in 1896 and 1897, and of this amount only 18,000,000 feet remain to be wintered in the boom, while 25,000,000 feet were left in the stream, up the river, or in yards.

Twenty-five years ago Bangor annually shipped from 200,000,000 to 275,000,000 feet of lumber to markets on both sides of the Atlantic, but since then its shipments have fallen off nearly one-half.

Pulp mills.

The pulp mills, which have replaced to a great extent this industry, have, however, been more profitable, so much so that new mills are constantly being added, and at the time of writing this report particulars are at hand of a projected new building at Millincockett, which is stated will be the largest pulp and paper mill in the world.

The mill when completed will contain eight machines, with a capacity of from 200 to 250 tons of newspaper daily, and will furnish employment for at least 650 men. The company is reported to have secured various spruce lands along the railroad lines, in addition to 250,000 acres of spruce lands situated on the West Branch waters, and it is estimated that this will furnish sufficient spruce land for 30 years.

Liquor traffic.

It is interesting to note that the total revenue collected (National and State) from the liquor traffic amounted to 25,764*l*. 16s. 8*d*., and the aggregate net profit of the agencies amounted to 1,893*l*. 4s. 5*d*. In this State the selling of liquor (except through the liquor agencies) is entirely illegal, and reliable statistics of the liquor trade, which is so extensively carried on, are not obtainable. It would appear, however, that the majority of liquor dealers first pay a United States stamp tax, which costs about 5*l.*, and this secures the purchaser against prosecution by the Federal authorities. In 1886 1,145 persons paid this tax. The fines collected by the courts from liquor dealers for the benefit of the several counties (16) amounted to 18,593*l.* The profits of the State liquor agencies to the State, and the combined net profits of town agencies by counties, for the year ending June 30, 1896, are shown as follows:—

	Amount.
	£ s.
State agency	172 0
Town agencies	1 733 4
Total	1,905 4

General notes.

I ventured in my report for 1897 to give the result of a careful canvass of Portland's imported goods. During the past year I have inquired into the imported trade in my district, and of the many replies received to my inquiries I have selected the answers of four firms, who replied to my questions as follows:—

(1) What is the percentage of foreign goods sold? 20 per cent., of which British manufacture equalled 5 per cent. Remarks upon trade and on goods of British manufacture. Satisfactory, and in demand; more could, we think, be sold if properly pushed. Silk? None. Wool? Only a few. Black dress goods? Of black crepons, cheviots, and mohair, perhaps about 600*l.* is sold annually by us. Mohair dress fabrics? Only a few in colours sold. Table damask napkins? 100 per cent., about 2,400*l.* per annum is sold by us. Towelling? About 25 per cent of what we use are British. Hose? 5 per cent are British. Nottingham laces? All we use, probably 400*l.* worth sold annually.

Prospect for improved business good.

(2) What is the percentage of foreign goods sold? 18 per cent., of which British manufacture equalled 7½ per cent. Remarks upon trade and on goods of British manufacture. Direct representatives are absolutely needed. Silk? Practically no British silk. Wool? 60 per cent. of dress goods sold are foreign, one-third are of British manufacture. Black dress goods? 50 per cent. of black goods sold are British. Table damask napkins? 25 per cent. of British manufacture. Towelling? 25 per cent. of British manufacture. Hose? We sell no British manufactured hosiery, the foreign goods being all German. Nottingham goods? 5 per cent. of our lace business is Nottingham goods.

(3) What is the percentage of foreign goods sold? 25 per cent., of which British manufacture equalled half of above. Remarks upon trade on goods of British manufacture. Needs pushing by someone directly interested in the manufacturers. Wool? In great favour, percentage not known. Black dress

goods? In great favour, percentage not known. Mohair dress fabrics? Very few used, and those all British. Table damask napkins? British preferable to any other. Towelling? British preferable to any other. Hose? All German. Nottingham laces? Nothing else as good.

We would suggest that the best man to sell goods is the one best acquainted with every detail; hence the manufacturer or someone in close touch with him would find it to his interest to meet and deal with the retailer direct, even if the orders have afterwards to be turned over to the jobber.

(4) What is the percentage of foreign goods sold? 25 per cent., of which British manufacture equalled 3 per cent. Remarks upon trade and on goods of British manufacture. Would say that more could be sold if properly canvassed. Table damask napkins? Probably 75 per cent. Irish, 15 per cent. Scotch, and 10 per cent German. Towelling? Probably 75 per cent. Irish, 15 per cent. Scotch, and 10 per cent. German. Nottingham laces? Use very few (American goods taking their place).

During the past year, I have received many inquiries from British manufacturers and exporters, but as only in one instance did I receive an acknowledgment of the receipt of the information asked for, I am unable to report whether the information furnished by me was of service or not.

LONDON:
Printed for Her Majesty's Stationery Office,
By HARRISON AND SONS,
Printers in Ordinary to Her Majesty.
(75 7 | 99—H & S 433)

No. 2349 Annual Series.

DIPLOMATIC AND CONSULAR REPORTS.

UNITED STATES.

REPORT FOR THE YEAR 1898

ON THE

TRADE, COMMERCE, &c., OF THE CONSULAR DISTRICT OF SAN FRANCISCO.

REFERENCE TO PREVIOUS REPORT, Annual Series No. 2152.

Presented to both Houses of Parliament by Command of Her Majesty,
SEPTEMBER, 1899.

LONDON:
PRINTED FOR HER MAJESTY'S STATIONERY OFFICE,
BY HARRISON AND SONS, ST. MARTIN'S LANE,
PRINTERS IN ORDINARY TO HER MAJESTY.

And to be purchased, either directly or through any Bookseller, from
EYRE & SPOTTISWOODE, EAST HARDING STREET, FLEET STREET, E.C., and
32, ABINGDON STREET, WESTMINSTER, S.W.; or
JOHN MENZIES & Co., 12, HANOVER STREET, EDINBURGH, and
90, WEST NILE STREET, GLASGOW; or
HODGES, FIGGIS, & Co., Limited, 104, GRAFTON STREET, DUBLIN.

1899.

[C. 9496—20.] *Price Twopence Halfpenny.*

CONTENTS.

	PAGE
SAN FRANCISCO—	
Introductory remarks	5
Trade and commerce—	
Return of exports and imports (articles, quantities, and values)	6
Exports—	
Wheat and flour	7
Preserved salmon	7
Preserved fruit and vegetables	7
Barley	8
Timber	8
Wine	8
Quicksilver	8
Hops	8
Brandy	8
Imports—	
Coal	8
Coke	9
Cement	9
Woollens, dress goods, and hosiery	10
Linens	10
Cloth goods, suitings, &c.	10
Return of exports and imports (countries and values)	11
Return of mining products	12
Shipping and navigation—	
Return of entries and clearances	13
Freights and charters	14
Catch of whaling fleet	15
Pilotage	15
Lumber rafts	15
Shipbuilding	15
New steamers for Pacific	16
Seamen's institute	16
„ wages	17

CONTENTS—continued.

	PAGE
SAN FRANCISCO—continued—	
Population, public health, and industries—	
Return of births, marriages, and deaths	17
Treatment of diphtheria	17
Adulteration of food	18
Analysis of gas and water	18
Attempt to restrict use of cigarettes	18
Hydraulic mining	18
Lower levels of Comstock to be drained	18
Return of principal mineral products	19
Labour market	19
Advice to intending settlers	20
Agriculture—	
Wheat	20
Barley	20
Hops	20
Fruit	20
Extension of orchards	21
Oranges	21
Lemons	21
Olives	21
Prunes	22
Raisins	22
Orchard pests	22
Importation of fruit and live plants	22
Wine crop	22
Beet sugar	23
Honey	23
Wool	23
Public works—	
Railway construction	24
General remarks—	
Real estate, stocks and bonds	24
Fire insurance	25
Bank clearings	25
Proposed commercial museum	26
LOS ANGELES trade report	26
SAN DIEGO trade report	33

No. 2349.   Annual Series.

Reference to previous Report, Annual Series No. 2152.

Report on the Trade, Commerce, Agriculture and other Matters of Interest of the Consular District of San Francisco for the Year 1898

By Mr. Consul-General Pickersgill.

(Received at Foreign Office, August 10, 1899.)

California did not share in the prosperity which so generally characterised the year 1898 in the United States. Owing to the drought of the previous winter the crop of cereals was extremely light, and as the European demand was supplied from other sources, the prices realised were not sufficiently high to compensate the farmers for the lessened production. The fruit crop also suffered for want of early rains, but prices advanced on account of the purchases made by the "canners." The wine crop was small and of inferior quality. Mining operations were restricted, and the gold output of the State decreased in consequence. {Introductory remarks.}

Exports show a heavy decline, which may largely be accounted for by the scanty wheat crop. The revised tariff inaugurated in 1897 was in operation the whole of last year, and was the main cause of the marked decrease in the imports.

Business in San Francisco was dull throughout the year, but received a temporary stimulus in some quarters by the purchase and shipment of Government supplies for the troops in Honolulu and the Philippine Islands. The bank clearings show an increase of over 14,000,000*l.*, but this cannot be accepted as a fair indication of the condition of trade during last year, owing to the unusually heavy transactions in securities. Food, clothing, and mining necessaries for Alaska and the Klondyke district continue to be procured in this market, but in reduced quantities, the excitement of a year ago having greatly subsided.

A considerable increase in the trade of San Francisco, and of the Pacific Coast, is regarded by business men as assured by recent developments. The extension of the Atchison, Topeka, and Santa Fé Railroad to this city will give increased facilities for reaching interior points and the markets of the Eastern States, and possibly lower rates; while the new steamer line to China and Japan, which is likely to be established in connection therewith, will undoubtedly have a stimulating effect on the growing trade with Oriental ports. Commerce with the Hawaiian Islands is

(470)

SAN FRANCISCO.

already controlled by San Francisco merchants, but considerable expansion of trade is looked for in that direction as a result of the annexation of the islands. The Philippine Islands are also confidently expected to open up extensive markets for Pacific Coast productions in the near future.

California was threatened with another visitation of drought in the early part of the present year, the rainfall up to the middle of March being much below the normal. Grave apprehension, however, gave way to bright confidence, on the fall of copious showers just in time to save the growing crops, and it is generally considered that the harvest will be fully up to the average.

Trade and commerce.

The following tables show the amount and principal articles of export and import for the years ended 1897–98 :—

RETURN of Principal Articles of Export from San Francisco during the Years 1898–97.

Articles.		1898.		1897.	
		Quantity.	Value.	Quantity.	Value.
			£		£
Wheat and flour	Centals	6,396,369	1,815,641	11,859,892	3,556,832
Tinned salmon	Cases	610,288	493,980	612,858	492,702
,, fruit and vegetables	,,	...	418,606	332,608	216,904
Barley	Centals	746,042	177,558	3,164,558	613,924
Timber	Feet	2,020,623	82,304	25,838,195	84,301
Wine	Gallons	1,048,266	81,769	883,445	79,443
Quicksilver	Flasks	5,952	48,211	5,464	42,073
Hops	Lbs.	1,595,934	35,733	578,706	13,104
Brandy	Gallons	13,190	4,314	8,773	2,086
Other articles		...	3,377,728	...	3,035,872
Total merchandise		...	6,535,844	...	8,147,241
Treasure		...	1,738,939	...	3,751,267
Grand total		...	8,274,783	...	11,898,508

RETURN of Principal Articles of Import to San Francisco during the Years 1898–97.

Articles.		1898.		1897.	
		Quantity.	Value.	Quantity.	Value.
			£		£
Sugar	Tons	118,592	1,899,532	146,910	1,934,188
Raw silk	Lbs.	3,141,328	1,895,581	4,325,560	2,366,659
Coal	Tons	775,800	1,070,604	867,500	1,041,000
Coffee	Lbs.	18,184,358	398,153	19,212,004	612,278
Tea	,,	8,103,892	219,237	14,172,700	398,202
Rice	Tons	20,132	160,125	18,759	252,121
Cement	Lbs.	120,182,513	78,637	87,903,830	58,523
Tin-plates	Boxes	83,404	39,274	277,270	143,181
Pig-iron	Tons	1,564	3,731	4,006	9,673
Other articles		...	1,447,751	...	1,353,533
Total merchandise		...	7,212,625	...	8,169,358
Treasure		...	7,498,559	...	2,756,460
Grand total		...	14,711,184	...	10,925,818

Exports.

Of exported merchandise there was a decrease during 1898, as compared with 1897, amounting to 1,611,397*l*., and a falling-off in exported treasure to the value of 2,012,328*l*.

Wheat and flour.
The returns of wheat exhibit a decrease of 5,285,774 centals during the same period, the shipments being even smaller than those of the memorably dry year of 1877. Great Britain took 3,005,075 centals at prices which varied from 1 dol. 80 c. to 1 dol. 15 c. per cental, and which, on the average, were lower than those of 1897. The flour sent abroad was less also, to the extent of 79,251 barrels, but a considerable quantity was despatched to the Philippine Islands by Government transports, of which no record was kept. Exports to Great Britain amounted to 74,720 barrels.

Tinned salmon.
There was also a decrease in the exportation of salmon during 1898. Great Britain and Australia were the chief buyers, the former having taken 508,656, and the latter 67,047 cases, while only comparatively small shipments were made to other countries. A large quantity, however, was despatched overland, of which particulars cannot be obtained.

The following is an estimate of the total Pacific Coast output of salmon in tins:—

	Quantity.
	Cases.
Columbia River	471,230
Sacramento River	27,150
Rogue River	13,459
Coast rivers and bays	72,044
Willapa and Gray's Harbours	33,100
Puget Sound	425,000
British Columbia	431,000
Alaska	960,000
Total	2,432,983*

* Or 116,783,184 1-lb. tins.

Preserved fruit and vegetables.
No figures are given by the custom-house indicating the quantity of tinned fruit and vegetables exported in 1898, but the value recorded is nearly double that of the preceding year, and yet the demand is not considered to have been fully met on account of the lack of produce suitable for tinning. Scarcity of fruit, unless extending to the total failure of a crop, does not affect the output of packers to the same degree as poorness of quality. They contract with their customers before the season opens, and being thus bound to supply the preserved article, are under the necessity of bidding high for the raw when crops are not plentiful. Deficiencies, therefore, are more readily noticed in connection with dried fruit than with tinned.

At the beginning of last season the stocks of the latter kind had run very low, and considerable excitement existed in the market when it was found that the crops were not satisfactory. The prices paid for fresh fruit were very much higher than those of 1897—except in the case of cherries, which were cheaper than usual—and there was a corresponding advance in the cost of the preserved product. Notwithstanding this rise, however, the demand for Californian fruit in England is said to have been the greatest ever known. For the first time in the history of the preserving industry a large quantity was sent overland to New York for shipment to Liverpool, and this is understood to have been sold for 10s. a case more than the average price in 1897.

Barley. Most of the Californian barley of 1898 went to Great Britain, but the total amount exported was less than that of any year since 1890.

Timber. Great Britain and Australia were the greatest purchasers of Californian timber during the year 1898. The former took 7,600,837 feet, and the latter 5,197,071 feet. As to the prices obtained, they were barely above the cost of cutting and shipping, although somewhat higher than in 1897. In the quantity exported there was a slight decrease.

Wine. A marked increase took place in the amount of wine sent from California by sea last year, although the consignments made to the Eastern States by the same route were less. Of the exportation by rail there is no public record. Prices, however, were low until the end of the year, when they began to improve as hostile interests in the trade became reconciled.

Quicksilver. The sea exportations of quicksilver show a fair increase upon those of 1897, but the quantity sent overland is considered to have been even larger. Still, consumption did not keep pace with production, which is said to have been greater in 1898 than in the preceding year by 16 per cent. One reason for this undoubtedly lay in the drought, which interfered very seriously with mining operations. Owing to a fear of the production and shipment of Spanish quicksilver being affected by the war, prices improved from 38 dol. 50 c. to 42 dol. 50 c., and closed at 40 dol. per flask.

Hops. Three times more hops were exported by sea last year than during the year preceding, Australia having purchased 1,043,529 lbs., and Great Britain, 270,885 lbs. As in the case of other products, no record is obtainable of the quantity sent by rail. The market was active at prices ranging from 10 to 19 c. per lb., and at the end of the year only a very small stock remained on hand. The indications, therefore, are towards higher prices.

Brandy. The quantity of brandy sent from California to the Eastern States by sea was 100,000 gallons more during 1898 than in 1897, and an increase was noticed also in the exportations to foreign countries, but prices were low in sympathy with those for wine.

Imports. During 1898 there was a decrease in imported merchandise to the extent of 956,733*l.*, but in the value of the treasure received there was an enormous increase, the total being 4,742,099*l.* in excess of the amount recorded for 1897. Australia contributed no less than 5,482,043*l.*; Japan, 1,353,165*l.*; and Mexico, 514,600*l.*

Coal. The importations of foreign coal in 1898 were as follows:—

SAN FRANCISCO.

From—	Quantity.
	Tons.
British Columbia	473,400
Australia	182,000
Great Britain	86,500
Other sources	33,900
Total	775,800

As compared with the returns for 1897, the figures show a decrease of 91,700 tons, but the importations of domestic coal, both by sea and land, are gaining in importance. The highest price paid for British coal was 7 dol. 50 c. per ton, as against 7 dol. 25 c. in 1897, while the lowest was 6 dol. 95 c., against 6 dol. 10 c.

More than half of the coke imported into California during 1898 came from Great Britain, while the remainder had its origin in Belgium, British Columbia, and Australia. The total amounted to 41,630 tons, which was an increase of 37 per cent. on the entries of 1897.

Coke.

The demand for cement last year was good, owing mainly to the United States Government requiring large quantities for fortifications, and prices were satisfactory also. Hereunder is shown the quantity imported during the last two years:—

Cement.

From—	Quantity.	
	1898.	1897.
	Lbs.	Lbs.
Belgium	55,890,713	40,015,610
Great Britain	37,416,600	30,191,656
Germany	23,515,200	17,694,800
France (of Belgian origin)	3,360,000	1,764
Total	120,182,513	87,903,830

It will be seen, on comparing the two sets of figures, that the British manufacturer's gain in the increased importation amounts only to 23·93 per cent., while his German and Belgian competitors have profited to the extent of 32·89 per cent. and 48 per cent. respectively.

The explanation of this rather startling contrast affords another illustration of what has now become an old story. Several years ago one of the largest dealers in cement here discovered that a new quality had been introduced from the Continent of Europe, and that it was meeting with the approval of consumers, on account of its greater fineness and somewhat lower price. It was to the advantage and convenience of this merchant to continue to take his supplies from England, his firm having its only European establishment there. He therefore notified the manufacturer of the danger to their joint interests, and recommended them to sift with a finer mesh and modify their price a little. Failing to make any impression by letter, he crossed the Atlantic and laid the state of affairs before them personally. But they remained, notwithstanding all his efforts, perfectly convinced that they were making as fine a cement as the world had any need of, and that it was good value for the money they asked. So, like a prudent man of business, he carried his firm's patronage elsewhere and is now importing from Germany only. When this bit of commercial history was related to me, it evoked the following comment from a neighbour:—"It is your manufacturers you Britishers want to educate rather than your merchants," and I reminded myself that I have now been, as a Consular representative, in three countries in which I have seen importers transfer custom to the Continent of Europe because the producers of the United Kingdom are too slow in adapting their goods to changing markets.

Woollens, dress goods, hosiery, and underwear.
The importations of plain woollen goods for ladies, tailor-made suits, and all kinds of serges show a marked decline, due no doubt to the prohibitory nature of the duty levied on them. Great Britain's trade with this market in such goods is now confined to the superior grade not made in this country, the bulk of the trade being supplied by the cheaper domestic article. The French manufacturers enjoy the reputation of surpassing the British in the matter of novelties in patterns, a fact which suggests that there is room for improvement in this respect. Tailor-made suits appear to have largely gone out of fashion, the demand this year being for light weight fabrics of a crape like appearance.

Germany is now supplying the major part of the cotton hosiery imported into this market, her merchants having succeeded in underselling all competitors. In underwear, however, Great Britain does a large trade here, particularly in the better class of flat goods. The ribbed article is supplied almost exclusively by Swiss makers. In the cashmere goods, also, the British make a most satisfactory show.

Linens.
While Germany is supplying the Pacific Coast with linen goods in no inconsiderable quantities, it is said that the United Kingdom retains the bulk of the trade, and there is further gratification in the fact that the British article is greatly preferred for the reason that it stands washing much better than any other. German merchants have made a feature of fancy tablecloths, with open-work borders, but as they are necessarily higher in price they do not command so ready a sale as the plainer sort.

Cloth goods, suitings, &c.
There is one branch of manufacture in which the British still maintain pre-eminence in this market, and that is cloth goods. A firm doing a large business therein reports that both in fine fancy suitings and trouserings, British goods lead the market, and that the superior diagonals and high class serges are the models of excellence. Cheap Bradford diagonals for shoe uppers are at present in great demand, while that texture known as "corkscrew"

is out of fashion. Scotch suitings still continue to hold a steady place, but domestic manufacturers are producing a close imitation. Speaking generally, British cloths of from medium to best quality are the goods which afford the greatest margin of profit under the present tariff. It is thought that piqué material could be made to advantage in the neighbourhood of Stroud, as the peculiar soft finish characteristic of West of England cloth can be imparted to this particular make. At present it comes from Sedan in France. British low-priced diagonals and goods of grey mixture, used principally by the manufacturers of ready made clothing, are, owing to the high duties, being largely supplanted by the domestic articles. American cloth makers are steadily improving their woollen goods, there being a marked improvement during the past five years in quality of material, in manufacture, and especially in the dyeing process.

TABLE showing Total Value of all Articles Exported from and Imported to San Francisco from and to Foreign Countries during the Years 1898–97.

Country.	Exports. 1898.	Exports. 1897.	Imports. 1898.	Imports. 1897.
	£	£	£	£
Great Britain	1,842,024	3,488,926	379,672	484,789
Hawaiian Islands	1,201,580	960,854	1,870,677	1,990,157
Japan	902,048	607,679	1,637,614	2,001,518
China	705,508	789,654	1,203,066	1,471,831
Australasia	468,931	513,882	136,179	152,131
Central America	364,212	485,238	383,859	539,656
Mexico	296,973	269,005	68,599	74,703
South Africa	241,693	335,898	..	..
Canada	200,800	122,359	402,198	357,937
Pacific Islands	101,873	74,642	88,617	104,507
South America	82,685	96,979	81,215	113,537
Asiatic Russia	61,400	75,485	22,707	22,208
East Indies	43,605	31,215	398,444	339,229
Germany	16,348	4,073	187,796	131,885
France	2,274	96,702	106,192	126,175
Belgium	1,865	163,376	173,139	168,957
Italy	..	..	32,172	29,470
Other countries	2,025	31,274	40,479	60,668
Total merchandise	6,535,844	8,147,241	7,212,625	8,169,358
Treasure	1,738,939	3,751,267	7,498,559	2,756,460
Grand total	8,274,783	11,898,508	14,711,184	10,925,818

NOTE.—The imports by rail included in the above totals of merchandise amounted to 355,308*l.* as against 344,876*l.* in 1897.

Remarks on the foregoing return.

It will be seen that as compared with 1897 there is a decrease amounting to 1,646,902*l.* in the exports to Great Britain. This diminution is mainly attributable to the heavy decline in wheat shipments consequent upon the partial failure of the crop. The majority of the vessels carrying grain consignments clear for Cork, there to await orders, and although in some instances the orders on arrival are to discharge at Continental ports, the value of their cargoes is included in the exports to Great Britain. Thus it is probable that the figures given in the above table are open to a considerable reduction.

The importations from Great Britain continue to show a decline, having diminished to the extent of 105,117*l.* as compared with 1897. Germany increased her trade with this market to the value of 55,911*l.*, and Belgium 4,182*l.* during the same period. As all three countries equally share the disadvantages of the customs tariff, I can only account for this disparity by the greater activity displayed by our commercial rivals in pushing the sale of their wares, and to better business methods employed by them. An instance illustrating this most important point will be found in the paragraph on cement.

Return of mining products.

The following estimate of the production of precious metals in the States and territory within the jurisdiction of this Consulate-General for the year 1898 is taken from Messrs. Wells, Fargo and Co.'s annual statement:—

	Gold Dust and Bullion, by Express.	Gold Dust and Bullion, by other Conveyances.	Silver Bullion, by Express.	Ores and Base Metal, by Freight.	Total.
	£	£	£	£	£
California	2,497,394	583,137	12,889	527,850	3,621,270
Nevada	319,925	240,032	121,118	38,033	719,108
Utah	241,132	192,522	20,265	1,642,459	2,096,378
Arizona	337,996	295,529	137,352	2,344,289	3,115,166
Total	3,396,447	1,311,220	291,624	4,552,631	9,551,922

According to this estimate the production of gold in California shows a decrease of 443,861*l.* as compared with the year 1897. This decline may be attributed to the great scarcity of water, which characterised the summer of 1898, compelling many of the miners to suspend operations until the autumnal rains set in.

The exports of silver from this port for China, Japan, and other Oriental countries amounted to 1,043,482*l.* during the past year, against 2,231,240*l.* in 1897.

Shipping and navigation.

The following table gives the number and nationality of the vessels which entered and cleared at this port during the past year:—

SAN FRANCISCO

Annex A.—RETURN of all Shipping at the Port of San Francisco during the Year 1898.

ENTERED.

Nationality.	Sailing. Number of Vessels.	Sailing. Tons.	Steam. Number of Vessels.	Steam. Tons.	Total. Number of Vessels.	Total. Tons.
British	126	223,222	80	141,951	206	365,173
American, from foreign countries	254	171,002	162	292,930	416	463,932
American, from Atlantic ports of Union	38	49,400	10	13,049	48	62,449
Hawaiian	26	28,855	18	34,251	44	63,106
Austro-Hungarian	...	...	25	61,530	25	61,530
Norwegian	2	2,952	23	52,907	25	55,859
French	11	13,208	...	...	11	13,208
Italian	8	13,010	...	...	8	13,010
German	7	10,450	...	...	7	10,450
Others	6	4,340	1	194	7	4,534
Total	478	516,439	319	596,812	797	1,113,251
,, for the year preceding	518	628,590	283	530,425	801	1,159,015

CLEARED.

Nationality.	Sailing. Number of Vessels.	Sailing. Tons.	Steam. Number of Vessels.	Steam. Tons.	Total. Number of Vessels.	Total. Tons.
British	132	229,807	80	142,014	212	371,821
American, from foreign countries	216	155,243	166	296,176	382	451,419
American, to Atlantic ports of Union	6	12,838	1	1,941	7	14,779
Hawaiian	25	27,473	22	38,885	47	66,358
Norwegian	1	1,456	22	50,270	23	51,726
Austro-Hungarian	...	...	23	45,521	23	45,521
French	13	15,370	1	1,101	14	16,471
German	10	12,424	...	...	10	12,424
Italian	6	9,427	...	...	6	9,427
Others	6	1,928	...	...	6	1,928
Total	415	465,966	315	575,908	730	1,041,874
,, for the year preceding	534	667,969	287	530,834	821	1,198,803

NOTE.—The entrances and clearances of American ships do not include the coasting trade, whaling, or fishing voyages.

Remarks on the foregoing return.

A comparison of the above return with that of the preceding year shows that although the entries of British ships were only less by three and the tonnage by 28,333 tons in 1898 than in 1897, there was a decrease of 37 vessels and 97,874 tons in the clearances.

This remarkable difference was occasioned partly by the scantiness of the Californian grain crop and partly by the lack of demand in Europe for wheat and barley, to which causes are to be attributed also the diminutions tabulated hereunder:—

	Entered.		Cleared.	
	Number of Vessels.	Tons.	Number of Vessels.	Tons.
American (trading to foreign countries) ..	38	80,296	61	87,072
German	6	12,142	5	11,629
Italian	2	1,574	3	3,971
Norwegian	4	..*	4	..*
American (to Atlantic ports of Union) ..	..	..	5	5,072

* Slight increase.

During 1898, however, the American vessels arriving from Atlantic ports of the Union doubled in number, and added 16,439 tons to their tonnage—an improvement, owing, in a great measure, to the war with Spain. France is credited with an increase of four ships and 2,853 tons in clearances, but her entries remained as before. Hawaii made a gain of two ships in and two out in the same 12 months.

The appearance of Austrian shipping in the return is accounted for by the charter of a steamer under that flag for the British Columbia coal trade.

Freights and charters. Hereunder are stated the lowest and highest rates paid for iron wheat-carrying ships in each month of 1898, based on the prices paid for ships in port to proceed to Cork for orders to the United Kingdom, Havre, Antwerp, or Dunkirk:—

Month.	Rate per Ton.	
	From—	To—
	£ s. d.	£ s. d.
January ..	..	1 10 0
February ..	1 5 0	1 11 3
March ..	1 2 6	1 8 9
April ..	0 17 0	0 18 9
May ..	..	..
June ..	..	..
July ..	1 5 0	1 7 6
August ..	..	1 3 9
September	..	1 2 6
October ..	1 2 6	1 7 6
November	1 5 0	1 6 3
December	..	1 6 3

At the beginning of July the charters for grain were very few and by the end of the month there was no demand at all for vessels to carry wheat and barley, on account of the dulness of the European markets. For the same reason freights continued to decline during August and September, but in October good business was done at advancing rates, especially in vessels chartered to load at northern ports, and it was brisk again at the beginning of November. Towards the close of that month, however, business declined once more, and during December it was very quiet, there being only one vessel engaged at the rate above quoted.

As reported at San Francisco, the catch of the Arctic whaling fleet during the last two years was as follows:—

Catch of whaling fleet.

Year.	Quantity.		
	Oil.	Bone.	Ivory.
	Barrels.	Lbs.	Lbs.
1897	5,929	142,326	5,223
1898	7,608	225,863	10,025

The case, referred to in last year's report, of the master of one of the China steamers who was prosecuted for violating the quarantine law of California by taking his ship to the wharf without obtaining pratique from the officer of the San Francisco Board of Health was carried, on appeal, to the Superior Court, and a decision was given recognising the authority of the Federal quarantine as paramount.

Quarantine.

Many complaints have been heard of the heavy charges on shipping at San Francisco, particularly with reference to the fees for pilotage, and efforts have been made to get these reduced. One difficulty in the way of improvement lay in the refusal of the pilots to allow their incomes to be ascertained by examination of their accounts. It was therefore enacted at the last session of the State Legislature that they shall make monthly returns to the Board of Pilot Commissioners, giving particulars respecting each vessel served, and stating exactly what fees have been received. By that means it is expected that sufficient information will be obtained to allow of the matter being dealt with further in the next session in 1901.

Pilotage.

The attempt made last year to transport lumber from the States of Oregon and Washington to this port by raft was only partially successful. Of three rafts which started, only one reached San Francisco intact, the others being broken up by rough weather and their contents lost. This method of conveying timber throws out of employment a considerable number of coasting schooners, and consequently is regarded with disfavour by shipping people generally. They feel the effect of it in their business, and complain of its being a source of danger to navigation. A movement is on foot to secure the interference of the Federal authorities in the matter.

Lumber rafts.

On account of the impetus given to trade with Alaska by the Klondike excitement, there was great activity in the San Fran-

Shipbuilding.

cisco shipbuilding yards last year. No fewer than 38 vessels were constructed in the bay. Most of them, however, were small steamers, and only three averaged 2,000 tons. The total tonnage produced amounted to 13,652 tons.

During the same period the Union Iron Works, where the "Oregon" was built, launched the battleship "Wisconsin" and the torpedo boat "Farragut," both belonging to the United States, and also a cruiser for Japan, named the "Chitose."

New steamers for the Pacific.

Trade between San Francisco and the East has greatly expanded since the United States occupied the Philippine Islands, and arrangements are being made to meet its requirements.

It is reported that the Pacific Mail Steamship Company has ordered in the Eastern States the construction of two vessels of 12,000 tons each, which is about double the size of the largest it now owns.

The Oceanic Steamship Company, who own a line to Honolulu and Sydney, is likewise contemplating an increase by the addition of two or perhaps three new vessels of 6,000 tons each. Much traffic is said to be diverted from San Francisco to other ports, on account of the inability of its present fleet to accept all the freight offered, and it is urged by the chairman of the company that a largely augmented carrying trade could be secured in Australia if the steamers connecting Sydney and Auckland were prepared to take it up. The probability is that when these new boats are finished there will be a fortnightly service to the British and American colonies named.

It has also been announced recently that the North German Lloyd Steamship Company has entered into an agreement with that of the Atchison, Topeka, and Santa Fé Railroad, by which the former is assured of such rates as will enable it to compete in the Pacific. The other trans-continental railroads have connections with China and Japan already, and if the project be carried into effect, the new steamers may be expected as soon as the Santa Fé Railway is extended to San Francisco.

The steamers of the Toyo Kisen Kaisha—a Japanese company mentioned in last year's report—are now actually running, the first vessel having arrived here from China and Japan at the beginning of January. They are the largest in the trade, and being well designed for carrying passengers and handling cargo, may be expected to secure a full share of business.

The Seamen's Institute.

The Seamen's Institute continues to exercise a good influence amongst the crews of British ships. Desertions of apprentices have become fewer since it was established, and the chaplain can always be depended on to respond with special effort to any appeal made to him on behalf of young sailors by persons interested in their welfare. In this branch of usefulness a charitable English lady at Port Costa co-operates most successfully, as far as her means will allow, and both the institute and its auxiliary are warmly recommended to the support of British shipowners. The Committee of Management will be glad to receive contributions to their funds.

Seamen's wages remained stationary at 4*l.* a month throughout the year 1898. No difficulty was experienced in obtaining crews, the demand being below the average for reasons already stated. On February 20 of the present year, the amended law regulating allotments came into force. which forbids, under a penalty of 20*l.*, the receiving of remuneration for providing seamen with employment, and makes it a misdemeanour, punishable by a fine and six months' imprisonment, to pay advance wages to seamen, but allows them to allot one month's wages to an original creditor in payment for board and clothing.

Previous to its alteration, the law permitted two months' wages to be allotted for that purpose. The sum available for exactions, therefore, has been reduced from 40 to 20 dol.; and the boarding-house keepers have to look beyond the sailor for their customary gain. They now oblige the shipowner to pay a bonus of 25 dol. for each man supplied; and the shipowners recoup themselves from the seaman by reducing his wages to 15 dol. In respect of a five months' voyage this arrangement successfully evades the law:—Former payment, 20 dol. for 5 months, minus allotment, 20 dol. for 2 months, equal 60 dol. received by seaman; present payment, 15 dol. for 5 months, minus allotment, 15 dol. for 1 month, equal 60 dol. received by seaman; the difference between the allotments, 40 dol. minus 15 dol., equal 25 dol., being paid by the shipowners direct to the boarding-house keepers.

On an estimated population of 360,000 the percentage of deaths in San Francisco is 18·17 per 1,000. The last official report of the Board of Health, which is made up for the year ending June 30, 1898, classifies the mortality as follows:—

	Number of Deaths.
General diseases	2,687
Local diseases	3,416
Violent deaths	441
Total	6,544

The number of marriages recorded last year was 3,019, and the birth registration was 5,359. It will be noticed that the deaths exceeded the births last year according to the official tables. But this unsatisfactory record is said to be due to the neglect of many physicians to report all births occurring in their practice, rather than to an excess of mortality over births.

In November, 1897, the local Health Department inaugurated a system whereby the poor of this city were furnished with antitoxin serum, for the treatment of diphtheria, free of charge. The attending physician was required to certify to the inability of the patient to procure it at his or her own expense. The physicians through whom the serum was distributed were requested to make reports regarding the progress of their patients so treated, and from this data a table was finally formulated, which shows that out of 144 cases only 16 deaths occurred. This is a marked decrease in the fatal terminations of this disease, and as the cases in point were very severe, being among the poorest classes, and in districts where the sanitary conditions were most unfavourable, the satisfactory result of the experiment is all the more remarkable.

Adulteration of food.

The Health Department's chemist reports that, during the year, 562 separate samples were analysed by him, and were principally prepared foods such as enter largely into the ordinary diet of the people. The result shows that adulteration and substitution are still practised to an alarming extent, although much good has been accomplished by the Department in its efforts to suppress the sale of impure articles of food.

Analysis of gas and water.

The large number of deaths from gas asphyxiation that have taken place in San Francisco during recent years, either by accident or with suicidal intent, have had the effect of directing official attention to the quality of the city's illuminant. An expert analysis shows that the gas furnished by one company contains an average of 16·44 per cent. of carbon monoxide, while that supplied by other makers contains this dangerous element to the extent of 24·33 per cent.

The water supply of San Francisco, considered from a chemical standpoint, is officially declared to be wholesome and free from injurious ingredients.

Attempt to restrict the use of cigarettes.

The excessive indulgence in cigarette smoking by boys of tender years has become a habit as general as it is pernicious, and in order to remove this menace to the health of the growing generation, measures to restrict the sale of cigarettes have been adopted by the authorities in many of the towns of the State. An ordinance prohibiting the sale of cigarettes within the city limits of Oakland, and the smoking of tobacco in that form by minors in public places, came into effect in October of last year. A similar law was passed by the authorities of the town of Alameda a few years ago. It is hoped that these measures will help to check the spread of this habit.

Hydraulic mining.

The annual report of the California Débris Commission for the year ending June 30, 1898, shows that 79 applications to mine were filed during the year, and 66 permits granted. Five permits were cancelled and two permits temporarily withdrawn during the same period. No failure of impounding barriers, of any importance, was brought to the notice of the Commission. The total amount of material mined by the hydraulic process, under permits, during the 12 months, is estimated at 512,022 cubic yards. As has been stated, the deficient rainfall in the winter of 1897–98 greatly restricted operations generally, and hydraulic mining was not the last to suffer. The storage of auriferous gravel available for future operations is estimated at 7,842,000 cubic yards.

Lower levels of the Comstock mines to be drained.

With the object of devising some plan for the draining of the lower levels of the Comstock mines, interested parties held several meetings last autumn in this city. It was made apparent that

SAN FRANCISCO.

by pumping out the water below the Sutro Tunnel it would be possible to resume the deep level mining abandoned in 1886. A report signed by 13 superintendents, acting on behalf of their respective companies, was finally adopted, and the work of freeing the lower Comstock levels of water is now progressing. By the use of modern apparatus it is said that the pumping process can be conducted for about one-twelfth of what it would have cost under the old system, and at the same time with more satisfactory results. When mining in the lower levels was discontinued, owing to the influx of water, many of the mines had only been partially opened and prospected, and it is in the belief that ore deposits in paying quantities and richness will be discovered that the present operations have been undertaken. Conservative mining men, however, do not speak very hopefully of the prospect.

The following figures, which have been compiled by the State Mineralogist, show the yield and value, for the year 1898, of the principal Californian mineral products:— *Principal mineral products of California.*

Articles.		Yield.	Value.
			Dollars.
Gold	..	..	15,906,478
Copper	Lbs.	21,543,229	2,475,168
Petroleum	Barrels	2,249,088	2,376,420
Quicksilver	Flasks	31,092	1,188,626
Borax	Tons	8,300	1,153,000
Clay, brick	M.	100,102	571,362
Asphalt	Tons	25,690	482,175
Rubble	,,	724,674	445,395
Silver	..	..	414,055
Macadam	Tons	452,691	369,082
Coal	,,	143,045	337,475
Lime	Barrels	297,860	254,010
Mineral waters	Gallons	1,429,809	213,817
Salt	Tons	93,421	170,855
Soda	,,	7,000	154,000
Cement	Barrels	50,000	150,000
Granite	Cubic feet	98,369	147,732
Bituminous rock	Tons	46,836	137,575

Owing to the great depression in trade, and a labour market greatly over-supplied, there continue to be large numbers of unemployed in this city, and I strongly dissuade skilled artisans as well as labouring men from coming to the Pacific Coast in the expectation of obtaining work. There are more men here now than can get steady employment, and even domestic servants experience considerable difficulty in procuring situations. In the field of clerical work there is absolutely no inducement, the supply being always far in excess of the demand. Despite repeated warnings, British subjects continue to come to this State without having first ascertained what opportunities it offers, with the result that there is much distress among them here. Not infrequently they are driven to the extremity of appealing to their friends for pecuniary assistance in order to get away, or *Labour market.*

as the only alternative, are compelled to accept menial labour should the opportunity present itself.

Advice to intending settlers.

In view of the numerous instances that have been brought to my notice of British subjects having made a failure of the fruit-growing business in California, and having ruined themselves by unwise investments in land, I am constrained to reiterate the advice given in former reports to intending settlers. That advice is, not to invest in farming property until they have resided in the State at least one or two years, and have had an opportunity of studying the conditions personally, and of acquiring some practical knowledge of the particular branch of husbandry in which they intend to engage. I cannot too strongly warn intending settlers of the importance of their observing this caution if they wish to escape the disasters which have overtaken so many of their inexperienced and confiding countrymen. Farms of almost every description may be rented or leased in any part of the State, and by adopting this method a prospective fruit-grower is enabled to find out by actual experience whether he has an aptitude for the business or not. At the same time he will get a more reliable idea of what returns he may expect from his contemplated investment than he would from any other source.

Agriculture. Wheat.

A commercial estimate puts the wheat crop of 1898 at 9,500,000 bushels, against the 30,500,000 bushels of 1897. In a few places, where moisture was abundant, harvests were good, but the severe drought proved most disastrous in the majority of wheat-growing districts, and bad was made worse by a fall in value, which naturally caused a general depression throughout the State, wheat being its staple product. The good prices obtained in 1897 enabled the farmer to pay off some of the interest owing to the banks, but last year's misfortune must have increased the indebtedness again.

Barley.

In the cereal which ranks next to wheat in California, namely barley, the lessening of the yield amounted to the difference between 26,250,000 bushels in 1897 and 5,250,000 bushels in 1898. This loss, however, was to some extent made good by an advance in prices. The barley grown here is of excellent quality for malting purposes, but a good deal is used in feeding stock.

Hops.

There was a deficiency in hops also. The demand, however, was great, and prices rose considerably. Some that were grown in Sonoma County sold for 19 c. a lb., which was the highest price ever paid on this coast.

Fruit.

The lack of sufficient rain, combined with successive heavy frosts, likewise caused the fruit crop of 1898 to fall much below the average, and in many parts of the State occasioned a complete failure. Canners were obliged to pay unprecedented prices, and had great difficulty in obtaining enough fruit of good quality to execute their orders. Pears, plums, peaches, and apricots were all very scarce, the crop of the last-named fruit being less by about one-third than it was in 1897. There was a paucity of berries too, and cherries were far from plentiful. Walnuts were not only few in quantity, but were poorer in quality than usual, and almonds were almost entirely wanting. Early in the season there was a prospect of a bountiful yield of raisin grapes, but it led to disappointment.

Wine also was not obtained as expected, and some of it has been discovered to be not altogether sound. In fact, nothing did well except oranges and lemons, of which the crops were very large, and, for the most part, of fine quality.

Extension of orchards.

But notwithstanding the low prices which have prevailed, almost without interruption for several seasons, interest in fruit culture has not abated. Every year extensive additions are made to the orchard area of California. According to the Assessors' Reports furnished to the Board of Equalisation in 1897, there were then 29,402,287 fruit trees in the State occupying an area of 452,252 acres, and including the undermentioned varieties:—

	Number of Trees.
French prunes	7,221,972
Peach	5,521,967
Orange	3,652,454
Apricot	2,744,910
Olive	2,162,740
Almond	1,603,485
Apple	1,576,796
Pear	1,519,956

Oranges.

The greater part of the orange crop is grown in Southern California, but large plantations have been made in the central and northern divisions of the State, and there is now hardly a county, except those of the extreme north and the mountainous region, which does not produce citrus fruit. The orange shipments of 1897–98 were the heaviest known in the history of the industry, but last season's crop will probably fall far below that record, partly on account of the cold weather which occurred at blossoming time, and partly because the orange, like most fruit trees, has its seasons of comparative rest.

Lemons.

When the 905,742 lemon trees, which were reported by the assessors to be existent in California a little over a year ago, come into full bearing, it is expected that they will over-supply the requirements of the entire country. There is not likely, therefore, to be any increase of the area devoted to lemon orchards. In fact some growers have already begun to graft their trees with oranges, and others will either follow suit or abandon the culture altogether.

Olives.

No reliable statistics of the California output of pickled olives or olive-oil are obtainable. The crop of 1898 was almost a total failure. Demand for the fruit and its product is growing in the country, but the popular taste is not yet educated in their use, and the industry suffers considerably through the market being glutted with spurious oils at prices with which the pure article cannot compete.

(470)

Prunes.

Whatever the season, wet or dry, hot or cold, a good prune crop may be depended on in California. That of 1898, although not so heavy as it would have been under conditions more favourable than those which prevailed, is estimated at from 55,000,000 lbs. to 75,000,000 lbs. The product is finding its way into the European markets, more than 6,000,000 lbs. having been shipped thither from San José, the principal centre of the business during the six months ended December 31, 1897. This export trade has been stimulated during the last four years by low prices, and was augmented in 1898 by the failure of the European crops. Consequently the importation of foreign prunes into the United States is declining.

Raisins.

The raisin yield of last year is estimated to have not exceeded 32,500 tons (of 2,000 lbs.), against 40,000 tons in 1897, and 52,500 tons in 1893. Various causes have been assigned for this falling-off, but it is generally believed to be the neglect of fertilisation, which during the early years of grape-growing was unnecessary, on account of the richness of the soil. Another is stated to be the injury done to vineyards, especially on the west side of the San Joaquim Valley, by the deposit of alkali from the water of the irrigating ditches. It is reported, however, that in spite of the poor crop, and notwithstanding the comparatively low price of raisins, both growers and packers have made money by combining their interests and working together.

Orchard pests.

Orchard pests have engaged the serious attention of Californian horticulturists for a number of years, and great success is said to have been attained by the introduction of insects which prey on the enemies of the fruit trees. It is claimed that this State is freer from such foes than any other in the Union. The pernicious "San José scale" has been almost entirely annihilated by internal parasites, and Australian lady-birds, introduced through the agency of the State Board of Horticulture, have practically exterminated the "cottony cushion scale." A like fate is overtaking the "black scale" at the jaws of another species of Australian lady-bird which has increased almost everywhere with astonishing results. Many orchard-growers, especially those on the coast and in the bay counties, have abandoned artificial means for destroying the "black scale," and leave the work to nature. The benefits derived from this method are considered so satisfactory that fruit-growers are hoping investigations will be continued until remedies have been found for all the pests from which they suffer.

Importation of fruit and live plants.

Great care is exercised in carrying out the State law which prohibits the entry of fruit or growing plants, unless they have been inspected and passed by officials appointed for the purpose. Every steamship and sailing-vessel from foreign ports is examined on arrival, as well as every importation of fruit or trees from other States, and large numbers of infected plants have been condemned and destroyed.

Wine crop.

The year 1898 was bad for grape-growers and winemakers, both with respect to the extent of the crop, which was small from scarcity of rain, and with regard to prices, which, notwithstanding the deficiency, were depressed on account of a commercial war between producers and merchants. An estimate of the vintage places it at 11,500,000 gallons of dry and 5,500,000 gallons of sweet wine, making a total of 17,000.000 gallons.

Compared with the yield of the preceding year this was a decrease of 15,250,000 gallons, but the net results obtained by shippers did not, as a rule, exceed from 6 c. to 8 c. per gallon until the close of the year, when prices advanced rapidly on the establishment of friendly relations between the parties who chiefly benefited thereby.

In counties where the grapes were harvested previous to the September rains—about 40 per cent. of the entire crop—wine was excellent. It was rich in colour and substance, resembling that of 1893, and promising well under the process of ageing. In other districts, owing to imperfect maturing of the grapes the vintage was generally high in acids.

The Wine-Makers' Corporation furnishes its members with all the special knowledge obtainable from experts, and the consequent advance in viticulture within the last two years is said to have been greater than the progress made in the decade preceding.

Beet sugar. Last year's drought was very disastrous to the growers of sugar beets, and the operations of the factories were much curtailed on account of the insufficiency of raw material. The season at the Alamitos refinery only lasted about 10 days, whereas in ordinary years it extends to about 17 weeks. A project to build a factory in the southern part of the State is said to have been abandoned, and it is not considered likely that capitalists will make further investments in this industry until the national policy in connection with the country's newly acquired possessions has been clearly developed.

Honey Every section of the State contributes to the honey output, but the industry finds its greatest expansion in Southern California, where from 600 to 1,000 colonies of bees may be seen in a single apiary. The harvest for 1898 was so small that the Secretary of the Bee-keepers' Association complained last autumn of having orders for over 600 tons of honey with not a ton on hand to execute them.

Wool The spring wool clip was not in good condition on account of the shortness of feed, but that of the autumn was extra good and resembled well-grown mountain wool much more than it had done for several years before. As to quantity, there was a large increase: 20,000,000 lbs. being considered an excessive estimate of the total yield. It is impossible to obtain a statement of the exportations overland, as the railway company has ceased to publish such statistics, but the shipments amounted to 1,451,554 lbs., and it was estimated at the close of the year that the unsold wool of the local market, including Nevada and Oregon as well as Californian stock, and unscoured as well as clean, was about 18,000,000 lbs.

(470)

Public works. Railway construction.

A transaction to which much importance is attached by the people of this State took place during the past year by which the Atchison, Topeka and Santa Fé Railroad Company acquired control of the San Francisco and San Joaquin Valley Railway. This latter road will form an important connection with the main line of the aforesaid trans-continental system as soon as the construction work between Stockton and Point Richmond (the San Francisco Bay terminus) is completed. The Valley road will then have fulfilled the purposes which its originators had in view, viz., the connecting of San Francisco with a trans-continental line in competition with the railroad already in operation, and increased shipping facilities and lower rates for the farmers of the San Joaquin Valley. The completion of the line to Bakersfield during the past year might be said to be the finishing touch to the latter project. It is expected that the connection with this city will be made this coming autumn. A block of land has been purchased in San Francisco for a freight depôt, and a ferry system will be inaugurated for the passenger traffic. One of the probable results of this railway extension will be the establishment of a new line of steamers between this port and the East, to be worked in connection with the Santa Fé. Arrangements are said to have been made with the Southern Pacific Company whereby the Santa Fé obtains running powers between the towns of Bakersfield and Los Angeles, thus obviating the necessity of the latter company constructing an independent line between these two points.

During the past year the Southern Pacific Company has added about 40 miles of new track to its system. The longest continuous stretch of road-bed constructed is the 16 miles extending from Ventura Junction, near San Buenaventura, to Nordhoff. This section was built by an independent company, but with the ultimate object, it is said, of being incorporated with the Southern Pacific—by which company it is being worked. Orders have been issued for the completion of the gap in the coast line between Surf and Elwood, which will give direct communication with Santa Barbara, and shorten the railway distance to that town by about 160 miles.

The Sierra Pacific Railroad, referred to in the last report, has extended its rails from Jamestown to Sonora. Surveyors are also at work on a proposed extension eastward of the latter town, the object being to tap the great timber belt of that section.

General remarks. Real estate, stocks and bonds.

The real estate market last year failed to show any improvement over 1897. In fact, the tendency was still downward. The number of sales was 2,645, showing a decline of 570, while their total valuation was only 2,149,420l., against 2,580,605l. in 1897. Both city and country property shared in the general torpidity of the market. The agricultural conditions invariably affect business of all classes in this city, and more particularly real-estate, but apart from this cause there is a growing tendency to seek stock and bond investments in preference to land. The annual report of the San Francisco Stock and Bond Exchange for the year ending September 19, 1898, shows that the transactions were the largest recorded for any one year in a period of 16 years, and were one-third more than for the previous year and double those of the year 1895-96.

The following tabulated statement gives the volume of business transacted in California during the last three years by the fire insurance companies locally represented. The figures for 1898 were obtained from a preliminary report by the State Insurance Commissioner:— *Fire insurance.*

Year.	Amount Written.	Premiums.	Losses Paid.	Ratio of Losses to Premiums.
	Dollars.	Dollars.	Dollars.	Per cent.
1898	453,680,964	6,657,887	3,578,294	53·8
1897	324,254,126	4,767,019	2,637,706	55·3
1896	336,334,238	3,817,315	2,645,595	69·3

The above comparisons show that the amount of fire insurance business done in 1898 was considerably greater than in either of the two preceding years, while the ratio of losses slightly declined. The cause of the increase is to be found in the circumstance that the long term (three years) policies, written at low rates in 1895, expired and were re-written last year.

The report of the manager of the clearing-house gives the bank clearings for the last two years as follows:— *Bank clearings.*

	Amount.
	£
Clearings for 1898	162,630,605
„ 1897	150,157,829
Increase for 1898	14,472,776

It should be stated that the gain in 1898 occurred entirely in the first half of the year, the latter six months showing a decrease of almost 3,000,000*l.* as compared with the same period in 1897. The augmentation was occasioned by the brisk condition of trade in the first half of 1898, due to the good prices realised on the grain crop of 1897. This brief season of prosperity enabled the farmers to pay off considerable indebtedness, and likewise had the beneficial effect of relieving the financial stringency which for some length of time had affected the commercial world. The clearings of the second half of 1898 were influenced by the dry season and the consequent injury to the cereal crops, resulting in restricted dealings on the part of the farmers. On the other hand, again, the clearing-house had the benefit of the unusually heavy trading in securities which marked the financial year, and the purchase in this city of large quantities of army supplies.

SAN FRANCISCO.

Proposed commercial museum at San Francisco.

Two members of the San Francisco Chamber of Commerce have recently been appointed to serve on the advisory board of the Philadelphia Commercial Museum, an institution designed for the fostering and promotion of American trade, and one which by its effective work has attained world-wide repute. The directors strongly recommend the establishment of a branch museum in San Francisco, to be conducted, on similar lines, in connection with the Chamber of Commerce, and by way of encouragement have offered to supply a large quantity of duplicate exhibits as a nucleus for the proposed display.

LOS ANGELES.

Mr. Vice-Consul Mortimer reports as follows:—

Introductory remarks.

Owing to the fact that the rainfall in 1897 was insufficient to produce good crops, business generally in this district was in a depressed condition during that year. In the latter part of 1898 local and national causes made it probable that there would be a marked revival in business, and the anticipations of a good year would certainly have been realised were it not that the rainfall was again deficient. The fact that Southern California has suffered from drought for two years in succession, has led scientific men to enquire into the cause, and a variety of theories have been advanced. The stream of warm water which flows northerly from the Equator along the East Coast of Japan, and which is known as the Japan Current, has, it is stated, changed its course for the past two winters, and, flowing several hundred miles further north than usual, has lost several degrees of heat, with the result that when it reached the California Coast it had become cold enough to check evaporation, and give California a cold, dry winter.

Japan Current.

In view of the facts, first, that there is no known cause why the current should have gone further north, and second, that there have been no accurate observations of the current for a series of years in regard to the temperature of the water off the California coast, I am unwilling to place much reliance on this theory. If, however, it can be definitely ascertained to be correct, it will be of the utmost importance to the California farmers. Advices could be cabled here in December, and the farmers would be saved the trouble and expense of planting their fields when the current was going too far towards the Arctic Circle. The average rainfall is 16 inches. The rainfall for the season 1897–98 was 7·13 inches, and the rainfall for the season of 1898–99 to April 30 is 4·90 inches. The crops, however, are somewhat better this year than last, owing to the fact that what rain there has been this season fell at exactly the right time, and it is in consequence probable that the farmers will have half a crop. Hay has been brought here from Kansas and sold at 5l. per ton, and a very large number of horses and other animals have been killed

Rainfall.

by their owners owing to lack of feed. The prolonged drought has had two good effects, however, first that inferior horses and stock generally have been killed, and the best kept which will materially improve the breed of animals in this district, and second, the lack of rainwater has directed attention to the development and storage of water. Storage reservoirs are being constructed in various places to hold the waste water from the mountains, and artesian wells have been sunk and water developed in this way sufficient for the irrigation of many thousands of acres of land.

Notwithstanding the drought, the general outlook for this district is very good. Work has been commenced on a harbour for this city, for the completion of which Congress has appropriated 600,000*l.* The work of constructing the railway from Los Angeles to Salt Lake City is progressing favourably, and when the harbour and this railway shall have been completed, the Eastern trade now controlled by North Pacific Coast ports will in a large measure be diverted to Los Angeles. Apart from these and other public improvements which are assured, it is at least probable that the Nicaragua Canal will be constructed. In the report of the Board of Engineers, when the construction of a harbour for this city was under consideration in 1894, I find the following expression of opinion by the Board:— *Harbour construction.*

Railways.

" Should the Nicaragua Canal be completed the importance of the proposed harbour will become still greater. At the present time the most convenient course for sailing vessels coming round the Horn is to go out into the mid-Pacific and strike the trade winds to make the port of San Francisco. With the completion of the canal, commerce will be principally transported by steam vessels of moderate draught, which will move north along the coast, and seek the nearest favourable and convenient port from which their freight can reach its market.

" A deep-water harbour on the southern coast would thus receive the Asiatic and Australian freight for shipment over the most favourable trans-continental lines, and accommodate a large portion of the commerce passing through the Nicaragua Canal which now goes round the Horn."

The completion of the railway to Salt Lake City will give Los Angeles a third competing trans-continental railway, whereas the other cities on the Pacific Coast have but one each.

When I made my first report on this district in 1883, the population of the city and county of Los Angeles was about 25,000, and this city was connected with the Eastern States by but one trans-continental railway. The population of this city and county is now over 250,000, and the population of the district dependent upon this city is between 600,000 and 700,000. There are two and there will shortly be three competing trans-continental railways, and there is every indication that the trade of the Pacific will centre here. As I have stated in former reports there are immense deposits of iron and coal within easy reach of this city on the road to Salt Lake, and the completion of this road *Population and industries.*

Coal and iron deposits

Clearing.

will, I think, result in the establishment here of manufacturing industries to supply the wants of China, Japan, and the islands of the Pacific.

The Los Angeles Clearing-house reports clearing (in round numbers) as follows:—

Year.	Value.
	£
1896	11,500,000
1897	11,460,000
1898	14,880,000

Value of property.

All properties are valued annually by the assessor of each county for purposes of taxation. These valuations are about one-third to one-half the amount at which owners are willing to sell. The assessed value of all property in the county of Los Angeles for the past two years has been as follows:—

Year.	Value.
	£
1897	20,080,000
1898	18,180,000

Building operations.

The Inspector of Buildings for this city reports that new buildings have been constructed in the past two years as follows:—

Year.	Value.
	£
1897	502,000
1898	430,000

Interest on investments.

The best investments in this district for persons satisfied with about 5 per cent. are gold bonds issued by the various cities and counties, both principal and interest has in all cases been paid at maturity, and the credit of this and other cities in this district is so good that the rate of interest on new issues of bonds has been reduced in the past 15 years from 10 per cent. to 4 and 5 per cent. Bonds of this city to the amount of 68,600*l.*, and bearing interest at 4 per cent. were sold a few months ago at a premium of nearly 4,000*l.* The principle on these bonds is repayable in 40 annual instalments. As only 40 to 60 days' notice of sale of bonds is given, persons in England desiring to invest would have to arrange with a bank or some agent here to keep them advised of intended sales.

The rate of interest on the best first mortgage security, which, 25 years ago was from 2 or 3 per cent. per month, compounded monthly, has steadily declined as the country filled up and capital was brought in. Seven per cent. can be obtained on good security on sums of from 200l. to 1,000l., and 5 to 6 per cent. on larger sums.

In my reports from 1892 to 1897 I devoted a great deal of space to advice to emigrants, and as conditions have not changed here on the points dealt with in these reports I would earnestly advise intending emigrants to purchase and read my reports for the years named. Owing to the drought for the last two years many of the farmers have not made a living, and many farms are for sale for a great deal less than their value, and, on this account, farmers who have capital will be able to purchase to advantage during the coming summer. In my report for 1889, and in prior and subsequent reports I have insisted that intending settlers are extremely unwise to purchase land in California (as many do) without personally inspecting it, and that new comers should reside here for at least a year before making any purchase, and I am still of this opinion. Owing to the present condition of Southern California, however, new-comers could readily rent land for a year with an option of purchase at a fixed price, and in this way could get the benefit of the low prices now prevailing here. The following extract from my report for 1890 is so true that I venture to repeat it:— *Advice to emigrants.*

"It is almost incredible the number of sons of professional men (chiefly clergymen) who apply to me for advice or assistance. Nearly every one of them tells me that his father could not afford to give him a start in life in England, and, in consequence, he had to emigrate. As a rule they do not succeed as well as comparatively uneducated Englishmen of the lower classes. It is much the same in Canada, and, I understand, in Australia, and I have come to the conclusion that English professional men blessed with a number of sons for whom they are unable to provide should be advised to send them away at 12 or 14 years of age, instead of 18 or 20, to finish their education in the colony or country in which their parents have determined to start them. Three or four years at school will teach them the habits of the natives, and they will then have a fair start in commencing for themselves."

As stated elsewhere in this report, work has been commenced on the breakwater at San Pedro, the port for this city. When completed, this will make San Pedro a safe and commodious harbour. 600,000l. has been appropriated by Congress for the work, and this will probably be sufficient to complete it. For the present foreign-going ships go to Port Los Angeles, 16 miles west of this city, where there is a wharf a mile in length. I am indebted to the Collector of Customs for the following return of shipping:— *Shipping and navigation.*

LOS ANGELES.

RETURN of all Shipping at the Port of Los Angeles, California, during the Year 1898.

ENTERED.

Nationality.	Sailing. Number of Vessels.	Tons.	Steam. Number of Vessels.	Tons.	Total. Number of Vessels.	Tons.
British	4	6,061	...	...	4	6,061
American	5	751	14	19,357	19	20,108
Other countries	2	3,419	20	39,132	22	42,551
Total	11	10,231	34	58,489	45	68,720
,, for the year preceding	5	7,386	37	70,094	42	77,480

NOTE.—This return does not include the coast trade.

CLEARED.

Nationality.	Sailing. Number of Vessels.	Tons.	Steam. Number of Vessels.	Tons.	Total. Number of Vessels.	Tons.
British	4	6,061	...	...	4	6,061
American	3	257	16	20,843	19	21,100
Other countries	2	3,419	18	37,156	20	40,575
Total	9	9,737	34	57,999	43	67,736
,, for the year preceding	5	7,386	38	70,259	43	77,645

Trade and commerce.

Owing to the drought of the past two years the purchasing power of the people has been materially reduced, and manufacturers must not, therefore, expect to increase their business in this district. For the present British merchants cannot sell staple goods in this market, and if they wish to increase their business in fancy goods and novelties they must adapt themselves to the requirements of this market, and above all things must send commercial travellers provided with samples and price-lists. Three or four firms dealing in different classes of goods could well afford to pay the expense of a competent man to represent them in Southern California, and in this way could build up a good deal of business which without personal efforts on their part will go elsewhere. Unless such efforts be made the business now done here by British merchants and manufacturers will decrease instead of increase, owing to the fact that the wholesale merchants here are not satisfied with the methods of distribution adopted by the British exporters, and, in consequence, push the sale of American goods which otherwise could be undersold by British merchants.

Oranges.

The citrus fruit exported from Southern California in the season of 1898 amounted to 14,835 carloads, of 10 tons each, and owing to the drought this season's crop will be about one-third less. The producers, however, will not suffer by the diminution in the crop, as, owing to the destruction of the Florida orange crop by frost, the California orange-growers are receiving much more for their crop this year than last.

In my reports from 1893 to 1896 I have given a great deal of information on orange growing which will be useful to persons who think of engaging in that industry. Owing to the drought, agriculture is in a very depressed condition in this district. The sources of supply of many of the artesian wells are diminishing, and some orange groves have been very much injured owing to lack of water for irrigation.

Vegetables. The export of vegetables from Southern California last year amounted to 824 carloads of 10 tons each. The reports of the trans-continental railways are a little in excess of these figures. I am indebted to the Collector of Customs for the statistics of exports and imports in Annexes B and C following.

RETURN of Principal Articles of Export from Los Angeles, California, during the Years 1897–98.

Articles.		1897.		1898.	
		Quantity.	Value.	Quantity.	Value.
			£		£
Wheat	Bushels	104,701	19,160	..	..
Other articles	..	..	3,373	..	1,723
Total	..	..	22,533	..	1,723

RETURN of Principal Articles of Import to Los Angeles, California, during the Years 1897–98.

Articles.		1897.		1898.	
		Quantity.	Value.	Quantity.	Value.
			£		£
Coal	Tons	106,889	68,453	115,593	82,600
Cement	Barrels	26,992	7,640	47,174	14,600
Total	..	..	76,093	..	97,200

LOS ANGELES.

TABLE showing Total Value of all Articles Exported from and Imported to Los Angeles, California, to and from Foreign Countries during the Years 1897-98.

Country.	Exports.		Imports.	
	1897.	1898.	1897.	1898.
	£	£	£	£
Great Britain	19,160		78,420	94,000
Other countries	3,373	1,723	19,137	30,300
Total	22,533	1,723	97,557	124,300

Population and industries. The population of Los Angeles is increasing steadily, and now numbers about 130,000. The street cars are worked by electricity, and the principal lines were recently purchased in the interest of the Southern Pacific Company.

The death rate in this city for 1898 was 15·60 per 1,000, on an estimated population of 103,000 in the last official census. A large percentage of the deaths were occasioned by affections of the lungs contracted elsewhere. The real population being about 130,000, the death rate is a good deal less than as stated above.

Mines. Valuable gold mines have been discovered recently in the vicinity of Randsburg, the mining camp referred to in my report for 1896. These mines, which are about 100 miles north of Los Angeles are reported in the press to be fabulously rich. A great deal of British capital is being invested in mines in this district. I have not sufficient knowledge of the mining enterprises which have been taken up by British capitalists to express an opinion as to the probability of their success or otherwise.

Electric power. The Southern California Power Company is now lighting this city, and working street cars and factories by electricity conveyed over a single wire from the Santa Ana River, a distance of 80 miles.

Public houses. The number of public-houses in this city (here called saloons) is now limited to 200. They pay a monthly license of 10l. each, and as the number is limited, the licenses sell at a premium.

Beet sugar industry. The Pacific Beet Sugar Company inform me that on account of the drought last year their factory was not worked, and add:—

"It was completed so that we would have been able to grind 1,000 tons of beets each 24 hours. We are now increasing the capacity so that we will be able to grind 2,000 tons of beets each 24 hours. We expect to have between 12,000 and 13,000 acres planted in beets this year, which will give an average yield of 15 tons to the acre."

There are a number of beet sugar factories in this vicinity, and the industry is becoming very important. It is stated in the press that with the exception of the Alamitos Sugar Company all the beet sugar factories in this district have passed into the hands of the Sugar Trust.

The Atchison, Topeka and Santa Fé Railway are extending their line to San Francisco, in competition with the Southern Pacific Company. The Southern Pacific Company is constructing a second line to San Francisco following the line of the coast. The work is being pushed on, and will probably be completed within a year. *Public works. Railway extension.*

As stated elsewhere in this report, the railway between Los Angeles and Salt Lake City is now under construction. It will probably be completed within the next five years. Its importance to this district cannot be over estimated as it will be the shortest line to the east, it will open up new markets for the fruit growers in the Great North-West, and will make this city a manufacturing centre. *Salt Lake Road.*

The climate of this district is very beneficial for persons suffering from affections of the lungs, and in the winter many visitors are attracted here from the Eastern States to escape the cold weather. The heat in summer is not excessive, and for invalids it is a better place of residence in summer than in winter. *Climate.*

In this report 2,000 lbs. is taken to be a ton, and dollars have been converted into pounds sterling at the rate of 5 dol. per 1*l*.

SAN DIEGO.

Mr. Vice-Consul Allen reports as follows:—

Business shows some slight improvement and may possibly grow in sympathy with the better conditions existing in the East. *Introductory remarks.*

Only one cargo of grain left for the United Kingdom during 1898, valued at 9,858*l*. 11*s*. This is in strong contrast to the previous year, when five cargoes valued at 69,567*l*. 8*s*. cleared the port. This difference was owing to the dry season of 1898, and general failure of grain crops in the southern portion of the State. No doubt a year with a good harvest will again induce shippers to charter vessels from this port which would otherwise leave here in ballast.

Cement imports show an increase of 4,577*l*.; one cargo coming from Hamburg, the remainder from the United Kingdom. German cement is, I am informed, being used entirely for the harbour fortifications. *Cement.*

Coal importations show a decrease of 5,049*l*. 4*s*., but as the new steamship company, of which mention is made elsewhere, will probably have to take in some of their coal at this port, the year 1899 will most likely show an increase. *Coal.*

The coal importations from British Columbia amounted to 21,150 tons, valued at 16,920*l*. 14*s*.

Nearly all of the imports with the exception of coal and

SAN DIEGO.

cement came by sail and rail from the East and San Francisco as in previous years.

Return of Principal Articles of Import to San Diego, California, U.S.A., during the Years 1897-98.

Articles.		1897.		1898.	
		Quantity.	Value.	Quantity.	Value.
			£ s.		£ s.
Coals	Tons	44,614	26,768 8	33,520	21,719 4
Cement	Casks	34,850	9,462 12	48,750	14,040 8
Other articles		...	12,580 12	...	4,070 16
Stock	Number	3,997	7,849 4	1,731	3,181 16
Guano	Tons	1,937	1,846 8	6,460	7,129 12
Bullion	Ozs.	5,146	14,777 8	3,325	10,642 16
Total		...	73,284 12	...	60,784 12
Lumber received from home ports	Feet	19,185,000	...	11,469,000	...

Return of Principal Articles of Export from San Diego, Calfornia, U.S.A., during the Years 1897-98.

Articles.		1897.		1898.	
		Quantity.	Value.	Quantity.	Value.
			£ s.		£ s.
Barley	Bushels	187,186	17.000 0	73,762	7,139 4
Wheat	,,	310,501	52,979 16	22,699	3,646 8
Agricultural implements	...	...	860 8	...	420 16
Fruit and nuts	...	...	325 8	...	327 4
Manufactured iron and steel	...	...	5,671 12	...	6,130 4
Wine	...	...	211 4	...	158 0
Powder and explosives	...	...	...	...	272 16
Lumber	Feet	244,000	1,014 0	...	1,484 16
Lime and cement	...	...	...	...	85 4
Coals	...	...	...	...	39 4
Other articles	...	...	10,096 4	...	8,723 8
Total	...	...	88,158 12	...	28,427 4

Table showing Total Value of all Articles Exported from and Imported to San Diego, California, to and from Foreign Countries during the Years 1897-98.

Country.	Exports		Imports	
	1897.	1898.	1897.	1898.
	£ s.	£ s.	£ s.	£ s.
Great Britain and British possessions	69,985 16	9,958 12	26,377 8	35,547 8
Mexico	16,297 8	17,231 4	30,107 12	20,997 8
Not classified	1,875 8	1,237 8	16,799 12	4,239 16
Total	88,158 12	28,427 4	73,284 12	60,784 12

SAN DIEGO.

The number of deep sea vessels which entered during 1898 amounted to seven. The total number of entries including the British steamer "St. Denis," trading between this port and Mexico amounted to 51. The Austro-Hungarian steamer "Siam" has been doing the carrying trade in British Columbia coal during the past year. This work might well be taken up by a British steamer.

Shipping and navigation. Opportunity for a British steamer.

A new steamship company under the title of the California and Oriental was established at the latter end of 1898, and will run monthly between this port and the East, viâ Honolulu, carrying cotton and flour to Japan and China, bringing in return tea, matting, rice, sugar, and Chinese and Japanese goods. The vessels employed are under the British flag, and it is confidently expected that this line will do much towards forwarding the interests of San Diego as a commercial city.

California and Oriental Steamship Company.

The expenditure by the Santa Fé Railway Company during the latter weeks of 1898 in preparation for the New California and Oriental Steamship Line amounts to about 20,000*l*. The additions consist of a large warehouse on the Santa Fé wharf, switches along California and Atlantic streets, and additional trackage at Twenty-Second Street. The Santa Fé wharf was also strengthened by new piles and re-planked at a cost of about 4,000*l*.

Seamen's wages ruled from 3*l*. to. 4*l*. per month.

Seamen's wages.

RETURN of all Shipping at the Port of San Diego during the Year 1898.

ENTERED.

Nationality.	Sailing. Number of Vessels.	Sailing. Tons.	Steam. Number of Vessels.	Steam. Tons.	Total. Number of Vessels.	Total. Tons.
British	7	11,793	44	13,288	51	25,081
American	61	1,016	100	111,769	161	112,785
Other countries	2	3,061	39	13,644	41	16,705
Total	70	15,870	183	138,701	253	154,571
,, for the year preceding	170	36,934	254	186,858	424	223,792

CLEARED.

Nationality.	Sailing. Number of Vessels.	Sailing. Tons.	Steam. Number of Vessels.	Steam. Tons.	Total. Number of Vessels.	Total. Tons.
British	7	11,803	44	13,288	51	25,091
American	63	10,213	7	6,290	70	16,503
Other countries	...	...	37	13,231	37	13,231
Total	70	22,016	88	32,809	158	54,825
,, for the year preceding	172	40,757	252	186,589	424	227,346

SAN DIEGO.

Population.
A census taken during 1898 shows the population of San Diego to be over 20,000.

The total amount devoted to new buildings during 1898 was not up to the average of the previous six years, and was about 28,000*l.*

Normal school building.
A State appropriation of 10,000*l.*, or the greater part of it, has been expended in the erection of the central portion of the new State Normal School. The building, when completed, will cost about 20,000*l.*

Work is progressing steadily on the water system of the Southern Californian Water Company, of which I made mention in my report of 1897.

Temperature and rainfall.
The mean temperature for the year was 61°. The highest temperature was 91°, and the lowest, 36°. The total rainfall for the calendar year was 4·67 inches.

The County Assessor's report shows the total assessed valuation of the county to be 3,763,117*l.*

Grain growing.
The annual report of the State Board of Agriculture begins with a review of general agriculture during the year 1898. Some space is devoted to the scanty rainfall and other unfavourable conditions, and the conclusion drawn as to grain-growing is that "the season 1898 can well be looked upon as one of great disaster to the farming community, while the business of the State has not suffered as much thereby as it would 10 years ago, as other productive industries and trade conditions have advanced to such an extent that California is not wholly dependent upon grain-growing as in former years." The Board in its report of the previous year had estimated a yield of wheat of 36,000,000 bushels, it now finds that the crop was not quite 12,500,000 bushels, or about 40 per cent. of the normal yield. Prices, however, are said to have been quite satisfactory, the bulk of the sales being at 1 dol. 20 c. per cental, or about 2*s.* 8*d.* per bushel.

Fruit growing.
In regard to fruit-growing (deciduous trees) during 1898, the report says that "early frosts, lack of rainfall, and a most unfavourable season as a whole, has not given to the Californian fruit-grower in general the results anticipated for the season, although the few that escaped disaster profited by the shortness of yield, and the carload shipments of fresh deciduous fruits reached within about 9 per cent. of the previous season." As to citrus fruits, the estimate is made that the present season's yield "will exceed 12,000 carloads, as against 15,000 carloads for last season."

Beet sugar.
Considerable space is devoted to beet-sugar, an industry which the reports says promises to "make California universally prosperous."

The State now has eight large sugar factories, and the prediction is made that "if the season of 1898 is favourable to the industry, over 100,000 acres of California's most fertile land will be devoted to the raising of the sugar beet." The report adds that during the past 10 years this State has produced over three-fourths of the total beet-sugar output of the United States.

Tobacco.
Reference is made to the increased interest in tobacco culture, and the State Board announces its purpose to republish the infor-

mation on this subject that was given in the report of 1895. In the meantime, the suggestion is advanced that farmers who purpose raising tobacco can obtain very full data from the Department of Agriculture.

Among the closing recommendations of the board is a suggestion that elementary agricultural science should be taught in the common schools, and that special training in this branch should be given for teachers in the Normal School.

<small>Elementary agricultural science and common schools.</small>

LONDON:
Printed for Her Majesty's Stationery Office,
By HARRISON AND SONS,
Printers in Ordinary to Her Majesty.
(75 9 | 99—H & S 470)

No. 2352 Annual Series.

DIPLOMATIC AND CONSULAR REPORTS.

UNITED STATES.

REPORT FOR THE YEAR 1898

ON THE

TRADE, &c., OF PHILADELPHIA.

REFERENCE TO PREVIOUS REPORT, Annual Series No. 1910.

Presented to both Houses of Parliament by Command of Her Majesty,
SEPTEMBER, 1899

LONDON:
PRINTED FOR HER MAJESTY'S STATIONERY OFFICE,
BY HARRISON AND SONS, ST. MARTIN'S LANE,
PRINTERS IN ORDINARY TO HER MAJESTY.

And to be purchased, either directly or through any Bookseller, from
EYRE & SPOTTISWOODE, East Harding Street, Fleet Street, E.C., and
32, Abingdon Street, Westminster, S.W.; or
JOHN MENZIES & Co., 12, Hanover Street, Edinburgh, and
90, West Nile Street, Glasgow; or
HODGES, FIGGIS, & Co., Limited, 104, Grafton Street, Dublin.

1899.

[C. 9496—23.]   *Price Three Halfpence.*

CONTENTS.

	PAGE
Shipping	3
Value of goods imported into Philadelphia	5
Table of comparative monthly values, 1897-98	5
Proposed deepening fairway channel in Delaware River	5
Shipyards	6
The Lake Shipbuilding Trust	7
Improvements on wharves at Port Richmond	7
Grain elevators	7
The Baldwin locomotive works	8
Pig-iron	9
Coal	14
Imports, general	15
Diplomatic, consular, and commercial instruction	15
National Export Exhibition of Philadelphia	15
Steel house decoration	16
Paper tiles	16
Shipping statistics	18

No. 2352.   Annual Series.

Reference to previous Report, Annual Series No. 1910.

Report on the Trade and Commerce of Philadelphia for the Year
1898

By Mr. Consul Powell.

(Received at Foreign Office, August 17, 1899.)

During the year 1898 the total number of British ships that entered the port of Philadelphia (including the carrying trade) amounted to 768 vessels, with the tonnage of 1,327,615 tons, and crews numbering 21,503 men, against 727 vessels, with the tonnage of 1,202,021 tons, and 19,800 men in crews, thus giving an increase in 1898 of 41 ships, with the tonnage of 125,594 tons, and 1,703 men in crews. *British shipping.*

This increase has been in spite of the falling-off in the fruit trade, which formerly was carried in British bottoms, but is now almost entirely borne in Norwegian and Danish vessels, and also to the entire stoppage of shipping to Cuba and Porto Rico during the Spanish–American war.

The number of vessels of other nationalities that entered and cleared at this port (exclusive of the coasting trade) in 1898 was as follows:— *Other shipping.*

Non-British Shipping at the Port of Philadelphia during the Year 1898.

Entered.

Flag.	Number of Vessels.	
	Sailing.	Steam.
American	85	9
Austro-Hungarian	..	3
Belgian	..	51
Danish	..	23
Dutch	9	13
French	5	5
German	23	63
Italian	22	1
Norwegian	10	103
Portuguese	6	..
Spanish	..	3
Swedish	..	4
Total	160	278

	Number of Vessels.	Tons.
With cargo	297	410,577
In ballast	141	220,308

Non-British Shipping at the Port of Philadelphia during the Year 1898.

Cleared.

Flag.	Number of Vessels.	
	Sailing.	Steam.
American	93	9
Austro-Hungarian	..	4
Belgian	..	51
Danish	..	18
Dutch	5	12
French	5	4
German	28	51
Italian	36	1
Norwegian	10	111
Portuguese	6	..
Spanish	..	3
Swedish	..	3
Total	183	267

	Number of Vessels.	Tons.
With cargo	421	588,560
In ballast	29	23,931

PHILADELPHIA.

TABLE showing the Value of Goods Imported into the **Port of Philadelphia** during the Year ending December 31, 1898.

Months.	American.	Foreign.	Total.
	Dollars.	Dollars.	Dollars.
January	109,148	1,924,954	2,034,102
February	110,128	2,517,320	2,627,448
March	345,587	3,397,026	3,742,613
April	47,542	3,119,322	3,166,864
May	69,025	3,331,266	3,400,291
June	9,311	3,493,310	3,502,621
July	12,804	3,915,415	3,928,219
August	24,522	2,538,525	2,563,047
September	52,733	2,792,747	2,845,480
October	35,478	3,914,621	3,950,099
November	87,816	2,370,439	2,458,255
December	69,342	3,228,326	3,297,668
Total	973,436	36,543,271	37,516,707

TABLE of Comparative Monthly Values for 1897 and 1898.

Month.	1897.	1898.
	Dollars.	Dollars.
January	2,347,363	2,034,102
February	3,101,002	2,627,448
March	5,659,539	3,742,613
April	7,189,460	3,166,864
May	5,486,578	3,400,291
June	6,916,879	3,502,621
July	2,390,388	3,928,219
August	1,696,210	2,563,047
September	1,945,567	2,845,480
October	2,485,015	3,950,099
November	2,259,134	2,458,255
December	2,168,891	3,297,668
Total	43,646,026	37,516,707

Attention just now is particularly called to the need of a deeper channel to the Delaware River, which is the maritime outlet to the States of Pennsylvania, Delaware, and a large part of New Jersey, comprising an acreage of over 54,000 square miles, with a population of nearly 7,000,000 people. *Proposed deepening of the fairway channel in the Delaware River.*

The State of Pennsylvania is the centre of the oil, coal, iron, and steel products of the Atlantic Slope, of which the city of Philadelphia is its leading manufacturing centre. It should also

(473)

be noted that in the year 1890 the State of Pennsylvania supplied 40 per cent. of the pig-iron manufactured in the United States, 62 per cent. of the manufactured steel, 60 per cent. of the petroleum products, and 37 per cent. of the bituminous and 100 per cent. of the anthracite coal. The value of the manufactured products of the city of Philadelphia alone in 1890 was 577,000,000 dol. (115,400,000*l*.), but although Philadelphia is the natural outlet for the products of the above-named States, the Delaware River has only a 24-foot channel, and is therefore seriously handicapped, while Baltimore has a 30-foot channel, Norfolk a 29-foot channel, New York a 30-foot channel, and Boston a 27-foot channel. The growing size of ocean vessels makes a deeper channel here an absolute necessity. There is further the need of a deeper channel for the development of League Island as a naval station, as well as in the interests of the important shipbuilding industry along the Delaware.

The cost of excavating a channel 30 feet deep and 600 feet wide from Philadelphia to the sea is estimated to cost 5,935,000 dol. (1,187,000*l*.).

In 1897 the value of the foreign commerce passing through Philadelphia was 95,406,000 dol. (19,081,200*l*.), according to the customs returns. The revenue collected on this amounted to 13,923,000 dol. (2,784,600*l*.).

In view of these facts the representatives of the trade of the port of Philadelphia are urging upon Congress that the project for the formation of a 30-foot channel may be adopted, and that contracts may be entered into by the Secretary of War for such materials and work as may be necessary to carry the project into effect, to be paid for as appropriations may from time to time be made by law, not exceeding in the aggregate 5,935,000 dol. (1,187,000*l*.).

Shipyards. Cramp's. At the yard of William Cramp, Shipping and Engine-building Company, almost all available space is taken up. 5,000 men were at work in March last, many more than in March, 1898, and the output is such that there will be employment for these men during the greater part of the present year.

The 5,000 ton steamship "Mexico," of the New York and Cuba line, will be the first of the vessels building to leave the ways, and the place vacated will be taken by one of the four steamers of the Oceanic Steamship Company, the contract for the building of which was recently made.

The Russian cruiser "Variag" will be launched early in the summer, and the battleship for the same nation, "Retvizan," probably early in the autumn.

The United States battleship "Alabama," is now fully two-thirds completed, and the work on her is now concentrated on fitting and securing the armour, and in finishing the interior details. The after barbette armour is almost all in place, and work is begun on the forward barbette. The side armour has yet to be fixed, nor has the armour arrived, but it is expected that the plates will be here shortly.

Material for the battleship "Maine" is arriving. The patterns for her stern and stem posts have been in the foundry for some time, and it is expected that work on her will now be carried forward rapidly and steadily.

Two stocks are vacant, but preparations are going forward for laying two more keels in them.

At Neafie and Levy's shipbuilding yard there is employed fully twice the number of men that were at work in March, 1898, indeed it is probable that this yard has never before furnished employment for so many men as at the present time. This company has now contracts enough to keep the yard working to its full capacity nearly the remainder of the year. *Neafie and Levy's Shipbuilding Yard.*

There are in process of building at the yard two tugs for the Philadelphia and Reading Railway Company, a yacht for Mr. P. A. B. Widener, and a tug for the Long Island City Railroad Company. The Company also have contracts for three torpedo boats for the United States Government, and for a passenger and freight steamer for the York River line. The company will increase its working staff by 250 or 300 men in the summer.

It is stated that a new shipbuilding yard and plant will be established during the course of this year on the Delaware River, the capital to amount to 12,000,000 dol. (2,400,000*l.*). *Proposed new shipbuilding yard on the Delaware.*

It is reported that the certificate of incorporation of the American Lake Shipbuilding Company, with a capital of 30,000,000 dol. (6,000,000*l.*) has been filed in the office of the Secretary of State at Trenton by the Counsel of the company. *The Lake Shipbuilding Trust.*

The purposes for which the organisation is formed, as stated in the certificate, are to be the building and equipping of ships and vessels, the transportation of goods, merchandise, and passengers, and the building of wharves, docks, and works of public and private utility. Provision is also made for manufacturing and mining of all kinds.

Better weather and the disappearance of the ice from the river and snow from the yards permitted great progress to be made with the improvements at the Richmond coal wharves of the Philadelphia and Reading Railway Company. *Improvements on the wharves at Port Richmond.*

In order to push the work forward as fast as possible, six dredgers are being employed to lift the mud from the river bottom between the old piers and to make a uniform depth of 30 feet.

The piers, when completed, will be nearly 700 feet long, and will have landing stages to accommodate two large ocean liners or four or even six smaller steamers.

There will be four railroad tracks so that much of the annoyance of shifting will be done away with. The width of the pier will be 180 feet between the string pieces.

The work of enlarging the grain elevator and flour shed to twice their original capacity is another improvement, and there should then be no further difficulty in handling the vast quantities of grain sent to the city from the West for export. *Grain elevators.*

(473)

PHILADELPHIA.

The 18 piers now used by the coal shipping department are also to be extended, and two of them are already in course of construction. When all are completed the section of river front from Cumberland Street to Allegheny Avenue will afford unusual shipping facilities by which vessels can be docked and loaded. There will be in all 38 piers.

To meet the increased demand the tracks of the Richmond coal line are being duplicated, and the work when completed will double the capacity of the coal yards and freight station.

It is expected that the Richmond yards and piers will become the terminal point for vessels sailing between this port and Cuba and Porto Rico.

The Baldwin Locomotive Works. Business at the Baldwin Locomotive Works continues to be very brisk, the output for 1898 being 755 locomotives. Of this number 348 or 46·09 per cent. were exported to the following countries:—Siberia, Russia, Finland, Brazil, Canada, New Zealand, Egypt, Mexico, Japan, Norway, Spain, Yucatan, Hawaii, Cuba, Newfoundland, United States of Colombia, Tasmania, San Domingo, Victoria, Venezuela, Nova Scotia, England, China, Peru, Denmark, Soudan, Barbados, British Columbia, and West Australia.

242 locomotives or 32·05 per cent. of the output, were compound engines and the rest single expansion; of the compound locomotives 235 were of the vauclain, four cylinder type, and seven were of the two-cylinder type.

The output also included nine electric locomotives.

The average number of men employed during the year 1898 was 4,888; the present prospect is that the output for the year 1899 will be still larger than that of 1898.

It will be seen by the above that the present output of these works is rather more than two locomotives a day, it may therefore be interesting to see the record of the Baldwin Locomotive Works for the 65 years of its existence.

Mr. Matthias W. Baldwin was a jeweller by trade which he carried on in the town of Philadelphia in 1817; however, the jewellery business having proved not sufficiently remunerative, in 1825 he formed a partnership with one, David Mason, a machinist, in the manufacture of bookbinders' tools and cylinders for calico printing. The business was so successful that steam power became necessary in carrying it on and an engine was bought for the purpose. This engine not proving altogether what was required for the purposes of their business, Mr. Baldwin decided to design and construct one especially adapted for their requirement.

In 1829–30 the use of steam as a motive power on railroads had begun to engage the attention of American engineers, a few locomotives had been imported from England, and one (which, however, was not successful) had been constructed at the West Point Foundry in New York City.

To gratify the public interest in the new motor, Mr. Franklin Peale, then proprietor of the Philadelphia Museum applied to

PHILADELPHIA.

Mr. Baldwin to construct a miniature locomotive for exhibition at that establishment. With the aid only of the imperfectly published descriptions and sketches of the locomotives which had taken part in the Rainhill competition in England, Mr. Baldwin undertook the work, and on April 25, 1831, the miniature locomotive was put in motion on a circular track made of pine boards covered with hoop-iron in the rooms of the museum, this was the commencement of the Locomotive Works which, still carrying the name of its indefatigable projector, are perhaps the largest locomotive works in the world.

The first practical locomotive, called "Old Ironside," was built in 1831, and was run upon the Philadelphia and Germantown line, a distance of 6 miles.

In 1896 the 15,000th locomotive was turned out at these works; 30 years were occupied in building the first 1,000 engines, whilst during 1898 the output for that single year was 755.

The present organisation, based on an annual output capacity of 1,000 locomotives (equal to $3\frac{1}{3}$ locomotives per day) is as follows:—

Number of men employed	5,800
Hours of labour per man, per day	10
Principal departments run continuously in shifts, hours per day	24
Horse power employed	5,000
Number of buildings comprised in works	24
Acreage of works	$17\frac{1}{4}$
Number of dynamos for furnishing power to drill presses, punching machines, shears, cranes, and for lighting	26
Number of electric lamps in service	3,000
Consumption of coal in net tons per week (approximate)	1,000
,, iron ,, ,, ,,	1,500
,, other materials in net tons per day (approximate)	40

All parts of locomotives and tenders, except the boiler and tank plates, the steel tires, chilled wheels, boiler tubes, and special patented appliances, are made in the works from the raw material.

The American Iron and Steel Association's complete returns of the production of pig-iron in 1898, as compiled by James M. Swank, show that pig-iron was made in that year in 19 different States, the same number as in 1897. The summary of Mr. Swank's report is as follows:— Pig-iron.

"The total production of pig-iron in 1898 was 11,773,934 gross tons, against 9,652,680 tons in 1897, an increase of 2,121,254 tons, or very nearly 22 per cent. Large as was the increase in tonnage in 1898 as compared with the production in 1897, it was not so large as the increased production in 1895 over the production of 1894. In 1894 we made 6,657,388 tons, and in 1895 we made 9,446,308 tons, an increase of 2,788,920 tons, or nearly 42 per cent. There have been other years in our history, notably 1880 and 1886, in which the percentage of increased production exceeded that of 1898. But 1898 was a great year, nevertheless, for the pig-iron industry of this country.

"Contrary to the general impression, the increased production of 1898 was not mainly in the last half of the year, the production in the last half was but little larger than in the first half, as the following table of half-yearly production will show:—

Period.	Quantity.			
	1895.	1896.	1897.	1898.
	Tons.	Tons.	Tons.	Tons.
1st half..	4,087,558	4,976,236	4,403,476	5,869,703
2nd half	5,358,750	3,646,891	5,249,204	5,904,231
Total	9,446,308	8,623,127	9,652,680	11,773,934

"The production in the second half of 1898 exceeded that of the first half by only 34,528 tons.

"The production of Bessemer pig-iron in 1898 was 7,337,384 tons, against 5,795,584 tons in 1897, an increase of 1,541,800 tons. The production of basic pig-iron in 1898 was 785,444 tons, against 556,391 tons in 1897, an increase of 229,053 tons. The production of basic pig-iron in 1898 was distributed as follows:—Allegheny County, Pa., 378,165 tons; other counties in Pennsylvania and New Jersey, 205,192 tons; Maryland and Virginia, 54,535 tons; Alabama, 100,294 tons; and Ohio and Illinois, Wisconsin, and Missouri, 47,267 tons. The production of spiegeleisen and ferromanganese in 1898 was 213,769 tons, against 173,695 tons in 1897, 131,940 tons in 1896, and 171,724 tons in 1895.

"The production of charcoal pig-iron in 1898 was 296,750 tons, against 255,211 tons in 1897, and 310,244 tons in 1896.

"The manufacture of pig-iron in this country with unmixed anthracite coal is a rapidly decaying industry. In 1897 we made only 21,149 tons of pig-iron with anthracite alone, and in 1898 we made only 22,274 tons. In both 1897 and 1898 New York did not make any pig-iron with anthracite coal, either mixed or unmixed.

"The stocks of pig-iron which were unsold in the hands of manufacturers or which were under their control in warrant yards or elsewhere on December 31, 1898, and which were not intended for their own consumption, amounted to 291,233 gross tons, against 571,577 tons which were similarly held on June 30, 1898, and 656,499 tons on December 31, 1897. These figures of unsold stocks do not include pig-iron sold and not removed from the furnace bank. Charcoal stocks were reduced during 1898 from 209,795 tons to 91,642 tons. The unsold stock at the close of 1898 was 2·4 per cent. of the total pig-iron production of the year. This was the lowest percentage on unsold stocks we have ever recorded at the close of any year in the last 25 years.

In addition to the stocks above noted as unsold on December 31, 1898, there should be added 124,100 tons in the yards of the American Pig-Iron Storage Warrant Company which had passed out of the hands of the makers, making 415,333 tons which may be said to have been then on the market, against 756,336 tons which were similarly held on June 30, 1898, and 874,978 tons on December 31, 1897. The total quantity of stocks in this company's warrant yards on December 31, 1898, was 150,800 tons, against 258,000 tons on June 30, 1898, and 275,800 tons on December 31, 1897.

Stocks on hand.

"On December 31, 1898, there were 202 furnaces in blast. Their weekly capacity at that date, as reported to us, was about 247,500 tons gross, or at the rate of 12,870,000 tons per annum.

"The whole number of furnaces out of blast on December 31, 1898, was 212. A large number of these furnaces cannot be expected to go in blast again under any conditions. Others may be expected to go in blast at an early date under the favourable conditions that now prevail? A few new furnaces that are already completed or nearly completed will go in blast this year under any conditions. Making a survey of the whole field, and eliminating all furnaces that are never likely to run again, we estimate the actual idle furnace capacity of the country to-day at 4,500,000 tons per annum, available in the next six months if there should be an extraordinary demand for pig-iron."

PHILADELPHIA.

Production by States.

The total production of pig-iron by States in 1898, and the condition of blast furnaces is as follows:—

States.	In Blast, June 30, 1898.	December 31, 1898. In.	Out.	Total.	Total Production for 1898 (includes Spiegeleisen).
					Tons.*
Massachusetts	1	1	2	3	3,661
Connecticut	1	1	4	5	6,336
New York	5	4	15	19	228,011
New Jersey	4	5	5	10	100,681
Pennsylvania	74	79	79	158	5,537,832
Maryland	3	2	6	8	190,974
Virginia	7	9	18	27	283,274
North Carolina	..	..	2	2	..
Georgia	1	1	3	4	13,762
Alabama	18	20	24	44	1,033,676
Texas	..	1	3	4	5,178
West Virginia	3	3	1	4	192,699
Kentucky	4	5	4	9	100,724
Tennessee	7	8	11	19	263,439
Ohio	30	34	21	55	1,986,358
Illinois	15	15	2	17	1,365,898
Michigan	6	6	6	12	147,640
Wisconsin	2	4	2	6	172,781
Minnesota	..	..	1	1	..
Colorado	1	2	1	3	} 141,010
Missouri	1	2	1	3	
Oregon	..	..	1	1	..
Total, 1898	183	202	212	414	11,773,934
„ 1897	146	191	232	423	9,652,680

* Gross tons of 2,240 lbs.

PHILADELPHIA.

TOTAL Stocks of unsold Pig-Iron on December 31, 1898.

States.	December 31, 1897.	June 30, 1898.	December 31, 1898.
	Gross tons.	Gross tons.	Gross tons.
New England	8,103	5,576	4,339
New York	36,444	27,322	25,005
New Jersey	7,730	10,525	1,853
Pennsylvania	208,860	196,599	108,805
Maryland	2,179	1,475	2,422
Virginia	70,509	35,825	18,882
North Carolina, Galveston, and Texas	16,791	15,491	14,266
Alabama	56,020	68,229	27,166
Kentucky	10,546	12,368	5,545
Tennessee	25,008	28,090	24,389
Ohio	76,238	62,554	28,910
Michigan, Indiana, and Minnesota	109,272	71,604	24,598
Illinois and Wisconsin	12,939		
Missouri and Colorado	14,663	} 35,919	5,953
Pacific States	1,187		
Total	656,489	571,577	291,233

To these stocks must be added 124,100 gross tons in the yards of the American Pig-Iron Storage Warrant Company, making the total stocks in the country, December 31, 1898, 415,333 tons.

PRODUCTION of Pig-Iron by States during the Years 1896–98.

Production of pig-iron.

States.	1896.	1897.	1898.
	Gross tons.	Gross tons.	Gross tons.
Massachusetts	1,873	3,284	3,661
Connecticut	10,187	8,336	6,336
New York	206,075	243,304	228,011
New Jersey	59,163	95,696	100,681
Pennsylvania	4,024,166	4,631,634	5,537,832
Maryland	79,472	193,702	190,974
Virginia	386,277	307,610	283,274
North Carolina	2,151	..	..
Georgia	15,593	17,092	13,762
Alabama	922,170	947,831	1,033,676
Texas	1,221	6,175	5,178
West Virginia	108,569	132,907	192,699
Kentucky	70,660	35,899	100,724
Tennessee	248,338	272,130	263,439
Ohio	1,196,326	1,372,889	1,986,358
Illinois	925,239	1,117,239	1,365,398
Michigan	149,511	132,578	147,640
Wisconsin	158,484	103,909	172,781
Missouri	12,548	23,883	} 141,010
Colorado	45,104	6,582	
Total	8,623,127	9,652,680	11,773,934

Coal.

The Anthracite Coal Operators' Association has been making a great effort to increase the export of anthracite coal, and the secretary of the Association sailed from New York to various European countries. It appears that he is visiting England, France, Germany, Sweden, Norway, Russia, Italy, and other countries of Europe which offer a promising opening for trade in this direction. The Anthracite Coal Operators' Association is being backed by other great interests in their effort at expansion in Europe.

The Philadelphia and Reading Railroad Company sold some anthracite coal abroad several years ago, but within the past seven or eight years the operations abroad appear to have been confined to small lots, sold independently. This has not been a profitable business owing to the freight rates.

The chief competition comes from the Welsh collieries, but it is stated that with a heavy trade once started, America would be able to compete successfully with the Welsh coalminers in countries which are far enough away from Wales to make the freight charges heavy. In Germany, for instance, American coal-owners, it is stated, could sell "steam sizes" of anthracite coal at a figure which would be lower than the prices of the Welsh fuel.

The output of anthracite coal for the State of Pennsylvania for the year 1898 was 46,947,354 tons, and the output of bituminous coal for the State of Pennsylvania for the year 1898 was 49,694,862 tons.

There does not appear, so far, to be any very valid reason at present for the "alarm," which is said to exist in Great Britain at the continued growth of the American coal trade in Europe; for during the seven months ending January, 1899, the amount of American coal exported to Great Britain was 6,200 tons to London, valued at 30,349 dol. (6,069*l*.), and only 17,158 tons, valued at 41,562 dol. (8,312*l*.), to the rest of Europe. This, however, is about double the amount sent last year, and those interested in coal in the United Kingdom should not lose sight of the fact that these amounts may be increased should opportunity arise.

The coal trade, however, to other parts of America is of real importance, this will be seen by the following table of the values of the export for the seven months (up to the end of January, 1899):—

	July to January.		
	1897.	1898.	1899.
	Dollars.	Dollars.	Dollars.
Mexico	318,290	484,016	624,086
Cuba	343,460	300,781	354,893
Other West Indian Isles	239,496	196,445	277,099
Brazil	43,006	46,062	106,650
Other South American countries	25,343	37,223	149,461

PHILADELPHIA.

The shipment of coal to Asia and Oceania increased from 10,160 dol. (2,032*l.*) in the seven months ending January, 1898, to 143,060 dol. (28,612*l.*) in the corresponding period in 1899.

Canada is the largest customer for coal with America, taking three-fourths of the export, or 6,340,000 dol. (1,268,000*l.*) in seven months ending January, 1899.

It may be useful to compare the total value of imports into Philadelphia of the various rival commercial nations. Thus:—

Imports, general.

	Value.
	Dollars.
United Kingdom	8,405,303
Germany	6,550,746
France	1,756,269
Netherlands	681,168
Dutch East Indies	7,448,672
British possessions	4,496,339
French possessions in Africa	221,442
Cuba	2,350,175
Russia	803,883

It is interesting to note that the University of Pennsylvania is about to include in its curriculum a two years' "diplomatic" course, comprising international and commercial law, in order to give an opportunity to students of acquiring the special knowledge necessary for entrance into the Diplomatic and Consular Service. In conjunction with this course will be one for the preparation of young men for commercial pursuits abroad.

Diplomatic, consular and commercial instruction.

To this end the Provost has organised a staff of instructors in the following subjects:—Diplomatic and international law, commercial law, governments and their laws, colonisation and colonial administrations, economics, finance and banking, with other allied subjects.

The students will be called upon to pass an examination at the end of the two years' course, which will obtain for them, if successful, a certificate of proficiency.

By this means it is the belief of the university authorities that they will be able to send out from time to time a body of men who will be fitted for entrance into the Diplomatic and Consular Service, in which merit alone would be recognised; while at the same time the commercial instruction would be assisting private enterprise by providing men fitted as agents or representatives abroad, who would be equipped to hold their own with the able commercial men employed by Great Britain and Germany.

A large quantity of samples from all parts of the world are being accumulated for exhibition at the National Export Exhibition, which will open in September next.

National Export Exhibition of Philadelphia.

It is interesting to note the varied descriptions of the samples of merchandise which the authorities of the Exhibition are collecting together for the instruction and guidance in the future of the American export merchant. These samples have been largely collected through the agency of the United States Consuls.

For instance, specimens of goods manufactured in Europe and sold in Turkey, or specimens of goods made in Turkey with which the Americans hope to compete have been received from the United States Consul at Smyrna. The specimens consist of Turkish jewellery of the styles most approved by Turkish ladies, revolvers as carried by Turks, hardware, and dry goods, chiefly made in Great Britain and Europe for the Turkish market. A box of samples of cloth, such as is mostly in demand by the Philippine Islanders has been received. These samples are almost all of European manufacture. 100 or more cases of similar nature have been forwarded from England, Germany, Australia, New Zealand, and South America. Additional shipments are on the way to Philadelphia. Thus, 20 cases of samples of goods which are in demand in Chinese markets, arrived a short time ago in San Francisco.

Commissioners of the Exhibition, aided by the Consular Service of the United States, selected and purchased the larger part of these samples abroad, and a representative collection of wares of foreign manufactures in demand all over the world has been secured. Congress voted the sum of 50,000 dol. for the purchase of "Samples in foreign countries of the character in favour and demand therein, together with necessary business data concerning said samples, to be displayed at said Exhibition for the instruction and benefit of American manufacturers and merchants, and thereby laying the foundation of a great system of national commercial education."

The Act provides that at the close of the Exhibition the samples should become the property of the Philadelphia Museum. The intention is that these samples shall completely and systematically illustrate the requirements of the different foreign markets. They are to show to American manufacturers just what competition they must meet from abroad, and by an examination of these foreign-made goods an accurate judgment can be formed as to how far adaptations and alterations must be made in similar articles manufactured here.

Steel house decoration. In consequence of the recent plasterers' strike in Great Britain, the export of metal walls and ceilings has been strongly suggested. The idea of these metal fronts to houses is that it does away in a great measure with plaster, and in the case of ceilings, removes the unsightly cracking and damp stains which so often appear.

The plated ceilings also, besides being extremely decorative, are a very great protection against fire. I venture to hope that before these American metal walls and ceilings can be placed on the market in Great Britain, some enterprising British firm may be equal to supplying the requirements of the British public.

Paper tiles. I am informed that there is a firm in this country who are turning out large quantities of paper tiles, which are used for roofing, but I am unfortunately not in a position to give details as to the process of manufacture. They are reported to be very hard and tough, and the glazing appears to be of the nature of Japanese lac. They are reported to be exceedingly cheap, and can be fashioned in any colour or shape to suit the purchaser.

Annex A.—RETURN of British Shipping at the Port of Philadelphia during the Year 1897.

Direct Trade in British Vessels from and to Great Britain and British Colonies.

Entered.

Total Number of Vessels.			Total Tonnage.			Total Number of Crews.	Total Value of Cargoes.
With Cargoes.	In Ballast.	Total.	With Cargoes.	In Ballast.	Total.		£
151	206	357	224,906	317,581	542,487	10,785	...

Cleared.

Total Number of Vessels.			Total Tonnage.			Total Number of Crews.	Total Value of Cargoes.
With Cargoes.	In Ballast.	Total.	With Cargoes.	In Ballast.	Total.		£
264	65	329	479,232	56,500	535,732	9,702	...

Indirect or Carrying Trade in British Vessels from and to other Countries.

Entered.

Countries whence Arrived.	Number of Vessels.			Tonnage.			Number of Crews.	Value of Cargoes.
	With Cargoes	In Ballast.	Total.	With Cargoes.	In Ballast.	Total.		£
Spain	87	12	99	134,337	19,994	154,331	2,444	...
France	5	22	27	8,811	47,947	56,758	766	...
United States of America	...	84	84	...	194,709	194,709	1,868	...
Germany	36	2	38	70,342	4,533	74,875	1,034	...
Holland	19	2	21	40,044	3,881	43,925	654	...
Mexico	2	9	11	1,584	12,640	14,224	262	...
Brazil	8	1	9	9,077	4,408	13,485	212	...
Portugal	...	8	9	3,145	9,358	12,503	196	...
Russia	13	...	13	18,109	...	18,109	309	...
Turkey	2	...	2	3,648	...	3,648	54	...
Chile	10	...	10	11,358	...	11,358	208	...
Argentine Republic	7	1	8	6,111	1,661	7,772	131	...
Italy	4	10	14	4,089	17,364	21,453	332	...
Denmark	6	3	9	3,531	5,539	9,070	171	...
Egypt	4	...	4	6,654	...	6,654	101	...
Belgium	1	...	2	1,730	1,625	3,355	52	...
Austria-Hungary	2	2	4	3,070	3,439	6,509	93	...
Hayti	4	...	4	2,651	...	2,651	70	...
United States of Colombia	...	1	1	...	1,934	1,934	29	...
Sandwich Islands	1	...	1	2,211	...	2,211	29	...
Total	212	158	370	330,502	329,032	659,534	9,015	...

Cleared.

Countries to which Departed.	Number of Vessels.			Tonnage.			Number of Crews.	Value of Cargoes.
	With Cargoes.	In Ballast.	Total.	With Cargoes.	In Ballast.	Total.		£
Spain	47	1	48	69,264	3,051	72,315	1,165	...
France	65	...	65	132,301	...	132,301	1,865	...
United States of America	...	90	90	...	145,740	145,740	2,437	...
Germany	15	...	15	22,870	...	22,870	344	...
Holland	41	...	41	79,040	...	79,040	1,136	...
Mexico	23	...	23	34,292	...	34,292	556	...
Denmark	41	...	41	71,219	...	71,219	1,050	...
United States of Colombia	2	...	2	3,309	...	3,309	55	...
Italy	7	...	7	12,753	...	12,753	189	...
Belgium	13	...	13	25,181	...	25,181	338	...
Japan	22	...	22	41,037	...	41,037	573	...
Sweden and Norway	11	...	11	15,070	...	15,070	283	...
Greece	3	...	3	4,772	...	4,772	75	...
Portugal	2	...	2	592	...	592	20	...
Austria-Hungary	1	...	1	2,075	...	2,075	29	...
Brazil	2	...	2	754	...	754	14	...
Egypt	1	...	1	1,606	...	1,606	22	...
Russia	2	...	2	2,165	...	2,165	43	...
Hayti	1	...	1	298	...	298	7	...
Venezuela	1	...	1	498	...	498	11	...
Total	300	91	391	519,096	148,791	667,887	10,212	...

PHILADELPHIA.

Annex B.—RETURN of British Shipping at the Port of Philadelphia during the Year 1898.

Direct Trade in British Vessels from and to Great Britain and British Colonies.

	Entered.							Cleared.						
	Total Number of Vessels.			Total Tonnage.			Total Number of Crews.	Total Value of Cargoes.	Total Number of Vessels.			Total Tonnage.			Total Number of Crews.	Total Value of Cargoes.
	With Cargoes.	In Ballast.	Total.	With Cargoes.	In Ballast.	Total.		£	With Cargoes.	In Ballast.	Total.	With Cargoes.	In Ballast.	Total.		£
	170	262	432	249,342	516,443	765,785	12,869	...	291	61	352	519,042	34,430	553,472	10,248	...

Indirect or Carrying Trade in British Vessels from and to other Countries.

Entered.

Countries whence Arrived.	Number of Vessels.			Tonnage.			Number of Crews.	Value of Cargoes.
	With Cargoes.	In Ballast.	Total.	With Cargoes.	In Ballast.	Total.		£
Spain	37	18	55	54,331	26,474	80,805	1,314	...
France	3	21	24	6,519	43,285	49,804	703	...
United States of America	...	82	82	...	137,575	137,575	2,092	...
Germany	20	9	29	45,371	17,444	62,815	824	...
Holland	47	4	51	92,650	7,964	100,614	1,528	...
Mexico	2	12	14	3,212	15,648	18,860	332	...
Brazil	3	2	5	3,953	3,810	7,763	108	...
Portugal	...	8	8	...	11,987	11,987	196	...
Russia	7	...	7	11,542	...	11,542	172	...
Turkey	3	...	3	4,523	...	4,523	71	...
Chile	8	...	8	12,390	...	12,390	202	...
Argentine Republic	5	...	5	2,126	...	2,126	44	...
Italy	4	17	21	5,820	24,910	30,730	486	...
Denmark	4	...	4	2,147	...	2,147	48	...
Egypt	2	...	2	3,097	...	3,097	48	...
Belgium	...	7	7	...	13,213	13,213	188	...
Hayti	8	...	8	6,678	...	6,678	200	...
Greece	2	...	2	3,054	...	3,054	47	...
Sweden and Norway	...	1	1	...	2,107	2,107	31	...
Total	155	181	336	257,413	304,417	561,830	8,684	...

Cleared.

Countries to which Departed.	Number of Vessels.			Tonnage.			Number of Crews.	Value of Cargoes.
	With Cargoes.	In Ballast.	Total.	With Cargoes.	In Ballast.	Total.		£
Spain	44	...	44	69,295	...	69,295	1,064	...
France	72	...	72	141,931	...	141,931	2,059	...
United States of America	...	68	68	...	122,444	122,444	1,988	...
Germany	26	...	26	54,003	...	54,003	718	...
Holland	47	...	47	89,791	...	89,791	1,237	...
Mexico	34	...	34	53,796	...	53,796	827	...
Denmark	46	1	47	76,906	538	77,444	1,190	...
United States of Colombia	1	...	1	1,903	...	1,902	25	...
Italy	4	...	4	8,934	...	8,934	155	...
Belgium	12	...	12	23,315	...	23,315	371	...
Japan	26	...	26	54,483	...	54,483	744	...
Sweden and Norway	7	...	7	11,274	...	11,274	184	...
Greece	1	...	1	1,371	...	1,371	23	...
Portugal	2	...	2	3,033	...	3,033	49	...
Brazil	4	...	4	4,755	...	4,755	77	...
Egypt	1	...	1	1,715	...	1,715	24	...
Russia	4	...	4	5,647	...	5,647	93	...
Hayti	1	...	1	149	...	149	7	...
Chile	1	...	1	1,461	...	1,461	24	...
Uruguay	1	...	1	2,412	...	2,412	44	...
China	1	...	1	2,182	...	2,182	30	...
Argentine Republic	2	...	2	2,532	...	2,532	37	...
Sandwich Islands	3	...	3	4,807	...	4,807	65	...
Total	340	69	409	615,695	122,982	738,677	11,035	...

PHILADELPHIA.

Annex C.—RETURN of British Shipping at the Port of Philadelphia during the Years 1897–98.

Direct Trade.

ENTERED.

	Total Number of Vessels.			Total Tonnage.			Total Number of Crews.
	With Cargoes.	In Ballast.	Total.	With Cargoes.	In Ballast.	Total.	
1897. Great Britain and colonies	151	206	357	224,906	317,581	542,487	10,785
1898. Great Britain and colonies	170	262	432	249,342	516,443	765,785	12,869
Increase in 1898	19	56	75	24,436	198,862	223,298	2,084

CLEARED.

	Total Number of Vessels.			Total Tonnage.			Total Number of Crews.
	With Cargoes.	In Ballast.	Total.	With Cargoes.	In Ballast.	Total.	
1897. Great Britain and colonies	264	65	329	479,232	56,500	535,732	9,702
1898. Great Britain and colonies	291	61	352	519,042	34,430	553,472	10,248
Increase in 1898	27	...	23	39,810	...	17,740	546
Decrease ,,	...	4	...	...	22,070	...	...

Indirect or Carrying Trade.

ENTERED.

	Total Number of Vessels.			Total Tonnage.			Total Number of Crews.
	With Cargoes.	In Ballast.	Total.	With Cargoes.	In Ballast.	Total.	
1897. Foreign countries	212	158	370	330,502	329,032	659,534	9,015
1898. Foreign countries	155	181	336	257,413	304,417	561,830	8,634
Increase in 1898	...	23	...	...	...	...	...
Decrease ,,	57	...	34	73,089	24,615	97,704	381

PHILADELPHIA.

CLEARED.

	Total Number of Vessels.			Total Tonnage.			Total Number of Crews.
	With Cargoes.	In Ballast.	Total.	With Cargoes.	In Ballast.	Total.	
1897. Foreign countries	300	91	391	519,096	148,791	667,887	10,212
1898. Foreign countries	340	69	409	615,695	122,982	738,677	11,035
Increase in 1898	40	...	18	96,599	...	70,790	823
Decrease ,,	...	22	...	...	25,809	...	...

TOTAL Returns of British Shipping at the Port of Philadelphia during the Years 1897–98.

ENTERED.

Year.	Total Number of Vessels.			Total Tonnage.			Total Number of Crews.
	With Cargoes.	In Ballast.	Total.	With Cargoes.	In Ballast.	Total.	
1897	363	364	727	555,408	646,613	1,202,021	19,800
1898	325	443	768	506,755	820,860	1,327,615	21,503
Increase	...	79	41	...	174,247	125,594	1,703
Decrease	38	...	...	48,653	...	...	...

CLEARED.

Year.	Total Number of Vessels.			Total Tonnage.			Total Number of Crews.
	With Cargoes.	In Ballast.	Total.	With Cargoes.	In Ballast.	Total.	
1897	564	156	720	998,328	205,291	1,203 619	19,914
1898	631	130	761	1,134,737	157,412	1,292,149	21,283
Increase	67	...	41	136,409	...	88,530	1,369
Decrease	...	26	...	...	47,879	...	...

LONDON:
Printed for Her Majesty's Stationery Office,
BY HARRISON AND SONS,
Printers in Ordinary to Her Majesty.
(75 9 | 99—H & S 473)